R. Gupta's®

Popular Master G

Sainik School

Entrance Exam

For Class VI

- Specialised Study & Practice Material Prepared by Experts
- Solved Previous Years' Papers • Solved MCQs

by

RPH Editorial Board

2023 EDITION

RAMESH PUBLISHING HOUSE, NEW DELHI

Published by
O.P. Gupta *for* Ramesh Publishing House

Admin. Office
12-H, New Daryaganj Road, Opp. Officers' Mess,
New Delhi-110002 ✆ 23261567, 23275224, 23275124

E-mail: info@rameshpublishinghouse.com
For Online Shopping: www.rameshpublishinghouse.com

Showroom
● Balaji Market, Nai Sarak, Delhi-6 ✆ 23253720, 23282525
● 4457, Nai Sarak, Delhi-6, ✆ 23918938

Book Code: R-951

ISBN: 978-93-86845-84-9

HSN Code: 49011010

Price: ₹ 360

Printed at: S.K. Graphic, Delhi

New Scheme of Examination

For Class VI (Objective Type Exam)

S. No.	Subject	No. of Questions	Marks	Total Marks
1.	Mathematics	50	3	150
2.	General Knowledge	25	2	50
3.	Language	25	2	50
4.	Intelligence	25	2	50
	Total	**125**		**300**

Note:

1. The exams will be OMR based (MCQs).

2. Though there will be only OMR based answer sheet for the entire paper, Question Paper on Intelligence will be handed over to the candidates only after a gap of two hours after commencement of the exam.

3. The subjects for class VI will be Mathematics, General Knowledge (Sc & SST), Language and Intelligence.

4. The question paper of Class VI will be set in English and all the recognised official languages.

CONTENTS

Previous Years' Paper (Solved)

Study Material

Previous Paper (Solved)
All India Sainik School Entrance Exam, 2022*
(CLASS-VI)

Section-A : LANGUAGE

Directions (Qs. No. 1 to 3): *Read the following passage carefully. Answer the following questions by choosing the correct option:*

The Seven Ancient Wonders of the World

The ancient Greeks made a list of places that people should see. The list was named 'the Seven Wonders of the World'. Only one of the ancient wonders can be found today in Giza, which is in Egypt. This is the Great Pyramid of Giza. It is one of the three great pyramids built around 2500 BC. The Hanging Gardens of Babylon are another ancient wonder. They are located on the banks of the River Euphrates. This area is near Baghdad in Iraq. A King built this garden for his wife.

The Statue of Zeus was built in Olympia, Greece in 457 BC. This statue was built to honour the Greek God Zeus. The statue was as tall as a four-storey building! In addition to Zeus, the Greeks built another very big statue, to honour the Greek Sun God, Helios. This wonder is known as the Colossus of Rhodes, built around 550 BC. The Temple of Artemis at Ephesus was considered the most beautiful structure on earth. Ephesus was an ancient city that was located in what is now Turkey. The Mausoleum at Halicarnassus was also constructed in Turkey. The only wonder built for practical use was the Pharos of Alexandria. This was a lighthouse off the coast of Egypt. It was once the tallest building in the world.

1. Which of the following statements is NOT TRUE about the passage?
   A. Colossus of Rhodes was built to honour Helios.
   B. Pharos of Alexandria was a lighthouse.
   C. The Great Pyramid of Giza was destroyed.
   D. The Hanging Gardens of Babylon were built by a king for his wife.

2. Which of the Seven Ancient wonders of the world, was as tall as a four-storey building?
   A. The Great Pyramid of Giza
   B. The Statue of Zeus
   C. The Mausoleum of Halicarnassus
   D. The Colossus of Rhodes

3. What is the meaning of the underlined word:
   'The Lighthouse at Halicarnassus'?
   A. A kind of fabric
   B. A country
   C. Building to guide the ships
   D. A temple

Do as directed:

4. Fill in the blank with the appropriate option.
   Rakesh is _____ excellent Science article.
   A. an   B. a
   C. the   D. no article

5. Fill in the blank with the appropriate option.
   My mother advised me to stay _____ home.
   A. in   B. at
   C. on   D. for

6. Fill in the blank with the correct option.
   It was a steep _____ from the hilltop.
   A. dissent   B. decent
   C. descent   D. desent

7. Rearrange the following words/phrases to make meaningful sentence by choosing the correct sequence.

waved (a)/ she (b)/ greeted (c)/ and (d)/ cheerfully (e)/ us (f)
A. (b), (c), (d), (f), (e), (a)
B. (c), (a), (d), (b), (e), (f)
C. (a), (d), (b), (f), (e), (c)
D. (b), (a), (d), (c), (f), (e)

8. Rearrange the following words/phrases to make meaningful sentence by choosing the correct sequence.

snowfall (a)/ heavy (b)/ the (c)/ everything (d)/ covered (e)   c b a e d
A. (c), (b), (a), (e), (d)   B. (b), (a), (e), (c), (d)
C. (d), (e), (c), (b), (a)   D. (c), (a), (b), (e), (d)

9. Choose the correct noun.

A _____ of soldiers marched into the battle-ground.
A. Troupe   B. Trupe
C. Troop   D. Truope

10. Choose the correct pronoun.

Is she the girl _____ won the first prize?
A. that   B. whom
C. which   D. who

11. Choose the correct Question Tag.

You paid the bill, _____?
A. won't you   B. didn't you
C. will you   D. doesn't you

12. Identify the type of sentence.

Mohan gave me a ten-rupee note.
A. Declarative   B. Imperative
C. Exclamatory   D. Interrogative

13. Choose the correct verb.

The water _____ from the tap last night.
A. dripping   B. drip
C. dripped   D. will drip

14. Choose the correct spellings:
A. Appointtment   B. Apointment
C. Appointmant   D. Appointment

15. Choose the word nearest in meaning to the underlined word.

There was a momentous moment in the cricket match.
A. Insignificant   B. Important
C. Sudden   D. Abrupt

16. Choose the option that is opposite of 'EARLIER'.
A. Former   B. Previous
C. Latter   D. Later

17. Choose the correct option.

Closest to the meaning of 'gigantic'.
A. Very small   B. Very good
C. Very bad   D. Very big

18. Choose the correct adjective.

Yesterday was the _____ day of our trip.
A. most worse   B. more worse
C. worst   D. worser

19. Choose the correct option.

A cobbler is a person who _____.
A. repairs taps   B. mends clothes
C. mends bulbs   D. repairs footwear

20. Choose the opposite of "literate".
A. Illiterate   B. Unliterate
C. Deliterate   D. Misliterate

21. Choose the appropriate option.

All my friends are good-natured. As they say, birds of a feather _____ together.
A. wing   B. clique
C. flock   D. group

22. Identify the adverb.

The doctor will see you later.
A. later   B. will
C. see   D. The

23. Choose the incorrect pair:
A. knife-knives   B. woman-women
C. deer-deer   D. mouse-mouses

24. Seeing the wounded bird, she _____ her mother.
A. was calling   B. called
C. call   D. calling

25. Fill in the blank with correct conjunction.

Manjeet cannot drive _____ he has a licence.
A. if   B. unless
C. although   D. yet

Section-B : MATHEMATICS

26. How many parts of the given figure should be shaded to represent $\frac{3}{7}$?

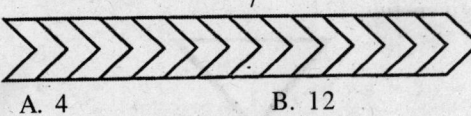

A. 4　　　　　　　B. 12
C. 8　　　　　　　D. 6

27. Convert the fraction $15\frac{1}{25}$ into a decimal number.
A. 150.4　　　　　B. 15.04
C. 1504　　　　　D. 1.504

28. What is the side of a cube, if its volume is 64 cu. cm?
A. 12 cm　　　　　B. 4 cm
C. 8 cm　　　　　D. 16 cm

29. Shreya has 32 red pens and 56 blue pens. She wants to make packs of equal number of pens our of them in such a way that each pack has pens of only one colour. How many pens would be there in the biggest pack?
A. 4　　　　　　　B. 8
C. 16　　　　　　D. 12

30. If ▲ + ▲ + ◖ = 420 and ◖ - ▲ = 90, then what is the value of ◖?
A. 100　　　　　　B. 200
C. 90　　　　　　D. 120

31. Fill in the blank with the correct option.
CCCXC + LIX = ____.
A. CCCCXLIX　　B. CDXLIX
C. CDCXLIX　　　D. CDXXXXIX

32. Which one of the following is the incorrect option?

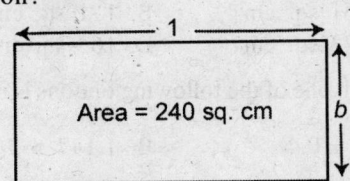

A. l = 19.2 cm, b = 12.5 cm
B. l = 16 cm, b = 15 cm
C. l = 54 cm, b = 5 cm
D. l = 32 cm, b = 7.5 cm

33. Identify the greatest fraction among the following:
$$\frac{2}{11}, \frac{2}{7}, \frac{2}{13}, \frac{2}{9}, \frac{2}{3}$$
A. $\frac{2}{11}$　　　　　B. $\frac{2}{9}$
C. $\frac{2}{7}$　　　　　D. $\frac{2}{3}$

34. What would be the price of seven chairs, if the price of one chair is ₹ 7642.45?
A. ₹ 53497.35　　B. ₹ 53497.15
C. ₹ 53499.15　　D. ₹ 53597.15

35. Select values of m, n to make the statement true.
$127 \times 15 = (m \times 15) + (n \times 15)$:
A. m = 100, n = 15　B. m = 120, n = 15
C. m = 15, n = 27　D. m = 100, n = 27

36. Solve: $\frac{6}{8} \div \frac{3}{2} \times \frac{4}{5}$.
A. $\frac{3}{5}$　　　　　B. $\frac{3}{8}$
C. $\frac{5}{8}$　　　　　D. $\frac{2}{5}$

37. Which one of the following are arranged in descending order?
A. $\frac{2}{5}, \frac{2}{7}, \frac{2}{13}, \frac{2}{9}, \frac{2}{3}$　　B. $\frac{6}{11}, \frac{14}{11}, \frac{10}{11}, \frac{4}{11}, \frac{2}{11}$
C. $\frac{7}{6}, \frac{7}{8}, \frac{7}{12}, \frac{7}{15}, \frac{7}{18}$　　D. $\frac{10}{9}, \frac{13}{9}, \frac{5}{9}, \frac{15}{9}, \frac{7}{9}$

38. An oil tank can hold 60 litres of oil. Another oil tank can hold thrice as much. What is the total capacity of both the tanks?
A. 180 litres　　　B. 240 litres
C. 120 litres　　　D. 300 litres

4

39. What would be the water image of [SEARCH >] ?

A. [SEARCH >]   B. [ƧEⱯꓵƆH >]

C. [< HƆЯⱯƎS]   D. [HƆЯⱯƎƧ >]

40. Sum of place values of the underlined digits in the given number is ____.

695281 5348573

A. 305071   B. 300551
C. 305017   D. 3005071

41. Anil had 78.6 m fabric which was just enough to make one set of uniform for 12 students. How much fabric would be used to make one uniform?

A. 6.05 m   B. 6.65 m
C. 6.55 m   D. 6.25 m

42. Raman started a journey 4 hours before Sameer. If Sameer started his journey at 2:15 p.m. at what time did Raman start his journey?

A. 09:15 hours   B. 11:15 hours
C. 10:15 hours   D. 14:15 hours

43. A dealer purchased 50 tables for ₹ 4570 each. Nine tables got damaged in transit. He sold the remaining tables of ₹ 5000 each. Choose the most appropriate statement for this case?

A. He was able to recover the cost of the damaged tables.
B. He made a profit of ₹ 25000.
C. He incurred a loss of ₹ 23500.
D. He made a profit of ₹ 23500.

44. In 563672, the place value of 6 at the ten thousands place is ____ times the place value of 6 at the hundreads place.

A. 1000   B. 100
C. 10   D. 10000

45. I am a five-digit even number. I have 9 at my tens place. The digit at the ten thousands place is three less than the digit at the tens place. The digit at the hundreds place is half the value of the digit at the ten thousand place. The digit at the thousand place is double the digit at the ones place. Who am I?

A. 68494   B. 61392
C. 64391   D. 68394

46. The area of a triangle whose base is 12 cm and the height twice the base, is ____.

A. 288 sq. cm   Ⓑ 144 sq. cm
C. 289 sq. cm   D. 298 sq. cm

47. How many acute angles are there inside the given figure?

A. 4   B. 6
C. 5   D. 7

48. In a particular year, 76,43,872 students appeared for an exam. Out of them if 42,37,602 were girls, how many were boys?

A. 43,06,270   B. 34,56,270
Ⓒ 34,06,270   D. 43,05,370

49. Which of the following numerals are arranged in ascending order?

A. 6821, 6812, 6261, 2861
B. 9075, 7905, 9701, 5907
C. 10529, 12049, 12509, 15249
D. 23124, 23213, 21467, 2764

50. Choose the smallest possible 7-digit number that you can form using each of the following digits 5, 1, 8, 0, 3.

A. 1310058   B. 1001358
C. 1130058   Ⓓ 1000358

51. Find the area of the shaded part of the figure.

A. 161 sq. cm   B. 171 sq. cm
C. 173 sq. cm   D. 163 sq. cm

52. Which one of the following options is incorrect?

A. $\dfrac{2}{5} = 0.4$ B. 1.147 > 1.039
C. 5.862 < 5.9   D. 3.21 > 3.222

53. What should be subtracted from 3 million to get 1765498?
A. 1,234,602   B. 1,234,502
C. 1,324,502   D. 1,234,402

54. If the classes for the senior students start everyday at 8:35 a.m. and end at 1:45 p.m. (with no breaks), find the total duration of the classes.
A. 4 hours 40 minutes
B. 310 minutes
C. 5 hours 20 minutes
D. 315 minutes

55. Identify the angle created by the minute hand and the hour hand at 2:30 p.m.
A. Acute   B. Obtuse
C. Straight   D. Right

56. Select the next figure in the pattern:

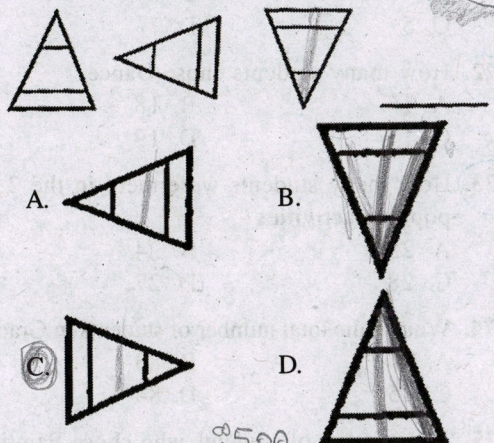

A.   B.

C.   D.

57. Rounding off 7348561 to the nearest hundreds is _____.
A. 7348000   B. 7348600
C. 7348560   D. 7348500

58. Choose the figure that will continue the series in the given figure.

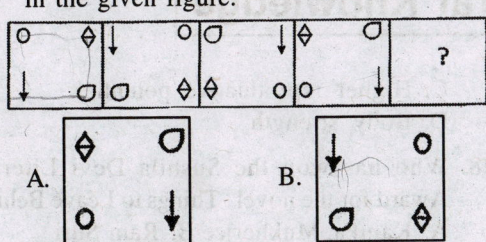

A.   B.

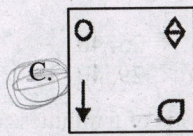
C.   D.

59. What is the fraction that the sum of the shaded regions represent?

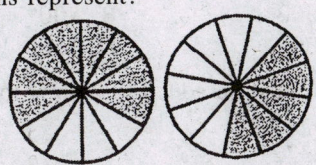

A. $\dfrac{10}{12}$ B. $\dfrac{1}{4}$

C. 1   D. $1\dfrac{1}{12}$

60. Which one of the following figures is not symmetrical along the dotted line?

A.    B.

C. **N**   D.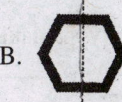

61. 128400 pens are to be filled in cartons, having 150 pens in each carton. How many cartons are required?
A. 856   B. 805
C. 846   D. 876

62. Which one of the following is not an equivalent fraction of $\dfrac{5}{7}$?
A. $\dfrac{15}{21}$ B. $\dfrac{45}{56}$
C. $\dfrac{25}{35}$ D. $\dfrac{10}{14}$

63. What is the weight of two dozen biscuits if each biscuit weights 4 g?
A. 24 g   B. 64 g
C. 48 g   D. 96 g

64. If the cost of fencing 1 m is ₹ 215, then find the cost of fencing a park with length 45 m and breadth 23 m.

A. ₹ 29240   B. ₹ 25340
C. ₹ 29440   D. ₹ 29540

65. A webinar has three intervals of 5 minutes each. What is the total duration of the intervals in seconds?
A. 1000   B. 800
C. 900   D. 1500

66. What must be added to 2.4624 to get 6.785?
A. 4.321
B. 4.3221
C. 4.3226
D. 4.3229

67. The product of the LCM and HCF of two numbers is 322. If one of the numbers is 23, What is the other?
A. 7   B. 14
C. 18   D. 46

68. Seventy six lakh four thousand eighty three is written as _____ in the international number system.
A. 7,640,083
B. 76,483
C. 760,483
D. 7,604,083

69. Prisha weighs 42 kg and Kyra weighs 39.5 kg. What is their total weight?
A. 82500 g   B. 8250 g
C. 81500 g   D. 8150 g

70. An athlete finishes 400 m race in 48 seconds. How many minutes has he spent in running if he ran five times on the same track at the same speed?
A. 4   B. 3.5
C. 5   D. 6

Directions (Qs. No. 71 to 75): *The following graph represents the activities taken up by Grade V students in a particular school. Study the graph and answer the following questions.*

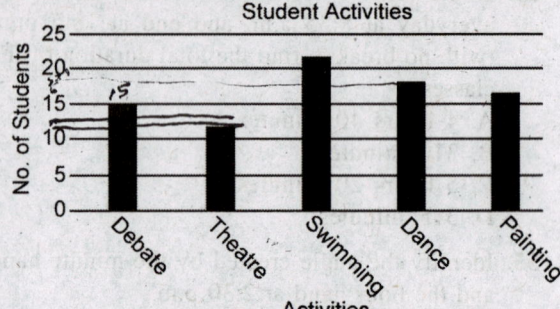

71. How many more students chose Swimming as compared to Debate?
A. 6   B. 8
C. 5   D. 7

72. How many students chose Dance?
A. 16   B. 18
C. 17   D. 19

73. How many students were there in the 2 least popular activities?
A. 25   B. 24
C. 28   D. 27

74. What is the total number of students in Grade V?
A. 80   B. 83
C. 85   D. 84

75. The number of students who chose Painting is _____ more than the number of students who choose Theatre.
A. 1   B. 2
C. 3   D. 4

Section–C : General Knowledge

76. Where did Buddha attain enlightenment?
A. Lumbini   B. Bodh Gaya
C. Sarnath   D. Kushinagar

77. What do tissues help in?
A. Faster development
B. Division of labour among cells

C. Higher reproductive potential
D. Body strength

78. Who has won the Sushila Devi Literature Award for the novel "Things to Leave Behind"?
A. Kanika Mukherjee B. Ram Suri
C. Namita Gokhale   D. Rita Chandra

79. The reading above _____ on Richter scale can cause severe damage.
A. 7　　　　　　　　B. 6
C. 5　　　　　　　　D. 4

80. What does white colour in the Indian National Flag represent?
A. Sacrifice　　　　B. Peace and Truth
C. Prosperity of life　D. None of these

81. Which sweet is deep-fried, dipped in sugar syrup, round shaped and usually orange in colour?
A. Gajar ka halwa　　B. Rasgulla
C. Bhakarwadi　　　　D. Jalebi

82. Salman Rushdie won the Booker Prize for which book?
A. The Satanic Verses
B. Midnight's Children
C. Fury
D. Shalimar the Clown

83. Who invented electric bulb?
A. Thomas Alva Edison
B. Alexander Graham Bell
C. Marie Curie
D. C.V. Raman

84. Which bacteria is responsible for the formation of curd?
A. Vibrio Cholerae
B. Lactobacillus Acidophillus
C. Streptococcus thermophillus
D. Bacillus radicicola

85. Which Vitamin deficiency leads to bleeding of gums, slow healing of wounds and aching limbs?
A. Vitamin A　　　　B. Vitamin B
C. Vitamin C　　　　D. Vitamin D

86. Which one of the following statements is true about fossil fuels?
A. They are renewable resources.
B. They are found within the top layers of the Earth's crust.
C. They are formed over the course of ten years.
D. They are the remains of once-living organisms.

87. Who was the Chief of Army during the Indo-Pak war, 1971?
A. General PP Kumaramangalam
B. Field Marshal SHFJ Manekshaw
C. General JN Chaudhari
D. General KS Thimayya

88. By what other name is the Water Cycle known as?
A. Water movement cycle
B. Air cycle
C. Hydrologic cycle
D. Tectonic cycle

89. Which classical dance form is named after the village it originated form?
A. Kuchipudi　　　　B. Kathakali
C. Bharatnatyam　　　D. Mohiniattam

90. Where is the famous Meenakshi Temple located?
A. Ujjain　　　　　　B. Varanasi
C. Madurai　　　　　D. Rameswaram

91. Where is the United Nations Headquarters located?
A. Vienna　　　　　　B. New York
C. Paris　　　　　　　D. Zurich

92. Which State/Union Territory is Nanda Devi located in?
A. Himachal Pradesh　B. Jammu and Kashmir
C. Uttarakhand　　　　D. Uttar Pradesh

93. Name the holy book of the Parsis.
A. Bible　　　　　　　B. Zend Avesta
C. Quran　　　　　　　D. Guru Granth Sahib

94. What is meant by seed coat?
A. Hard cover around the food stored
B. Hard cover around the baby plant
C. The protective outer coat of a seed
D. Hard cover around the roots of the plant

95. Pick out the incorrect statement.
A. Gravitation affects only part of the earth.
B. Gravitation pulls iron.
C. Gravitation prevents things from floating.
D. Aeroplane do not fly in the gravitational field.

96. Pick an example of water pollution.
A. An oil spill from a large ship
B. Animals walking along the beach

C. Drinking water out of a plastic bottle
D. Gasoline in a car

97. In which sport is the term 'Knock-Out' used?
A. Archery
B. Boxing
C. Golf
D. Billiards

98. Which part of the Earth supports its biodiversity?
A. Biosphere
B. Sanctuary
C. Ecosystem reserve
D. Biotic community

99. What is the major source of fresh water in India?
A. Ocean water
B. River water
C. Pond water
D. Ground water

100. What process is involved in Cloud Seeding, which is a technique that induce rain?
A. Adopting an agricultural practice that depends on clouds.
B. When water vapour in the atmosphere cools and condenses around a particle of dust or salt.
C. Making clouds and placing them in the sky.
D. Scattering clouds to form seed like structures.

Section–D : INTELLIGENCE

101. Which figure among the four alternatives (*a*), (*b*), (*c*), (*d*) would replace the question mark in figure.

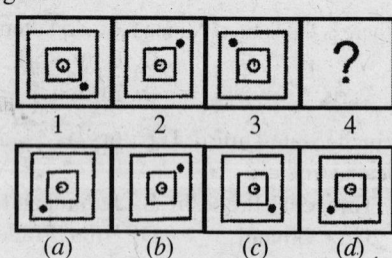

A. (*a*)
B. (*b*)
C. (*c*)
D. (*d*)

102. If 'A' means '÷', 'B' means '−', 'C' means '×' and 'D' means '+', then find the value of the following equation.

16 D 64 A 4 B 4 C 3 = ?
A. 20
B. 15
C. 9
D. 17

103. 37 boys are standing in a row. Akash is 14th from the right end. If he is shifted six places to the left, what is his position from the left end?
A. 20
B. 18
C. 11
D. 14

104. Find out the pair in which the words bear the same relationship to each other as the given one.

Austria : Vienna

A. Egypt : Cairo
B. Germany : London
C. USA : Orlando
D. Australia : Sydney

105. In a certain language 'FIGHT' is written as 'TGHFT', then how will 'PAPER' be written in that code?
A. RPEPA
B. REPPA
C. PEARP
D. PAEPR

106. Which of the following option is an odd one?
A. PQRS
B. LMNOP
C. BCDE
D. FGHI

107. Two positions of dice are shown below. Identify the number at the bottom when the top is '5'?

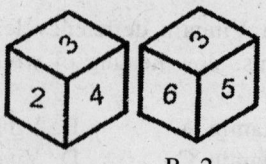

A. 3
B. 2
C. 6
D. 4

108. Surbhi is facing East. She turns 90° in the clockwise direction and moved 2 kilometers, then she turns 145° in clockwise direction and moved 1 kilometer. Which direction is she facing now?
A. North
B. East
C. North-West
D. South-East

109. Which character when placed at the sign of interrogation (?) shall complete the given pattern?

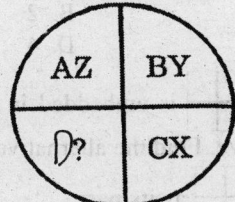

A. DW
B. DK
C. DE
D. DL

110. Which sequence of mathematical symbols can replace * in the given equation to balance the equation?

7 * 7 * 2 * 1 = 12

A. × ÷ –
B. + – ×
C. ÷ + –
D. × – ×

111. Choose the correct alternative.

Smoke : Pollution :: War : __?__
A. Peace
B. Victory
C. Treaty
D. Destruction

112. If in a certain language 'PARROT' is written as '123345' and 'SOAT' is written as '6425', then how would 'ROAST' be written in that code?
A. 34625
B. 32564
C. 32456
D. 34265

113. Fill in the blank with one of the options given below, which is in line with the sequence in the question.

PUE, QVF, RWG _____ TYI.
A. SXH
B. TSQ
C. ABN
D. STY

114. Which of the following words cannot be formed out of the word 'CONDUCT'?
A. Duct
B. Counted
C. Count
D. Donut

115. If GRAIN is related to WAREHOUSE, then Water is related to _____.
A. Estuary
B. River
C. Canal
D. Dam

116. What comes in the place of question mark (?) in the following number series?

4, 12, 36, 108, 324, ?
A. 520
B. 475
C. 680
D. 972

117. Choose the correct alternative from the options for the Assertion (A) and Reason (R) given below.

Assertion (A) : In India, people elect their own representatives.

Reason (R)   : India is a democratic country.

A. (A) is true, but (R) is false
B. (A) is false, but (R) is true
C. Both (A) and (R) are true
D. Both (A) and (R) are false

118. Which of the following diagrams best depicts the relationship between Table, Chair, Furniture?

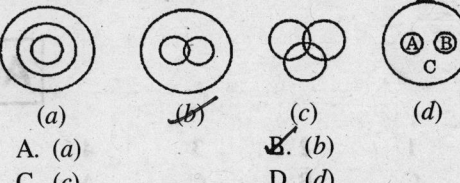

(a)   (b)   (c)   (d)

A. (a)
B. (b)
C. (c)
D. (d)

119. A bus for Delhi leaves every 30 minutes from a bus station. The station master told a passenger that a bus has already left 10 minutes ago and the next bus will leave at 9:35 am. At what time the station master gave this information to the passenger?
A. 9:20 am
B. 9:10 am
C. 9:15 am
D. 9:25 am

120. There are four buildings in a residential complex (a), (b), (c) and (d). Each one is of a different height. (d) is only shorter than (b). (a) is shorter than (d) and (c). Which one is the shortest of them all?
A. (a)
B. (b)
C. (c)
D. (d)

121. Replace the question mark (?) in the given series?

mm, OO, qq, SS, __?__
A. uu
B. Ss
C. UU
D. rr

122. If 35 out of 70 people are diabetic, which figure will depict the diabetic group?

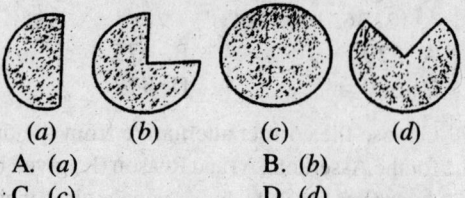

    (*a*)   (*b*)   (*c*)   (*d*)

A. (*a*)   B. (*b*)
C. (*c*)   D. (*d*)

123. Find the missing figures from the given alternatives.

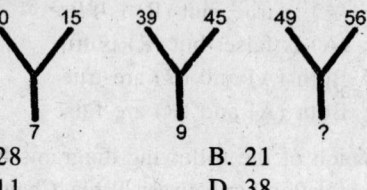

A. 28   B. 21
C. 11   D. 38

124. R is K's sister. P is K's brother. Q is T's father who is P's brother. H is K's mother. At least how many sons do Q and H have?
A. 3   B. 2
C. 1   D. 4

125. Figure is embedded in one of the four alternative. Find the alternative which contains figure as its part.

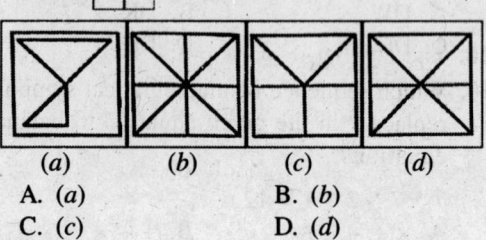

    (*a*)   (*b*)   (*c*)   (*d*)

A. (*a*)   B. (*b*)
C. (*c*)   D. (*d*)

ANSWERS

1	2	3	4	5	6	7	8	9	10
C	B	C	A	B	C	D	A	C	D

11	12	13	14	15	16	17	18	19	20
B	A	C	D	B	D	D	C	D	A

21	22	23	24	25	26	27	28	29	30
C	A	D	B	B	D	B	B	B	B

31	32	33	34	35	36	37	38	39	40
B	C	D	B	D	D	C	B	B	A

41	42	43	44	45	46	47	48	49	50
C	C	C	B	D	B	B	C	C	D

51	52	53	54	55	56	57	58	59	60
A	D	B	B	B	C	B	C	D	C

61	62	63	64	65	66	67	68	69	70
A	B	D	A	C	C	B	D	C	A

71	72	73	74	75	76	77	78	79	80
D	B	C	B	D	B	C	C	C	B

81	82	83	84	85	86	87	88	89	90
D	B	A	B	C	D	B	C	A	C

91	92	93	94	95	96	97	98	99	100
B	C	B	C	A	A	B	A	D	B

101	102	103	104	105	106	107	108	109	110
D	A	B	A	A	B	D	C	A	B
111	**112**	**113**	**114**	**115**	**116**	**117**	**118**	**119**	**120**
D	D	A	B	D	D	C	D	C	A
121	**122**	**123**	**124**	**125**					
A	A	C	A	B					

EXPLANATORY ANSWERS

26. The number of parts in the given figure = 14

$\therefore$ $\frac{3}{7}$ of part in figure = $14 \times \frac{3}{7} = 2 \times 3 = 6$

Hence, 6 parts should be shaded to represent $\frac{3}{7}$.

27. $15\frac{1}{2} = 15 + \frac{1}{25}$

$= 15 + 0.04 = 15.04.$

28. Volume of cube = 64 cu. cm.

$\therefore$ (side)^3 = (4)^3 cu. cm.

$\Rightarrow$ side = 4 cm.

29. $\because$ $32 = 8 \times 4$

$56 = 8 \times 7$

$\therefore$ The number of pens in the biggest pack

= HCF of 32 and 36 = 8.

30. Given,

▲ + ▲ + ◖ = 420

$\therefore$ $x + x + y = 420$

$\Rightarrow$ $2x + y = 420$ ...(i)

and ◖ − ▲ = 90

$\therefore$ $y - x = 90$ ...(ii)

Now subtrating (ii) from (i)

$2x + y - (y - x) = 420 - 90$

$\Rightarrow$ $2x + y - y + x = 330$

$\Rightarrow$ $3x = 330$

$\Rightarrow$ $x = 110$

putting the value of x in (ii), we get

$y - 110 = 90$

$\therefore$ $y = 110 + 90$

$\Rightarrow$ $y = 200$

Hence, ◖ $= y = 200.$

32. (A) Area = lb = 19.2 cm. × 12.5 cm.

= 240 sq. cm.

(B) Area = lb = 16 cm. × 15 cm.

= 240 sq. cm.

(C) Area = lb = 54 cm. × 5 cm.

= 270 sq. cm

(D) Area = lb = 32 cm. × 7.5 cm.

= 240 sq. cm.

Hence, option (C) is incorrect.

33. Numerator of each fraction are equal.

Smallest denominator is 3

Hence, greatest fraction = $\frac{2}{3}$.

34. Given,

Price of 1 chair = ₹ 7642.45

$\therefore$ Price of 7 chairs = 7 × ₹ 7642.45

= ₹ 53497.15.

35. $127 \times 15 = (m \times 15) + (n \times 15)$

$\Rightarrow$ $1905 = (m \times 15) + (n \times 15)$

(A) $(m \times 15) + (n \times 15)$

= $(100 \times 15) + (15 \times 15)$

= 1500 + 225 = 1725

(B) $(m \times 15) + (n \times 15)$

= $(120 \times 15) + (15 \times 15)$

= 1800 + 225 = 2025

12

(C) $(m \times 15) + (n \times 15)$

$\qquad = (15 \times 15) + (27 \times 15)$

$\qquad = 225 + 405 = 630$

(D) $(m \times 15) + (n \times 15)$

$\qquad = (100 \times 15) + (27 \times 15)$

$\qquad = 1500 + 405 = 1905$

Hence, after checking options

$\qquad m = 100$ और $n = 27$.

36. $\dfrac{6}{8} \div \dfrac{3}{2} \times \dfrac{4}{5} = \dfrac{6}{8} \times \dfrac{2}{3} \times \dfrac{4}{5} = \dfrac{2}{4} \times \dfrac{4}{5} = \dfrac{2}{5}$.

38. The total capacity of both the tanks

$\qquad = 60 + 3 \times 60$

$\qquad = 60 + 180 = 240$ litres.

40. In the given numbers

Place value of 5 $= 5 \times 1000 = 5000$

Place value of 1 $= 1 \times 1 = 1$

and place value of 3 $= 3 \times 100000 = 300000$

Place value of 7 $= 7 \times 10 = 70$

Hence, sum of place value

$\qquad = 5000 + 1 + 300000 + 70$

$\qquad = 305071$.

41. Fabric would be used to make one uniform

$\qquad = \dfrac{78.6}{12}$ m. $= 6.55$ m.

42. Time of Raman starting his journey

$\qquad = 2.15$ p.m. $- 4$ hours

$\qquad = 10.15$ hours.

43. C.P. of 50 tables $= ₹\ 4570 \times 50 = ₹\ 228500$

∵ The number of remaining tables after 9 tables got damge in transit

$\qquad = 50 - 9 = 41$

Now, S.P. of 41 table

$\qquad = ₹\ 5000 \times 41 = ₹\ 205000$

Hence, loss = C.P. – S.P.

$\qquad = ₹\ 228500 - ₹\ 205000$

$\qquad = ₹\ 23500$.

44. In 563672

The place value of 6 at the ten thousand place

$\qquad = 6 \times 10000 = 60000$

The place value of 6 at the hundreds place

$\qquad = 6 \times 100 = 600$

Hence, requird times $= \dfrac{60000}{600} = 100$.

45.

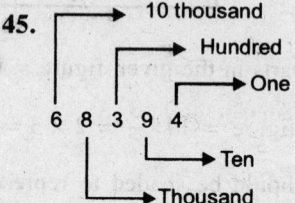

46. Given, Base of a triangle $= 12$ cm.

and Height $= 2 \times 12 = 24$ cm.

The area of triangle $= \dfrac{1}{2} \times$ base $\times$ height

$\qquad = \dfrac{1}{2} \times 12 \times 24$ sq. cm.

$\qquad = 12 \times 12 = 144$ sq. cm.

48. Number of boys $= 76,43,872 - 42,37,602$

$\qquad = 34,06,270$.

51. Area of the figure $= 25$ cm. $\times 9$ cm.

$\qquad = 225$ sq. cm.

The area of a the shaded part

$\qquad = 225 - (4 \times 7 + 6 \times 6)$

$\qquad = 225 - (28 + 36)$

$\qquad = 225 - 64 = 161$ sq. cm.

52. (A) $\dfrac{2}{5} = 0.4$ (Correct)

(B) $1.147 > 1.039$ (Correct)

(C) $5.862 < 5.9$ (Correct)

(D) $3.21 > 3.22$ (Incorrect)

53. Required answer $= 3$ million $- 1765498$

$\qquad = 30,00000 - 1765498$

$\qquad = 1234502$.

54. The total duration of the class

$$= 8{:}35 \text{ am to } 1{:}45 \text{ pm}$$

$= 8{:}35 \text{ am to } 12{:}00 \text{ pm} + 12 \text{ pm to } 1{:}45 \text{ pm}$

$= 25 \text{ minutes} + 3 \text{ hours} + 1 \text{ hour} + 45 \text{ minutes}$

$$= 4 \text{ hours} + 70 \text{ minutes}$$

$$= 5 \text{ hours} + 10 \text{ minutes}$$

$$= 5 \times 60 \text{ minutes} + 10 \text{ minutes}$$

$$= 300 \text{ minutes} + 10 \text{ minutes}$$

$$= 310 \text{ minutes}.$$

59. The sum of the shaded region

$$= \frac{8}{12} + \frac{5}{12} = \frac{8+5}{12}$$

$$= \frac{13}{12} = 1\frac{1}{12}.$$

61. The number of cartons $= \dfrac{128400}{150} = 856.$

62. (A) $\dfrac{15}{21} = \dfrac{3 \times 5}{3 \times 7} = \dfrac{5}{7}$

(B) $\dfrac{45}{56} = \dfrac{3 \times 15}{4 \times 14}$

(C) $\dfrac{25}{35} = \dfrac{5 \times 5}{5 \times 7} = \dfrac{5}{7}$

(D) $\dfrac{10}{14} = \dfrac{2 \times 5}{2 \times 7} = \dfrac{5}{7}$

Hence, $\dfrac{45}{56}$ is not an equivalent fraction of $\dfrac{5}{7}$.

63. Given, weight of 1 biscuit $= 4$ g.

$\therefore$ Weight of 2 dozen biscuits

$$= 2 \times 12 \times 4 = 96 \text{ g}.$$

64. Perimeter of park $= 2(l + b)$

$$= 2(45 \text{ m.} + 23 \text{ m.})$$

$$= 2 \times 68 = 136 \text{ m}.$$

Hence, the cost of fencing a park

$$= ₹ 215 \times 136$$

$$= ₹ 29240.$$

65. The total duration of the interval

$$= 3 \times 5 \text{ minutes} = 15 \text{ minutes}$$

$$= 15 \times 60 \text{ sec.} = 900 \text{ sec.}$$

66. Required answers $= 6.785 - 2.4624 = 4.3226.$

67. LCM $\times$ HCF of two numbers

$$= \text{First number} \times \text{Second number}$$

$\Rightarrow \qquad 322 = 23 \times \text{Second number}$

$\Rightarrow$ Second number $= \dfrac{322}{23} = 14.$

69. Total weight $= 42 \text{ kg.} + 39.5 \text{ kg.} = 81.5 \text{ kg.}$

$$= 81.5 \times 1000 \text{ g}.$$

$$= 81500.0 \text{ g}.$$

70. Athlete ran 5 times on the same track at the same speed

$$= 48 \times 5 \text{ sec}.$$

$$= 240 \text{ sec.} = \frac{240}{60} \text{ minutes}$$

$$= 4 \text{ minutes}.$$

71. The number of more students chose swimming as compared to Debate $= 22 - 15 = 7.$

72. The number of students chose Dance $= 18.$

73. The number of students in the 2 least popular activities

$$= 12 + 16 = 28.$$

74. The total number of students in Grade V

$$= 15 + 12 + 22 + 18 + 16 = 83.$$

75. Chose Painting – Chose Theatre

$$= 16 - 12 = 4.$$

102. Given, A $= \div$, B $= -$, C $= \times$, D $= +$

$\therefore$ 16 D 64 A 4 B 4 C 3 $= 16 + 64 \div 4 - 4 \times 3$

$$= 16 + 64 \times \frac{1}{4} - 4 \times 3$$

$$= 16 + 16 - 4 \times 3$$

$$= 16 + 16 - 12$$

$$= 32 - 12 = 20.$$

103.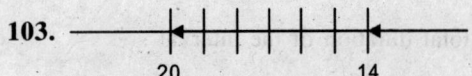

Given, number of boys in a row = 37

Akash is 14th from the right end

Akash is shifted 6 place to the left his position from right end = 14 + 6 = 20

Hence, Akash position from the left end

$$= 37 - 20 + 1 = 38 - 20 = 18.$$

105. Given,

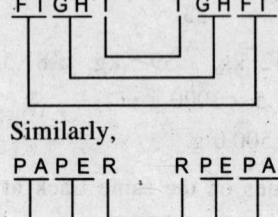

Similarly,

P A P E R   R P E P A

Hence, in a code 'PAPER' will be written as 'RPEPA'.

106. Option (B) is odd because of 5 letters.

107. In two position of dice taking from 3 clockwise.

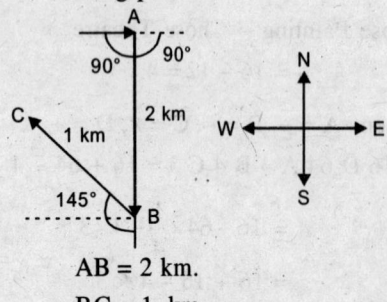

Hence The number of the bottom of 2 = 6

The number of the bottom of 4 = 5

The number of the bottom of 3 = 1

Hence, The number of the bottom of 5 = 4.

108. Here, Starting point = A

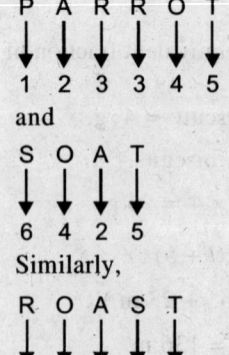

AB = 2 km.

BC = 1 km.

She is facing now in North-West direction.

109.

AZ BY CX [D W]

with −1 arrows over AZ, BY, CX and +1 arrows under them

Hence, ? = DW.

110. 7 * 7 * 2 * 1 = 12

(A) $7 \times 7 \div 2 - 1 = 12$

$$\Rightarrow 7 \times \frac{7}{2} - 1 = 12$$

$$\Rightarrow \frac{49-2}{2} = 12 \Rightarrow \frac{47}{2} = 12$$

(Equation is not balance)

(B) $7 + 7 - 2 \times 1 = 12$

$$\Rightarrow 7 + 7 - 2 = 12$$

$$\Rightarrow 14 - 2 = 12 \Rightarrow 12 = 12$$

(Equation is balance)

(C) $7 \div 7 + 2 - 1 = 12$

$$\Rightarrow \frac{7}{7} + 2 - 1 = 12$$

$$\Rightarrow 1 + 2 - 1 = 12 \Rightarrow 2 = 12$$

(Equation is not balance)

(D) $7 \times 7 - 2 \times 1 = 12$

$$\Rightarrow 49 - 2 = 12$$

$$\Rightarrow 47 = 12$$

(Equation is not balance)

112. Given,

P A R R O T
1 2 3 3 4 5

and

S O A T
6 4 2 5

Similarly,

R O A S T
3 4 2 6 5

Hence, in code ROAST will be written as 34265.

15

113.

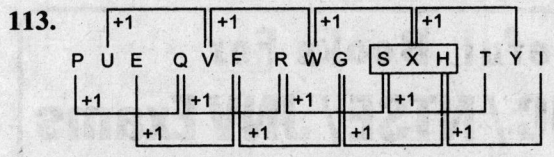

Hence, Missing term = S × H.

116.

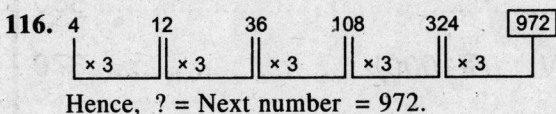

Hence, ? = Next number = 972.

119. Here, A bus leaves every 30 minutes
Hence, time of bus leave before 9:30 am
= 9:35 am – 30 minutes = 9:05 am
Hence, time the station master gave this information to the passanger
= 9:05 am + 10 minutes = 9:15 am.

120. Height of four buildings
B > D > C > A
Hence, A is shortest of them all.

16

R. Gupta's® Useful Books For
Sainik School/ACC / RIMC / NTSE / JNV Exams

- ACC Guide (Big Size) *(R-1329)* 560
- जवाहर नवोदय विद्यालय प्रवेश परीक्षा गाइड (कक्षा VI) *(R-1000)* 370
- Jawahar Navodaya Vidyalaya Entrance Exam (Class VI) *(R-1001)* 340
- Jawahar Navodaya Vidyalaya (Class IX) *(R-2020)* 310
- जवाहर नवोदय विद्यालय परीक्षा (कक्षा IX) गाइड *(R-2021)* 310
- राष्ट्रीय प्रतिभा खोज परीक्षा (कक्षा VIII) *(R-932)* 490
- NTSE Exam (Class VIII) Guide *(R-931)* 495
- NTSE Exam (Xth Class) Guide *(R-1551)* 660
- राष्ट्रीय प्रतिभा खोज परीक्षा (कक्षा X) गाइड *(R-1552)* 620
- Sainik School Entrance Test (Class VI) Guide *(R-951)* 330
- सैनिक स्कूल प्रवेश परीक्षा (कक्षा VI) गाइड *(R-722)* 330
- Sainik School Admission Test Guide (Class IX) *(R-955)* 480
- सैनिक स्कूल प्रवेश परीक्षा गाइड (कक्षा IX) *(R-778)* 480
- Military School Entrance Exam Guide *(R-207)* 310
- मिलिट्री स्कूल प्रवेश परीक्षा गाइड *(R-208)* 180
- RIMC Entrance Exam Guide *(R-216)* 260
- Rajkiya Pratibha Vikas Vidyalaya (RPVVS) Entrance Exam *(R-1023)* .. 320
- राजकीय प्रतिभा विकास विद्यालय (RPVVS) प्रवेश परीक्षा (वर्ग VI) *(R-825)* 320

RAMESH PUBLISHING HOUSE
12-H, New Darya Ganj Road, Opp. Officers' Mess, New Delhi-110002
For Online Shopping: www.rameshpublishinghouse.com

2202

All India Sainik Schools Entrance Exam (AISSEE)–2021*

Class-VI

Section A : Mathematics

1. Whole numbers are closed under which operation?
   A. Subtraction
   B. Division
   C. Multiplication
   D. All of these

2. The successor of 1 million is:
   A. 2 million
   B. 1000001
   C. 100001
   D. 10001

3. The points O, U, S, V, R, X, W, T, P, Q and Y on the number line are equidistant. The fraction represented by length OP is:

   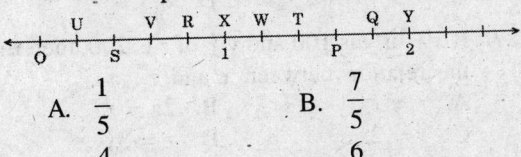

   A. $\dfrac{1}{5}$
   B. $\dfrac{7}{5}$
   C. $\dfrac{4}{5}$
   D. $\dfrac{6}{5}$

4. The two consecutive integers, between which the fraction $\dfrac{5}{7}$ lies, are:
   A. 0 and 1
   B. 5 and 7
   C. 5 and 6
   D. 6 and 7

5. Which of the following is the smallest fraction?
   A. $\dfrac{4}{5}$
   B. $\dfrac{5}{3}$
   C. $\dfrac{5}{6}$
   D. $\dfrac{5}{2}$

6. The HCF and LCM of two numbers are 6 and 864 respectively. If one number is 96, find the other number.
   A. 84
   B. 45
   C. 54
   D. 24

7. The HCF of two numbers is 12 and their difference is 12. Which of the following can be the numbers?
   A. 84, 96
   B. 66, 78
   C. 70, 82
   D. 62, 78

8. Find the smallest number that is divisible by each one of 9, 12 and 15.
   A. 60
   B. 90
   C. 120
   D. 180

9. A certain brand of soap-powder is sold at ₹ 15 per packet. It costs ₹ 144 a dozen. What is the profit in per cent on 8 dozen packets?
   A. 20
   B. 25
   C. 24
   D. 36

10. Find the greatest number that will divide 37, 56, 93 leaving remainder 1, 2 and 3 respectively.
    A. 9
    B. 18
    C. 15
    D. 12

11. If 10 men can do a piece of work in 4 days, how many men will be required to get the same work done in 5 days?
    A. 10
    B. 8
    C. 40
    D. 12

12. 21 goats eat as much as 15 cows. How many goats eat as much as 35 cows?
    A. 38
    B. 49
    C. 37
    D. 41

13. A mechanic earns ₹ 36,000 on 9 cars. How much will he earn in 1 day, if in a day he receives 27 cars?
    A. ₹ 1,08,000
    B. ₹ 1,80,000
    C. ₹ 1,00,800
    D. ₹ 1,00,080

14. If $x : y = 3 : 5$,
    find the ratio $3x + 4y : 8x + 5y$.
    A. 39 : 49   B. 29 : 50
    C. 29 : 49   D. 39 : 50

15. Find the value of m, if 3, 18, m, 42 are in proportion.
    A. 6   B. 54
    C. 7   D. 252

16. In an NCC Camp, 1200 trainees are participating out of which 900 are selected for Republic Day Camp. What is the ratio between the number of selected and non-selected cadets?
    A. 300 : 120   B. 4 : 1
    C. 3 : 1   D. 120 : 130

17. If a boy sells a book for ₹ 450, he makes a loss of 10%. To gain 10%, what should be the selling price?
    A. ₹ 500   B. ₹ 600
    C. ₹ 550   D. ₹ 525

18. A man sells one speaker for ₹ 7,500 at a profit of 20% and another speaker for ₹ 8,100 at a loss of 10%. Find his total loss or profit.
    A. Loss = ₹ 300   B. Loss = ₹ 350
    C. Profit = ₹ 300   D. Profit = ₹ 350

19. Simplify $(8 + 4 - 2) \times (17 - 12) \times 10 - 89$ = _____ .
    A. 3950   B. 411
    C. 412   D. 3949

20. Simplify $0.05 + 1.5 \times 5 \div 10 \times 0.5$ = _____ .
    A. 4.25   B. 42.5
    C. 0.425   D. 0.42

21. Simplify $7 + 5 - 2 \times (7 + 89) - 94 \div 2 + (33 \div 3 + 9 \times 2 - 7) \div 11$ = _____ .
    A. 254   B. − 225
    C. − 235   D. 245

22. The average weight of 20 boys in a class is 160 kg and that of the remaining 5 boys is 50 kg. Find the average weight of all the boys in the class.
    A. 138 kg   B. 183 kg
    C. 140 kg   D. 150 kg

23. The average marks obtained by 7 students in a group is 226. If the marks obtained by six of them are 340, 180, 260, 56, 275 and 307 respectively, find the marks obtained by the seventh student.
    A. 160   B. 162
    C. 163   D. 164

24. A library has an average of 510 visitors on Sundays and 240 on other days. The average number of visitors in a month of 30 days starting with Sunday is:
    A. 280   B. 285
    C. 290   D. 295

25. A batsman makes a score of 87 runs in the 17th match and thus increases his average by 3. Find his average after the 17th match.
    A. 36   B. 37
    C. 38   D. 39

26. Average of 1, 3, 5, 7, 9, 11, 13 is:
    A. 7   B. 8
    C. 7.5   D. 8.5

27. If $x\%$ of y is 100 and $y\%$ of z is 200, then find the relation between x and z.
    A. $z = x$ B. $2z = x$
    C. $z = 2x$ D. $z = 3x$

28. One-fourth of one-third of two-fifth of a number is 15. What will be 40% of that number?
    A. 140   B. 150
    C. 180   D. 200

29. If 15% of 40 is greater than 25% of a number by 2, then the number is:
    A. 14   B. 16
    C. 18   D. 20

30. Find the length of a rectangular playground in cm whose area is 700 sq.m and breadth is 25 m.
    A. 28   B. 280
    C. 2800   D. 2500

31. Reena took a loan of ₹ 1,200 with simple interest for as many years as the rate of interest. If she paid ₹ 432 as interest at the end of the loan period, what was the rate of interest?
    A. 3.6   B. 6
    C. 18   D. 10

32. Write the name of the angle formed when the clock time is 7:15 pm.
A. Acute angle   B. Right angle
C. Obtuse angle   D. Straight angle

33. The table below shows the maximum temperatures in New York City last year. Use the information in this table and answer the following:

What was the average maximum temperature (upto 2 decimal places) of three months May, July and September last year in New York City?

Month	Maximum temperature, in °C
January	3
March	9
May	21
July	29
September	24
November	11

A. 21.65°C   B. 24.66°C
C. 25.52°C   D. 26.23°C

34. In the morning, the temperature was −10°C and it decreased 3 degrees by the evening. What was the temperature in the evening?
A. −7°C   B. −23°C
C. −13°C   D. −12°C

35. A rectangular garden is 185 m long and 220 m wide. It has two roads in its centre of uniform width of 4 m, one parallel to its length and the other parallel to its breadth. Find the cost of levelling the roads at ₹ 1.25 per sq.m.
A. ₹ 3,900   B. ₹ 3,010
C. ₹ 4,010   D. ₹ 2,005

36. One decimeter is equal to:
A. 1×10^{-1} m   B. 1×10^{-2} m
C. 1×10^{2} m   D. 1×10^{3} m

37. In Roman numeration, if a symbol is repeated, its value is not multiplied as many times as it occurs.
A. True   B. False
C. Cannot say   D. Both are equal

38. The angle subtended by the diameter of a semicircle on any point on the circle is:
A. 45°   B. 180°
C. 90°   D. 60°

39. A big cube has each portion of 44 cm. Tiny cubes of 4 cm portion each are cut from that. Then how many tiny cubes will be formed that are surrounded by at least one cube?
A. 888   B. 729
C. 164   D. 33

40. A rectangular tank 15 cm long, 12 cm wide and 8 cm high was completely filled with water. Find the volume of water in the tank.
A. 180 cm^3 B. 1200 cm^3
C. 440 cm^3 D. 1440 cm^3

41. Which option shows fractions arranged in ascending order?
A. $\frac{5}{8} < \frac{7}{12} < \frac{3}{4} < \frac{13}{16}$ B. $\frac{5}{8} < \frac{7}{12} < \frac{13}{16} < \frac{3}{4}$
C. $\frac{5}{8} < \frac{3}{4} < \frac{13}{16} < \frac{7}{12}$ D. $\frac{7}{12} < \frac{5}{8} < \frac{3}{4} < \frac{13}{16}$

42. What is the value of
$945.341 - 1042.792 + 875.435 + 31.025$?
A. 908.004   B. 810.008
C. 795.659   D. 809.009

43. A man on tour travels first 160 km at 64 km/hr and the next 160 km at 80 km/hr. The average speed for the first 320 km of the tour is:
A. 35.55 km/hr   B. 36 km/hr
C. 71.11 km/hr   D. 71 km/hr

44. On dividing 2272 as well as 875 by a 3-digit number N, we get the same remainder. The sum of the digits of N is:
A. 10   B. 11
C. 12   D. 13

45. It takes Julia $\frac{1}{2}$ hour to wash, comb her hair and put on her clothes and $\frac{1}{4}$ hour to have her breakfast. How much time does it take Julia to be ready for school?

4

A. $\frac{3}{4}$ hour   B. 1 hour

C. $\frac{2}{4}$ hour   D. $\frac{5}{4}$ hour

46. Which of the following numbers in Roman Numerals is *incorrect*?
A. LXII   B. XCI
C. LC   D. XLIV

47. How many faces are there in a cuboid?
A. 6   B. 12
C. 8   D. 4

48. A flat surface which extends indefinitely in all directions is called a:

A. Plane   B. Line
C. Line segment   D. Point

49. The difference between two complementary angles is 10°. Calculate the values of both the angles.
A. 55°, 45°   B. 40°, 50°
C. 50°, 60°   D. 100°, 90°

50. The total weight of brinjal, lady-finger and onion is 48.057 kg. If brinjal and lady-finger weigh 5.35 kg and 24.52 kg respectively, find the weight of onion.
A. 17.187 kg   B. 18.187 kg
C. 17.180 kg   D. 18.180 kg

Section B : General Knowledge

51. Which device is used to measure the speed of vehicles?
A. Gravometer   B. Speedometer
C. Gyroscope   D. Kilometer

52. From which monument did India adopt its National Emblem?
A. Kapilavastu   B. Hastinapur
C. Sarnath   D. Panipat

53. In which of the following styles of dance is the story/theme always taken from Mahabharata and Ramayana?
A. Mohiniattam   B. Odissi
C. Bharatanatyam   D. Kuchipudi

54. Arrange the months based on our National Calendar (Saka Era) in correct serial order—
(a) Chaitra   (b) Vaishakha
(c) Jyaishtha   (d) Aashada
A. (a) (b) (c) (d)   B. (b) (c) (d) (a)
C. (d) (a) (c) (b)   D. (c) (d) (a) (b)

55. Which one of the following is a combat aircraft?
A. Tejas
B. Dhruv
C. Boeing C-17 Globemaster
D. Chetak

56. Which of the following cups/trophies is associated with football?
A. Davis Cup
B. Champions Trophy
C. Santosh Trophy
D. Deodhar Trophy

57. How do ants recognize ants from their group?
A. By colour   B. By face
C. By smell   D. By height

58. Which of the following is domesticated in poultry farms?
A. Goat   B. Sheep
C. Hen   D. Horses

59. The _____ cover the tongue and react to chemicals in food.
A. Taste Buds   B. Sphincters
C. Teeth   D. Skin

60. What does freezing do when preserving foods?
A. Keeps the food product hard
B. Keeps the flavours of the food fresh
C. Stops growth of micro-organisms
D. None of the above

61. Seeds of drumstick and maple are carried over long distances by wind because they possess:

A. winged seeds.
B. large and hairy seeds.
C. long and ridged fruits.
D. spiny seeds.

62. _____ is a traditional rainwater harvesting technique of Rajasthan.
A. Taanka   B. Khadin
C. Bavadi   D. Kuan

63. Which of the following will dissolve in water?
A. Soil   B. Chalk Powder
C. Sugar   D. Oil

64. Which of the following is a communicable disease?
A. Diabetes   B. Chicken pox
C. Alzheimers   D. Cancer

65. To climb the mountains, we have to
A. Bend forward   B. Bend backwards
C. Walk straight   D. Walk sideways

66. Name an astronomical observatory built in the 18th century by Rajput King Sawai Jai Singh of Rajasthan.
A. Red Fort   B. Qutub Minar
C. Jantar Mantar   D. Taj Mahal

67. _____ includes internal rocks, minerals, etc.
A. Atmosphere   B. Biosphere
C. Hemisphere   D. Geosphere

68. The remains of plants and animals that were buried millions of years ago are known as:
A. potential reserves   B. fossil fuels
C. biomass fuel   D. animate power

69. Rasgulla is a popular sweet of _____ .
A. West Bengal   B. Punjab
C. Kerala   D. Himachal Pradesh

70. Which of the following is a tribal community of India?
A. Pandits   B. Jaat
C. Bhil   D. Punjabi

71. Clouds are mostly made of:
A. snow   B. dust
C. water droplets   D. smog

72. For which of the following works has Vasdev Mohi been awarded the 29th Saraswati Samman?
A. Lost Children Archive
B. Chequebook
C. The Stranger Diaries
D. A Song for a New Day

73. Who was the first Indian to be the President of U.N. General Assembly?
A. Natwar Singh
B. V.K. Krishna Menon
C. Smt. Vijaya Lakshmi Pandit
D. Smt. Indira Gandhi

74. In which of the following parts of the human body are sweat glands absent?
A. Scalp   B. Armpits
C. Lips   D. Palms

75. What do we call the young one of a Kangaroo?
A. Foal   B. Colt
C. Joey   D. Cub

Section C : English Language

Directions (Qs. No. 76-78): *Read the following passage and answer the questions by choosing the most appropriate option:*

Zeus and Prometheus

From the very first, humans had trouble with the Greek Gods. Most Gods thought of humans as toys. But Gods made friends with the humans. One of those Gods was Prometheus. The first people created by the Gods lived happily together. They thought the Gods were wonderful. But their children were not as grateful or as content. The children argued among themselves, and sometimes even argued with the Gods. Zeus was very disappointed at mankind. He decided to punish mankind by depriving them of a very important tool — fire. Prometheus felt sorry for his human friends. Fire was important for many things such as heat and cooking. Prometheus stole a lightning bolt from Zeus and gave it to mankind. That's when man discovered fire.

Zeus was furious as Prometheus had defied Zeus. He ordered Prometheus be chained to a rock as punishment for stealing his lightning bolt, and for going behind his back to help the humans. To make Prometheus even more miserable, Zeus sent storms to beat angry waves against Prometheus, helplessly chained to his rock. Zeus made the sun shine really brightly now and then to burn his skin. It was Hercules who finally released the helpless God from his chains.

76. Which of the following statements is *not* true about Zeus and Prometheus?
    A. Most Greek Gods saw humans as a means of their entertainment.
    B. Prometheus was chained to a rock as he was a God.
    C. Zeus was an unforgiving God who did not like to be disobeyed.
    D. Hercules emerged as the saviour of Prometheus.

77. Why was Zeus angry and disappointed at humans?
    A. They kept asking him for fire.
    B. The humans misused his lightning bolt.
    C. The humans were quarrelsome and didn't respect the Gods.
    D. The humans were not intelligent enough to discover fire.

78. What is the meaning of the underlined word: 'Prometheus had defied Zeus'?
    A. Prometheus had worshipped Zeus all his life.
    B. Prometheus had defamed Zeus.
    C. Prometheus detested Zeus for his attitude.
    D. Prometheus had disregarded the authority of Zeus.

Directions (Qs. No. 79-81): *Fill in the blanks with the most appropriate option.*

79. The news is all _____ the internet.
    A. on
    C. over
    B. through
    D. near

80. We studied about _____ Roman Empire in school.
    A. a
    C. the
    B. an
    D. no article

81. There was no one else in the room _____ Collin.
    A. accept
    C. axcept
    B. except
    D. acept

Directions (Qs. No. 82 and 83): *Rearrange the following words/phrases to make meaningful sentences. Choose the correct sequence.*

82. the sun (A)/ you (B)/ of (C)/ must (D)/ stay out (E).
    A. ECADB
    C. BDECA
    B. ABCDE
    D. DECAB

83. I (A)/ immediately (B)/ salary (C)/ my (D)/ want (E).
    A. BAEDC
    C. DCAEB
    B. AEDCB
    D. EADCB

84. Do as directed:
    There are some diseases that are inherited. (Identify the kind of Noun)
    A. 'diseases' is a proper noun
    B. 'diseases' is an abstract noun
    C. 'diseases' is a collective noun
    D. 'diseases' is a common noun

85. After school you and _____ must discuss a few things. (Choose the correct pronoun)
    A. him
    C. I
    B. me
    D. we

86. It is quite warm, _____? (Use a Question Tag)
    A. is it
    C. isn't it
    B. wasn't it
    D. was it

87. Leave your bags at the gate. (Identify the type of sentence)
    A. Imperative
    C. Interrogative
    B. Declarative
    D. Exclamatory

88. Near the equator, the sun _____ greater quantities of water. (Choose the correct form of the verb)
    A. is evaporating
    C. has evaporated
    B. evaporates
    D. evaporate

89. Choose the correct spelling:
    A. appartment   B. aparttment
    C. apartment   D. apartmant

90. Today is the _____ day of my life.
    (Choose the correct adjective)
    A. more important   B. less important
    C. important   D. most important

91. Poets are known to fly in their thoughts.
    (Choose the word nearest in meaning to the underlined word)
    A. sore   B. sour
    C. soar   D. sure

92. Choose the most appropriate option:
    Which of the following options is the meaning of the word 'exhausted'?
    A. Very hot   B. Very polluted
    C. Very fresh   D. Very tired

93. A confectioner is a person who _____.
    A. sells tools   B. sells confetti
    C. sells sweets   D. sells clothes

94. The captain _____ along with the players.
    A. was present
    B. was presenting
    C. have been presenting
    D. has been presenting

95. Choose the word that means the opposite of MORTAL.
    A. Unmortal   B. Immortal
    C. Inmortal   D. Dismortal

96. A _____ of thieves was caught by the Police.
    A. swarm   B. pack
    C. team   D. batch

97. It has become his habit to _____ do his homework and then copy it from others.
    A. always   B. often
    C. frequently   D. never

98. There were several _____ at the conference.
    A. women   B. woman
    C. wemens   D. womans

99. 'To beat around the bush' means:
    A. to turn violent against a stranger.
    B. to avoid saying something because it is uncomfortable.
    C. to come to the main point of the conversation.
    D. to start a fire in the forest.

100. My father is a bookworm, he _____ books to films and sports.
    A. is prefer   B. prefer
    C. prefers   D. are prefer

Section D : Intelligence

101. What comes next in the given series?
    A, C, F, H, K, M, ...
    A. N   B. Y
    C. P   D. M

102. Rahul started walking straight towards East. He walks a certain distance and then turns towards his right and walks again. In which direction is he heading now?
    A. North   B. East
    C. South   D. West

103. From the given options, choose the odd one out.
    A. Bangladesh : Taka
    B. Brazil : Real

C. Cyprus : Dollar
D. Iran : Rial

104. Tanya is older than Eric.
    Cliff is older than Tanya.
    Eric is older than Cliff.
    If the first two statements are true, the third statement is:
    A. True   B. False
    C. Uncertain   D. None of these

105. What will come at the place of the question mark?
    10, 100, 200, 310,?
    A. 420   B. 410
    C. 430   D. 400

106. A is B's sister. C is B's mother. D is C's father. E is D's mother. Then how is A related to D?

A. Grandfather B. Grandmother
C. Daughter D. Grand-daughter

107. In a certain code language, COMPUTER is written as RFUVQNPC. How will MEDICINE be written in that code language?

A. MFEDJJOE B. EOJDEJFM
C. MFEJDJOE D. EOJDJEFM

108. If South-East becomes North, North-East becomes West and so on, what will West become?

A. North-East B. North-West
C. South-East D. South-West

109. In a class of 45 students, Amir's rank from the top is 16th. Ashok is 6 ranks below Amir. What is Ashok's rank from the bottom?

A. 23rd B. 32nd
C. 24th D. 30th

110. Which one set of letters when sequentially placed at the gaps in the given letter series shall complete it?

_ ab _ b _ aba _ _ abab.

A. abbaa B. bbaab
C. abaab D. aaaba

111. Look at this series : 2, 1, (1/2), (1/4), ... What number should come next?

A. 1/3 B. 1/8
C. 2/8 D. 1/16

112. Choose the correct alternative that has the same relation.

SCD, TEF, UGH, _____, WKL

A. CMN B. UJI
C. VIJ D. IJT

113. If 'WAY' is coded as 679, 'MAY' is coded as 579, then 'YAW' will be coded as:

A. 976 B. 769
C. 679 D. 579

114. If '+' means "Minus", '–' means "Multiply", 'x' means "Add", then what is the value of 10 × 5 + 3 – 2?

A. 24 B. 52
C. 9 D. 10

115. mend : sewing : : edit : _____

A. darn B. repair
C. manuscript D. makeshift

116. Fill in the blank.

rein : horse : : control panel : _____

A. pilot B. bit
C. plane D. rider

117. Choose the word which is least like the words in the group.

A. MS Paint B. Facebook
C. WhatsApp D. Twitter

118. Choose the word that is a necessary part of the underlined word.

Guitar

A. Band B. Teacher
C. Songs D. Strings

119.

Complete the second pair by selecting the appropriate alternative.

120. A man walks 6 km south, turns left and walks 4 km, again turns left and walks 5 km. Which direction is he facing now?

A. South B. North
C. East D. West

121. Which letter replaces the question mark?

A. N B. O
C. P D. M

122. The priest told the devotee, "The bell rings at regular intervals of 45 minutes. The last bell rang 5 minutes ago. The next bell is due to be rung at 7:45 am." At what time did the priest give this information to the devotee?

A. 6:55 am   B. 7:00 am
C. 7:05 am   D. 7:40 am

123. How many triangles are there in the figure given below?

A. 4   B. 12
C. 16   D. 10

124. In a code, 'BOMBAY' is coded as 'CNNABX', then what will be the code of 'DELHI'?

A. EDMJG
B. GMDEJ
C. DEGMJ
D. EDMGJ

125. Fill in the blank.
segregate : unify : : repair : _____

A. approach
B. push
C. damage
D. outwit

ANSWERS

1	2	3	4	5	6	7	8	9	10
C	B	C	A	A	C	A	D	B	B
11	12	13	14	15	16	17	18	19	20
B	B	A	C	C	C	C	D	B	C
21	22	23	24	25	26	27	28	29	30
B	A	D	B	D	A	C	C	B	C
31	32	33	34	35	36	37	38	39	40
B	C	B	C	D	A	B	C	B	D
41	42	43	44	45	46	47	48	49	50
D	D	C	A	A	C	A	A	B	B
51	52	53	54	55	56	57	58	59	60
B	C	C	A	A	C	C	C	A	C
61	62	63	64	65	66	67	68	69	70
A	A	C	B	A	C	D	B	A	C
71	72	73	74	75	76	77	78	79	80
C	B	C	C	C	B	C	D	C	C
81	82	83	84	85	86	87	88	89	90
B	C	B	D	C	C	A	B	C	D
91	92	93	94	95	96	97	98	99	100
C	D	C	A	B	B	D	A	B	C
101	102	103	104	105	106	107	108	109	110
C	C	C	B	C	D	D	C	C	D
111	112	113	114	115	116	117	118	119	120
B	C	A	C	C	C	A	D	B	B
121	122	123	124	125					
D	C	B	D	C					

EXPLANATORY ANSWERS

3. The fraction represented by length OP

$$= \frac{OP}{OY}$$

$$= \frac{OU + US + SV + VR + RX + XW + WT + TP}{OU + US + SV + VR + RX + XW + WT + TP + PQ + QY}$$

$$= \frac{8}{10} = \frac{4}{5}.$$

4. $\frac{5}{7} = 0.7$

∵ 0.7 lies between 0 and 1.

5. Here, LCM of 5, 3, 6 and 2 = 30

A. $\frac{4}{5} \times 30 = 24$

B. $\frac{5}{3} \times 30 = 50$

C. $\frac{5}{6} \times 30 = 25$

D. $\frac{5}{2} \times 30 = 75$

Hence, the smallest fraction = 4/5.

6. Given that, HCF = 6, LCM = 864

One number = 96

∵ Multiplication of two numbers

$$= HCF \times LCM$$

∴ $96 \times x = 6 \times 864$

⇒ $x = \frac{6 \times 864}{96} = \frac{864}{16} = 54.$

8. The required smallest number
   = LCM of 9, 12 and 15 = 180.

9. Selling price of per packet shoap powder

$$= ₹ 15$$

S.P. of 1 dozen packet

$$= 12 \times 15 = ₹ 180$$

S.P. of 8 dozen packets

$$= 8 \times 180 = ₹ 1440$$

and cost price of 8 dozen packets

$$= 8 \times 144$$

$$= ₹ 1152$$

Profit = S.P. – C.P.

$$= 1440 - 1152 = 288$$

∴ Profit per cent $= \dfrac{\text{Profit} \times 100}{\text{C.P.}}$

$$= \frac{288 \times 100}{1152} = \frac{28800}{1152}$$

$$= 25\%.$$

10. From checking options,

$$37 = 18 \times 2 + 1$$
$$56 = 18 \times 3 + 2$$
$$93 = 18 \times 5 + 3$$

According to the question,

The greatest number = 18.

11. Let the required number of men = x

∵ More men, less day → Indirect proportional

Men   Day

$$10 : x :: 5 : 4$$

⇒ $x \times 5 = 10 \times 4$

⇒ $x = \dfrac{10 \times 4}{5}$

$$= 2 \times 4 = 8$$

⇒ $x = 8$ men.

12. ∵   15 cows = 21 goats

∴   1 cow = $\dfrac{21}{15}$ goats

∴   35 cows = $35 \times \dfrac{21}{15}$ goats

$$= \frac{7 \times 21}{3}$$

$$= 7 \times 7 = 49 \text{ goats}$$

Hence, 49 goats eat as much as 35 cows.

13. More cars, more earn → direct proportion

cars   earning

$9 : 27 : : 36,000 : x$

$\Rightarrow \quad\quad 9 \times x = 27 \times 36000$

$\Rightarrow \quad\quad x = \dfrac{27 \times 36000}{9}$

$\quad\quad\quad\quad = 3 \times 36000 = ₹\ 108,000.$

14. Given, $x : y = 3 : 5$

$\Rightarrow \quad\quad \dfrac{x}{y} = \dfrac{3}{5}$

$\therefore \quad \dfrac{3x+4y}{8x+5y} = \dfrac{\dfrac{3x+4y}{y}}{\dfrac{8x+5y}{y}} = \dfrac{3\dfrac{x}{y}+4}{8\dfrac{x}{y}+5}$

$\quad\quad\quad = \dfrac{3 \times \dfrac{3}{5}+4}{8 \times \dfrac{3}{5}+5} = \dfrac{\dfrac{9}{5}+4}{\dfrac{24}{5}+5}$

$\quad\quad\quad = \dfrac{\dfrac{9+20}{5}}{\dfrac{24+25}{5}}$

$\quad\quad\quad = \dfrac{29}{49}$

Hence, $(3x + 4y) : (8x + 5y) = 29 : 49.$

15. The given that,

3, 18, m, 42 are in proportion

$\therefore\ 3 : 18 : : m : 42$

$\Rightarrow \quad\quad 3 \times 42 = 18 \times m$

$\Rightarrow \quad\quad m = \dfrac{3 \times 42}{18} = 7$

$\Rightarrow \quad\quad m = 7.$

16. The number of selected cadets = 900

and the number of non-selected cadets

$\quad\quad\quad\quad = 1200 - 900 = 300$

$\therefore\ $ Required ratio $= \dfrac{900}{300} = \dfrac{9}{3} = \dfrac{3}{1}$

$\quad\quad\quad\quad = 3 : 1.$

17. $\because$ Selling price = ₹ 450, loss = 10%

$\therefore$ Cost price $= 450 \times \dfrac{100}{100-10}$

$\quad\quad\quad = 450 \times \dfrac{100}{90} = 450 \times \dfrac{10}{9}$

$\quad\quad\quad = 50 \times 10 = ₹\ 500$

The selling price to gain 10%

$\quad\quad\quad = 500 \times \dfrac{100+10}{100}$

$\quad\quad\quad = 500 \times \dfrac{110}{100}$

$\quad\quad\quad = 500 \times \dfrac{11}{10} = 550$

Hence, the required selling price = ₹ 550.

18. The cost price of one speaker

$\quad\quad\quad = 7500 \times \dfrac{100}{100+20}$

$\quad\quad\quad = 7500 \times \dfrac{100}{120}$

$\quad\quad\quad = 7500 \times \dfrac{5}{6}$

$\quad\quad\quad = 1250 \times 5 = ₹\ 6250$

and, the cost price of another speaker

$\quad\quad\quad = 8100 \times \dfrac{100}{100-10}$

$\quad\quad\quad = 8100 \times \dfrac{100}{90}$

$\quad\quad\quad = 8100 \times \dfrac{10}{9}$

$\quad\quad\quad = 900 \times 10 = ₹\ 9000$

$\therefore\ $ Total cost price = 6250 + 9000

$\quad\quad\quad = ₹\ 15250$

and total selling price

$\quad\quad\quad = 7500 + 8100$

$\quad\quad\quad = ₹\ 15600$

Hence,   Profit = S.P. – C.P.

$\quad\quad\quad = 15600 - 15250 = ₹\ 350.$

19. $(8 + 4 - 2) \times (17 - 12) \times 10 - 89$

$= (12 - 2) \times (5) \times 10 - 89$

$= 10 \times 5 \times 10 - 89$

$= 500 - 89$

$= 411.$

20. $0.05 + 1.5 \times 5 \div 10 \times 0.5$

$= 0.05 + 1.5 \times 5 \times \dfrac{1}{10} \times 0.5$

$= 0.05 + 1.5 \times \dfrac{1}{2} \times 0.5$

$= 0.05 + 0.75 \times 0.5$

$= 0.05 + 0.375 = 0.425.$

21. $7 + 5 - 2 \times (7 + 89) - 94 \div 2$
$\qquad\qquad + (33 \div 3 + 9 \times 2 - 7) \div 11$

$= 7 + 5 - 2 \times (96) - 94 \div 2$
$\qquad\qquad + \left(33 \times \dfrac{1}{3} + 9 \times 2 - 7\right) \div 11$

$= 7 + 5 - 2 \times 96 - 94 \div 2 + (11 + 18 - 7) \div 11$

$= 7 + 5 - 2 \times 96 - 94 \times \dfrac{1}{2} + (29 - 7) \div 11$

$= 7 + 5 - 192 - 47 + 22 \times \dfrac{1}{11}$

$= 7 + 5 - 192 - 47 + 2 \times 1$

$= 7 + 5 - 192 - 47 + 2$

$= 14 - 192 - 47$

$= 14 - 239 = -225.$

22. The total weight of 20 boys

$\qquad\qquad = 20 \times 160$

$\qquad\qquad = 3200 \text{ kg}$

and the total weight of the remaining 5 boys

$\qquad\qquad = 5 \times 50 = 250 \text{ kg}$

∴ The total weight of all the boys in the class

$\qquad\qquad = (3200 + 250) \text{ kg}$

$\qquad\qquad = 3450 \text{ kg}$

Hence, the average weight of all the boys (20 + 5) in the class

$\qquad\qquad = \dfrac{3450}{20 + 5} = \dfrac{3450}{25} = 138.$

23. The total marks obtained by 7 students in a group $= 7 \times 226 = 1582$

and the total marks obtained by 6 of them

$= 340 + 180 + 260 + 56 + 275 + 307$

$= 1418$

Hence, the marks obtained by the seventh student

$= 1582 - 1418 = 164.$

24. The total number of visitors in a month of 30 days starting with Sunday

$= 5 \times 510 + 25 \times 240$

$= 2550 + 6000 = 8550$

Hence, the average number of visitors

$= \dfrac{8550}{30} = 285.$

25. Let the average score of 16 matches $= x$

then, According to the question,

$\qquad\qquad 16x + 87 = 17(x + 3)$

$\Rightarrow \qquad\quad 16x + 87 = 17x + 51$

$\Rightarrow \qquad\quad 17x - 16x = 87 - 51$

$\Rightarrow \qquad\qquad\qquad x = 36$

Hence, his average score after the 17th match

$\qquad\qquad\qquad = x + 3$

$\qquad\qquad\qquad = 36 + 3 = 39.$

26. Average of 1, 3, 5, 7, 9, 11, 13 is

$= \dfrac{1 + 3 + 5 + 7 + 9 + 11 + 13}{7}$

$= \dfrac{49}{7} = 7.$

27. Given that,

$\qquad\qquad x\% \text{ of } y = 100$

$\Rightarrow \qquad\qquad \dfrac{x}{100} \times y = 100$

$\Rightarrow \qquad\qquad\qquad xy = 10000$

$\Rightarrow \qquad\qquad\qquad y = \dfrac{10000}{x} \qquad \qquad ...(i)$

and $y\%$ of $z = 200$

$\Rightarrow \qquad \dfrac{y}{100} \times z = 200$

$\Rightarrow \qquad yz = 20000$

$\Rightarrow \qquad y = \dfrac{20000}{z} \qquad \qquad ...(ii)$

From (i) and (ii), we get,

$$\dfrac{10000}{x} = \dfrac{20000}{z}$$

$\Rightarrow \qquad \dfrac{1}{x} = \dfrac{2}{z}$

$\Rightarrow \qquad z = 2x.$

28. Let the number = x

Then, one-fourth of one-third of two-fifth of $x = 15$

$\therefore \quad \dfrac{1}{4} \times \dfrac{1}{3} \times \dfrac{2}{5} \times x = 15$

$\Rightarrow \quad \dfrac{1}{2} \times \dfrac{1}{3} \times \dfrac{1}{5} \times x = 15$

$\Rightarrow \qquad x = 15 \times 30 = 450$

$\Rightarrow \qquad x = 450$

Hence, 40% of that number

$\qquad = 40\% \text{ of } x$

$\qquad = x \times \dfrac{40}{100}$

$\qquad = 450 \times \dfrac{40}{100}$

$\qquad = 45 \times 4$

$\qquad = 180.$

29. Given that,

15% of 40 − 25% of a number = 2

$\therefore \quad 40 \times \dfrac{15}{100} - x \times \dfrac{25}{100} = 2$

$\Rightarrow \quad 2 \times \dfrac{15}{5} - x \times \dfrac{1}{4} = 2$

$\Rightarrow \quad 2 \times 3 - 2 = \dfrac{x}{4}$

$\Rightarrow \qquad 6 - 2 = \dfrac{x}{4}$

$\Rightarrow \qquad 4 = \dfrac{x}{4} \Rightarrow x = 16$

Hence, the number = x = 16.

30. Given that, area = 700 sq. m

and breadth = 25 m

$\because$ Area of a rectangular playground

$\qquad = \text{length} \times \text{breadth}$

$\therefore \qquad 700 = \text{length} \times 25$

$\Rightarrow \qquad \text{Length} = \dfrac{700}{25} = 28 \text{ m}$

$\Rightarrow \qquad \text{Length} = 28 \times 100 \text{ cm}$

$\qquad \qquad = 2800 \text{ cm}.$

31. Given that, P = ₹ 1200

Simple interest = ₹ 432,

time = rate = r

$\because$ Simple interest $= \dfrac{\text{P} \times \text{Rate} \times \text{Time}}{100}$

$\therefore \qquad 432 = \dfrac{1200 \times r \times r}{100}$

$\Rightarrow \qquad 432 = 12 \times r^2$

$\Rightarrow \qquad r^2 = \dfrac{432}{12} = 36$

$\Rightarrow \qquad r^2 = 36 = 6^2$

$\Rightarrow \qquad r = 6\%.$

32. The Clock time is 7 : 15 pm

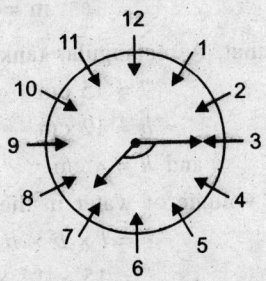

$\therefore$ The name of the angle formed = Obtuse angle.

33. The average maximum temperature of three months May, July and September

$$= \frac{21 + 29 + 24}{3} = \frac{74}{3}$$

$$= 24.66 \text{ °C}.$$

34. The temperature in the evening

$$= -10\text{°C} - 3\text{°C} = -13\text{°C}.$$

35. Given, A rectangular garden

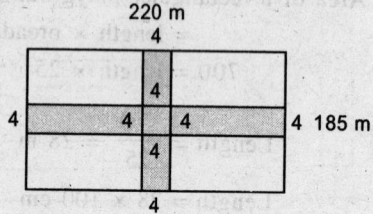

$l = 185$ m and $b = 220$ m

∵ Garden has two roads in its centre width of road = 4 m

Now, the area of the two roads

$$= 185 \times 4 + 220 \times 4 - 4 \times 4$$

$$= 740 + 880 - 16$$

$$= 1620 - 16 = 1604 \text{ sq. m.}$$

Hence, the cost of levelling the roads at ₹ 1.25 per sq. m.

$$= ₹ 1.25 \times 1604 = ₹ 2005.$$

36. ∵ 10 milimetre = 1 cm

10 cm = 1 decimeter

10 decimetre = 1 metre

∴ 1 decimetre $= \dfrac{1}{10}$ m

$$= 10^{-1} \text{ m} = 1 \times 10^{-1} \text{ m.}$$

40. Given that, A rectangular tank

$$l = 15 \text{ cm}$$

$$b = 12 \text{ cm}$$

and $h = 8$ cm

∴ The volume of water in the tank

$$= l \times b \times h$$

$$= 15 \times 12 \times 8 \text{ cm}^3$$

$$= 1440 \text{ cm}^3.$$

41. $\dfrac{5}{8} = 0.625,\quad \dfrac{7}{12} = 0.5833$

$$\dfrac{3}{4} = 0.75,\quad \dfrac{13}{16} = 0.8125$$

∵ $0.5833 < 0.625 < 0.75 < 0.8125$

∴ $\dfrac{7}{12} < \dfrac{5}{8} < \dfrac{3}{4} < \dfrac{13}{16}$.

42. $945.341 - 1042.792 + 875.435 + 31.025$

$$= 945.341 - 1042.792 + 906.46$$

$$= (945.341 + 906.46) - 1042.792$$

$$= 1851.801 - 1042.792 = 809.009.$$

43. Here, $t_1 = \dfrac{160}{64} = \dfrac{10}{4} = \dfrac{5}{2}$ hours

and $t_2 = \dfrac{160}{80} = 2$ hours

and distance = 320 km

∴ The average speed $= \dfrac{\text{Distance}}{t_1 + t_2}$

$$= \dfrac{320}{\dfrac{5}{2} + 2} = \dfrac{320}{\dfrac{9}{2}}$$

$$= \dfrac{320}{9} \times 2 = \dfrac{640}{9}$$

$$= 71.11 \text{ km/hr.}$$

45. Julia takes time to be ready for school

$$= \dfrac{1}{2} + \dfrac{1}{4}$$

$$= \dfrac{2 + 1}{4} = \dfrac{3}{4}.$$

49. 40°, 50°

∵ $50° - 40° = 10°$

and $40° + 50° = 90°$

∴ The two complementary angles are 40°, 50°.

50. The total weight of brinjal, ladyfinger and onion = 48.057 k.g.

and the total weight of brinjal and ladyfinger = 5.35 + 24.52 = 29.87

Hence, the weight of onion

= 48.057 − 29.87

= 18.187.

101.

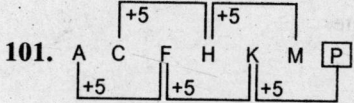

Here, the next term in the given series = P.

102.

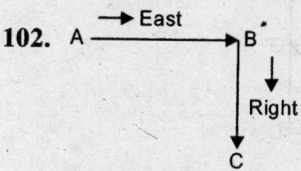

Here Starting point = A

Finally, in South direction is he heading now.

104. Tanya > Eric

Cliff > Tanya ⇒ Cliff > Tanya > Eric

Eric > Cliff

Given, the first two statements are true

∴ The third statement is false.

105.

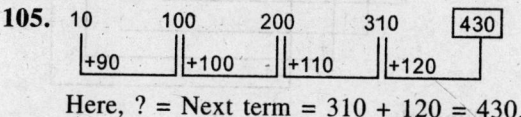

Here, ? = Next term = 310 + 120 = 430.

106.

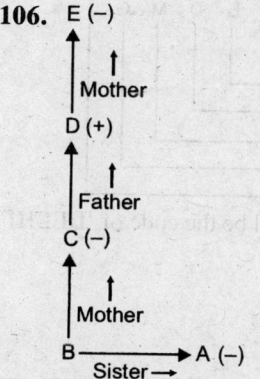

Here, A is Grand-daughter of D.

107.

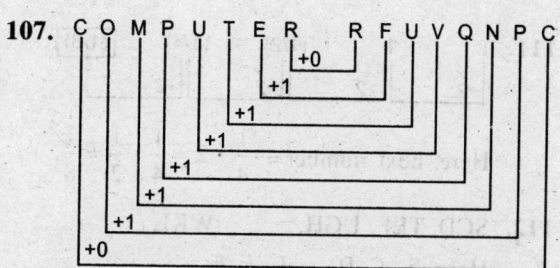

Similarly,

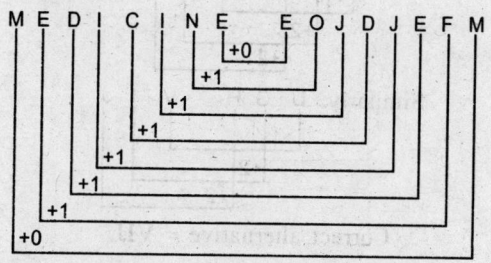

108. Here, given,

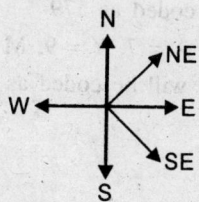

After changing,

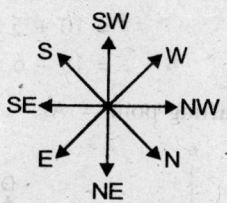

South-East becomes North

North-East becomes West

Hence, West becomes South-East.

109.

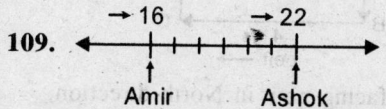

Here, Ashok's rank from the bottom

= 45 − (16 + 6) + 1

= 45 − 22 + 1

= 45 − 21

= 24th.

111.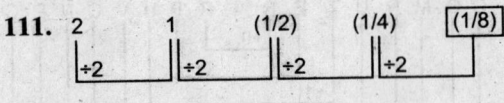

Here, next number $= \frac{1}{4} \div 2 = \frac{1}{4} \times \frac{1}{2} = \frac{1}{8}$.

112. SCD, TEF, UGH, _____ WKL

Here,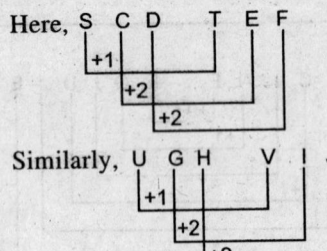

Similarly,

∴ Correct alternative = VIJ.

113. Given 'WAY' is coded as 679.

'MAY' is coded as 579

∴ W = 6, A = 7, Y = 9, M = 5

∴ 'YAW' will be coded as 976.

114. + = −,

− = ×,

× = +

$10 \times 5 + 3 - 2 = 10 + 5 - 3 \times 2$

$= 10 + 5 - 6$

$= 15 - 6 = 9.$

120. Here, Starting point = A

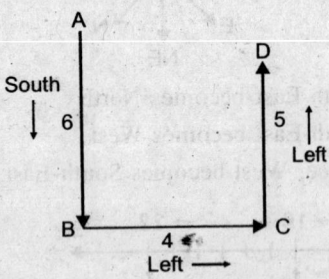

∴ He is facing now in North direction.

121. In each row,

E + H = 5 + 8 = 13 = M

N + A = 14 + 1 = 15 = O

I + D = 9 + 4 = 13 = M

Hence, ? = M.

122. Here, time to give information

= 7:45 AM − 45 minutes + 5 minutes

= 7:05 minutes

= 7:05 AM.

123.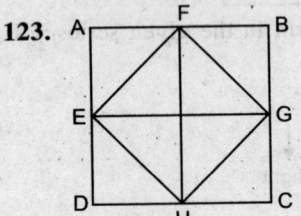

Here, Triangles:

ΔAEF, ΔEFO, ΔBFG, ΔFGO, ΔDEH, ΔEHO,
ΔCGH, ΔGHO, ΔFEG, ΔHEG, ΔEFH, ΔGFH

∴ The number of triangles = 12.

124. Here,

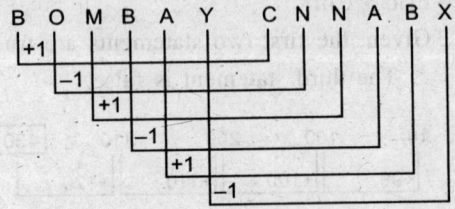

Similarly,

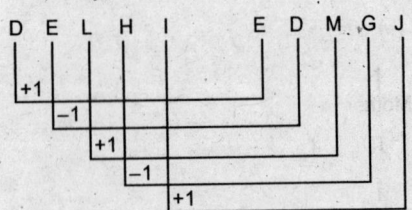

Hence, 'EDMGJ' will be the code of 'DELHI'.

Previous Paper (Solved)

All India Sainik School Entrance Exam, 2020*

(CLASS-VI)

PAPER-I : MATHEMATICS, GK AND LANGUAGE

Section-A : Mathematics

1. Find the difference between the greatest and the least number that can be written using the digits 6, 2, 7, 4, 3 each only once.
   A. 52965
   B. 53965
   C. 52956
   D. 52659

2. Estimate the product 5980 × 428 by rounding off each number to the nearest hundreds.
   A. 236000
   B. 240000
   C. 2400000
   D. 3000000

3. Three numbers are in the ratio of 3 : 4 : 5 and their LCM is 2400. Their HCF is:
   A. 120
   B. 60
   C. 80
   D. 40

4. Leela reads 25 pages of a book containing 100 pages. Lalita read $\frac{2}{5}$ of the same book. Who read less and by how much?
   A. Leela, 15 pages
   B. Lalita, 16 pages
   C. Leela, 20 pages
   D. Lalita, 20 pages

5. $\left(\dfrac{\sqrt{625}}{11} \times \dfrac{14}{\sqrt{25}} \times \dfrac{11}{\sqrt{196}} \right)$ is equal to
   A. 5
   B. 6
   C. 8
   D. 11

6. Naveen bought 3 m 20 cm cloth for his shirt and 2 m 5 cm cloth for his trousers. Find the total length of cloth bought by him.
   A. 5.7 m
   B. 5.25 m
   C. 4.25 m
   D. 5.00 m

7. The least common multiple of 3, 4 and 9 is:
   A. 36
   B. 12
   C. 27
   D. 45

8. An aeroplane covers a certain distance at a speed of 240 km/h in 5 hours. To cover the same distance in $1\frac{2}{3}$ hours, it must travel at a speed of?
   A. 300 km/h
   B. 360 km/h
   C. 600 km/h
   D. 720 km/h

9. 'A' can lay railway track between two given stations in 16 days and 'B' can do the same job in 12 days. With the help of 'C', they did the job in 4 days only. Then, 'C' alone can do the job in how many days?
   A. $9\frac{1}{5}$ days
   B. $9\frac{2}{5}$ days
   C. $9\frac{3}{5}$ days
   D. $9\frac{4}{5}$ days

10. In the figure, find the ratio of Number of triangles to the number of circles inside the rectangle and Number of squares to all the figures inside the rectangle.
    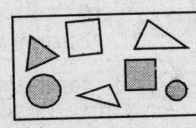
    A. $\frac{3}{2}, \frac{2}{7}$
    B. $\frac{3}{7}, \frac{2}{7}$
    C. $\frac{2}{7}, \frac{2}{7}$
    D. 3, 2

11. Ram, Rahul and Rohit shared a bag of marbles. The bag contained 272 marbles. How many marbles were left over after the friends shared them equally?
    A. 90
    B. 91
    C. 6
    D. 2

12. Cost of 4 dozens of bananas is ₹ 60. How many bananas can be purchased for ₹ 12.50?
    A. 10
    B. 15
    C. 12
    D. 18

13. The average weight of 16 boys in a class is 50.25 kg and that of the remaining 8 boys is 45.15 kg. Find the average weight of all the boys in the class.
    A. 47.55 kg
    B. 48 kg
    C. 48.55 kg
    D. 49.25 kg

14. Manju runs around a rectangular park of length 35 m and breadth 20 m. Meenu runs around a square park of side 30 m. Who covers less distance any by how much, if Meenu takes 4 rounds and Manju takes 3 rounds completely.
    A. Meenu, 150 m
    B. Manju, 120 m
    C. Manju, 150 m
    D. Meenu, 120 m

15. A photo frame is in the shape of quadrilateral with one diagonal longer than the other. Which of the following is the possible shape of the photo frame?
    A. Square
    B. Rectangle
    C. Rhombus
    D. None of these

16. The product of a non-zero whole number and its successor is always:
    A. Divisible by 3
    B. An odd number
    C. A prime number
    D. An even number

17. A sum fetched a total simple interest of ₹ 4016.25 at the rate of 9% in 5 years. What is the sum?
    A. ₹ 4462
    B. ₹ 8032
    C. ₹ 8900
    D. ₹ 8925

18. Find the angle measure between the hands of the clock when time shows 6 PM.
    A. 90°
    B. 45°
    C. 180°
    D. 270°

19. Find the volume of a cube of side 6 cm:
    A. 216 cm³
    B. 360 cm³
    C. 72 cm³
    D. 108 cm³

20. Write Roman numerical CDXXXIX in Arabic numeral.
    A. 439
    B. 449
    C. 529
    D. 539

21. The product of two numbers is 1296. If one number is 16 times the other, find the smaller number.
    A. 12
    B. 16
    C. 4
    D. 9

22. The measure of an angle is $\frac{3}{4}$ of 60°. What is the measure of its complementary angle?
    A. 30°
    B. 60°
    C. 45°
    D. 20°

23. Subtract the difference of 8.362 and 7.942 from the sum of 5.675 and 1.327.
    A. 6.582
    B. 4.348
    C. 3.982
    D. 4.384

24. Find the perimeter of the figure:

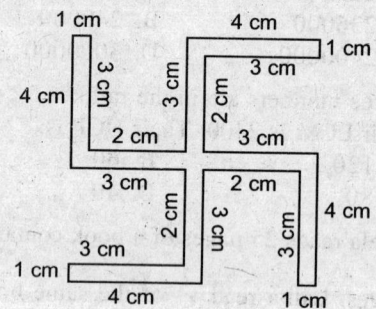

    A. 51 cm
    B. 52 cm
    C. 53 cm
    D. 54 cm

25. How much time will it take for an amount of ₹ 450 to yield ₹ 81 as interest at 4.5% per annum of simple interest?
    A. 3 years
    B. 4 years
    C. 6 years
    D. 5 years

26. In a triangle, if the second angle is 2 times the first angle and the third angle is 3 times the first angle, find the angles of the triangle.
    A. 30°, 60°, 90°
    B. 15°, 30°, 45°
    C. 45°, 45°, 90°
    D. 20°, 40°, 120°

27. The area of a circle is 616 cm². Find its diameter. $\left(\pi = \frac{22}{7}\right)$
    A. 28 cm
    B. 14 cm
    C. 56 cm
    D. 32 cm

28. Find the quotient when 53.016 is divided by 24.
  A. 2.29   B. 2.209
  C. 2.292   D. 2.029

29. A rectangular path of 60 m length and 3 m width is covered by square tiles of side 25 cm. Find the number of tiles used to make this path?
  A. 2250   B. 1440
  C. 2880   D. 1200

30. What is the value of A in 475 + 64% of 950 = 900 + A.
  A. 183   B. 233
  C. 1983   D. None of the above

31. What will be HCF of 216, 288 and 720?
  A. 12   B. 24
  C. 84   D. 72

32. Solve (106 × 106 − 94 × 94) = ?
  A. 2400   B. 2000
  C. 1904   D. 1906

33. If $\dfrac{2}{3}$ of 70% of 600 when subtracted from a number is 320, what is the number?
  A. 300   B. 600
  C. 720   D. 500

34. A mobile phone is sold for ₹ 1650 after purchasing it for ₹ 1500. What is the percentage of profit?
  A. 10   B. 15
  C. 20   D. 16

35. In the first test of mathematics a student gets 18 marks out of 25. In the second test of same weightage he got 22 marks. What percentage of marks did he get more in the second test?
  A. 4%   B. 8%
  C. 16%   D. None of the above

36. Average of 20 results is 18. If 3 is subtracted from each result, then what will be the new average?
  A. 21   B. 15
  C. 16   D. 17

37. Solve $\dfrac{\dfrac{7}{3} \times \dfrac{2}{3} \div \dfrac{3}{5}}{2 + 1\dfrac{2}{3}}$:
  A. $\dfrac{99}{70}$ B. $\dfrac{70}{99}$
  C. $\dfrac{33}{30}$ D. $\dfrac{70}{27}$

38. If 90.0675 is divided by 15, then quotient is:
  A. 6.0045   B. 6.0450
  C. 60.0450   D. 0.6045

39. How many seconds are there in 24 hours?
  A. 30   B. 60
  C. 3600   D. 86400

40. $\sqrt{1089 \div 121}$ value is:
  A. 3   B. 13
  C. 33   D. 53

41. If angles A, B and C in a triangle ABC are $3x$, $5x$ and $8x + 4$ respectively, then find all the three angles.
  A. 33, 55, 92   B. 70, 75, 35
  C. 90, 75, 15   D. 90, 95, 100

42. What are Prime factors of 37800?
  A. 2 × 2 × 3 × 3 × 5 × 5 × 7 × 7
  B. 2 × 2 × 2 × 3 × 3 × 3 × 5 × 5 × 7
  C. 8 × 27 × 25 × 7
  D. 2 × 4 × 25 × 27 × 7

43. (10% of 3.75 + 15% of 7.25) convert into decimal:
  A. 1.4625   B. 14.625
  C. 1.4652   D. 14.652

44. Which sequence correctly matches these angles with their measures.

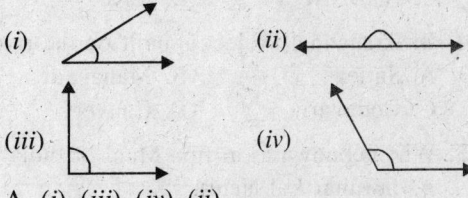

  A. (i), (iii), (iv), (ii)
  B. (i), (ii), (iii), (iv)
  C. (iv), (iii), (ii), (i)
  D. (i), (iv), (iii), (ii)

45. I am a prime number. If you subtract 2 from me, I become divisible by 7.
A. 29   B. 19
C. 31   D. 23

Directions (Qs. No. 46 to 50): *The following table has to be consulted.*

Name of the city	Temp. at 3 AM (°C)	Temp. at 3 PM (°C)
Chennai	21.1	29.9
Mumbai	19.0	35.1
Thiruvananthapuram	21.6	33.5
Kolkata	13.1	26.5
Bhopal	9.8	25.9
Srinagar	1.3	8.1
Guwahati	12.8	24.8
Jaipur	10.2	23.2

46. Which place had the highest temperature at 3 AM?
A. Chennai
B. Thiruvananthapuram
C. Srinagar
D. Jaipur

47. Which place is the coolest at 3 PM?
A. Kolkata   B. Srinagar
C. Mumbai   D. Bhopal

48. How much higher is the temperature in Mumbai from that of Srinagar at 3 PM?
A. 8.1   B. 35.1
C. 27   D. 29

49. How many degrees will the temperature at 3 AM need to rise for it to reach 40 degree celsius in Thiruvananthapuram.
A. 6.5   B. 18.4
C. 21.6   D. 33.5

50. How much lower is the temperature of Kolkata from that in Chennai at both times (3 AM and 3 PM)?
A. 8° and 3.3°   B. 3° and 8°
C. 8° and 8°   D. 3.3° and 3.3°

Section–B : General Knowledge

51. Black Soil is also known as?
A. Regur Soil   B. Red Soil
C. Laterite Soil   D. Mountain Soil

52. P.V. Sindhu is associated with which sports?
A. Badminton   B. Cricket
C. Football   D. Hockey

53. The Space Programme of Govt. of India is looked after by:
A. ISBT   B. NTRO
C. NABARD   D. ISRO

54. Bhakranangal Project is built on the river?
A. Sutlej   B. Mahanadi
C. Godavari   D. Cauvery

55. Who is known as a 'Iron Man' of India?
A. Jawahar Lal Nehru
B. Mahatma Gandhi
C. Sardar Vallabhbhai Patel
D. Subhash Chandra Bose

56. The longest river in South India is?
A. Mahanadi   B. Indus
C. Saraswati   D. Godavari

57. Which planet is known as a morning star as well as evening star?
A. Mars   B. Venus
C. Mercury   D. Earth

58. Which Article of constitution provides Indian Citizen 'Right to Equality'?
A. Article 12   B. Article 13
C. Article 17   D. Article 14

59. 'Narora' nuclear power plant is located in the state of?
A. Maharashtra   B. Tamil Nadu
C. Uttar Pradesh   D. West Bengal

60. Which of the following diseases spreads through contaminated food and water?
A. Malaria   B. Cholera
C. Dengue   D. Filaria

61. Which is biggest desert in the World?
    A. Kalhari Desert   B. Atakama Desert
    C. Sahara Desert   D. Gobi Desert

62. Manas national park is located in the state of?
    A. Assam   B. Arunachal Pradesh
    C. Himachal Pradesh   D. Andhra Pradesh

63. Which of these grows from the roots?
    A. Potato   B. Ginger
    C. Carrot   D. Sweet Potato

64. Sahyadris is also known as?
    A. Aravali   B. Western Ghats
    C. Himadri   D. Eastern Ghats

65. The gas filled in a weather balloons is:
    A. Neon   B. Helium
    C. Argon   D. Oxygen

66. Growing children need more of:
    A. Carbohydrates   B. Vitamins
    C. Proteins   D. Fats

67. Which gas is dissolved under pressure in soft drinks?
    A. Oxygen   B. Carbon dioxide
    C. Nitrogen   D. Hydrogen

68. Who is the lowest ranked Air Force Officer among these?
    A. Wing Commander   B. Group Captain
    C. Flying officer   D. Flight lieutenant

69. Which of the following is a national festival?
    A. Baisakhi   B. Republic day
    C. Pongal   D. Chhath puja

70. Dr. Amartya Sen won Nobel Prize in which field?
    A. Economics   B. Peace
    C. Chemistry   D. Literature

71. The imaginary line drawn half way between North Pole and South Pole is called:
    A. Tropic of Cancer   B. Equator
    C. Arctic Circle   D. Antarctic Circle

72. The largest island in the world is:
    A. Australia   B. New Zealand
    C. Greenland   D. Mozambique

73. The coldest place in world, lying in the south frigid zone is
    A. Greenland   B. Antarctica
    C. Australia   D. New Zealand

74. Who invented telephone in 1876?
    A. Alexander Graham Bell
    B. James Hickey
    C. Guglielmo Macron
    D. Logie Baird

75. 'Ghoomar' is a popular folk dance of which of the following states?
    A. Rajasthan   B. Madhya Pradesh
    C. Odisha   D. Uttar Pradesh

Section-C : Language

Directions (Qs. No. 76 to 80): *Read the following passage and answer the questions:*

Midas, the king, was a greedy person. He loved gold more than anything in the world. He had lots of wealth but he was never really a happy person.

One day God Bacchus came to Midas. Midas had once helped god Bacchus and in return Bacchus offered him a gift. "What shall I give you to make you happy," God asked him, Midas thought for a while and then said, "Please give me the power to turn everything I touch into gold." Bacchus laughed and said. "Your wish is granted. As soon as the Sun rises tomorrow, you will have the golden touch."

The next morning Midas woke up, and he had his golden touch. He touched his bed, the chairs, doors, windows and all became gold.

Suddenly, he felt very hungry. He sat at the table but as soon as the food touched his lips. It turned into gold. So did the water, it seemed he could no longer eat or drink. After some time, his daughter came to him, when he put his hand on her, she became a gold statue. In the end, Midas became very sad and prayed God Bacchus to take away the golden touch from him.

76. What kind of man was Midas?
    A. a greedy person   B. a great miser
    C. a brave man   D. wise man

77. Who came to Midas one day?
A. God Jesus
B. God Bacchus
C. God Zeus
D. God

78. Why did Bacchus offer him a gift?
A. because he had helped God once
B. because he had pleased Bacchus
C. because he had annoyed Bacchus
D. because he cared for Bacchus

79. What was Midas' wish?
A. To become rich
B. To turn anything into gold
C. To turn his daughter a golden doll
D. To become powerful

80. Who turned into gold statue when Midas touched?
A. daughter
B. son
C. uncle
D. aunt

Rearrange the following words/phrases to make meaningful sentences. Choose the correct sequence.

81. it (a)/ life is (b)/ what we (c)/ make (d)
A. abcd
B. cdab
C. dabc
D. bcda

82. gold (a)/ is not (b)/ glitters (c)/ all that (d)
A. abcd
B. cdba
C. dabc
D. dcba

83. playing (a)/ in the (b)/ park (c)/ children are (d)
A. abcd
B. bcda
C. dabc
D. cdab

Fill in the blanks with the appropriate option.

84. Either work hard _____ give up studies.
A. nor
B. or
C. and
D. but

85. He is afraid _____ the dog.
A. on
B. of
C. in
D. by

86. He _____ tea every morning.
A. drinks
B. is drinking
C. drank
D. drunk

87. The child has been missing _____ yesterday.
A. for
B. of
C. by
D. since

Do as directed.

88. John is my _____ brother. (Find out the correct adjective)
A. elder
B. bigger
C. old
D. young

89. French is _____ easy language. (Select the correct article)
A. a
B. an
C. the
D. none

90. Ashok _____ him yesterday. (Write the correct from of the verb)
A. meet
B. met
C. will meet
D. is meeting

Choose the most appropriate option.

91. Which word means nearly the same as 'sufficient'?
A. infinite
B. adequate
C. merry
D. surplus

92. Which word is the opposite of 'simple'.
A. complex
B. easy
C. obey
D. show

93. A list of books in a library.
A. monologue
B. dialogue
C. catalogue
D. diary

94. Find the feminine gender of 'horse'.
A. mare
B. doe
C. ewe
D. ram

95. Choose the word which means the opposite of 'RISE'.
A. fall
B. smooth
C. pride
D. rash

96. Choose the word which means same as 'GRIEF'.
A. cheerful
B. sorrow
C. happy
D. injury

97. One who does not believe in existence of God.
A. theist
B. pacifist
C. ascetic
D. atheist

98. The match has been postponed _____ it has been raining outside. (Supply Conjunction)
A. so
B. because
C. therefore
D. and

99. This is the boy _____ parents have died. (Supply correct Pronoun)
A. whose   B. who
C. whom   D. his

100. He doesn't help the poor, _____ ? (Use Question Tag)
A. did he   B. does he
C. doesn't   D. do he

PAPER–II : INTELLIGENCE TEST

101. If CATTLE is related to HERD then SHEEP is related to _____.
CATTLE : HERD :: SHEEP : ?
A. FLOCK   B. SWARM
C. SHOAL   D. MOB

102. Choose the alternative that has the same relationship to 09 as 07 has with 56.
07 : 56 :: 09 : ?
A. 54   B. 81
C. 72   D. 99

103. Choose the alternative that will continue the number series below:
5, 11, 17, 23, ?
A. 31   B. 29
C. 28   D. 35

104. If you fold the transparent paper along the dotted line in Figure 'X' which alternative figure from A, B, C and D would you get?

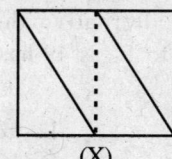
(X)

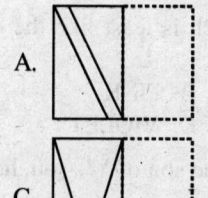
A.   B.
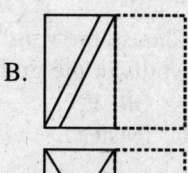

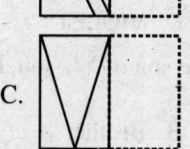
C.   D.
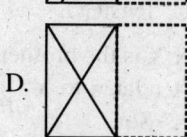

105. Choose the word which is least like the other words in the group.
A. BAKE   B. PEEL
C. FRY   D. ROAST

106. Which of the following diagrams indicate the best relation between India, Haryana and World?

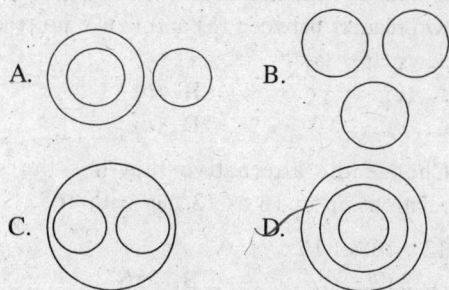

107. Choose the word which is least like the other words in the group.
A. VIRGO   B. PISCES
C. CANCER   D. ORION

108. If STATEMENT is coded as TNEMETATS then POLITICAL will be coded as:
A. LACITILOP   B. LCATILIOP
C. OPILITACL   D. LACITIPOL

109. Figure 'X' is embedded in any one of the four alternative, figures (a), (b), (c) and (d). Find the alternative which contains figure 'X' as its part.

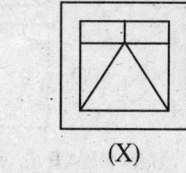
(X)

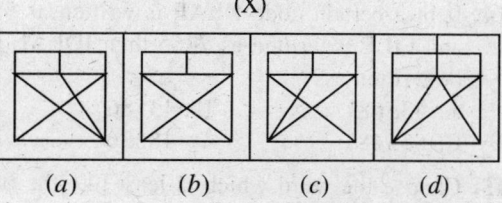
(a)   (b)   (c)   (d)
A. (a)   B. (b)
C. (c)   D. (d)

110. If 'A' means add, 'B' means subtract, 'C' means multiply and 'D' means divide, then what would be the answer of the equation?

15 D 5 C 2 A 3 =
A. 13   B. 11
C. 03   D. 09

111. Five men (a), (b), (c), (d) and (e) read a newspaper. The one who reads first gives it to (c). The one who reads last had taken from (a), (e) was not the first or last to read. There were two readers between (b) and (a). Who read the newspaper last?
A. (a)   B. (b)
C. (c)   D. (d)

112. Choose the alternative that has the same relationship to 16 as 12 has with 168.

12 : 168 :: 16 : ?
A. 232   B. 256
C. 224   D. 208

113. If you fold the transparent paper along the dotted line Figure 'X' which alternative figure would you get?

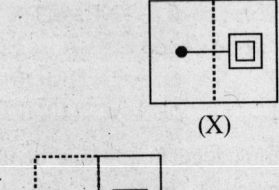

(X)

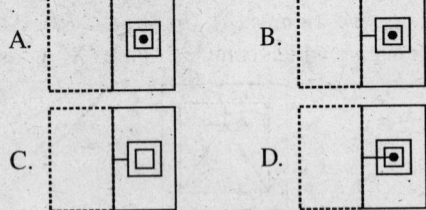

A.   B.

C.   D.

114. If in a certain code DEAF is written as 3587 and FILE is written as 7465 then IDEAL will be written as?
A. 43568   B. 43586
C. 63548   D. 48536

115. Choose the word which is least like the other words in the group.
A. PLASTIC   B. WOOL
C. PAPER   D. WOOD

116. If we arrange the given words in alphabetical order, which word would come at last place, choose the correct alternative?
A. ROBBER   B. RANDOM
C. RESTRICT   D. RESTAURANT

117. Choose the alternative that will continue the number series below:

11, 13, 17, 19, 23, 25, ?
A. 27   B. 29
C. 31   D. 33

118. Choose the correct alternative that has the same relation to BMJ as HSY is to EPV.

BMJ : ? :: EPV : HSY
A. DRM   B. YJG
C. EPM   D. EON

119. Which of the following diagrams indicates the best relation between Flower, Lotus and Rose?

A.   B.

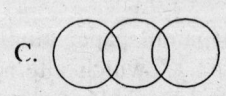
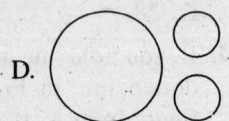
C.   D.

120. Choose the alternative that has the same relationship to 11 as 49 has with 07.

07 : 49 :: 11 : ?
A. 111   B. 90
C. 81   D. 121

121. Choose the word which is least like the other words in the group.
A. GREEN   B. PINK
C. INDIGO   D. VIOLET

122. If X is the brother of the son of Y's son, how is X related to Y?
A. Son   B. Brother
C. Grandson   D. Cousin

123. Area of rectangle is 48 m². If the length is 6 m then breadth = _____.
A. 13 m   B. 6 m
C. 10 m   D. 8 m

124. The priest told the devotee, "The temple bell is rung at regular intervals of 45 minutes. The last bell was rung 5 minutes ago. The next bell is due to be rung at 7 : 45 AM." At what time did the priest give this information to the devotee?

A. 7:00 AM   B. 7:05 AM
C. 6:55 AM   D. 7:40 AM

125. If in a certain code MBS is coded as ODU then BRL will be coded as?

A. DTN   B. DUN
C. CSM   D. CTN

ANSWERS

1	2	3	4	5	6	7	8	9	10
A	C	D	A	A	B	A	D	C	A
11	**12**	**13**	**14**	**15**	**16**	**17**	**18**	**19**	**20**
D	A	C	C	C	D	D	C	A	A
21	**22**	**23**	**24**	**25**	**26**	**27**	**28**	**29**	**30**
D	C	A	B	B	A	A	B	C	A
31	**32**	**33**	**34**	**35**	**36**	**37**	**38**	**39**	**40**
D	A	B	A	C	B	B	A	D	A
41	**42**	**43**	**44**	**45**	**46**	**47**	**48**	**49**	**50**
A	B	A	A	D	B	B	C	B	A
51	**52**	**53**	**54**	**55**	**56**	**57**	**58**	**59**	**60**
A	A	D	A	C	D	B	D	C	B
61	**62**	**63**	**64**	**65**	**66**	**67**	**68**	**69**	**70**
C	A	C	B	B	C	B	C	B	A
71	**72**	**73**	**74**	**75**	**76**	**77**	**78**	**79**	**80**
B	C	B	A	A	A	B	A	B	A
81	**82**	**83**	**84**	**85**	**86**	**87**	**88**	**89**	**90**
D	D	C	B	B	A	D	A	B	B
91	**92**	**93**	**94**	**95**	**96**	**97**	**98**	**99**	**100**
B	A	C	A	A	B	D	B	A	B
101	**102**	**103**	**104**	**105**	**106**	**107**	**108**	**109**	**110**
A	C	B	D	B	D	D	A	D	D
111	**112**	**113**	**114**	**115**	**116**	**117**	**118**	**119**	**120**
D	C	D	B	A	A	B	C	A	D
121	**122**	**123**	**124**	**125**					
B	C	D	B	A					

EXPLANATORY ANSWERS

1. Using the digits 6, 2, 7, 4, 3 each only once
Greatest number = 76432
Least number = 23467
∴ Difference = greatest number – least number
= 76432 – 23467
= 52965

2. 5980 × 428 = 2559440
In option (C) 2400000, the nearest hundreds.

3. Let three numbers are $3x$, $4x$, $5x$
Then LCM = $60x$ (LCM of $3x$, $4x$ and $5x$)
⇒ $2400 = 60x \Rightarrow x = 40$

∴ Three numbers are 3 × 40, 4 × 40, 5 × 40

∴   HCF = 40   [HCF = least common]

4. The number of pages of a book = 100

Lalita reads pages = $\dfrac{2}{5}$ of a book

$$= \dfrac{2}{5} \times 100 = 40$$

and Leela reads pages = 25

∴ Lalita reads pages – Leela reads pages
$$= 40 - 25 = 15$$

Here, Leela reads 15 pages less than Lalita.

5. $\dfrac{\sqrt{625}}{11} \times \dfrac{14}{\sqrt{25}} \times \dfrac{11}{\sqrt{196}}$

$$= \dfrac{25}{11} \times \dfrac{14}{5} \times \dfrac{11}{14}$$

$$\left[\sqrt{625} = 25, \sqrt{25} = 5, \sqrt{196} = 14 \right]$$

$$= \dfrac{25}{5} = 5$$

6. The total length of cloth = 3m 20 cm + 2 m 5 cm
$$= 5 \text{ m } 25 \text{ cm}$$
$$= 5.25 \text{ m}$$

$$25 \text{ cm} = \dfrac{25}{100} \text{ m} = 5.25 \text{ m}$$

7. $3 = 3 \times 1$

         $4 = 2 \times 2 = 2^2$

         $9 = 3 \times 3 = 3^2$

     LCM $= 2^2 \times 3^2$

           $= 4 \times 9 = 36.$

8. Speed of an aeroplane = 240 km/h

and   time = 5 hours

            [distance = speed × time]

∴ distance cover = 240 × 5 = 1200 km

Now, to cover the same distance in $1\dfrac{2}{3}$ hours

∴   Speed $= \dfrac{\text{Distance}}{\text{time}}$

$$= \dfrac{1200}{1\dfrac{2}{3}} = \dfrac{1200}{\dfrac{5}{3}}$$

$$= 1200 \times \dfrac{3}{5} = 24 \times 3 = 720 \text{ km/h}$$

∴   Speed = 720 km/h.

9. As, A can lay railway track in 16 days

So, A can lay railway track in 1 day $= \dfrac{1}{16}$

and B can lay railway track in 12 days

So, B can lay railway track in 1 day $= \dfrac{1}{12}$

Let C can lay railway track in x days

Then C can lay railway track in 1 day $= \dfrac{1}{x}$

∴ By question,

$$\dfrac{1}{16} + \dfrac{1}{12} + \dfrac{1}{x} = \dfrac{1}{4}$$

$$\Rightarrow \quad \dfrac{3+4}{48} + \dfrac{1}{x} = \dfrac{1}{4}$$

$$\Rightarrow \quad \dfrac{7}{48} + \dfrac{1}{x} = \dfrac{1}{4}$$

$$\Rightarrow \quad \dfrac{1}{x} = \dfrac{1}{4} - \dfrac{7}{48}$$

$$= \dfrac{12-7}{48} = \dfrac{5}{48}$$

$$\Rightarrow \quad \dfrac{1}{x} = \dfrac{5}{48}$$

$$\Rightarrow \quad x = \dfrac{48}{5} = 9\dfrac{3}{5} \text{ days}$$

Hence, (C) alone can do the job in $9\dfrac{3}{5}$ days.

10. The number of triangles inside the rectangle
$$= 3$$
and the number of circles inside the rectangle
$$= 2$$
∴ Ratio of the number of triangles and circles
$$= \dfrac{3}{2}$$
and the number of squares inside the rectangle
$$= 2$$
and, the number of all the figures inside the rectangle = 7

∴ Ratio of the number of squares and all figures = $\dfrac{2}{7}$

Hence, ratio is $\dfrac{3}{2}, \dfrac{2}{7}$

11. The number of Marbles in a bag = 272

∵ Ram, Rahul and Rohit shared then equally

∴
$$3 \,|\, \underline{272} \,|\, 90$$
$$\underline{-270}$$
$$2$$

∴ 272 = 3 × 90 + 2, Here, 272 – 30 × 90 = 2

∴ Marbles were left after share = 2.

12. ₹ 60 cost = 4 dozens of bananas

= 4 × 12 bananas

∵ ₹ 60 cost = 48 bananas

∴ ₹ 1 cost = $\dfrac{48}{60}$ bananas

∴ ₹ 12.50 cost = $\dfrac{48}{60} \times 1250$ bananas

$$= \dfrac{48}{6000} \times 12.50 = \dfrac{48}{600} \times 125$$

$$= \dfrac{4}{50} \times 125 = \dfrac{4}{2} \times 5$$

$$= 2 \times 5 = 10 \text{ bananas.}$$

Hence, 10 bananas can be purchased for ₹ 12.50.

13. As, the average weight of 16 boys = 50.25 kg

So, the total weight of 16 boys = 16 × 50.25 kg

and, the average weight of 8 boys = 45.15 kg

∴ The total weight of 8 boys = 8 × 45.15 kg

∴ The average weight of all the boys in the class

$$= \dfrac{\text{The total weight of all the boys}}{\text{The total number of all the boys}}$$

$$= \dfrac{16 \times 50.25 + 8 \times 45.15}{24}$$

$$= \dfrac{804.00 + 361.20}{24}$$

$$= \dfrac{1165.20}{24} = 48.55 \text{ kg.}$$

14. A rectangular park,

Length = 35 m

Breadth = 20 m

∴ Perimeter = 2(l + b)

= 2(35 + 20)

= 2 × 55 = 110 m

∴ Manju takes 3 rounds a rectangular park

∴ Manju covers distance = 3 × perimeter

= 3 × 110 m

= 330 m

And, A square park

Length of side = 30 m

∴ Perimeter = 4 × side = 4 × 30 = 120 m

Meenu takes 4 rounds a square park

∴ Meenu covers distance = 4 × perimeter

= 4 × 120 m = 480 m

Hence, Manju covers less distance by

= 480 – 330 m = 150 m.

15. A quadrilateral with one diagonal longer then the other.

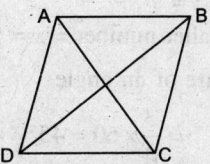

∴ Quadrilateral is a rhombus

Here, in figure

BD > AC, and all sides equal.

17. ∵ Simple interest = ₹ 4016.25

r = 9%, t = 5 years ∴ p = ?

∴ S.I. = $\dfrac{p \times t \times r}{100}$

⇒ 4016.25 = $\dfrac{p \times 5 \times 9}{100}$

∴ p = $\dfrac{4016.25 \times 100}{5 \times 9}$

∴ p = $\dfrac{401625}{5 \times 9} = \dfrac{80325}{9} = 8925$

Hence, p = sum = ₹ 8925.

18. The angle measure between the hands of the clock when time show 12 AM = 360°

and the angle measure between the hands in 12 hours = 360°

∴ 1 hour = $\dfrac{360°}{12} = 30°$

∴ 6 hours = 30° × 6 = 180°

∴ The angle measures between the hands when time shows 6 PM = 180°.

19. A side of cube = 6 cm
∴ The volume of a cube
$$= (\text{side})^3 = (6 \text{ cm})^3 = 216 \text{ cm}^3.$$

20. Roman numeral CDXXXIX
Arabic numeral 439.

21. Let the smaller number = x
Then, one number = 16 x
∴ $x \times 16x = 1296$
$\Rightarrow \qquad 16x^2 = 1296$
$\Rightarrow \qquad x^2 = \dfrac{1296}{16} = \dfrac{162}{2} = 81$
$\Rightarrow \qquad x^2 = 81$
$\Rightarrow \qquad x = \sqrt{81}$
$\Rightarrow \qquad x = 9$
Hence, smaller number = $x = 9$.

22. The measure of an angle
$$= \frac{3}{4} \times 60 = 45°$$
∴ Complementary of 45° = 90 – 45° = 45°.

23. (5.675 + 1.327) – (8.362 – 7.942)
$$= 7.002 - 0.42 = 6.582.$$

24. The perimeter of one part of figure

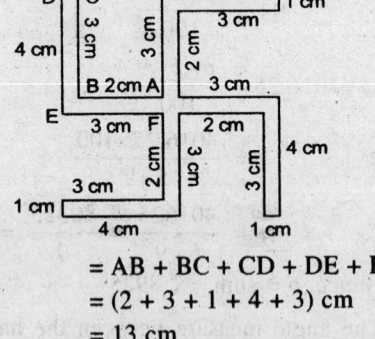

$$= AB + BC + CD + DE + EF$$
$$= (2 + 3 + 1 + 4 + 3) \text{ cm}$$
$$= 13 \text{ cm}$$
∴ The perimeter of the figure
$$= 4 \times 13 \text{ cm} = 52 \text{ cm}.$$

25. Here, p = ₹ 450, r = 4.5%,
Simple interest = ₹ 81
∴ $\qquad \text{time} = \dfrac{\text{S.I.} \times 100}{p \times r}$

$$= \frac{81 \times 100}{450 \times 4.5} = \frac{81 \times 1000}{450 \times 45}$$

$$= \frac{9 \times 100}{45 \times 5} = \frac{1 \times 20}{5} = 4 \text{ years.}$$

26. Let the first angle is $x°$ in a triangle
Then, the second angle = $2x$
and, the third angle = $3x$
As, sum of the angles in a triangle is 180°
So, $x° + 2x° + 3x° = 180°$
$\Rightarrow \qquad 6x° = 180°$
$\Rightarrow \qquad x° = \dfrac{180°}{6} = 30°$
$\Rightarrow \qquad x° = 30°$
∴ angles are $x = 30°, 2x = 60°, 3x = 90°$

27. The area of a circle = 616 cm²
∴ $\qquad \pi r^2 = 616 \text{ cm}^2$
$\Rightarrow \qquad \dfrac{22}{7} r^2 = 616 \text{ cm}^2$
$$r^2 = \frac{616}{\frac{22}{7}} = \frac{616}{22} \times 7 = 28 \times 7$$
$\Rightarrow \qquad r^2 = 28 \times 7 = 4 \times 7 \times 7$
$\Rightarrow \qquad r^2 = (2 \times 7)^2$
$\Rightarrow \qquad r = 2 \times 7 = 14 \text{ cm}$
∴ Diameter = $2r$ = 2 × 14 cm = 28 cm.

28. 53.016 is divide by 24
∴ $\dfrac{53.016}{24} = 2.209$
∴ quotient = 2.209

```
24 | 53.016 | 2.209
     -48
     ----
      50
     -48
     ----
      216
     -216
     ----
        ×
```

29. A rectangular path
length = 60 m = 60 × 100 = 6000 cm
and width = 3 m = 3 × 100 = 300 cm
∴ Area of path = $l \times b$ = 6000 × 300 cm²
$$= 18,00,000 \text{ cm}^2$$
and, Side of square tile = 25 cm
Area of tiles = (side)²
$$= (25)^2 = 625 \text{ cm}^2$$
The number of tiles used to make this path

$$= \frac{\text{area of park}}{\text{area of tile}}$$

$$= \frac{18,00,000}{625} = \frac{72,000}{25}$$

$$= \frac{720 \times 100}{25} = 720 \times 4 = 2880$$

Hence, the number of tiles = 2880.

30. $475 + 64\%$ of $950 = 900 + A$

$\Rightarrow 475 + 950 \times \dfrac{64}{100} = 900 + A$

$\Rightarrow 475 + 950 \times \dfrac{16}{25} = 900 + A$

$\Rightarrow 475 + 38 \times 16 = 900 + A$

$\Rightarrow 475 + 608 = 900 + A$

$\Rightarrow \quad 1083 = 900 + A$

$\Rightarrow \qquad A = 1083 - 900$

$\Rightarrow \qquad A = 183$

31. HCF of 216, 288 and 720

$$\begin{array}{r|r|l} 216 & 288 & 1 \\ & -216 & \\ \hline & 72 & 720 \,|\, 10 \\ & & -720 \\ \hline & & \times \end{array}$$

HCF = 72

32. $106 \times 106 - 94 \times 94 = 11236 - 8836 = 2400$

33. Let the number $= x$

Then, $x - \dfrac{2}{3}$ of 70% of $600 = 320$

$\Rightarrow x - \dfrac{2}{3} \times \dfrac{70}{100} \times 600 = 320$

$\Rightarrow x - \dfrac{2}{3} \times 70 \times 6 = 320$

$\Rightarrow x - 2 \times 70 \times 2 = 320$

$\Rightarrow x - 280 = 320$

$\Rightarrow \qquad x = 280 + 320$

$\Rightarrow \qquad x = 600$

Hence, the number of $x = 600$

34. Here, Selling price of a mobile phone = ₹ 1650
and Cost price = ₹ 1500

$\therefore \quad$ Profit = S.P. – C.P.

$\qquad = 1650 - 1500 = ₹ 150$

Now, the percentage of profit $= \dfrac{\text{Profit} \times 100}{\text{Cost price}}$

$$= \frac{150 \times 100}{1500} = \frac{150}{15} = 10\%$$

35. In the first test, 18 marks out of 25

$\therefore$ Percentage $= \dfrac{18}{25} \times 100 = 72\%$

And, in the second test, he got 22 marks of 25

$\therefore$ Percentage $= \dfrac{22}{25} \times 100 = 88\%$

$\therefore$ In second test he get more mark
$\qquad = 88 - 72 = 16\%$

36. Average of 20 results is 18
$\therefore$ All results $= 20 \times 18 = 360$
If 3 is subtracted from each result
Then, new results $= 360 - 60 = 300$

$\therefore$ The new average $= \dfrac{300}{20} = 15$

37. $\dfrac{\dfrac{7}{3} \times \dfrac{2}{3} \div \dfrac{3}{5}}{2 + 1\dfrac{2}{3}} = \dfrac{\dfrac{7}{3} \times \dfrac{2}{3} \times \dfrac{5}{3}}{2 + \dfrac{5}{3}}$

$$= \frac{\dfrac{70}{27}}{\dfrac{6+5}{3}}$$

$$= \frac{70}{27} \times \frac{3}{11} = \frac{70}{99}$$

38. If 90.0675 is divided by 15

Then, $\dfrac{90.0675}{15} = 6.0045$,

$$\begin{array}{r|l|l} 15 & 90.0675 & 6.0045 \\ & -90 & \\ \hline & 067 & \\ & -60 & \\ \hline & 75 & \\ & -75 & \\ \hline & \times & \end{array}$$

Hence, quotient = 6.0045

39. 24 hours = 24 × 60 min.
$\qquad = 24 \times 60 \times 60$ sec.
$\qquad = 24 \times 3600$ sec.
$\qquad = 86400$ sec.

40. $\sqrt{1089 \div 21} = \sqrt{\dfrac{1089}{121}} = \dfrac{33}{11} = 3$

41. The sum of all angles of a triangle is 180°

$\angle A + \angle B + \angle C = 180°$

$\Rightarrow 3x + 5x + 8x + 4 = 180°$

$\Rightarrow 16x + 4° = 180°$

$\Rightarrow 16x = 180° - 4° = 176°$

$\Rightarrow x = \dfrac{176°}{16} = 11°$

Hence, all the three angles are

$\angle A = 3x = 33°$,

$\angle B = 5x = 55°$,

$\angle C = 8x + 4 = 92°$

i.e., 33°, 55°, 92°

42.

2	37800
2	18900
2	9450
3	4725
3	1575
3	525
5	175
5	35
	7

Therefore, prime factor of 37800

$= 2 \times 2 \times 2 \times 3 \times 3 \times 3 \times 5 \times 5 \times 7$

43. 10% of 3.75 + 15% of 7.25

$= \dfrac{10}{100} \times 3.75 + \dfrac{15}{100} \times 7.25$

$= \dfrac{1}{100} \times 3.75 + 0.15 \times 7.25$

$= 0.1 \times 3.75 \times + 1.0875$

$= 0.375 + 1.0875$

$= 1.4625$

44. *(i)* 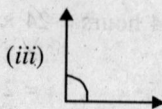   *(iii)*

(iv)    *(ii)*

45. $23 - 2 = 21$, $\dfrac{21}{7} = 3$

46. 21.6°C = Thiruvananthapuram had the highest temperature at 3AM.

47. Srinagar is the coolest at 3 PM = 8.1°C.

48. The temperature in Mumbai from that of Srinagar at 3 PM = 35.1° – 8.1°C = 27°C.

49. The temperature at 3 PM need to rise 40°C in Thiruvananthapuram = 45°C – 21.6° = 18.4°.

50. At 3 AM → Chennai – Kolkata

$= 21.1°C - 13.1°C = 8°C$

At 3 PM → Chennai – Kolkata

$= 29.9°C - 26.6°C = 3.3°C$

101. CATTLE : HERO :: SHEEP : ?

As, group of CATTLE is related to HERO

So, group of SHEEP is related to FLOCK.

102. 07 : 56 :: 09 : ?

Here, $07 \times 8 = 56$

Similarly, $09 \times 8 = 72$

103. 5   11   17   23   ?

+6   +6   +6   +6

$5 + 6 = 11$,

$11 + 6 = 17$,

$17 + 6 = 23$,

$23 + 6 = 29$

106. Haryana is an unit of India and India is an unit of world.

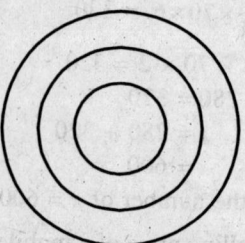

So, diagram idicate the best relation.

107. All expect Orion are Zodiac signs while orion is a constellaiton.

108.

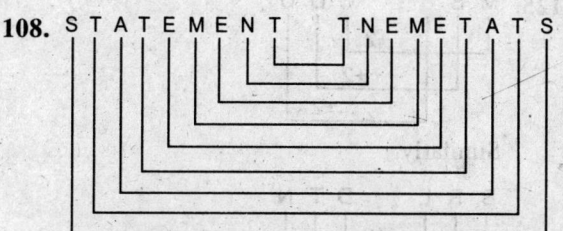

Similarly,

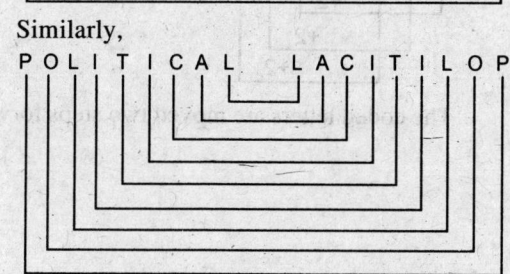

The letters of the word are written backward.

110. 15 D 5 C 2 A 3 = 15 ÷ 5 × 2 + 3
$$= 3 \times 2 + 3 = 6 + 3 = 9$$

111. Five men (*a*), (*b*) (*c*), (*d*) and (*e*) read a newspaper.

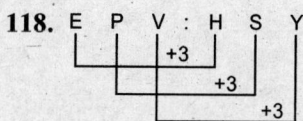

(*d*) reads the newspaper last.

112. 12 : 168 :: 16 : ?
As, 12 × 14 = 168
So, 16 × 14 = 224

114. Code DEAF is written as 3587
and FILE is written as 7465
∴ IDEAL will be written as 43586
As, I = 4, D = 3, E = 5, A = 8, L = 6

116. We arrange the given words in alphabetical order.
RANDOM ← RESTAURANT ← RESTRICT
← ROBBER

117.

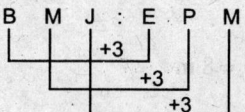

? = 25 + 4 = 29

118.

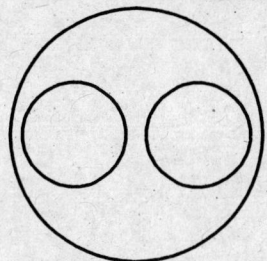

Similarly,

BMJ : EPM with +3, +3, +3

The word is coded by moving the letters two steps forward.

119. As, Lotus and Rose are flower
So, the diagram indicate the best relation between Flower, Lotus and Rose

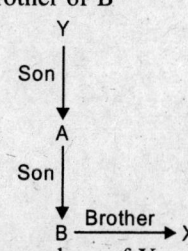

120. 07 : 49 :: 11 : ?
Here, $(07)^2 = 49$
Similarly, $(11)^2 = 121$

121. PINK colours is not in 7 colour

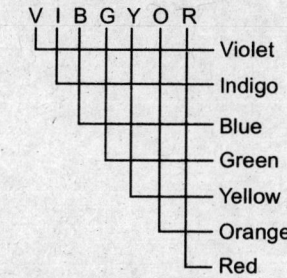

VIBGYOR — Violet, Indigo, Blue, Green, Yellow, Orange, Red

122. A is the son of Y,
B is the son of Y's son,
B is the grandson of Y
X is the brother of B

Y → Son → A → Son → B → Brother → X

Here, X is grandson of Y

123. Area of rectangle = 48 m², l = 6 m

$\Rightarrow \qquad l \times b = 48 \text{ m}^2$

$\Rightarrow \qquad 6 \times b = 48$

$\Rightarrow \qquad b = \dfrac{48}{6} = 8 \text{ m}$

$\Rightarrow \qquad b = 8 \text{ m}$

$\therefore$ Breadth = 8 m

124. Regular intervals = 45 minutes

The next bell be rung at 7 : 45 AM

The last bell was rung 5 minutes ago

$\therefore$ Present time = 7 : 05 AM

125.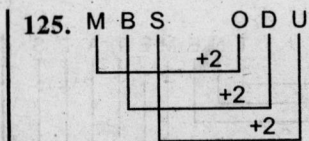

Similarly,

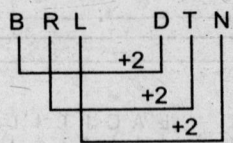

The coded letters are moved two steps forward.

All India Sainik School Entrance Exam, 2019*
(CLASS-VI)

PAPER-I : MATHEMATICS, GK AND LANGUAGE

Section-A : Mathematics

1. A student multiplied 7236 by 65 instead of multiplying by 56. By how much was his answer greater than the correct answer?
   A. 87555
   B. 65124
   C. 72360
   D. 65000

2. Simplify: $1 \div \left\{ \dfrac{1}{2} + \dfrac{1}{3} + \dfrac{1}{6} \div \left(\dfrac{3}{4} - \dfrac{1}{3} \right) \right\}$

   A. $\dfrac{30}{37}$
   B. $\dfrac{37}{30}$
   C. $\dfrac{15}{37}$
   D. $\dfrac{15}{30}$

3. Find the perimeter of the following figure
   A. 15 cm
   B. 15 cm^2
   C. 16 cm
   D. 25 cm^2

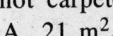

4. A floor is 5 m long and 4 m wide. A square carpet of side 3 m is laid on the floor. Find the area of the floor that is not carpeted.
   A. 21 m^2
   B. 29 m^2
   C. 11 m^2
   D. 21 cm^2

5. Find out the smallest number which is divisible by 6, 12, 18
   A. 360
   B. 180
   C. 120
   D. 60

6. Which of the following measures of angles given can be those of a isosceles triangle?
   A. 90, 45
   B. 60, 30
   C. 120, 40
   D. 90, 50

7. The length of a rectangle is 5 cm more than its breadth. If the perimeter of the rectangle is 50 cm than what is the area?
   A. 150 cm^2
   B. 250 cm^2
   C. 900 cm^2
   D. 800 cm^2

8. 12 persons can finish a piece of work in 15 days. In how many days will the same work be completed by 20 persons?
   A. 15 days
   B. 9 days
   C. 30 days
   D. 20 days

9. The LCM of two prime numbers is
   A. difference
   B. product
   C. sum
   D. none of the above

10. In a School of 1000 students, 330 come by bus, 400 come walking and the remaining are dropped by parents. What is the percentage of students that do not ride the bus to school?
    A. 67%
    B. 27%
    C. 50%
    D. 33%

11. A train from Station A to Station B covers a distance of 616 km at a uniform speed of 112 km/hr. It Halts at Station. B for 1 hour before starting back. How much time will it take to complete the journey and reach back to Station A (i.e. from A to B and back)?
    A. 11 hours
    B. 12 hours 45 minutes
    C. 12 hours
    D. 5 hours 30 minutes

12. A table was sold at 16% loss for ₹ 3360. Find the cost price of the table

A. ₹ 4000   B. ₹ 3392
C. ₹ 3600   D. ₹ 4296

13. There are 17 rooms in a school, every room has two fans and four LED bulbs. How many switches are required for the school if every fan requires a switch and one switch is required for every two bulbs?
    A. 34   B. 68
    C. 102   D. 17

14. The product of two decimal numbers is 12.194. If one of them is 4.69, what the other number is?
    A. 7.6   B. 2.6
    C. 9.8   D. 4.8

15. Rahul purchases a chair for ₹ 600 and uses ₹ 200 for repairs. If he sells it for ₹ 1000 then he has:
    A. no profit no loss
    B. 25% loss
    C. 25% profit
    D. cannot be calculated

16. The temperature dropped 15 degree celsius in the last 30 days. If the rate of temperature drop remains the same, how many degrees will the temperature drop in the next ten days?
    A. 10 degrees   B. 5 degrees
    C. 20 degrees   D. 15 degrees

17. From a basket of mangoes when counted in twos there was one extra, counted in threes there were two extra, counted in fours there were three extra, counted in fives there were four extra, counted in sixes there were five extra. But counted in sevens there were no extra. At least how many mangoes were there in the basket?
    A. 119   B. 110
    C. 111   D. 126

18. Which of the following two digit number when added to 27 gets reversed?
    A. 27   B. 24
    C. 47   D. 70

19. The ratio of income to expenditure of Radha is 7:5. If she saves ₹ 2000 a month, what is her annual income?
    A. ₹ 144000   B. ₹ 60000
    C. ₹ 95000   D. ₹ 84000

20. The ratio of the length to breadth of a rectangular lawn is 3 : 5. It costs ₹ 3200 to fence it at the rate of ₹ 2 a meter. What would be the cost of developing the lawn at the rate of ₹ 10 per square meter?
    A. ₹ 18,00,000   B. ₹ 15,00,000
    C. ₹ 19,00,000   D. ₹ 21,00,000

21. A, B and C divide an amount amongst themselves in the ratio of 4 : 7 : 9 respectively. If B's share in the amount is ₹ 2989, what is the total amount?
    A. ₹ 9820   B. ₹ 8540
    C. ₹ 2720   D. ₹ 8640

22. The average age of a class of 40 students is 18 years. When the teachers age is also included to calculate the average age becomes 19 years. What is the teacher's age?
    A. 59 years   B. 69 years
    C. 49 years   D. 39 years

23. What is the greatest number which when divides 3026 and 5053 leaves remainders 11 and 13 respectively?
    A. 15   B. 30
    C. 45   D. 60

24. Ravi purchased a chair at ₹ 500 and sold it at ₹ 550. What was his gain or loss percent?
    A. 10%   B. 20%
    C. 30%   D. 40%

25. A certain distance is being covered in 28 hours by walking with a speed of 5 km/h. If the speed is increased by 2 km/h then in how much time the same distance will be covered?
    A. 30 hours   B. 15 hours
    C. 20 hours   D. 25 hours

26. A piece of wire $\frac{7}{8}$ meter long broke into two pieces. One piece was $\frac{1}{4}$ meter long. How long is the other piece?
    A. $\frac{4}{8}$ m   B. $\frac{5}{8}$ m
    C. $\frac{6}{8}$ m   D. $\frac{7}{8}$ m

27. What is the missing number in the sequence 2, 5, 10, 14, 18, 23, 26, 32 ..... ?
A. 33
B. 34
C. 36
D. 37

28. 30 men can do a piece of work in 16 days. In how many days 8 men can do the same work?
A. 30 days
B. 40 days
C. 50 days
D. 60 days

29. Ram, Shyam and Mohan runs at speed of 75, 50 and 30 m/minute respectively. After how much time will they meet together for the first time running with the same speed?
A. 5 hours
B. 2 hours
C. 3 hours
D. $\frac{5}{2}$ hours

30. Represent 26 kg 5 gram using concept of decimals.
A. 26.05 kg
B. 26.005 kg
C. 26.5 kg
D. 26.0005 kg

31. At what rate, a sum of ₹ 6000 will amounts to ₹ 7800 in 5 years?
A. 3%
B. 4%
C. 5%
D. 6%

32. What will be the depth of a cubical pond whose volume is 729 m³?
A. 9 m
B. 6 m
C. 8 m
D. 5 m

33. Evaluate:
$3 \times 7 + 4 - 6 \div 3 - 7 + 45 \div 5 \times 4 + 49$
A. 101
B. 103
C. 99
D. 35

34. In what time a train whose length is 100 m moving with a speed of 60 km/h crosses a platform whose length is 150 m?
A. 15s
B. 14s
C. 18s
D. 20s

35. Ashu takes 12 days to complete the work. Pranav takes 10 days to complete the same work. Ashu, Pranav and Ramu take 5 days to complete the same work. How many days will Ramu take to complete the same work?
A. 70 days
B. 90 days
C. 60 days
D. 50 days

36. The LCM of two numbers is 28 times of their HCF. The sum of their LCM and HCF is 1740. If one number is 240 then what is the other number?
A. 420
B. 460
C. 500
D. 380

37. Four clocks rings at the time interval of 6s, 8s, 12s and 18s respectively. If they ring together at 12 am then how many times will they ring together within the time span of 6 minutes?
A. 6 times
B. 4 times
C. 7 times
D. 5 times

38. What is the least multiple of 23 which when divided by 18, 21 and 24 leaves remainders 7, 10 and 13 respectively?
A. 1240
B. 3013
C. 2364
D. 7628

39. A milkman has two cans of milk containing 75 litres and 45 litres of milk respectively. What will be the measure of largest vessel that can measure the milk of the two cans exactly?
A. 12 litres
B. 18 litres
C. 15 litres
D. 10 litres

40. A table was purchased at ₹ 1000 and was sold at ₹ 800. What was gain or loss% in this transaction?
A. 5%
B. 10%
C. 20%
D. 30%

41. The average weight of 6 boys gets increased by 5 kg if a boy with weight 20 kg is replaced by a new boy. What is the weight of new boy?
A. 41 kg
B. 50 kg
C. 65 kg
D. 49 kg

42. A man covers a distance of 40 km. He covers first 10 km at 10 km/h, second 10 km at 20 km/h, third 10 km at 30 km/h and last 10 km at 40 km/h. What is the average speed of man?
A. 18.2 km/h
B. 19.2 km/h
C. 19.0 km/h
D. 16.2 km/h

43. If area of rectangular garden of 5 m breadth is 300 sq. m, then what will be the length of garden?

A. 60 m B. 70 m
C. 80 m D. 90 m

44. If the square of a number is added to the square of 28 the result is 1808. What is the number?
A. 66 B. 50
C. 32 D. 16

45. Cost of a dozen pens is ₹ 180 and cost of 8 ball pens is ₹ 56. The ratio of the cost of a pen to the cost of a ball pen is
A. 15:7 B. 180:56
C. 1:1 D. 8:15

46. A truck requires 108 litres of diesel for covering a distance of 594 km. How much diesel will be required by the truck to cover a distance of 1650 km?
A. 3000 litres B. 108 litres
C. 300 litres D. 165 litres

47. Find the simple interest on ₹ 5000 at the rate of $7\frac{1}{2}$% for a period of 3 years
A. ₹ 5000 B. ₹ 6125
C. ₹ 2000 D. ₹ 1125

48. The angles of a triangle are in the ratio of 1:2:3. Find the values of the angles
A. 30, 60, 90 B. 15, 45, 120
C. 60, 60, 60 D. 45, 45, 90

49. One number exceeds another number by 36. The sum of numbers is 48 then the numbers are
A. 40, 08 B. 36, 12
C. 42, 06 D. 32, 16

50. At which one of the following times is the angle between the hands of a clock exactly one straight angle?
A. 12 AM B. 12 PM
C. 9.15 AM D. 6 AM

Section-B : General Knowledge

51. Out of the following list of Param Vir Chakra (PVC) Awardees who was awarded with PVC during Kargil War?
A. Lt Col Ardeshir Burzorji Tarapore
B. 2/Lt Arun Khetarpal
C. Capt Vikram Batra
D. Maj Somnath Sharma

52. Which state among the following has adopted Sanskrit as its one of the official languages?
A. Himachal Pradesh
B. Uttrakhand
C. Rajasthan
D. Uttar Pradesh

53. Who is the current Vice-President of India?
A. Shri Narendra Modi
B. Shri Venkaiah Naidu
C. Shri Arun Jaitley
D. Shri Ram Nath Kovind

54. A medical practitioner specializing in children and their diseases
A. Geologist B. Paediatrician
C. Cardiologist D. Neurologist

55. A group of stars is called a
A. Solar system B. Constellations
C. Planets D. Comets

56. Which gas when solidified is commonly known as Dry ice?
A. Carbon monoxide
B. Nitrous oxide
C. Carbon dioxide
D. Hydrogen peroxide

57. The members of the Rajya Sabha can have a maximum tenure of how long?
A. Five years B. Six years
C. Seven years D. Two years

58. P Gopichand is associated with which Sport?
A. Badminton B. Cricket
C. Football D. Hockey

59. Which of the following company does not sell mobiles?
A. Apple B. BSNL
C. HP D. Sony

60. A vehicle capable of travelling over land and water is called

A. Hovercraft   B. Rovercraft
C. Mowercraft   D. Car

61. The space programme of Government of India is looked after
A. ISBT   B. NTRO
C. NABARD   D. ISRO

62. The Motto of the Indian Navy is
A. Sarvatra Sarvottam Suraksha
B. Sham No Varunah
C. Valour and Wisdom
D. Nabhah Sparsham Deeptam

63. Which is the largest gland in human body?
A. salivary gland   B. lungs
C. liver   D. stomach

64. Who has written 'Sare Jahan Se Achchha'?
A. Rabindra Nath Tagore
B. Bankim Chandra Chatterjee
C. Muhammad Iqbal
D. Subash Chandra Bose

65. Which is the deepest ocean?
A. Indian Ocean   B. Arctic Ocean
C. Antarctic Ocean   D. Pacific Ocean

66. Who fixes the salaries and the allowances of the Speaker of Lok Sabha?
A. Council of Ministers
B. Presisent
C. Parliament
D. Judge of Supreme Court

67. Which article of constitution provides Indian citizen 'Right To Equality'?
A. Article 12   B. Article 13
C. Article 17   D. Article 14

68. 1024 Kilobytes is equal to:
A. 8 Bits
B. 1 Megabyte (MB)
C. 1 Gigabyte (GB)
D. 1 Byte

69. Hirakund dam is built on the river:
A. Cauvery   B. Mahanadi
C. Krishna   D. Sutlej

70. Deficiency of Iodine causes:
A. Goitre   B. Malaria
C. Cataract   D. Scurvy

71. Who is known as 'Iron man' of India?
A. Jawaharlal Nehru
B. Mahatma Gandhi
C. Sardar Patel
D. Subhas Chandra Bose

72. Which among of the following is not an Indian Sport?
A. Kabbadi   B. Kho-Kho
C. Hockey   D. Rugby

73. Those who study things that were made and used in the past these people are called ....
A. Biologist   B. Archaeologist
C. Geologist   D. Doctor

74. What is the ratio of width to the length of National Flag of India?
A. 4:5   B. 2:3
C. 1:1   D. 5:6

75. Where is Wagah-Border located?
A. Longewala, Rajasthan
B. Moreh, Manipur
C. Rann of Kutch, Gujarat
D. Amritsar, Punjab

Section-C : Language

Choose the most appropriate option given against each question.

76. Which word means nearly the same as "scream"?
A. find   B. stop
C. sell   D. shout

77. Which word means nearly the same as "happy"
A. conditions   B. disgusted
C. content   D. ambitious

Choose the appropriate option to complete the sentences

78. The men are working. Their .... are at home.
A. wife   B. husbands
C. husband   D. wives

79. Rahul works less .... than Mohan.
A. carefully   B. more careful
C. careful   D. careful as

80. It .... all day long yesterday.
    A. was rained   B. raining
    C. rained   D. has rained

Rearrange the following words/groups of words to make meaningful sentences. Choose the correct sequence given in the options.

81. (A) quite happy / (B) i was / (C) the first prize / (D) to receive.
    A. BADC   B. ABCD
    C. DCBA   D. BACD

82. (A) protect / (B) we must / (C) natural resources / (D) our.
    A. ABCD   B. BADC
    C. ACDB   D. DCAB

Choose the appropriate option to fill in the blanks:

83. One who leads an austere life
    A. Ruler   B. Auditor
    C. Ascetic   D. Carpenter

84. A person who presents a radio/television programme.
    A. Director   B. Actress
    C. Actor   D. Anchor

85. Pick the opposite gender of 'Lad'
    A. Lass   B. Queen
    C. Woman   D. Dame

86. Choose the opposite gender of 'Fox'
    A. Filly   B. Goose
    C. Witch   D. Vixen

Do as directed:

87. .... always stood third in her class (supply the correct pronoun)
    A. You   B. They
    C. He   D. She

88. All the candidates should bring .... own pen (supply the correct pronoun)
    A. Everyone   B. They
    C. Nobody   D. Their

89. Experience is the .... teacher (supply the correct adjective)
    A. Better   B. Good
    C. Best   D. Great

90. .... a beautiful scene it is ! (pick up the correct adverb)
    A. What   B. How
    C. Always   D. Never

91. Did you apply .... this post? (Supply the correct preposition)
    A. To   B. At
    C. For   D. Of

92. You should take care .... your health (supply the correct preposition)
    A. Of   B. In
    C. At   D. To

93. He is rich .... he is not happy (supply the correct conjunction)
    A. Yet   B. Though
    C. Because   D. But

94. Work hard .... you will fail (supply the correct conjunction)
    A. Or   B. Still
    C. Because   D. Either

95. The child .... for two hours (select the correct form of verb)
    A. Has been sleeping
    B. Have been sleeping
    C. Has slept
    D. Will sleep

Directions (Qs. No. 96 to 100): *Read the following passage and answer the questions:*

From far out in space, Earth looks like a blue ball. Since water covers three-fourths of the Earth's surface, blue is the colour we see most. The continents look brown, like small islands floating in the huge, blue sea. White clouds wrap around the Earth like a light blanket. The Earth is shaped like a sphere, or a ball. It is 25,000 miles around! It would take more than a year to walk around the whole planet. A spaceship can fly around the widest part of the sphere in only 90 minutes.

Even though spaceships have travelled to the Moon, people cannot visit the Moon without special suits. The Moon has no air or water. Plants and animals can't live there either. Astronauts first landed on the Moon in 1969. After that, there were six more trips to the Moon. They brought back Moon rocks, which scientists are still studying. There are holes, or craters, all over the Moon's surface. Scientists believe that meteorites smashed into the Moon millions of years ago and formed the craters.

The Sun is the closest star to Earth. A star is a hot ball of burning gas. The Sun looks very big because it is so close. But the Sun is just a medium-sized star. Billions of far-away stars are much bigger than our Sun. The burning gases from the Sun are so hot that they warm the Earth from 93 million miles away! Even though the Sun is always glowing, the night here on Earth is dark. That's because the Earth rotates, or turns around, every 24 hours. During the day, the Earth faces the Sun. Then we see light. During the night, the Earth turns away from the Sun. Then it faces the darkness of space. Each day we learn more about the Earth, the Moon, and the Sun.

96. Why is blue the colour we see most when looking at Earth from outer space?
A. Because most of the Earth is covered in land.
B. Because the Sun's rays make the Earth look blue.
C. Because most of the Earth is covered in water.
D. Because clouds wrap around the Earth.

97. What does 'formed' mean?
A. hit　　　　　B. made
C. broke　　　　D. stopped

98. What causes daylight on Earth?
A. The full Moon causes daylight.
B. Daylight is caused by the Earth facing away from the Sun.
C. The heat of the Sun's rays causes daylight.
D. Daylight is caused by the Earth facing toward the Sun.

99. Which of the following sentences BEST describes the Sun?
A. The Sun looks small because it is so far from Earth.
B. The Sun is a ball of burning gases that gives the Earth heat and light.
C. The Sun is a small star.
D. The Sun is not as hot as it looks.

100. Why did the astronauts bring rocks back from the Moon?
A. Because they didn't know if they would return to the Moon ever again.
B. Because they wanted to prove that they went to the Moon.
C. Because they wanted to remember how the Moon looked.
D. Because they wanted to study them and learn more about the Moon.

PAPER-II : INTELLIGENCE TEST

101. If you see the problem figure in the mirror, which figure out of the four figures A, B, C and D will be the mirror image of figure 'X'.

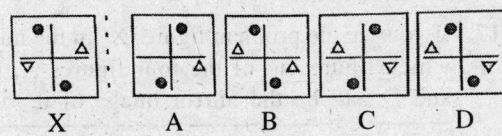

X　　　A　　　B　　　C　　　D

102. Choose the word which is least like the other words in the group.
A. PICTURE　　　B. POSTER
C. BOOK　　　　D. SCENERY

103. Which of the following diagram indicates the best relation between Travellers, Train and Bus?

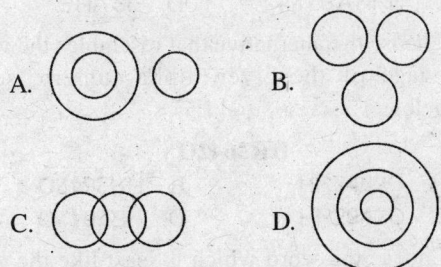

A.　　　　B.

C.　　　　D.

104. If CAR is to PETROL then TELEVISION is to ....
A. ANTENNA
B. TRANSMISSION
C. ENTERTAINMENT
D. ELECTRICITY

105. Which figure among the four figures A, B, C and D would replace the question mark in figure 'X'?

   X   A   B   C   D

106. A class of boys stands in a single line. One boy is nineteenth in order from both the ends. How many boys are there in the class?
   A. 27   B. 37
   C. 38   D. 39

107. If you fold the transparent paper along the dotted line Figure 'X' which alternative figure from A, B, C and D would you get?

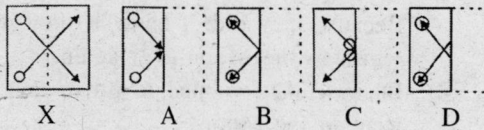

   X   A   B   C   D

108. If SCHOOL is to EDUCATION then BANK is to .... ?
   A. ATM   B. CHEQUE
   C. LOAN   D. LOCKER

109. If the given word is seen in mirror, which alternative would resemble its mirror image?

   SHARE
   A. ƎЯAHƧ   B. Ǝ ЯAHƧ
   C. ƎЯH AƧ   D. ƎƧAHƧ

110. Choose the alternative that resembles the water image of the given alpha-numeric series below:

   HR2642O
   A. OƧ4Ƨ2ЯH   B. HЯƧ6Ƨ4ƧO
   C. OƧ4Ƨ2ЯH   D. HЯƧ6Ƨ4ƧO

111. Choose the word which is least like the other words in the group.
   A. EARTH   B. SUN
   C. MERCURY   D. JUPITER

112. Which figure among the four alternatives A, B, C and D would replace the question mark in figure X?

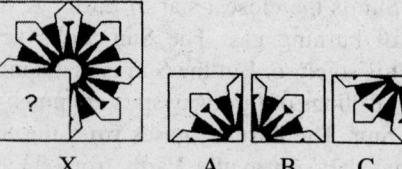

   X   A   B   C   D

113. If all directions are rotated clockwise by 90° angle i.e., North is changed to West, East to North and to on, then what will come in place of North West?
   A. SOUTH – WEST
   B. NORTH – EAST
   C. SOUTH – EAST
   D. EAST – WEST

114. Choose the word which can be formed from the given word:
   INFRASTRUCTURE
   A. RUPTURE   B. SCULPTURE
   C. FRACTURE   D. VULTURE

115. If you see the problem figure in the mirror along the dotted line, which figure out of the four figures A, B, C and D will be the mirror image of figure 'X'.

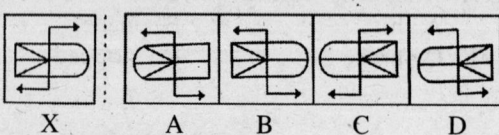

   X   A   B   C   D

116. Choose the word which is least like the other words in the group.
   A. STUDENT
   B. LAWYER
   C. MECHANIC
   D. ENGINEER

117. If you see the problem figure 'X' in the mirror, which figure out of the four figures A, B, C and D will be the mirror image of it.

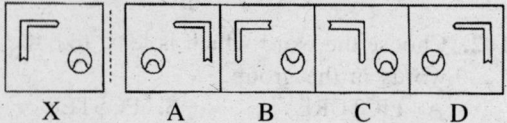

   X   A   B   C   D

118. If '+' means '÷', '÷' means '–', '–' means '×' and '×' means '+', then what would be the answer of the equation?
$$12 + 6 \div 3 - 2 \times 8 = ?$$

A. –2   B. 2
C. 4   D. 8

119. Figure 'X' is embedded in any one of the four alternative figures A, B, C or D. Find the alternative which contains figure 'X' as its part.

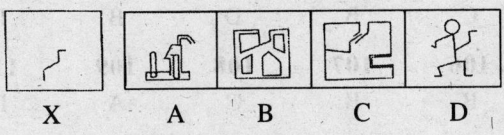

     X   A   B   C   D

120. If '÷' means '×', '×' means '+' , '+' means '–' and '–' means '÷', then what would be the answer of the equation?

$$16 \times 3 + 5 - 2 \div 4 = ?$$

A. 9   B. 10
C. 19   D. None of these

121. Nitin ranks eighteenth from the top in a class of 49 students. What is his rank from the last?
A. 18   B. 19
C. 31   D. 32

122. Which figure among the four alternatives A, B, C and D would replace the question mark in figure 'X'?

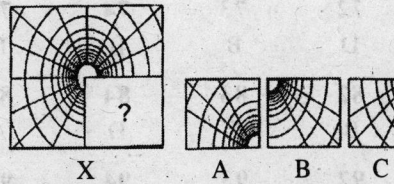

    X   A   B   C   D

123. Find out the figure which does not belong to the group of other figures.

   A   B   C   D

124. Find the missing number in the number series given below:

06, 11, 21, 36, 56, ...?

A. 42   B. 51
C. 81   D. 91

125. Find the missing number that has same relation to 26 as 37 has to 19.

19 : 37 : : 26 : ?

A. 52   B. 51
C. 46   D. 43

ANSWERS

1	2	3	4	5	6	7	8	9	10
B	A	A	C	B	A	A	B	B	A

11	12	13	14	15	16	17	18	19	20
C	A	B	B	C	B	A	C	D	B

21	22	23	24	25	26	27	28	29	30
B	A	C	A	C	B	B	D	D	B

31	32	33	34	35	36	37	38	39	40
D	A	A	A	C	A	C	B	C	C

41	42	43	44	45	46	47	48	49	50
B	B	A	C	A	C	D	A	C	C

51	52	53	54	55	56	57	58	59	60
C	B	B	B	B	C	B	A	B	A

61	62	63	64	65	66	67	68	69	70
D	B	C	C	D	C	D	B	B	A

10

71	72	73	74	75	76	77	78	79	80
C	D	B	B	D	D	C	D	A	C
81	82	83	84	85	86	87	88	89	90
A	B	C	D	A	D	D	D	C	A
91	92	93	94	95	96	97	98	99	100
C	A	D	A	A	C	B	D	B	D
101	102	103	104	105	106	107	108	109	110
C	C	C	D	A	B	B	C	A	D
111	112	113	114	115	116	117	118	119	120
B	C	A	C	D	A	A	C	D	A
121	122	123	124	125					
D	B	C	C	B					

EXPLANATORY ANSWERS

1. This answer greater than the correct answer
$$= 7236 \times 65 - 7236 \times 56$$
$$= 7236 (65 - 56)$$
$$= 7236 \times 9 = 65124.$$

2. $1 \div \left\{ \dfrac{1}{2} + \dfrac{1}{3} + \dfrac{1}{6} \div \left(\dfrac{3}{4} - \dfrac{1}{3} \right) \right\}$

According to BODMAS rule

$$= 1 \div \left\{ \dfrac{1}{2} + \dfrac{1}{3} + \dfrac{1}{6} \div \dfrac{5}{12} \right\}$$

$$= 1 \div \left\{ \dfrac{1}{2} + \dfrac{1}{3} + \dfrac{1}{6} \times \dfrac{12}{5} \right\}$$

$$= 1 \div \left\{ \dfrac{1}{2} + \dfrac{1}{3} + \dfrac{2}{5} \right\}$$

$$= 1 \div \left\{ \dfrac{15 + 10 + 12}{30} \right\} = 1 \div \left\{ \dfrac{37}{30} \right\} = \dfrac{30}{37}$$

3.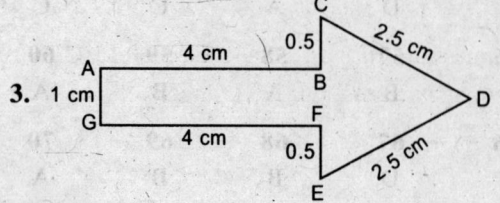

The perimeter of the figure
$$= AB + BC + CD + DE + EF + FG + GA$$
$$= 4 + 0.5 + 2.5 + 2.5 + 0.5 + 4 + 1$$
$$= 15 \text{ cm.}$$

4.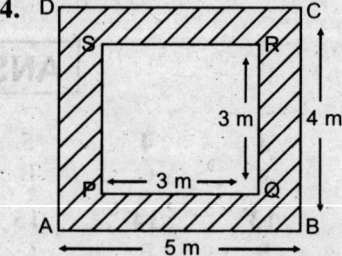

∴ The area of the floor that is not carpeted
= Area of Rectangle ABCD – Area of square PQRS
$$= l \times b - a^2$$
$$= 5 \times 4 - (3)^2$$
$$= 20 - 9 = 11 \text{ m}^2.$$

5. Required smallest No. which is divisible by
6, 12, 18 = LCM (6, 12, 18)
$$= 2 \times 2 \times 3 \times 3 = 36.$$
The answer will be multiple of 36, in the given option 180 is the smallest number.

2	6, 12, 18
2	3, 6, 9
3	3, 3, 9
3	1, 1, 3
	1, 1, 1

6. ∵ In Isosceles Triangle, two angles are same

Check the option

(a) 90, 45, i.e., $\angle A = 90°$, $\angle B = 45°$

$\qquad \angle C = 180 - (90 + 45)$

$\qquad\qquad = 180 - 135 = 45°$

∵ $\qquad\qquad \angle B = \angle C$

∴ Option (A) is the correct answer.

7. Let the breadth of the rectangle = x

Then, the length of the rectangle $(l) = x + 5$

Perimeter of the rectangle = 50 cm

$\qquad 2(l + b) = 50$

$\qquad l + b = 25$

$\qquad x + x + 5 = 25$

$\qquad 2x + 5 = 25$

$\qquad 2x = 20$

$\qquad x = 10$

∴ Breadth (b) = 10 cm

Length $(l) = 10 + 5 = 15$ cm

∴ Area = $l \times b$

$\qquad = 10 \times 15 = 150$ cm^2.

8. ∵ $\qquad W_1 = W_2$

∴ $\qquad M_1 \times D_1 = M_2 \times D_2$

$\qquad 12 \times 15 = 20 \times D_2$

∴ $\qquad D_2 = \dfrac{12 \times 15}{20} = 9$ days

Hence option (B) is the correct answer.

10. No. of students who do not ride the bus

$\qquad = 1000 - 330 = 670$

∴ Required percentage = $\dfrac{\text{No. of students who do not ride the bus}}{\text{Total student}} \times 100$

$\qquad = \dfrac{670}{1000} \times 100$

$\qquad = 67\%$.

11.

$$\overset{\longleftarrow\text{ 616 km }\longrightarrow}{\underset{\substack{\text{Station} \\ \text{A}}}{\bullet} \quad \underset{\text{112 km/hr}}{} \quad \underset{\substack{\text{Station} \\ \text{B}}}{\bullet}}$$

Total time taken = $\dfrac{\text{Distance AB}}{\text{Speed}} + 1h + \dfrac{\text{Distance BA}}{\text{Speed}}$

$\qquad = \dfrac{616}{112} + 1 + \dfrac{616}{112}$

$\qquad \left[\because \text{Time} = \dfrac{\text{Distance}}{\text{Speed}} \right]$

$\qquad = 5.5\ h + 1\ h + 5.5\ h$

$\qquad = 12\ h.$

12. ∵ $\quad \%\ \text{Loss} = \dfrac{\text{CP} - \text{SP}}{\text{CP}} \times 100$

$\qquad 16 = \dfrac{\text{CP} - 3360}{\text{CP}} \times 100$

$\qquad 16\ \text{CP} = 100\ \text{CP} - 336000$

$\qquad 84\ \text{CP} = 336000$

$\qquad \text{CP} = \dfrac{336000}{84} = ₹\ 4000.$

14. $4.69 \times$ Other No. = 12.194

∴ Other No. = $\dfrac{12.194 \times 1000}{4.69 \times 1000}$

$\qquad = \dfrac{12194}{4690} = 2.6.$

15. Total cost price of the chair = ₹ 600 + ₹ 200

$\qquad = ₹\ 800$

Selling price of the chair = ₹ 1000

∵ $\qquad \text{SP} > \text{CP} \rightarrow \text{Profit}$

Required profit % = $\dfrac{\text{SP} - \text{CP}}{\text{CP}} \times 100$

$\qquad = \dfrac{1000 - 800}{800} \times 100$

$\qquad = \dfrac{200 \times 100}{800}$

$\qquad = 25\%$ profit

16. Temperature dropped in 30 days = 15°C

Temperature dropped in 1 day

$\qquad = \dfrac{15}{30} = \dfrac{1}{2}$ °C/day

Temperature drop in the next 10 days

$$= \frac{1}{2} \times 10 = 5°C.$$

17. No. of mangoes in the basket 1

Which gives remainder 1 when divide by 2

Which gives remainder 2 when divide by 3

Which gives remainder 3 when divide by 4

Which gives remainder 4 when divide by 5

Which gives remainder 5 when divide by 6

Which gives remainder 0 when divide by 7

Check from the option

(A)
```
   2)119(59        3)119(39
     10              9
     19              29
     18              27
      1               2
```

```
   4)119(29        5)119(23
      8              10
      39             19
      36             15
       3              4
```

```
   6)119(19        7)119(17
      6              7
      59             49
      54             49
       5              ×
```

So, no. of mangoes will be 119.

18. Check the option

A. 27 + 27 = 54 (✗)

B. 24 + 27 = 51 (✗)

C. 47 + 27 = 74 (✓)

Hence (C) is the correct option.

19. Let Radha income and expenditure are $7x$ and $5x$ respectively.

Then,   Saving = Income − Expenditure

$$7x - 5x = 2000$$

$$2x = 2000$$

$$x = 1000$$

∴ Monthly income of Radha = $7x$

$$= 7 \times 1000 = 7000$$

Annual income of Radha = 12×7000

$$= 84000.$$

20. Let the length and breadth of rectangular lawn are $3x$ and $5x$ respectively

The perimeter of the lawn $2(l + b) = \dfrac{₹\,3200}{2}$

$$2(l + b) = 1600$$

$$2(3x + 5x) = 1600$$

$$16x = 1600$$

$$x = 100$$

∴ Length of the lawn = $3x$

$$= 3 \times 100 = 300 \text{ m}$$

Breadth of the lawn = $5x$

$$= 5 \times 100 = 500 \text{ m}$$

Area of the lawn = $l \times b$

$$= 300 \times 500$$

$$= 150000 \text{ m}^2$$

∴ Cost of developing the lawn

$$= 150000 \times 10$$

$$= 1500000.$$

21. Let the share of A, B and C are $4x$, $7x$ and $9x$ respectively

Given that

B's share = ₹ 2989

$$7x = 2989$$

$$x = 427$$

∴ Total amount = $4x + 7x + 9x = 20x$

$$= 20 \times 427$$

$$= ₹ 8540.$$

22. Required teacher's age = $41 \times 19 - 40 \times 18$

$$= 779 - 720$$

$$= 59 \text{ years}$$

$$\left[\because \text{Average Age} = \frac{\text{Total sum of age}}{\text{Total no. of student}} \right].$$

23. Required greatest no.

= HCF (|3026 −11|, |5053 − 13|)

= HCF (3015, 5040) = 45

3	3015		2	5040
3	1005		2	2520
5	335		2	1260
	67		2	630
			3	315
			3	105
			5	35
				7

$3015 = 3 \times 3 \times 5 \times 67$

$5040 = 2 \times 2 \times 2 \times 2 \times 3 \times 3 \times 5$

HCF (3015, 50, 40) = $3 \times 3 \times 5 = 45$.

24. Cost price of the chair = ₹ 500

Selling price of the chair = ₹ 550

$\because$ SP > CP → Profit

$$\% \text{ Profit} = \frac{SP - CP}{CP} \times 100$$

$$= \frac{550 - 500}{500} \times 100$$

$$= \frac{50}{500} \times 100 = 10\%$$

25. $\because$ Distance = Speed × Time

$= 5 \times 28 = 140$ km

New speed = 5 + 2 = 7 km/h

$\therefore \quad$ Time $= \dfrac{\text{Distance}}{\text{Speed}}$

Time $= \dfrac{140}{7} = 20$ h.

26. Length of other piece $= \dfrac{7}{8} - \dfrac{1}{4}$

$$= \frac{7-2}{8} = \frac{5}{8} \text{ meter.}$$

27.

28. $\because \qquad W_1 = W_2$

$\therefore \qquad M_1 \times D_1 = M_2 \times D_2$

$30 \times 16 = 8 \times D_2$

$$D_2 = \frac{30 \times 16}{8}$$

$D_2 = 60$ days.

29. Required time = LCM (75, 50, 30)

2	75, 50, 30
3	75, 25, 15
5	25, 25, 5
5	5, 5, 1
	1, 1, 1

$= 2 \times 3 \times 5 \times 5$

$= 150$ min

$= \dfrac{5}{2}$ hour.

30. $\because \qquad$ 1 kg = 1000 gm

$\therefore$ 26 kg 5 gram = 26 kg + $\dfrac{5}{1000}$ kg

$= 26 + 0.005$

$= 26.005$ kg.

31. $\because \qquad$ SI = Amount − Principle

$= 7800 - 6000$

$= ₹ 1800$

$\because \qquad SI = \dfrac{P \times r \times t}{100}$

$$1800 = \frac{6000 \times r \times 5}{100}$$

$$r = \frac{1800 \times 100}{6000 \times 5}$$

$r = 6\%$.

32. $\because \qquad$ Volume of cube = a^3

$\therefore \qquad a^3 = 729$

$a = 9$ m

$\because$ Depth of a cubical pond = 9 m.

33. $3 \times 7 + 4 - 6 \div 3 - 7 + 45 \div 5 \times 4 + 49$

According to BODMAS rule

$= 3 \times 7 + 4 - 2 - 7 + 9 \times 4 + 49$

$= 21 + 4 - 2 - 7 + 36 + 49$

$= 110 - 9 = 101.$

34. Require time $= \dfrac{\text{Distance}}{\text{Speed}}$

$= \dfrac{\text{Length of train} + \text{Length of platform}}{\text{Speed of train}}$

$= \dfrac{100 + 150}{60 \times \dfrac{5}{18}}$ $\left[\because 1 \text{ km/h} = \dfrac{5}{18} \text{m/s} \right]$

$= \dfrac{250 \times 18}{60 \times 5} = 15$ sec.

35. Ashu's 1 day work $= \dfrac{1}{12}$

Pranav's 1 day work $= \dfrac{1}{10}$

Ashu, Pranav and Ramu's 1 day work $= \dfrac{1}{5}$

$\therefore$ Ramu's one day work $= \dfrac{1}{5} - \left(\dfrac{1}{12} + \dfrac{1}{10} \right)$

$= \dfrac{12 - 5 - 6}{60}$

$= \dfrac{1}{60}$

$\therefore$ Ramu complete the work $= 60$ days.

36. Given that

$\quad$ LCM $(a, b) = 28 \times$ HCF (a, b) $\quad$ ...(1)

$\because \quad$ LCM $(a, b) +$ HCF (a, b)

$\quad\quad\quad = 1740$ $\quad$ ...(2)

From equations (1) and (2)

$\quad$ 28 HCF $(a, b) +$ HCF $(a, b) = 1740$

$\quad\quad\quad$ 29 HCF $(a, b) = 1740$

$\quad\quad\quad$ HCF $(a, b) = 60$

$\quad\quad\quad$ LCM $(a, b) = 28 \times 60$

$\quad\quad\quad\quad\quad\quad\quad = 1680$

$\because$ We know that

$\quad$ LCM $(a, b) \times$ HCF $(a, b) = a \times b$

$\quad\quad$ $60 \times 1680 = 240 \times b$

$\therefore \quad$ Second no. $b = \dfrac{60 \times 1680}{240}$

$\quad\quad\quad\quad\quad = 420.$

37. Clock rings again after LCM (6, 8, 12, 18) second

$\quad$ LCM (6, 8, 12, 18) $= 2 \times 2 \times 2 \times 3 \times 3$

$\quad\quad\quad\quad\quad\quad = 72$

2	6, 8, 12, 18
2	3, 4, 6, 9
2	3, 2, 3, 9
3	3, 1, 3, 9
3	1, 1, 1, 3
	1, 1, 1, 1

$\therefore$ In 6 minutes clock rings $= \dfrac{6 \times 60}{72} = 6$

$\quad\quad\quad\quad = 6 + 1$ (In starting)

$\quad\quad\quad\quad = 7$ times.

38. LCM (18, 21, 24) $= 2 \times 2 \times 2 \times 3 \times 3 \times 7$

$\quad\quad\quad\quad\quad\quad = 504$

Common remainder $\Rightarrow 18 - 7 = 11$

$\quad\quad\quad\quad\quad\quad \Rightarrow 21 - 10 = 11$

$\quad\quad\quad\quad\quad\quad \Rightarrow 24 - 13 = 11$

2	18, 21, 24
2	9, 21, 12
2	9, 21, 6
3	9, 21, 3
3	3, 7, 1
7	1, 7, 1
	1, 1, 1

In each case, remainder is equal i.e. 11

$\therefore$ We have to find of multiple 504, which is divisible by 23 after subtracting 11

$504 \times 1 - 11 = 493$ (✗)

$504 \times 2 - 11 = 997$ (✗)

$504 \times 3 - 11 = 1501$ (✗)

$504 \times 4 - 11 = 2005$ (✗)

$504 \times 5 - 11 = 2509$ (✗)

$504 \times 6 - 11 = 3013$ (✓)

∴ 3013 is the required No.

39. Required largest vessel = HCF (75, 45)

$$= 3 \times 5$$

$$= 15 \text{ litres.}$$

3	75
5	25
5	5
	1

3	45
3	15
5	5
	1

$75 = ③ \times ⑤ \times 5$

$45 = ③ \times 3 \times ⑤$

40. Cost price of the table = ₹ 1000

Selling price of the table = ₹ 800

∵   SP < CP → Loss

$$\% \text{ Loss} = \frac{CP - SP}{CP} \times 100$$

$$= \frac{1000 - 800}{1000} \times 100$$

$$= \frac{200}{10} = 20\% \text{ Loss.}$$

41. Let the initial average = x kg

and the weight of new boy = y kg

$6 \times x + y - 20 = 6(x + 5)$

$6x + y - 20 = 6x + 30$

$y - 20 = 30$

$y = 50$ kg

42. Average speed = $\dfrac{\text{Total distance}}{\text{Total time taken to cover the distance}}$

$$= \frac{40 \text{ km}}{\dfrac{10}{10}\text{h} + \dfrac{10}{20}\text{h} + \dfrac{10}{30}\text{h} + \dfrac{10}{40}\text{h}}$$

$$= \frac{40 \text{ km}}{1 + \dfrac{1}{2} + \dfrac{1}{3} + \dfrac{1}{4}}$$

$$= \frac{40 \times 12}{12 + 6 + 4 + 3} = \frac{40 \times 12}{25}$$

$$= \frac{480}{25} = 19.2 \text{ km/h.}$$

43. Let the length of the garden = x m

∵   Area = $l \times b$

$x \times 5 = 300$

$$x = \frac{300}{5} = 60 \text{ m.}$$

44. Let the number = x

Then, according to question

$x^2 + (28)^2 = 1808$

$x^2 + 784 = 1808$

$x^2 = 1808 - 784$

$x^2 = 1024$

$x = \sqrt[2]{1024}$

$x = 32.$

	32
3	1029
	9
62	124
2	124
	×

45. The cost of a dozen (12) pens = ₹ 180

The cost of a pen = $\dfrac{180}{12}$ = ₹ 15

The cost of 8 ball pens = ₹ 56

The cost of 1 ball pen = ₹ $\dfrac{56}{8}$ = ₹ 7

Required ratio = 15 : 7.

46. Diesel requires for covering 594 km distance

$$= 108 \text{ litres}$$

Diesel requires for covering 1 km distance

$$= \frac{108}{594} \text{ lit/km}$$

Diesel requires for covering 1650 km distance

$$= \frac{108}{594} \times 1650$$

$$= 300 \text{ litre.}$$

47. SI = $\dfrac{P \times r \times t}{100}$

$$= \frac{5000 \times \dfrac{15}{2} \times 3}{100}$$

$$= \frac{5000 \times 15 \times 3}{200}$$

$$= \frac{225000}{200} = ₹\ 1125$$

48. Let the angles of triangle are $x°$, $2x°$ and $3x°$ respectively

Then, the sum of three angles of a triangle

$$= 180°$$
$$x + 2x + 3x = 180°$$
$$6x = 180°$$
$$x = 30°$$

Then angles are 30°, 60° and 90°.

49. Let the numbers are x and y

Then, $\quad x - y = 36 \qquad$ ...(1)

$\qquad x + y = 48 \qquad$ ...(2)

Equation (1) + equation (2)

$$2x = 36 + 48$$
$$2x = 84$$
$$x = 42$$

$x = 42$ put in equation (1)

$$42 - y = 36$$
$$y = 42 - 36 = 6$$

∴ Numbers are 42 and 6.

50. At 9 : 15

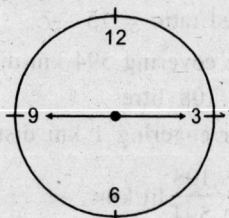

103.

Train   Travellers   Bus

106. 37 is a prime number.

111. Sun is a star, all others are planet.

113.

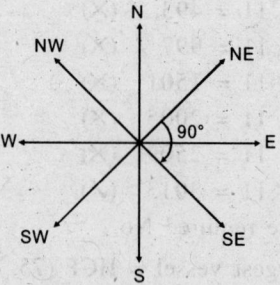

After rotation 90° clockwise

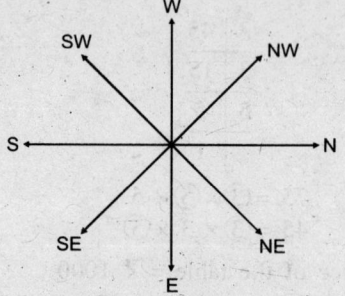

118. $12 + 6 \div 3 - 2 \times 8$

$$= \underline{12 \div 6} - 3 \times 2 + 8$$

According to BODMAS rule

$$= 2 - \underline{3 \times 2} + 8$$
$$= 2 - 6 + 8$$
$$= 10 - 6 = 4.$$

120. $16 \times 3 + 5 - 2 \div 4$

$$= 16 + 3 - \underline{5 \div 2} \times 4$$

According to BODMAS rule

$$= 16 + 3 - \frac{5}{2} \times 4$$
$$= 16 + 3 - \underline{5 \times 2}$$
$$= 16 + 3 - 10$$
$$= 19 - 10 = 9.$$

121. Total student = L + R − 1

$$49 = 18 + L - 1$$
$$L = 49 - 17$$
$$L = 32.$$

124. 6   11   21   36   56   81

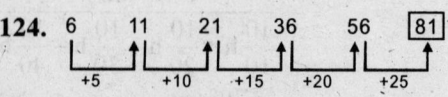

+5   +10   +15   +20   +25

125. 19 : 37 :: 26 : 51

× 2 − 1   × 2 − 1

All India Sainik School Entrance Exam., 2018*

(CLASS-VI)

PAPER-I : MATHEMATICS, GK AND LANGUAGE

Section-A : Mathematics

1. The greatest 8-digits number with given digits 5, 8, 7, 5, 2, 0, 6, and 1 is
   A. 88765210
   B. 87765210
   C. 88765521
   D. 87655210

2. Choose the correct option if numbers 52806, 52086, 52860, 52800 and 58260 are arranged in ascending order
   A. 52086, 52806, 52860, 52800, 58260
   B. 52800, 52860, 52086, 58260, 52806
   C. 52086, 52800, 52806, 52860, 58260
   D. 52800, 52806, 52860, 52086, 58260

3. A number that must be subtracted from 925564 to make it equal to the sum of 234251 and 352421 will be
   A. 238892
   B. 338882
   C. 338892
   D. 337892

4. The product of 10101 × 25 is
   A. 252725
   B. 252525
   C. 25025025
   D. 272725

5. The average age of 3 sisters is 15. If the ages of 2 sisters are 12 years and 15 years, the age of the third sister is
   A. 21 years
   B. 17 years
   C. 18 years
   D. 16 years

6. $\frac{7}{6}$ of a leap year = ... week
   A. 427
   B. 35
   C. 61
   D. 13

7. Write Roman numerals CDXLIX in Arabic numerals
   A. 569
   B. 449
   C. 549
   D. 469

8. Value of $(700 \div 10) - \{(12 \times 8) \div (34 - 10)\}$ is
   A. 69
   B. 68
   C. 67
   D. 66

9. 2 = ... %
   A. 200
   B. 0.02
   C. $\frac{2}{100}$
   D. 20

10. Vicky bought a bicycle for ₹ 3,000.00 and sold it for ₹ 2,700.00. What was his loss or gain per cent?
    A. 10% loss
    B. 10% gain
    C. 11.11% gain
    D. 11.11% loss

11. A train leaves Hyderabad at 01:15 PM on Friday and reaches Chennai at 07:30 AM on Saturday. The duration of the journey is
    A. 18 hrs 30 min
    B. 17 hrs 45 min
    C. 18 hrs 15 min
    D. 17 hrs 15 min

12. Karishma bought two necklace for ₹ 1,39,500.00. She sold one of them for ₹ 75,000.00 and the other one for ₹ 80,000.00. How much money did she gain?
    A. ₹ 25,500.00
    B. ₹ 15,500.00
    C. ₹ 20,500.00
    D. ₹ 15,000.00

13. A tall office building has 85 floors. Each floor has 48 windows. Each window is to be decorated with 64 tiny bulbs. How many bulbs would be needed to decorate all the windows?
    A. 261120
    B. 273920
    C. 456960
    D. 209920

14. The smallest 5-digit number that is divisible by 19 is

A. 10019   B. 10013
C. 10032   D. 10000

15. The greatest number that divides 38 and 68 leaving 8 as remainder in each case is
A. 10   B. 15
C. 60   D. 30

16. The decimal notation of 10 kg 2 dag 6 g is
A. 10.260 kg   B. 10.206 kg
C. 10.026 kg   D. 10.006 kg

17. Which of the following pair of angles are supplementary?
A. 46° and 44°   B. 113° and 67°
C. 245° and 115°   D. 90° and 180°

18. The perimeter of the rectangle and square are same. Length and breadth of the rectangle are 10 cm and 8 cm respectively. What is the area of the square?
A. 114 sq. cm   B. 36 sq.cm
C. 81 sq.cm   D. 64 sq.cm

19. Which of the following measures of three angles can be those of a triangle?
A. 52°, 69°, 79°   B. 30°, 69°, 71°
C. 132°, 169°, 59°   D. 32°, 69°, 79°

20. Which statement is true?
A. All hexagons are triangles because they have at least 3 sides.
B. All octagons are polygons because they have at least 3 sides.
C. All parallelograms are rectangles because they have 2 sets of parallel sides.
D. All rhombus are squares because they have 4 sides that are all the same length.

21. The fraction equivalent to 1.25 is:
A. $1\frac{1}{4}$ B. $12\frac{1}{2}$
C. $1\frac{1}{8}$ D. $12\frac{1}{4}$

22. The sum of two numbers is 11009. If one of them is 9999, the other number is
A. 1010   B. 1110
C. 2110   D. 21008

23. Simplify : 6 ÷ 6 + 6 × 6 – 6
A. 1   B. 7
C. 31   D. 36

24. Simplify: $1\frac{1}{24} - 1 + \frac{7}{36}$
A. $\frac{17}{72}$ B. $1\frac{17}{72}$
C. $\frac{7}{60}$ D. $\frac{5}{60}$

25. Sara poured $1\frac{1}{8}$ cups of lemonade each in 5 glasses. What was the total amount of lemonade Sara poured in 5 glasses?
A. $3\frac{7}{8}$ cups   B. $5\frac{1}{8}$ cups
C. $5\frac{5}{8}$ cups   D. $6\frac{1}{8}$ cups

26. Ritu has $\frac{1}{4}$ of a sack of rice. She divides the rice equally into 7 bags. What fraction of the full sack of rice is in each bag?
A. $\frac{1}{28}$ B. $\frac{1}{7}$
C. $\frac{2}{11}$ D. $\frac{11}{28}$

27. $1 + 0 + \frac{9}{100} + \frac{3}{1000} =$
A. 1.093   B. 1.903
C. 1.93   D. 1.0093

28. Which two quadrilaterals have both 2 pairs of parallel sides and 2 acute angles?

A.

B.

C.

D.

29. What is the sum of 20.08, 20.008, 20.088 and 20.888?
   A. 81.064   B. 81.604
   C. 80.064   D. 80.888

30. Round off 37504 to the nearest hundreds
   A. 37500   B. 37000
   C. 38000   D. 30000

31. A train is running at a speed of 75 kms/hour. How much time will it take to cover a distance of 350 kms?
   A. 4 hrs   B. 5 hrs
   C. 4 hrs 30 min   D. 4 hrs 40 min

32. A block of wood is in the form of a cube, its edge is 4 m. How many rectangular pieces of dimension 20 cm × 10 cm × 5 cm can be cut from the block?
   A. 640   B. 64
   C. 6400   D. 64000

33. In how many years, a sum of ₹ 500 at 5% per annum will amount to ₹ 600?
   A. 3 years   B. 4 years
   C. 5 years   D. 6 years

34. The average of four numbers is 30. If the sum of first three numbers is 85, the fourth number is:
   A. 35   B. 25
   C. 45   D. 55

35. What percent of 10 km is 10 m?
   A. 0.1%   B. 1.0%
   C. 10.0%   D. 40.0%

36. The number of square tiles, of side 15 cm, required for flooring a room of size 3.6 m × 4.5 m, will be:
   A. 720   B. 360
   C. 10800   D. 5400

37. The smallest odd number formed by using the digits 1, 2, 3, 4, and 5 is:
   A. 12345   B. 12435
   C. 12453   D. 12534

38. Which of the following numbers are arranged in ascending order?
   A. $\frac{1}{3}, \frac{1}{2}, 0.25$ B. $0.25, \frac{1}{2}, \frac{1}{3}$
   C. $0.25, \frac{1}{3}, \frac{1}{2}$ D. $\frac{1}{2}, \frac{1}{3}, 0.25$

39. A boat is flowing in still water at the speed of 18 km/hour. The speed of boat in m/sec is:
   A. 50 m/sec   B. 72 m/sec
   C. 7.2 m/sec   D. 5 m/sec

40. The value of 200°F in degree Celsius is ………. [Use C = 5/9 (F–32)]
   A. 80.3°C   B. 93.3°C
   C. 100.3°C   D. 105.3°C

41. Find the difference between the number 36490 and the number obtained by interchanging the places of 6 and 9:
   A. 2970   B. 3030
   C. 2070   D. 2790

42. Convert (3.75 of 5% + 7.25 of 10%) into decimals:
   A. 0.9152   B. 0.9521
   C. 0.9125   D. 09527

43. What is the next row of numbers?

28	84	112
38	114	152
48	144	192

   A. 58   174   232
   B. 58   184   244
   C. 68   204   272
   D. 68   214   292

44. A boy runs around a rectangular field of length 40 m and breadth 25 m. How much distance will he run if he takes 4 rounds of that field.
   A. 4000 m   B. 260 m
   C. 520 m   D. 400 m

45. A room is 15 m long and 10 m broad. Find the cost of carpeting its floor if 1 sq cm of carpet costs ₹ 2.00.
   A. ₹ 300   B. ₹ 300000
   C. ₹ 30000   D. ₹ 3000000

46. The cost of a pack of 15 balls is ₹ 300 and a pack of 12 shuttle cock is ₹ 96. If Raghu bought 1 ball and 1 shuttle cock, how much would he pay to shopkeeper?
   A. ₹ 24   B. ₹ 22
   C. ₹ 26   D. ₹ 28

47. The greatest number which divides 624 and 936 exactly is 312. Find the smallest number which is divisible by 624 and 936?
   A. 1820   B. 1872
   C. 1272   D. 1864

48. A person purchased an old bicycle for ₹ 450 and spends ₹ 50 on its maintenance. If he sold the old bicycle for ₹ 600 then his profit percentage is
  A. 15%   B. 18%
  C. 20%   D. 25%

49. Find the area of figure given below:

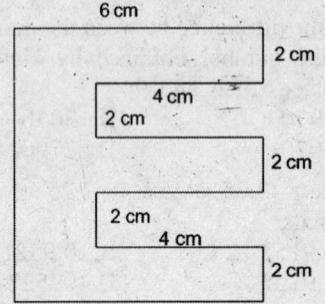

A. 56 sq cm
B. 48 sq cm
C. 44 sq cm
D. 60 sq cm

50. Amar spent $\frac{3}{8}$ of his time studying Science. He spent $\frac{2}{5}$ as much time studying English as Science. What fraction of Amar's study time was spent studying English?
  A. $\frac{1}{40}$ B. $\frac{3}{20}$
  C. $\frac{31}{40}$ D. $\frac{15}{16}$

Section-B : General Knowledge

51. Which feature helps a coconut fruit to float in water?
  A. a fibrous outer covering
  B. a spongy part
  C. presence of hook
  D. presence of spine

52. Which of the following is a non-communicable disease?
  A. chickenpox   B. beriberi
  C. common cold   D. measles

53. The rabies virus is carried by
  A. cockroaches   B. hens
  C. dogs   D. rabbits

54. Milk turning sour is a
  A. physical change   B. reversible change
  C. chemical change   D. none of these

55. The wearing off or carrying away of soil by the action of water or wind is called
  A. storm   B. flood
  C. soil erosion   D. deforestation

56. Whales and dolphins are classified as
  A. fishes   B. reptiles
  C. mammals   D. amphibians

57. The working of the internal organs of our body is controlled by this system
  A. reproductive   B. circulatory
  C. respiratory   D. nervous

58. A person might faint if his heart does not send enough blood to his
  A. feet   B. liver
  C. kidneys   D. brain

59. The upward push of water on a floating object is called
  A. buoyant force   B. volume
  C. density   D. pressure

60. The first artificial satellite launched by India in 1975 was
  A. Sputnic 1   B. Aryabhatta
  C. Charaka   D. Insat

61. Those who study earthquakes are called
  A. geologist   B. seismologists
  C. astronomers   D. astrologers

62. Which of the following gas is not a greenhouse gas?
  A. carbon dioxide   B. oxygen
  C. methane   D. CFC

63. The model of the earth is called a
    A. circle   B. sphere
    C. globe   D. marble

64. Agriculture cannot be practiced on mountains on a large scale as they
    A. are thinly populated
    B. have a shortage of land
    C. have a thin soil cover
    D. have unsuitable climate

65. The condition of the atmosphere at a given place and time is called
    A. season   B. climate
    C. altitude   D. weather

66. The highway of Central Africa is another name for
    A. River Nile   B. River Congo
    C. River Zimbani   D. River Kwango

67. Most of the grasslands of the world are found in the
    A. Tropical Zone   B. Temperate Zone
    C. Torrid Zone   D. Frigid Zone

68. Any sound louder than 90 decibels can cause
    A. asthma
    B. digestive problems
    C. typhoid
    D. loss of hearing

69. Aligarh Muslim University is associated with
    A. Rabindranath Tagore
    B. Tansen
    C. Kalidas
    D. Syed Ahmad Khan

70. The English Government introduced the policy of divide and rule to
    A. educate Indian
    B. encourage nationalism
    C. reform Indians
    D. suppress nationalism

71. Purna Swaraj means
    A. non-cooperation
    B. civil disobedience
    C. boycott
    D. complete Independence

72. The Lok Sabha can have a maximum of
    A. 12 members   B. 552 members
    C. 238 members   D. 543 members

73. The League of Nations was formed to prevent
    A. destruction   B. loss of lives
    C. droughts   D. another world war

74. The world has been made smaller due to
    A. wheels
    B. steam engines
    C. fast means of transport
    D. cars

75. Internet is a source of information on
    A. documentaries   B. e-mail
    C. any topic   D. a few topic

Section-C : Language

Read the following passage and answer the questions.

HORACE DENBY

Everyone thought that Horace Denby was a good and honest citizen. He was about fifty years old and unmarried, and he lived with a housekeeper who worried over his health. In fact, he was usually very well and happy, except for attacks of hay fever in summer. He made expensive locks and was successful enough at his business to have two helpers. Yes, Horace Denby was good and respectable – but not completely honest.

Fifteen years ago, Horace had served his first and only sentence in prison for stealing jewels. The priest at the prison had liked Horace – everyone did – and had tried to help him to live an honest life. But Horace did not want to become honest. He only wanted to make sure that his dishonesty never got him into trouble again.

76. Horace Denby was ....
    A. old   B. unmarried
    C. handicapped   D. both A & B

77. .... worried about the health of Horace.
    A. his wife   B. the priest
    C. his housekeeper   D. Horace

6

78. For stealing jewels, Horace was sent to prison
....
   A. only once   B. twice
   C. thrice   D. never

79. The profession of Horace was ....
   A. businessman   B. thief
   C. housekeeper   D. locksmith

80. Choose the word which means the opposite of EXPENSIVE.
   A. cheap   B. luxurious
   C. costly   D. heavy

81. Choose the word which means almost same as UNMARRIED.
   A. handsome   B. widow
   C. young   D. bachelor

Choose the most appropriate option given against each question.

82. A herd of cows or ....
   A. birds   B. elephant
   C. sheep   D. horse

83. This is my book and that is ....
   A. yours   B. your
   C. our   D. ours

84. Rajan's father and Rohan's father .... businessmen.
   A. are   B. have
   C. is   D. has

85. My friends .... been asking for the party photographs.
   A. do   B. does
   C. have   D. has

86. Rakesh .... his mother tongue very fluently.
   A. speak   B. speaking
   C. speaks   D. None of these

87. Ankit and his family .... in Europe for three weeks.
   A. have been travelling
   B. have travelling
   C. been travelling
   D. have travelled

88. Bharti .... yoga classes these days.
   A. attending
   B. has attending
   C. is attending
   D. has been attending

89. My house is .... as yours.
   A. big   B. as big
   C. bigger   D. biggest

90. This is the .... comics I have ever read.
   A. most interesting B. more interesting
   C. less interesting   D. None of these

Select one word from the options for the given definition.

91. A book or work of art whose author is unknown:
   A. anonymous   B. playwright
   C. novelist   D. poet

92. A person who believes in the existence of God:
   A. atheist   B. theist
   C. agnostic   D. pacifist

Select the most appropriate option for question tag.

93. I have completed my homework, ... ?
   A. have I   B. has I
   C. do I   D. haven't I

94. He does not do his work sincerely, ... ?
   A. does he   B. did he
   C. doesn't he   D. do he

Rearrange the following words/groups of words to make meaningful sentences. Choose the correct sequence given in the options.

95. (A) and grandpa / (B) my grandma / (C) too much / (D) love each other
   A. BDAC   B. BACD
   C. DBCA   D. BADC

96. (A) was very pretty / (B) in her childhood / (C) my grandma / (D) and beautiful
   A. CBAD   B. ADBC
   C. CADB   D. CDAB

Mark the option with the correct spelling of the given words:

97. A. address   B. adres
   C. adress   D. addres

98. A. appresiation B. appreciation
C. appreciason D. apreciation

Choose the appropriate option to fill in the blanks:

99. 'Books' is for 'book', ... is for 'ship'.
A. sheeps B. ships
C. shepherds D. sheep

100. 'Kids' is for 'kid', ... is for 'child'
A. childs B. child
C. children D. None of these

PAPER-II : INTELLIGENCE TEST

101. Find the missing number in the number series given below:

20, 30, 42, ?

A. 64 B. 56
C. 62 D. 54

102. Victory is to Joy as .... is to Sorrow.
A. Defeat B. Depression
C. Loneliness D. Cry

103. Find the missing number that has same relation to 289 as 13 has to 169.

169 : 13 : : 289 : ?

A. 19 B. 17
C. 27 D. 23

104. If TRAIN is written as WUDLQ then BUS would be written as ....
A. EXU B. DWU
C. EXV D. VXE

105. If FLOW is related to RIVER then STAGNANT is related to ....
A. Pool B. Rain
C. Stream D. Canal

106. Choose the word which is least like the other words in the group?
A. Ladder B. Staircase
C. Bridge D. Escalator

107. If we arrange the given words in alphabetical order, which word would come at the second place, choose the correct alternative?
A. Plane B. Plain
C. Plenty D. Player

108. Choose the alternative that resembles the water image of the given word below:

A1M3b

A. ∀1W3P B. ∀ИW3P
C. ∀⅃W3P D. ∀⅃WƐP

109. Choose the word which is least like the other words in the group.
A. Eyes B. Ear
C. Hand D. Scarf

110. Choose the alternative that will continue the number series below:

2, 3, 5, 7, 11, 13 ?

A. 15 B. 19
C. 17 D. 21

111. Which of the following diagram indicates the best relation between Country, Nepal and India?

A. 

B. 

C. 

D. 

112. Choose the alternative that will continue the number series below:

5, 11, 19, 29, ?, 55

A. 39 B. 41
C. 37 D. 43

113. A FISH is to GILLS then a MAN is to ....
A. Ear B. Eye
C. Lungs D. Nose

114. Which figure among the five alternatives A, B, C, D and E would replace the question mark in figure '4'?

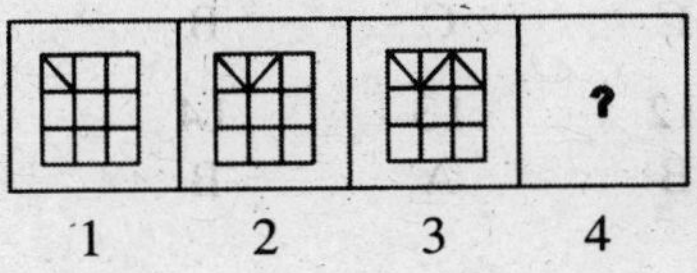

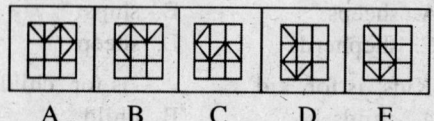

A B C D E

115. Choose the word which is least like the other words in the group.
A. Sun
B. Planets
C. Stars
D. Satellites

116. If Maya is the only daughter of Richa's grandmother's brother, how is Maya's daughter related to Richa?
A. Niece
B. Cousin
C. Aunt
D. Mother

117. O, P, Q, R, S and T are standing on a bench according to their height. P is taller than O but shorter than S. Only S is taller than T. R is shorter than P but taller than Q. Who is the shortest?
A. O
B. Q
C. P
D. Cannot be said

118. If '+' means '÷', 'x' means '−', '÷' means '+' and '−' means 'x', then what would be the answer of the equation?

$$16 \div 8 \times 6 - 2 + 12 = ?$$
A. 22
B. 24
C. 23
D. 20

119. Count the number of triangles present in the given figure.

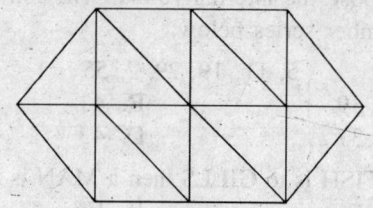

A. 16
B. 17
C. 18
D. 19

120. If DOG is to RABIES then MOSQUITO is to .... ?
A. Plague
B. Death
C. Malaria
D. Sting

121. It is 3 O'clock in a watch and it is rotated by 10 degree in a manner such that if the minute hand points towards the North–East, then hour hand will point towards which direction?
A. South
B. South-West
C. North-West
D. South-East

122. LOVE is to HATE then FRIEND is to ....?
A. Trust
B. Companion
C. Enemy
D. Despire

123. If the given alpha-numeric series is seen in mirror, which alternative would resemble its mirror image?

ANS43Q12
A. ΛИƧ4ƐOƖƐ
B. ƧƖΟƐ4ƧИΛ
C. ƧИΛƐ4ΟƧƐ
D. ƖƧWΛ4ƧИƧ

124. Given that A and B are a married couple. If X and Y are brothers and X is the brother of A. How is Y related to B?
A. Brother-in-law
B. Brother
C. Cousin
D. None of these

125. If '+' means '−', '−' means 'x'; 'x' means '÷' and '÷' means '+', then what would be the answer of the equation?

$$15 \times 5 \div 10 + 5 - 3 = ?$$
A. 9.5
B. 0
C. −2
D. 24

ANSWERS

1	2	3	4	5	6	7	8	9	10
D	C	C	B	C	C	B	D	A	A

11	12	13	14	15	16	17	18	19	20
C	B	A	B	B	C	B	C	D	B

21	22	23	24	25	26	27	28	29	30
A	A	C	A	C	A	A	C	A	A

31	32	33	34	35	36	37	38	39	40
D	D	B	A	A	A	A	C	D	B

41	42	43	44	45	46	47	48	49	50
A	C	A	C	D	D	B	C	C	B

51	52	53	54	55	56	57	58	59	60
A	B	C	C	C	C	D	D	A	B

61	62	63	64	65	66	67	68	69	70
B	B	C	C	D	B	B	D	D	D

71	72	73	74	75	76	77	78	79	80
D	B	D	C	C	D	C	A	D	A

81	82	83	84	85	86	87	88	89	90
D	C	A	A	C	C	A	C	B	A

91	92	93	94	95	96	97	98	99	100
A	B	D	A	D	C	A	B	B	C

101	102	103	104	105	106	107	108	109	110
B	A	B	C	A	C	A	C	D	C

111	112	113	114	115	116	117	118	119	120
A	B	C	A	C	B	D	C	A	C

121	122	123	124	125
D	C	B	A	C

EXPLANATORY ANSWERS

1. The greatest 8-digits number with given digits 5, 8, 7, 5, 2, 0, 6 and 1

$$= 87655210.$$

2. 52806, 52086, 52860, 52800, and 58260 are given numbers.

52086, 52800, 52806, 52860 and 58260 are in ascending order.

3. Sum of 234251 and 352421 = 586672

925564 – 586672 = 338892

Hence, 338892 that must be subtracted from 925564 to make it equal to the sum of 234251 and 352421.

4. $10101 \times 25 = 252525$

$$
\begin{array}{r}
10101 \\
25 \\
\hline
50505 \\
20202 \\
\hline
252525
\end{array}
$$

5. Total age of 3 sisters = 3×15

$= 45$ years

Sum of two sisters = $12 + 15$

$= 27$ years

∴ Age of the third sister = $45 - 27$

$= 18$ years.

6. $\dfrac{7}{6} \times 366$ days $= 7 \times 61$ days

$$= 427 \text{ days}$$

$$= \dfrac{427}{7} \text{ week}$$

$$= 61 \text{ week.}$$

7. The value of Roman numerals CDXLIX in Arabic numerals

$$= 400 + 40 + 9$$
$$= 449.$$

8. $(700 \div 10) - \{(12 \times 8) \div (34 - 10)\}$

$$= 70 - \{96 \div 24\}$$
$$= 70 - 4 = 66$$

9. $\quad 2 = 200\%$

$$\left[\because 200\% = \dfrac{200}{100} = 2 \right]$$

10. C.P. = ₹ 3000

S.P. = ₹ 2700

Loss = 3000 − 2700 = ₹ 300

Loss % $= \dfrac{300}{3000} \times 100 = 10\%.$

11. Duration of the Journey = 12 hrs + 6.15 hrs

$$= 18 \text{ hrs } 15 \text{ min.}$$

12. C.P. = ₹ 1,39,500

S.P. = ₹ 75,000 + ₹ 80,000

$$= ₹ 1,55,000$$

Gain = ₹ 1,55,000 − ₹ 1,39,500

$$= ₹ 15,500.$$

13. Required no. of bulbs

$$= 85 \times 48 \times 64$$
$$= 4080 \times 64 = 261120.$$

15. 38 − 8 = 30 and 68 − 8 = 60

HCF of 30 and 60 = 30

Hence, the required number = 30.

16. 10 kg + 2 dag + 6 g

$$= \left(10 + \dfrac{2}{100} + \dfrac{6}{1000} \right) \text{ kg} = 10.026 \text{ kg.}$$

18. Perimeter of rectangle = $2(l + b)$

$$= 2(10 + 8) = 36 \text{ cm.}$$

According to the question,

Perimeter of rectangle = Perimeter of square

$$\therefore \quad \text{Side of square} = \dfrac{36}{4} = 9 \text{ cm}$$

Area of the square = $9 \times 9 = 81$ cm^2.

19. Sum of three angles of a triangle = 180°

(A) $\quad 52° + 69° + 79° = 200°$

(B) $\quad 30° + 69° + 71° = 170°$

(C) $\quad 132° + 169° + 59° = 360°$

(D) $\quad 32° + 69° + 79° = 180°$

Hence, option (D) is correct.

21. $\quad 1.25 = \dfrac{125}{100} = \dfrac{5}{4} = 1\dfrac{1}{4}.$

22. Sum of two numbers = 11009

One number = 9999

$\therefore$ Other number = $\begin{array}{r} 11009 \\ -9999 \\ \hline 1010 \end{array}$

Hence, other number = 1010.

23. $6 \div 6 + 6 \times 6 - 6$

$$= 1 + 36 - 6 = 37 - 6 = 31.$$

24. $1\dfrac{1}{24} - 1 + \dfrac{7}{36}$

$$\Rightarrow \dfrac{25}{24} - 1 + \dfrac{7}{36}$$

$$= \dfrac{75 - 72 + 14}{72} = \dfrac{17}{72}.$$

25. Total amount of lemonade Sara poured in 5 glasses

$$= 1\dfrac{1}{8} \times 5 = \dfrac{9}{8} \times 5$$

$$= \dfrac{45}{8} = 5\dfrac{5}{8} \text{ Cups.}$$

26. Required rice in each bag $= \dfrac{1}{4} \div 7$

$$= \dfrac{1}{4} \times \dfrac{1}{7} = \dfrac{1}{28}.$$

27. $1 + 0 + \dfrac{9}{100} + \dfrac{3}{1000} = 1.093.$

29.
$$\begin{array}{r} 20.088 \\ 20.08 \\ 20.008 \\ 20.888 \\ \hline 81.064 \end{array}$$

Hence, required sum = 81.064.

30. Round off 37504 to the nearest hundreds
$$= 37500.$$

31. $\because \quad$ Speed $= \dfrac{\text{Distance}}{\text{Time}}$

$\therefore \quad$ Time $= \dfrac{\text{Distance}}{\text{Speed}}$

$$= \dfrac{350}{75} = \dfrac{14}{3} \text{ hrs.}$$

$$= 4\dfrac{2}{3} \text{ hrs} = 4 \text{ hrs } 40 \text{ minutes.}$$

32. Number of rectangular pieces

$$= \dfrac{\text{Volume of cube}}{\text{Volume of rectangular pieces}}$$

$$= \dfrac{400 \times 400 \times 400}{20 \times 10 \times 5}$$

$$= \dfrac{64000000}{1000} = 64000.$$

33. $\quad P = ₹\ 500$

$A = ₹\ 600$

$S.I. = A - P$

$= 600 - 500 = ₹\ 100$

Time $= \dfrac{S.I. \times 100}{P \times r}$

$$= \dfrac{100 \times 100}{500 \times 5} = 4 \text{ years.}$$

34. Total numbers of 4 numbers
$$= 4 \times 30 = 120$$

Sum of first-three numbers = 85

$\therefore$ The fourth number = $120 - 85 = 35$

35. Let $x\%$ of 10000 m = 10 m

$\Rightarrow \quad \dfrac{x}{100} \times 10000 = 10$

$\Rightarrow \quad 100x = 10$

$\Rightarrow \quad x = \dfrac{10}{100} = \dfrac{1}{10}\% = 0.1\%.$

36. Number of square tiles

$$= \dfrac{360 \times 450}{15 \times 15} = 720.$$

37. The smallest odd number formed by using the digits 1, 2, 3, 4 and 5 = 12345.

38. (A) $\dfrac{1}{3}, \dfrac{1}{2}, \dfrac{25}{100}$

$\Rightarrow \dfrac{1}{3}, \dfrac{1}{2}, \dfrac{1}{4}$ are not in ascending order

(B) $\dfrac{1}{4}, \dfrac{1}{2}, \dfrac{1}{3}$ are not in ascending order

(C) $\dfrac{1}{4}, \dfrac{1}{3}, \dfrac{1}{2}$ are in ascending order

(D) $\dfrac{1}{2}, \dfrac{1}{3}, \dfrac{1}{4}$ are not in ascending order

Hence, option (C) is correct.

39. 18 km/hr $= 18 \times \dfrac{5}{18}$ m/s = 5 m/s

Hence, the speed of boat = 5 m/s.

40. $\quad C = \dfrac{5}{9}(F - 32)$

$$= \dfrac{5}{9}(200 - 32)$$

$$= \dfrac{5}{9} \times 168 = \dfrac{5}{3} \times 56$$

$$= \dfrac{280}{3} = 93.3°C$$

Hence, the value of 200°F in degree Celsius
$$= 93.3°C.$$

41. $\quad$ Difference $= \begin{array}{r} 39460 \\ -36490 \\ \hline 2970 \end{array}$

42. $\dfrac{375}{100} \times \dfrac{5}{100} + \dfrac{725}{100} \times \dfrac{10}{100}$

$= \dfrac{1875}{10000} + \dfrac{7250}{10000} = \dfrac{9125}{10000} = 0.9125.$

43.

```
28          84          112
 |___ __↑ |___ __↑
    ×3        28 + 84

38          114         152
 |___ __↑ |___ __↑
    ×3        38 + 114

48          144         192
 |___ __↑ |___ __↑
    ×3        48 + 144

58          174         232
 |___ __↑ |___ __↑
    ×3        58 + 174
```

Hence, the next row of numbers is 58 174 232.

44. Perimeter of rectangular field
$= 2(l + b) = 2(40 + 25) = 130$ m
In 1 round distance $= 130$ m
In 4 rounds distance $= 130 \times 4$ m $= 520$ m.

45. Area of the room $= l \times b$
$= 1500 \times 1000$ cm^2
$= 1500000$ m^2
Cost of 1 cm^2 = ₹ 2
Cost of 1500000 cm^2 = ₹ 3000000
∴ Cost of carpeting its floor = 3000000

46. Cost of 15 balls = ₹ 300

Cost of 1 ball = ₹ $\dfrac{300}{15}$ = ₹ 20

Cost of 12 shuttle = ₹ 96

Cost of 1 shuttle = ₹ $\dfrac{96}{12}$ = ₹ 8

∴ Cost of 1 ball and 1 shuttle
$= ₹ 20 + ₹ 8 = ₹ 28.$

47. HCF × LCM = 1st no. × 2nd no.
$312 \times$ LCM $= 624 \times 936$

∴ LCM $= \dfrac{624 \times 936}{312}$

$= 2 \times 936 = 1872$
Hence, required smallest number = 1872.

48. Total C.P. = ₹ 450 + ₹ 50 = ₹ 500
Total S.P. = ₹ 600
Profit = S.P. – C.P.
$= 600 - 500 = ₹ 100$

Profit % $= \dfrac{\text{Profit}}{\text{CP}} \times 100$

$= \dfrac{100}{500} \times 100 = 20\%.$

49. Area of the given figure
$= 10 \times 6 - 4 \times 2 - 4 \times 2$
$= 60 - 16 = 44$ cm^2.

50. Let total time spent by Amar in study $= x$ hrs.

Time spent on Science $= \dfrac{3x}{8}$

Time spent on English $= \dfrac{3x}{8} \times \dfrac{2}{5} = \dfrac{3x}{20}$

Hence, $\dfrac{3}{20}$ of Amar's study time was spent studying English.

101. 20, 30, 42, ?
$20 + 10 = 30$
$30 + 12 = 42$
$42 + 14 = 56$

103. $(13)^2 = 169$
$(17)^2 = 289$

110. 2, 3, 5, 7, 11, 13 are prime numbers.
Hence, next prime number is 17.

112. $5 + 6 = 11$ $11 + 8 = 19$
$19 + 10 = 29$ $29 + 12 = 41$
$41 + 14 = 55.$

118. $16 \div 8 \times 6 - 2 + 12 = ?$
$16 + 8 - 6 \times 2 \div 12$

$= 16 + 8 - 6 \times 2 \times \dfrac{1}{12}$

$= 16 + 8 - 1 = 24 - 1 = 23.$

125. $15 \times 5 \div 10 + 5 - 3 = ?$
$= 15 \div 5 + 10 - 5 \times 3$

$= 15 \times \dfrac{1}{5} + 10 - 5 \times 3$

$= 3 + 10 - 15 = 13 - 15 = -2.$

All India Sainik School Entrance Exam., 2017
(CLASS-VI)

PAPER-I : MATHEMATICS AND LANGUAGE ABILITY

Part-A : Mathematics

Section-I

(Each question carries two marks)

1. Form the smallest and greatest 6-digit numerals by repeating any 2 digits from 7, 9, 5, 4.

2. Find the square root of 7921.

3. If a man can do a work in 32 days, in how many days will 24 men complete the same work?

4. Find the simple interest, if P = ₹ 400, R = 3.65% per annum and time = 150 days.

5. Round 48,540 and 23,467 to the nearest 1000 and find the difference.

6. Express 804.291 kg as decagrams.

7. Find the smallest number which when divided by 12 and 20 leaves no remainder.

8. Sonali and Priya are classmates. Sonali completed her homework in $\frac{5}{6}$ of an hour and Priya in $\frac{3}{4}$ of an hour. Who was faster?

9. Simplify $6\frac{3}{10} - 2\frac{3}{4} - 1\frac{2}{5}$

10. Two angles of a quadrilateral are each 90° and remaining two angles are such that one is 3 times the other. Find these two angles.

Section-II

(Each question carries three marks)

11. Find the ratio of 90 cm to 1.5 m.

12. Arrange the following in descending order: $\frac{3}{7}, \frac{3}{11}, \frac{3}{5}, \frac{3}{2}$ and $\frac{3}{17}$.

13. The number of girl students in each class of a co-educational middle school is depicted by the pictograph:

Observe this pictograph and answer the following questions:
(a) Which class has the maximum number of girl students?
(b) Is the number of girls in Class V less than the number of girls in Class III?
(c) How many girls are there in Class VII?

14. Akhilesh runs a coffee shop and sells 51 cups of coffee in 6 hours. If this is three-fourths of the total number of cups he sells in the whole day, find out the number of cups he sells in a day.

15. Simplify $4\frac{6}{8} - \left\{3\frac{1}{3} + \left(2\frac{1}{2} - 1\frac{1}{4}\right)\right\}$.

16. Find the greatest number which divides 149 and 101 leaving remainder 5 in each case.

17. Mrs. Singhal deposited ₹ 10,000 in a Post Office Saving at an interest of 3% per annum. How much amount will she receive at the end of 4th month?

18. Suppose your watch gains 4 seconds every 8 hours. How many seconds will it gain in a week?

19. A fruit seller had 2,00,000 apples. He packed them in boxes. Each box contains 176 apples. How many boxes were used and how many apples were left over?

20. Find the average of all prime numbers between 60 and 80.

Section-III

(Each question carries five marks)

21. Bob wants to cover the floor of a room 3 m wide and 4 m long by squared tiles. If each square tile is of side 0.5 m, then find the number of tiles required to cover the floor of the room.

22. Name the types of following triangles:
(a) Triangle with lengths of sides 7 cm, 8 cm and 9 cm.
(b) Δ ABC with AB = 8.7 cm, AC = 7 cm and BC = 6 cm.
(c) Δ PQR such that PQ = QR = PR = 5 cm.
(d) Δ DEF with m∠D = 90°.
(e) Δ XYZ with m∠Y = 90° and XY = YZ.

23. Find the smallest 4 digit number such that when it is divided by 12, 18, 21 and 28, it leaves remainder 3 in each case.

24. How much time will a 171 m long train take to cross 229 m long bridge, if it is running at a speed of 45 km/h?

25. Divide rupees 4000 among A, B, C, so that their shares may be in the ratio of 5 : 7 : 8.

26. Find the number of cubical boxes of cubical side 3 cm which can be accommodated in a carton of dimension 15 cm × 9 cm × 12 cm?

27. Fill in the blanks:
(a) There are only .... symbols in Roman numerals.
(b) The predecessor of the smallest 8 digit number is ....
(c) $\frac{4}{7}X$ .... = 84
(d) Length of a Rectangle = $\dfrac{?}{\text{Breadth}}$
(e) .... is the smallest prime number.

28. A crockery dealer ordered for 50 pieces of China tea sets for ₹ 18,000. When the goods arrived, he found that two tea sets were damaged. At what price per set should he sell the remaining tea sets to earn a total profit of ₹ 1200?

29. Vina's father baked a rectangular cake. In the evening $\frac{5}{6}$ of the cake was left. Vina ate half of it. What fraction of the cake did Vina eat?

30. (a) The product of two numbers is 2925. If LCM is 195, find HCF.
(b) Sohan bought rice at ₹ 4800.75 per quintal. Due to a fall in prices he could sell it as ₹ 4600.75 per quintal only. Find his total loss if he has bought 13.5 quintals rice.

ANSWERS

1. Greatest number = 997754
Smallest number = 445579.

2.

8	79 21	89
	64	
169	1521	
	1521	
	×	

∴ Square root of 7921 = 89.

3. ∵ 1 man can do a work in 32 days

∴ 24 men can do this work $\frac{32}{24} = \frac{4}{3}$ days

$= 1\frac{1}{3}$ days.

4. S.I. $= \dfrac{P \times r \times t}{100} = \dfrac{400 \times 365 \times 150}{100 \times 100 \times 365} = ₹ 6$

   Hence, Simple interest $= ₹ 6$.

5. $48540 = 49000$

          $23467 = 23000$

   Required difference $= 49000 - 23000$

                      $= 26000$.

6. 804.291 kg $= \dfrac{804291}{1000}$ kg

                 $= \dfrac{804291}{1000} \times 100$ deca gram

                 $= 80429.1$ deca grams.

7. LCM of 12 and 20 $= 60$

   Hence, the smallest number which when divided by 12 and 20 leaves no. remainder is 60.

8. Time taken by Sonali to complete her home

   work $= 60 \times \dfrac{5}{6}$ minutes $= 50$ min.

   Time taken by Priya to complete her home

   work $= 60 \times \dfrac{3}{4}$ minutes $= 45$ min.

   Hence, Priya is faster than Sonali.

9. $6\dfrac{3}{10} - 2\dfrac{3}{4} - 1\dfrac{2}{5} = \dfrac{63}{10} - \dfrac{11}{4} - \dfrac{7}{5}$

   $= \dfrac{126 - 55 - 28}{20} = \dfrac{126 - 83}{20} = \dfrac{43}{20} = 2\dfrac{3}{20}$.

10. Let remaining two angles are $x°$ and $3x°$

    $x° + 3x° + 90° + 90° = 360°$

    $\Rightarrow \quad 4x = 360 - 180 = 180$

    $\Rightarrow \quad x = \dfrac{180}{4} = 45°$

    $3x = 3 \times 45 = 135°$

    Hence, remaining two angles are 45° and 135°.

11. The ratio of 90 cm : 1.5 m

    $= \dfrac{90}{150} = \dfrac{3}{5} = 3 : 5$

12. Arrange in descending order of the following:

    $\dfrac{3}{7}, \dfrac{3}{11}, \dfrac{3}{5}, \dfrac{3}{2}$ and $\dfrac{3}{17}$

    $\dfrac{3}{2}, \dfrac{3}{5}, \dfrac{3}{7}, \dfrac{3}{11}, \dfrac{3}{17}$ are in descending order.

13. (a) The maximum number of girl students in class I $= 6 \times 4 = 24$ girls.

    (b) The number of girls in class V less than the number of girls in class III.

    In V class, no. of girls $= 10$

    In III class, no. of girls $= 5 \times 4 = 20$.

    (c) Number of girls in class VII $= 4 \times 3 = 12$.

14. Let, x cups he sells in a day

    According to the question,

    $\dfrac{3}{4}$ of $x = 51 \quad \Rightarrow \quad x = \dfrac{4 \times 51}{3} = 68$.

15. $4\dfrac{6}{8} - \left\{ 3\dfrac{1}{3} + \left(2\dfrac{1}{2} - 1\dfrac{1}{4} \right) \right\}$

    $= \dfrac{38}{8} - \left\{ \dfrac{10}{3} + \left(\dfrac{5}{2} - \dfrac{5}{4} \right) \right\}$

    $= \dfrac{38}{8} - \left\{ \dfrac{10}{3} + \left(\dfrac{10 - 5}{4} \right) \right\} = \dfrac{38}{8} - \left\{ \dfrac{10}{3} + \dfrac{5}{4} \right\}$

    $= \dfrac{38}{8} - \left\{ \dfrac{40 + 15}{12} \right\} = \dfrac{38}{8} - \dfrac{55}{12} = \dfrac{114 - 110}{24}$

    $= \dfrac{4}{24} = \dfrac{1}{6}$.

16. $149 - 5 = 144$

          $101 - 5 = 96$

    HCF of 144 and 96 $= 48$

    Hence, required greatest no. $= 48$.

17.   S.I. $= \dfrac{P \times r \times t}{100}$

                       $= \dfrac{10000 \times 3 \times 4}{100 \times 12} = ₹ 100$

    Amount $= 10000 + 100 = 10100$

    Hence, she will receive ₹ 10100 at the end of 4th month.

18. In 8 hrs watch gains 4 seconds

    In 24 hrs watch gains 12 seconds

    In 1 day watch gains 12 seconds

    In 7 days watch gains 12×7 seconds

                         $= 84$ seconds.

19. $200000 \div 176$ then we get

    quotient $= 1136$, remainder $= 64$

    Hence, no. of boxes $= 1136$ and 64 apples were left.

20. 61, 67, 71, 73 and 79 are prime numbers between 60 and 80

Average of all prime numbers

$$= \frac{61+67+71+73+79}{5} = \frac{351}{5} = 70.2$$

21. Required no. of tiles $= \frac{3 \times 4}{0.5 \times 0.5}$

$$= \frac{3 \times 4 \times 10 \times 10}{5 \times 5} = 48.$$

22. (a) Triangle with lengths of sides 7 cm, 8 cm and 9 cm is scalene triangle.

(b) $\triangle ABC$ with AB = 8.7 cm,
AC = 7 cm and BC = 6 cm
is scalene triangle.

(c) In $\triangle PQR$ where PQ = QR = PR = 5 cm
This type of triangle is equilateral triangle.

(d) In $\triangle DEF$, $\angle D = 90°$
This type of triangle is right triangle.

(e) In $\triangle XYZ$, $\angle Y = 90°$ and XY = YZ
This type of triangle is isosceles right triangle.

23. LCM of 12, 18, 21 and 28 = 252
The smallest 4 digit number = 1000
$\therefore$ 252 k + 3 is the smallest number of 4 digit number
$\therefore$ 252 × 4 + 3 = 1008 + 3 = 1011
Hence, the required no. = 1011.

24. Speed = 45 km/hr $= \frac{45 \times 1000}{60 \times 60} = \frac{25}{2}$ m/s

Distance = 171 m + 229 m = 400 m

Time taken $= \frac{400}{\frac{25}{2}} = \frac{400 \times 2}{25}$ seconds

$$= 16 \times 2 \text{ seconds}$$
$$= 32 \text{ seconds.}$$

25. A : B : C = 5 : 7 : 8

A's share $= \frac{5}{20} \times 4000 = ₹ 1000$

B's share $= \frac{7}{20} \times 4000 = ₹ 1400$

C's share $= \frac{8}{20} \times 4000 = ₹ 1600.$

26. No. of cubical boxes $= \frac{15 \times 9 \times 12}{3 \times 3 \times 3}$

$$= 5 \times 3 \times 4 = 60.$$

27. (a) There are only seven symbols in Roman numerals. [IVXLCDM]

(b) The predecessor of the smallest 8 digit number is 9999999.

(c) $\frac{4}{7} \times 147 = 84$

(d) Lenght of a rectangle $= \frac{\text{Area}}{\text{Breadth}}$

(e) 2 is the smallest prime number.

28. Cost price of 48 China tea sets = ₹ 18000

Cost of each China tea set $= \frac{18000}{48} = ₹ 375$

Selling price of 48 China tea sets
$$= 18000 + 1200 = ₹ 19200$$
Selling price of each China tea set

$$= \frac{19200}{48} = ₹ 400.$$

29. Portion of the cake left in the evening

$$= \frac{5}{6} \text{ portion.}$$

Portion of the cake ate by Vina $= \frac{1}{2}$ of $\frac{5}{6}$

$$= \frac{5}{6} \times \frac{1}{2} = \frac{5}{12}$$

30. (a) HCF $= \frac{\text{Product of two numbers}}{\text{LCM}}$

$$= \frac{2925}{195} = 15.$$

(b) Cost of 1 quintal rice = ₹ 4800.75
Selling price of 1 quintal rice = ₹ 4600.75
Loss per quintal = ₹ 200
Loss for 13.5 quintal = ₹ 200 × 13.5

$$= ₹ 200 \times \frac{135}{10}$$

$$= ₹ 2700.$$

PART-B : LANGUAGE ABILITY

1. Write 15 sentences on any *one* of the following topics: **(15)**
   Importance of Cleanliness or A Journey by Bus.

2. Read the following passage carefully and answer the questions that follow: **(15)**

   The Sahara Desert covers large parts of Africa. The desert is covered with sand dunes or sand seas. The desert also has several deeply dissected mountains and mountain ranges along with many volcanic mountains. Most of the rivers and streams that are found in Sahara are seasonal or intermittent, except the Nile river, which crosses the desert from its origins in central Africa to empty into Mediterranean.

   The central part of the Sahara is very dry, with little vegetation. The northern and southern reaches of the desert, along with the highlands, have areas of sparse grasslands and desert shrub, with trees and taller shrubs at places where moisture collects.

   (a) What is the meaning of word "seasonal"?
   (b) "The desert is covered by sand dunes or sand seas". What is the meaning of sand sea in the paragraph?
   (c) "The central part of Sahara is very dry, with little vegetation". What does it mean?
   (d) Give the meaning of "sparse".
   (e) What is the meaning of vegetation in paragraph?

3. Make your own sentences using the underlined words in the following paragraph. **(5 × 2 = 10)**

   Do you **support** a football or hockey team? Perhaps you follow the **success** of your national cricket team. You know every game has its own importance and follows its own **discipline.** To become a good player of any game you need to have **regular** practice of that game. Learinng basic skills of the game is very **essential.**
   (a) ....
   (b) ....
   (c) ....
   (d) ....
   (e) ....

4. Form meaningful sentences by rearranging the words in proper order: **(5 × 2 = 10)**
   (a) crying/she had/as/lost her/Manju was/pencil
   (b) at that hospital/Anil said that/was a doctor/his father
   (c) environmental/of everybody/protection/is responsibility/the
   (d) the/knocking/who/at/door/is
   (e) early to bed/good habit/and early to rise/is a

5. Give one word for the following: **(5 × 1 = 5)**
   (a) A person who carries our luggage
   ....
   (b) A person who spends money extravagantly
   ....
   (c) Young one of a horse
   ....
   (d) Happening once in two years
   ....
   (e) One who makes wooden furninture
   ....

6. Choose the correct word given in the brackets and fill in the blanks: **(5 × 2 = 10)**
   (a) Cleanliness is next to ....
   (God, Goddess, Godliness)
   (b) My father tells me to .... daily.
   (Play, played, playing)
   (c) Yesterday, a cyclone .... a small town near the beach. (hit/has hit)
   (d) I like .... blue candle the best.
   (a, an, the)
   (e) There is .... eucalyptus tree beside the house. (a, an, the)

7. Use the given word in separate sentences of your own to show the difference in the meaning of the words of the pair given below: **(5 × 2 = 10)**
   (a) Early, Yearly   (b) Greatness, Grateful
   (c) Pray, Prey   (d) Break, Brake
   (e) Lose, Loose

8. Give the Antonym (opposite) of the following words: **(5 × 1 = 5)**
   (a) Risky   (b) Doubtful
   (c) Negligent   (d) Deep
   (e) Differ

9. Change each of the following as directed: **(5 × 2 = 10)**
   (a) The news is too good to be true.
   (Remove "too")
   ....
   (b) She is your mother.
   (Change into interrogative)
   ....
   (c) Fire destroyed the town.

(Change the Voice)
....
(d) He said, 'I am very thirsty'
(Change into indirect speech)
....
(e) Raju is not as bad as Gaurav.
(Rewrite using comparative form of "good")
....

10. Imagine your name is Akash and you live at House No. 23, Dr Kalam Road, Jayanagar, Bangalore. Your sister, Deepika who lives at Shanti Nivas, Linking Road, Mumbai, has sent you a Rakhi on Rakshbandhan. Write a letter of thanks to her. **(10)**

ANSWERS

1. Importance of Cleanliness

It is rightly said, "Cleanliness is next only to godliness." Cleanliness is to our body what godliness is to our soul and mind. For the purity of our mind we should have noble thoughts. Similarly, for our good health, we must observe cleanliness in letter and spirit. Moreover, an unclean person or thing is very unsightly, unpleasant and a mere nuisance. Who wants to look at a filthy dog or a pig rolling in a heap of dung, though everybody would like the sight of a dancing peacock or a hopping sparrow? We should bathe daily and put on fresh well-washed clothes. We should keep our books neat and clean and our house spick and span. There should be no puddles which breed mosquitos and flies near our home as they are a source of many obnoxious diseases. Similarly, we should keep our roads, parks and village or town clean. Throwing of heaps of rubbish here and there or spitting everywhere can cause several diseases to ourselves and to others. Similarly, food should be fresh and covered and free from the approach of flies. Let the children be taught the habit of cleanliness from their very early life.

2. (a) Seasonal means relating to or characteristic of a particular season of the year.
   (b) Sand sea means a vast expanse of sand.
   (c) It means there is scarcity of water and plant in the central part of Sahara.
   (d) Sparse means thinly dispersed.
   (e) Vegetation means plants collectively.

3. (a) We must support the good cause.
   (b) Success depends upon you efforts.
   (c) We must follow the rules of discipline.
   (d) We must be regular in exercise.
   (e) It is essential to clear the test.

4. (a) Manju was crying as she had lost her pencil.
   (b) Anil said that his father was a doctor at that hospital.
   (c) The environmental protection is responsibility of everybody.
   (d) Who is knocking at the door?
   (e) Early to bed and early to rise is a good habit.

5. (a) Porter   (b) Spendthrift
   (c) Colt   (d) Biennial
   (e) Carpenter

6. (a) Godliness   (b) Play
   (c) hit   (d) the
   (e) a

7. (a) We must get up early in the morning. You have to pay the maintenance charges yearly.
   (b) Every one know him for this greatness. We are grateful to our teachers.
   (c) We pray to God every morning. The deer was an easy prey for the tiger.
   (d) Never break the rules of discipline. You must apply the brakes of your bicycle.
   (e) Never lose your temper. The brakes of your bicycle are loose.

8. (a) Safe   (b) Sure
   (c) Careful   (d) Shallow
   (e) Agree

9. (a) The news is so good that it cannot be true.
   (b) Is she your mother?
   (c) The town was destroyed in fire.
   (d) He told that he was very thirsty.
   (e) Raju is better than Gaurav.

10. House No. 23,
Dr Kalam Road,
Jayanagar, Bangalore.

August 7, 20....

My Dear Sister,

Hope this letter of mine will find you in good health and happiness. I received the precious Rakhi sent by you today. It looks really beautiful in my hand.

Thank you very much for the lovely Rakhi. I am sending you a small gift and hope you will like it.

Hope we will be together on the next Raksha Bandhan.

Love to Arpan and Regards to dear Jijaji.

Yours affectionately
AKASH

Postage

To

Ms Deepika,
Shanti Niwas,
Linking Road,
Mumbai

PAPER-II : INTELLIGENCE TEST*

Directions (Qs. 1-6) : *In each of the following series determine the order of the letters/numbers. Then from the given options select the one which will complete the given series.*

1. B D G K ? V
   (a) N   (b) P
   (c) Q   (d) M

2. dfe, jih, mln, ?, vut
   (a) oqp   (b) psr
   (c) prq   (d) rsp

3. QPO, SRQ, UTS, WVU, (?)
   (a) XVZ   (b) ZYA
   (c) YXW   (d) VWX

4. 4, 9, 19, 34, 54, ?, 109
   (a) 89   (b) 84
   (c) 74   (d) 79

5. 7776, 1296, 216, 36, 6, ?
   (a) 6   (b) 0
   (c) 3   (d) 1

6. 3, 15, 90, 630, 5040, ?
   (a) 35280   (b) 40320
   (c) 45360   (d) 10080

Directions (Qs. 7 and 8): *In the following questions select the right option which indicates the correct code for the word or letter given in the question.*

7. If BAD is coded as 7, HIS as 9, LOW will be coded as :
   (a) 50   (b) 8
   (c) 23   (d) 5

8. In a certain code LIBERATE is written as 56403170, TRIBAL will be written in the same code as :
   (a) 734615   (b) 736415
   (c) 136475   (d) 034615

9. Reena walked from A and B in the East 10 feet. Then she turned to the right and walked 3 feet. Again she turned to the right and walked 14 feet. How far is she from A?
   (a) 4 feet   (b) 5 feet
   (c) 24 feet   (d) 27 feet

10. Amit started walking positioning his back towards the sun. After some time, he turned left, then turned right and towards the left again. In which direction is he going now?
   (a) North or South   (b) East or West
   (c) North or West   (d) South or West

11. Pointing to a man, a lady said, "His brother's father is my grandfather's only son." How is the lady related to the man?
   (a) Mother   (b) Sister
   (c) Daughter   (d) Aunt

* Memory Based

12. Vidya is the wife of Gopi and Gopi is the brother of Akhil. Akhil is the uncle of Vijay. What is Vijay's relation with Vidya?
(a) Son   (b) Nephew
(c) Brother-in-law   (d) Brother

Directions (Qs. 13-17) : *In the questions given below one term is missing. Based on the relationship of the two given words/letters/numbers find the missing term from the given options.*

13. ACE : FGH : : LNP : ?
(a) QRS   (b) PQR
(c) QST   (d) MOQ

14. EIGHTY : GIEYTH : : OUTPUT : ?
(a) UTOPTU   (b) UOTUPT
(c) TUOUTP   (d) TUOTUP

15. 23 : 53 : : 8 : ?
(a) 66   (b) 57
(c) 27   (d) 19

16. PEARL : NECKLACE : : FLOWER : ?
(a) Plant   (b) Garden
(c) Petal   (d) Bouquet

17. ALPHABET : WORD : : WORD : ?
(a) Sound   (b) Music
(c) Sentence   (d) Dictionary

Directions (Qs. 18–24) : *In each of the following questions, there are four options. Three options are alike in certain manner. Only one option does not fit in. Choose the one which is different from the rest.*

18. (a) 18   (b) 12
(c) 30   (d) 20

19. (a) 336   (b) 213
(c) 436   (d) 819

20. (a) 28751   (b) 52638
(c) 85362   (d) 63852

21. (a) AEHJ   (b) EIJK
(c) DHKM   (d) CGJL

22. (a) Rabbit   (b) Crocodile
(c) Earthworm   (d) Snail

23. (a) Tree   (b) Leaf
(c) Bush   (d) Herb

24. (a) Doctor   (b) Teacher
(c) Engineer   (d) Diver

25. How many 7's are there in the following series which are preceded by 6 which is not preceded by 8?
8 7 6 7 8 6 7 5 6 7 9 8 6 1 6 7 7 6 8 8 6 9 7 6 8 7
(a) 2   (b) 3
(c) 4   (d) Only 1

26. If "+" means "÷"; "×" means "−"; "÷"means "×" and "−" means "+", what will be the value of the following expression?
$9 + 3 \div 4 - 8 \times 2 = ?$
(a) $6\dfrac{3}{4}$ (b) $-1\dfrac{3}{4}$
(c) $-6\dfrac{1}{4}$ (d) 18

27. If "−" means "÷"; "+" means "×"; "÷"means "−" and "×" means "+", then which of the following must be true?
(a) $1 \div 2 + 3 \times 6 - 8 = 12$
(b) $2 + 3 - 5 \times 8 \div 4 = 7$
(c) $5 + 6 \times 8 - 2 \div 3 = 31$
(d) $6 \div 1 + 2 - 8 \times 4 = 31$

28. If Thursday was the day after the day before yesterday five days ago, what is the least number of days ago when Sunday was three days before the day after tomorrow?
(a) Two days ago   (b) Three days ago
(c) Four days ago   (d) Five days ago

29. If the fifth day of a month is Friday, which of the following will be the Seventh day from 10th of that month?
(a) Tuesday   (b) Monday
(c) Wednesday   (d) Thursday

30. In a certain language 'mu mit es' means 'who is she' and 'elb mu es' means 'where is she'. What is the code for 'where' in this language?
(a) es   (b) elb
(c) mu   (d) mit

31. In a certain code language '069' means 'grapes are sweet', '476' means 'very sweet fruit' and '509' means 'grapes are ripe'. Which of the following digits means 'ripe' in that language?
(a) 0   (b) 5
(c) 9   (d) 7

32. If the odd numbers between 20 to 40 are arranged in a row, what will be the 6th number from the right?

(a) 27 (b) 31

(c) 33 (d) 29

Directions (Qs. 33–35) : *In each of the following questions, three out of four alternatives contain alphabet placed in a particular form. Find the one that does not belong to the group.*

33. (a) PEAR (b) TORE

(c) REAP (d) TEAR

34. (a) QePFoLA (b) OrDFkV

(c) TuMBiN (d) XZaWoB

35. (a) KQ14 (b) AY13

(c) MR11 (d) GW15

Directions (Qs. 36-40): *There are two sets of figure given. There is a definite relationship between first two. Establish a similar relationship between third and fourth by selecting a suitable figure from answer that would replace the question mark.*

36. Question Figures

Answer Figures

(a)   (b)   (c)   (d)

37. Question Figures

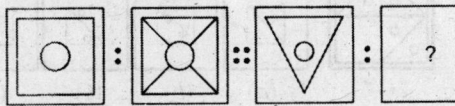

Answer Figures

(a)   (b)   (c)   (d)

38. Question Figures

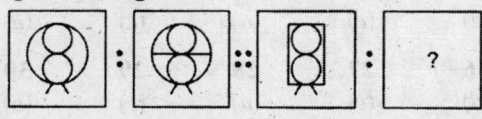

Answer Figures

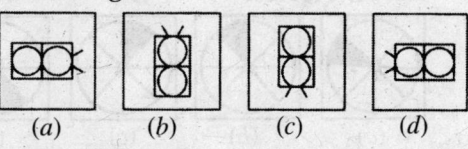

(a)   (b)   (c)   (d)

39. Question Figures

Answer Figures

(a)   (b)   (c)   (d)

40. Question Figures

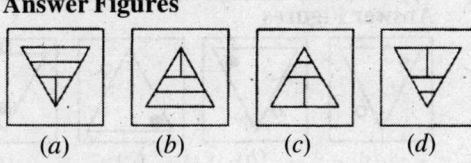

Answer Figures

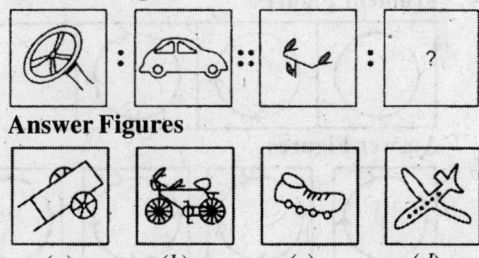

(a)   (b)   (c)   (d)

Directions (Qs. 41-45): *In each of the following questions, there are three figures and the space for the fourth figure is left blank. The problem figures are in a series. Find out one figure from among the answer figures which occupies the blank space for the fourth figure and completes the series. Indicate your answer in the answer sheet.*

41. Problem Figures

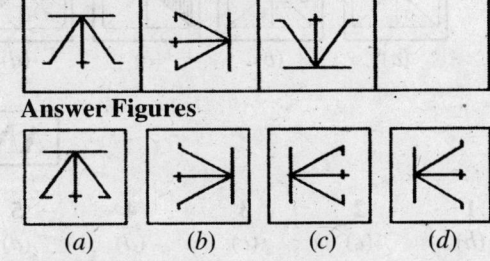

Answer Figures

(a)   (b)   (c)   (d)

42. Problem Figures

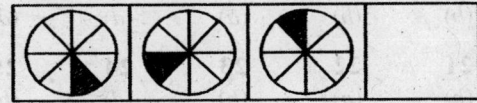

Answer Figures

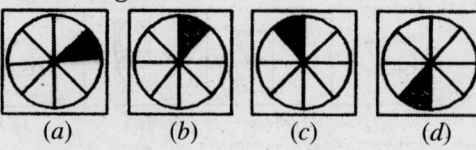

(a)　　　(b)　　　(c)　　　(d)

43. Problem Figures

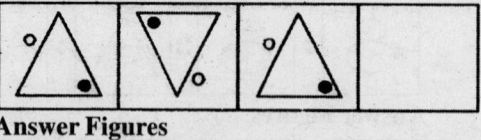

Answer Figures

(a)　　　(b)　　　(c)　　　(d)

44. Problem Figures

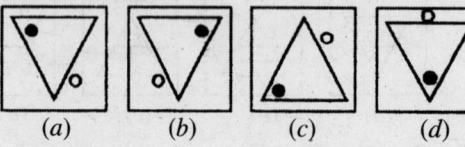

Answer Figures

(a)　　　(b)　　　(c)　　　(d)

45. Problem Figures

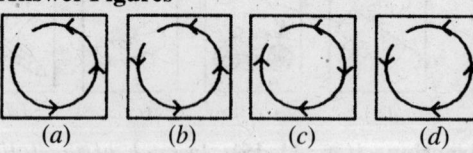

Answer Figures

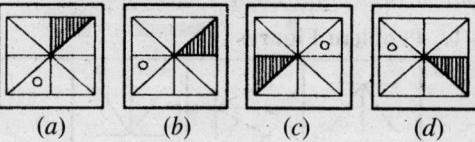

(a)　　　(b)　　　(c)　　　(d)

Directions (Qs. 46-50) : *There is a problem figure on the left-hand side, a part of which is missing. Observe the answer figures (a), (b), (c) and (d) on the right-hand side and find out the answer figure which, without changing the direction, fits in the missing part of the problem figure in order to complete the pattern in the problem figure. Indicate your answer by letter of the answer figure chosen by you in the box against the number corresponding to the questions in the answer sheet.*

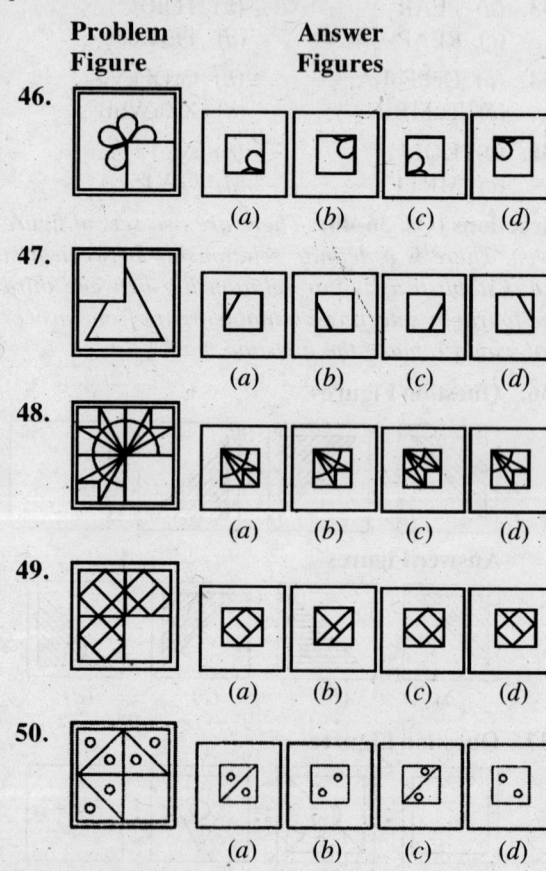

	Problem Figure	Answer Figures
46.		(a) (b) (c) (d)
47.		(a) (b) (c) (d)
48.		(a) (b) (c) (d)
49.		(a) (b) (c) (d)
50.		(a) (b) (c) (d)

ANSWERS

1	2	3	4	5	6	7	8	9	10
(b)	(c)	(c)	(d)	(d)	(c)	(d)	(b)	(b)	(a)

11	12	13	14	15	16	17	18	19	20
(b)	(b)	(a)	(d)	(d)	(d)	(c)	(a)	(c)	(a)

21	22	23	24	25	26	27	28	29	30
(b)	(a)	(b)	(d)	(b)	(d)	(c)	(a)	(c)	(b)

31	32	33	34	35	36	37	38	39	40
(b)	(d)	(b)	(b)	(c)	(d)	(a)	(c)	(c)	(b)
41	42	43	44	45	46	47	48	49	50
(c)	(a)	(a)	(b)	(b)	(d)	(c)	(b)	(d)	(a)

EXPLANATORY ANSWERS

1. The difference between the letters increases at each step after beginning with two.

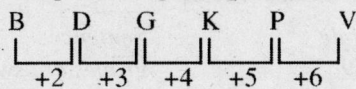

B D G K P V
+2 +3 +4 +5 +6

2.
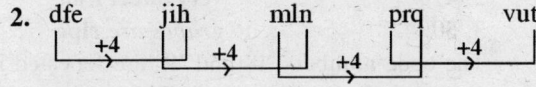

dfe jih mln prq vut
+4 +4 +4 +4

3. QPO SRQ UTS WVU YXW

6. The sequence in the series is ×5, ×6, ×7, ×8, ×9.

3 15 90 630 5040 45360
×5 ×6 ×7 ×8 ×9

7. The coded number is the sum of number digits signifying the position of the alphabet in the natural order.

B A D
↓ ↓ ↓
2nd 1st 4th *i.e.,* 2 + 1 + 4 = 7

Similarly,

H I S
↓ ↓ ↓
8th 9th 19th *i.e.,* 8 + 9 + 19 = 36
further, 3 + 6 = 9

Also,

L O W
↓ ↓ ↓
12th 15th 23rd *i.e.,* 12 + 15 + 23 = 50
further, 5 + 0 = 0

8. The letters of the word TRIBAL are picked from LIBERATE. So will be the coded numbers.

L I B E R A T E → given word
5 6 4 0 3 1 7 0 → codes

Similarly,

T R I B A L → word to be coded
7 3 6 4 1 5 → answer codes

9.
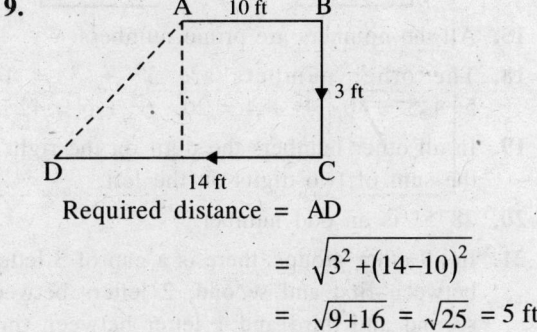

Required distance = AD
$$= \sqrt{3^2 + (14-10)^2}$$
$$= \sqrt{9+16} = \sqrt{25} = 5 \text{ ft}$$

11.
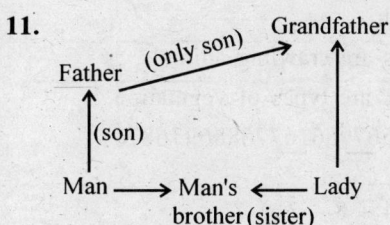

Man's brother's father is also the lady's father as he is the only son of lady's grandfather. So, the lady is man's sister.

12. The relationship chart based on problem is:

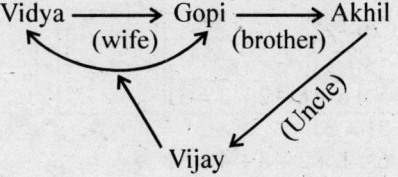

Vidya is wife of Gopi who is brother of Akhil. So, Vidya is sister-in-law of Akhil. If Akhil is uncle of Vijay then Gopi will naturally be the uncle of Vijay as it is not specified that any of the mentioned persons are Vijay's parents. Now, when Vijay is Gopi's nephew then he will also be Vidya's nephew.

13. The three letters are moved 5, 4, and 3 steps forward respectively.

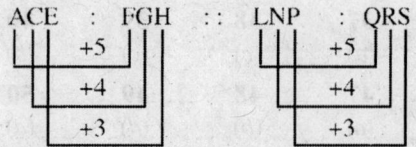

ACE : FGH :: LNP : QRS

14. The word is divided into two sections and the letters are written backwards.

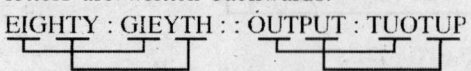

EIGHTY : GIEYTH : : OUTPUT : TUOTUP

15. All the numbers are prime numbers.

18. The other numbers are $3^2 + 3 = 12$, $5^2 + 5 = 30$, $4^2 + 4 = 20$, $6^2 + 6 = 42$

19. In all other numbers the digit on the right is the sum of two digits on the left.

20. 28751 is an odd number.

21. In all other groups, there is a gap of 3 letters between first and second, 2 letters between second and third and 1 letter between third and fourth.

22. All others are crawling animals.

23. All others are types of vegetation.

25. 8767867567986167768697687
       ‾1‾ ‾2‾ ‾3‾

26. $9 \div 3 \times 4 + 8 - 2$
    $12 + 8 - 2 = 18$

27. (a) $1 - 2 \times 3 + 6 \div 8 = 12$

    $\dfrac{-17}{4} = 12$

    (b) $2 \times 3 \div 5 + 8 - 4 = 7$

    $\dfrac{26}{5} = 7$

    (c) $5 \times 6 + 8 \div 2 - 3 = 31$

    $31 = 31$

    (d) $6 - 1 \times 2 \div 8 + 4 = 31$

    $\dfrac{-39}{4} = 31$

28. Day after the day-before-yesterday five days ago is the 6th day which is Thursday. And so, the 3rd day will be Sunday. Three days before the day-after-tomorrow is Yesterday which is the 1st day of the five days. So, two days ago was Sunday.

29. Seventh day from 10th is 17th.
5th day is Friday. Next Friday is on 12th
17 – 12 = 5, 5 days ahead of Friday will be Wednesday. So, 17th is Wednesday.

30.
Code	Sentence
1. *mu* mit *es*	who *is she*
2. **elb** *mu* es	**where** *is she*

The code words 'mu' and 'es' are repeated in Ist and IInd sentence. The only code left is 'elb' which means 'where'.

31.
Code	Sentence
1. **069**	*grapes are* sweet
2. **476**	very sweet fruit
3. **509**	*grapes are* **ripe**

The code numbers '0' and '9' are repeated in 1st and 3rd sentences. The only code remaining is '5' which stands for 'ripe'.

32. 21, 23, 25, 27, 29, 31, 33, 35, 37, 39
                    ↑‾‾‾‾‾‾‾‾‾‾‾‾‾‾‾‾
                   6th

33. All other groups contain E, A and R.

34. In all other groups, the small letters are vowels.

36. Second image is the mirror image of (vertically placed mirror along y-axis) first image.

37. Centre figure is get connected to vertices in next image.

38. A common tangent line passes through the intersection point of two circles.

39. A horizontal line and vertical line comes in picture in upper and lower portion of the figure respectively.

41. In every next figure the main design rotates 90° clockwise and two small lines move in and out.

42. In every next figure the shaded portion of the circle moves ahead two steps clockwise.

43. The first and third figures are similar. Hence, the answer figure will be similar to the second figure.

44. In every next figure an arrow-head is added in the anticlockwise direction.

45. In every next figure the circle and the shaded part is moving two steps clockwise.

All India Sainik School Entrance Exam., 2016
(CLASS-VI)

PAPER-I : MATHEMATICS AND LANGUAGE ABILITY

Time : 2 Hrs.   Max. Marks : 200

Part-A : Mathematics

Section-I

(Each question carries two marks.)

1. Estimate the difference of 879 and 338 to the nearest hundred.

2. Write 15 m as a percentage of 1000 km.

3. Find LCM of 120, 210 and 225.

4. Arrange $\frac{1}{3}, \frac{3}{10}, \frac{5}{6}, \frac{2}{5}$ in ascending order.

5. Find the sum of $1\frac{3}{5}$ and $2\frac{7}{10}$.

6. An aeroplane covers 1020 kms in an hour. How much distance will it cover in $4\frac{1}{6}$ hours.

7. Convert 131°F into Celsius scale.

8. Convert 2222 hours into days and hours.

9. One of the two equal angles of an Isosceles triangle measures 55°. Find the measure of all the angles of triangle.

10. Find the radius of a circle whose circumference is 79.2 cm. Given that $\pi = \frac{22}{7}$.

Section-II

(Each question carries three marks.)

11. Find the square numbers lying between 75 and 225.

12. Simplify: $125 - 25 \times 125 \div 25 + 25$.

13. Sudha scored 23 marks out of 30 in maths and 29 marks out of 50 in Hindi. In which subject did she perform better and by what percentage?

14. Find the HCF of 902, 1394 and 3321.

15. Jubaida took a loan of ₹ 4000 on 12% annual interest. After 3 years how much money she will have to return?

16. Find the square root of

    (a) $6\frac{9}{36}$ (b) $5\frac{41}{16}$

17. A baby elephant drinks around 12 litre of milk every day. How much milk will it drink in two years?

18. John plans to tile his kitchen floor with square tiles. Each side of the tile is 10 cm. His kitchen is 2.2 M long and 1.8 M wide. How many tiles will John need?

19. There are 24 Laddoos in 1 kg. How many Laddoos will be there in 8 kg? If 16 Laddoos can be packed in 1 box, how many boxes are needed to pack all the laddoos?

20. Find the mean of first ten even numbers.

Section-III

(Each question carries five marks.)

21. Annual Income of Rohan is ₹ 6,00,000. He spends ₹ 99,250 on food, ₹ 36,750 on clothes and ₹ 1,11,500 on other expenditures annually. What is his annual saving? What % of his income does he save in a year?

22. (a) Find the value of following angles:

(i) ∠BOC   (ii) ∠COD

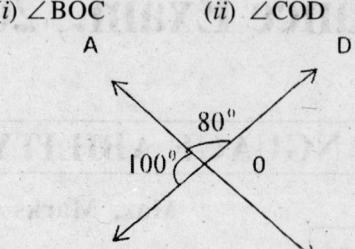

(b) Find HCF of 20 and 70 by prime factorization method.

23. Simplify:

$$0.2\big[3.5 - 0.3\{2.5 + 1.3(3.6 + 1.4)\}\big]$$

24. Find out perimeter and area of the given diagram.

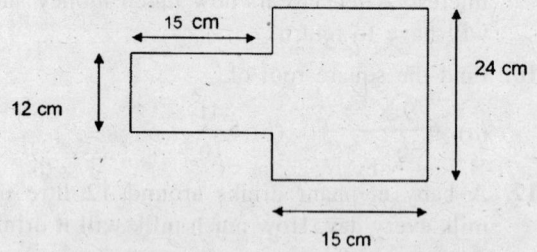

25. How many stones of 0.50 m² can be fixed in a court yard of length 15 m and width 10 m. if cost of fixing one stone is ₹ 2.50, what will be the expenditure on fixing stones in the courtyard?

26. An alloy contains 15% Carbon, 25% Zinc and rest is Copper. In 60 Kg alloy, find the quantity of each metal.

27. Fill in the blanks:

(a) $\dfrac{6}{21} = \dfrac{?}{7}$ (b) $.01 = \dfrac{1}{?}$

(c) Largest 7 digit number is ....

(d) Radius = $\dfrac{\text{Diameter}}{?}$

(e) In 75897, place value of 8 is ....

28. The denominator of a fraction is greater than its numerator by 3 . If 3 is subtracted from the numerator and 2 is added to its denominator, the new number become $\dfrac{1}{5}$. Find the original number.

29. Out of 40 students of a class, 60% passed in first division, 30% in second division and remaining in third division. Find out the number of students in each category?

30. (a) A shopkeeper sells a box costing ₹ 900 giving 15% discount. Find out the sale price of the box?

(b) The HCF and LCM of two number is 18 and 252 respectively. If one number is 126 find out another number?

EXPLANATORY ANSWERS

1.   879 − 338 = 541

            = 500 (Nearest hundred).

2. $15 = 1000 \times 1000 \times \dfrac{x}{100}$

⇒ $15 = 10000x$

⇒ $x = \dfrac{15}{10000} = 0.0015\%.$

3.

2	120, 210, 225
3	60, 105, 225
5	20, 35, 75
	4, 7, 15

L.C.M. = 2 × 3 × 5 × 4 × 7 × 15

        = 12600.

4. $\dfrac{1}{3}, \dfrac{3}{10}, \dfrac{5}{6}$ and $\dfrac{2}{5} = \dfrac{10, 9, 25, 12}{30}$

∴ $\dfrac{3}{10}, \dfrac{1}{3}, \dfrac{2}{5}, \dfrac{5}{6}$ are in ascending order.

5. $1\dfrac{3}{5} + 2\dfrac{7}{10} = \dfrac{8}{5} + \dfrac{27}{10} = \dfrac{16+27}{10} = \dfrac{43}{10} = 4\dfrac{3}{10}.$

6. ∵ In 1 hour aeroplane covers 1020 km

∴ In $\dfrac{25}{6}$ hours aeroplane will cover

      $= 1020 \times \dfrac{25}{6}$ km

      $= 170 \times 25$ km $= 4250$ km.

7. $\because$ $\dfrac{C}{5} = \dfrac{F-32}{9}$

$\Rightarrow$ $\dfrac{C}{5} = \dfrac{131-32}{9} = \dfrac{99}{9}$

$\Rightarrow$ $\dfrac{C}{5} = 11$

$\Rightarrow$ $C = 55°C$

Hence, $131°F = 55°C$.

8. $\dfrac{2222}{24} = 92$, $\dfrac{14}{24} \times 24 = 92$ days 14 hours.

9. Let, third angle $= x°$

$\angle A + \angle B + \angle C = 180°$

$\Rightarrow$ $55° + 55° + x° = 180°$

$\Rightarrow$ $x + 110° = 180°$

$\Rightarrow$ $x = 70°$

$\therefore$ $\angle A = 55°, \angle B = 55°, \angle C = 70°$.

10. $C = 2\pi r$

$\Rightarrow$ $79.2 = 2 \times \dfrac{22}{7} \times r$

$\Rightarrow$ $r = \dfrac{79.2 \times 7}{2 \times 22} = 1.8 \times 7 = 12.6$

Hence, radius of the circle $= 12.6$ cm.

11. The square numbers 81, 100, 121, 144, 169, 196 are lying between 75 and 225.

12. $125 - 25 \times 125 \div 25 + 25$

$= 125 - 25 \times 5 + 25$

$= 125 - 125 + 25 = 25$.

13. % of Maths $= \dfrac{23}{30} \times 100 = \dfrac{230}{3} = 76.6\%$

% of Hindi $= \dfrac{29}{50} \times 100 = 58\%$

Maths is better than Hindi

Difference $= 76.6\% - 58\% = 18.6\%$.

14.
```
            1
   902)1394(
       902    1
      ─────
       492)902(
           492    1
          ─────
           410)492(
               410    5
              ─────
               82)410(
                  410
                 ─────
                   ×
```

14 (right column).
```
        40
   82)3321(
      328    2
     ─────
      41)82(
         82
        ───
         ×
```
Hence required H.C.F. $= 41$.

15. $P = ₹\ 4000$

$r = 12\%$

$t = 3$ years

S.I. $= \dfrac{P \times r \times t}{100} = \dfrac{4000 \times 12 \times 3}{100} = 1440$

$A = P + $ S.I.

$= 4000 + 1440 = ₹\ 5440$

Hence, Jubaida will have to return ₹ 5440 after 3 years.

16. (a) $\sqrt{6\dfrac{9}{36}} = \sqrt{\dfrac{225}{36}} = \dfrac{15}{6} = \dfrac{5}{2} = 2.5$.

(b) $\sqrt{5\dfrac{41}{16}} = \sqrt{\dfrac{121}{16}} = \dfrac{11}{4} = 2.75$.

17. In 1 day baby elephant drinks $12l$ of milk

In 730 days baby elephant drink

$= 12 \times 730\ l$ of milk $= 8760\ l$ of milk.

18. Area of the kitchen floor $= 220 \times 180$ cm^2

Area of each tile $= 10 \times 10$ cm^2

$\therefore$ No. of tiles $= \dfrac{220 \times 180}{10 \times 10}$

$= 22 \times 18 = 396$.

19. In 1 kg $= 24$ Laddoos

In 8 kg $= 24 \times 8 = 192$ Laddoos

Required no. of boxes $= \dfrac{192}{16} = 12$.

20. Mean $= \dfrac{2+4+6+8+10+12+14+16+18+20}{10}$

$= \dfrac{110}{10} = 11$

Hence, mean of first ten even numbers $= 11$.

21. Annual income $= ₹\ 600000$

Annual expenditure $= ₹\ 99250$

$₹\ 36750$

$₹\ 111500$

$\overline{₹\ 247500}$

Annual saving = ₹ 6000000 – ₹ 247500

= ₹ 352500

% Saving = $\dfrac{352500}{600000} \times 100 = \dfrac{705}{12} = 58.75\%$.

22. (a)

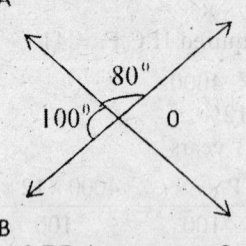

∵ AC and BD intersect at O

(i) ∠BOC = ∠AOD = 80°

                (Vertically opp. angles)

(ii) ∠COD = ∠AOB = 100°

                (Vertically opp. angles)

(b) $20 = 2 \times 2 \times 5$

         $70 = 2 \times 5 \times 7$

∴   H.C.F. = $2 \times 5 = 10$.

23. $0.2\big[3.5 - 0.3\{2.5 + 1.3(3.6 + 1.4)\}\big]$

$= 0.2\big[3.5 - 0.3\{2.5 + 1.3(5)\}\big]$

$= 0.2\big[3.5 - 0.3\{2.5 + 6.5\}\big]$

$= 0.2\big[3.5 - 0.3\{9\}\big]$

$= 0.2[3.5 - 2.7] = 0.2 \,[.8] = 0.16$.

24.

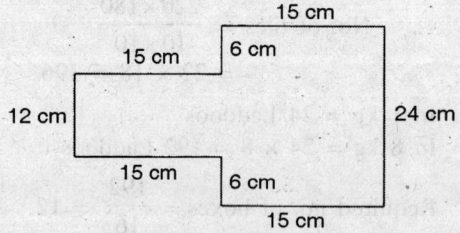

Perimeter = 12 + 15 + 6 + 15 + 24 + 15

                 + 6 + 15 = 108 cm

Area of the given figure

    = 12 × 15 + 15 × 24

    = 180 + 360 = 540 cm².

25. No. of stones = $\dfrac{15 \times 10 \times 100}{50} = 300$

∵   Cost of 1 stone = ₹ 2.50

∴ Cost of 300 stones = $\dfrac{250}{100} \times 300 = ₹ 750$.

26.   Carbon = 15%

         $= \dfrac{15}{100} \times 60$ kg

         = 9 kg

    Zinc = $\dfrac{25}{100} \times 60$ kg

         = 15 kg

    Copper = $\dfrac{60}{100} \times 60 = 36$ kg.

27. (a) $\dfrac{6}{21} = \dfrac{\boxed{2}}{7}$

(b) $.01 = \dfrac{1}{\boxed{100}}$

(c) Largest 7 digit number = 9999999

(d) Radius = $\dfrac{\text{Diameter}}{\boxed{2}}$

(e) In 75897, place value of 8 = 800.

28. Let,   numerator = x

∴   Denominator = $x + 3$

∴   Fraction = $\dfrac{x}{x+3}$

According to the question,

       $\dfrac{x-3}{x+3+2} = \dfrac{1}{5}$

$\Rightarrow$ $\dfrac{x-3}{x+5} = \dfrac{1}{5}$

$\Rightarrow$ $5x - 15 = x + 5$

$\Rightarrow$ $4x = 20 \Rightarrow x = 5$

∴ Fraction = $\dfrac{x}{x+3} = \dfrac{5}{8}$.

29. No of students in first division

       = 60% of 40

       $= \dfrac{60}{100} \times 40 = 24$

No. of students in second division

       = 30% of 40

       $= \dfrac{30}{100} \times 40 = 12$

No. of students in third division

       = 10% of 40

       $= \dfrac{10}{100} \times 40 = 4$.

30. (a) Discount = 15% of x

$$= \frac{15}{100} \times x = \frac{3x}{20}$$

$$\text{S.P.} = x - \frac{3x}{20} = \frac{17x}{20}$$

When M.P. ₹ x then S.P. $= \frac{17x}{20}$

When M.P. ₹ 900 then S.P. $= \frac{17x}{20 \times x} \times 900$

$$= 17 \times 45$$
$$= ₹\ 765$$

Hence, the sale price of the box = ₹ 765.

(b) ∵ H.C.F. × L.C.M. = First no. × 2nd no.

∴ 2nd number $= \dfrac{\text{H.C.F.} \times \text{L.C.M.}}{\text{First number}}$

$$= \frac{18 \times 252}{126} = 36$$

Hence, another number = 36.

PART-B : LANGUAGE ABILITY

1. Write 15 sentences on anyone of the following topics: **(15)**
My Friend or Aim of my life

2. Read the following passage carefully and answer the questions that follow: **(5 × 3 = 15)**

Florence Nightingale was born on the 15th May, 1820 at Florence in Italy and her parents called her after the name of the city where she was born. Her main ambition was to be a nurse and so she gave up all thoughts of marriage and personal happiness. She spent years visiting hospital after hospital. Day and night she visited every bed in the hospital to see that no patient was neglected and that all were as comfortable as possible. However hard she might have worked all day, every night she would take her lamp and move from bed to bed. 'The Lady with the Lamp' the soldiers called her and that is the name by which the world has remembered her ever since.

(a) Where was Florence Nightingale born?
(b) Why her parents named her Florence Nightingale?
(c) Why Florence Nightingale was called 'The Lady with the Lamp'?
(d) Give opposite of 'comfortable'?
(e) What did she do every night with a lamp in her hand?

3. Make a sentence of your own for each underlined word given in the following passage. (Do not copy any sentence from the given paragraph.) **(5 × 2 = 10)**

People who live in regions **covered** with forests and surrounded by hills generally believe that the **desert** is a vast **stretch** of dry, hot and sandy land. But those who have studied it, find the desert quite beautiful. It is not entirely **uninhabited** either. A **variety** of people, animals and plants make the desert their home.

(a) ....
(b) ....
(c) ....
(d) ....
(e) ....

4. Form meaningful sentences by rearranging the words in proper order: **(5 × 2 = 10)**
(a) a good/exercise/swimming/is
(b) Middle East/india/to/the/exporting/is/onions
(c) was/John/drinking /tea
(d) man/a strong /Sardar Patel/was
(e) named/Diamond/had/Newton/little dog/a

5. Give one word for the following: **(5 × 1 = 5)**
(a) One who knows everything
....
(b) A building in which monks live
....
(c) A person whose profession is to keep accounts ....
(d) All the customs and beliefs of a society
....
(e) Eater of flesh ....

6. Choose the correct article (a, an or the) and fill in the blanks. **(5 × 2 = 10)**
(a) Here is .... book I borrowed from you yesterday.

(b) Jordan drives .... Mazda.

(c) He goes to .... Delhi Golf Course on Sundays.

(d) James works as .... electrician.

(e) Raman sang .... song.

7. Use the given word in separate sentences of your own to show the difference in the meaning of the words of the pair given below:

(5 × 2 = 10)

(a) Principal, Principle (b) Cattle, Kettle

(c) Whether, Weather (d) Idle, Idol

(e) Floor, Flour

8. Change each of the following as directed:

(5 × 2 = 10)

(a) I met an old man.

(Change into Future Continuous)

....

(b) The driver stopped the train.

(Change into Passive Voice)

....

(c) The Sky grew dark.

(Change into negative sentence)

....

(d) Mr Verma teaches us grammar.

(Change into interrogative sentence)

....

(e) Peter said, "Imran will not be playing the match."

(Change into indirect sentence)

....

9. Give the Antonym (opposite) of the following words: (5 × 1 = 5)

(a) Arrest (b) Boon

(c) Heaven (d) Grateful

(e) Bravery

10. Write a letter to the Principal requesting him to organize an educational tour to Shimla.

(10)

EXPLANATORY ANSWERS

1. **Aim of my life**

It is rightly said that the chief aim of education is to broaden the horizon of human mind. But we know that in the modern world, we also have to make a living by taking up some profession. I have decided to become a teacher as I grow up. It is rightly said that a teacher is a nation builder. By becoming a teacher, I want to kill two birds with one stone. On the one hand, I want to make a decent living. The teachers are well-paid these days. They also command a high respect in society. On the other hand, my aim is to serve the society at large. I want to inculcate great moral values of life in the minds of young children. This I'll do while blending matter-of-fact and imaginative elements in my teaching. Fortunately, I'm a brilliant student and I hope I'll achieve my aim in life. Morever, both my father and mother are teachers and they are my good guides and a source of great inspiration to me.

2. (a) Florence Nightingale was born at Florence in Italy.

(b) Her parents named her Florence Nightingale after the name of the city where she was born.

(c) She was named so because she used to visit every bed in the hospital with a lamp.

(d) Uncomfortable.

(e) She moved with a lamp in her hand to see that all the patients were properly cared.

3. (a) She covered her face with a scarf.

(b) The camel is called the ship of the desert.

(c) There is a barren stretch of land in the village.

(d) The place is almost uninhabited.

(e) The student gave a variety of reasons to study at Sainik School.

4. (a) Swimming is a good exercise.

(b) India is exporting onions to the Middle East.

(c) John was drinking tea.

(d) Sardar Patel was a strong man.

(e) Newton had a little dog named Diamond.

5. (a) Omniscient (b) Monastery

(c) Accountant (d) Traditions

(e) Carnivorous

6. (a) the (b) a

(c) the (d) an

(e) a

7. (a) Who is the principal of your school?
What is the principle of your life?

(b) He was grazing the cattle in the field.
He poured tea from the kettle.

(c) She asked me whether I was going to school.
The weather is cozy now-a-days.

(d) Never sit idle, do something.
He was selected the Indian Idol last year.

(e) You must clean the floor everyday.
He grinds the wheat to make flour.

8. (a) I shall have been meeting an old man.
(b) The train was stopped (by the driver).
(c) The sky did not grow bright.
(d) Does Mr. Verma teach us grammar?
(e) Peter told that Imran would not be playing the match.

9. (a) Release   (b) Bane
(c) Hell   (d) Thankless
(e) Cowardice

10.
To

The Principal
Sainik School
New Delhi

Respected Sir,

    I am a new student of class VI in your school. Our class teacher has told us that every year on school organises an educational tour to some far off place. I request you to organise a tour to Shimla this year. Shimla is a famous tourist spot. It is popular for its scenic beauty. There is a lot for students to learn in Shimla about the mother nature.

    I hope you will accept my request.

Thanking you   Yours Obediently
                              XYZ.

Dated ....

PAPER-II : INTELLIGENCE TEST*

Time : 40 Minutes.   **Max. Marks : 100**

Directions (Qs. 1 to 6): *In the following questions, select the number(s)/letters from the given options for completing the given series.*

1. 27, 28, 25, 25, 23, 22, 21, ?
(a) 20   (b) 21
(c) 19   (d) 18

2. 80, 63, 72, 72, 64, 81, 56, ?
(a) 96   (b) 98
(c) 89   (d) 90

3. 0, 5, 22, 57, ?, 205
(a) 198   (b) 116
(c) 172   (d) 92

4. R K F ? B
(a) D   (b) C
(c) E   (d) B

5. LAZ, NEX, PIV, ?
(a) SLS   (b) QNS
(c) RMT   (d) RMS

6. -bbcaa-bcaa-bc-a-bca
(a) bacab   (b) abbab
(c) abcba   (d) bcaab

7. In a certain code LIBERATE is written as 56403170, TRIBAL will be written in the same code as:

(a) 734615   (b) 736415
(c) 136475   (d) 034615

8. In a certain language, (a) 'FOR' stands for 'old is gold'; (b) 'ROT' stands for 'gold is pure'; (c) 'ROM' stands for 'gold is costly'. How will 'pure old gold is costly' be written?
(a) TFROM   (b) FOTRM
(c) FTORM   (d) TOMRF

9. Facing the West direction, Priya jogs for 20 m, turns left and goes further 40 m. She turns left again and jogs for 20 m. Then she turns right to go 20 m to reach the park. How far is the park from her starting point and in which direction?
(a) 20 m South   (b) 40 m West
(c) 60 m South   (d) 100 m East

10. Pointing to a woman in the photograph a man said, "She is the daughter of my grand-mother's only son. How is the woman related to the man?
(a) Mother   (b) Daughter
(c) Sister-in-law   (d) Sister

11. If the following words are arranged in natural order, what will come in the last place in ascending order?
1. Captain

* Memory Based

2. Brigadier
3. Major
4. Lieutenant-General
5. Lieutenant

(a) Lieutenant-General (b) Brigadier
(c) Captain   (d) Major

12. What would be the proper order of the following :

1. Decameter   2. Meter
3. Kilometer   4. Centimeter
5. Milimeter

(a) 1 4 3 2 5   (b) 5 4 1 2 3
(c) 5 4 3 2 1   (d) 5 4 2 1 3

Directions (Qs. 13-17) : *In the questions given below one term is missing. Based on the relationship of the two given words/numbers find the missing term from the given options.*

13. Physicist : Physics : : ? : Anatomy
(a) Botany   (b) Botanist
(c) Body   (d) Biologist

14. Frequently : Always : : Selden : ?
(a) Often   (b) Rarely
(c) Occasionally   (d) Never

15. RRS : XMW : : ITB : ?
(a) PNE   (b) NOG
(c) RSW   (d) OOF

16. BYDW : FVHT : : GQIO : ?
(a) JLNP   (b) QSTR
(c) KMOL   (d) KNML

17. Which number will come in the place of question mark?
25 : 81 : : 36 : ?
(a) 121   (b) 93
(c) 65   (d) 103

Directions (Qs. 18-24): *In each of the following questions, there are four options. Three numbers/ words in these options, are alike in certain manner. Only one number/word does not fit in. Choose the one which is different from the rest.*

18. (a) Tutor   (b) Principal
(c) Pupil   (d) Professor

19. (a) Pond   (b) River
(c) Stream   (d) Brook

20. (a) Quotation   (b) Duty
(c) Tax   (d) Octroi

21. (a) 3215   (b) 9309
(c) 4721   (d) 2850

22. (a) 24   (b) 90
(c) 54   (d) 36

23. (a) 3730   (b) 6820
(c) 5568   (d) 4604

24. (a) 2587   (b) 7628
(c) 8726   (d) 2867

25. In the following list of numerals, how many 3s are followed by 3, but NOT preceded by 3?

2 4 6 3 3 1 5 7 8 3 3 3 3 4 6 2 3 3 3 3 9 7
2 3

(a) 1   (b) 2
(c) 3   (d) 4

26. If the + and × signs of the following equations are inter-changed, which will be the correct equation?
(a) $7 \times 5 + 3 = 20$ (b) $4 + 9 \times 1 = 42$
(c) $6 \times 5 + 8 = 46$ (d) $2 + 11 \times 4 = 28$

27. If '+' stands for multiplication, '×' stands for addition, '÷' stands for subtraction and '–' stands for division, then what will be the result of the following equation?
$7 \times 4 \div 10 \times 2 + 5 = ?$
(a) 7   (b) 0
(c) 11   (d) 15

28. If the day before yesterday was Thursday, when will Sunday be?
(a) Tomorrow
(b) Day after tomorrow
(c) Today
(d) Two days after today

29. If the seventh day of a month is three (3) days earlier than Friday, what day will it be on the nineteenth day of the month?
(a) Sunday   (b) Monday
(c) Wednesday   (d) Friday

Directions (Qs. 30 and 31): *In the following questions select the right option which indicates the correct code for the word or letter given in the question.*

30. If 'w' is coded as 'a', 's' as 'r' and 'r' as 'w', how will 'answer' be written?

   (*a*) wnsaes   (*b*) anraew

   (*c*) anrwas   (*d*) wnraes

31. In certain military code, SYSTEM is written as SYSMET, and NEARER as AENRER, what will be the code for FRACTION?

   (*a*) CRAFNOIT   (*b*) FRCAITNO

   (*c*) CARFNOIT   (*d*) FRACNOIT

32. A and B are two brothers. C is sister of B. D is sister of E. E is son of A. Who is D's uncle?

   (*a*) D   (*b*) E

   (*c*) B   (*d*) C

Directions (Qs. 33-35) : *In each of the following series determine the order of the letters. Then from the given options select the one which will complete the given series.*

33. B A F E J I P O ? U

   (*a*) V   (*b*) T

   (*c*) S   (*d*) Q

34. V R O K ? D

   (*a*) L   (*b*) I

   (*c*) H   (*d*) J

35. CFI, IKM, OPQ, ?

   (*a*) UUU   (*b*) UST

   (*c*) VUS   (*d*) TUV

Directions (Qs. 36-40): *The second figure in the first unit of the Problem Figures bears a certain relationship to the first figure. Similarly, one of the figures in the Answer Figures bears the same relationship to the first figure in the second unit of the Problem Figures. Locate the figure which would fit the question mark.*

36. Problem Figures

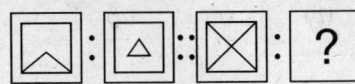

Answers Figures

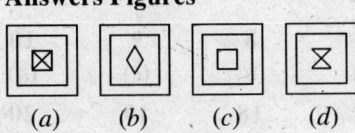

    (*a*)   (*b*)   (*c*)   (*d*)

37. Problem Figures

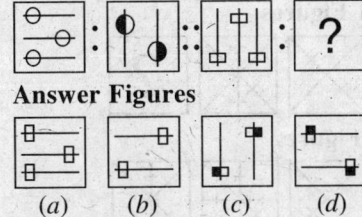

Answer Figures

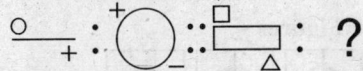

    (*a*)   (*b*)   (*c*)   (*d*)

38. Problem Figures

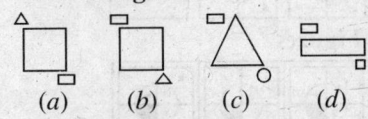

Answer Figures

    (*a*)   (*b*)   (*c*)   (*d*)

39. Problem Figures

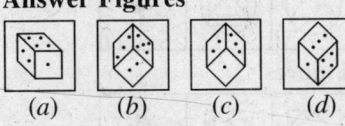

Answer Figures

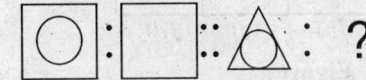

    (*a*)   (*b*)   (*c*)   (*d*)

40. Problem Figures

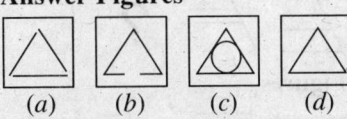

Answer Figures

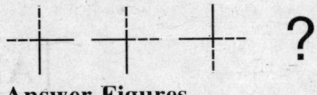

    (*a*)   (*b*)   (*c*)   (*d*)

Direction (Qs. 41-45): *Each of the following questions consist of problem figures followed by answer figures. Select a figure from amongst the answer figures which will continue the same series or pattern as established by the problem figures.*

41. Problem Figures

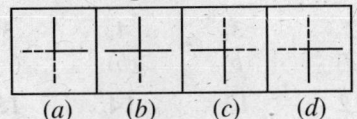

Answer Figures

    (*a*)   (*b*)   (*c*)   (*d*)

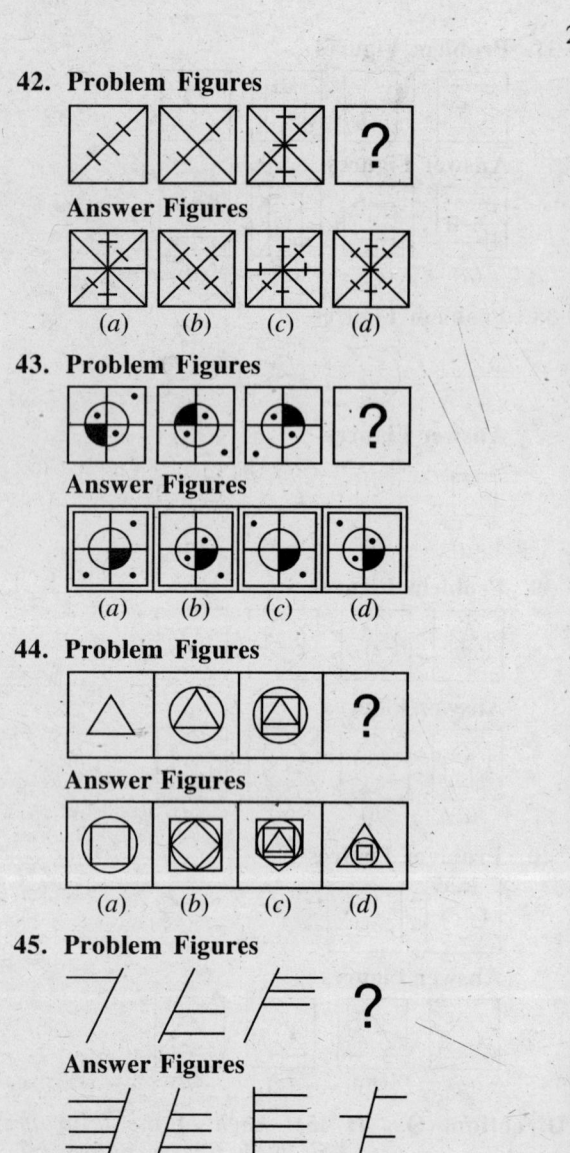

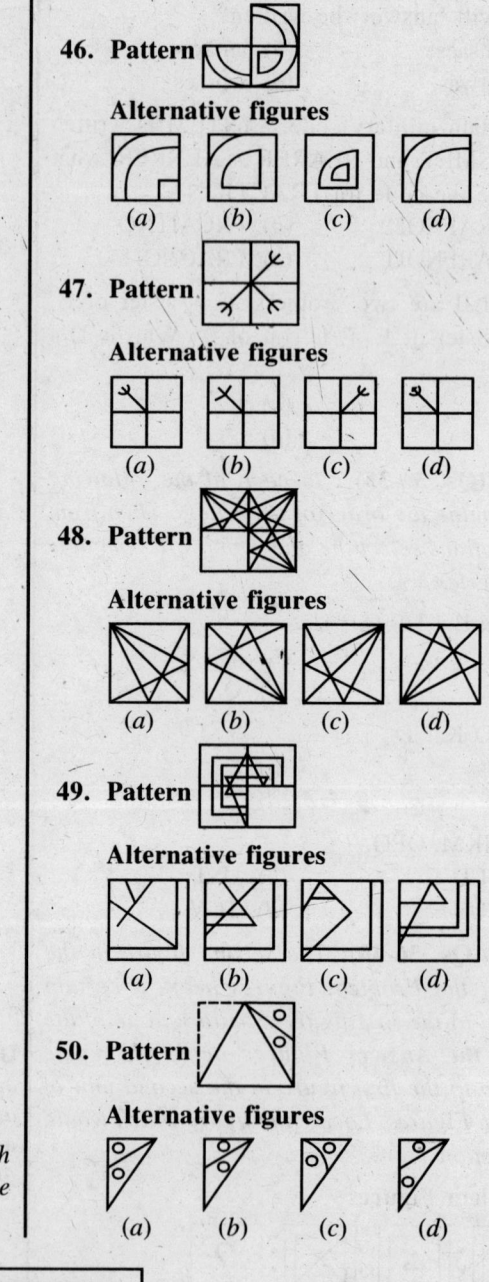

Directions (Qs. 46-50): *In each question, which one of the alternative figures will complete the given figure pattern?*

ANSWERS

1	2	3	4	5	6	7	8	9	10
(c)	(d)	(b)	(b)	(c)	(b)	(b)	(a)	(c)	(d)

11	12	13	14	15	16	17	18	19	20
(a)	(d)	(d)	(d)	(d)	(d)	(a)	(c)	(a)	(a)

21	22	23	24	25	26	27	28	29	30
(b)	(a)	(b)	(a)	(c)	(c)	(c)	(a)	(a)	(b)
31	32	33	34	35	36	37	38	39	40
(c)	(c)	(a)	(c)	(a)	(d)	(d)	(a)	(c)	(d)
41	42	43	44	45	46	47	48	49	50
(a)	(a)	(d)	(c)	(a)	(b)	(a)	(d)	(d)	(a)

SOME SELECTED EXPLANATORY ANSWERS

3. The series follows this sequence : cube of natural numbers starting from 1 minus odd numbers starting from 1.

$$0 \quad 5 \quad 22 \quad 57 \quad 116 \quad 205$$
$$\downarrow \quad \downarrow \quad \downarrow \quad \downarrow \quad \downarrow \quad \downarrow$$
$$1^3-1 \quad 2^3-3 \quad 3^3-5 \quad 4^3-7 \quad 5^3-9 \quad 6^3-11$$

4. The difference between the letters is reduced by two at each step.

R K F C B
  −7   −5   −3   −1

6. The series is abbca, abbca, abbca, abbca.

7. The letters of the word TRIBAL are picked from LIBERATE. So will be the coded numbers.

L I B E R A T E → given word
5 6 4 0 3 1 7 0 → codes

Similarly,

T R I B A L → word to be coded
7 3 6 4 1 5 → answer codes

9. (40 + 20) = 60 metres South

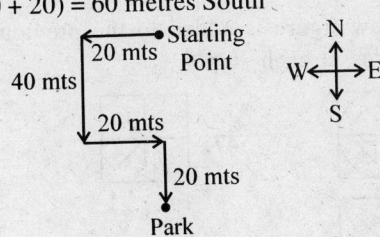

10.

Man's Grandmother

Grandmother's only son

Man (sister) Daughter

'My grandmother's only son' is the father of the man, and 'daughter of my grandmother's only son' is the sister of the man.

11. The arrangement of ranks in ascending order is—Lieutenant, Captain, Major, Brigadier, **Lieutenant-General.**

12. The proper order of measurement in increasing order is—Milimeter, Centimeter, Meter, Decameter, Kilometer.

13. Physicist deals with the subject Physics and biologist with subject anatomy.

14. The related words are near opposites.

16. The letters are moved +4, −3, +4, −3 steps respectively

BYDW : FVHT :: GQIQ : KNML

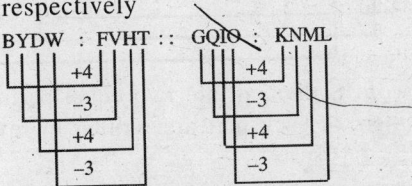

+4
−3
+4
−3

17. All the numbers are squares of different numbers.

$$25 \; : \; 81 \; :: \; 36 \; : \; 121$$
$$\downarrow \qquad \downarrow \qquad \downarrow \qquad \downarrow$$
$$5^2 \qquad 9^2 \qquad 6^2 \qquad 11^2$$

18. All others are instructors. Pupil learns from the instructor.

19. All others are running forms of water.

20. All others are forms of taxes.

21. In other numbers, no digit is repeated.

22. In other numbers, the sum of both the digits is 9.

23. In all other numbers, two digits are same.

24. Other numbers are made with digits 2, 6, 7 and 8.

25. 2 4 6 3 3 1 5 7 8 3 3 3 4 6 2 3 3 3 3 9 7 2 3

26. After interchanging the signs the equations are:
(a) 7 + 5 × 3 = 22 which is wrong

24

(b) $4 \times 9 + 1 = 37$ which is wrong

(c) $6 + 5 \times 8 = 46$ which is correct

(d) $2 \times 11 + 4 = 26$ which is wrong

27. $7 + 4 - 10 + 2 \times 5$
$7 + 4 - 10 + 10 = 11.$

28. Thursday —Day-before-yesterday
Friday —Yesterday
Saturday —Today
Sunday — Tomorrow

29. 7th day is 3 days earlier than Friday so, 10th day is Friday, so also is 17th.

∴ 19th day will be 2nd day ahead of Friday, *i.e.,* Sunday.

30. Alphabet whose codes are given
w → a
s → r
r → w

All other alphabet will remain unchanged, so, 'answer' will be coded as :

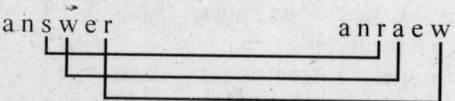

31. The word is divided into two equal parts and the letters of each part are written in reverse order.

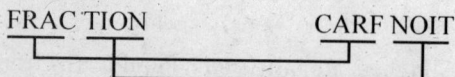

Similarly,

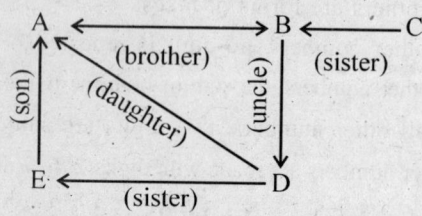

32. The relationship chart based on the problem is:

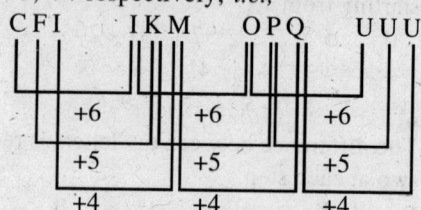

When D is sister of E, who is son of A then D is daughter of A. Brother of A is B and so, B is D's uncle.

33. Each vowel (AEIOU) is preceded by the letter that comes next to it in the natural alphabetical series.

B A   F E   J I   P O   V U

34. The letters are in reverse series and the difference is four and three alternately.

V   R   O   K   H   D
  −4   −3   −4   −3   −4

35. The three alphabet in one group correspond to the alphabet in the next group in the manner +6, +5, +4 respectively, *i.e.,*

C F I   I K M   O P Q   U U U
       +6   +6   +6
       +5   +5   +5
       +4   +4   +4

38. The element at the bottom is moved to the diagonal corner, the element in the top is enlarged and moved to the centre and element in the middle is reduced and moved to the bottom right corner.

40. The inner shape in the first figure is removed to get the second figure.

41. The cross is turned 90° clockwise at each step.

43. The complete figure is turned 90° clockwise at each step.

44. A new figure is added to the previous set of figures at each step.

46.    47.

48.

49.

50.

SAINIK SCHOOL ENTRANCE EXAM., 2015
(CLASS-VI)

PAPER-I : MATHEMATICS AND LANGUAGE

Time : 2 Hrs.   Max. Marks : 200

Part-A : Mathematics

Section-I

(Each question carries two marks.)

1. What is the LCM of two numbers if their HCF is 2 and the product is 112?

2. Write the Hindu-Arabic numerals for MDCL.

3. John had $2\frac{1}{2}$ Cake. His friends ate $1\frac{2}{3}$ of the Cake. How much of the Cake is left?

4. The dimensions of a rectangular field are 36 m and 24 m. Find the cost of fencing of the field if cost of wire is ₹ 4.50 per meter.

5. Find the average of first 9 prime numbers.

6. Simplify : $\dfrac{\frac{1}{5} \div \frac{1}{5} \text{ of } \frac{1}{5}}{\frac{1}{5} \text{ of } \frac{1}{5} \div \frac{1}{5}}$

7. A train covers 20 m in a second. Convert the speed of train in Km/h.

8. Form the greatest and smallest 4 digit numbers with digits 9, 3, 7 and 1.

9. Mayank bought a ball for ₹ 20. He sold it for ₹ 30 and again bought it back for ₹ 40. Again he sold it for ₹ 50. Did he gain or lose? By how much did he gain or lose?

10.

In the above figure if
$\angle AOC = x$
$\angle COD = 2x$
$\angle BOD = 3x$
Then find each angle in degree.

Section-II

(Each question carries three marks.)

11. Solve : $\dfrac{2}{7}$ of $\left[2 + \{2(11 + \overline{4 - 2})\}\right] - 2$

12. What percent is 200 grams of 4.5 kg?

13. If the simple interest on ₹ 12800 for a period of 2 years is ₹ 3840, then find the rate of interest per annum.

14. If the circumference of a circular park is 88 m, then find the area of the park.

15. Arrange the following in ascending order :
$\dfrac{3}{7}, \dfrac{4}{5}, \dfrac{7}{9}, \dfrac{1}{2}$ and $\dfrac{3}{5}$.

16. Mohan, a student of Class-V secured 315 marks out of 450. Find marks in percentage.

17. In the given figure, what is the value of angles BAC ($x°$) and CAD ($y°$)?

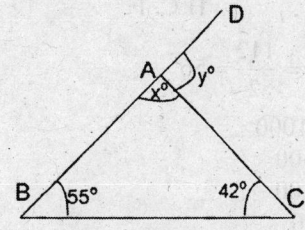

18. Sachin saved ₹ 400 each in the first and second months, ₹ 800 and ₹ 600 in the third and fourth months respectively. Find average monthly saving over the four months.

19. If average (mean) of the following marks obtained by students of Class-V is 35.
26 45 37 43 49 20 *x* 22 and 30.
Find unknown mark *i.e. x*.

20. Find : 1 – 2 + 3 – 4 + 5 – 6 + ... + 19 – 20.

Section-III

(Each question carries five marks.)

21. A rectangle and a square have the same perimeter 100 m. Find the side of the square if the rectangle has a breadth 2 m less than that of the square. Find breadth, length and area of the rectangle.

22. Rakesh completes one round of a running track in 8 minutes and Saroj completes it in 6 minutes. How long will it take for both to arrive again at their starting point together, if they start running at the same time and maintain their speed?

23. Akshita's dad needed a loan of ₹ 20,000 to buy a new car. Mr. Das, the Bank Manager agreed to give him the loan at 3% per annum. If the loan was to be paid back after 5 years, what total amount must he return to the bank?

24. Find the value of '*x*' for following figure if AB ∥ CD.

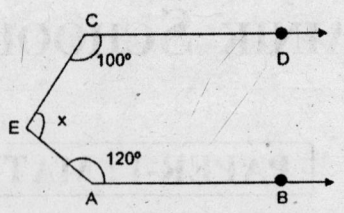

25. A Supermarket sells 19 oranges for ₹ 114, 6 Apples for ₹ 48, 22 Pomegranates for ₹ 154 and 17 Mangoes for ₹ 153. Which one of the fruits is the cheapest?

26. A rectangular grassy lawn measuring 48 m by 35 m is to be surrounded externally by a path, which is 2.5 m wide. Find the cost of leveling the path at the rate ₹ 4.50 per Sq. m.

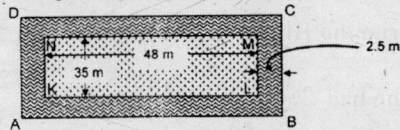

27. One number exceeds another number by 36. If sum of both number is 48. Find the numbers.

28. Find the smallest number, having four different prime factors.

29. What sum of money will produce ₹ 143 interest in $3\frac{1}{4}$ years at $2\frac{1}{2}$% simple interest?

30. A brick measures 20 cm by 10 cm by $7\frac{1}{2}$ cm. How many bricks will be required for a wall 25 m long, 2 m high and $\frac{3}{4}$ m thick?

EXPLANATORY ANSWERS

1. LCM = $\dfrac{\text{Product of numbers}}{\text{H.C.F.}}$

   $= \dfrac{112}{2} = 56$

2. M — 1000
   D — 500
   C — 100
   L — 50

3. Remaining Cake $= \dfrac{5}{2} - \dfrac{5}{3} = \dfrac{15-10}{6} = \dfrac{5}{6}$

4. Perimeter of the rectangular field $= 2(l + b)$
   $= 2(36 + 24) = 120$ m.
   Cost of fencing of the field
   $= ₹\dfrac{9}{2} \times 120$
   $= ₹ 9 \times 60 = ₹ 540$

5. Average of first 9 prime numbers
   $= \dfrac{2+3+5+7+11+13+17+19+23}{9}$
   $= \dfrac{100}{9} = 11.1$

6. Simplify $\dfrac{\dfrac{1}{5} \div \dfrac{1}{5} \text{ of } \dfrac{1}{5}}{\dfrac{1}{5} \text{ of } \dfrac{1}{5} \div \dfrac{1}{5}}$

$= \dfrac{\dfrac{1}{5} \div \dfrac{1}{5} \times \dfrac{1}{5}}{\dfrac{1}{5} \times \dfrac{1}{5} \div \dfrac{1}{5}} = \dfrac{\dfrac{1}{5} \div \dfrac{1}{25}}{\dfrac{1}{25} \div \dfrac{1}{5}} = \dfrac{\dfrac{1}{5} \times \dfrac{25}{1}}{\dfrac{1}{25} \times \dfrac{5}{1}} = \dfrac{5}{\dfrac{1}{5}}$

$= \dfrac{5}{1} \times \dfrac{5}{1} = 25$

7. Speed of the train = 20 m/s

$\qquad = 20 \times \dfrac{18}{5}$ km/hr

$\qquad = 72$ km/hr

8. The greatest number = 9731
The smallest number = 1379

9. Total CP = 20 + 40 = ₹ 60
Total SP = 30 + 50 = ₹ 80
SP > CP ∴ he got profit.
Profit = SP – CP = 80 – 60 = ₹ 20

10.

$x + 2x + 3x = 180°$
$\Rightarrow 6x = 180° \Rightarrow x = 30°$
$\angle AOC = 30°, \angle COD = 2 \times 30 = 60°$
$\angle BOD = 3 \times 30 = 90°$

11. $\dfrac{2}{7}$ of $\left[2 + \{2(11 + \overline{4 - 2})\}\right] - 2$

$= \dfrac{2}{7}$ of $\left[2 + \{2(11 + 2)\}\right] - 2$

$= \dfrac{2}{7}$ of $\left[2 + \{26\}\right] - 2$

$= \dfrac{2}{7}$ of $\left[28\right] - 2$

$= \dfrac{2}{7} \times 28 - 2$

$= 8 - 2 = 6$

12. Required % $= \dfrac{200}{4500} \times 100$

$\qquad = \dfrac{40}{9} = 4.4\%$

13. Rate of interest $= \dfrac{SI \times 100}{p \times t} = \dfrac{3840 \times 100}{12800 \times 2}$

$\therefore \qquad r = 15\%$

14. $\qquad C = 2\pi r$

$\Rightarrow \qquad 88 = 2 \times \dfrac{22}{7} \times r$

$\Rightarrow \qquad r = \dfrac{88 \times 7}{44} = 14$ m.

Area of the circular park $= \pi r^2$

$\qquad = \dfrac{22}{7} \times 14 \times 14$

$\qquad = 22 \times 28 = 616$ m².

15. $\dfrac{3}{7} = 0.4$

$\dfrac{4}{5} = 0.8$

$\dfrac{7}{9} = 0.7$

$\dfrac{1}{2} = 0.5$

$\dfrac{3}{5} = 0.6$

$\therefore \dfrac{3}{7}, \dfrac{1}{2}, \dfrac{3}{5}, \dfrac{7}{9}, \dfrac{4}{5}$ are in ascending order.

16. Out of 450 marks Mohan got 315 marks.
Out of 100 marks Mohan got

$\qquad = \dfrac{315}{450} \times 100 = 70\%$

17.

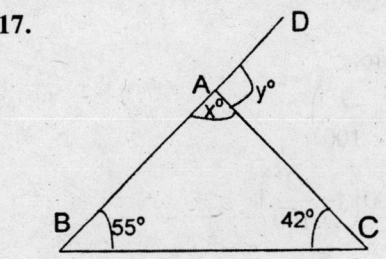

In Δ ABC,

$x + 55° + 42° = 180°$

$\Rightarrow x = 180° - 97° = 83°$

$x + y = 180°$ (linear pair)

$\therefore y = 180° - 83° = 97°$

18. Average monthly saving

$= \dfrac{400 + 400 + 800 + 600}{4}$

$= \dfrac{2200}{4} = ₹ 550$

19. $\dfrac{x + 26 + 45 + 37 + 43 + 49 + 20 + 22 + 30}{9} = 35$

$\Rightarrow x + 272 = 35 \times 9 = 315$

$\Rightarrow x = 315 - 272 = 43$

20. $1 + 3 + 5 + 7 + 9 + 11 + 13 + 15 + 17 + 19$
$-(2 + 4 + 6 + 8 + 10 + 12 + 14 + 16 + 18 + 20)$
$= 100 - 110 = -10$

21.

100 m	100 m
rectangle	square

$\therefore$ Perimeter of square = perimeter of rectangle
$= 100$ m

$\therefore$ Side of square $= \dfrac{100}{4} = 25$ m

Breadth of rectangle $= 25 - 2 = 23$ m

Now $\quad 2(l + b) = 100$

$l + b = 50$

$\Rightarrow \quad\quad l + 23 = 50 \Rightarrow l = 27$ m

Length of rectangle = 27 m

$\therefore$ Area of rectangle $= l \times b = 27 \times 23$
$= 621$ m^2

22. L.C.M. of 8 and 6 = 24

$\begin{array}{c|cc} 2 & 8, & 6 \\ \hline & 4, & 3 \end{array}$

L.C.M. $= 2 \times 4 \times 3 = 24$

Hence, both will arrive together after 24 min.

23. P = ₹ 20,000

$r = 3\%$

$t = 5$ years

$A = p\left(1 + \dfrac{r}{100}\right)^t$

$= 20000\left(1 + \dfrac{3}{100}\right)^5$

$= 20000 \times \dfrac{103}{100} \times \dfrac{103}{100} \times \dfrac{103}{100} \times \dfrac{103}{100} \times \dfrac{103}{100}$

$= \dfrac{23184069486}{1000000} = 23184.069486$

$\therefore$ Required total amount paid = ₹ 23184

24.

$\because$ AB $\parallel$ CD

$\therefore \angle FCE = 180 - 100 = 80°$

and $\angle EAG = 180 - 120 = 60°$

$\angle CEH = 80°$ (alternate angle)

$\angle AEH = 60°$ (alternate angle)

$\therefore x = 80° + 60° = 140°$

25. Cost of 1 Orange $= \dfrac{114}{19} = ₹ 6$

Cost of 1 Apple $= \dfrac{48}{6} = ₹ 8$

Cost of 1 Pomegranate $= \dfrac{154}{22} = ₹ 7$

Cost of 1 Mango $= \dfrac{153}{17} = ₹ 9$

Hence, Orange is the cheapest fruit.

26. 48 m + 5 m = 53 m

35 m + 5 m = 40 m

Area without path = 48 × 35 = 1680 m^2

Area with path = 53 × 40 = 2120 m^2

$\therefore$ Area of path = 2120 - 1680 = 540 m^2

Cost of leveling the path $= 540 \times \dfrac{9}{2}$.

$= 270 \times 9 = ₹ 2430$

27. Let one number = x

$\therefore$ other number = $x + 36$

$x + x + 36 = 48$

$\Rightarrow \quad\quad 2x = 48 - 36 = 12$

$\Rightarrow \quad\quad x = 6, \quad x + 36 = 6 + 36 = 42$

$\therefore$ Numbers are 6 and 42.

28. Required number $= 2 \times 3 \times 5 \times 7 = 210$.

29. $P = \dfrac{S.I. \times 100}{R \times T} = \dfrac{143 \times 100 \times 2 \times 4}{13 \times 5}$

$= 88 \times 20 = ₹ 1760$

30. Volume of Wall $= l \times b \times h$

$= 2500 \times 200 \times \dfrac{3}{4} \times 100$

$= 2500 \times 150 \times 100 \text{ cm}^3$

Volume of each brick $= l \times b \times h$

$= 20 \times 10 \times \dfrac{15}{2}$

$= 1500 \text{ cm}^3$

$\therefore$ Number of bricks $= \dfrac{2500 \times 150 \times 100}{1500}$

$= 25000$

PART-B : LANGUAGE ABILITY

1. Write 15 sentences on any one of the following topics— **(15 Marks)**
(a) My Favourite Sportsperson
(b) Festivals of India

2. Read the following passage carefully and answer the questions that follow: **(15 Marks)**

Ants are the most interesting of all insects because they are so like human beings in many ways. They live in families, build their own houses, and have a king and a 'queen'. Each ant has its own work to do and it does its work well. The very young ants who have just come out of their cocoons are generally the nurses. When they are older and their skins are harder, they are ready to leave the nest and do other kinds of work. Some of the ants hunt for food. Most other kinds of insects go about looking for food, but it is always for themselves alone. But the ants think of the nest. They bring in food for the queen and other workers as well as for themselves.

(a) How are ants similar to human beings?
(b) What jobs are done by the very young ants?
(c) When do these very young ants leave the nest?
(d) Which word in the passage conveys the meaning – "a cover that keeps someone safe and warm".
(e) How are ants different from most other kinds of insects?

3. Make a sentence of your own for each underlined word given in the following passage. (Do not copy any sentence from the given paragraph.) **(10 Marks)**

Laughter is indicative of joy. A man who **laughs** radiates **happiness** and wins friends. Laughter can be the best tonic. A man who cannot laugh fails to **attract** friends, loses his **health** and deprives himself of any **pleasure** of life.

(a) ....
(b) ....
(c) ....
(d) ....
(e) ....

4. Rearrange the jumbled words to form meaningful sentences. **(10 Marks)**
(a) newspapers/very important/day to day life/in our/have become
(b) others/at/you/not/laugh/should
(c) smiles/full of/tears/is/life/and
(d) a/standing/the/fox/was/clever/tree/under
(e) the/west/in/the/sets/sun

5. Give one word for the following: **(5 Marks)**
(a) A doctor who does operations

....
(b) A bunch of flowers

....
(c) A person who works with machines

....
(d) Happening once a year

....
(e) A house or shelter for a dog

....

6. Choose the correct word/phrase from the brackets and fill in the blanks: **(10 Marks)**
(a) He .... a new bicycle last week.
(bought, have bought, had bought)

(b) It .... since early morning. (rained, is raining, has been raining)

(c) He .... TV most evening. (is watch, watches, is watching)

(d) I .... a lot of work today. (do, have done, had done)

(e) He .... fast when the accident happened. (is driving, was driving, drove)

7. Use each of the word in separate sentences of your own to show the difference in the meaning of the words of the pairs given below:

(10 Marks)

(a) Dairy, Diary   *(b)* There, Their
(c) Tail, Tale   *(d)* Peace, Piece
(e) Weight, Wait

8. Write opposite words for the following:

(5 Marks)

(a) Win   *(b)* Refuse
(c) Cruel   *(d)* Ascending
(e) Give

9. Change each of the following as directed:

(10 Marks)

(a) It is going to rain.
(Change into Interrogative)
....

(b) Mr Mukherji knows Chinese.
(Change into negative)
....

(c) He knows me well.
(Change verb to past tense)
....

(d) You are very smart.
(Change into Exclamatory)
....

(e) The cat killed the mouse.
(Change into Passive Voice)
....

10. Your elder brother has sent you a birthday gift. Write a letter of Thanks to him.

(10 Marks)

EXPLANATORY ANSWERS

1. (b)   **Festivals of India**

India is a land of festivals. The most famous festival in the Christian world is Christmas. The Mohammedans observe Id-ul-Fitr as one of their most important festivals. In India the most famous festival is the Diwali which though chiefly a Hindu festival, is celebrated by other communities also because of their beliefs. Diwali comes in October or November. The Dussehra which precedes the Diwali by twenty days is another famous festival which is celebrated all over India. Holi which comes in February or March, is also celebrated all over India, but most vehemently in North India. Baisakhi which often comes off on 13th April, marks the beginning of harvest season and advent of the Hindu new Calendar. The harvest festival of Kerala is Onam which comes off in September. In Tamil Nadu, Pongal is the harvest festival which comes off in September. There are other festivals like Pushkar Mela at Pushkar in Rajasthan. It is celebrated in November. Vishwakarma Day is celebrated by the artisans on the day next to Diwali. Desert Festival is celebrated at Jaisalmer in Rajasthan during February. Surajkund Crafts Mela is held in Haryana in the same month

i.e. February. There are Gurpurbs celebrated by the Sikhs. Similarly there are other festivals like Lohari, Basant, etc., and social days for other communities. There are also celebrations on more or less scale on days like Purnima, Amavas, Ekadishi, etc. In Kashmir we have the famous Amarnath Yatra and "Chhari Mubarak" March.

2. *(a)* Because they live in families, build their own houses, and do work like human beings.

(b) The very young ants do the jobs of nurses.

(c) When they are older and their skins are harder, then they leave the nest.

(d) Cocoon.

(e) Ant collect food for other ants also while most other kinds of insect do it just for themselves only.

3. *(a)* Never laugh at poor and deprived poeple.

(b) Laughter is a sign of happiness.

(c) Those who laugh often, attract more friends.

(d) Laughter also improves the health.

(e) Laughter, happiness and pleasure are good for healthy life.

4. (a) Newspapers have become very important in our day to day life.
   (b) You should not laugh at others.
   (c) Life is full of tears and smiles.
   (d) The clever fox was standing under a tree.
   (e) The sun sets in the west.

5. (a) Surgeon
   (b) Bouquet
   (c) Engineer, Mechanic, Machinist
   (d) Annual
   (e) Kennel

6. (a) bought   (b) has been raining
   (c) watches   (d) have done
   (e) was driving

7. (a) We go to Mother Dairy to fetch milk.
       I maintain a daily diary for record.
   (b) There is a snake in the grass.
       Their car broke down on the way.
   (c) The dog was wagging its tail.
       He narrated a long tale of a king.
   (d) All religions teach us to live in peace.
       I also ate a piece of cake there.

   (e) Your body weight should be normal.
       After a long wait I left the place.

8. (a) Lose   (b) Accept
   (c) Kind   (d) Descending
   (e) Take

9. (a) Is it going to rain?
   (b) Mr Mukherji doesn't know Chinese.
   (c) He knew me well.
   (d) How smart!
   (e) The mouse was killed by the cat.

10. Examination Hall,
    TUV City
    6 March, ...
    My dear Brother,

    I thank you very much for the watch that you have just sent as my birthday gift. It is really a beautiful watch. It keeps correct time. I will never be late for college now. My friends also like it very much.

    I request you to attend my birthday party in person the next year. Don't forget to bring the kids.
    Your affectionate brother,
    ABC.

PAPER-II : INTELLIGENCE TEST

Time : 40 Minutes.   **Max. Marks : 100**

Directions (Qs. 1 to 5): *Out of the four choices: (A), (B), (C) and (D) given in each problem three are similar in one way. However one choice is not like the other three. Choose the choice which is different from the rest and write the answer in the answer box.*

1. (a) Open & Close   (b) Hate & Dislike
   (c) Rise & Fall   (d) Go & Come

2. (a) R5A1T6   (b) B2A1D4
   (c) C3E5A1   (d) H8B2D4

3. (a) Far and Near
   (b) Last and First
   (c) Distance and Fare
   (d) High and Low

4. (a) You   (b) He
   (c) She   (d) Am

5. (a) 699   (b) 789
   (c) 773   (d) 798

Directions (Q. 6 to 9): *In each of the following questions, arrange the letters of each word then find fourth letter.*

6. ENKAL (A BODY PART)   ....

7. HCDNGRHAIA (A UNION TERRETORY)
                            ....

8. HEPES (AN ANIMAL)   ....

9. NEGOAR (A FRUIT)   ....

10. (a) Lion and Roar
    (b) Elephant and Trumpet
    (c) Snake and Hiss
    (d) Dogs and Cook

11. (a) Cow and Goat
    (b) Horse and Mare

(c) Dog and Bitch

(d) Cock and Hen

Directions (Qs. 12 to 15): *Choose the right answer and write the answer in the answer box.*

12. Uncle is to Aunt as Cook is to
    (a) Fowl   (b) Hen
    (c) Chicken   (d) Duck

13. Wood is to table as .... is to coat
    (a) Shirt   (b) Wear
    (c) Trouser   (d) Cloth

14. Boy is to Girl as nephew is to ....
    (a) Uncle   (b) Niece
    (c) Brother in law   (d) Aunt

15. Fish is to Bird as submarine is to
    (a) Ship   (b) Train
    (c) Aeroplane   (d) Car

16. Disease : Pathology : : Planet : ?
    (a) Sun   (b) Stars
    (c) Astrology   (d) Astronomy

17. Waiting : Boredom : : Education : ?
    (a) Class
    (b) Enlightenment
    (c) Schooling
    (d) Cunning

18. Light : Sun : : Heat : ?
    (a) Electricity   (b) Moon
    (c) Fire   (d) Star

Directions (Qs. 19 to 22): *Below are given numbers/ alphabets/figures followed by 4 answer choices marked as A, B, C and D. Choose a correct answer option, which will continue the series.*

19. 246, 357, 468, 579 ....
    (a) 759   (b) 690
    (c) 678   (d) 459

20. A/2, 4/C, E/6 ....
    (a) 8/G   (b) 8/K
    (c) 7/G   (d) G/8

21. B, D, G, K ....
    (a) P   (b) A
    (c) O   (d) N

22. 1243, 2354, 3465, ...
    (a) 4576   (b) 4675
    (c) 4796   (d) 4367

23. C - 3, E - 6, G - 12, I - 24, K - 48, ?
    (a) S - 48   (b) M - 96
    (c) L - 96   (d) O - 48

24. 3, 6, 8, 16, 18, ...
    (a) 28   (b) 36
    (c) 54   (d) 34

25. KPA, LQB, MRC, NSD, ?
    (a) UOT   (b) OTE
    (c) EOT   (d) TOE

26. If CHAIR is coded as FKDLU, then RAID is coded as:
    (a) ULGD   (b) ULKG
    (c) ULDG   (d) UDLG

27. If "grey" is called "brown", "white" is called "pink", "red" is called "grey", "black" is called "red", "brown" is called "white", what is the colour of "coal"?
    (a) brown   (b) red
    (c) black   (d) pink

28. If $5 \times 8 = 28$, $3 \times 7 = 12$, $8 \times 6 = 35$, then find the value of 13×13?
    (a) 169   (b) 130
    (c) 140   (d) 144

29. If TOUR is written as 1234, CLEAR is written as 56784 and SPARE is written as 90847, find the code for CARE?
    (a) 1247   (b) 4847
    (c) 5247   (d) 5847

30. If RAJI has been coded as TCLK, then what would be the code for KLCT?
    (a) MENV   (b) RAJI
    (c) MNFV   (d) MNEV

Directions (Qs. 31 & 32): *Choose the word, which will come third in the dictionary and write the answer in answer box.*

31. (a) Battalion   (b) Barrister
    (c) Banana   (d) Balance

32. (a) Dear   (b) Decide
    (c) Diagram   (d) Departure

33. If ÷ means ×, × means +, + means – and – means ÷. Find the value of 16 × 3 + 5 – 2 ÷ 4
(a) 19   (b) 10
(c) 9   (d) 13

34. What is common in hydrometer, lactometer and manometer?
(a) They are units of measurement
(b) They are instruments
(c) They are scales
(d) They are equipments used in physics

35. What is common in Bauxite, Iron, Tungsten and Monazite?
(a) They are all minerals
(b) They are all metals
(c) They are all chemicals
(d) None of these

Directions (Qs. 36-40): *In each of the following sets of figures, select the one that is different from the rest.*

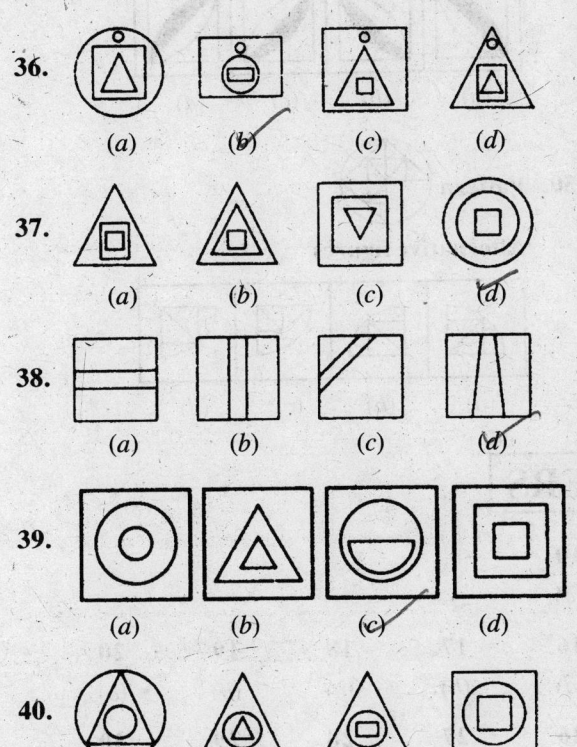

36.
(a)   (b)   (c)   (d)

37.
(a)   (b)   (c)   (d)

38.
(a)   (b)   (c)   (d)

39.
(a)   (b)   (c)   (d)

40.
(a)   (b)   (c)   (d)

Directions (Qs. 41-45): *Each of the following questions consists of unmarked figures followed by four figures mark (a), (b), (c) and (d). Select a figure from the marked figures which will continue the series established by the unmarked figures.*

41. Problem Figures

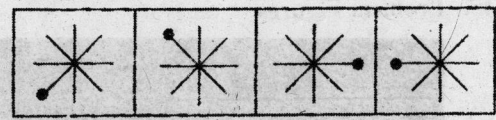

Answer Figures

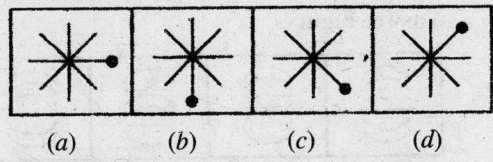

(a)   (b)   (c)   (d)

42. Problem Figures

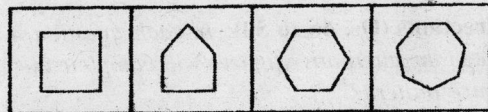

Answer Figures

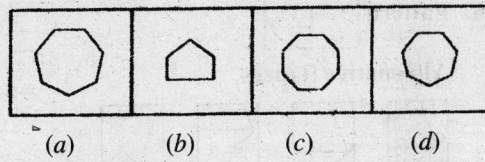

(a)   (b)   (c)   (d)

43. Problem Figures

Answer Figures

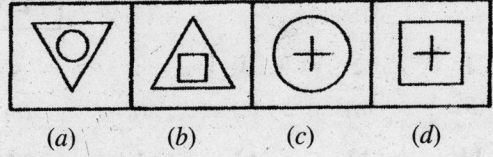

(a)   (b)   (c)   (d)

44. Problem Figures

| ○ | ○ ○ | ○ ○ | ○ ○ ○ |
| △ △ | △ △ | △ △ △ | △ △ △ |

Answer Figures

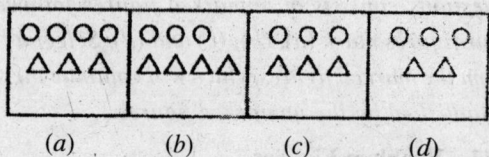

(a)   (b)   (c)   (d)

45. Problem Figures

Answer Figures

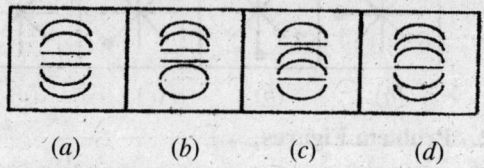

(a)   (b)   (c)   (d)

Directions (Qs. 46 to 50): *In each question, which one of the alternative figures will complete the given figure pattern?*

46. Pattern

Alternative figures

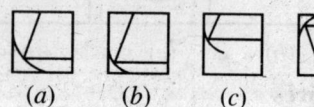

(a)   (b)   (c)   (d)

47. Pattern

Alternative figures

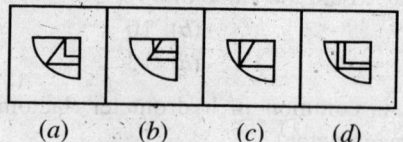

(a)   (b)   (c)   (d)

48. Pattern

Alternative figures

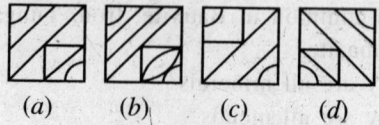

(a)   (b)   (c)   (d)

49. Pattern

Alternative figures

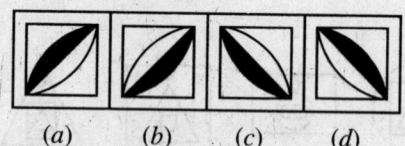

(a)   (b)   (c)   (d)

50. Pattern

Alternative figures

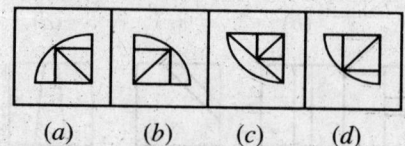

(a)   (b)   (c)   (d)

ANSWERS

1	2	3	4	5	10				
(b)	(a)	(c)	(d)	(c)	(d)				
11	12	13	14	15	16	17	18	19	20
(a)	(b)	(d)	(b)	(c)	(d)	(b)	(c)	(b)	(a)
21	22	23	24	25	26	27	28	29	30
(a)	(a)	(b)	(b)	(b)	(d)	(b)	(d)	(d)	(d)

31	32	33	34	35	36	37	38	39	40
(c)	(b)	(c)	(b)	(a)	(a)	(a)	(d)	(c)	(c)

41	42	43	44	45	46	47	48	49	50
(c)	(c)	(d)	(b)	(d)	(a)	(b)	(c)	(b)	(c)

SOME SELECTED EXPLANATORY ANSWERS

2. The given term is english alphabet and its position

			Latter	Position
B2A1D4	→		A —	1
			B —	2
			D —	4
C3E5A1	→		C —	3
			E —	5
			A —	1
H8B2D4	→		H —	8
			B —	2
			D —	4

Hence, worng term is R5A1T6

5. Except '773' other three numbers are divisible by '3'.

6. ENKAL → ANKLE → 4th letter is L.

7. HCDNGRHAIA → CHANDIGARH → 4th letter is N.

8. HEPES → SHEEP → 4th letter is E.

9. NEGOAR → ORANGE → 4th letter is N.

19.
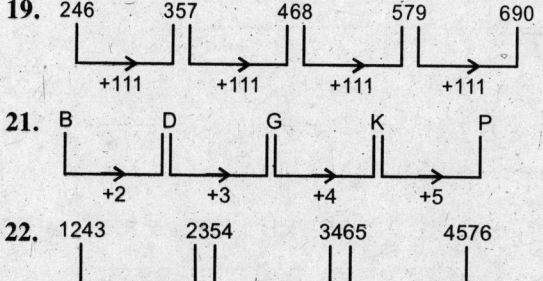

21.

22.
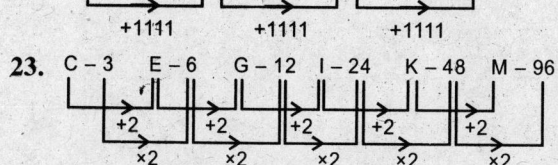

23. C – 3   E – 6   G – 12   I – 24   K – 48   M – 96

24.
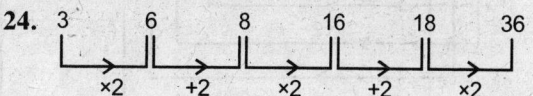

25.
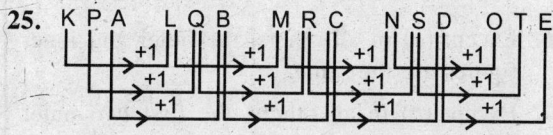

26.
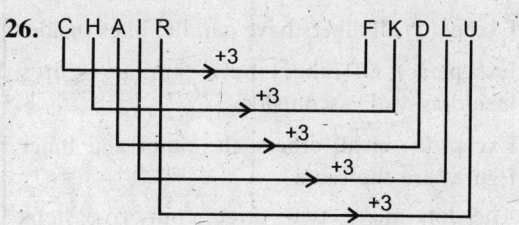

Similarly,

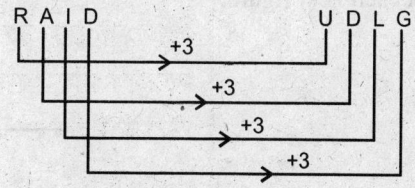

28.
$5 \times 8 = (5 - 1) \times (8 - 1) = 4 \times 7 = 28$
$3 \times 7 = (3 - 1) \times (7 - 1) = 2 \times 6 = 12$
$8 \times 6 = (8 - 1) \times (6 - 1) = 7 \times 5 = 35$

Similarly,
$13 \times 13 = (13 - 1) \times (13 - 1) = 12 \times 12 = 144$

29.

Letters :	T	O	U	R	C	L	E	A	S	P
Code :	1	2	3	4	5	6	7	8	9	0

Hence, Code for 'CARE' is 5847.

30.

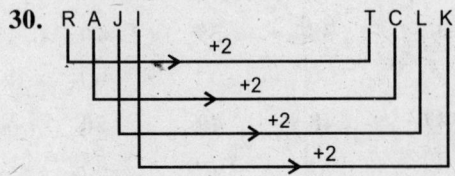

Similarly,

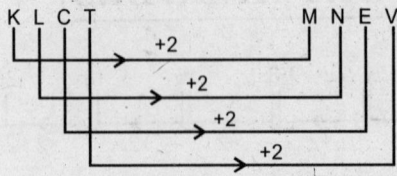

36. Except (*a*) in all others, the outer and inner figures are the same.

37. Except (*a*) in all others, the first two outer figures are same.

38. Except (*d*) all others have parallel lines inside.

39. Except (*c*) all others have similar figures inside as well as outside.

40. Except (*c*) in all others, the outer and inner figures are the same.

41. The dots move, two, three, four, five steps respectively in a clockwise direction.

42. The number of sides in each figure increases by one in each next figure.

43. The inner figure becomes the outer one and the outer figure disappears and another figure comes inside in each subsequent figure.

44. The number of circles and the number of triangles increase in every alternate figure.

45. One line in each figure changes to a curve up and down alternately.

46.

47.

48.

49.

50.

English Language

1. English Grammar

Part of speech	Definition or Function	Examples
Noun	Name of a person, place, animal, quality or thing	Ram, boy, dog pen, sun, Delhi, truth, honesty
Pronoun	Used in place of a noun	I, you, he she, they
Articles & Determiners	Point out indefinite and definite nouns	a, an, the, few, some
Adjective	Describes a noun or pronoun	big, honest, wooden valuable, quiet, deep, soft, narrow
Adverb	Describes a verb, an adjective or another adverb	silently, widely, softly, quietly, very, carefully
Verb	Tells about action or state of something or someone	is, am, was, have, do, like, walk, work, make, throw, tell
Conjuction	Joins words, clauses or sentences	and, but, when, yet, while, else
Preposition	Links a noun or pronoun to another word	at, to, after, on for, under, over, with
Interjection	Expresses sudden feelings or emotions	Ah!, Alas!, oh!, ouch!, hi!, well!, Hurrah!

NOUNS

A word which denotes a person, a thing, an animal or a place is said to be a noun.

There are two noun numbers in English — the *Singular* and the *Plural*.

Singular Numbers : A noun that denotes one person or one thing, is said to be in the Singular number. For example — book, pencil, bird, dog, hen etc. are in singular number.

Plural Number : A noun that denotes more than one person or one thing is said to be in plural number. For example — boys, pens, lions, girls, men etc. are in plural number.

REMEMBER

Singular	Plural
Cat	Cats
Book	Books
Pen	Pens
Room	Rooms
Tree	Trees
Bus	Buses
Bush	Bushes
Box	Boxes
Glass	Glasses
Dish	Dishes
Judge	Judges
Tax	Taxes
Watch	Watches
Calf	Calves
Thief	Thieves
Knife	Knives

Singular	Plural
Scarf	Scarves
Wife	Wives
Leaf	Leaves
Wolf	Wolves
Half	Halves
Monarch	Monarchs
Roof	Roofs
Hoof	Hoofs
Gulf	Gulfs
Staff	Staffs
Radio	Radios
Bamboo	Bamboos
Folio	Folios
Hero	Heroes
Volcano	Volcanoes
Mango	Mangoes
Potato	Potatoes
Photo	Photos
Piano	Pianos
Baby	Babies
Fly	Flies
Country	Countries
Lady	Ladies
Boy	Boys
Monkey	Monkeys
Ox	Oxen
Child	Children
Man	Men
Woman	Women
Tooth	Teeth
Axis	Axes
Basis	Bases
Foot	Feet
Goose	Geese
Englishman	Englishmen
Radius	Radii
Vertex	Vertices
Stimulus	Stimuli

1. Note the plurals of the following nouns:

Singular	Plural	Singular	Plural
copy	copies	cry	cries
baby	babies	duty	duties
body	bodies	country	countries
family	families	diary	diaries
fly	flies	fairy	fairies

Singular	Plural	Singular	Plural
city	cities	spy	spies
army	armies	storey	storeys
bay	bays	monkey	monkeys

2. The following nouns do not undergo any change in plural form, in general:

Singular	Plural	Singular	Plural
deer	deer	sheep	sheep
thousand	thousand	pair	pair
hundred	hundred	score	score
dozen	dozen	gross	gross

Note: We can write:

(a) thousands of men; (b) two pairs of shoes; (c) dozens of mangoes; (d) scores of people etc. But—

(a) two thousand rupees; (b) three hundred men; (c) five dozen eggs, etc.

3. The following nouns are usually used in plural forms. They take a plural verb after them:

eatables	fetters	surroundings
riches	alms	spectacles
trousers	pants	scissors
premises	thanks	annals
congratulations	goods	shorts
tongs	pains	arms
breeches	(for troubles)	

4. The following are the nouns which are plural in appearance but are usually used in singular number. They are followed by a singular verb:

news	politics	physics
mathematics	economics	ethics
politics	classics	gallows
statistics	athletics	innings
mechanics	summons	mumps

5. Collective nouns often used as plurals:

public	police	cattle
audience	clergy	folk
people	poultry	nation
elite	gentry	glitterati

6. The nouns that are usually used in singular forms:

advice	hair	rice
fuel	alphabet	machinery
offspring	issue	furniture
mischief	stationery	luggage
bedding	information	abuse

7. Material nouns are always used in singular number:

gold	copper	milk
water	silk	wool

Note: They may be used in plural with a different meaning.

copper coins (coppers), chains or fetters (irons), cans made of tin (tins).

GENDERS

The difference in sex is denoted by Gender in grammar. The various genders are as follows:

1. **Masculine Gender :** A noun that denotes a male is said to be of the masculine gender, as man, uncle, ox, boy etc.
2. **Feminine Gender :** A noun that denotes a female is said to be of feminine gender, as woman, aunt, princess, cow etc.
3. **Common Gender :** Nouns which denote both males and females are said to be of the common gender, as friend, cousin, person, parent, baby etc.
4. **Neuter Gender :** A noun that denotes the name of object without life is said to be of neuter gender, as file, table, pencil.

REMEMBER

Masculine	Feminine
Boy	Girl
Son	Daughter
Brother	Sister
Murderer	Murderess
Sorcerer	Sorceress
Son-in-law	Daughter-in-law
Father-in-law	Mother-in-law
Man-servant	Maid-servant
Land-lord	Land-lady
Bachelor	Maid
Gentleman	Lady
Monk	Nun
Earl	Countess
Lad	Lass
Sir	Madam
Duke	Dutchess
Emperor	Empress
Milk-man	Milk-maid
Pea-cock	Pea-hen

Masculine	Feminine
Step-father	Step-mother
Hero	Heroine
Viceroy	Vicerine
Mr.	Mrs.
Governor	Governess
Master	Mistress
Wizard	Witch
Heir	Heiress
Host	Hostess
Lion	Lioness
Mayor	Mayoress
Actor	Actress
Buck	Doe
Colt	Filly
Dog	Bitch
Horse	Mare
Count	Countess
Hunter	Huntress
Prince	Princess
Abbot	Abbess
God	Goddess
Author	Authoress
Ox	Cow
Widower	Widow
Grand-father	Grand-mother
He-goat	She-goat
Milk-man	Milk-woman
Bridegroom	Bride
Tiger	Tigress
Priest	Priestess
Poet	Poetess
Shepherd	Shepherdess
Nephew	Niece
Stag	Hind

PRONOUNS

The repetition of a noun in a sentence or a set of sentences is really boring. So, instead of repeating the noun, we can use a word (for that noun) called the pronoun.

"A pronoun is a word that we use instead of a noun".

Example:
This is *Sachin*. *He* plays cricket.

Note: *He* is the pronoun used in place of *Sachin*.

Kinds of Pronouns

1. **Personal Pronouns :** A pronoun which is used instead of the name of a person is known as a 'Personal Pronoun'. A list of the 'Personal pronouns' is listed below :

   I, my, mine, me, we   (First Person)
   You, your, yours   (Second Person)
   He, his, him, she, her, hers, it,
   its, they, their, theirs, them   (Third Person)

2. **Demonstrative, Indefinite and Distributive Pronouns :**

   (a) **Demonstrative Pronouns :** Pronouns used to point out the objects to which they refer are called Demonstrative Pronouns.

   Examples :
   (i) *This* is a present from my uncle.
   (ii) *These* are merely excuses.
   (iii) Bombay mangoes are better than *those* of Bangaluru.

   (b) **Indefinite Pronouns :** All pronouns which refer to persons or things in a general way and do not refer to any particular person or thing are called Indefinite Pronouns.

   Examples :
   (i) *Somebody* has stolen my watch.
   (ii) *Few* escaped unhurt.
   (iii) Did you ask *anybody* to come?

   (c) **Distributive Pronouns :** Each, either, neither are called distributive pronouns because they refer to persons or things one at a time. For this reason they are always singular and followed by the verb in singular.

   Examples :
   (i) *Each* of the men received a reward.
   (ii) *These* men received *each* a reward.
   (iii) *Either* of you can go.

3. **Relative Pronouns :** A relative pronoun refers or relates to some noun going before, which is called its Antecedent.

Examples :
(i) I met Hari *who* used to live here.
(ii) I have found the pen *which* I had lost.
(iii) Here is the book *that* you lent me.

4. **Interrogative Pronouns :** These pronouns, are used for asking questions.

   Examples :
   (i) *Whose* book is this?
   (ii) *What* will all the neighbours say?
   (iii) *Which* do you prefer, tea or coffee?

   Note : Interrogative pronouns can also be used in asking indirect questions. Consider the following examples :
   (i) I asked *who* was speaking.
   (ii) Tell me *what* you have done.
   (iii) Say *which* you would like best.

Behaviour of the Pronouns

1. If three pronouns are used together in the same sentence they are arranged in the following order:

   2   +   3   +   1
   ↓   ↓   ↓
   Second   Third   First
   Person   Person   Person

   Examples :
   I, you and he must help *that* poor man.
                          (Incorrect)
   You, he and I must help *that* poor man.
                          (Correct)

2. When two or more singular nouns are joined by 'and', the pronoun used for them should be plural.

   Examples :
   Mohan and Sohan are, friends. *They* play football. *They* live at Lajpat Nagar.

3. But if these nouns joined by 'and' and refer to the same person or thing, the pronoun used should be singular.

   Examples :
   (i) Delhi, the beautiful city and the capital of India, is famous for *its* historical monuments.
   (ii) The manager and owner of the firm expressed *his* views on the demands of the workers.

4. When two nouns are used with 'as well as', the pronoun agrees with the first subject.
   Examples :
   (i) Mohan as well as his friends is doing *his* work.
   (ii) The students as well as their teacher are doing *their* work.

5. When two singular nouns joined by 'and' are preceded by *each* or *every,* the pronoun used must be singular and should agree in gender with the second noun.
   Examples :
   (i) Every man and every woman will do *her* best for the nation.
   (ii) Each boy and each girl did *her* work.

6. When two nouns are joined by using 'with', the pronoun agrees with the noun coming before 'with'.
   Examples :
   (i) The boy with *his* parents has gone to see a movie.
   (ii) The children with *their* parents have gone to picnic.

7. When two different nouns are joined by either.......... or; neither .... nor, the pronoun is used according to the number and gender of the second noun.

Examples :
(i) Either your sister or you have done *your* work.
(ii) Neither the students nor the teacher was in *his* class.

8. The pronoun coming after 'than' must be in the same case as that coming before 'than'.
   Examples :
   (i) She plays better than *me*.   (Incorrect)
       She plays better than *I*.   (Correct)
   (ii) His elder brother is more intelligent than *him*.   (Incorrect)
       His elder brother is more intelligent than *he*.   (Correct)

9. 'Many a' always takes a singular pronoun and singular verb.
   Example :
   Many a soldier has met *his* death in the battle field.

10. 'Who', 'Whose', 'Whom' are used only for persons.
    Examples :
    (i) *Who* is knocking at the door?
    (ii) *Whose* pen is this?
    (iii) *Whom* do you want?

11. 'Which' is used for things.
    Example :
    Which game do you like?

MULTIPLE CHOICE QUESTIONS

Directions: *In the following questions choose the correct options to fill in the blanks.*

1. The place was so dirty that ..... wished to run away from there.
   A. everybody   B. anybody
   C. few   D. some

2. ..... was there to help me.
   A. Somebody   B. Anything
   C. Anybody   D. Nobody

3. Is there .... to eat?
   A. some   B. something
   C. any   D. few

4. ..... of the students were making a great noise.
   A. Anyone   B. Somebody
   C. Many   D. Nobody

5. ..... of the students can solve this sum.
   A. Someone   B. Anybody
   C. Somebody   D. None

6. ...... of us should try our best to make India a heaven.
   A. Any   B. Somebody
   C. Anybody   D. All

7. ...... of us do not know the real meaning of our lives.
   A. Any   B. Something
   C. Several   D. Many

8. My .... black.
   A. hairs are   B. hair is
   C. hairs shall   D. hair will

9. She saw two .... on the last Sunday.
   A. thiefs   B. theifs
   C. thieves   D. theives

10. My sister is a ....
   A. bacheloress   B. bachelor
   C. unmarried   D. spinster

11. One is supposed to do ....
   A. our duty   B. their duty
   C. one's duty   D. his duty

12. Take anything .... you want.
   A. that   B. which
   C. than   D. then

13. I cannot tolerate ....
   A. separated you
   B. your separation
   C. separation from you
   D. you separated

14. He is .... faithful partner.
   A. Yours   B. You
   C. Your   D. Your's

15. Ajay is more smart than ....
   A. her   B. hers
   C. herself   D. she

16. Vivek works harder than ....
   A. me   B. I
   C. her   D. his

17. They should help ....
   A. the poor people   B. the poor
   C. the poor persons   D. the poor peoples

18. .... are mad.
   A. All his sons   B. His all sons
   C. Sons all his   D. All sons his

19. The poor fellow .... to fate.
   A. resigned
   B. resigned himself
   C. resigned itself
   D. resigned themselves

20. Nobody will help you but ....
   A. I   B. me
   C. ours   D. his

21. It is a good chance, You must avail .... this opportunity.

A. of   B. yourself of
C. for   D. from

22. The person who is elected .... my relative.
   A. is   B. he is
   C. his   D. him

23. He made ....
   A. yours mention   B. mention of you
   C. mention for you   D. mention about you

24. .... I know, he is quite faithful.
   A. As far as   B. So far as
   C. So far this   D. So far so

25. It is a duty of a person to take .... for his family.
   A. pain   B. pains
   C. pain-killers   D. pained

26. She does not love .... husband.
   A. his   B. her
   C. its   D. their

27. Let .... work together.
   A. him and me   B. he and I
   C. he and him   D. I and me

28. Copper, Silver and Gold ....
   A. each will do   B. either will do
   C. any one will do   D. any will do

29. Jessica and Roma are very irregular .... habits.
   A. in her   B. in their
   C. in its   D. in every

30. One likes to enjoy .... who was a great poet.
   A. The sonnets of Shakespeare
   B. Shakespeare's sonnets
   C. Sonnets
   D. Shakespeare

31. That is the boy .... everybody loves.
   A. whom   B. who
   C. that   D. whose

32. That is the girl .... won the first prize.
   A. whom   B. who
   C. whose   D. which

33. That is the man .... purse was lost.
   A. who   B. whom
   C. whose   D. their

ANSWERS

1	2	3	4	5	6	7	8	9	10
A	D	B	C	D	D	D	B	C	D
11	12	13	14	15	16	17	18	19	20
C	A	C	C	D	B	B	A	B	B
21	22	23	24	25	26	27	28	29	30
B	A	B	A	B	B	A	C	B	A
31	32	33							
A	B	C							

ARTICLES

The family of the articles has only three members. They are : A, An and The. However, they fall under two groups :

(a) Definite Article (b) Indefinite Article

'The' is known as definite article whereas 'a' and 'an' are known as indefinite articles.

Use of the Definite Article 'The'

'The' is used before

1. The superlative degree, e.g.,
   He is the ablest man of the town.
   (ablest is a superlative degree)

2. The name of states, countries etc. having a descriptive name, e.g.,
   (i) The J & K is a small state. (J & K is a descriptive name)
   (ii) He lives in the U.S.A. (U.S.A. is a descriptive name)
   (But the Delhi and the America are wrong because neither Delhi nor America is a descriptive name)

3. The names of the scriptures, e.g.,
   The Gita is a holy book. (Gita is a scripture)

4. Name of newspapers:
   The Tribune is published from Chandigarh.

5. Name of rivers, canals, seas, oceans, bays, gulfs, groups of islands etc. e.g.,
   (i) The Ganga is a holy river.
   (ii) The Indian Ocean is the deepest ocean.
   (iii) The Persian Gulf is a narrow gulf.

6. The name of famous buildings, e.g.,
   The Taj is one of the best buildings in India.

7. The names of nationals, sects and communities, e.g.,
   (i) The English defeated the Germans in the World War.
   (ii) The rich should help the poor.
   (iii) The Hindus believe in the caste system.

8. Proper nouns used as common nouns, e.g.,
   (i) Kalidas is the Shakespeare of India.
   (ii) Delhi is the London of India.

9. Famous historical events, e.g.,
   The Industrial Revolution changed the face of England.

10. The directions and the celestial bodies, e.g.,
    The sun rises in the east.

11. Titles, e.g.,
    Akbar, the Great was loved by his subjects.

Do not use 'the'

1. Before languages:
   The English is an international language. (Incorrect)
   English is an international language. (Correct)

2. Before the names of games:
   The hockey is a popular game. (Incorrect)
   Hockey is a popular game. (Correct)

Use of the Indefinite Articles 'A' and 'An'

'A' is used before :

1. All singular common nouns beginning with a consonant, e.g.,
   (i) A boy sings a song.

(ii) A black and a white cow were grazing in the field.

2. If a word begins with a vowel but gives the sound of a consonant, 'a' should be used before it, *e.g.*,
   (i) He was helped in his work by a European.
   (ii) He is a one-eyed man.
   (iii) It is a useful work.

'An' is used as follows :

1. All singular common nouns beginning with a vowel (*i.e.*, a, e, i, o, u), *e.g.*,
   (i) He is an artist.
   (ii) He is an old man.
   (iii) I intend to buy an umbrella.

2. If a word starts with a consonant but gives the sound of a vowel, 'an' should be used before it, *e.g.*,
   (i) Brutus is an honourable man.
   (ii) He is an honour to his profession.
   (iii) He is an L.L.B.

(iv) He is an M.A.
(v) You will reach there in an hour.

Demonstratives, that, these and those

1. The demonstrative adjectives and pronouns are for objects nearby the speaker:
   this (singular), those (plural)
   and for objects far away from the speaker.
   That (singular), those (plural)

2. Demonstratives are the only adjectives that agree in number with their nouns. *e.g.*,
   (i) That hat is nice.
   (ii) Those hats are nice.

3. When there is the idea of selection, the pronoun 'one' (or 'ones') often follows the demonstrative. *e.g.*,
   I want a book. I'll get this (one).
   If the demonstrative is followed by an adjective, 'one' (or 'ones') must be used.
   I want a book. I'll get this big one.

MULTIPLE CHOICE QUESTIONS

Directions: *In the following questions choose the correct options to fill in the blanks.*

1. .... will have to be paid for this material.
   A. Half rupee   B. Half a rupee
   C. A half rupee   D. An half rupee

2. .... is taking keen interest in India.
   A. The USA   B. USA
   C. An USA   D. A USA

3. Only .... can save our country.
   A. the Hitler   B. a Hitler
   C. Hitler   D. an Hitler

4. I can run for ....
   A. hundred miles   B. the hundred miles
   C. a hundred miles D. an hundred miles.

5. .... man-eater has been killed.
   A. The   B. A
   C. An   D. Either A or B

6. What .... fine idea!
   A. the   B. an
   C. a   D. No article

7. .... earth is moving around the sun.
   A. An   B. A

C. The   D. No article

8. This is .... first example while I got.
   A. the   B. a
   C. an   D. No article

9. This is .... house which was built during earthquake.
   A. a   B. an
   C. the   D. No article

10. .... America is a rich country.
    A. The   B. An
    C. A   D. No article

11. .... U.S.A. is a developed country.
    A. A   B. An
    C. The   D. No article

12. .... Bible is a holy book.
    A. A   B. The
    C. An   D. No article

13. .... rich should help the poor.
    A. The   B. A
    C. An   D. No article

14. .... Gold is a costly metal.
    A. The   B. A
    C. An   D. No article

15. Kalidas is .... Shakespeare of India.
A. a
B. an
C. the
D. No article

16. I cannot do .... difficult work.
A. a such
B. the such
C. such the
D. such a

17. How foolish .... plan it is!
A. a
B. an
C. the
D. No article

18. An ink is .... useful article.
A. an
B. a
C. the
D. No article

19. There are .... husband and wife.
A. a
B. an
C. the
D. No article

20. He is learning .... French
A. the
B. a
C. an
D. No article

ANSWERS

1	2	3	4	5	6	7	8	9	10
B	A	B	C	D	C	C	A	C	D

11	12	13	14	15	16	17	18	19	20
C	B	A	D	C	D	A	B	D	D

ADJECTIVES & ADVERBS

ADJECTIVE

An Adjective is a word which adds something to the meaning of a noun or a pronoun. *e.g.,*

 (i) He talks slowly.
 (ii) Mridula is an *intelligent* girl.
 (iii) He has a *black* goat.
 (iv) He is a *brilliant* student.
 (v) She is a *clever* girl.
 (vi) It is a *beautiful* picture.

In the sentences given above, the words in italics are adjectives.

ADVERB

An Adverb is a word which qualifies the meaning of a Verb, an Adjective or another Adverb. *e.g.,*

 (i) He talks slowly.
 (ii) He is a very good student.
 (iii) He talks very slowly.

In sentence (*i*), *slowly* qualifies the verb *talks*.
In sentence (*ii*), *very* qualifies the adjective *good*.
In sentence (*iii*), *very* qualifies the adverb *slowly*.

Adjectives have three degrees of comparison:

1. Positive Degree : It expresses the common form of an adjective.
   Example :
   Ram is a *tall* boy.
   In the above sentence *tall* is an adjective and expresses the common form.

2. Comparative Degree : It expresses the more of the same form.
   Example :
   Ram is *taller* than Mahesh.
   In the above sentence *taller* is an adjective that expresses the more of the common form of the adjective *tall*.

When and How to Use Comparative Degree?

(a) Comparative Degree is used when two persons or two groups of persons or things are compared.
   Examples :
   (i) He is *wiser* than his younger brother.
   (ii) This glass is *cleaner* than the other.

(b) When two different qualities in the same person are compared, more is used instead of 'er' to form the comparative. The formula used in this case should be:
   More + Positive Degree
   She is *fairer* than polite.   (Incorrect)
   She is *more fair* than polite.   (Correct)

(c) When selection of one out of two persons or things is meant, the degree of comparison is followed by *of* and *the* is used before it.
   Example :
   Zia is abler of *the* two sisters.

(d) If two comparatives are used in the same sentence to impress upon an idea, both should be preceded by the definite article.

Examples :

(i) The higher you go, *the* cooler it is.

(ii) The more we get, *the* more we desire.

(e) When one person or thing is compared with another of the same kind, other is used after the comparative degree. In such sentences other is normally preceded by *any* or *all*.

Examples :

(i) Kalidas is greater than *any* dramatist. (Incorrect)

Kalidas is greater than *any* other dramatist. (Correct)

(ii) Lead is heavier than *all* metals. (Incorrect)

Lead is heavier than *all* other metals. (Correct)

(f) Senior, junior, superior, inferior, prior, anterior (earlier than) and posterior (later than) are always followed by 'to'.

Examples :

(i) Ram is senior *to* Mohan by three years.

(ii) That pen is inferior *to* that.

(iii) He is junior *to* me in rank.

(iv) This event was posterior *to* that.

Note: Never use *than* after the above mentioned adjectives.

Important Information

(a) 'Preferable' is also used as an adjective of the comparative degree. As such, it is always followed by *to* and not *a*.

Death is preferable than dishonour. (Incorrect)

Death is preferable *to* dishonour. (Correct)

(b) To intensify the Degree of comparison, we use *far* or *much* before the comparative.

Examples :

(i) This book is *far* better than that.

(ii) His performance was *much* better than Mohan's.

Warning : Always avoid the use of double comparatives.

Don't say : Ram is more cleverer than his younger brother.

Say: Ram is cleverer than his younger brother.

3. **Superlative Degree :** It expresses the most of the common form of an adjective.

Example :

He is the ablest man of the town.

How and when to use the Superlative Degree?

(a) The Superlative Degree is used when more than two persons or things are compared.

(b) The Superlative Degree is generally preceded by 'the' and followed by 'of' in most of the cases or otherwise.

(c) When an adjective of the superlative degree is preceded by a Possessive Adjective or a Noun in the Possessive case, 'the' should not be used before it.

Example :

Which is Kalidas' best play?

It will be a blunder to use 'the' before the Superlative Degree in such cases.

Don't say : Which is Kalidas' the best play.

(d) To intensify the degree of comparison, *by far* is used before the superlative degree.

Example :

India is *by far* the most beautiful country of the world.

Note: Always avoid the use of double superlatives.

Don't say : He is the most strongest boy in the class.

Say : He is the strongest boy in the class.

Use of some Important Adjectives

1. (a) '**Some**' is used as follows:

(i) With countable nouns where it means: a little, a small quantity.

(ii) In a question which shows some request.

Examples :

(i) There is some water in the bottle.

(ii) Some of the students were absent yesterday.

(iii) Will you have some milk?

(iv) Will you buy some fruit for me?

(b) '**Any**' is used as follows:

(i) In negative sentences.

(ii) In interrogative sentences.

(iii) After 'Hardly', 'Scarcely' and 'Barely'.

(iv) After 'If'.

Examples :

(i) There is not any sugar in the pot.

(ii) We haven't any rice in the house.

(iii) I have hardly any money.

(iv) There are scarcely any plants in this field.

(v) If there is any danger, blow the whistle.

2. (a) **Older :** Older (and oldest) are used for persons animals and things. But 'Older' and 'Oldest' refer to the persons who do not belong to the same family.

Examples :

(i) Radha is older than Shyama.

(ii) John is the oldest member of the staff.

(b) **Elder** (and **eldest**) are used in respect of the members of the same family like sons, daughters, brothers, sisters.

Examples :

(i) My elder sister is a lecturer.

(ii) Meenakshi is the eldest of the three sisters.

Note :

(i) 'Elder' is not followed by 'than'.

(ii) 'Elder' and 'Eldest' cannot be used for things.

3. (a) **'Few'** is negative and is the opposite of 'Many'. It means 'not many'.

(b) **'A few'** is positive and means 'some at least'. It is the opposite of 'None'.

(c) **'The few'** means 'minority' and suggests 'whether there is'.

Examples :

(i) We have few holidays in school.

(ii) Only a few boys will fail in the examination.

(iii) The few poems that he wrote are very popular.

4. (a) **Further** means 'something additional'.

(b) **Farther** means 'a greater distance'.

Examples :

(i) Further discussion will be held in the office of the principal.

(ii) Amritsar is farther from Delhi than Ambala.

5. (a) **Little** is negative. It means, 'not much', or 'hardly any'.

(b) **A little** is positive. It means 'some quantity'.

(c) **The little** denotes quantity. It means, 'not much but all that is, or whatever quantity there is'.

Examples :

(i) There is little hope of his success.

(ii) He knows a little of everything.

(iii) I have spent the little money I had.

(iv) The little knowledge of shoe-making proved very useful to me.

6. (a) **'Much'** expresses 'quantity'.

(b) **'Many'** expresses 'number'.

(c) **'Many a'**—'Singular noun' and 'Singular verb' are used with 'many a'.

Examples :

(i) There is not *much* water in the jug.

(ii) *Many* boys are absent today.

(iii) *Many* a battle has been fought on the soil of India.

7. (a) **'Less'** denotes 'in a small degree'.

(b) **'Fewer'** denotes 'number'.

Examples :

(i) He devotes less time to his studies.

(ii) There are no fewer than ten chairs in this room.

8. (a) **'Each'** is used for a single number of 'two persons' or 'things'.

(b) **'Every'** is used for a single number of 'many persons' or 'things'.

Examples :

(i) Each boy must take part in games.

(ii) There are only two poets. Each poet recited his poem.

(iii) Every man dies in this world.

(iv) Every man is expected to do his duty.

9. (a) **'Either'** means one of the two or both.

(b) **'Neither'** is negative of the either.

Examples :

(i) You may buy either of these two chairs.

(ii) Neither of them could speak on the stage.

10. (a) **'Later'** expresses 'late in time'.
    (b) **'Latter'** means 'second in position or order'.
    Examples :
    (i) My father reached later than I expected.
    (ii) The latter position was better than the former.

Use of some Important Adverbs

1. (a) **Also, Too, Enough:** 'Also' and 'too' suggest 'addition' and 'excess' while 'enough' is placed after the verb it qualifies. *e.g.,*
    (i) He taught English. Also, he edited the school magazine.
    (ii) He is a writer and also he is a painter.
    (iii) He is too obstinate to listen to any reason.
    (iv) This is too difficult a piece for the junior students.
    (v) Sarla was kind enough to help the poor.
    (vi) He is brave enough to help the truth.
    (b) **Fairly and Rather:** Both suggest the meaning 'moderately'. But, mainly 'fairly' is used with the words that denote a positive meaning and rather is used with the words that denote a negative meaning, *e.g.,*
    (i) Rita did fairly well in that competition, but her performance was rather poor in sports.
    (ii) Mona is fairly rich, but she is rather stingy.
    Note: 'Rather' can also be used in a positive sense.
    (i) This is a rather interesting job.
    (ii) That boy is rather smart.
    (c) **Hardly, Barely, Scarcely:** These words mostly convey the negative suggestions and are almost similar. *e.g.,*
    (i) I have hardly any strength now.

(ii) There was barely any supply to the township.
(iii) There were scarcely a hundred guests present.
Note: With slight variance in the meaning, the words given above convey the idea of 'very little', 'not enough', 'lack of quantity and number'.

(d) **Yet, Still:** These adverbs can often be used to connect the sentence units:
    (i) Mona was sick; yet she went on doing her work.
    (ii) He has been defeated many times in the contest; still he wants to be a competitor.
(e) **Alone:**
    (i) He alone (none else) is capable of handling that fire,
    (ii) He hunted all alone in the forest. (not in any company)

Special Note:
(a) Apart from their conventional positions the adverbs might be used in different positions with different meanings and angles.
    (i) He had only four books.
    (ii) John only contacted his friend in need.
    (iii) He greeted me only.
    (iv) Only he greeted me there.
(b) Some adverbs can be inverted *i.e.* placed in the beginning of the sentence and then be followed by an interrogative form. The most common of these adverb are: so, seldom, never, nowhere, under no circumstances, hardly, scarcely etc. *e.g.,*
    (i) So big was the bus that it could not enter the narrow lane.
    (ii) Hardly had he reached the station when he received the message.

MULTIPLE CHOICE QUESTIONS

Directions: *In the following questions choose the correct options to fill in the blanks.*

1. The girl whom you met is the .... sister of Ravi.

A. eldest   B. elder
C. older   D. oldest

2. The historical place is ....
A. seeing worth

B. worthy of seeing
C. worth seeing
D. worthy seeing

3. These flowers smell ....
   A. sweet   B. sweetly
   C. more sweetly   D. sweetest

4. .... aspirant cannot pass the entrance examination.
   A. Each   B. Every
   C. All   D. No

5. Harivansh Rai .... second Shakespeare.
   A. is a   B. is
   C. is the   D. is an

6. .... student in the class got prizes.
   A. Each and every   B. Every and each
   C. Every   D. Never

7. It is .... picture than the one we saw last Monday.
   A. interesting   B. much interesting
   C. more interesting D. most interesting

8. She is clever ....
   A. that her mother is
   B. as her mother is
   C. to her mother is
   D. than her mother is

9. They will get ....
   A. Red, green and black paper
   B. Red, green black paper
   C. Red and green and black paper
   D. Red green black paper

10. Health is .... wealth.
    A. preferable to
    B. more preferable than
    C. more preferable to
    D. most preferable then

11. .... water that was in the jug evaporated.
    A. Little   B. The little
    C. Small   D. A small

12. He has not sung .... songs.
    A. much   B. most
    C. more   D. many

13. Srishti has searched .... office.
    A. whole the   B. the whole
    C. a whole   D. some whole

14. Premchand was .... best and .... famous writer.
    A. a, the most   B. the, a most
    C. the, more   D. the, the most

15. William Shakespeare is famous as ....
    A. a poet and a dramatist
    B. a poet and dramatist
    C. the poet and the dramatist
    D. a poet and the dramatist

16. What does .... leader suggest?
    A. other   B. another
    C. others   D. anothers

17. He .... money.
    A. has few   B. have few
    C. has little   D. have little

18. The .... boys are rewarded.
    A. first two   B. two first
    C. firsts two   D. two's first

19. He is .... brave.
    A. stronger than
    B. stronger then
    C. more strong then
    D. more strong than

20. No sooner said ....
    A. so done   B. and done
    C. than done   D. but done

21. She returned .... than I had thought.
    A. quickly   B. more quicker
    C. more quickly   D. quicker

22. He is .... foolish person.
    A. rather the   B. a rather
    C. rather a   D. rather

23. This pen .... rupees.
    A. costs twenty
    B. twenty costs only
    C. costs only twenty
    D. only costs twenty

24. It is .... pride.
    A. nothing else but
    B. nothing else than
    C. else nothing than
    D. but

25. This tea is .... to drink.
    A. too hot   B. very hot
    C. enough hot   D. much hot

16

ANSWERS

1	2	3	4	5	6	7	8	9	10
A	C	A	B	A	C	C	C	A	A
11	12	13	14	15	16	17	18	19	20
B	D	B	D	B	B	C	A	D	C
21	22	23	24	25					
C	C	C	A	A					

DETERMINERS

Determiners are actually Adjectives. They are always followed by nouns.

Determiners are of the following kinds:

1. **Demonstrative Determiners**
   e.g., this, that, these, those

2. **Possessive Determiners**
   e.g., my, our, your, his, her, its, their

3. **Quantitative Determiners**
   e.g., some, any, much, enough, sufficient, whole, a little, the little, little, all, both

4. **Numerical Determiners**
   e.g., a few, some, few, the few, any, several, many, no, etc.
   One, two, three ...   (Cardinals)
   First, second, third ...   (Ordinals)

5. **Distributive Determiners**
   e.g., either, neither

6. **Articles**
   Indefinite: a, an
   Definite: the

MULTIPLE CHOICE QUESTIONS

Directions: *In the following questions choose the correct options to fill the blanks.*

1. Give me .... rice.
   A. some   B. few
   C. a few   D. any

2. .... sheep grazing on the slope of the hill had gone away.
   A. Any   B. The few
   C. This   D. Much

3. Have you got .... magazines to read?
   A. all   B. much
   C. some   D. little

4. I have .... money that I want to spend on shares.
   A. any   B. much
   C. less   D. some

5. There is .... owl on the branch of the tree.
   A. a   B. the
   C. an   D. some

6. My brother is .... MBA.
   A. a   B. an
   C. the   D. any

7. Have you got .... cheese?
   A. some   B. many
   C. a few   D. few

8. No, I have not got .... cheese.
   A. many   B. few
   C. any   D. some

9. There is only .... milk left in the bottle.
   A. enough   B. few
   C. much   D. a little

10. There is .... hope of his recovery.
    A. any   B. little
    C. many   D. few

11. .... dogs were barking at the strangers.
    A. Some   B. Any
    C. Much   D. Less

12. The girl bought her father .... juice.
  A. few   B. some
  C. any   D. many

13. You should take .... honey everyday.
  A. any   B. many
  C. a little   D. a few

14. .... boy was punished by the teacher.
  A. Either   B. All
  C. Any   D. Many

15. .... girl was asked to join the army.
  A. None   B. Neither
  C. All   D. Any

16. .... water in the jug has been drunk by Mohan.

  A. The little   B. The few
  C. A few   D. Few

17. I shall play .... piano at the party.
  A. some   B. any
  C. the   D. few

18. .... labourers were found dead in the mine.
  A. Any   B. Fewer
  C. Many   D. Less

19. Could I borrow .... umbrella?
  A. our   B. your
  C. yours   D. my

20. My brother is standing in the .... row.
  A. any   B. many
  C. some   D. first

ANSWERS

1	2	3	4	5	6	7	8	9	10
A	B	C	D	C	B	A	C	D	B

11	12	13	14	15	16	17	18	19	20
A	B	C	A	B	A	C	C	B	D

THE VERB

A Verb is a word that tells something about the action or state of or happenning to a person or thing.

A Verb tells the following:

1. What a person or thing does. *e.g.,*
  (i) Sachin goes to school daily.
  (ii) The bell *rang* loudly.
  (iii) Many birds *fly* in the sky.
  (iv) She *sang* a song.

2. What a person or thing is. *e.g.,*
  (i) India *is* the biggest democracy in the world.
  (ii) Ram Mehar *is* very rich.
  (iii) They *are* happy.

3. What is done to a person or thing. *e.g.,*
  (i) You *are liked* by all.
  (ii) Two thieves *were arrested.*
  (iii) Four students *were punished* by the teacher.

4. What happens to a person or thing. *e.g.,*
  (i) His maternal uncle *died* last week.
  (ii) Two ships *sank* yesterday.
  (iii) Leaves *turn* yellow in autumn.

5. What a person or thing has, had, and so on. *e.g.,*
  (i) I *have* a new car.
  (ii) He *had* a scooter last year.

(iii) He *has* several cows and goats.

It goes without saying that a verb is the most important part of a sentence. No sentence is complete without a Verb.

Important Information

1. If two or more singular nouns are joined by 'and' the verb used will be plural.

  Example:
  (i) He and I *were* going to the market.
  (ii) Ram and Mohan *are* friends.

2. If two singular nouns joined by 'and' points out to the same thing or person, the verb used must be singular.
  Example:
  (i) Rice and curry *is* the favourite food of the Punjabis.
  (ii) The Collector and District Magistrate *is* away.

3. In case two subjects are joined by 'as well as' the verb agrees with the first subject.
  Example :
  (i) Kanta as well as *her* children is playing.
  (ii) Children as well as their mother *are* playing.

In the case of first sentence the verb 'is' agrees with Kanta and in the case of second sentence the verb 'are' agrees with the children.

4. 'Neither', 'Either', 'Every', 'Each', 'Everyone', and 'Many a' are followed by a singular verb.
Example :
(i) Either of the plans *is* to be adopted.
(ii) Neither of the two brothers *is* sure to pass.
(iii) Every student *is* expected to be obedient.
(iv) Everyone of them *desires* this.
(v) Many a person *is* drowned in the sea.

5. If two subjects are joined by 'Either .... or' / 'Neither .... nor', the verb agrees with the subject near to 'or' or 'nor'.

Example :
(i) Either my brother or I *am* to do this work.
(ii) Neither he nor they *are* prepared to do this work.

6. 'A great many' is always followed by a 'plural noun' and a 'plural verb'. *e.g.,*
A great many *students have* been declared successful.

7. Similarly if two subjects are joined by 'with', 'together with', 'no less than', in addition to 'and not', etc. the verb agrees with the first subject.
Example :
(i) The boy with his parents *has* arrived.
(ii) He, no less than I, *is* to blame.

8. Nouns, plural in form, but singular in meaning, take a singular verb.
Example :
This news *was* broadcast from television yesterday.

MULTIPLE CHOICE QUESTIONS

Directions: *In the following questions choose the correct options to fill in the blanks.*

1. The bus with all its passengers .... lost.
A. were   B. was
C. are   D. would

2. You as well as I .... responsible for this work.
A. am   B. are
C. was   D. is

3. Raghava like all his companions .... a spoiled child.
A. are   B. were
C. is   D. will be

4. Pen and ink .... required for me.
A. are   B. were
C. is   D. has required

5. Every girl and every boy .... attended the seminar.
A. have   B. has
C. is   D. are

6. Not only she but all her sisters ...... been married.
A. has   B. have
C. is   D. are

7. There .... nothing but miseries in life.
A. is   B. are
C. were   D. will be

8. Neither prose nor poem .... given.
A. were   B. was
C. has   D. have

9. Either he or I .... wrong.
A. is   B. are
C. am   D. were

10. Either Sulekha or Rekha .... coming here.
A. are   B. is
C. were   D. have

11. .... the child or his parents to blame?
A. Is   B. Are
C. Were   D. Has

12. You and I .... neighbours.
A. am   B. are
C. was   D. has

13. The house with all its belongings ..... sold away.
A. were   B. are
C. was   D. must

14. Either water or juice .... required.
A. is   B. are
C. were   D. has

15. There were not as many tables as .... required.
A. was   B. were
C. is   D. are

16. They each .... a book.
    A. have   B. are
    C. has   D. is
17. He and I .... class friends.
    A. is   B. am
    C. was   D. are
18. She as well as I .... guilty.
    A. is   B. are
    C. am   D. must be
19. Purushottam .... not read more on this chapter.
    A. needs   B. has been need
    C. need   D. had been need
20. He came .... to his aunt.
    A. run   B. running
    C. to run   D. in run
21. She dislikes .... meat.
    A. eat to   B. to eat

C. eating   D. to eating
22. He likes ....
    A. sing to   B. singing
    C. to sing   D. to singing
23. We are ready .... the match.
    A. play to   B. to playing
    C. playing   D. to play
24. .... is injurious to health.
    A. Smoking   B. To smoke
    C. To smoking   D. Smoke to
25. He loves .... raw vegetables.
    A. eaten   B. eating
    C. to eating   D. eat to
26. He seemed .... finished his homework.
    A. have to   B. to have
    C. having   D. to having

ANSWERS

1	2	3	4	5	6	7	8	9	10
B	B	C	C	B	B	A	B	C	B
11	12	13	14	15	16	17	18	19	20
A	B	C	A	B	A	D	A	C	B
21	22	23	24	25	26				
C	B	D	A	B	B				

CONJUNCTIONS

A conjunction is a word which connects words, clauses or sentences.

Look at the following sentences:
(i) He bought apples *and* mangoes.
(ii) God made the country *and* man made the town.
(iii) The door was open *but* there was no one in the house.
(iv) He knows that I am here *and* that I want to see him.

In the sentence (i), *and* connects two words—*apples* and *mangoes*.

In the sentence (ii), *and* connects two sentences—*God made the country* and *man made the town.*

In the sentence (iii), *but* connects two sentences—*The door was open* and *there was no one in the house.*

In the sentence (iv), *and* connects two clauses—*that I am here* and *that I want to see him.*

The main coordinating conjunctions are:
and, but, for, or, nor, also, either ..... or, neither ...., nor.

There are some conjunctions which are used in pairs. They are:
either .... or, ... neither .... nor, both .... and, though .... yet, whether .... or, not only .... but also.

Example: *Either* take it *or* leave it.
It is *neither* useful *nor* ornamental.
They *both* like *and* respect me.
Though he is suffering from high fever, *yet* he does not cry.
He does not care *whether* you go *or* stay.
He is *not only* doltish, *but also* obstinate.

The conjunctions which are used in pairs in this way, are called correlative conjunctions, or merely correlatives.

Use of Important Conjunctions

1. **As soon as :** As soon as denotes simultaneous time.

    Example : *As soon as* he saw his enemy, he took to his heels.

2. **No sooner .... than :**
    (a) 'No sooner' is always followed by 'than'.
    (b) Please remember that 'No sooner' is always followed by 'do/does/did'. As such only first form of the verb should be used after the subject.

    Example :

    No sooner did he see his enemy *than* he took to his heels.

3. **Hardly :** 'Hardly' is followed by 'when'.

    Examples :
    (i) *Hardly* had I left the house *when* it started raining.
    (ii) We had *hardly* come into the room *when* his father began chastising him.

    Note :
    (i) Hardly is never followed by than.
    (ii) 'Scarcely' can also be used in the sense and manner of 'Hardly'.

4. **Lest :** Lest is used in the sense of 'so that .... not.' It is always followed by 'should.' Lest is negative in sense. Hence 'not' should never be used with it.

    Example :

    Work hard *lest* you *should* fail.

    Note : 'Lest' is always followed by 'should' and not 'may'.

5. **Unless :** Unless expresses condition. It is also used in the negative sense. Use of 'not' is not allowed with unless because unless is already in the negative sense.

    Example :

    Unless you labour hard you will not pass.

6. **Until :** 'Until' expresses time. It means 'till not'.

    Example :

    Wait here *until* I return.

    Note : Until is in the negative sense. So 'not' should not be used with it.

    Example :
    Wait here *until* I do not return.   (Incorrect)
    Wait here *until* I return.   (Correct)

7. **As well as :** When two subjects are joined by 'as well as', the verb always agrees with the first subject.

    Examples :
    (i) The teacher *as well as* students *is* playing.
    (ii) Students *as well as* the teacher *are* playing.

    Note : 'Both' and 'as well as' cannot be used together in the same sentence.

    Examples :
    Both Sita as well as Kanta are beautiful.
       (Incorrect)
    Sita as well as Kanta is beautiful. (Correct)
    Both Sita and Kanta are beautiful. (Correct)

8. **As if :** 'As if' is used in the sense of pretension. While using 'as if' in a sentence, we should see that even the third person singular subject gets 'were'.

    Example :
    He talks *as if* he *were* mad.

9. **Till :** Till expresses time. Till is always used in the affirmative.

    Example :
    We did not come back *till* sunset.

10. **Rather than :** 'Rather than' is used in the sense of 'preference'. 'Rather' is always followed by 'than'.

    Example :
    I would *rather* die *than* submit.

11. **As long as/so long as :** Both express time during which an action or event takes place.

    Example :
    As long as there is life, there is hope.

12. **However :** It is both a subordinate and co-ordinate clause.

    Examples :
    (i) Mala worked hard, she *however*, failed.
    (ii) *However* hard he may work, he cannot pass.

13. **Such as :** 'Such as' gives us the sense of 'like'. 'Such' is always followed by 'as'.

    Example :
    Life is *such* a puzzle *as* cannot be solved.

MULTIPLE CHOICE QUESTIONS

Directions: *In the following questions choose the correct options to fill in the blanks.*

1. Neither he .... his friend is good.
   A. or
   B. and
   C. but
   D. nor

2. The officer asked the peon .... why he was late.
   A. that
   B. if
   C. but
   D. No word needed

3. Both Ajay .... Vijay are intelligent.
   A. or
   B. nor
   C. and
   D. No word needed

4. No Sooner did the thief see the public .... he ran away.
   A. then
   B. and
   C. but
   D. than

5. Abhinav .... his brothers was going to Mumbai.
   A. but
   B. yet
   C. No word needed
   D. together with

6. He behaves .... he were the captain of the team.
   A. as if
   B. as
   C. No word needed
   D. that

7. Either Rupali .... Sonali is going to attend the meeting.
   A. and
   B. but
   C. nor
   D. or

8. Neither Nirmal .... Ashwinee is going to listen the speech.
   A. and
   B. but
   C. nor
   D. or

9. Ravi .... Prakash are going to Kolkata.
   A. or
   B. nor
   C. but
   D. and

10. Rice .... curry is my usual breakfast.
    A. and
    B. but
    C. then
    D. than

11. Hardly had he left .... his brother came.
    A. then
    B. than
    C. when
    D. that

12. I would rather have a copy .... a book.
    A. then
    B. than
    C. when
    D. that

13. He is no other .... my friend.
    A. then
    B. than
    C. when
    D. but

14. He saw a snake ....he awoke.
    A. then
    B. when
    C. than
    D. No word needed

15. Ten years have passed .... my grandmother died.
    A. since
    B. when
    C. then
    D. than

16. She is .... good .... bad.
    A. either, not
    B. neither, or
    C. neither, nor
    D. neither, than

17. The cellphone is both cheap .... best.
    A. than
    B. and
    C. then
    D. or

18. No sooner did the rogue see the police .... he disappeared.
    A. then
    B. than
    C. so
    D. because

19. Srishti will go .... Sanju goes.
    A. if
    B. than
    C. then
    D. although

20. She is wise .... timid.
    A. and
    B. yet
    C. but
    D. however

21. Make hay .... the sun shines.
    A. though
    B. while
    C. after
    D. before

22. He is so weak .... he cannot walk.
    A. but
    B. that
    C. then
    D. so

23. Although he is rich, ... he is unhappy.
    A. but
    B. yet
    C. so
    D. still

24. Wait here .... I come back.
    A. till
    B. until
    C. before
    D. after

25. He is my friend .... I shall help him.
  A. so
  B. hence
  C. that is why
  D. therefore

26. He must go away .... he will be beaten.
  A. otherwise   B. and
  C. or   D. else

27. God loves good men .... good men love God.

  A. and   B. or
  C. that   D. those

28. He was late .... he was not punished.
  A. but   B. yet
  C. still   D. therefore

29. Walk slowly ...., you may fall.
  A. and   B. or
  C. so   D. otherwise

30. Work hard, ... you will fail.
  A. and   B. or
  C. otherwise   D. else

ANSWERS

1	2	3	4	5	6	7	8	9	10
D	D	C	D	D	A	D	C	D	A
11	**12**	**13**	**14**	**15**	**16**	**17**	**18**	**19**	**20**
C	B	B	B	A	C	B	B	A	C
21	**22**	**23**	**24**	**25**	**26**	**27**	**28**	**29**	**30**
B	B	B	A	B	C	A	C	D	D

PREPOSITIONS

A Preposition is a word which is placed before a noun or a pronoun to show its relation to some other word in the sentence. *e.g.,*

    (i) I saw a goat *in* the field.
    (ii) I am fond *of* tea.

In sentence (i), the word *in* shows the relation between two things—*goat* and *field*.

In sentence (ii), the word *of* shows the relation between the attribute expressed by the adjective *fond* and *tea*.

The words *in* and *of* are here used as prepositions.

The noun or pronoun which is used with a preposition is called its object. The noun or pronoun is in the objective case. It is governed by the preposition. Now it is absolutely clear that in sentence (i), the noun *field* is in the objective case. The word *field* is governed by the preposition *in*.

A preposition may have two or more objects. *e.g.,*

The road runs over *hill* and *plain.*

Here, the words *hill* and *plain* are used as objects.

Use of Important Prepositions

1. Among, Between
'Among' is used for more than two persons or things; 'Between' is used only for two.
Examples :
  (i) Distribute these sweets *among* the poor students of the class.
  (ii) Distribute these books *between* Ram and Shyam.

2. Among, In
'Among' is used before collective plural nouns. 'In' is used before collective singular nouns.
Examples :
  (i) I found him standing *among* the crowd.
  (ii) I saw him in the crowd.

3. Beside, Besides
'Beside' means 'by the side of'. 'Besides' means 'in addition to'.
Examples :
  (i) The daughter was sitting *beside* her mother.
  (ii) *Besides* his relatives, he invited his friends also.

4. In, Within
'In' means at the expiry of a period of time in future, 'Within' means before the expiry of a period of time in any tense.

Examples :

(i) She will return *in* a week.

(ii) I shall finish my work *within* a weak.

5. On, Upon

'On' is used for things at rest; 'Upon' is used for things in motion.

Examples :

(i) He is sitting *on* the floor.

(ii) The dog sprang *upon* the table.

6. By, With

'By' denotes the agent or doer, 'With' denotes the instrument with which anything is done.

Examples :

(i) The bird was killed *by* the hunter with an arrow.

(ii) He beat the dog *with* a stick.

(iii) I shall reach here *by* five o'clock.

7. After, In

'After' means at the end of a period of time in the past. 'In' means at the end of a period of time in future.

Examples :

(i) I shall return your book *in* a week.

(ii) He returned the book *after* a week.

8. For, From, Since

'For' is used before a noun denoting a period of time with all the tenses. 'From' is used before a noun or phrase denoting a point of time, it is used in all the tenses. 'Since' is used before a noun or phrase denoting some point of time and is always produced by a verb in the perfect continuous tense or third form of a verb.

Examples :

(i) We have been playing cards *for* two hours.

(ii) She stayed with her uncle *from* the 15th of March to the 15th of May.

(iii) I have been reading this book *since* morning.

9. Above, Over

'Above' means 'higher from', Over is used in the following four senses :

(i) In the sense of 'above' :
    At noon, the sun is *over* our heads.

(ii) In the sense of 'beyond' :
    I cannot get *over* my disappointment.

(iii) In the sense of 'Superiority' :
    God *over* all blesses for ever more.

(iv) In the sense of 'Conclusion' :
    It is all *over* with me.

10. At, Towards

'At' denotes the idea of aim, 'Towards' denotes the idea of destination.

Examples :

(i) He threw the stone *at* the cat.

(ii) He went *towards* the house.

11. At, In, On

'At' is used as follows:

(i) 'At' is used with small towns and villages.

Examples :

(a) He was born *at* Sonepat.

(b) He lives *at* village Bangra. (Bangra is a village)

(ii) 'At' is used before a noun denoting a definite point of time.

Example :

He called on me *at* 9 p.m. yesterday.

'In' is used as follows:

(iii) 'In' is used with the names of big cities, provinces and countries.

Examples :

(a) His father lives *in* England.

(b) His younger brother lives *in* Calcutta.

(iv) 'In' is used before the names of months and years.

Example :

His elder sister was born *in* 1972 *in* the month of May.

'On' is used with dates and names of days.

Examples :

(a) I joined college *on* the 26th April.

(b) He will leave for Kolkata *on* Wednesday next.

Important Information

(i) 'In' is also used in the following phrases: In the morning; In the evening, In winter, In summer.

(ii) 'In' also denotes a place inside anything. He travelled *in* a crowded bus.

(iii) 'At' is used in the following phrases :
At home, At the station, At work, At play.

12. Below, Beneath

Below means 'of lower level in position, dignity and expectation' etc. *Beneath* means 'under'.

Examples :

(i) It is *below* my dignity to talk to her.

(ii) They rested *beneath* the shade of a tree.

13. In, Into, To

'In' expresses Rest or Motion inside anything. 'Into' expresses Motion towards the inside of anything or change from one medium to another. 'To' denotes motion from one place to another.

Examples :

(i) The boys are *in* the room.

(ii) Translate this passage from English *into* Hindi.

(iii) Every morning he goes *to* the temple.

14. Till, By, Of, Off

- 'Till' means upto or not earlier than.
- 'By' means not later than.
- 'Of' shows cause, source, separation, quality, contents, possession, apposition, point of reference, space in time etc.
- 'Off' shows separation at a near distance, and detached condition.

Consider the following examples:

(i) I shall work *till* 5 a.m.

(ii) Madhu died *of* cancer.

(iii) The nib *of* the pen is made *of* gold.

(iv) He presented me a bottle *of* perfume.

(v) Our principal is a man *of* principle.

(vi) He lived in the house *of* his friend.

(vii) *By* this time tomorrow, I'll have finished my job.

(viii) My house is *off* the road.

(ix) The book fell *off* the table.

(x) He got *off* the bus there.

MULTIPLE CHOICE QUESTIONS

Directions: *Tick the correct preposition for the blank in each of the following sentences.*

1. He applied ...... the manager.
   A. for   B. to
   C. with   D. by

2. Trust ...... God and do the right.
   A. in   B. for
   C. to   D. with

3. She is worthy ...... a prize.
   A. with   B. for
   C. to   D. of

4. Mr. Gomes has no taste ...... music.
   A. of   B. for
   C. with   D. to

5. You are hard ...... hearing.
   A. at   B. of
   C. with   D. for

6. He is sure ...... his success
   A. for   B. with
   C. on   D. of

7. Preeti was warned ...... the danger ahead.
   A. for   B. at
   C. of   D. about

8. I am thankful ...... you for a good advice.
   A. for   B. with
   C. to   D. of

9. Deepak would not surrender ...... the police.
   A. with   B. to
   C. for   D. on

10. The small plant in your lawn is very sensitive ...... touch.
    A. on   B. with
    C. to   D. about

11. Divya was sure to succeed ..... the examination.
    A. for   B. in
    C. to   D. with

12. Geeta was jealous ...... Ravina's beauty.
    A. to   B. with
    C. for   D. of

13. He was ignorant ..... what was happening there.
    A. for   B. of
    C. to   D. with
14. Your pen is inferior ...... mine.
    A. than   B. with
    C. from   D. to
15. Reenu is no match ...... Meenu.
    A. to   B. for
    C. with   D. upon
16. It is necessary ...... you to apply for this job.
    A. on   B. with
    C. for   D. to

17. Be loyal ...... your country.
    A. for   B. to
    C. on   D. with
18. Mukesh is junior ...... me.
    A. than   B. to
    C. from   D. of
19. Deepika was innocent ...... the crime.
    A. of   B. with
    C. from   D. to
20. I am desirous..... joining the Indian cricket team.
    A. for   B. of
    C. to   D. on

ANSWERS

1	2	3	4	5	6	7	8	9	10
B	A	D	B	B	D	D	D	B	D

11	12	13	14	15	16	17	18	19	20
B	D	B	D	B	D	B	B	A	B

SYNONYMS

A synonym is a word which conveys a meaning similar to the given word.

REMEMBER

Words	Synonyms
Add	Increase
Adequate	Enough
Adjust	Adapt
All	Aggregate
Allow	Permit
Abode	Dwelling
Apt	Proper
Assess	Appraise
Accuse	Calumniate
Abashed	Timid
Annoy	Displease
Ample	Enough, Sufficient
Amplify	Increase
Apathetic	Unenthusiastic
Accost	Address
Authentic	True

Words	Synonyms
Adjust	Fit
Approve	Assent, Allow, Accept
Adapt	Conform
Adversary	Opponent, Rival, Competitor
Beat	Whack
Benign	Kind
Breeze	Zephyr
Baffle	Puzzle
Booty	Spoil
Beauty	Charm
Beast	Animal
Bandit	Robber
Blaze	Shine
Bond	Tie
Bend	Twist
Bate	Diminish
Beg	Plead
Barbaric	Wild, Savage
Bashful	Shy, Reserved

Words	Synonyms	Words	Synonyms
Begin	Start	Dwell	Live, Dilate
Blend	Mix, Mingle	Declare	Pronounce
Bizarre	Funny	Drunk	Flushed
Below	Under	Deficient	Lacking
Bedevil	Confuse	Damn	Condemn, Curse
Bemoan	Lament	Decrease	Diminish
Babble	Nonsense	Destruction	Devastation
Blame	Fault	Efficient	Competent
Behaviour	Demeanour	Ethnic	Racial
Call	Accost	Enthral	Enslave
Copy	Imitate	Earnest	Serious
Close	Shut	Envious	Jealous
Caress	Love	Ending	Final
Camp	Stay	Egg	Incite
Connect	Attach	Extempore	At once
Cut	Injure, Curtail	Extensive	Far-ranging
Cling	Stick	Extra	Surplus
Conical	Funny	Existence	Life
Convey	Carry	Exceed	Overstep
Conspicuous	Prominent	Enormous	Vast
Cheerful	Happy, Pleasant	Excessive	Superfluous
Curtail	Decrease	Free	Unhindered
Cheerless	Sad, Dejected	Frigid	Cold
Curious	Strange	Feed	Cater
Circumstance	Factor, Situation, Condition	Fame	Reputation
		Frame	Make
Competent	Capable	First	Initial
Congruent	Overlapping	Frighten	Terrorise, Intimidate
Cope	Deal, Endure	Fervent	Fervid
Confident	Sure	Fall	Decline
Complex	Intricate	Feeble	Frail
Cajole	Coax, Flatter	Fickle	Changeable
Cunning	Crafty	Finish	Conclude
Delectable	Joyful, Delightful	Fraud	Deception
Devilish	Diabolical	Forgiving	Placable
Delicate	Soft	Grow	Develop
Devil	Fiend	Greed	Avidity
Delay	Postpone	Greet	Welcome
Dislike	Repugnance	Grave	Serious
Destroy	Ruin	Group	Constellation

Words	Synonyms	Words	Synonyms
Given	Bestowed	Lofty	High
Gratitude	Thankfulness	Lenient	Soft, Gentle
Have	Possess	Lacking	Deficient, Wanting
Hire	Rent	Lessen	Decrease
Hit	Strike	Middleclass	Bourgeois
Handsome	Beautiful	Mitigate	Lessen, Abate
Hinder	Prevent	Modesty	Humility, Lowliness
Heap	Pile	Mix	Mingle, Blend
Hope	Expect	Mixture	Mingling
Hard	Harsh	Mixed	Assorted
Help	Aid	Modify	Decrease
Hymn	Song	Mean	Imply
Henpecked	Enslaved	Multifarious	Varied
Hoodwink	Mystify, Cheat	Miscarry	Abort
Humble	Polite, Urbane, Modest	Note	Notice
Harass	Vex, Trouble	Noble	Stately
Impart	Instil	Native	Indigenous
Intact	Untouched	Needful	Necessary
Instal	Establish	Notify	Declare
Indict	Impeach	Nervous	Shaky, Tremulous, Timid
Imitate	Ape	Natural	Spontaneous
Instigate	Incite	Near	Close
Initiate	Start, Introduce	Normal	Natural
Inimical	Unfriendly	Offend	Displease
Insufferable	Intolerable	Oppress	Persecute, Tyrannize
Impartiality	Justice	Opponent	Adversary
Jolly	Merry	Obstruct	Hinder, Check
Joyful	Delectable	Offence	Fault
Join	Conjoin	Offender	Villain
Kind	Benign	Overstep	Exceed
Kill	Murder	Overlapping	Congruent
Kindred	Similar	Occult	Mystic
Kinship	Relationship	Profane	Unholy
Keen	Sharp	Patience	Forbearance
Knowledge	Scholarship	Pornographic	Obscene
Lazy	Slothful	Plenitude	Abundance
Large	Substantial, Gargantuan	Prominent	Important
Listless	Careless, Lackadaisical	Prodigal	Spender
Lax	Loose	Procrastinate	Postpone
Little	Small	Promote	Develop, Honour
Lifelike	Realistic	Persecute	Tyrannise

Words	Synonyms	Words	Synonyms
Profess	Claim	Unbeaten	Unsubdued
Pliant	Flexible	Use	Utilize, Practise
Plebian	Common	Underhand	Unfair, Undue
Polished	Sophisticated	Unfair	Unjust
Quake	Shake	Unravel	Reveal, Divulge
Quit	Leave	Unimportant	Common
Queer	Eccentric	Unconcerned	Apathetic
Quell	Suppress	Unimitated	Inimitable
Quantify	Allot	Unfortunate	Unlucky
Reply	Answer	Understand	Perceive, Comprehend
Relinquish	Retire	Vain	Proud, Haughty, Conceited, Shameless
Read	Peruse	Vale	Valley, Dale, Dell
Relation	Reference	Vice	Fault
Render	Do	Virtue	Quality
Remainder	Residuals	Veracity	Reality
Repeat	Reiterate	Value	Price, Prize
Repentant	Contrite	Vex	Tease
Retaliative	Retaliatory	Vibrate	Quiver, Shake
Rumour	Hearsay	Violent	Excessive
Reveal	Divulge	Vivid	Clear, Lucid
Ritualistic	Ceremonious	Victory	Triumph
Soft	Delicate	Vulgar	Indecent
Sort	Kind, Choose, Select	Virtuous	Honest
Selfish	Egoistic	Variegated	Varied, Multifarious
Sensual	Earthly	Well	Good
Suppress	Quell, Check	Yell	Cry, Shout
Stimulate	Provoke	Yonder	There
Tasteless	Insipid	Yearn	Wish, Desire
Travel	Journey	Yoke	Slavery
True	Authentic, Faithful, Truthful	Zest	Earnestness, Enthusiasm
Turbulence	Turmoil	Zealous	Earnest
Tragedy	Calamity		
Tasteful	Tasty, Delicious		
Touching	Painful		
Thankful	Grateful		
Tremendous	Great, Huge		
Tough	Strong		
Terminate	Conclude, End		
Theory	Doctrine		
Tell	Relate		
Tremble	Shake, Shiver		
Urge	Spur		

ANTONYMS

A antonym is a word which conveys a meaning opposite to the given word.

REMEMBER

Words	Antonyms
Abhor	Love
Abnormal	Normal
Able	Unable
Acceptable	Unacceptable
Adequate	Inadequate
Amusing	Boring

Words	Antonyms	Words	Antonyms
Angry	Calm	Hard	Soft
Apex	Bottom	Hate	Love
Attract	Repel	Honest	Dishonest
Bad	Good	Idle	Busy
Barren	Fertile	Immoral	Moral
Beautiful	Ugly	Include	Exclude
Bitter	Sweet	Incorrect	Correct
Brave	Cowardly	Intelligent	Unintelligent
Brief	Lengthy	Kind	Cruel
Bright	Dull	Like	Dislike
Calm	Violent	Long	Short
Careful	Careless	Lucid	Vague
Clear	Vague, Cloudy	Major	Minor
Cold	Hot	Naive	Experienced
Cruel	Kind	Nadir	Apex
Dear	Cheap	Neat	Clumsy
Deep	Shallow	Obedient	Disobedient
Difficult	Easy	Obscure	Clear
Direct	Indirect	Oppose	Support
Dishonest	Honest	Optimistic	Pessimistic
Disobey	Obey	Out	In
Encourage	Discourage	Patience	Impatience
Enormous	Tiny	Peaceful	Belligerent
Excellent	Bad	Pious	Impious
Expensive	Cheap	Polite	Impolite
Eat	Fast	Potent	Impotent
Fair	Unfair	Prominent	Unimportant
Fake	Authentic	Proper	Improper
False	True	Pure	Impure
Famous	Notorious	Quick	Slow
Fool	Genius	Quiet	Disturbance
Generous	Miserly	Real	False, Unreal
Genius	Fool	Reject	Select, Choose
Genuine	Unauthentic	Reliable	Unreliable
Gigantic	Tiny	Respect	Disrespect
Glad	Depressed	Right	Wrong
Good	Bad	Robust	Feeble, Weak
Great	Little	Sad	Happy
Happy	Sad		

Words	Antonyms
Secret	Open
Sensible	Insensible
Severe	Mild
Sharp	Blunt
Simple	Complex
Sociable	Unsociable
Tall	Short
Tidy	Untidy
Uncanny	Canny
Violent	Calm
Vivid	Vague

Words	Antonyms
Volatile	Calm
Voracious	Moderate
Vulgar	Elegant
Waive	Demand
Wane	Wax
Warm	Cold
Wary	Careless
Yielding	Obstinate
Zeal	Apathy
Zenith	Nadir
Zest	Aversion

MULTIPLE CHOICE QUESTIONS

Directions (Qs. 1 to 20): *In the following questions choose the word which best expresses the meaning of the given word.*

1. ABSURD
   A. Foolish B. Simple
   C. Courageous D. Silly

2. ABANDON
   A. Lose B. Profit
   C. Vacate D. Foil

3. CAJOLE
   A. Pause B. Lenient
   C. Blast D. Lure

4. COMBAT
   A. Fight B. Conflict
   C. Shoot D. Quarrel

5. LAMENT
   A. Condone B. Console
   C. Complain D. Contribution

6. DEBACLE
   A. Disgrace B. Defeat
   C. Collapse D. Decline

7. SHIVER
   A. Fear B. Tremble
   C. Shake D. Ache

8. TORTURE
   A. Terror B. Harassment
   C. Torment D. Tranquility

9. LAUDABLE
   A. Lovable B. Commendable
   C. Profitable D. Oblivious

10. FIXED
    A. Sterile B. Static
    C. Stubborn D. Parennial

11. QUEER
    A. Unfamiliar B. Cute
    C. Curious D. Strange

12. SUFFICIENT
    A. Fit B. Proper
    C. Adequate D. Vast

13. GLOSS
    A. Brightness B. Soothing
    C. Rubbing D. Miracle

14. LONGING
    A. Prune B. Apathy
    C. Curtail D. Craving

15. JEER
    A. Applaud B. Magnanimity
    C. Avoid D. Scoff

16. ZENITH
    A. Minimum B. Nadir
    C. Plant D. Peak

17. GARB
    A. Distort B. Dress
    C. Trivial D. Rage

18. ABHOR
- A. Rude
- B. Reconcile
- C. Crave
- D. Detest

19. YIELD
- A. Shum
- B. Incisive
- C. Retain
- D. Surrender

20. YOKE
- A. Twist
- B. Release
- C. Link
- D. Extra

Directions (Qs. 21 to 38): *In the following questions choose the word which best expresses the opposite of the given word.*

21. TRAGIC
- A. Dramatic
- B. Strong
- C. Gentle
- D. Comic

22. ORAL
- A. Verbal
- B. Sane
- C. Minor
- D. Written

23. ADMIRE
- A. Hate
- B. Unlike
- C. Dislike
- D. Enough

24. VIOLENT
- A. Gentle
- B. Savage
- C. Haughty
- D. Decline

25. ADVERSITY
- A. Windfall
- B. Inprosperity
- C. Prosperity
- D. Slave

26. GENUINE
- A. Spurious
- B. Obscure
- C. Countless
- D. Apathetic

27. GRUDGE
- A. Essence
- B. Guile
- C. Goodwill
- D. Ill-will

28. STIFF
- A. Soft
- B. Courteous
- C. Lively
- D. Flexible

29. VANITY
- A. Conceit
- B. Pride
- C. Ostentious
- D. Humility

30. FRONT
- A. Upper
- B. Unusual
- C. Back
- D. Rear

31. ATTRACT
- A. Lured
- B. Longing
- C. Repel
- D. Disguise

32. COMFORT
- A. Discomfort
- B. Discontent
- C. Uncomfort
- D. Miscomfort

33. WELCOME
- A. Repel
- B. Accept
- C. Resist
- D. Fight

34. TACTFUL
- A. Naive
- B. Loose
- C. Strict
- D. Uncivilized

35. DUTIFUL
- A. Harmful
- B. Watchful
- C. Forgetful
- D. Remiss

36. RIGID
- A. Flux
- B. Adoptable
- C. Yielding
- D. Adaptable

37. RARE
- A. Petty
- B. Poor
- C. Small
- D. Common

38. ZEAL
- A. Despair
- B. Calmness
- C. Passiveness
- D. Indifference

ANSWERS

1	2	3	4	5	6	7	8	9	10
D	C	D	A	C	C	B	C	B	B
11	12	13	14	15	16	17	18	19	20
D	C	A	D	D	D	B	D	D	C
21	22	23	24	25	26	27	28	29	30
D	D	C	A	C	A	C	D	D	D
31	32	33	34	35	36	37	38		
C	A	C	A	D	D	D	D		

2. One Word Substitution

There are many single words in English language which can be perfectly used for a number of words. These words help in expressing ideas in a short and correct manner for the right occasion. Such words not only increase the vocabulary but also enable you to economise in the use of words to a great extent.

Multiple Word Expression	Substitution
One who always looks towards the bright side of things	Optimist
One who always looks towards the dark side of things	Pessimist
The time when one develops from a child into an adult	Adolescence
The process of growing more plants in order to form a forest.	Afforestation
The science which deals with farming	Agriculture
From some other country or place etc.	Alien
A term, etc. giving more than one meaning	Ambiguous
A vehicle which is used to carry sick persons	Ambulance
An animal which can live both in water and on land	Amphibian
A lawless situation when there is no government	Anarchy
Belonging to the history of thousands of years old	Ancient
Once a year	Annual
A very old object but still valuable	Antique
Words of opposite meanings	Antonyms
Words of similar meanings	Synonyms
Signatures of a famous person	Autograph
A government led by one person with absolute authority	Autocracy
A written work of one's own life history	Autobiography
A person who has never been married	Bachelor
A person usually having no hair on his head	Bald
A place where one can deposit money and get interest	Bank
A person who cuts our hair	Barber
A building/group of buildings where soldiers live	Barracks
A person who makes buns and biscuits	Baker
A person who lives by asking people for food and money without doing any useful job	Beggar
The crime of having married to two persons at the same time	Bigamy
The branch of science which deals with the study of plants	Botany
Able to speak two languages	Bilingual

Multiple Word Expression	Substitution
Able to speak more than two languages	Polyglot
The branch of science which deals with the living organisms	Biology
A powerful snow storm	Blizzard
A great successful book or movie	Blockbuster
A short news on the radio or TV	Bulletin
A system in which the most important works are organised by the government officials	Bureaucracy
A person who has no vision in his eyes	Blind
A page or a series of pages on which the information of days, weeks, months, etc. is given	Calendar
A person who eats human flesh	Cannibal
A complete list of items often arranged alphabetically	Catalogue
A sudden disaster	Catastrophe
A period of 100 years	Century
A branch of science which deals with chemicals	Chemistry
A printed leaf usually issued by banks that we sign to carry certain financial deal	Cheque
A person who makes or mends shoes	Cobbler
A group of people chosen by others to make decisions on their own	Committee
A building in which nuns live	Convent
An animal which feeds on other animals	Carnivorous
A person who does criticism	Critic
A person who cannot hear	Deaf
A condition in which one loses a lot of water from one's body because of vomiting, etc.	Dehydration
A system of government in which the people cast their votes to elect their leaders	Democracy
The study of skin problems	Dermatology
A long piece of land covered with sand	Desert
The art of managing relationships between countries	Diplomacy
A piece of information about the words in a book form	Dictionary
A piece of information about the telephone numbers of the people in a book form	Directory
A person in charge of a newspapers, magazine etc.	Editor
A person who thinks he is better than the others	Egoist
To leave your country and settle in some other country	Emigrate
A book or series of books giving almost all knowledge about an area or some persons etc.	Encyclopaedia
Study of insects	Entomology
Time when day and night are of the same duration	Equinox
To sell things out of the country	Export
To purchase things from some other country	Import
A plant or animal no longer in existence	Extinct
A situation when there is a shortage of food for a long period of time	Famine
An amount of money that we pay for some action or services	Fee
Related to women	Feminine
An animal strong and aggressive	Ferocious

Multiple Word Expression	Substitution
A piece of land where plants grow easily from the soil that is favourable to them	Fertile
A work of literature having some imaginary events	Fiction
A large amount of water covering certain area	Flood
A person who sells flowers	Florist
A religious ceremony for burying or cremating a dead person	Funeral
A substance which kills fungus	Fungicide
A person studying or having studied the diseases and the related things of female reproductive system	Gynaecologist
The murder of the person of the same group race or country	Genocide
A substance which kills germs	Germicide
A situation in which many people die because of fire during war	Holocaust
The act of killing a person deliberately	Homicide
A word having the pronunciation as the other word but differs in meaning	Homophone
A word having the same spelling as the other word but pronounced in some other way	Homonym
A person who is attracted towards the person of the same sex	Homosexual
Go across and parallel to the ground	Horizontal
A substance which kills the insects	Insecticide
That cannot be corrected	Incorrigible
That cannot be defeated	Invincible
That cannot be eaten	Inedible
That cannot be seen	Invisible
A place in a school or college where books are kept for the benefit of students, teachers etc.	Library
A place in a school or college where scientific experiments are performed	Laboratory
An official who is a judge in the lowest court	Magistrate
A piece of music or a book before it is printed	Manuscript
Related to men	Masculine
One who believes in the existence of God	A theist
One who does not believe in the existence of good	An atheist
That can be believed	Credible
That cannot be believed	Incredible
That which dissolves in a solvent	Soluble
That which does not dissolve in a solvent	Insoluble
Hard writing that can be read	Legible
Hard writing that cannot be read	Illegible
A person who does jobs beneficial to mankind	Philanthropist
A person who goes on foot	Pedestrian
A person who fights for his own country	Patriot
An act of killing oneself	Suicide
A woman whose husband is dead	Widow
A man whose wife is dead	Widower
A person who eats vegetarian and non-vegetarian diets	Omnivorous

35

Multiple Word Expression	Substitution
Something which is everywhere at the same time	Omnipresent
One who knows everything	Omniscient
A child who does not have parents	Orphan
An award etc. given after the death of the person	Posthumous
The place where animals are kept for amusement and to increase the knowledge of the public	Zoo
The science which deals with the study of animals	Zoology

MULTIPLE CHOICE QUESTIONS

Directions: *In questions given below, out of the four alternatives, choose the one which can be substituted for the given words/sentences.*

1. Something that relates to everyone in the world:
   A. General   B. Common
   C. Usual   D. Universal

2. An expression of mild disapproval:
   A. Warning   B. Denigration
   C. Impertinence   D. Reproof

3. One who is not easily pleased by anything:
   A. Maiden   B. Medieval
   C. Precarious   D. Fastidious

4. Murder of a king:
   A. Infanticide   B. Matricide
   C. Genocide   D. Regicide

5. A remedy for all diseases:
   A. Stoic   B. Marvel
   C. Panacea   D. Recompense

6. A dramatic performance:
   A. Mask   B. Mosque
   C. Masque   D. Mascot

7. Study of birds:
   A. Orology   B. Optology
   C. Ophthalmology   D. Ornithology

8. Ready to believe:
   A. Credulous   B. Credible
   C. Creditable   D. Incredible

9. Incapable of being seen through:
   A. Ductile   B. Opaque
   C. Obsolete   D. Potable

10. One who eats everything:
    A. Omnivorous   B. Omniscient
    C. Irresistible   D. Insolvent

11. A place where bees are kept is called:
    A. An apiary   B. A mole
    C. A hive   D. A sanctuary

12. One who cannot be corrected:
    A. Incurable   B. Incorrigible
    C. Hardened   D. Invulnerable

13. One who is in charge of a museum:
    A. Curator   B. Supervisor
    C. Caretaker   D. Warden

14. Continuing fight between parties, families, clans, etc.:
    A. Enmity   B. Feud
    C. Quarrel   D. Skirmish

15. A voice loud enough to be heard:
    A. Audible   B. Applaudable
    C. Laudable   D. Oral

16. A paper written by hand:
    A. Handicraft   B. Manuscript
    C. Handiwork   D. Thesis

17. Habitually silent or talking little:
    A. Servile   B. Unequivocal
    C. Taciturn   D. Synoptic

18. To slap with a flat object:
    A. Chop   B. Hew
    C. Gnaw   D. Swat

19. A person who speaks many languages:
    A. Linguist   B. Monolingual
    C. Polyglot   D. Bilingual

20. A light sailing-boat built specially for racing:
    A. Canoe   B. Yacht
    C. Frigate   D. Dinghy

21. A fixed orbit in space in relation to earth:
    A. Geological   B. Geo-synchronous
    C. Geo-centric   D. Geo-stationary

22. A style in which a writer makes a display of his knowledge:
    A. Pedantic   B. Verbose
    C. Pompous   D. Ornate

23. A religious discourse:
    A. Preach   B. Stanza
    C. Sanctorum   D. Sermon

24. A place that provides refuge:
    A. Asylum   B. Sanatorium
    C. Shelter   D. Orphanage

25. Detailed plan of a journey:
    A. Travelogue   B. Travelkit
    C. Schedule   D. Itinerary

26. A person who insists on something:
    A. Disciplinarian   B. Stickler
    C. Instantaneous   D. Boaster

27. A drawing on transparent paper:
    A. Red print   B. Blue print
    C. Negative   D. Transparency

28. One who believes that all things and events in life are predetermined, is a:
    A. Fatalist   B. Puritan
    C. Egoist   D. Tyrant

29. A school boy who cuts classes frequently is a:
    A. Defeatist   B. Sycophant
    C. Truant   D. Martinet

30. The act of violating the sanctity of the church is:
    A. Blasphemy   B. Heresy
    C. Sacrilege   D. Desecration

31. A place where monks live as a secluded community:
    A. Cathedral   B. Diocese
    C. Convent   D. Monastery

32. One who is fond of fighting:
    A. Bellicose   B. Aggressive
    C. Belligerent   D. Militant

33. Tending to move away from the centre or axis:
    A. Centrifugal   B. Centripetal
    C. Axiomatic   D. Awry

34. Words inscribed on tomb:
    A. Epitome   B. Epistle
    C. Epilogue   D. Epitaph

35. Leave or remove from a place considered dangerous:
    A. Evade   B. Evacuate
    C. Avoid   D. Exterminate

36. Original inhabitants of a country:
    A. Abroge   B. Aborger
    C. Aborgory   D. Aborigins

37. Government by the officials:
    A. Theocracy   B. Plutocracy
    C. Bureaucracy   D. Democracy

38. Incapable of being exhausted:
    A. Inexhaustible   B. Inaexhaustible
    C. Exhaustable   D. Non-tired

39. A person of good understanding, knowledge and reasoning power:
    A. Expert   B. Intellectual
    C. Snob   D. Literate

40. One absorbed in his own thoughts and feelings rather than in things outside:
    A. Scholar   B. Recluse
    C. Introvert   D. Intellectual

ANSWERS

1	2	3	4	5	6	7	8	9	10
D	D	D	D	C	C	D	A	B	A
11	12	13	14	15	16	17	18	19	20
A	B	A	B	A	B	C	D	A	B
21	22	23	24	25	26	27	28	29	30
D	A	D	A	D	B	D	A	C	C
31	32	33	34	35	36	37	38	39	40
D	A	A	D	B	B	C	A	B	C

3. Sentence Completion

It is such an exercise which starts with the primary schools and continues in the highest level of competitive examinations. One must practise it regularly to score well.

Directions: *Pick out the most effective word(s) from the given words to fill in the blanks to make the sentence meaningfully complete.*

1. The student ...... that book from the library to study at home.
   A. issued   B. borrowed
   C. hired   D. lent

2. I wish I ...... a king.
   A. was   B. am
   C. should be   D. were

3. He ...... to listen to my arguments and walked away.
   A. denied   B. disliked
   C. objected   D. refused

4. The flow of blood was so ...... that the patient died.
   A. intense   B. adequate
   C. profuse   D. extensive

5. When I met her yesterday, it was the first time I ...... her since Christmas.
   A. saw   B. have seen
   C. had seen   D. have been seing

6. Can you pay ...... all these articles?
   A. for   B. of
   C. off   D. out

7. I ...... you to be at the party this evening.
   A. expect   B. hope
   C. look forward to D. desire

8. ...... being a handicapped person, he is very cooperative and self-reliant.
   A. Because   B. Although
   C. Since   D. Despite

9. The child broke ...... from his mother and ran towards the painting.
   A. away   B. after
   C. down   D. with

10. With his ...... income, he finds it difficult to live a comfortable life.
    A. brief   B. sufficient
    C. meagre   D. huge

11. He could ...... a lot of money in such a short time by using his intelligence and working hard.
    A. spend   B. spoil
    C. exchange   D. accumulate

12. Though the brothers are twins, they look ......
    A. alike   B. handsome
    C. indifferent   D. different

13. Unfavourable weather conditions can ..... illness.
    A. cure   B. detect
    C. treat   D. enhance

14. No sooner did the bell ring, ... the actor started singing.
    A. when   B. than
    C. after   D. before

15. If I ...... realised it, I would not have acted on his advice.
    A. was   B. had
    C. were   D. have

16. Why don't you ...... your work in advance before commencing it.
   A. start
   B. complete
   C. finish
   D. plan

17. ...... the doctor's advice he started taking some daily exercise.
   A. In
   B. To
   C. On
   D. Towards

18. Do you ...... giving that book to me for a few days?
   A. desire
   B. mind
   C. call
   D. observe

19. Our volunteers will ...... your donations either in cash or kind and give you a receipt.
   A. lend
   B. gave
   C. return
   D. collect

20. If you need some money, I will ...... the amount from my bank and give you.
   A. deposit
   B. return
   C. withdraw
   D. require

21. ...... he wanted to attend his friend's party, he could not attend it.
   A. As
   B. But
   C. Since
   D. Although

22. The boss considered the situation and ...... only three days leave to him.
   A. granted
   B. submitted
   C. sanction
   D. asked

23. If you want to do well, you must follow a strict ...... in your studies.

   A. discipline
   B. belief
   C. view
   D. report

24. It was very difficult to dig as the ground was very ....
   A. thin
   B. soft
   C. rigid
   D. hard

25. That rule is applicable ...... everyone.
   A. to
   B. for
   C. about
   D. with

26. Besides other provisions, that shopkeeper deals ...... cosmetics too.
   A. with
   B. in
   C. at
   D. for

27. The ruling party will have to put its own house ...... order.
   A. in
   B. on
   C. to
   D. into

28. He has ...... people visiting him at his house because he fears it will cause discomfort to neighbours.
   A. forbidden
   B. warned
   C. stopped
   D. request

29. Nowadays, why ...... people so scared of each other?
   A. were
   B. is
   C. had
   D. are

30. If the perceptions of two individuals do not ...... there is bound to be problems.
   A. reflect
   B. differ
   C. match
   D. express

ANSWERS

1	2	3	4	5	6	7	8	9	10
B	D	D	C	C	A	A	D	A	C
11	12	13	14	15	16	17	18	19	20
D	D	D	B	B	D	C	B	D	C
21	22	23	24	25	26	27	28	29	30
D	A	A	D	A	B	A	C	D	C

4. Words Commonly Confused

There are many words in English which may look or sound similar but there is lot of difference in their meanings and usage. Some examples are : Their-There, Here-Hear, Principal-Principle, Week, Weak, Sweet-Sweat, Wheather-Whether, Tail-Tale, Due-Dew, Decent-Descent, Dear-Deer, Expect-Except, Accept-Except, Waist-Waste, Plain-Plane etc.

Directions: *In the following questions choose the correct word to fill the blank.*

1. She comes of a .... family.
   A. respectable   B. respectful
   C. respected   D. respecting

2. It began to .... as I reached my office.
   A. reign   B. rain
   C. region   D. rein

3. The teacher told the students to be ....
   A. quiet   B. quite
   C. quit   D. quest

4. The .... has gone to attend the meeting.
   A. principle   B. principal
   C. principles   D. principals

5. .... makes a man perfect.
   A. Practice   B. Practise
   C. Practicing   D. Practising

6. Uttar Pradesh is the most .... state of India.
   A. popular   B. populous
   C. population   D. populist

7. The bird had a .... of bread in its beak.
   A. piece   B. peace
   C. pice   D. paise

8. As she read the letter, her face turned ....
   A. pail   B. pale

   C. pile   D. pill

9. Man is the maker of his own ....
   A. destination   B. destiny
   C. desert   D. destitute

10. Try this medicine, it will prove ....
    A. effectual   B. effective
    C. efficient   D. effluent

11. Maninder has employed an .... boy for his office works.
    A. errand   B. errant
    C. error   D. ergent

12. The soldiers wanted to .... over their victory in the battle.
    A. exalt   B. exult
    C. exit   D. exist

13. When I asked him to accompany us, he .... illness.
    A. fained   B. feigned
    C. find   D. fined

14. The books are lying on the .... piece.
    A. mantal   B. mantle
    C. marital   D. martial

15. Sohan lives a .... life.
    A. luxurious   B. luxuriant
    C. lux   D. luxury

16. She is a lady of .... birth.
   A. lowly
   B. low
   C. lower
   D. lowest

17. We should not be ....of other's wealth.
   A. jealous
   B. zealous
   C. jealousy
   D. zeal

18. It is two days .... from Delhi to Kerala by train.
   A. journey
   B. voyage
   C. walk
   D. passage

19. My father makes a .... selection of books before buying.
   A. judicial
   B. judicious
   C. judgement
   D. judiciary

20. Marconi had an .... mind.
   A. ingenious
   B. ingenuous
   C. enormous
   D. envious

21. It is .... to spend more than what you earn.
   A. impudent
   B. inprudent
   C. important
   D. impotent

22. Orders for his arrest were issued by the .... court.
   A. imperial
   B. imperious
   C. immoral
   D. immortal

23. During the voyage she suffered from sea ....
   A. sickness
   B. illness
   C. weakness
   D. harness

24. Akbar was a .... ruler.
   A. human
   B. humane
   C. humus
   D. humid

25. Gandhiji was a .... leader.
   A. famish
   B. famous
   C. fable
   D. facial

26. The boys broke the window ... of the class room.
   A. pain
   B. pane
   C. pen
   D. pine

27. My new trousers are very ....
   A. lose
   B. loose
   C. lodge
   D. loss

28. She has learnt her ....
   A. lesson
   B. lessen
   C. legion
   D. lesion

29. Brutus is an .... man.
   A. honorary
   B. honourable
   C. honorarium
   D. honorific

30. I have to replace the .... of my shoe.
   A. heal
   B. heel
   C. hill
   D. hell

ANSWERS

1	2	3	4	5	6	7	8	9	10
A	B	A	B	A	B	A	B	B	B

11	12	13	14	15	16	17	18	19	20
B	B	B	B	A	B	A	A	B	A

21	22	23	24	25	26	27	28	29	30
B	A	A	B	B	B	B	A	B	B

5. Spotting Errors

The most common errors in English are of grammar and usage of words. By regular practice, the errors can be easily spotted and minimised.

MULTIPLE CHOICE QUESTIONS

Directions: *In the following questions some of the sentences have errors and some are correct. Find out in each which part of given sentence has an error, the number of that part is your answer. If a sentence is free from errors, then your answer is D i.e., No error. Ignore the errors of punctuation, if any.*

1. (A) Either Ram or/(B) you is responsible/(C) for this action./(D) No error.

2. (A) The student flatly denied/(B) that he had copied/(C) in the examination hall./(D) No error.

3. (A) By the time you arrive tomorrow/(B) I have finished/(C) my work./(D) No error.

4. (A) The captain with the members of his team/(B) are returning/(C) after a fortnight./(D) No error.

5. (A) After returning from/(B) an all-India tour/(C) I had to describe about it./(D) No error.

6. (A) The teacher asked his students/(B) if they had gone through/(C) either of the three chapters included in the prescribed text./(D) No error.

7. (A) Do you know/(B) how old were you/(C) when you came here?/(D) No error.

8. (A) Beware of/(B) a fair-weather friend/(C) who is neither a friend in need nor a friend indeed./(D) No error.

9. (A) Copernicus proved/(B) that Earth/(C) moves round the Sun./(D) No error.

10. (A) The property/(B) was divided/(C) among the two brothers./(D) No error.

11. (A) I am quite certain/(B) that the lady is not only greedy/(C) but miserly./(D) No error.

12. (A) The brilliant success in the examination/(B) as well as his record in sports/(C) deserves high praise./(D) No error.

13. (A) I cannot find/(B) where has he gone/(C) though I have tried my best./(D) No error.

14. (A) If I was/(B) the Prime Minister of India/(C) I would work wonders./(D) No error.

15. (A) If it weren't/(B) for you,/(C) I wouldn't be alive today./(D) No error.

16. (A) He looked like a lion/(B) baulked from/(C) its prey./(D) No error.

17. (A) Widespread flooding/(B) is affecting/(C) large areas of the villages./(D) No error.

18. (A) If we really set to/(B) we can get the whole house/(C) cleaned in an afternoon./(D) No error.

19. (A) It's arrogant for you/(B) to assume you'll/(C) win every time./(D) No error.

20. (A) The two books are the same/(B) except for the fact that this/(C) has an answer in the back./(D) No error.

21. (A) Your husband doesn't/(B) believe that you are older/(C) than I./(D) No error.

22. (A) I could not/(B) answer to/(C) the question./(D) No error.

23. (A) Two years passed/(B) since/(C) my cousin married./(D) No error.

24. (A) I am learning English/(B) for ten years/(C) without much effect./(D) No error.

25. (A) Ramesh has agreed/(B) to marry with the girl/(C) of his parent's choice./ (D) No error.

26. (A) When he was arriving./(B) the party was/(C) in full swing./(D) No error.

27. (A) The most studious boy/(B) in the class/(C) was made as the captain./(D) No error.

28. (A) I am participating/(B) in the two-miles race/(C) tomorrow morning./(D) No error.

29. (A) When the boy committed a mistake/(B) the teacher made him to do/(C) the sum again./ (D) No error.

30. (A) Whenever a person lost anything/(B) the poor folk around/(C) are suspected./(D) No error.

ANSWERS

1	2	3	4	5	6	7	8	9	10
B	D	B	B	C	C	D	D	B	C
11	12	13	14	15	16	17	18	19	20
C	D	B	A	C	C	C	A	A	C
21	22	23	24	25	26	27	28	29	30
C	B	A	A	B	A	C	B	B	A

EXPLANATORY ANSWERS

1. Replace 'is' by 'are'.
2. No error.
3. Replace 'have' by 'would have'.
4. Replace 'are' by 'is'.
5. Replace 'had to describe' by 'described'.
6. Replace 'either' by 'any'.
7. No error.
8. No error.
9. Omit 'that'.
10. Replace 'among' by 'between'.
11. Add 'also'.
12. No error.
13. Replace 'has he' by 'he has'.
14. Replace 'was' by 'were'.
15. Replace 'wouldn't be' by 'would not have been'.
16. Replace 'its' by 'his'.
17. Replace 'areas' by 'area'.
18. Replace 'set to' by 'set on'.
19. Replace 'for' by 'of'.
20. Replace 'in' by 'on'.
21. Replace 'I' by 'me'.
22. Omit 'to'.
23. Replace 'passed' by 'have passed'.
24. Replace 'am' by 'have been'.
25. Omit 'with'.
26. Replace 'was arriving' by 'arrived'.
27. Omit 'as'.
28. Replace 'in' by 'at'.
29. Omit 'to'.
30. Replace 'lost' by 'loses'.

6. Transformation of Sentences

A sentence may be written in many different ways conveying the same meaning. This is called transformation of sentences. Practise various methods of transformation given below:

REMOVING 'TOO'

By replacing 'too' with 'so that'
1. He is too weak to walk.
   He is so weak that he cannot walk.
2. The book was too tough to comprehend.
   The book was so tough that it could not be comprehended.

Note: Sentence No. 1 is in the Present Tense so 'cannot' has been used in it; Sentence No. 2 is in the Past Tense, so, 'could not' has been used in it.

INTERCHANGE OF DEGREE OF COMPARISON

Degree of Comparison of Adjectives
Read the following sentences:
1. She is as clever as a fox. (Positive)
   A fox is not cleverer than her. (Comparative)

Note: In Positive Degree 'as' is used but in Comparative Degree a Negative sentence is used. If the negative has been used with the Positive Degree, it will be removed from the comparative degree.

2. He is not so weak as his brother. (Positive)
   He is stronger than his brother. (Comparative)
3. Shimla is the coldest tourist spot in India. (Superlative)
   Shimla is colder than any other tourist spot in India. (Comparative)
   No other tourist spot is as cold as Shimla. (Positive)
4. Rohit is one of the most intelligent boys in our class. (Superlative)
   Rohit is more intelligent than most other boys in our class. (Comparative)
   Very few boys in our class are so intelligent as Rohit. (Positive)
5. Gold is not the most expensive metal. (Superlative)
   A few metals are more expensive than gold. (Comparative)
   Some metals are at least as expensive as gold. (Positive)

6. Lead is the heaviest of all metals.   (Superlative)
Lead is heavier than any other metal.   (Comparative)
No other metal is so heavy as lead.   (Positive)

CHANGING IMPERATIVE SENTENCES INTO ASSERTIVE

Read the following sentences:

1. Walk fast.   (Imperative)
You are ordered to walk fast.   (Affirmative)

2. Let us take a cup of tea.   (Imperative)
It is proposed that we should take a cup of tea.   (Affirmative)

3. Please bring me a glass of water.   (Imperative)
You are requested to bring me a glass of water.   (Affirmative)

4. Work hard.   (Imperative)
You are advised to work hard.   (Affirmative)

5. Don't smoke.   (Negative imperative)
You are forbidden to smoke.   (Assertive)

INTERCHANGE OF AFFIRMATIVE AND NEGATIVE SENTENCES

Read the following sentences:

1. He runs slow.   (Affirmative)
He does not run fast.   (Negative)

2. He loves himself the most.   (Affirmative)
He does not love anybody more than himself.   (Negative)

3. Mr Sharma is a busy man.   (Affirmative)
Mr Sharma is not an idle man.   (Negative)

4. She is as brilliant as you.   (Affirmative)
You are not more brilliant than her.   (Negative)

5. He spoke angrily.   (Affirmative)
He did not speak calmly.   (Negative)

INTERCHANGE OF INTERROGATIVE AND ASSERTIVE SENTENCES

Read the following sentences:

1. Why to speak ill of anybody?   (Interrogative)
We should not speak ill of anybody.   (Assertive)

2. Who can win his fate?   (Interrogative)
No one can win his fate.   (Assertive)

3. Where will you find such beautiful shoes?   (Interrogative)
You will not find such beautiful shoes anywhere.   (Assertive)

4. How can he die without paying my debt?   (Interrogative)
He cannot die without paying my debt.   (Assertive)

5. When will he learn manners?   (Interrogative)
He will never learn manners.   (Assertive)

6. What can be done now?   (Interrogative)
Nothing can be done now.   (Assertive)

INTERCHANGE OF EXCLAMATORY AND ASSERTIVE SENTENCES

Read the following sentences:

1. What a beautiful flower it is!   (Exclamatory)
   It is a very beautiful flower.   (Assertive)

2. How beautiful the Taj is!   (Exclamatory)
   I am surprised that the Taj is very beautiful.   (Assertive)

3. O for a one-rupee coin!   (Exclamatory)
   A one-rupee coin is urgently desired.   (Assertive)

4. Would that I were rich!   (Exclamatory)
   I wish that I were rich.   (Assertive)

5. O that I were rich!   (Exclamatory)
   I wish that I were rich!   (Assertive)

INTERCHANGE OF PARTS OF SPEECH

Read the following sentences with special attention to the words given in bold:

1. This way you will **minimize** the risk.   (Verb)
   This way you will bring the risk to the **minimum level**.   (Adjective)

2. She fought **courageously**.   (Adverb)
   She showed a great **courage** in the fight.   (Noun)

3. She does not speak the **truth**.   (Noun)
   She is not **truthful**.   (Adjective)

4. He fought **bravely**.   (Adverb)
   He fought with **bravery**.   (Noun)

5. He **ran** fast.   (Verb)
   He ran a fast **race**.   (Noun)

6. He showed **generosity** towards his opponent.   (Noun)
   He was **generous** towards his opponent.   (Adjective)

CHANGING OF SIMPLE SENTENCES INTO COMPOUND ONES

Read the following sentences:

1. Besides being abused he was charged with misbehaving with others.   (Simple)
   He was not only abused but also charged with misbehaving with others.   (Compound)

2. You must run fast to catch the bus.   (Simple)
   Run fast or you may miss the bus.   (Compound)

3. Having finished her kitchen work, Mrs Sharma sat against the T.V. set.   (Simple)
   Mrs Sharma finished her kitchen work and sat against the T.V. set.   (Compound)

4. In spite of bitter cold, they managed to climb the hill.   (Simple)
   It was bitter cold, yet they managed to climb the hill.   (Compound)

5. In spite of being strong, he dare not oppose his opponents.   (Simple)
   He is strong but still he dare not oppose his opponents.   (Compound)

CHANGING OF SIMPLE SENTENCES INTO COMPLEX ONES

Read the following sentences:

1. In spite of being on crutches, he managed to catch the thief. (Simple)
   Though he was on crutches, he caught the thief. (Complex)
2. She is too weak in mathematics to solve even a simple sum. (Simple)
   She is so weak in mathematics that she cannot solve even a simple sum. (Complex)
3. The girl in all black is my classmate. (Simple)
   The girl, who is in all black, is my classmate. (Complex)
4. Because of/Owing to his negligence he lost his credibility. (Simple)
   He lost his credibility because he was negligent. (Complex)
5. He was happy at having been able to make an impressive speech. (Simple)
   He was happy that he was able to make an impressive speech. (Complex)
6. Put the ring at the place of your finding. (Simple)
   Put the ring where you found it. (Complex)

CHANGING OF COMPOUND SENTENCES INTO COMPLEX SENTENCES

Read the following sentences:

1. He is intelligent, but he is unkind. (Compound)
   Although he is intelligent, he is unkind. (Complex)
2. Buy a ticket or you cannot go inside the hall. (Compound)
   You cannot go inside the hall unless you buy a ticket. (Complex)
3. He could not attend the meeting, for he was ill. (Compound)
   He could not attend the meeting because he was ill. (Complex)
4. Work hard or you won't be able to earn a lot. (Compound)
   If you don't work hard, you cannot earn a lot. (Complex)
5. It was fog all around, yet he managed to cross the uneven stretch of land. (Compound)
   Although it was fog all around, he managed to cross the uneven stretch of land. (Complex)

USE OF TIME-CLAUSES

Read the following phrases:

1. As soon as
2. No sooner did .... than
3. Hardly had .... when
4. Scarcely had .... when or before

These are used to express two actions taking place immediately one after the other. *e.g.,*

1. As soon as the cat saw the dog, it started to run.
2. No sooner did the cat see the dog than it started to run.
3. Hardly had the cat seen the dog when it started to run.
4. Scarcely had the cat seen the dog when it started to run.

MULTIPLE CHOICE QUESTIONS

Directions: *Select the correct transformation of the given sentences.*

1. She is too proud to listen to you.
   A. She is very proud to listen to you.
   B. She feels too proud to listen to you.
   C. She is so proud listening to you.
   D. She is so proud that she will not listen to you.

2. He ran so slowly that he could not catch the train.
   A. He ran so slowly to catch the train.
   B. He ran very slowly to catch the train.
   C. He ran too slowly to catch the train.
   D. He ran too slow to catch the train.

3. I like him because he is good person.
   A. He is a good person. I like him.
   B. He is a good person for which I like him.
   C. He is a good person as I like him.
   D. He is a good person for I like him.

4. In spite of working hard, he failed.
   A. He worked hard but he failed.
   B. He worked hard as he failed.
   C. He worked hard so he failed.
   D. He worked hard for which he failed.

5. Unless you work hard, you cannot pass.
   A. If you work hard, you cannot pass.
   B. Work hard if you cannot pass.
   C. You cannot pass without working hard.
   D. You should work hard, you can pass.

6. As soon as the thief saw the policeman, he started to run fast.
   A. No sooner did the thief see the policeman when he started to run fast.
   B. No sooner did the thief see the policeman than he started to run fast.
   C. No sooner did the thief saw the policeman when he started to run fast.
   D. No sooner did the thief saw the policeman than he started to run fast.

7. No sooner did I walk out of the house than it began to rain.
   A. Hardly did I walked out of the house when it began to rain.
   B. Hardly had I walked out of the house than it began to rain.
   C. Hardly had I walked out of the house then it began to rain.
   D. Hardly had I walked out of the house when it began to rain.

8. Hardly had the passenger boarded the bus when it punctured.
   A. Scarcely had the passenger boarded the bus than it punctured.
   B. Scarcely had the passenger boarded the bus then it punctured.
   C. Scarcely had the passenger boarded the bus when it punctured.
   D. Scarcely had the passenger boarded the bus but it punctured.

9. Scarcely had the ship berthed in America when it began to blow hard.
   A. No sooner did the ship berth in America than it began to blow hard.
   B. As soon as the ship berthed in America then it began to blow hard.
   C. Hardly had the ship berthed in America then it began to blow hard.
   D. Scarcely had the ship berthed in America then it began to blow hard.

10. No sooner did she alight from the train than the guard whistled.
    A. Scarcely had she alighted from the train then the guard whistled.
    B. Scarcely had she alighted from the train than the guard whistled.
    C. Scarcely had she alighted from the train when the guard whistled.
    D. Scarcely did she alight from the train when the guard whistled.

Directions: *In the following questions, one out of the given four alternatives is the correct transformation of the given statement, pick that one.*

11. You must be present in the meeting.
    This statement can be converted into Negative as:
    A. Nobody should be absent from the meeting.
    B. You must not be absent from the meeting.
    C. Anybody cannot be absent from the meeting.
    D. You must not walk out of the meeting.

12. It is a beautiful bird.
    This statement can be converted into Exclamatory as:
    A. Is it a beautiful bird?
    B. How is it a beautiful bird?
    C. Who says it is not a beautiful bird?
    D. What a beautiful bird it is!

13. It does not matter if we lose the match.
    This statement can be converted into Interrogative as:
    A. What does it matter if we lose the match?
    B. Does it not matter if we lose the match?
    C. Who says it does not matter if we lose the match?
    D. How can we lose the match?

14. How happy I am!
    This statement can be converted into Assertive as:
    A. Am I happy?
    B. I cannot say I am happy.
    C. I am very happy.
    D. How is it that I am happy?

15. There is none who cannot buy a bicycle.
    This statement can be converted into Affirmative as:
    A. Nobody can buy a bicycle.
    B. Any one can buy a bicycle.
    C. Some people cannot buy a bicycle.
    D. It is useless to buy a bicycle.

16. You are forbidden to pluck flowers.
    This statement can be converted into Negative as:
    A. You should not pluck flowers.
    B. You are allowed to pluck flowers.
    C. You are not allowed to pluck all the flowers.
    D. You should give up the habit of plucking flowers.

17. He will definitely come here.
    This statement can be converted into Interrogative as:
    A. When will he come here?
    B. With whom will he come here?
    C. How will he come here?
    D. Will he not come here?

18. What a comfortable life he leads!
    This sentence can be converted into an Assertive sentence as:
    A. I do not understand why he leads a comfortable life.
    B. He leads a very comfortable life.
    C. How does he lead a comfortable life.
    D. Nobody knows how his life has become comfortable.

19. You should not absent yourself from the class any day.
    This negative sentence can be con-verted into an Affirmative one as:
    A. You should be present in the class every day.
    B. You should absent yourself from the class only rarely.
    C. It is improper for you to be absent from the class.
    D. You can come to the class any day you like.

20. What is the cause for worry?
    This interrogative sentence can be converted into an Assertive sentence as:
    A. There is some cause for worry.
    B. There is not much cause for worry.
    C. There is no cause for worry.
    D. Never think of a cause for worry.

21. You should give full information.
    This statement can be converted into Negative as:
    A. Everybody should not give full information.
    B. Nobody is allowed to give full information.
    C. You should not hide anything.
    D. You should not give full information only.

22. You dare not speak against me in public.
This statement can be converted into Interrogative as:
A. Dare you speak against me in public?
B. Is it proper for you to speak against me in public?
C. Can anybody speak against somebody in public?
D. Speaking against anybody in public is nobody's business.

23. A sailor should not be afraid of water.
This statement can be converted into Exclamatory as:
A. Should a sailor be afraid of water?
B. A sailor and afraid of water!
C. How afraid of water a sailor is!
D. A sailor cannot be afraid of water.

24. Oh! What an interesting book that was.
This statement can be converted into Assertive as:
A. What an interesting book it was!
B. It was a very interesting book.
C. A very interesting book was read by me.
D. It was not an interesting book at all.

25. What can be done now?
This interrogative sentence can be converted into an Assertive one as:
A. Nothing can be done now.
B. You can do everything now.
C. They can do something now.
D. Something can be done now.

26. It is useless to give any advice to an obstinate person.
This statement can be converted into Negative as:
A. It is useless to ask an obstinate person not to seek advice.
B. It is of no use giving advice to an obstinate person.
C. An obstinate person does not like the person who gives him any advice.
D. Some people do not make any use of advice given to obstinate persons.

27. Good people do not hate others.
This statement can be converted into Interrogative as:
A. Do good people never hate others?
B. Why do not good people hate others?
C. When do good people say that they hate others.
D. Do good people hate others?

28. Isolation is very horrible for a child.
This statement can be converted into Exclamatory as:
A. How horrible for a child isolation is!
B. How for a child isolation is horrible!
C. How horrible is for a child isolation!
D. How isolation is horrible for a child!

29. What a lame excuse!
This statement can be converted into Assertive as:
A. A lame excuse it is.
B. How lame this excuse is.
C. Why do you make a lame excuse?
D. It is a very lame excuse.

30. True friends help each other not just once or twice.
This statement can be converted into Affirmative as:
A. True friends help each other several times.
B. True friends help each other even unasked.
C. True friends help each other if they can.
D. True friends are helpful to each other.

Directions (Qs. 31-40): *Do as directed.*

31. Uttar Pradesh is the largest State in India. *(Choose the correct sentence in which positive degree is used).*
A. Uttar Pradesh is as large as any other State in India.
B. No other State in India is as large as Uttar Pradesh.
C. Uttar Pradesh is larger than any other State in India.
D. None of these

32. She is most beautiful girl I have ever seen. *(Choose the correct sentence in which comparative degree is used).*

A. She is more beautiful than any other girl I have ever seen.
B. She is more beautiful than many other girls I have ever seen.
C. She is much beautiful than any other girl I have ever seen.
D. None of these

33. Alas! There is no one to help him. *(Choose the correct sentence in which assertive form is used).*
A. It is matter of sorrow that no one will help him.
B. It is matter of sorrow that there is no one to help him.
C. It is sad that he has no help.
D. None of these

34. I was not sure that he will come. *(Choose the correct sentence in which affirmative form is used).*
A. I was doubtful whether he comes.
B. I was doubtful if he comes.
C. I was doubtful whether he will come.
D. None of these

35. No other metal is as precious as gold. *(Choose the correct sentence in which superlative degree is used)*
A. Gold is the most precious metal.
B. Gold is more precious than any other metal.
C. Gold is the most precious of any metal.
D. None of these

36. None of her children are as fair as she is. *(Choose the correct sentence in which comparative degree is used)*

A. She is not as fair as any of her children.
B. She is fairer than her children.
C. She is fairer than all her children.
D. None of these

37. He is the smartest boy in his class. *(Choose the correct sentence in which positive degree is used)*
A. No other boy in the class is as smart as he is.
B. No other boy is as smart as he is.
C. He is smarter than other boys in the class.
D. None of these

38. He **ran** fast. *(Choose the correct sentence in which the bold word is replaced with a noun)*
A. He ran faster.
B. He ran fastest.
C. He ran.
D. He ran a fast race.

39. He fought **bravely**. *(Choose the correct sentence in which the bold word is replaced with a noun)*
A. He fought.
B. He fought brave.
C. He fought with bravery.
D. He fought with brave.

40. She doesnot speak the **truth**. *(Choose the correct sentence in which the bold word is replaced with an adjective)*
A. She not speaks truth.
B. She is no truthful.
C. She is not truthful.
D. She is not true speaker.

ANSWERS

1	2	3	4	5	6	7	8	9	10
D	C	B	A	C	B	D	C	A	C
11	**12**	**13**	**14**	**15**	**16**	**17**	**18**	**19**	**20**
B	D	A	C	B	A	D	B	A	C
21	**22**	**23**	**24**	**25**	**26**	**27**	**28**	**29**	**30**
C	A	B	B	A	B	D	A	D	A
31	**32**	**33**	**34**	**35**	**36**	**37**	**38**	**39**	**40**
B	A	B	C	A	C	A	D	C	C

7. Idioms, Phrases and Proverbs

- An idiom is a group of words established by usage as having a meaning different from the individual words.

- A phrase is a small group of words standing together as an idiomatic expression.

- A proverb is a brief statement or a short sentence often with a moral and usually containing similes or metaphors drawn from daily life.

   Learn and practise as many as you can.

IDIOMS AND IDIOMATIC PHRASES

ABC (basic principles)
She does not know the ABC of photography.

To cut a sorry figure (present oneself in a bad way)
She cut a sorry figure on the stage.

Cut loose (Keep away)
India should cut loose from bad politics.

To give a red carpet reception (to give a warm welcome)
The PM was given a red carpet reception in America.

To dance to one's tune (to follow someone submissively)
He always dances to his brother's tune.

To turn a deaf ear to (to disregard)
She turned a deaf ear to her parents' advice.

To call a spade a spade (to speak the truth)
Gandhiji always called a spade a spade.

To bring to book (to scold)
The naughty boy was brought to book by the teacher.

From hand to mouth (without any saving)
The poor factory worker is living from hand to mouth.

Once in a blue moon (seldom)
She visits her brother once in a blue moon.

To cut short (to reduce)
Smoking will cut short your life.

By hook or by crook (by any means fair or foul)
He wants to get money by hook or by crook.

In the good books of (be good in one's mind)
Jack is in the good books of his teachers.

At sixes and sevens (in disorder)
The drawing room articles were lying at sixes and sevens on the floor.

To grease the palm of (to bribe)
Rohit greased the palm of the clerk and got the file moved.

Through thick and thin. (under all circumstances)
We'll stand by you through thick and thin.

At one's beck and call (ready to obey)
He had a dozen men at his beck and call.

To die by inches (to die a painful death)
The old man died by inches.

To eat one's words (to retract one's statement)
You'll have to eat your words because you have spoken without thinking.

To burn the midnight oil (to work hard)
You'll have to burn the midnight oil if you want to get good marks.

Fair and square (clean)
One must be fair and square in one's dealing.

To poke one's nose into (to meddle with)
It is bad to poke your nose into others' affairs.

To fall flat (to have no effect)
His father's advice fell flat on him.

To make a clean breast of (to confess)
He made a clean breast of his involvement in the bomb blast.

To get the better of (overcome)
Anger got the better of him.

A wet blanket (a discouraging person)
Don't allow Rakesh to accompany you to the hunting trip because he is a wet blanket.

A big gun (an important person)
Mr Smith is a big gun in our city.

In black and white (in written)
Don't give him anything in black and white.

Neck and neck (even)
There is a neck and neck fight between the two boxers.

At a stone's throw (at a short distance from)
My school is at a stone's throw from my house.

Cut-throat competition (a stiff competition)
There is a cut-throat competition among the publishers in the market.

Black sheep (a traitor)
Later on Mr XYZ proved a black sheep.

By dint of (by means of)
By dint of hard work, she earned a lot of money.

A man of word (a person who keeps his promise)
Mr Sharma is a man of word.

A man of a few words (a remarkable person)
Gandhiji was a man of a few words.

In cold blood (mercilessly)
The old woman was murdered in cold blood.

At arm's length (to keep away)
We should always keep bad boys at arm's length

Keep the ball rolling (to maintain the progress of some activity)
After the death of his father he had to take the charge of his office to keep the ball rolling.

A bolt from the blue (a sudden and unexpected event)
The news of my friend's death came to me like a bolt from the blue.

(i) **Break ones back** (to work hard to get something)
He broke his back to earn his livelihood.

(ii) **To break somebody's back** (to give too much work to him to do)
She broke his back by giving him so much hard work to do.

Break the back of (accomplish the hardest part of a certain job)
There is nothing to be worried about as we've already broken the back of the problem.

Beat about the bush (to go on talking on some worthless topic)
Stop this beating about the bush, come to the main task.

Throw cold water on (to discourage)
She tried to throw cold water on his plan but he was well-determined.

Hard of hearing (somewhat deaf)
She is a bit hard of hearing.

Come what may (no matter what happens)
I'll do it, come what may.

Beyond one's means (beyond one's budget)
He is living beyond his means, therefore, he is sure to get ruined.

A man of letters (a scholar)
Radha Krishnan was a man of letters.

Chips of the same block (having the same taste)
They are the chips of the same block.

The long and short of (in brief)
The long and short of his lecture is that we should live like brothers.

In full swing (in full force)
The studies of the students are going on in full swing.

To burn one's fingers (to get oneself in trouble)
You have burnt your fingers by speaking against him.

A hard nut to crack (a puzzling problem)
To get a win over American basket ball team is a hard nut to crack for India.

To turn over a new leaf (to change the course of life)
He has turned over a new leaf in his life.

A yeoman's service (service which is beneficial to the human beings)
He did yeoman's service through his life.

To have one's own axe to grind (to have vested interest)
He has his own axe to grind in this matter.

To take to one's heels (to run away)
The thief took to his heels as soon as he saw the policeman.

A snake in the grass (a hidden foe)
Beware of him because he seems to be a snake in the grass.

To move heaven and earth (to make too much effort)
The young man moved heaven and earth to find a job.

To be caught red handed (to be caught at the time of committing a crime)
The clerk was caught red handed when he was accepting bribe from Mr ABC.

To receive with open arms (to give a warm welcome)
The new president of the club was received with open arms by the members.

Acid test (hard test)
The election will be an acid test for the ruling party.

A wolf in sheep's clothing (a hypocrite)
You should not keep company with him because he is a wolf in sheep's clothing.

To be born with a silver spoon in one's mouth (to be born in a rich family)
Mr. J. L. Nehru was born with a silver spoon in his mouth.

At the eleventh hour (at the last moment)
The war was about to start but fortunately at the eleventh hour a messenger came to the PM with a message of peace.

Drop someone a line (send a letter, etc.)
Please drop me a line of your well-being.

Dull the edge of (reduce the intensity of)
Take this pill and it will dull the edge of pain.

A fool of the first water (one completely foolish)
Being a fool of the first water he could not solve even the simplest sum.

To come to light (to be known)
A new disease has recently come to light.

To be the apple of one's eye (be very dear)
He is the apple of his parent's eye.

A bone of contention (to be the cause of quarrel)
Kashmir is the bone of contention between India and Pakistan.

To make fun of (laugh at)
The children made fun of the waiter in the hotel.

To let the cat out of the bag (to divulge a secret)
It was Sohan who let the cat out of the bag by telling the real matter.

A great card (an important person)
Mr. Sood is a great card in the ministry of finance.

To open a new chapter (to start some habit, etc.)
By writing, you've opened a new chapter in your life.

Under a cloud (be in trouble or in a state of disgrace or suspicion)
His company seemed to be under a cloud as it had no funds to pay the wages to the workers.

In a crack (all of a sudden or rapidly)
The thief left the place in a crack.

A green hand (not very much experienced)
We shall pay a little to a green hand.

To make the flesh creep (to terrify)
The story made my flesh creep.

To lose ground (to retreat)
After fighting for some time the Pakistani army began to lose ground.

All in all (completely)
Rajesh is all in all in this office.

An apple of discord (to be the cause of conflict)
Kashmir is an apple of discord between India and Pakistan.

To bring to book (to punish)
The student was brought to book by the teacher.

A bed of roses (a comfort)
Life is not a bed of roses.

To show a clean pair of heels (to run away)
The thief showed a clean pair of heels as soon as he saw the policeman approaching.

A white elephant (of no use)
This sort of glib talker always proves a white elephant in the end.

In the twinkling of an eye (quickly)
The monkey ate up grams in the twinkling of an eye.

To gain ground (to be established)
He gained ground in India in a few years.

Slow and steady (slowly but continually)
Slow and steady wins the race.

A red letter day (An important day)
15th August is a red letter day for the Indians.

To get wind of (to get information)
I got wind of his secret plans.

VERBAL PHRASES

Act upon (to follow)
I acted upon my father's advice.

Act upto (to perform within limits)
He acted upto his conscience.

Act beyond (to perform crossing limits)
We should not act beyond our capacity.

Act for (to perform in place of someone else)
The vice principal acted for the principal.

Back up (to make a queue)
The vehicles began to back up.

Back down (withdraw claim in the presence of opposition)
The leader backed down from his previous statement.

Back off (draw back from some plan or action)
They backed off from building a flyover.

Back out (withdraw from a promise, etc.)
The government backed out of its promise of pension scheme.

Break down (stop working) My car broke down on the highway.

Break into (enter in certain premises by breaking the door, etc.)
Last night a thief broke into my neighbour's.

Break off (stop all of a sudden)
She broke off and began to think over about her/his hand.

Break out (spread)
Cholera has broken out in the town.

Break out of (escape from)
A prisoner broke out of the prison last night.

Break up (disperse)
The cloud of fog began to break up as the sun rose.

Break something up (Cause something to break into small pieces)
She broke up the chocolate to distribute it among the girls.

Break with (Cut off connection after quarrelling with someone)
He has broken with his brother.

Call on (pay a visit to somebody)
I'll call on Mohan's today.

Call out (to start)
The workers have called out a strike.

Call off (to stop the strike etc.)
The workers have called off the strike.

Call at (to visit someone's house)
I called at his house yesterday.

Call in (send for)
Please call in the doctor.

Carry on (continue)
Please carry on your work.

Carry something out (perform a task)
Our company is carrying out a big deal with a foreign company.

Carry something over (postpone)
The fancy dress competition had to be carried over till Monday)

Carry someone off (kill somebody)
Cancer carried her off on the day of her 20th birthday.

Come of age (get established)
As our company has come of age, so, there is no problem in selling our goods.

Come of (belong to)
She comes of a royal family.

Come over (surmount)
We at last came over all our problems.

Come off (to take place)
The marriage of my brother comes off in the next month.

Come round (agree)
At last he came round to my views.

Come under (fall in the category of)
All these animals come under the same species.

Come down with (suffer from)
She came down with whopping cough.

Come from (be the native of)
She came from London.

Come about (happen)
The explosion came about when the worker struck the match to light a cigarette.

Cut off (die)
The princess was cut off in the prime of her life.

Cut down (reduce)
The prices of consumer goods should be cut down.

Cut someone out (exclude someone)
His father cut him out of his will.

Fall in
She fell in love with the prince.

Fall down (fail)
The deal fell down for lack of transparency.

Fall out (quarrel)
She fell out with his elder brother.

Fall through (fail)
The project fell through for lack of funds.

Get away (escape)
She got away with her life.

Get by (to accomplish something with great difficulty)
She is not rich. She has just enough to get by.

Get on (perform)
How are you getting on with your studies?

Get out (become known)
The news got out that the PM was paying a visit to Russia.

Get over (overcome)
At last I got over all obstacles.

Get up (rise)
When do you get up in the morning?

Give up (stop)
He gave up smoking.

Give out (emit)
Garlic gives out a pungent smell.

Give in (collapse)
The bridge gave in under the heavy load.

Give away (distribute)
The Principal gave away the prizes.

Give out (announce)
It was given out that the President of India would visit the place soon.

Go off (explode)
The gun went off suddenly.

Go on (continue)
She went on about how she flew the aeroplane.

Go through (examine)
I'll go through this book later on.

Go up (be built)
The construction of the house is going up.

Grind on (continue for a long time in a tedious way)
The discussion over political issues ground on.

Grind something out (produce something a tedious way)
She will grind some more short stories.

Look out (be careful)
Look out! There is a snake.

Look down upon (hate)
We should not look down upon the poor.

Look at (watch)
Look at the blackboard.

Look after (take care of)
We ought to look after our old parents.

Look into (investigate)
The new police inspector will look into the matter.

Look up (rise)
The prices of consumer goods are looking up.

Look back (think of the past)
It made her feel desolate when she looked back on things of the past.

Make up (to fulfil)
I'll make up my deficiency in Mathematics.

Make out (understand)
I could not make out what she said.

Make up one' mind (to resolve)
I have made up my mind to settle in the USA.

Make off (leave hurriedly)
She made off without informing anybody.

56

Make something over (transfer)
She should make her property over to her sons.

Make over (hand over)
He made over the charge of the file to Mr Robert.

Pull back (retreat)
The government has pulled back from its previous policy.

Pull something down (demolish)
The authorities concerned pulled down a few buildings which were illegally built on government land.

Pull out (pluck)
The child pulled out a few petals of the flower.

Pull through (recover)
The patient will pull through.

Push on (continue a journey)
It was getting darker but we pushed on.

Push at (exert force)
He pushed at the bell, but it did not ring.

Push for (demand persistently)
The workers have been pushing for the installation of new machines for five years.

Put out (extinguish)
She put out the light.

Put on (wear)
He put on an overcoat.

Put off (postpone)
The plan had to be put off.

Put by (spare something for future)
We must put by some money for future.

Put up with (stay)
Your aunt is out of town for a couple of days, you may put up with us till she comes.

Put something down (record something)
She put a new idea down on the paper.

Take after (resemble)
He takes after his father.

Take off (remove)
He took off his shoes.

Take something out (obtain)
You may take out some money from Rohit if you want to purchase this car.

Take to (fall into the habit of)
He took to gambling.

Turn something down (reject something)
The judge turned down his appeal.

Turn on (attack)
The thief turned on him with a knife.

PROVERBS

A friend in need is a friend indeed
It is incumbent upon a true friend to help and stand by his friend in distress. The true friend must not desert him when he is in difficulty but do his best to help him in every possible way.

A tree is known by its fruit
This adage denotes that a person is judged and known by his deeds.

He who will have the fruit must climb the tree
This is a maxim which signifies that nothing can be achieved unless you make sincere or adequate efforts in the right direction.

Necessity is the mother of invention
When a man needs something very badly, he bends all his energy and channelises all his resources in order to find, trace, discover or invent what is needed.

Absence makes the heart grow fonder
Absence increases or sharpens love or affection.

Actions speak louder than words
It is not what you say but what you do that can be eloquent.

Birds of a feather flock together
People having similar tastes and characters associate with one another. Hence, man may be known by the friends he has.

A bird in hand is worth two in the bush
A thing which is certain is worth two which are uncertain. It is better to be in possession of one thing, even if it is very small or insignificant, than to have hope or expectation based on something that is of greater value but is remote and doubtful.

An apple a day keeps the doctor away
This adage emphasises the value of fruit for good health.

A good apple is often rotten at the core
Appearances are, off and on, deceptive.

Ask much to get little
Let your ambitions always be high and you are sure to achieve something.

Every ass loves to hear himself bray
We all like to praise ourselves and our actions.

A bad workman quarrels with his tools
A bad workman puts the blame for his inefficiency upon his implements or circumstances.

An empty bag will not stand upright
Nobody can work without food.

Reckless youth makes rueful age
If we spend our youth recklessly, we shall repent of it in our old age.

All work and no play makes Jack a dull boy
Excess of anything is bad. It causes disastrous effects.

Do not put all your eggs in one basket
Do not stake all your money on a single business, concern, venture, etc., you should spread your resources over a variety of transactions.

Beggars cannot be choosers
If you are in a weak situation, you cannot lay down conditions. You cannot be exacting in demands or terms.

Among the blind, the one-eyed is king
Among those who are less gifted, the one who has some talent or experience gains supremacy.

Do not judge a book by its cover
Appearance are often deceptive and misleading.

Blood is thicker than water
Ties of kinship have a stronger influence than any other bond.

Do not cast pearls before swine
Do not talk of beautiful or subtle or higher things to those who are unable to appreciate them. Do not waste valuable things on those who cannot appreciate or judge their value.

A cat has nine lives
A cat is supposed to be very tenacious of life.

When the cat is away, the mice play
When the superior or master is absent, the subordinates stop work and do what they like.

Character is destiny
A man's character determines his fate and fortune.

Spare the rod and spoil the child
The surest way of spoiling a child is by allowing his faults to go unpunished.

Do not count your chickens before they are hatched
Do not assume that you will have a thing, or do not make plans about it, before the conditions are realised or the event has taken place. You should wait till your difficulties are over. Thereafter, you can boast of success.

Too many cooks spoil the broth
The work done in an enterprise, project, etc. is spoilt if too many people are employed in it.

Give the devil his due
You should give credit to a person or cause or even to an enemy in the name of justice.

Death is the grand leveller
Death makes all men—famous, notorious, insignificant, rich, poor, wise, foolish, good, bad, happy, miserable—equal by reducing them to dust and ashes.

What cannot be cured must be endured
We must submit with good grace to a situation, which cannot be remedied or altered, after we have done our best.

It is no use crying over spilt milk
It is absolutely useless to indulge in regrets for what has been done and cannot be remedied.

Cut your coat according to your cloth
You should live within your income. Make what you possess serve your needs. Make your plans fit the circumstances.

A short cut is often a wrong cut

A short cut is not necessarily the safest and quickest way to our destination.

Better an open enemy than a false friend

We are on our guard against an open enemy, but a false friend can stab us in the back.

Failures are stepping stones to success

Failures can be an incentive to greater courage and endeavour.

Like father, like son

The son is likely to turn out like the father.

All that glitters is not gold

Fine outward appearances are often delusive. They hide what is of no value. Things are not what they seem.

Speech is silver but silence is golden

Speech produces much that is delightful and valuable. But there are times when the most important and precious thing is to say nothing. Speech may be good but silence is better.

Love is blind

One who is in love is generally unable to see any defect in his beloved.

True love never grows old

True love is ageless as well as timeless.

No man can serve two masters

A person cannot satisfactorily devote himself to two different causes having different and opposed aims.

A hungry man is an angry man

A man who is hungry gives vent to his discomfort.

Give every man your ear, but few your voice

Listen to everyone, but express your opinion to only a chosen few.

One man's meat is another man's poison

What is beneficial to or liked by one person is harmful to or disliked by another.

Marry in haste and repent at leisure

Those who rush into anything often regret their haste later.

Might is right

There are occasions when force gets the better of justice.

Out of sight, out of mind

A person who is absent is soon forgotten.

Money begets money

Money goes where money is. The rich become richer.

Money makes the mare go

Great things can be done with money.

Never do things by halves

You should make it a point to complete whatever you undertake.

Never say die

You should never give up hope.

It is never too late to learn

A man can begin to acquire knowledge at any age.

Penny wise and Pound foolish

A man who economises while spending small amounts often foolishly squanders large amounts.

The pot should not call the kettle black

A man should not accuse another of faults of which he himself is guilty.

Practise what you preach

You should carry out what you urge on others.

Pride must have a fall

A proud person will, sooner or later, come to grief.

Prevention is better than cure

To take precaution against an event is better than remedying it afterwards.

There is no rose without a thorn

However good or attractive a thing may appear, it has its drawbacks.

Slow and steady wins the race

You can make great progress if you proceed slowly and steadily. Those who are impatient or who work by fits and starts rarely succeed.

A rolling stone gathers no moss

A person who is constantly moving and changing from one place or occupation to another will never gain a steadily established position or income.

Nothing succeeds like success

The fact that a thing is known to be successful causes it to become even more so. Success is an incentive to greater effort.

A stitch in time saves nine

Prompt action at the beginning of some trouble eventually saves a lot of time, energy and expense.

Time is the best counsellor

Time teaches us many lessons that are very useful and effective in our life.

Look before you leap

You should carefully consider the possible dangers and difficulties before entering on or rushing into a course of action or enterprise.

Better late than never

It is better to be late for a function rather than to miss it altogether. It is better that a thing should be done after a long delay than that it should not be done at all.

A little learning is a dangerous thing

Inadequate knowledge may mislead one and lead to wrong conclusions, actions, principles, and so on.

Let sleeping dogs lie

Do not disturb a state of affairs that at present is dormant, causing no harm, but has potentialities for trouble, if interfered with.

Out of debt, out of danger

One who pays his debts can face the future boldly.

Familiarity breeds contempt

Too frequent contact with a person is likely to diminish our respect for him.

When glory comes, memory departs

When a person attains fame and glory, he is liable to forget his former status in life and his early associates.

MULTIPLE CHOICE QUESTIONS

Directions: *Some idioms/phrases/proverbs are given below with their probable meanings. Select the options with their correct meanings.*

1. **Pay off old scores**
   A. To repay the debt   B. To have revenge
   C. To invite   D. Secretly spend

2. **Turn turtle**
   A. To cheat
   B. To be lopsided
   C. To frustrate
   D. To dance to the tune

3. **Wash one's hands of**
   A. To refuse
   B. To assist
   C. To abuse
   D. To refuse to be liable

4. **Under duress**
   A. Under compulsion
   B. Willing
   C. To elicit information
   D. To demand

5. **To turn the tables**
   A. To ruin someone
   B. To turn the situation to one's own side
   C. To reverse the situation
   D. To move from one point to another

6. **On the cards**
   A. Possibly
   B. Probably
   C. Openly
   D. Likely

7. **To leave someone in the lurch**
   A. To come to compromise with someone
   B. Constant source of annoyance to someone
   C. To put someone at ease
   D. To desert someone in his difficulties

8. **To play second fiddle**
   A. To be happy, cheerful and healthy
   B. To reduce importance of one's senior
   C. To support the role and view of another person
   D. To do backseat driving

9. Day and night, he **'yearns for'** his beloved, means
   A. He weeps for his beloved
   B. He remembers his beloved
   C. He admires his beloved
   D. He keenly desires to meet his beloved

10. **'Call off'** means
    A. To finish   B. To withdraw
    C. To postpone   D. To cry

11. **'Carry out'** means
    A. To take from one place to another
    B. To continue
    C. To obey
    D. To make efforts

12. **In the same boat**
    A. A worn out choice
    B. Indifferent
    C. In identical circumstances
    D. Having same choice

13. **In one's good book**
    A. A costly book
    B. A priceless treasure
    C. In one's favour
    D. An enchanting beauty

14. **Keep a straight face**
    A. To do make up
    B. To change clothes
    C. Assume responsibility
    D. To remain serious

15. **To be above board**
    A. To have a good height
    B. To be honest in any business deal
    C. To have no debts
    D. To try to be beautiful

16. **On the face of it**
    A. To agree   B. From an action
    C. More than enough D. Apparently

17. **Let the bygones be bygones**
    A. In one's favour   B. To pretend
    C. To forget the past D. Other choice

18. **To split hairs**
    A. Major distinctions
    B. Hair with two ends
    C. To make minute distinction
    D. Without distinction

19. **'Bread and butter'** means
    A. Both bread and butter
    B. Something essential
    C. Livelihood
    D. Relevant things

20. **'Acid Test'** means
    A. To taste acid
    B. To make an effort
    C. To be quick
    D. A difficult part of work

21. **'Hard and fast'** means
    A. Strict   B. Solid
    C. Fast moving   D. Some hard surface

22. **'Part and parcel'** means
    A. The part of a parcel
    B. An essential part
    C. A missing parcel
    D. Some part of a machine sent by parcel

23. **'Null and void'** means
    A. Something invalid
    B. Something that can be avoided
    C. Something that can be nullified
    D. Something evil

24. **To make clean breast of**
    A. To gain prominence
    B. To praise oneself
    C. To confess without reserve
    D. To destroy before it blooms

25. **'Trump card'** means
    A. A powerful means of achieving an object
    B. Resourcefulness
    C. The best gamble to attain success
    D. None of these

26. **'Tall talk'** means
    A. A discussion continued for a long time
    B. A high sounding talk
    C. A meaningful talk
    D. A useless talk

27. **'Small talk'** means
    A. Gossip
    B. A discussion carried on for a long time
    C. A brief discussion
    D. None of these

28. Throw out of gear
A. To replace
B. Hinder, disturb
C. To decide
D. Take up tune

29. To and fro
A. Back and forth
B. Puzzled
C. Amazed
D. Reprove

30. To bell the cat
A. To do an easy job
B. To be indifferent to
C. To undertake a difficult job
D. To clarify

31. To be under cloud
A. Puzzle
B. Enjoy the favour
C. Talk thoughtlessly
D. To be under suspicion

32. A labour of love
A. A tragic end
B. A funny thing
C. Not fruitful
D. Work done without payment

33. Follow suit
A. Follow an example
B. Wear a new dress
C. Irrelevant
D. A smart person

34. 'Foul play' means
A. Bad intentions
B. A play not well acted
C. A play not liked by the audience
D. None of these

35. To pick holes
A. To find some reason to quarrel
B. To destroy something
C. To criticise someone
D. To cut some part of an item

36. To smell a rat
A. To see signs of plague epidemic
B. To get bad smell of a dead rat
C. To suspect foul dealings
D. To be in a bad mood

37. To put a spoke in one's wheel
A. To encourage
B. Act without restraint
C. Risk something
D. To obstruct one's progress

38. To pull one's leg
A. To give up
B. Take care of
C. To befool
D. To walk fast

39. To play with fire
A. Grasp the truth
B. To handle a dangerous thing
C. To ridicule
D. To flee away

40. To reckon with
A. Take up time
B. Make an inventory
C. To deal with
D. Submit to punishment

ANSWERS

1	2	3	4	5	6	7	8	9	10
B	B	D	A	C	D	D	C	D	B
11	**12**	**13**	**14**	**15**	**16**	**17**	**18**	**19**	**20**
C	C	C	D	B	D	C	C	C	D
21	**22**	**23**	**24**	**25**	**26**	**27**	**28**	**29**	**30**
A	B	A	C	C	B	A	B	A	C
31	**32**	**33**	**34**	**35**	**36**	**37**	**38**	**39**	**40**
D	D	A	A	C	C	D	C	B	C

8. Reordering Words

The words form a sentence and convey their meaning only when they are arranged in a proper order. One must study and practise it regularly.

Directions (Qs. 1–30): *In the following questions, some parts of the sentence have been jumbled up. You are required to rearrange these parts which are labelled 1, 2, 3, 4 and 5 to produce the correct sentence. Choose the option with proper sequence.*

1. (1) any cost (2) house at (3) a new (4) shift to (5) I must.
   - A. 54132
   - B. 54231
   - C. 54321
   - D. 54123

2. (1) immediately (2) must be (3) attended to (4) patient (5) the.
   - A. 54312
   - B. 54123
   - C. 54231
   - D. 54213

3. (1) hungry (2) me that (3) I looked (4) my sister (5) told.
   - A. 45123
   - B. 45312
   - C. 45231
   - D. 45321

4. (1) be seated (2) me to (3) he welcomed (4) requested (5) me and.
   - A. 35124
   - B. 35421
   - C. 35142
   - D. 35241

5. (1) unhappy (2) I did (3) I was (4) though (5) not grumble.
   - A. 43152
   - B. 43125
   - C. 43512
   - D. 43215

6. (1) the experience (2) I was (3) by (4) disheartened (5) in fact.
   - A. 52413
   - B. 52134
   - C. 52431
   - D. 52341

7. (1) of the (2) shone faintly (3) town (4) the lights (5) below.
   - A. 54231
   - B. 54123
   - C. 54312
   - D. 54132

8. (1) been forced (2) of milk (3) the consumption (4) to reduce (5) I have.
   - A. 51423
   - B. 51432
   - C. 51324
   - D. 51243

9. (1) the company (2) in the hostel (3) life in (4) was enjoyable (5) of friends.
   - A. 31542
   - B. 31524
   - C. 31245
   - D. 31425

10. (1) his expenses (2) he drastically (3) on various (4) cut down (5) items.
    - A. 24351
    - B. 24531
    - C. 24135
    - D. 24153

11. (1) at others (2) in glass houses (3) throw stones (4) people living (5) should not.
    - A. 42351
    - B. 42153
    - C. 42531
    - D. 42513

12. (1) the crown (2) lies (3) that wears (4) uneasy (5) the head.
    - A. 42153
    - B. 42513
    - C. 42315
    - D. 42531

13. (1) every qualification (2) except sincerity (3) for the post (4) had (5) he.
    - A. 25314
    - B. 25134
    - C. 25431
    - D. 25413

14. (1) this book (2) besides being (3) from mistake also (4) beautifully printed (5) is free.
    - A. 12435
    - B. 12354
    - C. 12453
    - D. 12543

15. (1) immediately (2) on (3) he (4) leaving (5) insisted.
A. 35241   B. 23541
C. 12345   D. 34215

16. (1) the accounts (2) in checking (3) me (4) he assisted.
A. 3214   B. 1234
C. 2413   D. 4321

17. (1) talking something (2) which (3) they were (4) not understand (5) I could.
A. 31425   B. 31524
C. 31254   D. 31542

18. (1) mental (2) extraordinary (3) alertness (4) blessed with (5) he is.
A. 54132   B. 54213
C. 54321   D. 54123

19. (1) leaving for (2) few minutes (3) we are (4) in a (5) the market.
A. 31254   B. 31524
C. 31452   D. 31542

20. (1) war (2) to be (3) moving towards (4) seems (5) the country.
A. 54321   B. 54123
C. 54231   D. 54213

21. (1) only (2) reached Delhi (3) I (4) morning (5) this.
A. 32415   B. 32145
C. 32541   D. 32154

22. (1) confined (2) to bed (3) fever (4) he is (5) with.
A. 41532   B. 41253
C. 41325   D. 41235

23. (1) car there (2) the policeman (3) parking his (4) prevented him (5) from.
A. 43521   B. 53214
C. 24531   D. 35412

24. (1) with success (2) some day (3) be crowned (4) efforts will (5) your.
A. 54213   B. 54312
C. 54123   D. 54312

25. (1) reach (2) time they (3) by the (4) the train will have left (5) the railway station.
A. 31254   B. 31245
C. 32154   D. 12543

26. (1) cannot (2) second fiddle (3) to others (4) John (5) play.
A. 41523   B. 45123
C. 42315   D. 32154

27. (1) of the (2) have rotten (3) pillars (4) nine tenth (5) away.
A. 43125   B. 42315
C. 41325   D. 41352

28. (1) this exam (2) to clear (3) my best (4) try (5) I will.
A. 12345   B. 25341
C. 15243   D. 54321

29. (1) for this (2) really hard (3) you (4) have to (5) work.
A. 12345   B. 23541
C. 34521   D. 43251

30. (1) impossible (2) nothing is (3) if (4) you work (5) hard
A. 12345   B. 34521
C. 43215   D. 23514

ANSWERS

1	2	3	4	5	6	7	8	9	10
C	D	C	B	B	C	D	B	A	C

11	12	13	14	15	16	17	18	19	20
C	D	D	C	A	D	C	B	D	C

21	22	23	24	25	26	27	28	29	30
D	B	C	D	C	A	C	D	C	B

9. Spelling Errors

There are thousands of words in English language. It is difficult to remember the spellings and meanings of all at once. Try to learn as many as you can. Use a dictionary regularly.

Directions: *Find the correctly spelt words.*

1. A. Damage   B. Dammage
   C. Damaige   D. Dammege

2. A. Efficiant   B. Effecient
   C. Efficient   D. Eficient

3. A. Schedule   B. Schdule
   C. Schedale   D. Schedeule

4. A. Occurad   B. Occurred
   C. Ocurred   D. Occured

5. A. Grieff   B. Grief
   C. Grieef   D. Grrief

6. A. Guarantee   B. Garuntee
   C. Guaruntee   D. Gaurantee

7. A. Meddicine   B. Medicine
   C. Medicene   D. Medicinne

8. A. Benefeted   B. Benefitted
   C. Benifited   D. Benefited

9. A. Acommodation   B. Acomodation
   C. Accomodation   D. Accommodation

10. A. Querrelsome B. Quarrelsame
    C. Quarrelsome D. Querralsome

11. A. Sympathetic B. Smypathetic
    C. Sympothetic D. Sympethetic

12. A. Prograssive B. Progressive
    C. Progresive   D. Prograsive

13. A. Uncivilized B. Uncevilized
    C. Uncivillized D. Uncevelized

14. A. Extravagant B. Extreragent
    C. Extreregant D. Extravegent

15. A. Missunderstood B. Miesunderstood
    C. Misunderstood   D. Misunderstod

16. A. Belligerent B. Beligirent
    C. Belligarant D. Belligerrent

17. A. Astonished   B. Astronished
    C. Astoneshed   D. Asstonished

18. A. Sincerely   B. Sencerely
    C. Sincerelly   D. Sincerrely

19. A. Rigourous   B. Rigerous
    C. Rigorous   D. Regerous

20. A. Satellite   B. Sattellite
    C. Satelite   D. Sattelite

21. A. Pesanger   B. Passenger
    C. Pessenger   D. Pasanger

22. A. Humurous   B. Humorous
    C. Humoreus   D. Humorrous

23. A. Exeggerate   B. Exaggerate
    C. Exadgerate   D. Exagerate

24. A. Fariegn   B. Forein
    C. Foriegn   D. Foreign

25. A. Excesive   B. Excessive
    C. Exccessive   D. Exccesive

26. A. Forcaust   B. Forcast
    C. Forecast   D. Forecaste

27. A. Paralleled   B. Paralelled
    C. Parralleled D. Parallelled

28. A. Ocasion   B. Occassion
    C. Occasion   D. Ocassion

29. A. Boquet   B. Bouquet
    C. Bouquete   D. Bouquette

30. A. Chettering   B. Chaterring
    C. Chattering   D. Chatering

31. A. Discourage   B. Disscourage
    C. Discourege   D. Discaurage

32. A. Curageous   B. Courageous
    C. Courrageous   D. Couregeous

33. A. Abandon   B. Abanddon
    C. Abendon   D. Abbandon

34. A. Embarassment
    B. Emberrassement
    C. Embarrassment
    D. Embbaresment

35. A. Eccintric   B. Eccentrie
    C. Eccentric   D. Eccintrie

36. A. Occasional   B. Occassional
    C. Occesional   D. Occessional

37. A. Querrel   B. Querral
    C. Quarrel   D. Quarel

38. A. Contrebution   B. Contribution
    C. Contributtion D. Conterbution

39. A. Desgrace   B. Disgrece
    C. Disgrice   D. Disgrace

40. A. Harassment   B. Herassment
    C. Harasment   D. Harassmient

41. A. Imaginative   B. Imeginative
    C. Imagenative D. Imaginetive

42. A. Suficient   B. Suficiant
    C. Sufficient   D. Sufficiant

43. A. Adequate   B. Edequate
    C. Adaquete   D. Edaquete

44. A. Experianced B. Experianced
    C. Experienced D. Experrienced

45. A. Flatering   B. Fletering
    C. Flattering   D. Fletaring

46. A. Cuttriveted   B. Culltrivated
    C. Cultivated   D. Caltivated

47. A. Praiceworthy B. Peiseworthy
    C. Praiseworthy D. Praisaworthy

48. A. Profesional   B. Professionel
    C. Professional   D. Profissional

49. A. Ameteur   B. Amateur
    C. Amataur   D. Amateor

50. A. Unfevourable B. Unfevaurable
    C. Unfavourable D. Unfivourable

ANSWERS

1	2	3	4	5	6	7	8	9	10
A	C	A	B	B	A	B	B	D	C

11	12	13	14	15	16	17	18	19	20
A	B	A	A	C	A	A	A	C	A

21	22	23	24	25	26	27	28	29	30
B	B	B	D	B	C	A	C	B	C

31	32	33	34	35	36	37	38	39	40
A	B	A	C	C	A	C	B	D	A

41	42	43	44	45	46	47	48	49	50
A	C	A	C	C	C	C	C	B	C

10. Narration

The words spoken by a speaker are known to be in Direct Speech.

The words spoken by somebody and expressed by someone else with some modification are known as Indirect Speech. *e.g.,*

    (a) Rohit says to me, "You do not understand me."   (Direct speech)

    (b) Rohit tells me that I do not understand him.   (Indirect speech)

MULTIPLE CHOICE QUESTIONS

Directions (Qs. 1 to 20): *Pick out the correct alternative that completes the incomplete sentence which is changed into indirect narration.*

1. She said to me, "I shall see you as soon as I get time."
   She told me:
   A. that she will see me as soon as she will get time.
   B. that she would see me as soon as she would get time.
   C. she would see me whenever she got time.
   D. that she would see me whenever she gets time.

2. She told me, "Your plane will leave if you do not go at once."
   She told me that:
   A. my plane would leave if I did not go at that time.
   B. her plane would leave if I do not go at once.
   C. my plane would leave if I do not go at that very time.
   D. my plane will leave if I did not go at that time.

3. My mother said to me, "Don't quarrel among yourselves."

My mother:
   A. forbade me to quarrel among ourselves.
   B. asked me not to quarrel among ourselves.
   C. asked me that not to quarrel among ourselves.
   D. asked me to quarrel not among ourselves.

4. Her father said to her mother, "Excuse the daughter."
   Her father:
   A. requested her mother to excuse the daughter.
   B. asked her mother to excuse the daughter.
   C. asked her mother to have excused to daughter.
   D. asked her mother to have been excused.

5. He said to his friend, "Wait here till father comes."
   He requested his friend:
   A. to wait here till father had come.
   B. that to wait there till his friend come.
   C. to wait there till father came.
   D. to wait here until his friend come.

6. She said to her maid, "Run and catch the thief."
   She ordered her maid:
   A. run and catch the thief.
   B. that to run and to catch the thief.
   C. ran and caught the thief.
   D. to run and catch the thief.

(951) *English–9-I*

7. Anita said Sunita, "What are you doing?"
   Anita asked Sunita:
   A. what she will be doing.
   B. that what she is doing.
   C. that what she was doing.
   D. what she was doing.

8. She said to me, "Are you meeting me today?"
   She enquired of me:
   A. whether I am meeting her that day.
   B. whether I was meeting her today.
   C. whether I was meeting her that day.
   D. I was meeting her that day.

9. Nitish said to me, "When did you buy this pen?"
   Nitish asked me:
   A. when I was to buy that pen.
   B. when I would buy that pen.
   C. when I had bought that pen.
   D. when I was buying that pen.

10. She said to me, "Are you going to market?"
    She enquired of me:
    A. I am going to market.
    B. I was going to market.
    C. if I was going to market.
    D. if I had been going to the market.

11. Kamini said to me, "Why did not you change your clothes?"
    Kamini asked me:
    A. why I had not changed my clothes.
    B. why I did not change my clothes.
    C. why I would not change my clothes.
    D. why I have not been changing my clothes.

12. Umesh asked me, "Have you read that novel?"
    Umesh asked me:
    A. if he was reading that novel.
    B. if he had read that novel.
    C. if I had read that novel.
    D. if I was reading that novel.

13. She said to me, "I shall forgive you."
    A. She told me that she will forgive me.
    B. She told me that she was going to forgive me.
    C. She told me that she will not forgive me.
    D. She told me that she would forgive me.

14. I said to her, "It was very hot last night."
    I told her:
    A. that it had been very hot the previous night.

B. that it was very hot the previous night.
C. that it has been very hot the last night.
D. that it had been very hot this night.

15. She said to me, "I thank you for the help you have given."
    She:
    A. told me that she thanked me for the help I had given.
    B. thanked me for the help I have given.
    C. thanked to me for the help I have given.
    D. thanked me for the help I had given.

16. Mohini said to me, "Trust in God."
    Mohini advised me:
    A. that I should trust in God.
    B. should trust in God.
    C. trusted in God.
    D. to trust in God.

17. I said to him, "Let us go to school."
    I told him:
    A. we would go to school.
    B. we shall go to school.
    C. that we would go to school.
    D. that we should go to school.

18. Rajni said, "May God bless you?"
    Rajni:
    A. exclaimed with wish that God might bless me.
    B. expressed a wish that God might bless me.
    C. asked God to bless me.
    D. shouted with joy to bless me.

19. My mother said to me, "Do not have so many friends."
    My mother forbade me:
    A. to have so many friends.
    B. not to have so many friends.
    C. to have been so many friends.
    D. to possess so many friends.

20. Ram said, "Pay attention to me."
    Ram asked:
    A. pay attention to him.
    B. paid attention to him.
    C. having paid attention to him.
    D. to pay attention to him.

21. She said, "Shall I thread the needle?"
    She:
    A. asked if she should thread the needle.

B. asked if she shall thread the needle.

C. requested if she should thread the needle.

D. says that if she would thread the needle.

22. We said, "What a place it is!"
We:
A. said that it was a very fine place.
B. said that is a very fine place.
C. said that the place is fine.
D. exclaimed with joy that the place was very fine.

23. My father said, "The earth is round".
My father:
A. said that the earth was round.
B. says that the earth is round.
C. said that the earth is round
D. ordered that the earth is round.

24. The teacher said, "Don't make a noise".
The teacher:
A. says to us not to make a noise.
B. asked us not to make a noise.
C. requested us not to make a noise.
D. asked us not to made a noise.

25. He said, "Bring a chair at once".
He:
A. ordered to bring a chair at once.
B. requested to bring a chair at once.
C. told to bring a chair at once.
D. says to bring a chair at once.

Directions (Qs. 26 to 30): *A sentence correctly changed into indirect narration is followed by four sentences in the direct narration. Pick out from the alternatives one which, when changed into indirect narration will be the same as the indirect sentence preceding the alternatives.*

26. The driver asked the mechanic if he would repair his car.

A. "Repair the car," the driver ordered the mechanic.
B. "Please repair the car," the driver asked the mechanic.
C. "O, please repair the car," the driver asked the mechanic.
D. "Will you repair my car?" the driver asked the mechanic.

27. She thanked me and asked me not to disturb her.
A. "Thank you. Do not disturb me," she said.
B. "Dear friend thank you, do not disturb," she said.
C. "Disturb not, thank you," she said.
D. "Thank you, please ask not to disturb," she said.

28. In a tone of anger she asked her boyfriend why he had come.
A. "You fool, why have you come," she said.
B. "Oh, why have you come?" said she.
C. "You damned, why have you come," she said.
D. "You, you, O you why have you come?" she said.

29. Calling him a coward, the girl asked him to come out.
A. "Come out, you coward," said the girl.
B. "Come out," said the girl to the coward.
C. The girl said, "Alas coward come."
D. The girl said, "Come out."

30. He called her a naughty girl.
A. "Oh! naughty girl," said he.
B. "You naughty girl," said he.
C. He said, "naughty girl."
D. "Naughty," boy said to her.

ANSWERS

1	2	3	4	5	6	7	8	9	10
B	A	A	B	C	D	D	C	C	C

11	12	13	14	15	16	17	18	19	20
A	C	D	A	A	A	D	B	A	D

21	22	23	24	25	26	27	28	29	30
A	D	C	B	A	D	A	C	A	B

11. Active & Passive Voice

A sentence in active voice focuses on the person or thing doing the action. A sentence in passive voice focuses on the person or thing affected by the action. *e.g.*,

The idol was built. (Active voice)

Someone built the idol. (Passive voice)

Transformation of voice

● Voice and Tense are closely associated with each other.

● Tense remains the same while transforming the voice.

MULTIPLE CHOICE QUESTIONS

Directions (Qs. 1 to 20): *In the following questions, a sentence has been given in Active/Passive Voice. Out of the four alternatives suggested, select the one that Best Expresses the same sentence in Passive/Active Voice.*

1. Circumstances will oblige me to go.
   A. I will oblige the circumstances and go.
   B. I shall be obliged to go by the circumstances.
   C. Under the circumstances, I should go.
   D. I shall be obliged by the circumstances to go.

2. We waste much time on trifles.
   A. Much time was wasted on trifles.
   B. Much time will be wasted on trifles.
   C. Much time is wasted by us on trifles.
   D. Much time is wasted on trifles.

3. Mohan gave the beggar an old shirt.
   A. An old shirt was given to Mohan by the beggar.
   B. An old shirt was given to the beggar by Mohan.
   C. The beggar is given an old shirt by Mohan.
   D. An old shirt is given to the beggar by Mohan.

4. They have made him a king.
   A. A king has been made by him.
   B. He was made a king by them.
   C. They have been made king by him.
   D. He has been made a king by them.

5. Who taught you English?
   A. By whom English was taught to you?
   B. By whom you were taught English?
   C. By whom was English taught to you?
   D. By whom are you taught English?

6. Was he knocking at the door?
   A. Was the door being knocked at by him?
   B. Was the door being knocked by him?
   C. Was the door knocked by him?
   D. Was the door knocking at him?

7. What was Rani doing?
   A. What was done by Rani?
   B. What was Rani being done?

C. What was being done by Rani?

D. What was being doing Rani?

8. Why were you wasting your Time?

A. Why was your time being wasted?

B. Why was your time being wasted by you?

C. Why was your time wasted by you?

D. Why was your time wasted?

9. She has laid out a small garden.

A. A small garden has been laid by her.

B. A small garden has laid out her.

C. A small garden being laid by her.

D. A small garden has been laid out by her.

10. She had already solved all the sums.

A. All the sums had already been solved by her.

B. All the sums have already been solved by her.

C. All the sums have been solved by her.

D. All the sums are solved by her.

11. He will have posted the letter.

A. The letter has been posted by him.

B. The letter will be posted by him.

C. The letter will have been posted by him.

D. The letter is posted by him.

12. They will have sold all the books by 4 P.M.

A. All the books will be sold by 4 P.M.

B. All the books will have been sold by 4 P.M.

C. All the books were being sold by 4 P.M.

D. All the books must be sold by 4 P.M.

13. Do you speak English?

A. Is English spoken by you?

B. Does English spoken by you?

C. Is English being spoken by you?

D. Does English being spoken by you?

14. Had they seen me before?

A. Had myself been seen by them before?

B. Had me being seen by them before?

C. Had I been seen by them before?

D. Had I being seen by them before?

15. May I take this pen?

A. May this pen will be taken by me?

B. May this pen shall be taken by me?

C. May this pen should be taken by me?

D. May this pen be taken by me?

16. Can we send it by air?

A. Can this be sent by air?

B. Can it be sent by air?

C. Can it go by air?

D. Can it be send by air?

17. Who wrote this book?

A. By whom was this book written?

B. By whom is this book written?

C. By whom was this book being written?

D. By whom is this book being written?

18. What did you buy?

A. What is bought by you?

B. What is being bought by you?

C. What was bought by you?

D. What was being bought by you?

19. Whom do you want?

A. Who is wanted by you?

B. Who is being wanted by you?

C. You are wanted by whom?

D. You are being wanted by whom?

20. When will you raise this question?

A. When this question will be raised by you?

B. When will this question be raised by you?

C. When this question is being raised by you?

D. When is this question being raised by you?

Directions (Qs. 21 to 35): *In each of the following questions, a sentence is given in Active Voice. Below it are given four alternatives suggesting the Passive Voice form of the above sentence. Choose the correct alternative.*

21. Who did this?

A. This was done by whom?

B. By whom was this done?

C. Who has done this?

D. By whom this was done?

22. One should keep ones promises.

A. Promises should be kept.

B. Ones promises should be kept by one.

C. Promises must be kept.

D. Ones promises one should keep.

23. Give the order.
 A. Order given.
 B. Order be given.
 C. Let the order be given.
 D. Order may be given by you.

24. You will have to do it.
 A. It will be done by you.
 B. It will have to be done by you.
 C. It has to be done by you.
 D. It would have to be done by you.

25. Keep to the left.
 A. You are ordered to keep to the left.
 B. You ought to keep to the left.
 C. You are advised to keep to the left.
 D. You must keep to the left.

26. They will arrange a party.
 A. A party will have to be arranged by them.
 B. A party they will have to arrange.
 C. A party will be arranged by them.
 D. A party by them will be arranged.

27. Someone has picked my pocket.
 A. My pocket is picked.
 B. My pocket has picked.
 C. My pocket has been picked.
 D. My pocket was picked.

28. He kept me waiting.
 A. I kept waiting for him.
 B. I kept waiting by him.
 C. I was waiting for him.
 D. I was kept waiting by him.

29. Why do you tell a lie?
 A. Why is a lie told by you?
 B. Why is told a lie by you?
 C. Why is told by you a lie?
 D. Why has a lie been told by you?

30. I have written a letter.
 A. A letter is written by me.
 B. A letter has been written by me.
 C. A letter was written by me.
 D. A letter had been written by me.

ANSWERS

1	2	3	4	5	6	7	8	9	10
D	C	B	D	C	A	C	B	D	A
11	**12**	**13**	**14**	**15**	**16**	**17**	**18**	**19**	**20**
C	B	A	C	D	B	A	C	A	B
21	**22**	**23**	**24**	**25**	**26**	**27**	**28**	**29**	**30**
B	A	C	B	C	C	C	D	A	B

12. Comprehension Passages

The objective of language comprehension test is to ascertain the ability of the candidates to understand the passage properly. Therefore candidates are required to take notice of the following points:

1. Read the full passage very attentively and intelligently.
2. Try to comprehend the gist of it.
3. Make a mental note of all the important details and points given in the passage.
4. Read the passage for the second time in case you have not been able to understand it satisfactorily.
5. Divide the time proportionately for all the passages.
6. Answer the questions on the basis of facts, as given in the paragraph.
7. Don't waste much time in answering the questions of any one passage.
8. Check all the answers once again, very carefully, to see whether any question is left unanswered by mistake.

MODEL QUESTIONS (FOR PRACTICE)

Directions: *Each of the following passages is followed by five questions. Read the passage carefully and then answer the questions that follow each. For each question, four probable answers A, B, C and D are given. Only one out of these is correct. Choose the correct answer.*

PASSAGE-1

The use of words like 'welcome', 'thank you', 'please', etc., at the right moment reflects a polite nature. The civic sense also lies within the scope of good manners. We should not shout or talk loudly in public places like hospitals and libraries and create disturbance. We should not cheat people or make fun of them. Cleanliness is also necessary. We must not throw the waste on roads and make use of dustbins. We should not harm the public property as it belongs to all of us. While in a queue, discipline should be maintained. We must give fair chance to others.

1. Expressions like 'welcome' 'thank you' and 'please' reflect:
   A. happiness   B. discipline
   C. civic sense   D. polite nature

2. While in a library, we should:
   A. respect others   B. avoid arguments
   C. talk in low tone   D. be courteous

3. A public property belongs to:
   A. nobody
   B. all of us
   C. government
   D. one who maintains it

4. Discipline is:
   A. the rule of proper conduct or action
   B. the rule of road sense
   C. making use of dustbins
   D. forming a queue

5. The most appropriate title for this passage would be:
   A. Polite Nature
   B. Courtesy
   C. Good Manners
   D. Civic Sense

PASSAGE-2

There is an old proverb 'Early to bed and early to rise makes a man healthy and wise.' I am in the habit of getting up early in the morning and have formed the habit of taking long morning walks in the past two years. It is a light exercise and best for physical fitness. The morning air which is fresh and pure is beneficial for the lungs. The early rays of the rising sun are good for healthy skin. 'Health is wealth' and doctors also recommend morning walk to their patients for gaining sound health and freshness of energy.

1. What is good for lungs?
   A. Sunrays   B. Fresh air
   C. Sound sleep   D. Light exercise

2. What is a light exercise?
   A. Early to bed
   B. Early to rise
   C. Morning walk
   D. Gaining sound health

3. What is good for skin?
   A. Fresh air
   B. Morning air
   C. Morning walk
   D. Rising sun's rays

4. What is best for physical fitness?
   A. Light exercise
   B. Long morning walk
   C. Early to rise
   D. Fresh and pure air

5. Long morning walk:
   A. bring sound sleep
   B. ensures physical fitness

   C. ensures healthy skin
   D. keeps healthy, wealthy and wise

PASSAGE-3

Mahatma Gandhi lived a splendid long life and has set great moral standards before us. He showed to the world the true way to peace. He wished to see India prosper but he became a martyr for the noble cause of Hindu-Muslim unity at the time of partition when a religious fanatic, Nathuram Godse, shot him dead on January 30, 1948. His last words were 'Hey Ram'. He lived and died for his country and countryman.

1. Mahatma Gandhi showed the world the true way to:
   A. prosperity   B. love
   C. truth   D. peace

2. Mahatma Gandhi became a martyr for the noble cause of:
   A. truth
   B. non-violence
   C. freedom of India
   D. Hindu-Muslim unity

3. Mahatma Gandhi was shot dead:
   A. before India achieved independence
   B. by a mad man
   C. by an intolerant religious person
   D. by a non-religious person

4. Mahatma Gandhi set great moral standards. It means:
   A. he was a great religious teacher
   B. he was a great moralist
   C. he made India morally stronger
   D. moral was everything to him

5. Gandhiji lived and died for his country and countryman. It means:
   A. he was born in India and died in India
   B. he was a patriot
   C. he was a great moralist
   D. he sacrified his life for India and her people

PASSAGE-4

On one hot day a crow felt very thirsty. He flew from one place to another in search of water. After long hours of labour he found a pitcher. Eagerly, he perched on the mouth of the pitcher. He found that the water was at the bottom of the vessel. He tried his best to dip his beak but did not succeed. He did not know what to do. Suddenly some pebbles lying nearby gave him an idea. One by one he dropped the pebbles with his beak into the pitcher. The level of water slowly came up to the mouth of the pitcher. The crow then drank the water and quenched his thirst.

1. The crow found a pitcher:
   A. as it flew
   B. after many hours of labour
   C. full of water
   D. which was empty

2. What is the moral of the passage?
   A. No pains, no gains
   B. God helps those who help themselves
   C. Necessity is the mother of invention
   D. Try and try again, you will succeed at last

3. The crow flew from place to place:
   A. in search of pitcher
   B. in search of pebbles
   C. in search of water
   D. in search of a vessel

4. The pitcher, the crow found:
   A. was full of water
   B. was dry
   C. had little water in the bottom
   D. had water up to its mouth

5. As the crow dropped pebbles into the pitcher, what happend?
   A. The pitcher broke down
   B. The water leaked one of the pitcher
   C. The level of water into the pitcher rose up slowly
   D. Water level immediately rose to the mouth of the pitcher

PASSAGE-5

Once upon a time a crane and a fox lived in a forest. They were good friend. One day the fox invited the crane to a feast. He made a tasty food and served it before the crane on a plate. The crane could not eat anything because of the long beak. But the fox licked all his food. The crane felt insulted. He decided to teach the fox a lesson.

Next day he invited the fox. He prepared the same tasty food and placed it in front of the fox inside a narrow glass. The crane ate easily while the fox looked on. Now, it was the fox's turn to remain hungry.

1. What is the moral of the passage?
   A. Beware of the wicked
   B. One good turn deserves another
   C. Be contented with what you have
   D. Tit for tat

2. The crane could not eat tasty food because the:
   A. food was served in a shallow plate
   B. food was very hot
   C. food was served in a long jar
   D. crane was not hungry

3. The fox had to remain hungry because:
   A. the food served was not enough in quantity
   B. the food was served inside a narrow glass
   C. the food served was not tasty
   D. the food was all liquid

4. Why did the crane feel insulted?
   A. Because he was invited to feast but he could not eat anything
   B. Because the food was served in a shallow plate and he could not eat
   C. Because the food was too hot
   D. Because the fox gulped all the food quickly

5. The crane successfully taught a lesson to the fox when he invited the fox to a feast and served the food:
   A. in a narrow glass
   B. in a large plate
   C. in a broken plate
   D. in a long jar

PASSAGE-6

The family set down at the table and began to talk about the summer holidays. They had to decide a place to visit during the vacation. Should they go to their village or to a hill station? The parents preferred the village while the children wished to go the hill station. After few moments of discussion the elders decided to visit both the places. First they shall go to the village for a week and then stay at the hill station for the remaining days. For the first time the family shall be together during the holidays. The children were happy with the holiday plan.

1. The purpose for which the family set down at the table was:
   A. to decide a place to visit during the vacation
   B. to educate the children how to carry articles during a visit to a hill station
   C. to decide the date when they should start their journey
   D. to tell the children that they will visit a hill station during this vacation

2. The final plan was to visit:
   A. their village
   B. a hill station
   C. their village as well as a hill station
   D. their home town

3. The final decision was made by:
   A. the boys   B. the girls
   C. the women   D. the elders

4. They decided first to go to their village and stay there for:
   A. a day   B. a week
   C. ten days   D. a fortnight

5. Why were children happy?
   A. Because a hill station was included in their holiday plan
   B. Because a visit to their village was excluded from their holiday plan
   C. Because their choice prevailed
   D. Because they were going all alone to the hill station

PASSAGE-7

Once Govind intended to go on pilgrimage with his family. He asked Mirind to accompany. But for his trade's reason, he did not go with him. So Govind thought it safe to leave the box of his jewellery with him, as it was dangerous to leave it in a lone house or take it on the journey. So he went to him with the box. He took him to a lonely place under a tree and handed it over to him. He told Mirind, "Keep it safe with you. I shall return from the journey after six month then I shall take it back from you." Mirind said, "Don't worry, I shall keep it as safe as own."

1. Govind intended to go:
   A. for a business trip
   B. to a hill station
   C. on a long journey to a sacred place
   D. to his home town for a long period

2. Why did Govind leave his box of jewellery with Mirind?
   A. Because it was not safe to take the box with him on a long journey
   B. Because Mirind was his fast friend
   C. Because the box was very heavy
   D. Because his house was unsafe

3. Why did Govind take Mirind to a lonely place?
   A. To tell him that the box contained valuable jewellery
   B. So that no third person could see box
   C. To show him what was within the box
   D. To tell him that the box will remain with him

4. Where did Govind hand over the box of jewellery to Mirind?
   A. At Mirind's house
   B. At his own house
   C. In a lonely place
   D. In a lonely place under a tree

5. It was not safe to leave the box in a lone house. Here the word 'lone house' means:
   A. a house in a deserted place
   B. a house where none lives
   C. a house without door and lock
   D. a house near the forest

PASSAGE-8

Zahir-ud-din Babar was the first Mughal emperor of India. A descendent of Timur on father's side and Changez Khan on his mother's side, Babar was a brave warrior. After defeating Ibrahim Lodhi in the First Battle of Panipat in 1526 he entered Delhi and soon gained control over Agra. After many more battles with Rajputs he extended his empire over Punjab, Uttar Pradesh and north Bihar. He died at a young age of 48 years in 1530 at his capital Agra without getting much time to consolidate his victories.

1. Zahir-ud-din Babar was the first:
   A. Muslim ruler of India
   B. Mughal ruler of India
   C. Afghan ruler of India
   D. Turk ruler of India

2. Babar was born in the years:
   A. 1480   B. 1482
   C. 1492   D. 1962

3. Babar first occupied:
   A. Punjab   B. Agra
   C. Delhi   D. Panipat

4. Babar was a brave warrior. Here brave warrior means:
   A. courageous soldier
   B. a kind hearted soldier
   C. a clever fighter
   D. a victorious general

5. Babar extended his empire over Punjab and Uttar Pradesh after many more battles with the:
   A. Afghans   B. Rajputs
   C. Mughals   D. Lodhies

PASSAGE-9

Our National Flag is tricolour. It has three equal horizontal strips. The strip at the top is saffron, in the middle is white and at the bottom is green. The ratio of width to length of the flag is 2 : 3. In the centre of the white strip is a wheel in navy blue. The wheel represents the *chakra*. Its design is similar to the wheel which appears on the abacus of the Sarnath Lion Capital of Ashoka. Its diameter approximates to the width of the white strip. The wheel has 24 spokes. It was adopted by Constituent Assembly on July 22, 1947. We love our national flag. We respect it. We are ready to sacrifice our life to protect its honour. It represents the nation. So it is a symbol of national honour.

1. In our national flag the wheel is located in the centre of:
   A. saffron strip   B. white strip
   C. green strip   D. blue strip

2. In our national flag which of the strips is at the bottom in our national flag:
   A. blue   C. saffron
   B. white   D. green

3. Why do we love our national flag?
   A. Because it is tricolour
   B. Because it has three strips
   C. Because it has a wheel at the centre
   D. Because it is a symbol of national honour

4. Our national flag was approved by:
   A. President
   B. Lok Sabha
   C. Parliament
   D. Constituent Assembly

5. The diameter approximates to the width of the white strip. Here the word 'approximates' means:
   A. is more or less equal
   B. is exactly equal
   C. is not equal
   D. is related

PASSAGE-10

Distance in large cities are long. All the people do not have their own means of transport. They have to depend upon the state or private buses. The number of bus users is very large. Every bus stop is, therefore, crowded. The number of buses is not adequate. Thus people suffer the torture of long wait at the bus stop. Some bus stops are quite orderly. People form queues and get into the buses turn by turn. However, often this order is forgotten and confusion spreads when the bus comes and the law of jungle prevails.

1. Why are the bus stops crowded?
   A. Because they are small is size
   B. Because the number of passengers is very large
   C. Because they are situated at some busy centre
   D. Because people do not form queues

2. Long wait at the bus stop is the result of:
   A. over-crowding in the buses
   B. late running of buses
   C. shortage of buses
   D. slow speed of buses

3. Some bus stops are quite orderly where:
   A. there is no crowd
   B. the number of buses is adequate

C. people do not have to wait for long

D. people form queues and enter the buses one by one

4. Most of the people who travel by buses are:
A. non-working
B. do not have their own vehicles
C. have to go a long distance
D. live in large cities

5. What happens when people do not have their own transport?
A. They have to wait for a bus at a bus stop
B. They have to depend upon the state or private buses
C. They have to travel long distances
D. They form queues and get into buses one by one

PASSAGE-11

A certain king once fell ill and doctors said that only a sudden fright would restore his health but the king was not a man for anyone to play tricks on, except his fool. One day, when the fool was with him in his boat he cleverly pushed the king into water but he was rescued and put to bed. The fright, the bath and bed cured the diseased king, but he was so angry with the fool that he turned him out of the country.

1. What did the doctor say about the king?
A. Only a sudden fright would restore the king's health
B. Only fool would cure the king
C. Only a boat trick could cure the king
D. The king had suffered a sudden fright

2. He cleverly pushed the king into water but *he* was rescued and put to bed. In this sentence *he* refers to:
A. the king   B. the fool
C. the doctor   D. the river

3. When the fool pushed the king into water they were:
A. in the palace   B. in the bed
C. in the garden   D. in a boat

4. Who played the trick on the king?
A. The doctor   B. The boatman
C. The fool   D. The fright

5. The fool who cured the king was:
A. rewarded
B. thrown into water
C. turned out of the country
D. put into jail

ANSWERS

Passage 1.	1	2	3	4	5
	D	C	B	A	C
Passage 2.	1	2	3	4	5
	B	C	D	B	B
Passage 3.	1	2	3	4	5
	D	D	C	B	D
Passage 4.	1	2	3	4	5
	B	C	C	C	C
Passage 5.	1	2	3	4	5
	D	A	B	B	A
Passage 6.	1	2	3	4	5
	A	C	D	B	A

Passage 7.	1	2	3	4	5
	C	A	B	D	B
Passage 8.	1	2	3	4	5
	B	B	C	A	B
Passage 9.	1	2	3	4	5
	B	D	D	D	A
Passage 10.	1	2	3	4	5
	B	C	D	B	B
Passage 11.	1	2	3	4	5
	A	A	D	C	C

13. Question Tags

It is a common practice in conversation to make a statement and ask for confirmation; as,

'It's very cold, isn't it?'

The later part ('isn't it?') is called a question tag.

The pattern is:

(i) auxiliary + n't + subject, if the statement is positive, e.g.,

It's raining, isn't it?
Raju broke the glass, didn't he?
She can swim well, can't she?
Your sister cooks well, doesn't she?
You are free, aren't you?

(ii) auxiliary + subject, if the statement is negative, e.g.,

You aren't busy, are you?
They haven't come yet, have they?
Sam doesn't work hard, does he?
She can't swim, can she?

The subject of the question tag is always a pronoun, never a noun.

Note the peculiarities in the following:

I am right, ain't I?
I am right, aren't I?
Let's go to the mall, shall we?
Wait a moment, can you?
Have some more tea, will you?
Somebody has called, haven't they?
There is a temple in that street, isn't there?
There are some girls in your class, aren't there?

MULTIPLE CHOICE QUESTIONS

Direction: *Select the most appropriate options for question tags in the following questions:*

1. It's very cold today, ...?
   A. is it
   B. isn't it
   C. was it
   D. wasn't it

2. You like her, ...?
   A. don't you
   B. do you
   C. are you
   D. aren't you

3. Rohan will come. ....?
   A. shall he
   B. will he
   C. won't he
   D. would he

4. We must hurry, ...?
   A. do we
   B. don't we
   C. must we
   D. mustn't we

5. He will never give up, ...?
   A. will he
   B. won't he
   C. would he
   D. should he

6. Your father is a teacher, ...?
   A. is he
   B. isn't he
   C. does he
   D. doesn't he

7. You have tea for breakfast, ...?
   A. did you
   B. didn't you
   C. have you
   D. haven't you

8. I didn't hurt you, ...?
   A. did I
   B. didn't I
   C. had I
   D. do I

78

9. You aren't going out, ...?
   A. do you   B. don't you
   C. are you   D. aren't you

10. They have sold the car, ...?
    A. have they   B. had they
    C. did they   D. haven't they

11. I needn't get up early today, ...?
    A. did I   B. didn't I
    C. need I   D. needn't I

12. It isn't ready yet, ...?
    A. isn't it   B. is it
    C. does it   D. doesn't it

13. Arpan has passed the exam, ...?
    A. hasn't he   B. has he
    C. had he   D. hadn't he

14. They will go home soon, ...?
    A. will they   B. won't they
    C. would they   D. wouldn't they

15. He didn't write it himself, ...?
    A. do he   B. don't he
    C. did he   D. didn't he

16. Can you sing, ...?
    A. could you   B. couldn't you
    C. can you   D. can't you

17. Do you like tea, ...?
    A. do you   B. don't you
    C. did you   D. are you

18. Are you happy with me, ...?
    A. aren't you   B. are you
    C. do you   D. did you

19. Is it going to rain ....?
    A. was it   B. wasn't it
    C. is it   D. isn't it

20. Am I in your seat, ...?
    A. ain't I   B. am I
    C. do I   D. did I

21. Does your father drive, ...?
    A. does he   B. doesn't he
    C. did he   D. didn't he

22. Did you go to school yesterday, ...?
    A. do you   B. don't you
    C. did you   D. didn't you

23. Will they be at the hotel, ...?
    A. won't they   B. wouldn't they
    C. were they   D. weren't they

24. Is he staying with his uncle, ...?
    A. doesn't he   B. didn't he
    C. isn't he   D. wasn't he

25. Has she met you, ...?
    A. has she   B. hasn't she
    C. had she   D. hasn't she

26. Kids like playing, ...?
    A. don't they   B. do they
    C. do kids   D. don't kids

27. Dad has left already, ...?
    A. has dad   B. hasn't dad
    C. has he   D. hasn't he

28. My mom came yesterday, ...?
    A. hasn't mom   B. has mom
    C. hasn't she   D. has she

29. They are playing well, ...?
    A. are they   B. aren't they
    C. do they   D. don't they

30. Mr. John knows ten languages, ...?
    A. doesn't he   B. does he
    C. doesn't Mr. John   D. does Mr. John

31. Tom has come to see you, ...?
    A. has he   B. hasn't he
    C. has Tom   D. hasn't Tom

32. Ram doesn't like tea, ...?
    A. does he   B. doesn't he
    C. does Ram   D. doesn't Ram

33. You haven't done well, ...?
    A. haven't you   B. have you
    C. had you   D. hadn't you

34. Your father doesn't look his age, ...?
    A. does he   B. doesn't he
    C. didn't he   D. did he

35. Ria didn't complain, ...?
    A. does she   B. doesn't she
    C. did she   D. did Ria

36. He can't speak French fluently, ...?
    A. could he   B. can he
    C. couldn't he   D. can't he

37. Rohan didn't attend the party, ...?
  A. did he
  B. didn't he
  C. did Rohan
  D. didn't Rohan

38. Sam lied, ...?
  A. didn't Sam
  B. did Sam
  C. didn't he
  D. did he

39. Mini has promised to obey you, ...?
  A. has she
  B. hasn't she
  C. has Mini
  D. hasn't Mini

40. Why have you spoiled my book, ...?
  A. haven't you
  B. have you
  C. hadn't you
  D. had you

41. The kid will hurt himself, ...?
  A. will he
  B. won't he
  C. will kid
  D. won't kid

42. I suppose he is lying, ...?
  A. does he
  B. doesn't he
  C. is he
  D. isn't he

43. You are in the queue, ...?
  A. aren't you
  B. are you
  C. were you
  D. weren't you

44. That's your Jacket, ...?
  A. is it
  B. does it
  C. isn't it
  D. doesn't it

45. It isn't your coat, ...?
  A. isn't it
  B. is it
  C. does it
  D. doesn't it

46. Those are your gloves, ...?
  A. aren't they
  B. don't they
  C. didn't they
  D. weren't they

47. Those aren't your books, ...?
  A. don't they
  B. do they
  C. aren't they
  D. are they

48. It is your hat, ...?
  A. is it
  B. isn't it
  C. does it
  D. doesn't it

49. These aren't your shoes, ...?
  A. are they
  B. aren't they
  C. are these
  D. aren't these

50. It rains a lot here, ...?
  A. is it
  B. isn't it
  C. does it
  D. doesn't it

ANSWERS

1	2	3	4	5	6	7	8	9	10
B	A	C	D	A	B	D	A	C	D

11	12	13	14	15	16	17	18	19	20
C	B	A	B	C	D	B	A	D	A

21	22	23	24	25	26	27	28	29	30
B	D	A	C	B	A	D	C	B	A

31	32	33	34	35	36	37	38	39	40
B	A	B	A	C	B	A	C	B	A

41	42	43	44	45	46	47	48	49	50
B	D	A	C	B	A	D	B	A	D

MATHEMATICS

Number: A number answers the question "how many time" a unit is taken, as two pens, eight bulls.

Natural Numbers: Counting numbers are called Natural Numbers. For example 1, 2, 3, 4, 5, ... 8, 9 .... 14, 15, ... *etc.,* are natural numbers.

Prime Number: A number is a prime number which is divisible by 1 or itself. For example 2, 3, 5, 7, 11, 13, 17, 19, 23, 29, ... *etc.,* are prime numbers.

Odd Numbers: Number which are not divisible by 2 are called Odd Numbers. For example 1, 3, 5, 7, 9, 11, 13, 15 .... *etc.,* are odd numbers.

Digits: There are ten digits 1, 2, 3, 4, 5, 6, 7, 8, 9 and 0. The symbols 1 to 9 are called significant digits as each of them has a value of its own. The symbol 0, called zero, which has no value of its own is called in significant digit. It has a value in combination.

Roman Notation: The symbol I, V, X, L, C, D, M denote 1, 5, 10, 50, 100, 500 and 1000 respectively

REMEMBER

- Number 2 is the only even prime number.
- Number 9 is the greatest one digit number.
- Number 10 is the least two digit number.
- Number 99 is the greatest two digit number.
- Number 100 is the least three digit number.
- If a number ends in the digits 0, 2, 4, 6 or 8 it can be divided by 2.
- If a number ends in 0, it is divisible by 10 or 5.
- If the number can be divided by 2 and by 3, it can be divided by 6.
- if one's last digit is 0 or 5, the number can be divided by 5.
- If the sum of the digits can be divided by 3 the number can be divided by 3.
- If the number formed by the last two digits is divisible by 4, the number is divisible by 4.

- When an expression involves all (or some of) the signs +, −, ×, ÷ the operations of multiplication and division must be performed before those of addition and subtractions. Use the rule DMAS. First division operation must be performed then multiplication, Addition and at last the operation of subtraction is to be performed.
- In a division sum, we have four quantities— Dividend, Divisor, Quotient and Remainder. Dividend = (Divisor × Quotient) + Remainder.

SOLVED EXAMPLES

1. What is the difference between the place value of 5 and 3 in the number 15030?

Solution:
Place value of 5 in 15030 = 5000
Place value of 3 in 15030 = 30
Their difference = 5000 − 30 = 4970.

2. Find the difference between the greatest 3-digits number and the least 3-digits number.

Solution:
Greatest three digits number = 999
Least three digits number = 100
Difference = 999 − 100 = 899.

3. Which least number should be added to the least number of 4-digits so that resulting may be exactly divisible by 89?

Solution:
Least 4 digits number = 1000

$$\begin{array}{r} 11 \\ 89\overline{)1000} \\ \underline{89} \\ 110 \\ \underline{89} \\ 21 \end{array}$$

Hence , required number = 89 − 21 = 68.

4. Find the greatest two digits number divisible by 8.

Solution:

Greatest two digits number = 99

$$\begin{array}{r} 12 \\ 8\overline{)99} \\ \underline{8} \\ 19 \\ \underline{16} \\ 3 \end{array}$$

Hence, greatest two digits number divisible by 8 is 99 – 3 = 96.

5. Find the greatest prime factor of 1212.

Solution:

$$\begin{array}{r|r} 2 & 1212 \\ \hline 2 & 606 \\ \hline 3 & 303 \\ \hline 101 & 101 \\ \hline & 1 \end{array}$$

It is evident that the greatest prime factor of 1212 is 101.

6. If a number is multiplied by 15, and then 50 is added to it, then it becomes 155, what is the number?

Solution:

Suppose the number is x

∴ By hypothesis

$15x + 50 = 155$

or, $15x = 155 - 50 = 105$ or, $x = \dfrac{105}{15} = 7$.

7. A number is reduced by 5 and then multiplied by 3. The result is 111. Find the number.

Solution:

Let the required number be x.

By hypothesis,

$(x - 5) \times 3 = 111$ or, $3x - 15 = 111$

or, $3x = 111 + 15$ or, $3x = 126$

∴ $x = \dfrac{126}{3} = 42$

Hence, the number is 42.

8. What should be subtracted from— 21.924 + 9.005 + 17.683 to get 15?

Solution:

If the required number is x, then 21.924 + 9.005 + 17.683 – x = 15

or, 48.612 – x = 15

or, $x = 48.612 - 15 = 33.612$.

9. Find the sum of all prime numbers between 10 and 20.

Solution:

Prime numbers between 10 and 20 are 11, 13, 17, and 19.

Sum = 11 + 13 + 17 + 19 = 60.

10. Convert 18 into factors.

Solution:

$$\begin{array}{r|r} 2 & 18 \\ \hline 3 & 9 \\ \hline & 3 \end{array}$$

Factors of 18 = 2 × 3 × 3.

11. Find the place value of 9 and 4 in the number 46, 928.

Solution:

Place value of 9 in the number 46,928 = 900

Place value of 4 in the number 46,928 = 40,000

12. Find the sum of the greatest and the least numbers formed by using the digits 3, 6, 0 and 7.

Solution:

Least number = 3,067

Greatest number = 7,630

Sum = 10,697

13. Simplify: 4 × 8 × 5 – 4 × 40

Solution:

4 × 8 × 5 – 4 × 40 = 160 – 160 = 0.

14. Simplify: 279 – (25 + 7) ÷ 8

Solution:

279 – (25 + 7) ÷ 8

= 279 – (32) ÷ 8

= 279 – 4 = 275.

15. Simplify: 2 + [4 – {4 – (4 – 4) × 8}]

Solution:

2 + [4 – {4 – (4 – 4) × 8}]

= 2 + [4 – {4 – 0 × 8 }]

= 2 + [4 – {4}]

= 2 + [4 – 4]

= 2 + 0

= 2.

Explanation

When there is a bracket within a bracket it will be found most, convenient to remove the inner most bracket first then the next inner most and so on.

EXERCISE

1. Find the difference between the greatest five digits number and the least five digits number.
   A. 89999   B. 89099
   C. 89078   D. 89708

2. Find the greatest number of 4-digits which is exactly divisible by 91.
   A. 9819   B. 9919
   C. 9991   D. 9199

3. Find the place value of 6 in 7609.
   A. 600   B. 609
   C. 6   D. 7609

4. Find the greatest 3-digits number which is divisible by 5.
   A. 999   B. 996
   C. 995   D. 993

5. Find the sum of all numbers between 20 and 40 which are divisible by 7.
   A. 48   B. 96
   C. 72   D. 84

6. A number when divided by 5 gives 12 as quotient and leaves 3 as remainder. What will be the remainder if the number is divisible by 7?
   A. 1   B. 2
   C. 0   D. 3

7. Simplify: $(36 + 64) \times 25 + (36 + 64) \times 15$.
   A. 4000   B. 3200
   C. 3600   D. 5000

8. Simplify: $(3 + 3 + 3) \div 3$
   A. 1   B. 2
   C. 3   D. 0

9. Find the greatest number of 4-digits which is exactly divisible by 43?
   A. 9976   B. 9796
   C. 9967   D. 9769

10. Write the largest and smallest number using all the digits 0, 1, 2, ... 9 each digit occuring only once in the number. Find their sum.
    A. 10899999999   B. 98099999999
    C. 80999999999   D. 20899999999

11. Simplify $135 - [\, 75 + (4 \times 25 - 2 \times 25)]$
    A. 8   B. 9
    C. 7   D. 10

12. Evaluate $81 \times 24 + 19 \times 24 - 2,400$.
    A. 1   B. 2
    C. 0   D. 3

13. Evaluate $3 + 33 + 333 \div 3 - 21 \times 7$.
    A. 0   B. 2
    C. 3   D. 1

14. Add LX + CXII + VIII.
    A. 160   B. 180
    C. 125   D. 150

15. What is the greatest number which can be formed with the digits 7, 0, 0, 2?
    A. 7020   B. 7200
    C. 2007   D. 7002

16. Write the largest and the smallest number with the digits 5, 3, 7. Find also the difference between them.
    A. 396   B. 369
    C. 386   D. 368

17. A number when divided by 6 gives 8 as quotient and leaves 2 as remainder. Find the number.
    A. 60   B. 40
    C. 45   D. 50

18. Find the sum of all numbers between 10 and 25 which are divisible by 4.
    A. 64   B. 72
    C. 56   D. 84

19. Find the sum of all prime numbers between 15 and 25.
    A. 48   B. 52
    C. 56   D. 59

20. Find the sum of all odd numbers less than 15.
    A. 49   B. 48
    C. 47   D. 46

21. Gopal's age is 8 years. If his father is 63 years older than him, what is his father's age?
    A. 69 years   B. 68 years
    C. 71 years   D. 72 years

22. Multiply 9 by 89 and subtract 342 from the product. Divide the result by 17. Write the answer.
A. 25　　　　　　　B. 26
C. 27　　　　　　　D. 28

23. Multiply 19 by 45 and add 453. Divide the result by 12. Write the answer.
A. 109　　　　　　B. 119
C. 121　　　　　　D. 99

24. If $x = 5$; $y = 4$; $z = 6$, find $2x + 3y + 5z$.
A. 48　　　　　　　B. 49
C. 51　　　　　　　D. 52

25. If $a = 3$; $b = 4$; $c = 5$, find $4a - 5b + 3c$.
A. 2　　　　　　　B. 4
C. 7　　　　　　　D. 5

26. What least number should be added to 174 so that the resulting number be divisible by 12?
A. 2　　　　　　　B. 6
C. 4　　　　　　　D. 8

27. What is the smallest number which must be added to 357 to make it exactly divisible by 9?
A. 1　　　　　　　B. 2
C. 3　　　　　　　D. 4

28. What is the smallest number which must be subtracted from 57 to make it exactly divisible by 9?
A. 3　　　　　　　B. 2
C. 1　　　　　　　D. 4

29. What least number must be added to 19 to make it exactly divisible by 3?
A. 1　　　　　　　B. 2
C. 4　　　　　　　D. 3

30. The product of two numbers is 10519. If one number is 67, find the other number.
A. 142　　　　　　B. 152
C. 153　　　　　　D. 157

ANSWERS

1	2	3	4	5	6	7	8	9	10
A	B	A	C	D	C	A	C	A	A

11	12	13	14	15	16	17	18	19	20
D	C	A	B	B	A	D	B	D	A

21	22	23	24	25	26	27	28	29	30
C	C	A	D	C	B	C	A	B	D

EXPLANATORY ANSWERS

1. Greatest 5 digit number = 99999

Least 5 digit number = 10000

$$
\begin{array}{r}
\text{Difference} = 99999 \\
- 10000 \\
\hline
89999
\end{array}
$$

2.
$$
\begin{array}{r}
109 \\
91\overline{)9999} \\
91 \\
\hline
899 \\
819 \\
\hline
80
\end{array}
$$

Hence, the greatest number of 4-digits which is divisible by 91 = 9999 – 80 = 9919.

4.
$$
\begin{array}{r}
199 \\
5\overline{)999} \\
5 \\
\hline
49 \\
45 \\
\hline
49 \\
45 \\
\hline
4
\end{array}
$$

Hence, greatest number of three digits divisible by 5 = 999 – 4 = 995.

5. Sum of the numbers between 20 and 40 divisible by 7 = 21 + 28 + 35 = 84

6. Required number = 5 × 12 + 3 = 63

$$63 \div 7 = 9$$

Hence, remainder = 0

∴ Remainder when the number is divided by 7 = 0.

7. $(36 + 64) \times 25 + (36 + 64) \times 15$

$= 100 \times 25 + 100 \times 15$

$= 2500 + 1500 = 4000$

8. $(3 + 3 + 3) \div 3$

$= 9 \div 3 = 3.$

9.
```
        232
   43)9999
        86
        ___
        139
        129
        ___
        109
         86
        ___
         23
```
Hence, greatest number of four digits divisible by 43 = 9999 − 23 = 9976.

10. Largest number = 9876543210

Smallest number = 1023456789

Sum = 10899999999

11. $135 - [75 + (4 \times 25 - 2 \times 25)]$

$= 135 - [75 + (100 - 50)]$

$= 135 - [75 + 50]$

$= 135 - 125 = 10.$

12. $81 \times 24 + 19 \times 24 - 2,400$

$= 1944 + 456 - 2,400$

$= 2400 - 2400 = 0.$

13. $3 + 33 + 333 \div 3 - 21 \times 7$

$= 3 + 33 + 111 - 147$

$= 147 - 147 = 0.$

14. LX + CXII + VIII

$= 60 + 112 + 8$

$= 180.$

16. Largest number = 753

Smallest number = 357

Difference = 753 − 357 = 396.

17. Let number = x

Dividend = Quotient × divisor + remainder

⇒ $x = 8 \times 6 + 2$

$= 50$

Hence, number = 50.

18. Numbers between 10 and 25 which are divisible by 4

12, 16, 20 and 24

⇒ Sum = 12 + 16 + 20 + 24

$= 72.$

19. Prime numbers between 15 and 25 are

17, 19, 23

⇒ Sum = 17 + 19 + 23

$= 59.$

20. Odd numbers less than 15 are

1, 3, 5, 7, 9, 11, 13

⇒ Sum = 1 + 3 + 5 + 7 + 9 + 11 + 13

$= 49.$

21. Gopal's father age = 63 + 8 = 71 years.

∵ Gopal age = 8 years

Father is 63 years older than Gopal.

Hence, father's age = 63 + 8 = 71 years.

22. $9 \times 89 = 801$

$801 - 342 = 459$

$459 \div 17 = 27.$

23. $19 \times 45 = 855$

$855 + 453 = 1308$

$1308 \div 12 = 109.$

24. $2x + 3y + 5z = 2 \times 5 + 3 \times 4 + 5 \times 6$

$= 10 + 12 + 30$

$= 52.$

25. $4a - 5b + 3c = 4 \times 3 - 5 \times 4 + 3 \times 5$

$= 12 + 15 - 20$

$= 27 - 20$

$= 7.$

8

26.

$$12\overline{)174}\ (14$$

12
54
48
6

If we add 6 in 174 then it is divided by 12.

174 + 6 = 180 which is divisible by 12.

Hence, required no. = 6.

27.

$$9\overline{)357}\ (39$$

27
87
81
6

If we add 3 in 357 then it is divisible by 9.

Hence, the required no. = 3.

28.

$$9\overline{)57}\ (6$$

54
3

If we subtract 3 from 57, then it is divisible by 9.

Hence, the required no. = 3.

29.

$$3\overline{)19}\ (6$$

18
1

If we add 2 in 19, then it is divisible by 3.

Hence, the required no. = 2.

30. Other no. = $\dfrac{\text{Product of two numbers}}{\text{One number}}$

$= \dfrac{10519}{67} = 157.$

2 H.C.F. AND L.C.M.

Highest Common Factor (H.C.F.) : Highest common factor of two or more numbers is the greatest number which divides each of them exactly. For example 6 is the highest common factor of 18 and 24.

Lowest Common Multiple (L. C. M.): Lowest common multiple of two or more numbers is the smallest number which is exactly divisible by them. For example 24 is a common multiple of 2, 3, 6, 8 and 12.

SOLVED EXAMPLES

1. Find the H. C. F. of 18 and 24.

Solution:

$$18\overline{)24}(1$$
$$\underline{18}$$
$$6\overline{)18}(3$$
$$\underline{18}$$
$$\times$$

Hence, H. C. F. = 6.

2. Find the H. C. F. of 30, 45 and 55.

Solution:

$$30\overline{)45}(1$$
$$\underline{30}$$
$$15\overline{)30}(2$$
$$\underline{30}$$
$$\times$$

Hence, H. C. F. of 30 and 45 is 15.

$$15\overline{)55}(3$$
$$\underline{45}$$
$$10\overline{)15}(1$$
$$\underline{10}$$
$$5\overline{)10}(2$$
$$\underline{10}$$
$$\times$$

Thus, H. C. F of 30, 45 and 55 is 5.

3. Find the measure of the greatest length which can measure 24m, 32m, and 44m, completely.

Solution:

The greatest length which can measure 24m, 32m, and 44m exactly is the H. C. F of these lengths.

$$24\overline{)32}(1 \qquad 8\overline{)44}(5$$
$$\underline{24} \qquad\qquad \underline{40}$$
$$8\overline{)24}(3 \qquad 4\overline{)8}(2$$
$$\underline{24} \qquad\qquad \underline{8}$$
$$\times \qquad\qquad \times$$

Hence, greatest length is 4m.

4. Find the greatest number which will divide 39 and 84 so as to leave remainder 3 in each case.

Solution:

39 – 3 = 36; 84 – 3 = 81

According to the given condition the number will divide 36 and 81 exactly.

$$36\overline{)81}(2$$
$$\underline{72}$$
$$9\overline{)36}(4$$
$$\underline{36}$$
$$\times$$

Hence, greatest number is 9.

5. Find the greatest number which will divide 410, 751 and 1030 so to leave the remainder 7 in each case.

Solution:

410 – 7 = 403; 751 – 7 = 744; 1030 – 7 = 1023.

$$403\overline{)744}(1$$
$$\underline{403}$$
$$341\overline{)403}(1$$
$$\underline{341}$$
$$62\overline{)341}(5$$
$$\underline{310}$$
$$31\overline{)62}(2$$
$$\underline{62}$$
$$\times$$

$$31\overline{)1023}(33$$
$$\underline{93}$$
$$\times 93$$
$$\underline{93}$$
$$\times$$

Thus, the greatest number is 31.

6. Find the least number which when divided by 9, 12, 16 and 20 leaves 3 as remainder in each case.

Solution:

$$
\begin{array}{r|llll}
2 & 9, & 12, & 16, & 20 \\ \hline
2 & 9, & 6, & 8, & 10 \\ \hline
3 & 9, & 3, & 4, & 5 \\ \hline
& 3, & 1, & 4, & 5
\end{array}
$$

L. C. M. = $2 \times 2 \times 3 \times 3 \times 4 \times 5 = 720$.

Hence, the required number = $720 + 3 = 723$.

7. What is the least number which when divided by 12, 18, 36 and 45 leaves remainder 8, 14, 32 and 41 respectively?

Solution:

$$12 - 8 = 4$$
$$18 - 14 = 4$$
$$36 - 32 = 4$$
$$45 - 41 = 4$$

In other words, the difference between the numbers and the corresponding remainders is the same in all the cases *i.e.*, 4.

$$
\begin{array}{r|llll}
2 & 12, & 18, & 36, & 45 \\ \hline
2 & 6, & 9, & 18, & 45 \\ \hline
3 & 3, & 9, & 9, & 45 \\ \hline
3 & 1, & 3, & 3, & 15 \\ \hline
& 1, & 1, & 1, & 5
\end{array}
$$

L. C. M. = $2 \times 2 \times 3 \times 3 \times 5 = 180$

Required number = $180 - 4 = 176$.

8. Find the length of the largest possible square slab which can be used in paving the floor 5 m., 12 cm. long and 3 m., 36 cm. broad.

Solution:

Length of the floor = 5 m. 12 cm. = 512 cm.

Breadth of the floor = 3 m. 36 cm. = 336 cm.

Length of the side of this square slab = H. C. F. of 512 cm. and 336 cm.

$$
\begin{array}{r}
336\overline{)512}(1 \\
\underline{336} \\
176\overline{)336}(1 \\
\underline{176} \\
160\overline{)176}(1 \\
\underline{160} \\
16\overline{)160}(10 \\
\underline{160} \\
\times
\end{array}
$$

Thus, the length of each side of the square slab = 16cm.

9. L. C. M of two numbers is 100 and their H. C. F. is 5. If one number is 25, find the other number.

Solution:

First number × Second number

= L. C. M × H. C. F.

$\Rightarrow$ 25 × Second number = 100 × 5

$\therefore$ Second number $= \dfrac{100 \times 5}{25} = 20$

Remember: Product of two numbers is equal to the product of their L. C. M and H. C. F *i.e.*, first number × second number

= L. C. M × H. C. F.

10. Find the greatest 3-digits number which is exactly divisible by 3, 4, 6 and 10.

Solution:

$$
\begin{array}{r|llll}
2 & 3, & 4, & 6, & 10 \\ \hline
3 & 3, & 2, & 3, & 5 \\ \hline
& 1, & 2, & 1, & 5
\end{array}
$$

L. C. M = $2 \times 3 \times 2 \times 5 = 60$

$60 \times 1 = 60$

$60 \times 2 = 120$

$60 \times 3 = 180$

$60 \times 4 = 240$

Further $60 \times 8 = 480$

$60 \times 10 = 600$

$60 \times 15 = 900$

$60 \times 16 = 960$

Hence, the required number is 960.

11. Find the L. C. M of 9, 12, and 18.

Solution:

$$
\begin{array}{r|lll}
2 & 9, & 12, & 18 \\ \hline
3 & 9, & 6, & 9 \\ \hline
3 & 3, & 2, & 3 \\ \hline
& 1, & 2, & 1
\end{array}
$$

L. C. M = $2 \times 3 \times 3 \times 2 = 36$.

12. Find the least number which is exactly divisible by 15, 20 and 30.

Solution:

It is clear that the least number divisible by the given numbers will be the L. C. M of the given numbers.

```
5 | 15, 20, 30
2 | 3,  4,  6
3 | 3,  2,  3
    1,  2,  1
```

L. C. M = $5 \times 2 \times 3 \times 2 = 60$

Hence, the least number which is exactly divisible by 15, 20 and 30 is 60.

13. Find the L. C. M of 12, 15, 21, 24.

Solution:

```
2 | 12, 15, 21, 24
2 |  6, 15, 21, 12
3 |  3, 15, 21,  6
     1,  5,  7,  2
```

∴ L. C. M = $2 \times 2 \times 3 \times 5 \times 7 \times 2 = 840$.

14. Find the least number which when added to 5 becomes exactly divisible by 16, 18 and 24.

Solution:

```
2 | 16, 18, 24
2 |  8,  9, 12
2 |  4,  9,  6
3 |  2,  9,  3
     2,  3,  1
```

L. C. M = $2 \times 2 \times 2 \times 3 \times 2 \times 3 = 144$

Required number = $144 - 5 = 139$.

15. Find the sum of all numbers less than 1000 which are exactly divisible by 2, 3, 4, 5, 6 and 7.

Solution:

```
2 | 2, 3, 4, 5, 6, 7
3 | 1, 3, 2, 5, 3, 7
    1, 1, 2, 5, 1, 7
```

L. C. M = $2 \times 3 \times 2 \times 5 \times 7 = 420$

$420 \times 1 = 420$; $420 \times 2 = 840$.

It is clear that 420 and 840 are exactly divisible by 2, 3, 4, 5, 6 and 7 and are less than 1000. Hence, their sum = $420 + 840$ = 1260.

16. Traffic light at one particular crossing changes after every 40 seconds. The Traffic light at the next crossing changes after every 32 seconds. At a certain time, they change together. After what time will they again change together?

Solution:

```
2 | 40, 32
2 | 20, 16
2 | 10,  8
     5,  4
```

L. C. M = $2 \times 2 \times 2 \times 5 \times 4 = 160$

Thus, the light will change together after 160 seconds.

EXERCISE

1. L.C.M and H.C.F of two numbers are 960 and 16 respectively. If one number is 120, find the other.
A. 128   B. 125
C. 132   D. 127

2. Find the H.C.F of 30 and 42.
A. 3   B. 6
C. 10   D. 14

3. Find the least common multiple of 126 and 105.
A. 360   B. 420
C. 630   D. 720

4. Find the smallest number which when divided by 35, 36, 72 and 80 leaves a remainder 1 in each case.
A. 4096   B. 5121
C. 5231   D. 5041

5. Find the H.C.F. of 99, 108, 405 and 315.
A. 6   B. 3
C. 9   D. 15

6. Find the least square number which is exactly divisible by 4, 5, 6, 15 and 18.
A. 700   B. 800
C. 600   D. 900

7. Find the least number which when divided by 14, 15, 16 and 18 leaves no remainder.
A. 5040 B. 4870
C. 4580 D. 5160

8. Find the greatest number which when divides 729 leaves 9 as remainder and leaves 5 as remainder when it divides 901.
A. 12 B. 16
C. 24 D. 18

9. Find the sum of all 3-digit numbers which are exactly divisible by 72, 80, and 120.
A. 360 B. 420
C. 720 D. 640

10. Find the greatest number of 3-digits which is exactly divisible by 27, 63 and 42.
A. 756 B. 840
C. 760 D. 616

11. HCF of 11, 0.121, 0.1331 is:
A. 0.0011 B. 0.121
C. 0.1331 D. 12.21

12. The L.C.M of 22, 54, 108, 135 and 198 is:
A. 330 B. 1980
C. 5940 D. 11880

13. HCF of 8^{-2}, 8^{-3}, 8^{-4}, 8^{-5} is:
A. 8^{-2} B. 8^{-3}
C. 8^{-4} D. 8^{-5}

14. The sum of two numbers is 528, and their HCF is 33. How many pairs of such numbers can be formed?
A. 4 B. 5
C. 8 D. 2

15. HCF of 4^5, 4^{11} and 4^{15} is:
A. 4^5 B. 4^{11}
C. 4^{15} D. 4

16. The HCF of 2^3, 3^2, 4 and 15 is:
A. 2^3 B. 3^2
C. 1 D. 360

17. HCF of 15, 45, 90 is:
A. 12 B. 13
C. 13 D. 15

18. The GCM of 9/45, 15/20, 16/20 and 15/25 is:
A. 1/20 B. 1/40
C. 1/60 D. 1/15

19. GCM of 3556 and 3444 is:
A. 25 B. 26
C. 27 D. 28

ANSWERS

1	2	3	4	5	6	7	8	9	10
A	B	C	D	C	D	A	B	C	A

11	12	13	14	15	16	17	18	19
A	C	D	A	A	C	D	A	D

EXPLANATORY ANSWERS

1. First number × Second number
= L.C.M × H.C.F.

$120 \times$ Second number $= 960 \times 16$

∴ Second number $= \dfrac{960 \times 16}{120}$

$= 8 \times 16$

$= 128.$

2. H.C.F of 30 and 42.

$$30\overline{)42}(1$$
$$\underline{30}$$
$$12\overline{)30}(2$$
$$\underline{24}$$
$$6\overline{)12}(2$$
$$\underline{12}$$
$$\times$$

H.C.F of 30 and 42 = 6.

3.

3	105, 126
7	35, 42
	5, 6

$3 \times 7 \times 5 \times 6 = 630$

Hence, L.C.M = 630

4.

2	35, 36, 72, 80
2	35, 18, 36, 40
2	35, 9, 18, 20
3	35, 9, 9, 10
3	35, 3, 3, 10
5	35, 1, 1, 10
	7, 1, 1, 2

L.C.M $= 2 \times 2 \times 2 \times 3 \times 3 \times 5 \times 7 \times 2 = 5040$

Hence, the required number = 5040 + 1
$$= 5041$$

5. H.C.F of 99, 108, 405 and 315

```
99) 108 (1
    99
    9) 99 (11
       99
        ×
```

```
9) 405 (45
   36
   45
   45
    ×
```

```
9) 315 (35
   27
   45
   45
    ×
```

H.C.F = 9.

6.

2	4, 5, 6, 15, 18
3	2, 5, 3, 15, 9
5	2, 5, 1, 5, 3
	2, 1, 1, 1, 3

L.C.M $= 2 \times 3 \times 5 \times 2 \times 3 = 180$

$180 \times 2 = 360, 180 \times 3 = 540, 180 \times 5 = 900$

Hence, the required number which is a perfect square is 900.

7.

2	14, 15, 16, 18
3	7, 15, 8, 9
	7, 5, 8, 3

L.C.M $= 2 \times 3 \times 7 \times 5 \times 8 \times 3 = 5040.$

8. $729 - 9 = 720, 901 - 5 = 896$

```
720) 896 (1
     720
     176) 720 (4
          704
          16) 176 (11
              176
               ×
```

The greatest number is 16.

9.

2	72, 80, 120
2	36, 40, 60
2	18, 20, 30
3	9, 10, 15
5	3, 10, 5
	3, 2, 1

L.C.M $= 2 \times 2 \times 2 \times 3 \times 5 \times 3 \times 2 = 720$

But $720 \times 2 = 1440$ which is not a three digit numbe

Thus, sum of all 3 digit number = 720.

10.

3	27, 63, 42
3	9, 21, 14
7	3, 7, 14
	3, 1, 2

L.C.M $= 3 \times 3 \times 7 \times 3 \times 2 = 378$

Thus, the greatest number of three digits = $378 \times 2 = 756$.

11. HCF of 11, 121, 1331 is 11.

So, HCF of 11, 0.121 and 0.1331 is = 0.0011.

12. Method 1

2	22, 54, 108, 135, 198
11	11, 27, 54, 135, 99
9	1, 27, 54, 135, 9
3	1, 3, 6, 15, 1
	1, 1, 2, 5, 1

14

So, LCM = $2 \times 11 \times 9 \times 3 \times 2 \times 5 = 5940$

Method 2

Factors of 22 = 2×11

Factors of 54 = $2 \times 3 \times 3 \times 3 = 2 \times 3^3$

Factors of 108 = $2 \times 2 \times 3 \times 3 \times 3 = 2^2 \times 3^3$

Factors of 135 = $5 \times 3 \times 3 \times 3 = 5 \times 3^3$

Factors of 198 = $2 \times 3 \times 3 \times 11 = 2^1 \times 3^2 \times 11^1$

So, LCM = Max. power of 2 × Max. power of 3 × Max. power of 5 × Max. power of 11

= $2^2 \times 3^3 \times 5 \times 11 = 5940$

13. HCF of the given numbers = 8^{-5}

14. **Trick:**

Let the numbers be $33a$ and $33b$

Now, $33a + 33b = 528$

$\Rightarrow \quad 33(a + b) = 528 \qquad a + b = 16$

The possible values of a and b are (1, 15); (3, 13) ; (5, 11) and (7, 9).

So, the possible pairs of numbers are (33, 495); (99, 429); (165, 363); (231, 297).

15. HCF of the given numbers = 4^5

Minimum power of 4.

16. **Trick:**

HCF of 2^3, 3^2, 4 and 15

Here by factorization method we see that 1 is the HCF of given numbers

$$\left. \begin{array}{ll} 2^3 & = 2^3 \\ 3^2 & = 3^2 \\ 4 & = 2^2 \\ 15 & = 3 \times 5 \end{array} \right\} = 1$$

HCF of 2^3, 3^2, 4 and 15

17. By Factorization Method

Factors of 15 = 3×5

Factors of 45 = $3^2 \times 5$

Factors of 90 = $3^2 \times 5 \times 2$

So, HCF = $3 \times 5 = 15$.

18. GCM of the given fractions

$$= \frac{\text{G.C.M of } 9, 15, 16, 15}{\text{L.C.M of } 45, 20, 20, 25} = \frac{1}{900}$$

19. **Trick:**

$$
\begin{array}{r}
\text{HCF} = \quad 3444 \overline{)3556} (1 \\
-3444 \\
\hline
112) 3444 (30 \\
-360 \\
\hline
84) 112 (1 \\
-84 \\
\hline
28) 84 (3 \\
84 \\
\hline
\times
\end{array}
$$

HCF = 28.

3 FRACTIONS

A fraction is represented by two numbers written one above the other and separated by a horizontal line. For example $\frac{2}{3}, \frac{5}{7}, \frac{4}{2}$ are all fractions.

In the fraction $\frac{2}{3}$; 2 is called the numerator and 3 the denominator.

Rule: When two fractions have the same denominator, the greater fraction is that which has the greater numerator. For example $\frac{6}{8}$ is greater than $\frac{3}{8}$. When two fractions have same numerator, the greater fraction is that which has the smaller denominator.

If two or more fractions with different denominators are to be compared, they must be reduced to equivalent fractions whose denominators are equal to the L. C. M of the denominators of the given fractions.

SOLVED EXAMPLES

1. Simplify: $5\frac{1}{4} + 3\frac{1}{8} \div 1\frac{1}{4} - 1\frac{1}{4}$

Solution:

$$5\frac{1}{4} + 3\frac{1}{8} \div 1\frac{1}{4} - 1\frac{1}{4}$$

$$= \frac{21}{4} + \frac{25}{8} \div \frac{5}{4} - \frac{5}{4}$$

$$= \frac{21}{4} + \frac{25}{8} \times \frac{4}{5} - \frac{5}{4}$$

$$= \frac{21}{4} + \frac{5}{2} - \frac{5}{4}$$

$$= \frac{21 + 10 - 5}{4} = \frac{26}{4} = \frac{13}{2} = 6\frac{1}{2}.$$

2. Write the following fractions in descending order $\frac{7}{12}, \frac{11}{18}, \frac{5}{8}$.

Solution:

$$\frac{7}{12}, \frac{11}{18}, \frac{5}{8}$$

L. C. M of 12, 18, 8 = 72.

$$\therefore \frac{7}{12}, \frac{11}{18}, \frac{5}{8} = \frac{42, 44, 45}{72}$$

Hence, the required order is $\frac{5}{8}, \frac{11}{18}, \frac{7}{12}$.

3. Write the following fractions in ascending order $\frac{1}{3}, \frac{2}{7}, \frac{4}{21}$.

Solution:

L. C. M of 3, 7, 21 = 21

$$\therefore \frac{1}{3}, \frac{2}{7}, \frac{4}{21} = \frac{7, 6, 4}{21}$$

Thus, the required order is $\frac{4}{21}, \frac{2}{7}, \frac{1}{3}$.

4. Arrange in descending order of magnitude the following fractions—

$$\frac{19}{22}, \frac{9}{11}, \frac{13}{33}, \frac{17}{11}$$

Solution:

L. C. M of 22, 11, 33, 11 = 66.

$$\therefore \frac{19}{22}, \frac{9}{11}, \frac{13}{33}, \frac{17}{11} = \frac{57, 54, 26, 102}{66}$$

Hence, the required order is $\frac{17}{11}, \frac{19}{22}, \frac{9}{11}$ and $\frac{13}{33}$.

5. Simplify:

(A) $5\frac{2}{3} - 1\frac{4}{9}$ (B) $4\frac{3}{8} \times 2\frac{6}{8}$ (C) $11\frac{2}{5} \div 6\frac{1}{3}$

Solution:

(A) $5\frac{2}{3} - 1\frac{4}{9} = \frac{17}{3} - \frac{13}{9}$

$= \frac{51 - 13}{9} = \frac{38}{9} = 4\frac{2}{9}.$

(B) $4\frac{3}{8} \times 2\frac{6}{7} = \frac{35}{8} \times \frac{20}{7} = \frac{25}{2} = 12\frac{1}{2}.$

(C) $11\frac{2}{5} \div 6\frac{1}{3} = \frac{57}{5} \div \frac{19}{3}$

$= \frac{57}{5} \times \frac{3}{19} = \frac{9}{5} = 1\frac{4}{5}.$

6. $\frac{4}{5}$th of an estate is worth ₹ 16,800. Find $\frac{3}{7}$th of the estate.

Solution:

$\frac{4}{5}$th of estate = ₹ 16,800

$\therefore$ 1 estate $= ₹\ 16,800 \times \frac{5}{4} = ₹\ 21,000$

Hence, $\frac{3}{7}$ of estate

$= ₹\ 21,000 \times \frac{3}{7} = ₹\ 9,000.$

7. Simplify: $\frac{1}{5} \times \frac{5}{6} \times \frac{6}{7} + \frac{3}{7} \div \frac{1}{2}$

Solution:

$\frac{1}{5} \times \frac{5}{6} \times \frac{6}{7} + \frac{3}{7} \div \frac{1}{2}$

$= \frac{1}{7} + \frac{3}{7} \div \frac{1}{2} = \frac{1}{7} + \frac{3}{7} \times \frac{2}{1}$

$= \frac{1}{7} + \frac{6}{7} = \frac{1+6}{7} = \frac{7}{7} = 1.$

8. Find the value of $\frac{7}{8} - \frac{2}{3} + \frac{5}{4}$

Solution:

$\frac{7}{8} - \frac{2}{3} + \frac{5}{4} = \frac{21 - 16 + 30}{24} = \frac{35}{24}$

$= 1\frac{11}{24}.$

9. Out of certain sum of money a boy spends $\frac{2}{3}$ and then $\frac{1}{6}$ of the remainder. He had ₹ 25 left. What had he at first?

Solution:

Let the sum be Re. 1

Amount spent $= \frac{2}{3} \times 1 = ₹\frac{2}{3}$

Remainder $= 1 - \frac{2}{3} = \frac{1}{3}$

Amount spent afterwards $= \frac{1}{6} \times \frac{1}{3} = ₹\ \frac{1}{18}$

Reminder $= \frac{1}{3} - \frac{1}{18} = \frac{6-1}{18} = ₹\ \frac{5}{18}$

$\therefore \frac{5}{18}$ of the sum = ₹ 25

$\therefore$ The sum $= \frac{18}{5} \times 25 = ₹\ 90.$

10. Simplify:

$1 + [1 - \{1 - (4-3)\}] \div \frac{1}{3}$

Solution:

$1 + [1 - \{1 - (4-3)\}] \div \frac{1}{3}$

$= 1 + [1 - \{1 - 1\}] \div \frac{1}{3}$

$= 1 + [1 - 0] \div \frac{1}{3}$

$1 + 1 \times \frac{3}{1} = 1 + 3 = 4.$

11. A sum of money increased by its seventh part amounts to ₹ 32. Find the sum.

Solution:

$1 + \frac{1}{7} = \frac{7+1}{7} = \frac{8}{7}$

$\therefore \frac{8}{7}$ of the sum = ₹ 32

$\therefore$ The whole sum $= ₹\ \frac{32 \times 7}{8} = ₹\ 28.$

12. What fraction should be added in $\frac{1}{2} + \frac{2}{3}$ to get $3\frac{1}{2}$?

Solution:

$3\frac{1}{2} - \left(\frac{1}{2} + \frac{2}{3}\right) = \frac{7}{2} - \frac{(3+4)}{6}$

$= \frac{7}{2} - \frac{7}{6} = \frac{21-7}{6} = \frac{14}{6} = \frac{7}{3}$

Thus, $\frac{7}{3}$ should be added to $\left(\frac{1}{2} + \frac{2}{3}\right)$ to get $3\frac{1}{2}$.

EXERCISE

1. Simplify: $\frac{1}{2} \div \left\{ 2\frac{1}{4} - \left(\frac{1}{3} + \frac{1}{2}\right) \right\}$

   A. $\frac{2}{15}$ B. $\frac{6}{17}$

   C. $\frac{7}{15}$ D. $\frac{9}{17}$

2. Simplify: $10 - 2\frac{1}{3} \times 3 + 3\frac{3}{4} \div 2\frac{1}{2}$

   A. $3\frac{1}{2}$ B. $5\frac{1}{2}$

   C. $4\frac{1}{2}$ D. $2\frac{1}{2}$

3. Simplify: $\frac{12}{15}$ of $10\frac{1}{8} \div \frac{20}{49}$ of $\frac{35}{36}$

   A. $20\frac{103}{250}$ B. $19\frac{101}{250}$

   C. $18\frac{103}{250}$ D. $21\frac{103}{250}$

4. Add: $30 + \frac{3}{10} + \frac{3}{100} + \frac{3}{1000}$
   A. 30.303   B. 30.333
   C. 303.33   D. 3033.3

5. Simplify: $8\frac{1}{3} \div \left\{ 3\frac{1}{2} + \frac{2}{3}\left(\frac{1}{3} + \frac{3}{2}\right) \right\}$

   A. $1\frac{13}{17}$ B. $2\frac{7}{17}$

   C. $1\frac{11}{17}$ D. $2\frac{11}{17}$

6. Find the value of $\frac{2a}{b+c}$, if

   $a = \frac{1}{3}, b = \frac{1}{4}, c = \frac{1}{2}$

   A. $\frac{5}{9}$ B. $\frac{7}{9}$

   C. $\frac{8}{9}$ D. $\frac{4}{9}$

7. $\frac{1}{3}$ part of a certain amount was given to Ashok and rest to Anil. If Anil got ₹ 524, what did Ashok get?
   A. ₹ 252   B. ₹ 272
   C. ₹ 242   D. ₹ 262

8. If $\frac{4}{5}$ of an estate is worth ₹ 1,680, find the value of half of the estate.
   A. ₹ 1050   B. ₹ 1060
   C. ₹ 1040   D. ₹ 1055

9. The sum of two numbers is 19. If $\frac{1}{3}$rd of the first number is 5. Find $\frac{1}{2}$ of the second number.
   A. 1   B. 2
   C. 3   D. 4

10. Ramesh give $\frac{1}{3}$rd of his savings to his wife and $\frac{2}{5}$th to his son. Now he had ₹ 24000 left with him. Find Ramesh's total saving.
    A. ₹ 80,000   B. ₹ 70,000
    C. ₹ 90,000   D. ₹ 60,000

11. $\dfrac{2}{7}$ part of a village population is uneducated. If the number of uneducated is 2674, find the population of the village.
A. 9359   B. 9195
C. 9395   D. 9539

12. Ramesh spends $\dfrac{5}{6}$ th part of his monthly income. If his annual saving be ₹ 624, find his annual income.
A. ₹ 2444
B. ₹ 2844
C. ₹ 3744
D. ₹ 3544

13. Divide ₹ 91 among three brothers in such a way that the eldest gets twice as much as the youngest and $1\dfrac{1}{2}$ times as much as the middle brother. Find the share of the eldest brother.
A. ₹ 38   B. ₹ 40
C. ₹ 44   D. ₹ 42

14. Weight of an empty glass is $\dfrac{1}{5}$ th of the weight of the glass full of milk. If the weight of a glass full of milk is 750 grams. How much milk will it contain when half full?
A. 300 gm   B. 250 gm
C. 350 gm   D. 275 gm

ANSWERS

1	2	3	4	5	6	7	8	9	10
B	C	A	B	A	C	D	A	B	C

11	12	13	14
A	C	D	A

EXPLANATORY ANSWERS

1. $\dfrac{1}{2} \div \left\{ 2\dfrac{1}{4} - \left(\dfrac{1}{3} + \dfrac{1}{2} \right) \right\}$

$= \dfrac{1}{2} \div \left\{ \dfrac{9}{4} - \left(\dfrac{2+3}{6} \right) \right\}$

$= \dfrac{1}{2} \div \left\{ \dfrac{9}{4} - \dfrac{5}{6} \right\}$

$= \dfrac{1}{2} \div \left\{ \dfrac{27-10}{12} \right\} = \dfrac{1}{2} \div \dfrac{17}{12}$

$= \dfrac{1}{2} \times \dfrac{12}{17} = \dfrac{6}{17}$

2. $10 - 2\dfrac{1}{3} \times 3 + 3\dfrac{3}{4} \div 2\dfrac{1}{2}$

$= 10 - \dfrac{7}{3} \times 3 + \dfrac{15}{4} \div \dfrac{5}{2}$

$= 10 - \dfrac{7}{3} \times 3 + \dfrac{15}{4} \times \dfrac{2}{5}$

$= 10 - \dfrac{7}{3} \times 3 + \dfrac{3}{2}$

$= \dfrac{10}{1} - \dfrac{7}{1} + \dfrac{3}{2} = \dfrac{20-14+3}{2} = \dfrac{9}{2} = 4\dfrac{1}{2}$

3. $\dfrac{12}{15}$ of $10\dfrac{1}{8} \div \dfrac{20}{49}$ of $\dfrac{35}{36}$

$= \dfrac{12}{15} \times \dfrac{81}{8} \div \dfrac{20}{49} \times \dfrac{35}{36}$

$= \dfrac{81}{10} \div \dfrac{25}{63} = \dfrac{81}{10} \times \dfrac{63}{25} = \dfrac{5103}{250}$

$= 20\dfrac{103}{250}$

4. $30 + \dfrac{3}{10} + \dfrac{3}{100} + \dfrac{3}{1000} = \dfrac{30000 + 300 + 30 + 3}{1000}$

$= \dfrac{30333}{1000} = 30.333$

5. (B) $8\dfrac{1}{3} \div \left\{ 3\dfrac{1}{2} + \dfrac{2}{5}\left(\dfrac{1}{3} + \dfrac{3}{2}\right) \right\}$

$= \dfrac{25}{3} \div \left\{ \dfrac{7}{2} + \dfrac{2}{3}\left(\dfrac{2+9}{6}\right) \right\}$

$= \dfrac{25}{3} \div \left\{ \dfrac{7}{2} + \dfrac{2}{3}\left(\dfrac{11}{6}\right) \right\} = \dfrac{25}{3} \div \left\{ \dfrac{7}{2} + \dfrac{2}{3} \times \dfrac{11}{6} \right\}$

$= \dfrac{25}{3} \div \left\{ \dfrac{7}{2} + \dfrac{11}{9} \right\} = \dfrac{25}{3} \div \left\{ \dfrac{63 + 22}{18} \right\}$

$= \dfrac{25}{3} \div \dfrac{85}{18} = \dfrac{25}{3} \times \dfrac{18}{85} = \dfrac{30}{17} = 1\dfrac{13}{17}$

6. $\dfrac{2a}{b+c}$, if $a = \dfrac{1}{3}$, $b = \dfrac{1}{4}$, $c = \dfrac{1}{2}$

$= \dfrac{2 \times \dfrac{1}{3}}{\dfrac{1}{4} + \dfrac{1}{2}} = \dfrac{\dfrac{2}{3}}{\dfrac{1+2}{4}} = \dfrac{\dfrac{2}{3}}{\dfrac{3}{4}} = \dfrac{2}{3} \times \dfrac{4}{3} = \dfrac{8}{9}$

7. Ashok's share $= \dfrac{1}{3}$

$\therefore$ Anil's share $= 1 - \dfrac{1}{3} = \dfrac{2}{3}$

When Anil gets $\dfrac{2}{3}$ Ashok gets $\dfrac{1}{3}$

$\therefore$ When Anil gets ₹ 524. Ashok will get

$= \dfrac{524}{2} = ₹\ 262.$

8. $\dfrac{4}{5}$ of an estate $= ₹\ 1680$

$\therefore$ Whole estate $= \dfrac{5}{4} \times 1680$

$\therefore \dfrac{1}{2}$ of estate $= \dfrac{1}{2} \times \dfrac{5}{4} \times 1680$
$= 5 \times 210 = ₹\ 1050.$

9. $\dfrac{1}{3}$ rd of the first number $= 5$

$\therefore$ First number $= 15$

Sum of the two number $= 19$

$\therefore$ Second number $= 19 - 15 = 4$

$\therefore \dfrac{1}{2}$ of the second number $= \dfrac{1}{2} \times 4 = 2$.

10. Total money given $= \dfrac{1}{3} + \dfrac{2}{5} = \dfrac{5+6}{15} = \dfrac{11}{15}$

Money left $= 1 - \dfrac{11}{15} = \dfrac{4}{15}$

When saving is ₹ $\dfrac{4}{15}$, total money $= ₹\ 1$

$\therefore$ When savings is ₹ 1, total money $= \dfrac{15}{4}$

$\therefore$ When savings is ₹ 24000, total money

$= \dfrac{15 \times 24000}{4} = ₹\ 90,000.$

11. When $\dfrac{2}{7}$ part is uneducated whole population
$= 1$

$\therefore$ When 1 is uneducated whole population

$= \dfrac{7}{2}$

$\therefore$ When 2674 are uneducated, whole population

$= \dfrac{7}{2} \times 2674 = 7 \times 1337 = 9359$.

12. Ramesh spends $\dfrac{5}{6}$ th part of his monthly

income. It means Ramesh saves $\left(1 - \dfrac{5}{6}\right) =$

$\dfrac{1}{6}$ th of his monthly income.

It means that it Ramesh's annual income is

₹ 1, his savings $= ₹\dfrac{1}{6}$.

$\therefore$ Ramesh's annual income $= 6 \times 624 =$
₹ 3744.

13. Let the middle brother gets ₹ 1

$\therefore$ Eldest brother will get ₹ $\dfrac{3}{2} \times 1 = ₹\dfrac{3}{2}$

∴ Youngest brother will get

$$₹\frac{1}{2} \times ₹\frac{3}{2} = ₹\frac{3}{4}$$

Ratio between their shares $= \frac{3}{2} : 1 : \frac{3}{4} = 6 : 4 : 3$

Total $= 6 + 4 + 3 = 13$

∴ Eldest brother's share $= \frac{6 \times 91}{13} = ₹\,42.$

14. Let the weight of the glass full of milk be 1 gm.

∴ Weight of the empty glass $= \frac{1}{5}$ gm.

∴ Weight of the milk $= 1 - \frac{1}{5} = \frac{4}{5}$ gm.

When the weight of the glass full of milk is 1 gm, weight of the milk contained in the glass $= \frac{4}{5}$ gm.

When the glass is full of milk,
Weight of milk contained in

$$= \frac{4}{5} \times 750 = 4 \times 150 = 600 \text{ gm}.$$

∴ Weight of the milk when glass is half full

$$= 600 \times \frac{1}{2} = 300 \text{ gm}.$$

DECIMAL FRACTIONS

A decimal fraction is a fraction which has 10 or any power of 10 for its denominator and is expressed in decimal system of notation. For example $\frac{3}{10}, \frac{3}{100}$ etc., are decimal fractions.

$$\frac{3}{10}, = 0.3; \quad \frac{3}{100} = 0.03; \quad \frac{3}{1000} = 0.003;$$

$$\frac{3}{100000} = 0.00003$$

SOLVED EXAMPLES

1. Find the continued product of $.4 \times .04 \times .004$.
Solution:

$$.4 \times .04 \times .004 = .000064$$

2. Simplify: $\dfrac{.0203 \times 2.92}{.0073 \times 14.5 \times .7}$

Solution:

$$\frac{.0203 \times 2.92}{.0073 \times 14.5 \times .7} = \frac{203 \times 292}{73 \times 145 \times 7}$$

$$= \frac{4}{5} = 0.8$$

3. Fill in the blanks $3.5 \times \text{-----} = .035$

Solution:

We have to find a number which when multiplied by 3.5 results .035

∴ Required number

$$= \frac{.035}{3.5} = \frac{35}{3500} = \frac{1}{100} = .01$$

4. Simplify $4.7 \times 13.5 + 5.3 \times 13.5$

Solution: $4.7 \times 13.5 + 5.3 \times 13.5$
$$= (4.7 + 5.3) \times 13.5$$
$$= 10 \times 13.5$$
$$= 135$$

5. Simplify: $.1 \times .1 \times .1 - .01 \times .01 \times .01$

Solution:

$.1 \times .1 \times .1 - .01 \times .01 \times .01$
$=.001 - .000001$
$=.000999.$

6. Add: $3.34 + 2.10 + 4$

Solution:

$3.34 + 2.10 + 4 = 3.34 + 2.10 + 4.00 = 9.44$

7. Simplify: $0.077 \div 7 - 0.005 \div 5$

Solution:

$0.077 \div 7 - 0.005 \div 5$

$$= 0.077 \times \frac{1}{7} - 0.005 \times \frac{1}{5}$$

$$= 0.011 - 0.001 = 0.010 = 0.01$$

EXERCISE

1. Which of the following is equivalent to $\frac{15}{25}$?

   A. $\frac{150}{25}$ 　　　　B. $\frac{15}{250}$

   C. $\frac{3}{5}$ 　　　　　D. $\frac{60}{75}$

2. $\frac{5}{6}$ of an hour is equal to
   A. half an hour
   B. 40 minutes
   C. 50 minutes
   D. 55 minutes

3. Which of the following is the largest fraction?

   $$\frac{3}{15}, \frac{5}{20}, \frac{8}{64}, \frac{25}{1000}$$

   A. $\frac{3}{15}$ 　　　　B. $\frac{5}{20}$

   C. $\frac{8}{64}$ 　　　　D. $\frac{25}{1000}$

4. Six times x increased by 12 is equal to

   A. $\frac{x}{2}$ 　　　　　B. $2x$
   C. $6x + 12$ 　　　D. $12x + 6$

5. Five times y diminished by 20 is equal to
   A. $5y - 20$ 　　　B. $5y + 20$
   C. $y/4$ 　　　　　D. $4y$

6. The number less than 15 by 7 is
   A. $15x - 7$ 　　　B. $15/7$
   C. 15 　　　　　D. 8

7. If 21 is add to four times a number, the result is 57. The number is
   A. 7 　　　　　B. 8
   C. 9 　　　　　D. 10

8. A number, the sum of whose fourth and fifth parts exceeds their third part by 28, is
   A. 120 　　　　B. 240
   C. 220 　　　　D. 160

9. The sum of 1/2, 1/4 and 1/8 of a number is 28. The number is
   A. 28 　　　　　B. 32
   C. 36 　　　　　D. 42

10. In decimal system, $9\frac{1}{8}$ may be represented as
    A. 9.18 　　　　B. 9.125
    C. 9.025 　　　　D. 9.225

11. Divide $0.\dot{6}$ by 0.75
    A. $0.\dot{8}$ 　　　　B. 0.75
    C. 0 　　　　　D. $0.\dot{6}7\dot{5}$

12. What is the value of $\frac{1}{0.04}$?

    A. 25 　　　　　B. 2.5

    C. $\frac{2}{5}$ 　　　　　D. $\frac{1}{40}$

13. The fractional form of $0.\overline{47}$ is

    A. $\frac{46}{99}$ 　　　　B. $\frac{46}{90}$

    C. $\frac{47}{99}$ 　　　　D. $\frac{47}{90}$

14. If $213 \times 16 = 3408$, then $1.6 \times 21.3 = ?$
    A. 340.8 　　　　B. 34.08
    C. 3.408 　　　　D. 0.3408

15. $\dfrac{0.0203 \times 2.92}{0.0073 \times 14.5 \times 0.7} = ?$
    A. 3.25 　　　　B. 2.40
    C. 1.45 　　　　D. 0.8

16. $\dfrac{5 \times 1.6 - 2 \times 1.4}{1.3} = ?$
    A. 4 　　　　　B. 1.4
    C. 1.2 　　　　D. 0.4

ANSWERS

1	2	3	4	5	6	7	8	9	10
C	C	B	C	A	D	C	B	B	B

11	12	13	14	15	16
A	A	C	B	D	A

EXPLANATORY ANSWERS

1. $\dfrac{15}{25} = \dfrac{3 \times 5}{5 \times 5} = \dfrac{3}{5}$

2. $\dfrac{5}{6}$ of 1 hr. $= \dfrac{5}{6} \times 60$ minutes $= 50$ minutes.

3. $\dfrac{3}{15} = \dfrac{1}{5}, \dfrac{8}{64} = \dfrac{1}{8}, \dfrac{5}{20} = \dfrac{1}{4}, \dfrac{25}{1000} = \dfrac{1}{40}$

   Now, the fractions are $\dfrac{1}{5}, \dfrac{1}{4}, \dfrac{1}{8}, \dfrac{1}{40}$

   $\therefore$ The largest fraction is $\dfrac{1}{4} = \dfrac{5}{20}$

4. $x \times 6 + 12 = 6x + 12$

5. $5 \times y - 20 = 5y - 20$

6. $15 - 7 = 8$

7. Let the number be x

   $\therefore 4x + 21 = 57$ or, $4x = 57 - 21 = 36$

   Hence, $x = \dfrac{36}{4} = 9$.

8. Let the number be x

   $\therefore \quad \dfrac{x}{4} + \dfrac{x}{5} = \dfrac{x}{3} + 28$

   $\Rightarrow \quad \dfrac{9x}{20} = \dfrac{x}{3} + 28$

   $\Rightarrow \quad \dfrac{9x}{20} - \dfrac{x}{3} = 28$

   $\Rightarrow \quad \dfrac{27x - 20x}{60} = 28$

   $\therefore \quad x = \dfrac{28 \times 60}{7} = 240$.

9. Let the number be x

   $\therefore \quad \dfrac{x}{2} + \dfrac{x}{4} + \dfrac{x}{8} = 28,$

   $\Rightarrow \quad \dfrac{7x}{8} = 28$

   $\therefore \quad x = \dfrac{28 \times 8}{7} = 32$.

10. $9\dfrac{1}{8} = 9 + \dfrac{1}{8} = 9 + .125 = 9.125$

11. $0.\dot{6} \div 0.75 = \dfrac{6}{9} \div \dfrac{75}{100} = \dfrac{2}{3} \div \dfrac{3}{4} = \dfrac{2}{3} \times \dfrac{4}{3}$

    $= \dfrac{8}{9} = 0.\dot{8}$

12. $\dfrac{1}{0.04} = \dfrac{100}{4} = 25$

13. $0.\overline{47} = \dfrac{47}{99}$

14. Here, $213 \times 16 = 3408$

    Then, $1.6 \times 21.3 = \dfrac{16}{10} \times \dfrac{213}{10} = \dfrac{3408}{100} = 34.08$

15. $\dfrac{0.0203 \times 2.92}{0.0073 \times 14.5 \times 0.7} = \dfrac{203 \times 292 \times 10^{-6}}{73 \times 145 \times 7 \times 10^{-6}}$

    $= \dfrac{4}{5} = 0.8$

16. $\dfrac{5 \times 1.6 - 2 \times 1.4}{1.3} = \dfrac{8 - 2.8}{1.3} = \dfrac{5.2}{1.3} = \dfrac{52}{13} = 4$.

The average value of a number of quantities of the same kind is equal to their sum divided by their number.

$$\text{Average of quantities} = \frac{\text{Sum of the quantities}}{\text{Number of quantities}}$$

SOLVED EXAMPLES

1. Find the average of 3, 6, 9 and 6.

Solution:

$$\text{Average} = \frac{3+6+9+6}{4} = \frac{24}{4} = 6.$$

2. Find the average of first five counting numbers.

Solution:

First five counting numbers are 1, 2, 3, 4 and 5.

$$\therefore \text{ Their average} = \frac{1+2+3+4+5}{5} = \frac{15}{5} = 3.$$

3. A cricket player scores 13, 0, 19, 17 and 6 runs in different matches. Find his average score.

Solution:

Average

$$= \frac{13+0+19+17+6}{5} = \frac{55}{5} = 11 \text{ runs.}$$

4. The average score of five children is 35 runs. The average score of first three children is 41. Find the average score of the last two children.

Solution:

Average score of five children = 35 runs

Total score of five children = 35 × 5 = 175

Average score of first three children = 41

Total score of first three children
= 41 × 3 = 123

$\therefore$ Total score of last two children
= 175 – 123 = 52

Hence, average score of last two children

$$= \frac{52}{2} = 26 \text{ runs.}$$

5. The average of three numbers is 9. If the average of first two numbers is 12, find the third number.

Solution:

$\because$ Average of three numbers = 9

$\therefore$ Sum of three numbers = 9 × 3 = 27

$\because$ Average of two numbers = 12

$\therefore$ Sum of two numbers = 12 × 2 = 24

$\therefore$ Third number = 27 – 24 = 3.

6. The weights of 5 boys in a class are 49.6 kg., 39.8 kg., 40.8 kg., 45.2 kg., and 24.6 kg. respectively. Find their average weight.

Solution:

Total weight of 5 boys

$$= \frac{49.6 + 39.8 + 40.8 + 45.2 + 24.6}{5}$$

$$\therefore \text{ Average weight} = \frac{200}{5} = 40 \text{ kg.}$$

7. The average weight of 9 boys in a class is 42 kg. Another boy joined the class and the new average was found to be 42.5 kg. Find the weight of the new boy.

Solution:

$\because$ Average weight of 9 boys = 42 kg.

$\therefore$ Sum of the weight of 9 boys
= 42 × 9 = 378 kg.

$\because$ Now total number of boys = 9 +1 = 10

$\because$ Average weight of 10 boys = 42.5 kg.

$\therefore$ Sum of the weights of 10 boys
= 42.5 × 10 = 425 kg.

$\therefore$ Weight of the new boy = 425 – 378 = 47 kg.

8. Average score in 10 matches of a cricket player was 45.6 runs. If average score in first six matches was 48 runs, find the average score in last four matches.

Solution:

∵ Average score in 10 matches = 45.6 runs.

∴ Total score in 10 matches = 45.6 × 10

= 456 runs.

∵ Average score in 6 matches = 48

∴ Total score in 6 matches = 48 × 6 = 288

∴ Sum of the runs scored in last 4 matches

= 456 – 288 = 168

∴ Average score in last 4 matches = $\dfrac{168}{4} = 42$

= 42 runs.

EXERCISE

1. The average of the fractions $1\frac{1}{2}, 2\frac{1}{3}, 3\frac{1}{3}$ and $4\frac{5}{6}$ is

   A. 2   B. $2\frac{1}{2}$

   C. 3   D. 4

2. The average of first nine multiples of 3 is
   A. 12.0   B. 12.5
   C. 15.0   D. 18.5

3. The average of 13 numbers is 68, the average of first 7 numbers is 63 and the average of last 7 numbers is 70. What is the 7th number?
   A. 43   B. 45
   C. 47   D. 49

4. Average age of 8 persons increased by 2 years, when two men whose ages are 20 and 24 years are replaced by two women. What is the average age of women?
   A. 30 years   B. 31 years
   C. 28 years   D. 33 years

5. A batsman has a certain average of runs for 16 innings. In the 17th innings, he makes a score of 85 runs thereby increasing his average by 3. What is the average after the 17th inning?
   A. 33 runs   B. 34 runs
   C. 37 runs   D. 36 runs

6. The average of 50 numbers is 38. If two numbers namely 45 and 55 are discarded, the average of the remaining numbers is
   A. 36.5   B. 37
   C. 37.5   D. 37.52

7. The average of 6 observations is 12. A new seventh observation is included and the new average is decreased by 1. The seventh observation is
   A. 1   B. 3
   C. 5   D. 6

8. The average of marks obtained by 120 candidates was 35. If the average of marks of passed candidates was 39 and that of failed candidates was 15, the number of candidates who passed the examination is
   A. 100   B. 110
   C. 120   D. 150

9. The average of three numbers is 42. The first is twice the second and the second is twice the third. The difference between the largest and the smallest number is
   A. 18   B. 36
   C. 54   D. 72

10. The average age of 30 students in a class is 12 years. The average age of a group of 5 of the students is 10 years and that of another group of 5 of them is 14 years. The average age of the remaining students is
    A. 8 years   B. 10 years
    C. 12 years   D. 14 years

11. Out of four numbers, the average of first three is 15 and that of the last three is 16. If the last number is 19, the first is
    A. 15   B. 16
    C. 18   D. 19

12. The average age of 24 students in a class is 10. If the teacher's age is included, the average increases by one. The age of the teacher is
   A. 25   B. 30
   C. 35   D. 40

13. The average weight of a class of 40 students is 40 kg. If the weight of the teacher be included, the average weight increases by 500 gms. The weight of the teacher is
   A. 40.5 kg   B. 60 kg
   C. 60.5 kg   D. 62 kg

14. The average weight of 8 persons is increased by 2.5 kg when one of them whose weight is 56 kg is replaced by a new man. The weight of the new man is
   A. 66 kg   B. 75 kg
   C. 76 kg   D. 86 kg

15. The average age of the boys in a class is 16 years and that of the girls is 15 years. The average age for the whole class is:
   A. 16 years   B. 15.5 years
   C. 15 years   D. Data inadequate

16. The average of six numbers is 3.95. The average of two of them is 3.4, while the average of other two is 3.85. What is the average of remaining two numbers?

A. 4.8   B. 4.7
C. 4.6   D. 4.5

17. The average of five numbers is 27. If one number is excluded, the average becomes 25. The excluded number is
   A. 35   B. 30
   C. 27   D. 25

18. The average score of a cricketer for ten matches is 38.9 runs. If the average for the first six matches is 42, then find the average for the last four matches?
   A. 35   B. 34.25
   C. 33.5   D. 33.25

19. The average age of 35 students in a class is 16 years. The average age of 21 students is 14. What is the average age of remaining 14 students?
   A. 19 years   B. 18 years
   C. 17 years   D. 15 years

20. The average weight of 16 boys in a class is 50.25 kgs and that of the remaining 8 boys 45.15 kgs. Find the average weight of all the boys in the class.
   A. 49.25 kgs   B. 48.55 kgs
   C. 48 kgs   D. 47.55 kgs

ANSWERS

1	2	3	4	5	6	7	8	9	10
C	C	C	A	C	C	C	A	C	C

11	12	13	14	15	16	17	18	19	20
B	C	C	C	D	C	A	B	A	B

EXPLANATORY ANSWERS

1. Average $= \frac{1}{4}\left(\frac{3}{2}+\frac{7}{3}+\frac{10}{3}+\frac{29}{6}\right)$

$= \left(\frac{9+14+20+29}{24}\right)$

$= \frac{72}{24} = 3$

2. Average $= \frac{3(1+2+3+4+5+6+7+8+9)}{9}$

$= \frac{135}{9} = 15$

3. Average of 13 numbers = 68
∴ Total of 13 numbers = 13 × 68 = 884
Average of last 7 numbers = 70

$\therefore$ Total of last 7 numbers = $7 \times 70 = 490$

$\therefore$ Average of first 6 numbers = $884 - 490 = 394$

$\therefore$ Average of first 7 numbers = 63

$\therefore$ Total of first 7 numbers = $63 \times 7 = 441$

$\therefore$ 7th number = $441 - 394 = 47$

4. Total increase in the age of 8 persons
   $$= 2 \times 8 = 16 \text{ years}$$
   Total age of two men being replaced
   $$= 20 + 24 = 44 \text{ years}$$
   Total of the age of two women
   $$= 44 + 16 = 60 \text{ years}$$
   $\Rightarrow$ The average age of women = $\dfrac{60}{2} = 30$ years.

5. Average increase in the score of 17 innings
   $$= 3 \text{ runs}$$
   Total increase in the score of 17 innings
   $$= 3 \times 17 = 51 \text{ runs}$$
   $\therefore$ His average of 16 innings
   $$= 85 - 51 = 34 \text{ runs}$$
   Hence, average after the 17th innings
   $$= 34 + 3 = 37 \text{ runs}$$

6. Total of 50 numbers = $50 \times 38 = 1900$
   Total of 48 numbers = $1900 - (45 + 55) = 1800$
   $\therefore$ Average = $\dfrac{1800}{48} = 37.5$

7. Seventh observation = $(7 \times 11 - 6 \times 12) = 5$

8. Let the number of candidates who passed = x
   $\Rightarrow 39 \times x + 15 \times (120 - x) = 120 \times 35$
   $\Rightarrow 24x = 4200 - 1800$
   $\therefore x = \dfrac{2400}{24} = 100$

9. Let the third number = x
   Then, second number = $2x$ and first number = $4x$
   $\therefore \dfrac{x + 2x + 4x}{3} = 42$
   $\Rightarrow \dfrac{7x}{3} = 42$
   $\Rightarrow x = \dfrac{42 \times 3}{7}$
   $\Rightarrow x = 18$
   So, (largest) – (smallest) = $(4x - x) = 3x = 54$

10. Let, the required average age be x
    Then, $5 \times 10 + 5 \times 14 + 20 \times x = 30 \times 12$
    $\Rightarrow 20x = 360 - 120$
    $\Rightarrow 20x = 240$
    $\Rightarrow x = 12$

11. Sum of four numbers = $(15 \times 3 + 19) = 64$
    Sum of last three numbers = $(16 \times 3) = 48$
    $\therefore$ First number = $(64 - 48) = 16$

12. Age of the teacher = $(25 \times 11 - 24 \times 10)$ years
    $= (275 - 240)$ years $= 35$ years.

13. Weight of the teacher
    $= (41 \times 40.5 - 40 \times 40)$ kg
    $= (1660.5 - 1600)$ kg $= 60.5$ kg

14. Total increase = (8×2.5) kg $= 20$ kg
    Weight of new man = $(56 + 20)$kg $= 76$ kg

15. The average age of the boys = 16 years
    The average age of the girls = 15 years
    Hence, number of boys and girls are not given so it is quite impossible to find out the average age for the whole class. Therefore, data is inadequate.

16. Required average of remaining two numbers
    $$= \frac{6 \times (3.95) - (2 \times 3.4 + 2 \times 3.85)}{2}$$
    $$= \frac{23.70 - 14.50}{2} = \frac{9.20}{2} = 4.6$$

17. The excluded number = $5 \times 27 - 4 \times 25$
    $$= 135 - 100 = 35$$

18. Average of last 4 matches
    $$= \frac{10 \times 38.9 - 6 \times 42}{4} = \frac{389 - 252}{4} = \frac{137}{4}$$
    $$= 34.25$$

19. The average age of remaining 14 students =
    $$\frac{35 \times 16 - 21 \times 14}{14} = \frac{560 - 294}{14} = \frac{266}{14} = 19$$

20. The average weight of all the boys in the class
    $$= \frac{16 \times 50.25 + 8 \times 45.15}{16 + 8}$$
    $$= \frac{804 + 361.20}{24} = \frac{1165.20}{24}$$
    $$= 48.55 \text{ kgs}$$

The square root of a number is one of two equal factors which if multiplied together, produce that number. For example:

$2 \times 2 = 4$

Hence, 2 is the square root of 4 and 4 is the square of 2.

or, $\sqrt{4} = 2$

and $(2)^2 = 4$

SOLVED EXAMPLES

1. Find the square root of 36

Solution:

$$\begin{array}{r|l} & 6 \\ \hline 6 & 36 \\ & 36 \\ \hline & \times \end{array}$$

$\therefore \sqrt{36} = 6$.

2. Find the square root of 289.

Solution:

$$\begin{array}{r|l} & 17 \\ \hline 1 & 289 \\ & 1 \\ \hline 27 & 189 \\ & 189 \\ \hline & \times \end{array}$$

$\therefore \sqrt{289} = 17$.

3. A gardener planted 81 apple plants. There was as many rows as there were plants. Find the number of plants in a row.

Solution:

The number of rows is the square root of 81.

$$\begin{array}{r|l} & 9 \\ \hline 9 & 81 \\ & 81 \\ \hline & \times \end{array}$$

Hence, the number of rows = 9.

4. Add $\sqrt{16} + \sqrt{625}$

Solution:

$$\begin{array}{r|l} & 4 \\ \hline 4 & 16 \\ & 16 \\ \hline & \times \end{array}$$

$\therefore \sqrt{16} = 4$

$$\begin{array}{r|l} & 25 \\ \hline 2 & 625 \\ & 4 \\ \hline 45 & 225 \\ & 225 \\ \hline & \times\times\times \end{array}$$

$\therefore \sqrt{625} = 25$

$\therefore \sqrt{16} + \sqrt{625} = 4 + 25 = 29$.

5. A man plants his orchard with 5,625 trees, and arranges them to that there are as many rows as there are trees in a row; how many rows are there?

Solution:

According to the given condition, number of rows in the orchard is equal to the number of trees in each row. Therefore, number of rows will be equal to square root of 5,625.

$$\begin{array}{r|l} & 75 \\ \hline 7 & 5625 \\ & 49 \\ \hline 145 & 725 \\ & 725 \\ \hline & \times \end{array}$$

$\therefore \sqrt{5,625} = 75$

Therefore, number of rows in the orchard = 75.

6. Find the square root of 22,801

Solution:

```
        151
    1 | 22801
        1
   25 | 128
        125
  301 |  301
         301
          ×
```

$\therefore \sqrt{22801} = 151$.

7. Find the square root of $4\frac{29}{49}$.

Solution:

$4\frac{29}{49} = \frac{225}{49}$

$\sqrt{\frac{225}{49}} = \frac{\sqrt{225}}{\sqrt{49}} = \frac{15}{7} = 2\frac{1}{7}$.

8. Find the least number which must be added to 624 to make it a perfect square.

Solution:

```
        24
    2 | 624
        4
   44 | 224
        176
         48
```

Now $25^2 = 625$

Therefore, the least number to be added is $625 - 624 = 1$.

9. Find the square root of .4 to two places of decimal.

Solution:

```
         .63
    6 | .4000
        36
  123 |  400
         369
          31
```

$\therefore \sqrt{.4} = .63$.

10. Find the least number which must be subtracted from 258 to make it a perfect square.

Solution:

```
        16
    1 | 258
        1
   26 | 158
        156
          2
```

Extracting the square root we get a remainder 2.

Hence, 2 is the least number which ought to be subtracted from 258 to make it a perfect square.

EXERCISE

1. The largest number of five digits which is a perfect square, is :
A. 99999   B. 99764
C. 99976   D. 99856

2. The value of $\sqrt{2}$ up to three places of decimals is :
A. 1.410   B. 1.412
C. 1.413   D. 1.414

3. $\dfrac{(\sqrt{7} + \sqrt{5})}{\sqrt{7} - \sqrt{5}}$ is equal to :
A. $6 + \sqrt{35}$ B. $6 - \sqrt{35}$
C. 2   D. 1

4. The least number by which 294 must be multiplied to make it a perfect square, is :
A. 2   B. 3
C. 6   D. 5

5. The least number to be added to 269 to make it a perfect square , is :
A. 31   B. 16
C. 7   D. 20

6. What is the smallest number by which 3600 be divided to make it a perfect cube?
A. 9   B. 50
C. 300   D. 450

7. The smallest number of 4 digits, which is a perfect square is :
A. 1000   B. 1016
C. 1024   D. 1036

8. $\sqrt{10} \times \sqrt{250} = ?$
A. 46.95   B. 43.75
C. 50.25   D. 50

9. $\sqrt{?}/200 = 0.02$
A. 0.4   B. 4
C. 16   D. 1.6

10. $\sqrt{.04} = ?$
A. .02   B. .2
C. .002   D. 1.2

11. The greatest number of four digits which is a perfect square, is :
A. 9996   B. 9801
C. 9900   D. 9604

12. $\sqrt[3]{?}/200 = 0.02$
A. 0.4   B. 64
C. 16   D. 1/64

13. If $\sqrt{256} \div \sqrt[3]{x} = 2$, then x is equal to :
A. 64   B. 128
C. 512   D. 1024

14. $112/\sqrt{196} \times \sqrt{576}/12 \times \sqrt{256}/8 = ?$
A. 8   B. 12
C. 16   D. 32

15. $(2\sqrt{27} - \sqrt{75} + \sqrt{12})$ is equal to :
A. $\sqrt{3}$ B. $2\sqrt{3}$
C. $3\sqrt{3}$ D. $4\sqrt{3}$

16. $\sqrt{50} \times \sqrt{98}$ is equal to :
A. 65.95   B. 63.75
C. 70.25   D. 70

17. The largest four-digit number which is a perfect cube, is :
A. 9999   B. 9261
C. 8000   D. 8467

18. If $\sqrt{2} = 1.4142$, the square root of $\dfrac{(\sqrt{2}-1)}{\sqrt{2}+1}$ is equal to :
A. 0.732   B. 0.3652
C. 1.3142   D. 0.4142

19. $\dfrac{\sqrt{121} \times 0.9}{1.1 \times 0.11} = ?$
A. 2   B. $\dfrac{900}{11}$
C. 9   D. 11

20. $\sqrt{25}/15625 = \sqrt{?}/30625$
A. 2   B. 3.5
C. 96.04   D. 1225

21. $\sqrt{3.61/10.24} = ?$
A. 29/32   B. 19/72
C. 19/32   D. 29/62

22. $\dfrac{\sqrt{32} + \sqrt{48}}{\sqrt{8} + \sqrt{12}} = ?$
A. $\sqrt{2}$ B. 2
C. 4   D. 8

23. $\dfrac{1}{\sqrt{9} - \sqrt{8}} = ?$
A. $1/2\,(3 - \sqrt{2})$ B. $1/3 + 2\sqrt{2}$
C. $(3 - 2\sqrt{2})$ D. $(3 + 2\sqrt{2})$

ANSWERS

1	2	3	4	5	6	7	8	9	10
D	D	A	C	D	D	C	D	C	B

11	12	13	14	15	16	17	18	19	20
B	B	C	D	C	D	B	D	B	C

21	22	23
C	B	D

EXPLANATORY ANSWERS

1. Largest number of 5 digits is 99999.

$$3 \overline{)\, 99999 \,} (\, 316$$
$$\underline{-9}$$
$$61 \overline{)\, 99 \,} ($$
$$\underline{-61}$$
$$626 \overline{)\, 3899 \,} ($$
$$\underline{\;3756\;}$$
$$-143$$

So, required number = (99999 − 143) = 99856.

2.
$$1 \overline{)\, 2.000000 \,} (\, 1.414$$
$$\underline{-1}$$
$$24 \overline{)\, 100 \,} ($$
$$\underline{-96}$$
$$281 \overline{)\, 400 \,} ($$
$$\underline{-281}$$
$$2824 \overline{)\, 11900 \,} ($$
$$\underline{-11296}$$

So, $\sqrt{2} = 1.414$.

3. $\dfrac{\sqrt{7}+\sqrt{5}}{\sqrt{7}-\sqrt{5}} = \dfrac{\sqrt{7}+\sqrt{5}}{\sqrt{7}-\sqrt{5}} \times \dfrac{\sqrt{7}+\sqrt{5}}{\sqrt{7}+\sqrt{5}}$

$= \dfrac{\left(\sqrt{7}+\sqrt{5}\right)^2}{7-5} = \dfrac{7+5+2\sqrt{7}\times\sqrt{5}}{2}$

$= \dfrac{12+2\sqrt{35}}{2} = 6 + \sqrt{35}$.

4. $294 = 7 \times 7 \times 2 \times 3$. To make it a perfect square it must be multiplied by 2×3, *i.e.,* 6.

5.
$$1 \overline{)\, 269 \,} (\, 16$$
$$\underline{-1}$$
$$26 \overline{)\, 169 \,} ($$
$$\underline{-156}$$
$$13$$

Required number to be added = $(17)^2 - 269 = 20$.

6. $3600 = 2 \times 2 \times 2 \times 2 \times 3 \times 3 \times 5 \times 5$.
To make it a perfect cube, we must divide it by $2 \times 5 \times 5 \times 3 \times 3 = 450$

7. Smallest number of 4 digits = 1000

$$3 \overline{)\, 1000 \,} (\, 31$$
$$\underline{-9}$$
$$61 \overline{)\, 100 \,} ($$
$$\underline{-61}$$
$$39$$

So, required number = $(32)^2 = 1024$.

8. $\sqrt{10} \times \sqrt{250} = \sqrt{2500} = 50$.

9. Let $\sqrt{x}/200 = 0.02$

Then, $\sqrt{x} = 200 \times 0.02 = 4$

So, $x = 16$.

10. $\sqrt{.04} = \sqrt{4/100} = 2/10 = 0.2$

11. Greatest number of four digits = 9999
Now, $9999 = (99)^2 + 198$
So, $(99)^2 = 9999 - 198 = 9801$,
So, required number = 9801.

12. Let $\sqrt[3]{x}/200 = 0.02$

Then, $\sqrt[3]{x} = 200 \times 0.02 = 4$

So, $x = 4 \times 4 \times 4 = 64$.

13. $\sqrt{256}/\sqrt[3]{x} = 2 \Rightarrow 16 = 2\sqrt[3]{x}$

$\Rightarrow \sqrt[3]{x} = 8 \Rightarrow x = 512$

14. Given expression
$= (112/14 \times 24/12 \times 16/8) = 32$

15. $2\sqrt{27} - \sqrt{75} + \sqrt{12}$

$= 2\sqrt{9 \times 3} - \sqrt{25 \times 3} + \sqrt{4 \times 3}$

$= 6\sqrt{3} - 5\sqrt{3} + 2\sqrt{3} = 3\sqrt{3}$

16. $\sqrt{50} \times \sqrt{98} = \sqrt{4900} = 70$

17. Clearly, 9261 is a perfect cube.

18. $\dfrac{\sqrt{2}-1}{\sqrt{2}+1} = \dfrac{\sqrt{2}-1}{\sqrt{2}+1} \times \dfrac{\sqrt{2}-1}{\sqrt{2}-1} = \dfrac{\left(\sqrt{2}-1\right)^2}{1}$

So $\sqrt{\dfrac{\sqrt{2}-1}{\sqrt{2}+1}} = \sqrt{2} - 1 = 1.4142 - 1 = 0.4142$.

19. Given expression $= \dfrac{\sqrt{121} \times 0.9}{1.1 \times 0.11}$

$$= \dfrac{11 \times 9 \times 1000}{11 \times 11 \times 10} = \dfrac{900}{11}$$

20. $\dfrac{\sqrt{25}}{15625} = \dfrac{\sqrt{x}}{30625} \Rightarrow \sqrt{x} = \dfrac{30625 \times 5}{15625} = 9.8$

$\therefore \quad x = 96.04.$

21. $\sqrt{3.61/10.24} = \sqrt{361/1024}$

$$\dfrac{\sqrt{19 \times 19}}{\sqrt{32 \times 32}} = \dfrac{19}{32}.$$

22. $\dfrac{\sqrt{32} + \sqrt{48}}{\sqrt{8} + \sqrt{12}} = \dfrac{\sqrt{16 \times 2} + \sqrt{16 \times 3}}{\sqrt{4 \times 2} + \sqrt{4 \times 3}}$

$$= \dfrac{4\sqrt{2} + 4\sqrt{3}}{2\sqrt{2} + 2\sqrt{3}} = \dfrac{4\left(\sqrt{2} + \sqrt{3}\right)}{2\left(\sqrt{2} + \sqrt{3}\right)} = \dfrac{4}{2} = 2.$$

23. $\dfrac{1}{\sqrt{9} - \sqrt{8}} = \dfrac{1}{\sqrt{9} - \sqrt{8}} \times \dfrac{\sqrt{9} + \sqrt{8}}{\sqrt{9} + \sqrt{8}}$

$$= \dfrac{3 + 2\sqrt{2}}{9 - 8} = 3 + 2\sqrt{2}.$$

6 UNITARY METHOD

The method by which we find the value of a unit is called Unitary Method.

SOLVED EXAMPLES

1. If one dozen note-books cost ₹ 42, find the cost of 5 note-books.

Solution:

1 dozen = 12 pieces

∵ Cost of 12 note-books = ₹ 42

∴ Cost of one note-book $= \dfrac{42}{12}$

∴ Cost 5 note-books $= \dfrac{42 \times 5}{12} = ₹ 17.50$.

2. A bullet travels at a speed of 99 meters per second. How many seconds will it take to travel 1 km 89 m.?

Solution:

1 km 89 m. = 1089 m.

Speed = 99 m/second

∵ The bullet travels 99 m. in one second

∴ It will travel 1 m. in $\dfrac{1}{99}$ second

∴ It will travel 1089 m. in

$\dfrac{1}{99} \times 1089 = 11$ seconds.

3. 4 men complete a piece of work in 3 days. In how many days one man will complete the same work?

Solution:

It is evident that one man will do the work in more days than 4 men.

∵ 4 men complete a work in 3 days

∴ 1 man will complete the work in 4 × 3 = 12 days.

4. A fort had provisions for 1200 men for 20 days. If 400 men joined the fort on the first day. How long would the food last at the same rate?

Solution:

1200 + 400 = 1600

∵ 1200 men can eat the food in 20 days

∴ 1 man can eat the food in 20 × 1200 days

∴ 1600 men can eat the food in

$\dfrac{20 \times 1200}{1600} = 15$ days.

5. The cost of 5 tables is the same as the cost of 7 chairs. If the cost of one table is ₹ 210 find the cost of a chair.

Solution:

Cost of 5 tables = Cost of 7 chairs.

∵ Cost of 1 table = ₹ 210

∴ Cost of 5 tables = 210 × 5 = ₹ 1050

∴ Cost of 7 chairs = 1050

∴ Cost of 1 chair = 1050 ÷ 7 = ₹ 150.

6. If 36 bags of wheat can be loaded in a truck. In how many trucks can 3,456 bags of wheat be loaded?

Solution:

∵ 36 bags can be loaded in 1 truck

∴ 1 bag can be loaded in $\dfrac{1}{36}$ truck

∴ 3,456 bags can be loaded in $= \dfrac{1}{36} \times 3456$

= 96 trucks.

7. 30 men can reap a field in 8 days. How many men can reap the field in 12 days?

Solution:

∵ For reaping in 8 days, men required = 30 men

∴ For reaping in 1 day men required = 30 × 8 men

∴ For reaping in 12 days men required

$= \dfrac{30 \times 8}{12} = 20$ men.

8. Ram can finish a work in 15 days and Shyam can finish it in 25 days. In how many days will they finish the work if working together?

Solution:

∵ Ram can finish the work in 15 days.

∴ Ram's 1 day's work $= \dfrac{1}{15}$

Similarly, Shyam's 1 day's work $= \dfrac{1}{25}$

∴ (Ram + Shyam)'s 1 days's work

$$= \dfrac{1}{15} + \dfrac{1}{25} = \dfrac{5+3}{75} = \dfrac{8}{75}$$

Hence, (Ram + Shyam) together will finish the work in $\dfrac{75}{8}$ days $= 9\dfrac{3}{8}$ days.

9. If two horses are worth 3 oxen and 5 oxen are worth 120 sheep and one sheep is worth ₹ 50, what is the price of a horse?

Solution:

∵ Price of 1 sheep = ₹ 50

∴ Price of 120 sheep = 50 × 120 = ₹ 6,000

∴ Price of 5 oxen = ₹ 6,000

∴ Price of 1 ox $= \dfrac{6000}{5} = ₹ 1,200$

∴ Price of 3 oxen = 1,200 × 3 = ₹ 3,600

∴ Price of 2 horses = ₹ 3,600

∴ Price of 1 horse $= \dfrac{3600}{2} = ₹ 1,800.$

10. Cost of 5 pencils is ₹ 25.50. Find the cost of 4 pencils.

Solution:

∵ Cost of 5 pencils = ₹ 25.50

∴ Cost of 1 pencil $= \dfrac{25.50}{5} = ₹ 5.10$

∴ Cost of 4 pencils = 5.10 × 4
= ₹ 20.40.

11. Find the cost of 465 quintals of Rice at ₹ 152 per quintal.

Solution:

∵ Cost of 1 quintal of Rice = ₹ 152

∴ Cost of 465 quintals of Rice = 465 × 152
= ₹ 70,680.

12. How many packets of 25 gm. each can be made out of 3 kg. of washing powder?

Solution:

3 kg. = 3,000 gm

∵ 25 gm. = 1 packet

∴ 1 gm. $= \dfrac{1}{25}$ packet

∴ 3000 gm $= \dfrac{1}{25} \times 3,000$ packet = 120 packets.

13. If 8 men can do a job in 10 days, then in how many days 4 men will do the same job?

Solution:

∵ 8 men can do a job in 10 days.

∴ 1 man can do the job in 10 × 8 = 80 days

∴ 4 men can do the same job in $\dfrac{80}{4} = 20$ days.

14. If 12 men or 18 women can reap a field in 7 days. In what time can 4 men and 8 women reap the same field?

Solution:

∵ 12 men = 18 women

∴ 1 man $= \dfrac{18}{12}$ women

∴ 4 men + 8 women

$$= 4 \times \dfrac{18}{12} \text{ women} + 8 \text{ women}$$

$$= 6 + 8 = 14 \text{ women}$$

∵ 18 women can reap a field in 7 days

∴ 1 woman can reap in 7 × 18 days

∴ 14 woman can reap that field in

$\dfrac{7 \times 18}{14}$ days = 9 days.

15. If 6 men or 9 boys can do a work in 8 days, then in how many days 8 men and 12 boys will finish the same work?

Solution:

∵ 6 men = 9 boys

∴ 1 man $= \dfrac{9}{6}$ boys

∴ 8 men $= \dfrac{3}{2} \times 8 = 12$ boys

Or, 8 men + 12 boys = 12 boys + 12 boys
= 24 boys

Now 9 boys can finish the work in = 8 days

1 boy can finish the work in = 8 × 9 = 72 days

∴ 24 boys can finish the work in $\dfrac{72}{24} = 3$ days

16. A fort has provision for 1,000 soldiers for 30 days. If 200 more soldiers join the camp, how long will the provision last?

Solution:

Original number of soldiers = 1,000

New soldiers = 200

Total soldiers = 1000 + 200 = 1,200

Now provision for 1,000 soldiers can last for
$$= 30 \text{ days}$$

provision for 1 soldier can last for
$$= 30 \times 1000 \text{ days}$$

and provision for 1200 soldiers can last for
$$= \frac{30 \times 1000}{1200} \text{ days} = 25 \text{ days.}$$

17. A can do a piece of work in 10 days and B can do it in 15 days. How long will they take if they work together?

Solution:

∵ A can do a piece of work in 10 days

∴ A will do $\frac{1}{10}$ of the work in 1 day

∴ B can do the same work in 15 days

∴ B will do $\frac{1}{15}$ of the work in 1 day

∴ Working together A and B will do $\left(\frac{1}{10} + \frac{1}{15}\right)$ of the work in 1 day $= \frac{3+2}{30} = \frac{5}{30}$ of the work in 1 day

∴ Working together A and B will finish the work in $= \frac{30}{5} = 6$ days.

18. If the cost of 3 quintal 30 kg. rice be ₹ 429, find the cost of 3 quintal rice.

Solution:

3 quintal 30 kg. = 330 kg.

3 quintal = 300 kg.

∵ Cost of 330 kg. rice = ₹ 429

∴ Cost of 1 kg. rice $= \frac{429}{330}$

∴ Cost of 300 kg. rice $= \frac{429}{330} \times 300 = ₹ 390.$

EXERCISE

1. Suresh can do a job in 6 days and Dinesh can do the same job in 8 days . Working together in how many days they will complete the same job?

A. $3\frac{2}{5}$ days   B. $3\frac{3}{7}$ days

C. $2\frac{1}{3}$ days   D. $3\frac{1}{5}$ days

2. 12 men or 18 women can reap a field in 14 days. How many days will 8 men and 16 women take to reap it?

A. 5 days   B. 7 days

C. 9 days   D. 8 days

3. How many meters of cloth at the rate of ₹ 50 per meter will be exchanged by a cloth merchant for $2\frac{1}{2}$ gm, gold at the rate of ₹ 2000 per 10 gm.?

A. 10 m   B. 8 m

C. 12 m   D. 9 m

4. A labour was engaged for 25 days on the condition that for every day, he works he will be paid ₹ 12 and for every day he is absent he will be fined ₹ 2. He received only ₹ 132. How many days did he not do the work?

A. 8 days   B. 10 days

C. 9 days   D. 12 days

5. A garrison of 1200 men has provision for 15 days. How long will the provisions last if the garrison be increased by 600 men?

A. 8 days   B. 10 days

C. 9 days   D. 11 days

6. A library charges 10 paise for the first day and 5 paise for each additional day that a book is overdue. If the borrower paid 65 paise for late charges, for how many days was the book over due?

A. 12 days   B. 9 days
C. 10 days   D. 8 days

7. If 24 men can do a piece of work in 24 days working 7 hours a day. In how many days will 42 men finished the same work, working 8 hours a day?
   A. 15 days   B. 11 days
   C. 12 days   D. 14 days

8. A grocer mixes 28 kg. of tea costing ₹ 15 per kg. with 12 kg. of tea costing ₹ 18 per kg. Find the cost of the mixture per kg.
   A. ₹ 16.20   B. ₹ 15.90
   C. ₹ 18.45   D. ₹ 14.80

9. If 30 men do a piece of work in 27 days, in what time can 18 men do another piece of work 3 times as great?
   A. 135 days   B. 140 days
   C. 125 days   D. 128 days

10. A man bought goods worth ₹ 480. He paid sales tax at the rate of ₹ 2 per hundred on his purchase. What was the total amount that he paid?
    A. ₹ 529.50   B. ₹ 499.80
    C. ₹ 489.60   D. ₹ 478.60

11. A boy gets ₹ 2 for every correct aim at a target and loses ₹ 0.50 for every aim missed. In a game of 8 trials he missed the aim 3 times. How much amount did he get?
    A. ₹ 9.50   B. ₹ 8.50
    C. ₹ 10.50   D. ₹ 7.50

12. A boy runs a km. in 7 min. 10 seconds. How long will he take to run 400 m.?
    A. 2 min 52 seconds B. 2 min 32 seconds
    C. 2 min 42 seconds D. 2 min 22 seconds

13. The cost of 4 chairs is the same as the cost of 3 tables. If the cost of one chair be ₹ 48, find the cost of one table.

A. ₹ 62   B. ₹ 72
C. ₹ 68   D. ₹ 64

14. Find the cost of 30 note-books at the rate of ₹ 20 per dozen.
    A. ₹ 45   B. ₹ 48
    C. ₹ 50   D. ₹ 55

15. A farmer had fodder for 40 animals for 60 days. He bought some more animals and the fodder lasted for 50 days. How many more animals did he buy?
    A. 6 animals   B. 8 animals
    C. 5 animals   D. 9 animals

16. 36 boys can do a piece of work in 49 days. How many extra boys should be engaged so that the work may be finished in 21 days?
    A. 48 boys   B. 44 boys
    C. 52 boys   D. 46 boys

17. A man spends ₹ 72 in 12 days. Find out by unitary method, in how many days he will spend ₹ 48?
    A. 6 days   B. 5 days
    C. 8 days   D. 10 days

18. An aeroplane travels 3,060 km. in 10 hours. How much time will it take to fly 1,683 km?
    A. $4\frac{1}{2}$ hrs   B. $5\frac{1}{2}$ hrs
    C. $6\frac{1}{2}$ hrs   D. $3\frac{1}{2}$ hrs

19. If 13 boxes of apples cost ₹ 845, find the cost of 49 boxes?
    A. ₹ 3185   B. ₹ 3165
    C. ₹ 3155   D. ₹ 3175

20. If 40 oranges cost ₹ 14, find the cost of 14 oranges.
    A. ₹ 4.75   B. ₹ 4.65
    C. ₹ 4.80   D. ₹ 4.90

ANSWERS

1	2	3	4	5	6	7	8	9	10
B	C	A	D	B	A	C	B	A	C

11	12	13	14	15	16	17	18	19	20
B	A	D	C	B	A	C	B	A	D

EXPLANATORY ANSWERS

1. In 1 day Suresh will do $\frac{1}{6}$ of the work

   In 1 day Dinesh will do $\frac{1}{8}$ of the work

   Working together they will do $\frac{1}{6} + \frac{1}{8}$

   $= \frac{4+3}{24} = \frac{7}{24}$ of the work

   Thus, they will take $\frac{24}{7}$ days $= 3\frac{3}{7}$ days to complete the work if they work together.

2. $\because$ 12 men = 18 women

   $\therefore$ 8 men $= \frac{18 \times 8}{12}$ women = 12 women

   8 men and 16 women = 12 women + 16 women
   $= 28$ women

   Now 18 women can reap a field in 14 days
   $\therefore$ 28 women will reap the field in

   $= \frac{18 \times 14}{28} = 9$ days.

3. Cost of 10 gm. gold = ₹ 2000

   Cost of 1 gm. gold $= \frac{2000}{10}$

   $\therefore$ Cost of $\frac{5}{2}$ gm. gold $= \frac{2000 \times 5}{2 \times 10} = $ ₹ 500

   $\because$ Cost of 1 m. cloth = ₹ 50

   $\therefore$ We can get $\frac{500}{50} = 10$ metre cloth for ₹ 500

   Thus, we can get 10 m. cloth for the exchange of gold.

4. Let the labour was absent for x days
   Total no of working days = 25 – x
   Money received by the labourer
   $= (25 - x) \times 12 = $ ₹ $(300 - 12x)$.
   Money paid by the labourer as fine $= x \times 2$
   $= $ ₹ $2x$

   $300 - 12x - 2x = 132$
   $\therefore \qquad -14x = 132 - 300$
   $\therefore \qquad -14x = -168$
   $\therefore x = 12$
   Thus, labourer was absent for 12 days.

5. $1200 + 600 = 1800$
   1200 men finished the food in 15 days
   $\therefore$ 1 man will finish the food in
   $= 15 \times 1200$ days
   $\therefore$ 1800 men will finish the food in

   $= \frac{15 \times 1200}{1800}$

   $= 10$ days.

6. Total fine = ₹ 0.65
   Fine for first day = ₹ 0.10
   Fine for the remaining days = .65 – .10 = 0.55
   No of days for which he paid fine after first

   day $= \frac{.55}{.05} = 11$

   Thus, total days = 11 + 1 = 12.

7. Let 42 men finish the work in x day 24 men finish a work in 24 × 7 hours.
   $\therefore$ 42 men will finish the work in

   $= \frac{24 \times 7 \times 24}{42} = 96$ hours.

   $\therefore \qquad x \times 8 = 96$

   $\therefore \qquad x = \frac{96}{8} = 12$ days.

8. Cost of 28 kg. of tea at the rate of ₹ 15 per kg. = 28 × 15 = ₹ 420
   Cost of 12 kg. of tea at the rate of ₹ 18 per kg. = 12 × 18 = ₹ 216
   Total weight of the tea = 28 + 12 = 40 kg.
   total cost = 420 + 216 = 636
   $\therefore$ Cost of the mixture per kg.

   $= \frac{636}{40} = $ ₹ 15.90.

9. $\because$ 30 men do a work in 27 days
   $\therefore$ 1 man will do the work = 27 × 30
   $\therefore$ 18 men will do the work in

   $= \frac{27 \times 30}{18} = 45$ days

   But they have to do thrice of the work.
   Hence they will take 45 × 3 = 135 days.

10. Sales tax paid $= \dfrac{2 \times 480}{100} = ₹\,9.60.$

∴ Total amount paid $= 480 + 9.60$
$= ₹\,489.60.$

11. No. of trials = 8
No. of correct aims = 8 − 3 = 5
No. of missed aims = 3
Thus, the boy will get $(5 \times 2 - 0.50 \times 3)$
$= 10 - 1.50$
$= ₹\,8.50$

12. 7 minutes 10 seconds $= (60 \times 7 + 10)$ seconds
$= 430$ seconds

1 km = 1000 metres
Now for running 1000 m. the boy takes 430 seconds
∴ For running 1m. the boy will take

$= \dfrac{430}{1000}$ seconds

∴ For running 400 m. the boy will take

$= \dfrac{430 \times 400}{1000} = 172$ seconds

$= 2$ minutes 52 seconds.

13. Cost of 4 chairs = Cost of 3 tables
Cost of one chair = ₹ 48
∴ Cost of 4 chairs = 4 × 48
∴ Cost of 3 table = 4 × 48

∴ Cost of one table $= \dfrac{4 \times 48}{3} = ₹\,64.$

14. Cost of 12 note-books = ₹ 20

∴ Cost of 1 note-book $= \dfrac{20}{12}$

∴ Cost of 30 note-books

$= \dfrac{20 \times 30}{12} = ₹\,50$

15. Number of animals $= \dfrac{40 \times 60}{50} = 48$

Thus, he bought 48 − 40 = 8 extra animals.

16. In 49 days 36 boys do the work

∴ In 1 days 36 × 49 boys will do the work

∴ In 21 days $= \dfrac{36 \times 49}{21} = 84$ boys will do
the work
Thus, (84 − 36) = 48 extra boys should be engaged.

17. A man spends ₹ 72 in 12 days

A man spends ₹ 48 in $\dfrac{12}{72}$ days

A man spends ₹ 1 in $\dfrac{12}{72} \times 48$ days = 8 days.

18. An aeroplane travels 3060 km in 10 hrs

An aeroplane travels 1 km in $\dfrac{10}{3060}$ hrs

An aeroplane travels 1683 km in

$\dfrac{10}{3060} \times 1683$ hrs

$= \dfrac{11}{2}$ hrs $= 5\dfrac{1}{2}$ hrs.

19. ∵ Cost of 13 boxes of apples = ₹ 845

∴ Cost of 1 box of apples $= ₹\,\dfrac{845}{13}$

∴ Cost of 49 boxes of apples $= ₹\,\dfrac{845}{13} \times 49$

$= 65 \times 49 = ₹\,3185.$

20. ∵ Cost of 40 oranges = ₹ 14

∴ Cost of 1 orange $= ₹\,\dfrac{14}{40}$

∴ Cost of 14 orange $= ₹\,\dfrac{14}{40} \times 14 = \dfrac{49}{10}$

$= ₹\,4.90.$

 **PERCENTAGE**

A fraction, whose denominator is 100, is called a percentage and the numerator of the fraction is called the rate percent. It is usually denoted by %.

SOLVED EXAMPLES

1. Find 15% of ₹ 200

Solution:

$$15\% \text{ of } ₹ 200 = \frac{15 \times 200}{100}$$
$$= ₹ 30$$

2. Vikas had ₹ 250. He spent ₹ 50 on the books. Find his per cent expenditure.

Solution:

∵ Out of ₹ 250, the expenditure = ₹ 50

∴ Out of ₹ 1, the expenditure $= \dfrac{50}{250}$

∴ Out of ₹ 100, the expenditure

$$= \frac{50 \times 100}{250} = 20\%.$$

3. Find [5% of ₹ 400 + 10% of ₹ 350]

Solution:

5% of ₹ 400 + 10% of ₹ 350

$$= \frac{5 \times 400}{100} + \frac{10}{100} \times 350$$

$$= 20 + 35 = ₹ 55.$$

4. Find 15% of 75

Solution:

$$15\% \text{ of } 75 = \frac{15}{100} \times 75 = \frac{45}{4} = 11.25$$

Hence, 15% of 75 is 11.25.

5. Population of a town increases 25% per year. If the population of the town this year is 3,50,000, find the population of the town after two years.

Solution:

Increase in population = 25%

It means that if the population of the town is 100, its population will be 125 after one year

∴ If population of the town is 3,50,000 this year

Its population after one year will be

$$= \frac{125 \times 3,50,000}{100} = 4,37,500$$

∴ Population of the town after one more year

$$= \frac{125}{100} \times 437500$$

$$= 546875.$$

6. The population of a certain town has increased from 70,000 to 75,000. Find the increas per cent.

Solution:

Increase in population = 75000 − 70000 = 5000

Percentage increase $= \dfrac{5000 \times 100}{70,000} = \dfrac{50}{7}\%$

$$= 7\frac{1}{7}\%.$$

7. In a school, there are 300 students. Out of them, there are 40% girls. Find the number of boys and girls in the school.

Solution:

Girls students = 40%

Number of girls $= \dfrac{40}{100} \times 300 = 120$

∴ Number of boys = 300 − 120 = 180.

8. Neeraj's salary is 15% more than Dheeraj's salary. If Dheeraj's salary is ₹ 1200, find Neeraj's salary.

Solution:

Neeraj's salary is 15% more than Dheeraj's salary.

If Dheeraj's salary is ₹ 100 Neeraj's salary

$$= ₹ 115$$

∴ If Dheeraj's salary is Re 1, Neeraj's salary

$$= ₹ \frac{115}{100}$$

∴ When Dheeraj's salary is ₹ 1200, Neeraj's

salary $= \frac{115 \times 1200}{100} = ₹ 1380.$

9. When a solid is immersed in water, standing to a height of 24 cm. in vessel, the water level was raised $\frac{1}{4}$ of its height. What is the percentage of increase in height? What is the present height?

Solution:

Height of water level = 24 cm.

Water level raised $= \frac{1}{4} \times 24 = 6$ cm.

Hence, percentage increase in water level

$= \frac{6}{24} \times 100 = 25\%$

Also, present water level = 24 cm. + 6 cm.

= 30 cm.

10. A's salary is 90% of B's salary. If B's salary be ₹ 14560, find A's salary.

Solution:

∵ A's salary is 90% of B's salary, It means that if B's salary is ₹ 100, A's salary = ₹ 90

∴ When B's salary is Re. 1, A's salary $= \frac{90}{100}$

∴ When B's salary is ₹ 14560, A's salary

$$= \frac{90 \times 14560}{100} = ₹ 13104.$$

11. A shopkeeper marks an article for ₹ 250. He gives 12% discount for cash payment. How much does a customer have to pay while paying in cash?

Solution:

Marked price = ₹ 250

Discount $= \frac{12}{100} \times 250 = ₹ 30$

∴ Customer will pay = 250 – 30 = ₹ 220.

12. A shirt originally priced at ₹ 80 is reduced to ₹ 70. What is the decrease percent?

Solution:

Reduction = 80 – 70 = ₹ 10

On ₹ 80, the reduction = ₹ 10

On Re. 1, the reduction $= \frac{10}{80}$

On ₹ 100, the reduction $= \frac{10}{80} \times 100 = \frac{25}{2}\%$

$$= 12\frac{1}{2}\%.$$

EXERCISE

1. Find the sum whose 20% is ₹ 240.
   A. ₹ 1200　　　　B. ₹ 800
   C. ₹ 1000　　　　D. ₹ 1600

2. After spending 69% of her money, a lady has ₹ 93 left. How much had she first?
   A. ₹ 250　　　　B. ₹ 350
   C. ₹ 300　　　　D. ₹ 800

3. A boy spends 30% of his pocket money and had ₹ 4.90 left. How much pocket money did he get?
   A. ₹ 8　　　　B. ₹ 6
   C. ₹ 5　　　　D. ₹ 7

4. Out of 200 candidates who appeared in a certain examination, 25% were not successful. How many candidates were successful?
   A. 150　　　　B. 145
   C. 140　　　　D. 160

5. A shopkeeper marks an article for ₹ 300. He gives 5% discount for cash payment. How much does a customer has to pay while paying in cash?
   A. ₹ 275　　　　B. ₹ 285
   C. ₹ 265　　　　D. ₹ 280

6. A's salary is 50% more than B's salary. If B's salary is ₹ 1500, find the salary of A.

A. ₹ 2500. B. ₹ 2400
C. ₹ 2250 D. ₹ 2350

7. A man bought goods worth ₹ 60. He paid sales tax at the rate of 9% of his purchases. What was the total amount that he paid?
A. ₹ 61.50 B. ₹ 62.40
C. ₹ 64.50 D. ₹ 65.40

8. 6% of the soldiers of an army were killed in a war. If 282 soldiers are still alive, find the number of soldier killed in the war.
A. 15 B. 18
C. 16 D. 17

9. The price of butter is ₹ 25 per kg. Find the cost of 4 kg. butter if the price increases by 40% per kg.
A. ₹ 140 B. ₹ 145
C. ₹ 150 D. ₹ 135

10. The population of a city has increased from 50,000 to 60,000. Find the increase per cent.
A. 18% B. 20%
C. 25% D. 15%

11. Find 8% of ₹ 400 + 5% of ₹ 200.
A. ₹ 38 B. ₹ 42
C. ₹ 45 D. ₹ 40

12. A earns 20% more than B. If B earns ₹ 40, find the earnings of A.
A. ₹ 40 B. ₹ 50
C. ₹ 45 D. ₹ 48

13. A candidate who gets 220 marks fails by 11 marks. Maximum marks are 700. Find the pass percentage.
A. 33% B. 34%
C. 36% D. 32%

14. A labourer gets ₹ 10 per day. He saves 20% of his monthly earnings. Find his savings in a year.
A. ₹ 690 B. ₹ 720
C. ₹ 735 D. ₹ 700

15. The population of a village is 4,500. If 11/18th of them are males and the rest females; find the percentage of females.
A. $38\frac{8}{9}\%$ B. $37\frac{8}{9}\%$
C. $39\frac{8}{9}\%$ D. $35\frac{8}{9}\%$

16. A trader weights 800 gm. in place of a kg. weight. Find the error per cent committed by the trader.
A. 15% B. 18%
C. 20% D. 25%

17. An agent sells goods of value ₹ 1600. What is his commission at 25%?
A. ₹ 375 B. ₹ 425
C. ₹ 300 D. ₹ 400

18. A chair which cost, ₹ 30 last year, cost 10% less at present. What is the cost of the chair at present?
A. ₹ 27 B. ₹ 25
C. ₹ 28 D. ₹ 30

19. A man saves 20% of his salary. If he saves ₹ 50 per month, what is his salary?
A. ₹ 225 B. ₹ 250
C. ₹ 275 D. ₹ 245

20. The population of a town is 32,000. It increases 15 per cent annually. What will it be in 2 years?
A. 40440 B. 42000
C. 42320 D. 41430

ANSWERS

1	2	3	4	5	6	7	8	9	10
A	C	D	A	B	C	D	B	A	B

11	12	13	14	15	16	17	18	19	20
B	D	A	B	A	C	D	A	B	C

EXPLANATORY ANSWERS

1. Let the sum be ₹ x

   $\therefore \dfrac{20x}{100} = 240$

   $\therefore x = \dfrac{240 \times 100}{20} = 1200$

   $\therefore x = ₹ 1200.$

2. Expenditure = 69%
   Saving = 100 – 69 = 31%
   If savings are ₹ 31 total amount = ₹ 100
   $\therefore$ When savings are ₹ 93 total amount

   $= \dfrac{100 \times 93}{31} = ₹ 300$

3. Expenditure = 30%
   Saving = 100 – 30 = 70%
   When he saves ₹ 4.90 his pocket money

   $= \dfrac{100 \times 4.90}{70} = ₹ 7$

4. Number of successful candidates

   $= \dfrac{75 \times 200}{100} = 150$

5. Discount = 5%
   It means that an article of ₹ 100 will be sold for ₹ 95
   $\therefore$ Article worth ₹ 300 will be sold for

   $= \dfrac{95 \times 300}{100} = ₹ 285$

6. A's salary = 50% more than B's salary
   $\therefore$ When B earns ₹ 100, A earns ₹ 150
   $\therefore$ When B's salary is ₹ 1500, A's salary

   $= \dfrac{150 \times 1500}{100} = ₹ 2250$

7. Sales Tax. $= \dfrac{9}{100} \times 60 = ₹ 5.40$

   $\therefore$ Total amount paid = 60 + 5.40 = ₹ 65.40

8. Soldiers killed = 6%
   Soldiers alive = 100 – 6 = 94%
   When 94 soldiers are alive number of soldiers killed = 6

   When number of soldiers alive is 282, number of soldiers killed in the war $= \dfrac{6 \times 282}{94} = 18$

9. Increase in price = 40%
   Original price of 1 kg. butter = ₹ 25

   New price of 1 kg. butter $= \dfrac{140 \times 25}{100} = ₹ 35$

   Cost of 4 kg. butter = 35 × 4 = ₹ 140

10. Increase in population = 6000 – 5000 = 1000

    $\therefore$ Increase per cent $= \dfrac{1000 \times 100}{5000} = 20\%$

11. 8% of ₹ 400 + 5% of ₹ 200

    $= \dfrac{8}{100} \times 400 + \dfrac{5}{100} \times 200$
    = 32 + 10 = ₹ 42

12. A's earning = 20% more than B's earning
    $\therefore$ When B earns ₹ 100, A earns ₹ 120
    When B earns ₹ 40, A earns

    $= \dfrac{120 \times 40}{100} = ₹ 48$

13. Pass marks = 220 + 11 = 231
    In 700 full marks, pass marks = 231
    $\therefore$ In 100 full marks, pass marks

    $= \dfrac{231 \times 100}{700} = 33\%$

14. Monthly earning = 30 × 10 = ₹ 300

    Monthly saving $= \dfrac{20 \times 300}{100}$

    $\therefore$ Labourer's yearly saving = 12 × 60 = ₹ 720.

15. Population of the village = 4500

    No. of males $= \dfrac{11}{18} \times 4500 = 2750$

    $\therefore$ No. of females = 4500 – 2750 = 1750
    $\therefore$ Percentage of females

    $= \dfrac{1750 \times 100}{4500} = 38\dfrac{8}{9}\%$

16. 1 kg. = 1000 gms.
    Error = 1000 – 800 = 200 gms.

42

On weighing 1000 gms. error = 200 gms.

∴ Per cent error = $\dfrac{200 \times 100}{1000} = 20\%$

17. Commission = 25%

∴ Agents commission = $\dfrac{25 \times 1600}{100} = ₹\ 400.$

18. Reduction = 10%
Cost of the chair at the present

$= \dfrac{90 \times 30}{100} = ₹\ 27.$

19. When man's saving is ₹ 20 his income
= ₹ 100

∴ When man's saving is ₹ 50 his income

$= \dfrac{100 \times 50}{20} = ₹\ 250$

20. Increase in population = 15% per year.
∴ Population of the town = 32000
∴ Population of the town after 1 year

$= \dfrac{115 \times 32000}{100} = 36800$

∴ Population of the town after 2 years

$= \dfrac{115 \times 36800}{100} = 42320.$

 **SIMPLE INTEREST**

Simple Interest: If the interest is paid, as it falls due, it is called simple interest. It is denoted by S.I.

Suppose I borrow a sum of ₹ 200 from a money lender and return it after one year. After the end of one year, I return the sum of ₹ 200 to the money lender with some extra money say ₹ 20. The sum of money borrowed by me is called "Principal". ₹ 20 is called simple interest and ₹ 220 is called amount. I paid ₹ 20 as simple interest on ₹ 200.

If A stands for amount; P stands for Principal; I stands for Simple interest; T stands for Time (in years); R stands for Rate per cent per year (per annum); the following relations may be remembered.

REMEMBER	
1. $I = \dfrac{P \times R \times T}{100}$	2. $R = \dfrac{100 \times I}{P \times T}$
3. $P = \dfrac{100 \times I}{R \times T}$	4. $P = \dfrac{100A}{100 + RT}$
5. $T = \dfrac{100 \times I}{P \times R}$	6. Amount = P + I

SOLVED EXAMPLE

1. In how many years, will ₹ 4,000 amount to ₹ 4,480 at 6% per annum?

Solution:

Here P = ₹ 4,000; R = 6%; T = ?

A = ₹ 4,480

∴ I = ₹ 4480 – 4000 = ₹ 480

Hence, $T = \dfrac{I \times 100}{P \times R} = \dfrac{480 \times 100}{4,000 \times 6} = 2$ years.

2. Find the interest on ₹ 500 for 4 years at 6% per annum.

Solution:

P = ₹ 500. R = 6%, T = 4 years.

∴ Simple Interest $= \dfrac{P \times R \times T}{100}$

$= \dfrac{500 \times 6 \times 4}{100} = ₹ 120.$

3. ₹ 1,800 amounts to ₹ 2,250 in $2\dfrac{1}{2}$ years. Find the rate percent.

Solution:

P = ₹ 1,800

A = ₹ 2,250

∴ I = A – P

$= 2250 – 1800 = ₹ 450$

Time $= 2\dfrac{1}{2}$ years $= \dfrac{5}{2}$ years.

$R = \dfrac{100 \times S.I}{P \times T} = \dfrac{100 \times 450 \times 2}{1,800 \times 5} = 10\%.$

4. Simple interest on a sum at $3\dfrac{1}{2}\%$ per annum in 4 years is ₹ 70. Find the sum.

Solution:

Here P = ?; I = ₹ 70, T = 4 year

$R = 3\dfrac{1}{2}\% = \dfrac{7}{2}\%$

∴ $P = \dfrac{I \times 100}{R \times T} = ₹ \dfrac{70 \times 100}{\dfrac{7}{2} \times 4}$

$= \dfrac{70 \times 100}{14} = ₹ 500.$

5. At what rate per cent, simple interest will a certain sum of money double itself in 20 years?

Solution:

Let the principal be ₹ 100

Amount = ₹ 200

∴ Interest = 200 – 100 = ₹ 100

T = 20 years.

∴ $R = \dfrac{100 \times I}{P \times T} \Rightarrow R = \dfrac{100 \times 100}{100 \times 20}$

= 5%.

6. What sum of money lent for 3 years at 4% per year will amount to ₹ 392?

Solution:

Time = 3 years, R = 4%

Let principal be ₹ 100

$I = \dfrac{P \times R \times T}{100}$

$I = \dfrac{100 \times 4 \times 3}{100} = ₹ 12$

∴ Amount = ₹ 100 + 12 = ₹ 112

∴ When amount is ₹ 112, principal = ₹ 100

∴ When amount is ₹ 392, principal

$= \dfrac{100 \times 392}{112}$

= ₹ 350.

7. Prakash deposited ₹ 400 in a bank and at the end of 5 years received ₹ 80 as interest. What is the rate percent?

Solution:

P = ₹ 400, T = 5 year, S.I. = ₹ 80

$R = \dfrac{100 \times S.I}{P \times T} = \dfrac{100 \times 80}{400 \times 5} = 4\%.$

8. In what time will ₹ 500 amount to ₹ 1,000 at 5% per year?

Solution:

P = ₹ 500, Amount = ₹ 1000

∴ I = A – P = 1000 – 500 = ₹ 500

R = 5%

$Time = \dfrac{100 \times I}{P \times R} = \dfrac{100 \times 500}{500 \times 5} = 20 \text{ years}.$

9. At what rate per cent, simple interest ₹ 1 will amount to ₹ 9 in 60 years?

Solution:

P = ₹ 1, T = 60 years, R = ?

A = ₹ 9

∴ I = 9 – 1 = ₹ 8

Hence, $R = \dfrac{I \times 100}{P \times T} = \dfrac{8 \times 100}{1 \times 60}$

$= \dfrac{40}{3}\% = 13\dfrac{1}{3}\%.$

10. A man borrowed ₹ 875 for a period of $3\dfrac{1}{2}$ years at the rate of 5% simple interest per annum. After the fixed time he cleared of his debt by paying ₹ 200 in cash and a bicycle. Find the price of the bicycle.

Solution:

$P = ₹ 875, R = 5\%, T = \dfrac{7}{2} \text{ years}$

$I = \dfrac{PRT}{100}$

$I = \dfrac{875 \times 5 \times 7}{100 \times 2} = \dfrac{1,225}{8} = 153.125$

= ₹ 153.13 (nearly)

Amount = Principal + Interest

= ₹ 875 + ₹ 153.13

= ₹ 1,028.13

Cash Payment = ₹ 200

∴ Price of bicycle = 1,028.13 – 200

= ₹ 828.13.

11. Find the simple interest on ₹ 1,000 from 2nd July to 12 September, 2006 at 4% per year.

Solution:

Number of days from 2nd July to 12 September, 2006:

July + August + September = 30 + 31 + 12

= 73 days.

Principal = ₹ 1000, Rate = 4%

$Time = \dfrac{73}{365} \text{ year} = \dfrac{1}{5} \text{ year}$

$$\because \text{S. I} = \frac{P \times R \times T}{100}$$

$$\therefore \text{S. I} = \frac{1000 \times 4 \times 1}{5 \times 100}$$

$$\therefore \text{S. I} = ₹ 8$$

Amount = P + S. I = 1000 + 8 = ₹ 1008.

12. In what time, will the interest on ₹ 2,600 amount to ₹ 288 at 8% per annum?

Solution:

P = ₹ 2,600, R = 8%, S. I = ₹ 288

$$\text{Time} = \frac{100 \times \text{S. I}}{P \times R} = \frac{100 \times 288}{2,600 \times 8} = \frac{18}{13} \text{ years}$$

$$= 1\frac{5}{13} \text{ years.}$$

13. Pramod took ₹ 1,100 from Ajay at 8% interest per year. How much will he return to Ajay after six months?

Solution:

Here, P = ₹ 1,100; R = 8%

$$T = 6 \text{ months} = \frac{1}{2} \text{ years}$$

$$\therefore I = \frac{P \times R \times T}{100} = \frac{1100 \times 8 \times 1}{100 \times 2} = ₹ 44.$$

14. Find the principal that shall earn interest of ₹ 60 at 6% per annum in 5 years.

Solution:

I = ₹ 60, R = 6%, T = 5 years.

$$P = \frac{100 \times I}{R \times T} \Rightarrow P = \frac{100 \times 60}{6 \times 5} = ₹ 200.$$

15. Prabhat deposited ₹ 1,000 in a bank which gives simple interest at 6% per annum. He withdrew ₹ 650 after 3 years. How much is left in his account after 3 years?

Solution:

P = ₹ 1,000, R = 6%, T = 3 years.

$$\text{Simple Interest} = \frac{P \times R \times T}{100}$$

$$= \frac{1000 \times 6 \times 3}{100} = ₹ 180$$

Amount = 1000 + 180 = ₹ 1,180

Thus, after 3 years Prabhat was having ₹ 1,180 in his account

$\because$ Prabhat withdrew ₹ 650 from the bank

$\therefore$ Remaining money in his account

$$= ₹ 1180 - ₹ 650 = ₹ 530.$$

EXERCISE

1. What sum of money lent out at 9% for 3 years will produce ₹ 81 simple interest?
   A. ₹ 225
   B. ₹ 250
   C. ₹ 300
   D. ₹ 325

2. What sum of money will amount to ₹ 900 in 4 years at 5%?
   A. ₹ 650
   B. ₹ 750
   C. ₹ 675
   D. ₹ 775

3. A money lender lends money, collecting 5 paise per rupee per month. Find the rate of interest per annum per cent.
   A. 60%
   B. 50%
   C. 40%
   D. 70%

4. A sum of ₹ 200 is deposited in the post office at the rate of $5\frac{1}{2}$% simple interest per annum. What will be the total amount after 2 years?
   A. ₹ 550
   B. ₹ 345
   C. ₹ 255
   D. ₹ 222

5. Find the simple interest on ₹ 1500 for 219 days at 6% per year.
   A. ₹ 54
   B. ₹ 64
   C. ₹ 50
   D. ₹ 60

6. Find the simple interest on ₹ 120 for 7 months at 5% per annum.
   A. ₹ 2.50
   B. ₹ 3.50
   C. ₹ 4.50
   D. ₹ 5.50

7. Find the interest on ₹ 600 for 2 years at the rate of 2 paise per rupee per month.
   A. ₹ 275
   B. ₹ 278
   C. ₹ 288
   D. ₹ 285

8. A sum of money invested at 5 per cent simple interest amounts to ₹ 1,380 in $2\frac{1}{2}$ years at the rate of 6% per year. Find the sum.
   A. ₹ 1000
   B. ₹ 1100
   C. ₹ 1300
   D. ₹ 1200

9. A money lender lends money, collecting 2 paise per rupee per month. Find the rate of interest per cent per year.
   A. 15%
   B. 24%
   C. 25%
   D. 18%

10. If in 10 years ₹ 150 amounts ₹ 200, find the rate of simple interest.

    A. $3\frac{1}{3}\%$
    B. $4\frac{1}{2}\%$

    C. $3\frac{1}{2}\%$
    D. $4\frac{1}{3}\%$

11. In how many years will a sum of ₹ 400 yield an interest of ₹ 112 at 14% per annum.
    A. 3 years
    B. 4 years
    C. 2 years
    D. 5 years

12. Satyendra borrowed ₹ 450 from Raju. After two years, he cleared the account by paying ₹ 549 to Raju. Find the rate of interest.
    A. 8%
    B. 9%
    C. 10%
    D. 11%

13. Abhishek borrowed ₹ 750 for a period of 6 years at the rate of 4% per annum. After fixed time, he cleared of his debt by paying ₹ 300 in cash and a radio set. Find the price of the radio set.

A. ₹ 580
B. ₹ 630
C. ₹ 625
D. ₹ 595

14. Kalam borrowed ₹ 500 from a bank. If the bank charges interest at 6% per year, how much amount shall Kalam pay after 2 years?
    A. ₹ 560
    B. ₹ 575
    C. ₹ 600
    D. ₹ 540

15. A sum of money amounts to ₹ 910 at 5% per year in 6 years. Find the principal.
    A. ₹ 500
    B. ₹ 600
    C. ₹ 700
    D. ₹ 400

16. A sum of ₹ 800 is deposited in a bank at the rate of 5% simple interest per annum. In how many years will this sum become ₹ 1,000?
    A. 4 years
    B. 5 years
    C. 3 years
    D. 6 years

17. Manoj borrowed ₹ 1,500 at 8% per annum from his friend and returned the whole amount after 10 months. What amount did he repay?
    A. ₹ 1200
    B. ₹ 1400
    C. ₹ 1500
    D. ₹ 1600

18. Find the principal that shall earn interest of ₹ 60 at 6% per annum in 5 years.
    A. ₹ 200
    B. ₹ 250
    C. ₹ 180
    D. ₹ 225

19. In what time will ₹ 50 amount to ₹ 55 at 4 per cent per annum simple interest?

    A. $3\frac{1}{2}$ years
    B. $2\frac{1}{2}$ years

    C. $4\frac{1}{2}$ years
    D. $5\frac{1}{2}$ years

20. What is the rate of simple interest when ₹ 1,875 amounts to ₹ 2,325 in 4 years?
    A. 3%
    B. 4%
    C. 6%
    D. 5%

ANSWERS

1	2	3	4	5	6	7	8	9	10
C	B	A	D	A	B	C	D	B	A

11	12	13	14	15	16	17	18	19	20
C	D	B	A	C	B	D	A	B	C

EXPLANATORY ANSWERS

1. Simple Interest = ₹ 81, R = 9%, T = 3 years

$$P = \frac{100 \times S.\,I}{T \times R}$$

$$= \frac{100 \times 81}{3 \times 9} = 300$$

∴ P = ₹ 300.

2. Let the sum be ₹ 100, T = 4 years, R = 5%

Simple Interest $= \dfrac{100 \times 5 \times 4}{100} = ₹\ 20$

Amount = 100 + 20 = ₹ 120

∴ If amount is ₹ 900 sum

$$= \frac{100 \times 900}{120} = ₹\ 750.$$

3. 5 P per month = 5 × 12 = 60 P per year.

∴ Rate % $= \dfrac{60}{100} \times 100 = 60\%$

4. P = ₹ 200, R $= \dfrac{11}{2}$%, T = 2 years

∴ Simple Interest $= \dfrac{200 \times 11 \times 2}{2 \times 100} = ₹\ 22$

A = P + S.I.

= ₹ 200 + ₹ 22

∴ Amount = ₹ 222

5. P = ₹ 1500, R = 6%, T $= \dfrac{219}{365}$ years.

∴ Simple Interest $= \dfrac{1500 \times 6 \times 219}{365 \times 100} = ₹\ 54.$

6. P = ₹ 120, R = 5%, T $= \dfrac{7}{12}$ years.

∴ S. I $= \dfrac{120 \times 5 \times 7}{12 \times 100} = ₹\ 3.50.$

7. Rate = 2 Paise per rupee per month

= 24 Paise per rupee per year

$$= \frac{24}{100} \times 100 = 24\%$$

∴ S. I $= \dfrac{600 \times 2 \times 24}{100} = ₹\ 288.$

8. Let the sum be Rs. 100

Simple Interest $= \dfrac{100 \times 5 \times 6}{2 \times 100} = ₹\ 15$

∴ Amount = 100 + 15 = ₹ 115

When amount is ₹ 1380 sum

$$= \frac{100 \times 1380}{115} = ₹\ 1200.$$

9. Rate of interest per cent = 2 Paise × 12 per rupee per year

= 24 Paise per rupee per year

$$= ₹\ \frac{24}{100} \times 100 \text{ per year}$$

= 24%

10. P = ₹ 150, Amount = ₹ 200

∴ S. I = 200 – 150 = ₹ 50

Time = 10 years

$$R = \frac{100 \times S.\,I}{P \times T} \Rightarrow R = \frac{100 \times 50}{150 \times 10} = 3\frac{1}{3}\%$$

11. P = ₹ 400; Interest = ₹ 112, Rate = 14%

$$T = \frac{100 \times S.\,I}{P \times R} \Rightarrow T = \frac{100 \times 112}{400 \times 14} = 2 \text{ years}$$

12. P = ₹ 450, A = ₹ 549

Simple Interest = 549 – 450 = ₹ 99

Time = 2 years

$$R = \frac{100 \times S.\,I}{P \times T}$$

$$R = \frac{100 \times 99}{450 \times 2} = 11\%$$

13. P = ₹ 750, R = 4%, T = 6 years.

Simple Interest $= \dfrac{750 \times 4 \times 6}{100} = ₹\ 180$

Amount = 750 + 180 = ₹ 930

Now ₹ 300 + Cost of radio set = ₹ 930

∴ Cost of radio set = 930 – 300

= ₹ 630

14. S.I. $= \frac{p \times r \times t}{100} = \frac{500 \times 6 \times 2}{100} = ₹ 60$

Amount = P + S.I. = 500 + 60 = ₹ 560.

15. Let P = ₹ 100

S.I. $= \frac{100 \times 5 \times 6}{100} = ₹ 30$

Amount = 100 + 30 = ₹ 130

When amount ₹ 130 then P = ₹ 100

When amount ₹ 910 then P $= \frac{100}{130} \times 910$

∴ P = ₹ 700.

16. Amount = ₹ 1000

Principal = ₹ 800

∵ Simple interest = 1000 − 800 = ₹ 200

Time $= \frac{S.I. \times 100}{p \times r} = \frac{200 \times 100}{800 \times 5} = 5$ years.

17. S.I. $= \frac{p \times r \times t}{100} = \frac{1500 \times 8 \times 10}{100 \times 12} = ₹ 100$

Amount = 1500 + 100 = ₹ 1600.

18. P $= \frac{S.I. \times 100}{r \times t} = \frac{60 \times 100}{5 \times 6} = ₹ 200.$

19. $t = \frac{S.I. \times 100}{p \times r} = \frac{5 \times 100}{50 \times 4} = \frac{5}{2} = 2\frac{1}{2}$ years.

20. S.I. = Amount − principal

= 2325 − 1875 = ₹ 450

$r = \frac{S.I. \times 100}{p \times t} = \frac{450 \times 100}{1875 \times 4} = 6$

∴ $r = 6\%$.

When goods are sold for more than what they cost, they are said to be sold at profit or gain, but when they are sold for less than what they cost they are said to be sold at a loss.

∴ Profit = Selling Price – Cost Price
Loss = Cost Price – Selling Price.

REMEMBER

(i) Profit % = $\dfrac{\text{Profit}}{\text{C. P.}} \times 100$

(ii) Loss % = $\dfrac{\text{Loss}}{\text{C. P.}} \times 100$

(iii) S.P = C.P. $\times \dfrac{100 + \text{Gain}}{100}$, C.P. $\times \dfrac{100 - \text{Loss}}{100}$

(iv) C.P. = S.P. $\times \dfrac{100}{100 + \text{Gain}}$, S.P. $\times \dfrac{100}{100 - \text{Loss}}$

SOLVED EXAMPLE

1. A toy was purchased for ₹ 15 and was sold for ₹ 8. Find percent gain or loss.

Solution:

Cost price of toy = ₹ 15
Selling Price of the toy = ₹ 8
Loss = ₹ 15 – ₹ 8 = ₹ 7

Percent Loss = $\dfrac{₹\,7}{₹\,15} \times 100$

$= \dfrac{140}{3}\% = 46\dfrac{2}{3}\%.$

2. A man bought 75 metres of cloth at ₹ 18 per metre. At what rate per metre should he sell the cloth so as to gain ₹ 150.

Solution:

C.P. of the cloth = 75 × 18 = ₹ 1,350
Gain = ₹ 150
S.P. = 1,350 + 150 = ₹ 1500

It means that he should sell 75 metre cloth for ₹ 1,500

Rate per metre = $\dfrac{1500}{75} = ₹ 20.$

3. C.P. = ₹ 300; S.P. = ₹ 400. Find Profit or loss per cent.

Solution:

Profit = 400 – 300 = ₹ 100

Profit % = $\dfrac{\text{Profit}}{\text{C.P.}} \times 100$

$= \dfrac{100 \times 100}{300} = \dfrac{100}{3} = 33\dfrac{1}{3}\%.$

4. A man losses 10% by selling a watch for ₹ 630. Find the cost price of the watch.

Solution:

Loss = 10 %
∵ When S.P. is ₹ 90, C.P. = ₹ 100

∴ When S.P. is ₹ 630, C.P. = $\dfrac{100}{90} \times 630$

$= ₹ 700.$

5. By selling a plot of land for ₹ 17,220 Rajesh gains 5%. For how much, he should have sold the plot to gain 15% in transaction?

Solution:

S.P. = ₹ 17,220
Profit = 5%
∵ When S.P. is ₹ 105, C.P. = ₹ 100

∴ When S.P. is ₹ 1, C.P. = $\dfrac{100}{105}$

∴ When S.P. is ₹ 17,220, C.P. = $\dfrac{100}{105} \times 17,220$

$= ₹ 16,400$

∴ C.P. for the plot of land = ₹ 16,400
Gain = 15%

∴ S.P. = $\dfrac{115}{100} \times 16,400 = ₹ 18,860.$

951 (Math)—7

6. Vikas bought a transistor for ₹ 500 and sold it for ₹ 550. What is loss or gain per cent?

Solution:

$$C.P. = ₹\ 500$$
$$S.P. = ₹\ 550$$
$$Profit = ₹\ 50$$

$$Profit\ \% = \frac{50}{500} \times 100 = 10\%.$$

7. Devendra purchased a motor cycle for ₹ 10,000. He paid ₹ 150 for road tax and ₹ 100 as license fee. What price must he shell it to gain 20 %?

Solution:

Actual cost price of the motor cycle
$$= 10,000 + 150 + 100$$
$$= ₹\ 10,250$$
$$Gain = 20\%$$

$$S.P. = \frac{120}{100} \times 10,250 = ₹\ 12,300.$$

8. A watch maker bought an old watch for ₹ 80. He spent ₹ 10 on its repair and then sold it for ₹ 117. Find his gain or loss percent.

Solution:

C.P. of the watch = ₹ 80

Expenditure or repairs = ₹ 10

$$Actual\ C.P. = ₹\ 80 + ₹\ 10$$
$$= ₹\ 90$$
$$S.P. = 117$$
$$\therefore \qquad Profit = ₹\ 117 - ₹\ 90$$
$$= ₹\ 27$$

Hence, profit percentage $= \frac{27}{90} \times 100 = 30\%$

9. Rajendra bought a bicycle for ₹ 1050. For how much should he sell the bicycle so as to gain 10%.

Solution:

Gain = 10%

∵ When C.P. is ₹ 100, S.P. = ₹ 110

∴ When C.P. is ₹ 1050, S.P. $= \frac{110}{100} \times 1050$
$$= 1155$$

Hence, he must sell the bicycle for ₹ 1155.

10. Some mangoes were bought at the rate of 1.50 per dozen and sold at the rate of 2.25 per dozen. If there is profit of ₹ 2.25, how many mangoes were bought?

Solution:

C.P. = ₹ 1.50 per dozen

S.P. = ₹ 2.25 per dozen

Profit = 2.25 – 1.50 then, no. of mangoes
$$= ₹\ 0.75\ per\ dozen.$$

∴ When profit was ₹ 0.75 one dozen mangoes were purchased.

∴ When profit is ₹ 2.25 then no. of mangoes
purchased $= \dfrac{2.25}{.75} = 3$

= 3 dozen mangoes were purchased.

11. If the cost price of 15 articles be equal to selling price of 12 articles, find the profit or loss percent?

Solution:

Let C.P. of an article be ₹ 1

∴ Cost price of 15 articles = ₹ 15

Cost of 12 articles = ₹ 12

But selling price of 12 articles = Cost price of 15 articles

∴ Selling price of 12 articles = ₹ 15

Profit = 15 – 12 = ₹ 3

On ₹ 12, profit = ₹ 3

∴ On ₹ 100, profit $= \dfrac{3}{12} \times 100 = 25\%.$

12. By selling a shirt for ₹ 55. Dinesh losses 20%. For how much should he sell the shirt to gain 20%?

Solution:

Here S.P. = ₹ 55, Loss = 20%

$$C.P. = S.P. \times \frac{100}{100 - loss}$$

$$= 55 \times \frac{100}{100 - 20} = \frac{55 \times 100}{80} = \frac{275}{4}$$

Thus, C.P. of the shirt $= ₹\ \dfrac{275}{4}$

Now profit = 20%

$$S.P. = C.P. \times \frac{100 + Gain}{100}$$

$$S.P. = \frac{275}{4} \times \frac{100 + 20}{100} = \frac{275}{4} \times \frac{120}{100} = \frac{165}{2}$$

$$= ₹\ 82.50.$$

EXERCISE

1. By selling an article for ₹ 165, a man losses 4%. Find the S.P. of the article in order to gain 28%.
   A. ₹ 220   B. ₹ 180
   C. ₹ 225   D. ₹ 195

2. A merchant lost ₹ 51 by selling 17 bags of rice for ₹ 1,020. What was his cost per bag?
   A. ₹ 75   B. ₹ 68
   C. ₹ 63   D. ₹ 65

3. Ramesh buys 50 metre cloth at the rate of ₹ 120 per metre. At what rate should he sell the cloth in order to get 20% gain?
   A. ₹ 180   B. ₹ 144
   C. ₹ 150   D. ₹ 154

4. A man buys two pens at ₹ 20 each. He sells one at a gain of 5% and other at a loss of 5%. Find his profit or loss per cent?
   A. Gain ₹ 5
   B. Loss ₹ 24
   C. Gain ₹ 25
   D. Neither Profit nor loss

5. An electronics dealer buys a radio for ₹ 475 and spends ₹ 25 on its repairs. If he sells the radio for ₹ 600, find his profit per cent?
   A. 20%   B. 8%
   C. 12%   D. 9%

6. An article which cost ₹ 70 was sold at a gain of 10%. What was the selling price?
   A. ₹ 77   B. ₹ 88
   C. ₹ 65   D. ₹ 80

7. By selling 60 oranges for ₹ 30 a man loses 25%. Find the cost price of 30 oranges.
   A. ₹ 25   B. ₹ 30
   C. ₹ 20   D. ₹ 15

8. John bought horse for ₹ 450. He sold it to Mohan at a profit of 10%. Mohan sold it to Murray at a gain of 20%. Find the cost price of horse for Murray.
   A. ₹ 580   B. ₹ 594
   C. ₹ 610   D. ₹ 625

9. A shop keeper sell 50 m. cloth for ₹ 450 and losses 10%. If he sells the cloth at the rate of ₹ 12 per metre, find his loss or gain per cent?
   A. Loss 25%   B. Gain 25%
   C. Gain 20%   D. Loss 20%

10. A profit of 25% is made when an article is sold for ₹ 625. Find the profit per cent if the article is sold for ₹ 550.
    A. 15%   B. 18%
    C. 8%   D. 10%

11. Calculate the gain per cent if a watch bought for ₹ 60 was sold at ₹ 75.
    A. 25%   B. 20%
    C. 15%   D. 22%

12. Sunil purchased a motor–cycle for ₹ 28,500. He spent ₹ 500 on repairs. He sold the motor–cycle at a gain of 15%. Find the selling price of the motor–cycle.
    A. ₹ 10520   B. ₹ 10350
    C. ₹ 10820   D. ₹ 10440

13. A man loses 12% by selling his watch for ₹ 440. Find the cost price of the watch.
    A. ₹ 300   B. ₹ 400
    C. ₹ 500   D. ₹ 550

14. A man bought 5 apples for ₹ 3 and sold each for ₹ 1.20. What was his loss or gain?
    A. Gain ₹ 10   B. Loss ₹ 4
    C. Gain ₹ 3   D. Loss ₹ 4

15. Sohan sold his television for ₹ 5,067 and lost 10%. If he sold television for ₹ 5,630, find his gain or loss per cent?
    A. 20%
    B. 30%
    C. 25%
    D. Neither loss nor gain

16. A shop-keeper purchased 27 balls at ₹ 4 per ball and sold them for ₹ 120. Find his gain or loss per cent.

    A. Gain $11\frac{1}{9}\%$ B. Loss $9\frac{1}{9}\%$

    C. Gain 15%   D. Loss 18%

17. A man bought 6 oranges for a rupee and sold them at a profit of 20%. How many oranges for a rupee did he sell?
A. 6 Oranges   B. 5 Oranges
C. 4 Oranges   D. 3 Oranges

18. Cost price of 10 articles is equal to selling price of 8 articles. Find the gain or loss per cent.
A. 15%   B. 20%
C. 25%   D. 30%

19. A shopkeeper buys a fan for ₹ 225. He wants to earn a profit of 8 per cent. At what price should he sell it?
A. ₹ 243   B. ₹ 250
C. ₹ 255   D. ₹ 240

20. A man purchased an old car for ₹ 6,200 and he spent ₹ 1700 on repairs. He resold the car for ₹ 8,200. How much profit he got?
A. ₹ 400   B. ₹ 500
C. ₹ 200   D. ₹ 300

ANSWERS

1	2	3	4	5	6	7	8	9	10
A	C	B	D	A	A	C	B	C	D

11	12	13	14	15	16	17	18	19	20
A	B	C	C	D	A	B	C	A	D

EXPLANATORY ANSWERS

1. S.P. for an article = ₹ 165

Loss = 4%

When S.P. is ₹ 96, C.P. for the article = ₹ 100

∴ When S.P. is ₹ 165, C.P. for the article

$$= \frac{100 \times 165}{96} = \frac{25 \times 55}{8}$$

Gain = 28%

When C.P. for the article is ₹ 100

S.P. = ₹ 128

When C.P. for the article is $\frac{25 \times 55}{8}$ then

$$S.P. = \frac{128 \times 25 \times 55}{100 \times 8} = ₹ 220$$

2. S. P. for 17 bags of rice = ₹ 1020

Loss = ₹ 51

∴ C. P. for the 17 bags of rice = 1020 + 51
$$= ₹ 1071$$

Cost of one bag $= \frac{1071}{17} = ₹ 63$

3. Cost price of 50 metre cloth at the rate of ₹ 120 per metre = ₹ 6000

Gain = 20%

∴ Selling price $= \frac{120 \times 6000}{100} = ₹ 7200$

It means that 50 metre cloth should be sold for ₹ 7200

∴ Selling price for 1 metre cloth

$$= \frac{7200}{50} = ₹ 144$$

4. C.P. for the first pen = ₹ 20

Gain = 5%

∴ S.P. for the first pen $= \frac{105 \times 20}{100} = ₹ 21$

C.P. for the second pen = ₹ 20

Loss = 5%

∴ S.P. for the second pen $= \frac{95 \times 20}{100} = ₹ 19$

C.P. for both the pens = ₹ 40

S.P. for both the pens = 21 + 19 = ₹ 40

There is no loss or gain.

5. C.P. for radio = ₹ 475

Repair charges = ₹ 25

Actual cost price for radio = ₹ 500

Selling price = ₹ 600

Profit = ₹ 600 – ₹ 500 = ₹ 100

Profit per cent $= \dfrac{100 \times 100}{500} = 20\%$

6. Cost price = ₹ 70

   Profit = 10%

   ∴ When C.P. is ₹ 100, S.P. = ₹ 110

   When C.P. is ₹ 70, S.P. $= \dfrac{110 \times 70}{100} = ₹ 77.$

7. S.P. for 60 oranges = ₹ 30

   Loss = 25%

   ∵ C.P. for 60 oranges $= \dfrac{100 \times 30}{75} = ₹ 40$

   ∴ C.P. for 30 oranges $= \dfrac{40 \times 30}{60} = ₹ 20$

8. C.P. for John = ₹ 450

   Profit = 10%

   ∴ Selling price of the horse of John

   $= \dfrac{110 \times 450}{100} = ₹ 495$

   ∴ C.P. of the horse of Mohan = ₹ 495

   Profit = 20%

   S.P. of the horse for Mohan $= \dfrac{120 \times 495}{100}$

   $= ₹ 594$

   ∴ C.P. of the horse for Murray = ₹ 594.

9. S. P. for 50 m. cloth = ₹ 450

   Loss = 10%

   ∴ C.P. for 50 m. cloth $= \dfrac{100 \times 450}{90} = ₹ 500$

   Selling price for 50 m. cloth at the rate of ₹ 12 per meter

   $= 50 \times 12$

   $= ₹ 600$

   ∴ Gain = 600 – 500

   $= ₹ 100$

   Gain % $= \dfrac{100 \times 100}{500}$

   $= 20\%.$

10. Selling price for an article = ₹ 625

    Gain = 25%

    Cost price for the article $= \dfrac{100 \times 625}{125} = ₹ 500$

    Now selling price = ₹ 550

    ∴ Profit = ₹ 550 – ₹ 500

    $= ₹ 50$

    ∴ Profit % $= \dfrac{50 \times 100}{500}$

    $= 10\%.$

11. C.P. = ₹ 60

    S.P. = ₹ 75

    ∴ Profit = 75 – 60

    $= ₹ 15$

    On ₹ 60 profit = ₹ 15

    ∴ On ₹ 100 profit $= \dfrac{15 \times 100}{60} = 25\%$

12. Total cost price of motor cycle

    $= ₹ 8500 + ₹ 500$

    $= ₹ 9000$

    Gain = 15%

    ∴ When C.P. is ₹ 100 S. P. = ₹ 115

    ∴ When C.P. is ₹ 9000, S. P. $= \dfrac{115 \times 9000}{100}$

    $= ₹ 10350.$

13. S.P. of the watch = ₹ 440

    Loss = 12%

    When S.P. is ₹ 88, C.P. = ₹ 100

    ∴ When S.P. is ₹ 440,

    C.P. $= \dfrac{100 \times 440}{88} = ₹ 500.$

14. C.P. for 5 apples = ₹ 3

    S.P. for 5 apples = 1.20 × 5 = ₹ 6

    Gain = 6 – 3 = ₹ 3.

15. S.P. for a television = ₹ 5067

    Loss = 10%

    when S.P. is ₹ 5067; C.P. $= \dfrac{100 \times 5067}{90}$

    $= ₹ 5630$

    Cost price of the television = ₹ 5630

    ∴ Selling price of the television = ₹ 5630

    It means, there will be no loss or gain in this transaction.

16. C.P. for 27 balls = 27 × 4

$$= ₹\ 108$$

S.P. for 27 balls = ₹ 120

$$\text{Profit} = ₹\ 120 - ₹\ 108$$

$$= ₹\ 12$$

$$\text{Profit} = \frac{12 \times 100}{108}$$

$$= 11\frac{1}{9}\%.$$

17. C.P. for 6 oranges = ₹ 1

Profit = 20%

$$\therefore \text{ S.P. for 6 oranges} = \frac{120 \times 1}{100} = ₹\ 1.20$$

It means he sold 6 oranges for ₹ 1.20

$$\therefore \text{ In a rupee he sold} = \frac{6 \times 1}{1.20} = 5 \text{ oranges}.$$

18. Let the cost price of an article be ₹ 1

∴ Cost price of 10 article = ₹ 10

Cost price of 8 article = ₹ 8

But

given that selling price for 8 article

$$= \text{Cost price for 10 articles}$$

∴ S.P. for 8 articles = ₹ 10

∴ Profit = 10 − 8

$$= ₹\ 2$$

∴ Profit on ₹ 8 is ₹ 2

$$\therefore \text{ Profit on } ₹\ 100 = \frac{2 \times 100}{8} = 25$$

∴ Profit % = 25%.

19. C.P. of the fan = ₹ 225

$$\text{Profit} = \frac{8}{100} \times 225$$

$$= ₹\ 18$$

S.P. of the fan = 225 + 18

$$= ₹\ 243.$$

20. C.P. of the car = 6200 + 1700

$$= ₹\ 7900$$

S.P. of the car = ₹ 8200

$$\text{Profit} = 8200 - 7900$$

$$= ₹\ 300.$$

10 RATIO AND PROPORTION

RATIO

It is the relation between two numbers or quantities of the same kind, which shows what multiple part or part one quantity is of the other. Thus the ratio of ₹ 4 and ₹ 5 is represented by the fraction 4/5 or by the notation 4:5.

REMEMBER

If we divide the given ratio by any number (except 0) the ratio remains unaltered. Similarly if we multiple a given ratio by any number the ratio will not change.
$24 : 36 = 4 : 6 = 2 : 3$

PROPORTION

Consider two ratios 2 : 5 and 6 : 15. We observe that 2 : 5 = 6 : 15. These two ratios are said to be in proportion. Hence, we can say that a statement which states that two ratio are equal is called proportion.

$4 : 7 = 12 : 21$

4 and 21 are called extremes and 7 and 12 are known as means.

We see that $4 \times 21 = 84$

$7 \times 12 = 84$

We can say that product of extremes is equal to product of means.

SOLVED EXAMPLE

1. Find the ratio of 500 gm. and 2 kg.

Solution:

2 kg. = 2000 gm.

Reqd. ratio = 500 gm. : 2 kg.

= 500 gm. : 2000 gm.

= 1 : 4.

2. Find the ratio of 42 and 105.

Solution:

42 : 105 = 6 : 15

= 2 : 5.

3. Write the ratio 2 : 5 in different way.

Solution:

2 : 5 = 4 : 10

= 6 : 15.

4. Find the ratio of 5 m. and 550 cm.

Solution:

We know that the ratio between two quantities is possible only if both the quantities are of the same type.

∵ 5 m. = 500 cm.

∴ 5 m. : 550 cm. = 500 : 550

= 100 : 110

= 10 : 11.

5. Find the angles of a triangle which are in the ratio of 1 : 2 : 3

Solution:

Sum of three angles of a triangle = 180°

Ratio of angles = 1 : 2 : 3

Sum of angles = 1 + 2 + 3 = 6

∴ First angle $= \dfrac{1}{6} \times 180° = 30°$

∴ Second angle $= \dfrac{2}{6} \times 180° = 60°$

Third angle $= \dfrac{3}{6} \times 180° = 90°$

Hence, angles of a triangle are 30°, 60° and 90°.

6. How many days will 12 men take to do a piece of work if 10 men do the same work in 24 days?

Solution :

Let 12 men do the work in x days

12 : 10 = 24 : x

∴ $12 x = 10 \times 24$

55

$$\therefore x = \frac{10 \times 24}{12} = 20$$

$\therefore x = 20$ days.

7. Find x if $2 : 5 = 4 : x$

Solution:

We know that the product of extrems is equal to product of means.

$\therefore 2x = 5 \times 4$

$$\therefore x = \frac{5 \times 4}{2} = 10$$

$\therefore x = 10$.

8. A train runs a distance of 35 km. in 50 minutes. How long will it take to run 98 km.?

Solution:

Let the train takes x minutes.

$35 : 98 = 50 : x$

$\therefore 35 x = 50 \times 98$

$$\therefore x = \frac{50 \times 98}{35}$$

$\therefore x = 140$ minutes.

9. The ratio of income and expenditure of 9 family is $9 : 8$ if income of the family is ₹ 3,600, find its savings.

Solution:

Income of the family = ₹ 3,600

Ratio of the income and expenditure = $9 : 8$

Hence, if ₹ 9 is the income, expenditure = ₹ 8

or if ₹ 1 is the income, expenditure = ₹ $\frac{8}{9}$

or if ₹ 3,600 is the income, expenditure

$$= ₹ \frac{8}{9} \times 3,600 = ₹ 3,200$$

Hence, savings = ₹ 3,600 – ₹ 3,200

$$= ₹ 400.$$

10. If 24 men can do a work in 16 days, how long will it take 36 men to do the same work?

Solution:

Let 36 men can do the work in x days

$36 : 24 = 16 : x$

$\therefore 36 x = 24 \times 16$

$$\therefore x = \frac{24 \times 16}{36}$$

$$\therefore x = \frac{32}{3} \text{ days}.$$

11. 4 kg. wheat cost ₹ 10, find the cost of 6 kg. of wheat.

Solution:

Let cost of 6 kg. of wheat be ₹ x

$4 : 6 = 10 : x$

$4x = 10 \times 6$

$$\therefore x = \frac{10 \times 6}{4}$$

$\therefore x = ₹ 15$

$\therefore$ The cost of 6 kg. of wheat will be ₹ 15.

EXERCISE

1. Find x if $\dfrac{8}{12} = \dfrac{14}{x}$.

   A. 18   B. 19

   C. 20   D. 21

2. Find x if $\dfrac{24}{x} = \dfrac{15}{20}$.

   A. 28   B. 32

   C. 30   D. 34

3. If 12 oranges cost ₹ 4, what will 18 oranges cost?

   A. ₹ 6   B. ₹ 7

   C. ₹ 8   D. ₹ 5

4. A man has provisions for 750 mens for 30 days. For how many days will the same provisions lost for 360 men?

   A. 50 days   B. $55\frac{1}{2}$ days

   C. $62\frac{1}{2}$ days   D. 60 days

5. The ratio between two quantities is $4 : 5$. If second quantity is 45. Find the first.

   A. 30   B. 36

   C. 32   D. 16

6. The ratio between two quantities is 5 : 14. If first quantity is 35. Find the second.
   A. 90   B. 92
   C. 94   D. 98

7. If 10, 20, x, 40 are in equal proportion, then what is the value of x?
   A. 18   B. 20
   C. 24   D. 22

8. Ratio between income and expenditure of a certain family is 9 :7. If income of the family is ₹ 3,600, find its expenditure.
   A. ₹ 2400   B. ₹ 2600
   C. ₹ 2800   D. ₹ 3000

9. Raju distributes ₹ 91 amongst three brothers in such a way that the eldest gets twice as much as the youngest and $1\frac{1}{2}$ times as much as the middle brother. Find the share of the eldest brother.
   A. ₹ 28   B. ₹ 21
   C. ₹ 32   D. ₹ 42

10. A, B and C has ₹ 1,371. The ratio of the money between A and B was 3 : 5. If C has ₹ 171, calculate A's share.
    A. ₹ 400   B. ₹ 450
    C. ₹ 425   D. ₹ 350

11. In a mixture of alcohol and water, the ratio between alcohol and water is 2 : 3. If the mixture contains 30 litres of alcohol, find the quantity of water in the mixture.
    A. 45 l B. 42 l
    C. 36 l D. 54 l

12. A man had ₹ 30,000. He gave to his daughter, son and nephew in the ratio 5 : 4 : 3. Find the total number of rupees each got.
    A. ₹ 800   B. ₹ 900
    C. ₹ 1000   D. ₹ 1100

13. Find the value of x if 2 : 3 = 4 : x
    A. 2   B. 3
    C. 4   D. 6

14. Find the ratio of 60 cm : 1 metre.
    A. 3 : 5   B. 5 : 3
    C. 5 : 6   D. 6 : 5

15. 5 kg. of sugar cost ₹ 12 . Find the cost of 6 kg. of sugar.
    A. ₹ 13.20   B. ₹ 14.40
    C. ₹ 13.80   D. ₹ 14.60

16. 33 cows can graze a field in 12 days. How many cows will graze the same field in 9 days?
    A. 28 cows   B. 36 cows
    C. 44 cows   D. 55 cows

17. 5 men do a piece of work in 12 days. In how many days will 6 men complete the same work?
    A. 8 days   B. 10 days
    C. 12 days   D. 9 days

18. Abhay's monthly income is ₹ 1,550 and monthly expenditure ₹ 1,200. What is the ratio between his monthly income and expenditure?
    A. 31 : 24   B. 19 : 24
    C. 23 : 24   D. 29 : 24

19. Ratio between income and expenditure of a certain family is 9 : 7. If the income of the family is ₹ 45,000, find its expenditure.
    A. ₹ 28000   B. ₹ 30000
    C. ₹ 35000   D. ₹ 32000

20. The ratio of the number of boys and girls in a school is 4 : 3. If there are 360 girls in the school, find the number of boys in the school. Also find the total strength of the school.
    A. 480, 840   B. 380, 940
    C. 460, 860   D. 430, 890

ANSWERS

1	2	3	4	5	6	7	8	9	10
D	B	A	C	B	D	B	C	D	B

11	12	13	14	15	16	17	18	19	20
A	C	D	A	B	C	B	A	C	A

EXPLANATORY ANSWERS

1. $\dfrac{8}{12} = \dfrac{14}{x}$

   $\therefore 8x = 14 \times 12$

   $\therefore x = \dfrac{14 \times 12}{8} = 21$

   $\therefore x = 21.$

2. $\dfrac{24}{x} = \dfrac{15}{20}$

   $\Rightarrow \quad 15x = 24 \times 20$

   $\Rightarrow \quad x = \dfrac{24 \times 20}{15}$

   $\qquad = 32.$

3. $\because$ Cost of 12 oranges = ₹ 4

   $\therefore$ Cost of 18 oranges = ₹ $\dfrac{4}{12} \times 18 =$ ₹ 6

4. Let the provisions last for x days

   $360 : 750 = 30 : x$

   $\therefore 360\,x = 750 \times 30$

   $\therefore x = \dfrac{750 \times 30}{360}$

   $\therefore x = 62\dfrac{1}{2}$ days.

5. Let first quantity = $4x$

   and second quantity = $5x$

   According to the question,

   $\qquad 5x = 45$

   $\Rightarrow \qquad x = 9$

   $\therefore$ First quantity = $4 \times 9 = 36.$

6. Let the second quantity be x

   $5 : 14 = 35 : x$

   $\therefore 5x = 14 \times 35$

   $\therefore x = \dfrac{14 \times 35}{5} = 98$

   $\therefore x = 98.$

7. $\because 10 : 20 :: x : 40$

   $\Rightarrow \quad \dfrac{10}{20} = \dfrac{x}{40}$

   $\Rightarrow \quad 20x = 10 \times 40$

   $\Rightarrow \quad x = \dfrac{10 \times 40}{20}$

   $\qquad = 20.$

8. Let income = ₹ $9x$

   and expenditure = ₹ $7x$

   According to the question,

   $\qquad 9x = 3600$

   $\Rightarrow \quad x = 400$

   $\therefore$ Expenditure of the family

   $\qquad = 7 \times 400$

   $\qquad =$ ₹ 2800.

9. Let eldest's share = ₹ x

   $\therefore$ Middle's share = $\dfrac{2}{3}x$

   and youngest's share = ₹ $\dfrac{x}{2}$

   $x + \dfrac{2x}{3} + \dfrac{x}{2} = 91$

   $\Rightarrow \quad \dfrac{6x + 4x + 3x}{6} = 91$

   $\Rightarrow \quad 13x = 6 \times 91$

   $\Rightarrow \quad x = \dfrac{6 \times 91}{13}$

   $\qquad = 42$

   Hence, share of the elest brother = ₹ 42.

10. $\dfrac{A}{B} = \dfrac{3}{5}$

    $\Rightarrow \quad B = \dfrac{5A}{3}$

    $\because$ C's share = ₹ 171

    $A + B + C = 1371$

    $A + \dfrac{5A}{3} + 171 = 1371$

    $\Rightarrow \quad A + \dfrac{5A}{3} = 1200$

$\Rightarrow \quad \dfrac{3A + 5A}{3} = 1200$

$\Rightarrow \qquad 8A = 3 \times 1200$

$\Rightarrow \qquad A = \dfrac{3 \times 1200}{8}$

$\qquad\qquad\quad = 3 \times 150$

$\qquad\qquad\quad = 450$

Hence, A's share = ₹ 450.

11. Let the mixture contains x litres water.

$2 : 3 = 30 : x$

$\therefore 2x = 3 \times 30$

$\therefore x = \dfrac{3 \times 30}{2} = 45$

$\therefore x = 45.$

Hence, the mixture contains 45 litres of water.

12. Let daughter's share = ₹ $5x$

son's share = ₹ $4x$

nephew's share = ₹ $3x$

$\qquad 5x + 4x + 3x = 30000$

$\Rightarrow \qquad 12x = 30000$

$\Rightarrow \qquad x = \dfrac{30000}{12}$

$\qquad\qquad\quad = 2500$

Hence, son's share = 4×2500 = ₹ 1000.

13. $\because \qquad \dfrac{2}{3} = \dfrac{4}{x}$

$\Rightarrow \qquad 2x = 3 \times 4$

$\Rightarrow \qquad x = \dfrac{3 \times 4}{2} = 6.$

14. Required ratio = $\dfrac{60}{100} = \dfrac{6}{10} = \dfrac{3}{5} = 3 : 5.$

15. Let the cost of 6 kg. of sugar be ₹ x

$5 : 6 = 12 : x$

$\therefore 5x = 6 \times 12$

$\therefore x = \dfrac{6 \times 12}{5} = \dfrac{72}{5}$

$\therefore x = $ ₹ 14.40

Thus, the cost of 6 kg. of sugar will be ₹ 14.40.

16. $\because$ 33 cows can graze a field in 12 days

$\therefore$ 1 cow can graze that field in 33×12 days

$\therefore$ x cows can graze that field in $\dfrac{33 \times 12}{x}$ days.

$\qquad \dfrac{33 \times 12}{x} = 9$

$\Rightarrow \qquad 9x = 33 \times 12$

$\Rightarrow \qquad x = \dfrac{33 \times 12}{9}$

$\qquad\qquad\quad = 44$

Hence, 44 cows can graze that field in 9 days.

17. $\because$ 5 men can do a work in 12 days

$\therefore$ 1 man can do this work in 5×12 days

$\therefore$ 6 men can do that work in $\dfrac{5 \times 12}{6} = 10$ days

Hence, 6 men can do the same work in 10 days.

18. Required ratio = $\dfrac{1550}{1200} = \dfrac{155}{120} = \dfrac{31}{24} = 31 : 24.$

19. Let income of the family = ₹ $9x$

and expenditure of the family = ₹ $7x$

According to the question,

$\qquad 9x = 45000$

$\Rightarrow \qquad x = 5000$

Hence, expenditure = 7×5000 = ₹ 35000.

20. Let there be x boys in the school

$4 : 3 = x : 360$

$\therefore 3x = 4 \times 360$

$\therefore x = \dfrac{4 \times 360}{3} = 480$

Hence, there are 480 boys in the school.

Strength of the school = 480 + 360 = 840.

# 11 TIME AND DISTANCE

REMEMBER

- Time = $\dfrac{\text{Distance}}{\text{Speed}}$,
- Speed = $\dfrac{\text{Distance}}{\text{Time}}$
- Distance = Speed × Time
- If two trains are moving in opposite directions, their relative speed is equal to the sum of their speeds.
- If the trains are moving in the same direction their relative velocity is equal to the difference of their speeds.

SOLVED EXAMPLE

1. A train starts on Monday from a city at 5 p. m. and reaches the other city at 5 p. m. on Wednesday. If the distance between two cities is 1440 km, find the speed of the train.

Solution:

Time taken by train to reach from one city to the second city = 5 p. m. Monday to
5 p. m. Wednesday
= 2 days
= 2 × 24 = 48 hours

Distance between two cities = 1440 km

Hence, speed of the train = $\dfrac{1440}{48}$,
= 30 km / hr.

2. A boy runs a distance of 3 metres in one second. What is his speed in km. per hour?

Solution:–

∵ Distance run by the boy in 1 sec.
= 3 metres

∴ Distance run by the boy in 3600 sec.
= 3 × 3600 metres = 10800 metres

or, distance run by the boy in 1 hour
= 10800 metres

= $\dfrac{10800}{1000}$ km. = 10.8 km.

Hence, speed of the boy is 10.8 km./hr.

EXERCISE

1. A train covers a distance of 480 km. in 8 hours. How much distance will be covered in 2 hours?
   A. 140 km   B. 120 km
   C. 115 km   D. 125 km

2. A man travels 4 kms. 500 metres in $\frac{1}{2}$ hour, find his speed per hour?
   A. 9 km/hr   B. 6 km/hr
   C. 8 km/hr   D. 10 km/hr

3. If Rajdhani Express covers a distance of 441 km. between New Delhi and Lucknow in 4 hours and 30 minutes, what is its speed per hour?

A. 90 km/hr   B. 88 km/hr
C. 98 km/hr   D. 120 km/hr

4. A train can do a journey in 6 hours if it travels at 40 km. per hour. At what speed does it travel in order to complete the journey in 5 hours?
   A. 40 km/hr   B. 42 km/hr
   C. 45 km/hr   D. 48 km/hr

5. A bus covers a distance of 190 km. in 6 hours and 20 minutes. Find the average speed.
   A. 30 km/hr   B. 25 km/hr
   C. 40 km/hr   D. 45 km/hr

6. A cyclist covers a distance of 0.9 kilometre in 3 minutes. Find his speed in kilometre per hour.
A. 15 km/hr
B. 18 km/hr
C. 21 km/hr
D. 20 km/hr

7. A train leaves Delhi at 4:10 p.m. and reaches Agra at 7:25 p.m. The average speed of the train is 40 km. per hour. What is the distance in km. from Delhi to Agra?
A. 90 km
B. 110 km
C. 140 km
D. 130 km

8. A man is walking at a speed of 10 km. per hour. After every kilometre, he takes rest for 5 minutes. How much time will he take to cover a distance of 5 km.?
A. 40 min
B. 45 min
C. 50 min
D. 48 min

9. Which of the two speeds is greater : 20 m. per second or 90 km. per hour.?
A. 90 km/hr
B. 20 m/s
C. Both are equal
D. Neither 90 km/hr nor 20 m/s

10. The distance between Bhopal and Nagpur is 390 kilometres Andhra Express covers this distance in 6 hours and 40 minutes. Find the speed of the train.
A. 52.5 km/hr
B. 58.5 km/hr
C. 54.5 km/hr
D. 56.5 km/hr

11. If a train covers 180 km. distance in 4 hours 30 min, find the average speed of the train.
A. 40 km/hr
B. 30 km/hr
C. 35 km/hr
D. 45 km/hr

12. A cyclist rides 24 km at 16 km/h and further 36 km at 15 km/hr. Find his average speed for the journey.
A. 15.38 km/hr
B. 15.5 km/hr
C. 16 km/hr
D. 16.5 km/hr

13. A car is running at a speed of 108 km/hr. Find the distance covered by it in 15 seconds.
A. 450 m
B. 475 m
C. 500 m
D. 550 m

14. How long will a boy take to run round a square field of side 35 meters, If he runs at the rate of 9 km/hr?
A. 56 sec.
B. 54 sec.
C. 52 sec.
D. 50 sec.

15. A person crosses a 600 m long street in 5 minutes. Find his speed in km/hr.
A. 10
B. 8.4
C. 7.2
D. 3.6

16. A man walking at the rate of 5 km/hr crosses a bridge in 15 minutes. What is the length of the bridge in meters?
A. 1250
B. 1000
C. 750
D. 600

17. How long will a train 60 m long travelling at 40 km/hr take to pass through a station whose platform is 90 m long?
A. 12.5 seconds
B. 13.5 seconds
C. 14.5 seconds
D. 15.5 seconds

18. Two trains of equal lengths take 10 seconds and 15 seconds respectively to cross a milestone. If the length of each train be 120 metres, in what time (in seconds) will they cross each other travelling in opposite direction?
A. 20 sec
B. 15 sec
C. 12 sec
D. 10 sec

19. A train is running at the rate of 40 kmph. A man is also going in the same direction parallel to the train at the speed of 25 kmph. If the train crosses the man in 48 seconds, the length of the train is:
A. 100 m
B. 200 m
C. 300 m
D. 400 m

20. A train 700 m long is running at 72 kmph. If it crosses a tunnel in 1 minute, the length of the tunnel is:
A. 700 m
B. 600 m
C. 550 m
D. 500 m

ANSWERS

1	2	3	4	5	6	7	8	9	10
B	A	C	D	A	B	D	C	A	B

11	12	13	14	15	16	17	18	19	20
A	A	A	A	C	A	B	C	B	D

EXPLANATORY ANSWERS

1. Speed of the train $= \dfrac{480}{8} = 60$ km/hr

   Distance covered in 2 hours
   = Speed × time
   = 60 × 2
   = 120 km.

2. Speed of the man $= \dfrac{\text{Distance}}{\text{Time}}$

   $= \dfrac{9}{2} \div \dfrac{1}{2}$

   $= \dfrac{9}{2} \times \dfrac{2}{1}$

   = 9 km/hr.

3. Distance = 441 km

   Time = 4 hrs 30 min = $4\dfrac{1}{2}$ hrs = $\dfrac{9}{2}$ hrs.

   Speed $= \dfrac{441}{\dfrac{9}{2}} = \dfrac{441 \times 2}{9} = 98$ km/hr.

4. Distance = Speed × Time = 40 × 6 = 240 km

   Now, time = 5 hrs, distance = 240 km

   Speed of the train $= \dfrac{240}{5} = 48$ km/hr.

5. Average speed of the bus $= \dfrac{\text{Distance}}{\text{Time}}$

   $= \dfrac{190}{\dfrac{19}{3}} = \dfrac{190 \times 3}{19}$

   = 30 km/hr.

6. Speed $= \dfrac{\text{Distance}}{\text{Time}}$

   $= \dfrac{\dfrac{9}{10}}{\dfrac{3}{60}} = \dfrac{9}{10} \times \dfrac{60}{3} = 18$ km/hr.

7. Time taken = 7 : 25 pm – 4 : 10 pm
   = 3 : 15 hrs.

   Distance = Speed × time

   $= 40 \times \dfrac{13}{4}$ km.

   = 130 km.

   Hence, distance from Delhi to Agra = 130 km.

8.

5 min	5 min	5 min	5 min	
6 min	6 min	6 min	6 min	6 min
1 km	1 km	1 km	1 km	1 km

   Required time taken to cover the distance 5 km

   = 6 + 6 + 6 + 6 + 6
   = 30 min.

   and 5 + 5 + 5 + 5 = 20 min
   = (30 + 20) min
   = 50 minutes.

9. 20 m/s $= 20 \times \dfrac{18}{5}$ km/hr = 72 km/hr

   Speed = 90 km/hr (given)

   Clearly, 90 km/hr is greater than 72 km/hr

   Hence, 90 km/hr is greater speed.

10. Speed of the train $= \dfrac{\text{Distance}}{\text{Time}}$

$$= \frac{390}{\frac{20}{3}} = \frac{390 \times 3}{20}$$

$$= \frac{117}{3}$$

$$= 58.5 \text{ km/hr.}$$

11. Speed $= \dfrac{180}{\frac{9}{2}} = 180 \times \dfrac{2}{9} = 40$ km/hr.

12. Required average speed

$$= \frac{24 + 36}{\frac{24}{16} + \frac{36}{15}} = \frac{60}{\frac{3}{2} + \frac{12}{5}} = \frac{60 \times 10}{39}$$

$$= 15.38 \text{ km/hr.}$$

13. Required distance $= 108 \times \dfrac{15}{60 \times 60}$ km

$$= \frac{9}{20} \text{ km} = \frac{9}{20} \times 1000 = 450 \text{ m.}$$

14. 9 km/hr $= 9 \times \dfrac{5}{18} = \dfrac{5}{2}$ m/s

Time taken $= \dfrac{4 \times 35}{5/2} = 4 \times 7 \times 2 = 56$ sec.

15. Speed $= \dfrac{600\text{m}}{5 \times 60\text{s}} = 2\text{m/s} = 2 \times \dfrac{18}{5}$ km/hr

$$= \frac{36}{5} = 7.2 \text{ km/hr.}$$

16. 5 km/hr $= 5 \times \dfrac{5}{18}$ m/s $= \dfrac{25}{18}$ m/s

Hence, length of a bridge $= \dfrac{25}{18} \times 15 \times 60$

$$= 1250 \text{ m.}$$

17. Speed $= 40$ km/hr $= 40 \times \dfrac{5}{18}$ m/s

So, Time $= \dfrac{(60 + 90)}{40 \times 5} \times 18$

$$= \frac{150 \times 18}{40 \times 5}$$

$$= 13.5 \text{ seconds.}$$

18. Speed of first train $= \dfrac{120}{10} = 12$ m/s

Speed of second train $= \dfrac{120}{15} = 8$ m/s

Their relative speed $= 12 + 8 = 20$ m/s

Hence, required time $= \dfrac{120 + 120}{20} = \dfrac{240}{20} = 12$ sec.

19. Length of train = Relative speed × time

$$= (40 - 25)\left(\frac{5}{18}\right) \times 48$$

$$= \frac{15 \times 5 \times 48}{18}$$

$$= 200 \text{ m.}$$

20. Let length of the tunnel be x m

Speed $= (72 \times 5/18)$ m/sec

$$= 20 \text{ m/sec}$$

Time = 60 sec

$\therefore \qquad 60 = \dfrac{700 + x}{20}$

$\Rightarrow \qquad 700 + x = 1200$

$\Rightarrow \qquad x = 500$ m

12 AREA AND PERIMETER

The area of a plane figure is the surface enclosed by its sides. The unit of area is square metres.

REMEMBER

Area of a square $= (\text{Side})^2$

Side of a square $= \sqrt{\text{Area}}$

Area of four walls $= 2\,(\,\text{Length} + \text{Breadth})$
$\times\, \text{Height}$

Perimeter of a square $= 4 \times \text{Side}$

Side of a square $= \dfrac{\text{Perimeter}}{4}$

Area of a rectangular region $= \text{Length} \times \text{Breadth}$

Perimeter of a rectangular region $= 2\,(\text{Length} + \text{Breadth})$

Length of a rectangle $= \dfrac{\text{Area}}{\text{Breadth}}$

Breadth of a rectangle $= \dfrac{\text{Area}}{\text{Length}}$

Diagonal of a rectangle
$$= \sqrt{(\text{Length})^2 + (\text{Breadth})^2}$$

Volume of a cuboid $= \text{Length} \times \text{Breadth} \times \text{Height}$

Area of all the six surfaces of a cuboid
$$= 2\,[\,l \times b + b \times h + l \times h\,]$$

Area of a semi-circle $= \dfrac{1}{2}\,\pi\,r^2$

Diameter of a circle $= 2 \times \text{radius}$

Perimeter of a circle $= 2\,\pi \times \text{radius}$

Area of a circle $= \pi \times (\text{radius})^2 = \pi\,r^2$

Area of a triangle $= \dfrac{1}{2} \times \text{base} \times \text{height}$

Surfaces area of six faces $= 6\,l^2$

Volume of a cube $= l^3$

SOLVED EXAMPLE

1. A square garden is 46 m. long. Find its area and perimeter.

Solution:

$\because$ Area of a square $= (\text{Side}) \times (\text{Side})$

$\therefore$ Area of the square $= 46 \times 46 \text{ m}^2$

$$= 2,116 \text{ m}^2.$$

$\because$ Perimeter of a square $= 4 \times \text{Side}$

$\therefore$ Perimeter of the square $= 4 \times 46 \text{ m}.$

$$= 184 \text{ m}.$$

2. The area of a rectangular region is 40,182 square metres. If its length be 362 m. find its perimeter.

Solution:

$$\text{Breadth} = \frac{\text{Area}}{\text{Length}} = \frac{40,182}{362} = 111 \text{ m}$$

$\therefore$ Perimeter $= 2\,(\text{Length} + \text{Breadth})$

$$= 2\,(362 + 111)$$

$$= 946 \text{ m}.$$

3. Find the area of a rectangular field whose length is 35 metres and breadth is 25 metres.

Solution:

Length = 35 m. ; Breadth = 25 m.

Area of the rectangular field $= 35 \times 25$

$$= 875 \text{ m}^2.$$

4. Find the area and perimeter of rectangle with sides of 9 cm. and 3 cm.

Solution:

Length of rectangle = 9 cm.

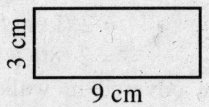

3 cm

9 cm

Breadth of rectangle = 3 cm.

∴ Area of rectangle = 9 × 3 sq. cm.

= 27 sq. cm.

Also, perimeter of rectangle

= 2 (Length + Breadth) = 2 (9 + 3) cm

= 2 × 12 cm. = 24 cm.

5. Find the area of four walls of a room if its length is 19 metres and breadth is 16 metres if the height of walls is 9 metres.

Solution:

Length (l) = 19 m.

Breadth (b) = 16 m.

Height (h) = 9 m.

Area of four walls = 2 ($l + b$) h

= 2 (19 + 16) × 9

= 2 × 35 × 9

= 630 sq. m.

6. Find the area and perimeter of a rectangle whose sides are 5 m and 4 m.

Solution:

Area of a rectangle = Length × Breadth

Area of a rectangle = 5 × 4 = 20 m^2

Perimeter of the rectangle

= 2 (Length + Breadth)

= 2 (5 + 4)

= 18 m.

7. Area of a square kitchen garden is 16,900 square meters. Find its perimeter.

Solution:

Side of the square = $\sqrt{\text{Area of the square}}$

= $\sqrt{16,900}$

∴ Side of the square = 130 m.

Perimeter of the square = 4 × Side

∴ Perimeter of the square = 4 × 130

= 520 m.

8. Find the area of a semi circular plate of diameter 14 cm.

Solution:–

d = 14 cm., r = 7 cm.

Area of a semi circle = $\frac{1}{2} \pi r^2$

= $\frac{1}{2} \pi \times 7^2$

= $\frac{1}{2} \times \frac{22}{7} \times 7 \times 7$

= 77 cm^2.

9. The floor of a room is rectangular in shape. Its length is 6 metres and breadth 5 metres. If the area of its four walls is 110 sq. metres, what is its height?

Solution:

2 (Length + breadth) × height = Area of four walls

2 (6 +5) × height = 110

∴ 2 × 11 × height = 110

∴ Height = $\frac{110}{2 \times 11}$ = 5 metres.

10. The perimeter of a rectangle is 240 metres and the ratio of the length to the breadth is 5 : 3. Find the area of the rectangle.

Solution:

5 + 3 = 8

Sum of the length and breadth

= $\frac{1}{2}$ × perimeter

= $\frac{1}{2}$ × 240 = 120 m

When sum of length and breadth of the rectangle is 8 m, its length = 5 m.

∴ When the sum is 120 m, length = $\frac{5 \times 120}{8}$

= 5 × 15 = 75 m.

∴ When sum of its length and breadth is 8 m its breadth = 3 m.

∴ When sum of its length and breadth is 120

its breadth = $\frac{3 \times 120}{8}$ = 45 m.

∴ Area of the rectangle = 75 × 45

= 3,375 m^2.

11. Floor of a room is $8\frac{1}{2}$ m. × 5 m. How many bricks 20 × 10 cm. will be required to make the brick floor?

Solution:

Length of room = $8\frac{1}{2}$ m. = $\frac{17}{2}$ m.

Breadth of room = 5 m.

Area of room = $\frac{17}{2} \times 5 = \frac{85}{2}$ sq. m.

Length of brick = 20 cm. = $\frac{20}{100}$ m. = $\frac{1}{5}$ m.

Breadth of brick = 10 cm. = $\frac{10}{100}$ m. = $\frac{1}{10}$ m.

Area of a brick = $\frac{1}{5} \times \frac{1}{10} = \frac{1}{50}$ sq. m.

Hence, number of bricks reqd. = $\frac{85}{2} \div \frac{1}{50}$

$$= \frac{85}{2} \times \frac{50}{1} = 2125.$$

12. Find the volume of a cuboid 5 cm. long. 4 cm. wide and 3 cm. high.

Solution:

Volume of the cuboid = $l \times b \times h$

$$= 5 \times 4 \times 3$$

$$= 60 \text{ cubic cm.}$$

13. How much distance does a boy cover in walking round 5 times around a rectangular field 80 m long and 50 m. wide?

Solution:

Walking around once around a rectangular field = Perimeter of the field

Perimeter of the rectangular field

= 2 (Length + Breadth)

= 2 (80 + 50) = 260 m.

Total distance covered in walking round 5 times around the field = 5 × 260 = 1300 m.

14. A rectangular hall 12 meters long 8 metres broad is surrounded by a verandah 2 metres wide. Find the area of the verandah.

Solution:

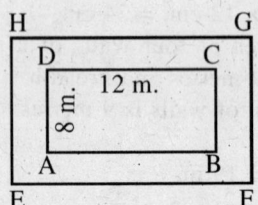

Area of the verandah = Area of EFGH – Area of ABCD.

= 16 × 12 – 12 × 8

= 192 – 96

= 96 sq. metres.

15. How many bricks 10 cm. long 7 cm. wide are needed to pave a rectangular floor 14 m. long and 12.5 m. wide?

Solution:

Area of the floor = 14 × 12.5 sq. m.

$$= 14 \times 12.5 \times 100 \times 100 \text{ cm}^2$$

$$= 17,50,000 \text{ cm}^2$$

Area of one brick = 10 × 7 cm² = 70 cm²

Number of bricks needed = $\dfrac{1750000}{70}$

$$= 25000.$$

EXERCISE

1. A rectangular field is 80 metres long and 60 metres wide. A 2 metres wide path runs round it. Find the area of the path.
   A. 576 m²   B. 536 m²
   C. 566 m²   D. 586 m²

2. Area of rectangular field is 726 sq. m. If the ratio between its length and breadth be 3 : 2, find the length and breadth.
   A. 33m, 22m
   B. 44 m, 11m
   C. 22 m, 11 m
   D. 30 m, 25 m

3. The perimeter of a rectangle is 30 metres and the ratio of the length to the breadth is 7 : 3, find the area of rectangle.
   A. 46.25 m²   B. 47.25 m²
   C. 48.25 m²   D. 49.25 m²

4. A rectangular photograph is 12 cm. long and 9 cm. broad. What length of the wooden frame would be needed for framing it? What will be the cost of the frame if one meter of the wood cost rupee one?
   A. 42 cm, 42 p   B. 40 cm, 40 p
   C. 38 cm, 42 p   D. 44 cm, 44 p

5. Find the perimeter of a square field whose area is 169 square metres.
   A. 39 m
   B. 48 m
   C. 52 m
   D. 44 m

6. How many bricks 20 cm. long and 10 cm. wide will be required to pave a floor 10 metres long and 8 metres wide?
   A. 4000
   B. 3500
   C. 5000
   D. 4500

7. A rectangular field is 75 metres long and 27 metres wide. Area of a square field is equal to the area of this rectangular field. Find the perimeter of the square field.
   A. 160 m
   B. 170 m
   C. 180 m
   D. 165 m

8. One side of a square garden is 560 metres. What is the cost of fencing it at the rate of ₹ 12 for 10 metres.
   A. ₹ 2688
   B. ₹ 2484
   C. ₹ 2577
   D. ₹ 2644

9. A floor of a room is square in shape and its area is 25 sq. m. What is the area of its four walls, if the height of the room is 4 m.?
   A. 60 m^2
   B. 70 m^2
   C. 75 m^2
   D. 80 m^2

10. The area of a rectangular field is 1,053 square metres. Its length is 39 metres. What is its breadth?
    A. 25 m
    B. 27 m
    C. 19 m
    D. 31 m

11. Find the area and perimeter of a square garden whose one side measures 38 metres.
    A. 1444 m^2, 152 m
    B. 1455 m^2, 142 m
    C. 1488 m^2, 162 m
    D. 1477 m^2, 172 m

12. A hall is 16 metres long 14 metres broad and 10 m. high. Each wall has a door 5 metres long and 4 metres wide and a window 3 metres long and 2 metres wide. Find the area of the four walls of the room.
    A. 484 m^2
    B. 486 m^2
    C. 496 m^2
    D. 502 m^2

13. Find the cost of carpet 28 m. long, 22 m wide, at ₹ 4.35 per square metres.
    A. ₹ 2679.60
    B. ₹ 2669.50
    C. ₹ 2689.64
    D. ₹ 2696.60

14. Perimeter of a rectangular field 50 m long and 30 m. broad is equal to the perimeter of a square field. Find the area of the square field.
    A. 1200 m^2
    B. 1400 m^2
    C. 1500 m^2
    D. 1600 m^2

15. Perimeter of a square field is 36 metres. Find its area.
    A. 61 m^2
    B. 71 m^2
    C. 81 m^2
    D. 88 m^2

16. The perimeter of a rectangle is 60 metres and the ratio of the length to the breadth is 7 : 3, find the area of the rectangle.
    A. 169 m^2
    B. 196 m^2
    C. 184 m^2
    D. 189 m^2

17. The perimeter of rectangular field is 480 meters and the ratio between the length and breadth is 5 : 3, find the area of the rectangle.
    A. 13500 m^2
    B. 12800 m^2
    C. 14200 m^2
    D. 11500 m^2

18. Area of a square garden is 16,900 square metres. A path 1 metre wide runs round it. Find the area of the path.
    A. 529 m^2
    B. 524 m^2
    C. 532 m^2
    D. 520 m^2

19. One side of a square garden is 85 decametres. What is the cost of fencing it at the rate of 25 paise per metre?
    A. ₹ 820
    B. ₹ 830
    C. ₹ 840
    D. ₹ 850

20. One side of a square tile is 10 cm. How many tiles are required for a wall 2.5 m long and 2 m. high?
    A. 500
    B. 400
    C. 475
    D. 525

ANSWERS

1	2	3	4	5	6	7	8	9	10
A	A	B	A	C	A	C	A	D	B

11	12	13	14	15	16	17	18	19	20
A	C	A	D	C	D	A	B	D	A

EXPLANATORY ANSWERS

1. Area of the rectangular field = 80 × 60

= 4800 sq. m.

80 + 4 = 84; 60 + 4 = 64

Area of the path = 84 × 64 – 80 × 60

= 5376 – 4800

= 576 sq. m.

2. Lenght : Breadth = 3 : 2

Let the length of the field be $3x$ and its breadth be $2x$

$\Rightarrow 3x \times 2x = 726$

$\therefore \quad 6x^2 = 726$

$\therefore \quad x^2 = 121$

$\therefore \quad x = \sqrt{121} = 11$

$\therefore$ Length of the rectangular field

= 3 × 11 = 33 m.

$\therefore$ Breadth of the rectangular field

= 2 × 11 = 22 m.

3. Perimeter of the rectangle = 30 metre

$\therefore$ Length + Breadth = 15 metre

But Length : Breadth = 7 : 3

$\therefore$ Length $= \dfrac{7 \times 15}{10} = \dfrac{21}{2} = 10.5$ m.

$\therefore$ Breadth $= \dfrac{3 \times 15}{10} = 4.5$ m.

$\therefore$ Area of the rectangle = 10.5 × 4.5

= 47.25 sq. m

4. Perimeter of the wooden frame

= 2 (12 + 9) = 42 cm.

Hence, 42 cm. long wood is needed for the frame.

Now cost of 1 m. wood = ₹ 1

$\therefore$ Cost of 42 cm. wood $= \dfrac{42}{100} = ₹\, 0.42$

or 42 p.

5. Area of the square field = 169 sq. m.

$\therefore$ One side of the square field

$= \sqrt{169}\,\text{m.} = 13\,\text{m.}$

Perimeter of a square = 4 × Side

Perimeter of the square field = 4 × 13 = 52 m.

6. Surface area of one brick = 20 × 10

= 200 sq. m.

Area of the floor = 10 × 8 sq. m.

= 10 × 8 × 100 × 100 sq. cm.

Number of bricks required

$= \dfrac{10 \times 8 \times 100 \times 100}{200} = 4000.$

7. Area of the rectangular field = 75 × 27 sq. m

= 2025 sq. m

Area of the square field = 2025 sq. m

One side of the square field $= \sqrt{2025} = 45$ m.

$\therefore$ Perimeter of the square field = 4 × Side

= 4 × 45 = 180 m.

8. One side of the square garden = 560 m.

$\therefore$ Perimeter of the square garden = 4 × 560

Cost of 10 m. fencing = ₹ 12

$\therefore$ Cost of fencing for 4 × 560 m $= \dfrac{12 \times 4 \times 560}{10}$

= ₹ 2688

9. Area of the square floor = 25 sq. m.

One side of the square floor $= \sqrt{25} = 5$ m.

Height = 4 m.

Area of the four walls = 2 × h ($l + b$)

= 2 × 4 (5 + 5)

= 80 sq. m.

10. Length × Breadth = Area

Length = 39 m. Area = 1053 sq. m.

$\therefore$ Breadth $= \dfrac{\text{Area}}{\text{Length}} = \dfrac{1053}{39} = 27$ m.

11. One side of the square garden = 38 m

∴ Area of the square garden = 38 × 38

= 1444 sq. m.

Perimeter of the square garden

= 38 × 4 = 152 m.

12. Area of the 4 doors = 4 × 5 × 4 = 80 sq. m.

Area of the 4 windows = 4 × 3 × 2 = 24 sq. m.

Total area of the 4 doors and 4 windows

= 104 sq. m.

Area of the four walls

= 2 × 10 (16 + 14) − 104

= 600 − 104

= 496 sq. m.

13. Area of the carpet = 28 × 22 sq. m.

Cost of carpet = 28 × 22 × 4.35 = ₹ 2679.60

14. Perimeter of a rectangular field = 2 $(l + b)$

= 2 (50 + 30) = 160 m.

∴ Perimeter of the square field = 160 m.

∴ One side of the square field $= \dfrac{160}{4} = 40$

∴ Area of the square field = 40 × 40

= 1600 sq. m.

15. Perimeter of a square = 4 × Side

4 × Side = 36

Side = 9 m.

Area of a square = $(Side)^2$

∴ Area of the square field = 9 × 9 = 81 sq. m.

16. Let length of rectangle = $7x$

Breadth of rectangle = $3x$

Perimeter = 2(7x + 3x)

⇒ 20x = 60

⇒ x = 3

Length = 21 m and Breadth = 9 m

Area = 21 × 9 = 189 m².

17. 2(5x + 3x) = 480

16x = 480

⇒ $x = \dfrac{480}{16}$

= 30

l = 5 × 30 = 150 m

b = 3 × 30 = 90 m

Area = 150 × 90 = 13500 m².

18. Area of the square garden = 16900

∴ Side of square = $\sqrt{16900}$ = 130 m

Area with path = $(132)^2$

= 17424 m²

Area of the path = 17424 − 16900

= 524 m²

19. Side of square = 850 m

Perimeter = 4 × 850 m

Cost of fencing = $4 \times 850 \times \dfrac{1}{4}$

= ₹ 850.

20. No. of tiles = $\dfrac{5 \times 100 \times 200}{2 \times 10 \times 10}$ = 500.

13 VOLUMES

REMEMBER

(i) Volume of sphere $= \dfrac{4}{3} \pi r^3$, where r is the radius of the sphere.

(ii) Volume of a cube $= (l)^3$, where l is the edge of the cube.

(iii) Volume of cone $= \dfrac{1}{3} \pi r^2 h$, where r is the radius of the base and h height.

(iv) Volume of a cylinder $= \pi r^2 h$ where r is the radius of the base and h is the height of cylinder.

(v) Volume of a cuboid (rectangular solid) $= l \times b \times h$, where l, b and h denote length, breadth and height respectively.

(vi) Surface area of the sphere $= 4\pi r^2$

(vii) Curved Surface Area of cylinder $= 2\pi rh$

(viii) Total Surface area of a cuboid $= 2\,(l.b + b.h + l.h)$

(ix) Area of the slant side of cone $= \pi rl$, where l is the side and is equal to $\sqrt{r^2 + h^2}$

SOLVED EXAMPLE

1. A soap cake is 8 cm. long, 5 cm. broad and 2.5 cm. high. How many such soap cakes can be placed inside a cardboard whose length, breadth and height are 56 cm., 35 cm. and 25 cm. respectively?

Solution:

Volume of one soap cake $= 8 \times 5 \times \dfrac{5}{2}$ cm^3

$$= \dfrac{200}{2} = 100 \text{ cm}^3$$

Volume of cardboard $= 56 \times 35 \times 25$ cm^3

Hence, the number of soap cakes in the cardboard
$= 56 \times 35 \times 25 \div 100$ cm^3

$$= \dfrac{56 \times 35 \times 25}{100} = 490.$$

2. A tank is 6 m. long, 5 m. wide and 4 m. high. How much water can it hold?

Solution:

Length of tank = 6 cm.

Breadth of tank = 5 cm.

Height of tank = 4 cm.

∴ Volume of tank $= 6 \times 5 \times 4$ m^3 = 120 cu. metres

Hence, quantity of water in tank = 120 cu. metres

EXERCISE

1. How many cubes having 2 cm. edge will be required to make a cube having 4 cm. edge?
   A. 6   B. 4
   C. 8   D. 2

2. The area of the floor of a rectangular room is 10 sq. m. Its height is 4 metre. What is the volume of air in that room?
   A. 30 cc   B. 40 cc
   C. 28 cc   D. 35 cc

3. A soap cake is 7 cm. long, 5 cm. broad and 2.5 cm. high. How many soap cakes may be put in a card board 56 cm. long 40 cm. broad and 25 cm. high?
   A. 540   B. 620
   C. 580   D. 640

4. A solid (rectangular) 10 cm. long, 8 cm. wide and 6 cm. thick weigh 9 kg. Find the weight of another solid of the same metal whose

length is 20 cm., width 4 cm. and thickness 3 cm.

A. 4.5 kg   B. 3.8 kg
C. 5.5 kg   D. 4.8 kg

5. From a log of wood being 3 metres long 1 metre broad and 50 cm. high. How many pieces of 25 cm. long, 20 cm. broad and 10 cm. high can be cut?

A. 125   B. 230
C. 300   D. 340

6. A rectangular tank $6\frac{1}{2}$ m. long and 3 m. broad contain 2 m. high full of water. Water of this tank is transferred to another tank 6 m. long and 5 m. broad. Find the height of water in this tank.

A. 1.2 m   B. 1.3 m
C. 1.4 m   D. 1.5 m

7. Find the volume of a cube whose one side is 6 cm.

A. 36 cm^3 B. 64 cm^3
C. 125 cm^3 D. 216 cm^3

8. The length, breadth and height of a cuboid are 1 m., 50 cm. and 25 cm. respectively. Find its volume.

A. $\frac{1}{4}$ m^3 B. $\frac{1}{6}$ m^3
C. $\frac{1}{9}$ m^3 D. $\frac{1}{8}$ m^3

9. Find the volume of a cuboid whose length, breadth and height are 1 m., 15 cm. and 25 cm. respectively.

A. 32500 cm^3 B. 37500 cm^3
C. 34500 cm^3 D. 36500 cm^3

10. A tank is 8 metres long, 5 metres broad and 2 metres high. How much water can be contained in it?

A. 80 m^3 B. 70 m^3
C. 60 m^3 D. 52 m^3

11. A drum $\frac{5}{8}$ part is full. If 75 litres more are required to fill the drum completely, find the capacity of the drum.

A. 180 l B. 220 l
C. 200 l D. 250 l

12. A wall 8 m long 6 m high and 22.5 cm thick is made up of bricks each measuring (25 cm × 11.25 cm × 6 cm). The number of bricks required is :

A. 6000   B. 5600
C. 6400   D. 7200

13. The maximum length of rod that can be kept in a rectangular box of dimensions 8 cm × 6 cm × 2 cm, is:

A. $2\sqrt{13}$ cm   B. $2\sqrt{14}$ m
C. $2\sqrt{26}$ cm   D. $10\sqrt{2}$ m

14. A rectangular block 6 cm × 12 cm × 15 cm is cut up into exact number of equal cubes. The least possible number of cubes will be :

A. 6   B. 11
C. 33   D. 40

15. Three cubes of iron whose edges are 6 cm, 8 cm and 10 cm respectively are melted and formed into a single cube. The edge of the new cube formed is :

A. 12 cm   B. 14 cm
C. 16 cm   D. 18 cm

16. The surface area of a cube is 600 cm^2. The length of its diagonal is :

A. 10/$\sqrt{3}$ cm   B. 10/$\sqrt{2}$ cm
C. $10\sqrt{3}$ cm   D. $10\sqrt{2}$ cm

17. A beam 9 m long, 40 cm wide and 20 cm high is made up of iron which weighs 50 kg per cubic metre. The weight of the beam is :

A. 56 kg   B. 48 kg
C. 36 kg   D. 27 kg

18. Given that 1 cu cm of marble weighs 25 gms, the weight of a marble block 28 cm in width and 5 cm thick is 112 kg. The length of the block is :

A. 36 cm   B. 37.5 cm
C. 32 cm   D. 26.5 cm

19. The volume of a wall, 5 times as high as it is broad and 8 times as long as it is high, is 12.8 cu metres. The breadth of the wall is :
A. 30 cm   B. 40 cm
C. 22.5 cm   D. 25 cm

20. In a shower 5 cm of rain falls. The volume of water that falls on 1.5 hectares of ground is :
A. 75 cu m   B. 750 cu m
C. 7500 cu m   D. 75000 cu m

ANSWERS

1	2	3	4	5	6	7	8	9	10
C	B	D	A	C	B	D	D	B	A

11	12	13	14	15	16	17	18	19	20
C	C	C	D	A	C	C	C	B	B

EXPLANATORY ANSWERS

1. Number of cubes $= \dfrac{4\times4\times4}{2\times2\times2} = 8.$

2. Volume of air in the room
= Area × Height
$= 10 \times 4$
= 40 C.C.

3. No. of soap cakes $= \dfrac{56\times40\times25\times10}{7\times5\times25}$
$= 8 \times 8 \times 10$
= 640.

4. Volume of first solid $= 10 \times 8 \times 6 = 480$ cm^3
Volume of 2nd solid $= 20 \times 4 \times 3 = 240$ cm^3
∵ Weight of 480 cm^3 = 9 kg
∴ Wight of 240 cm^3 $= \dfrac{9}{480} \times 240 = \dfrac{9}{2}$ kg
= 4.5 kg.

5. Required no. of pieces $= \dfrac{300\times100\times50}{25\times20\times10}$
= 300.

6. Height of water in the tank $= \dfrac{13\times3\times2}{2\times6\times5}$
$= \dfrac{13}{10}$ m = 1.3 m.

7. Volume of cube $= 6 \times 6 \times 6 = 216$ cm^3.

8. Volume of cuboid $= l \times b \times h$
$= 100 \times 50 \times 25$ cm^3
$= \dfrac{100\times50\times25}{100\times100\times100}$ m^3
$= \dfrac{1}{8}$ m^3.

9. Volume of cuboid $= 100 \times 15 \times 25$
$= 37500$ cm^3

10. Volume of cuboid $= l \times b \times h$
$= 8 \times 5 \times 2 = 80$ m^3.

11. Let the capacity of the drum $= x\, l$
∵ $\dfrac{5}{8}$ part of drum is full.
∴ Remaining $= x - \dfrac{5}{8}x = \dfrac{8x-5x}{8} = \dfrac{3x}{8}$
According to the question,
$\dfrac{3x}{8} = 75$
⇒ $3x = 8 \times 75$
⇒ $x = \dfrac{8\times75}{3}$
= 200
Hence, capacity of the drum = 200 l.

12. Number of bricks $= \dfrac{800 \times 600 \times 22.5}{25 \times 11.25 \times 6}$

$\qquad\qquad\qquad = 6400.$

13. Required length $= \sqrt{(8^2 + 6^2 + 2^2)}$ cm

$\qquad\qquad\qquad = \sqrt{104} = 2\sqrt{26}$ cm

14. Volume of rectangular block $= (6 \times 12 \times 15)$
$\qquad\qquad\qquad = 1080$ cm^3
The side of largest cube = HCF of 6 cm,
12 cm, 15 cm = 3 cm
Volume of cube $= (3 \times 3 \times 3)$ cm^3 = 27 cm^3
Number of cubes = (1080/27) = 40.

15. Volume of the new cube $= [6^3 + 8^3 + (10)^3]$
$\qquad\qquad\qquad = 1728$ cu cm

Let the edge of new cube be a cm
Then, $a^3 = 1728 = (4 \times 4 \times 4 \times 3 \times 3 \times 3)$
$\Rightarrow \quad a = 12$ cm

16. $6a^2 = 600 \Rightarrow a^2 = 100$ or $a = 10$ cm

So, diagonal $= \sqrt{3}a = 10\sqrt{3}$ cm.

17. Volume $= (9 \times \dfrac{40}{100} \times \dfrac{20}{100})$ cu m $= \dfrac{18}{25}$ cu m

So, weight of the beam $= \left(\dfrac{18}{25} \times 50\right)$ kg

$\qquad\qquad\qquad = 36$ kg.

18. Let length $= x$ cm

Then, $x \times 28 \times 5 \times \dfrac{25}{1000} = 112$

So, $x = \dfrac{112 \times 1000}{28 \times 5 \times 25} = 32$ cm
So, length of block = 32 cm

19. Let, breadth $= x$ metres . Then,
$\qquad\qquad$ height $= 5x$ metres
and $\quad$ length $= 40x$ metres
So, $\quad x \times 5x \times 40x = 12.8$

or $\qquad\qquad x^3 = \dfrac{12.8}{200}$

$\qquad\qquad\qquad = \dfrac{128}{2000}$

$\qquad\qquad\qquad = \dfrac{64}{1000}$

So, $x = \dfrac{4}{10}$ m $= \left(\dfrac{4}{10} \times 100\right)$ cm = 40 cm

20. $\qquad$ Area $= (1.5 \times 10000)$ sq . metres
$\qquad\qquad\quad = 15000$ sq metres.
$\qquad$ Depth $= 5/100$ m $= 1/20$ m
So, $\;$ Volume $= $ (Area $\times$ Depth)
$\qquad\qquad\quad = (15000 \times 1/20) = 750$ cu m.

Geometry is a science which deals with solids, surfaces, lines and points etc.

Line: Mark two points A and B on your paper. You will find that it is possible to draw a straight path through A and B. It is called the line AB and is considered to extend indefinitely in both directions. So we mark two arrows on a line as shown in the figure.

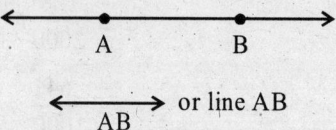

or line AB

Ray: If a line is drawn through A and the line is extended idefinitely in one direction only but not in other direction then it is called a ray. As for example, in the following diagram, the line is extended in the right direction of A but not to the left.

Ray is shown as AB. Here the arrow AB is shown only in one direction. It means that A is an end point and the arrow shows that it is extended indefinitely.

Segment: The portion between A and B including points A and B is called segment of AB or segment AB.

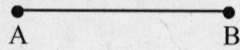

$\overline{AB}$ or Line Segment AB

Solid: It is a limited portion of space, *i.e.*, space occupied by a body.

Surface: It is the boundary of a solid.

Concurrent lines: If three or more lines are converging at a point, they are called concurrent lines.

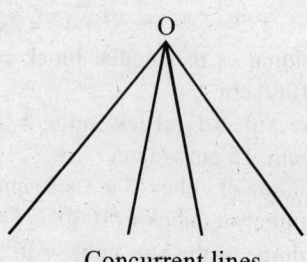

Concurrent lines

Intersecting lines: If two lines meet at a point, they are called intersecting lines.

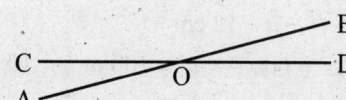

In the above figure, AB and CD are two intersecting lines intersecting at the point O.

Angle: It is the union of two rays which have the same end point.

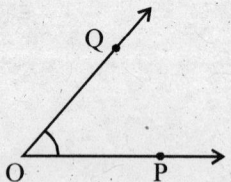

If through a point O in a plane, two rays OP and OQ are drawn in different directions; the figure so formed is angle OP and OQ are known as the arms of the angle and the point O is known as the Vertex of the angle. This angle can be denoted as $\angle$ O or $\angle$ Q O P or $\angle$ P O Q.

The unit of an angle is degrees.

Right Angle: An angle of 90° is known as the right angle. In the figure, $\angle$ CBA is the right angle.

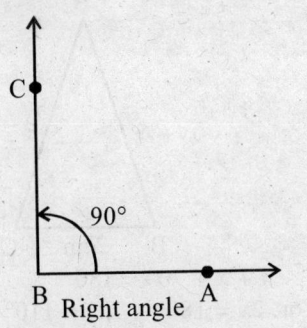

90°

B Right angle A

Straight Angle: An angle of 180° is called a straight angle.

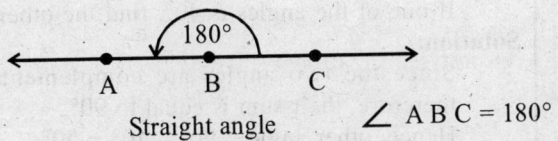

180°

A B C

Straight angle   ∠ A B C = 180°

Acute Angle: An angle which is less then 90° is known as an acute angle. For example, angles such as 30°, 50°, 75°, 86°, etc. are all acute angles.

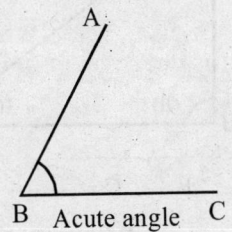

A

B   Acute angle   C

Obtuse Angle: An angle more than 90° and less than 180° is called an obtuse angle. For example, angle of 100°, 130°, 175° etc. are obtuse angles.

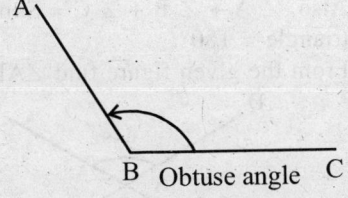

A

B   Obtuse angle   C

Reflex Angle: An angle more than 180° and less than 360° is called a reflex angle. For example, angles of 190°, 205°, 329°, 340° etc. are reflex angles.

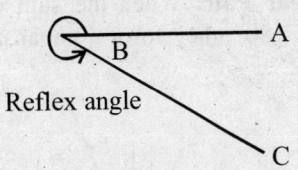

B   A

Reflex angle

C

Supplementary Angles: If the sum of two angles is 180°, each angle is known as the supplementary angle of the other.

For example, if the measurements of two angles are 145° and 35° respectively these two angles are supplementary to each other because the sum of 145° and 35° is 180°.

Complementary Angles: If the sum of two angles is equal to 90° each angle is known as complementary angles of the other.

For example, if the measurements of two angles are 20° and 70°, then these two angles are complementary to each other because the sum of 20° and 70° is equal to 90°.

Adjacent Angles: Two angles having same vertex and one arm in common are called adjacent angles.

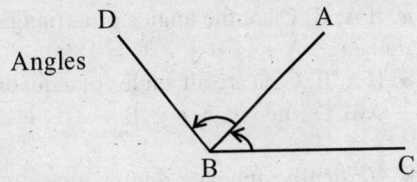

D   A

Angles

B   C

In the above figure, ∠ ABC and ∠ ABD are adjacent angles.

Triangle: A figure formed by the three straight lines is called a triangle. In the figure, ABC is a triangle formed by the straight lines AB, BC and CA.

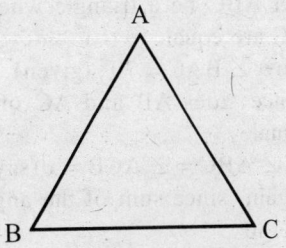

A

B   C

Linear Pair: When the sum of two adjacent angles is 180°, they form a linear pair.

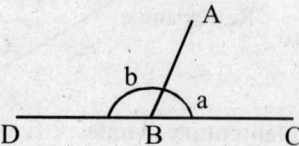

In the above figure, $\angle a + \angle b = 180°$. Thus we say that $\angle a$ and $\angle b$ form a linear pair.

Quadrilateral: A figure formed by four straight lines is called a quadrilateral. In the figure, ABCD, a quadrilateral is formed by the straight lines AB, BC, CD, DA.

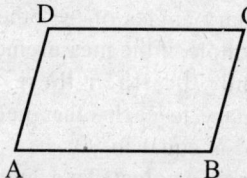

REMEMBER

- If A, B, C are the angles of a triangle ABC, then $\angle A + \angle B + \angle C = 180°$
- If A, B, C, D are all angles of a quadrilateral ABCD, then $\angle A + \angle B + \angle C + \angle D$
$$= 360°$$
- Vertically opposite angles are equal.

SOLVED EXAMPLE

1. Two sides of a triangle are equal. The angle opposit to third side is 70°. Find the measures of other two angles.

Solution:

Let ABC be a triangle where sides AB and AC are equal.

Now $\angle BAC = 70°$ (given)

Since sides AB and AC of the triangle are equal.

$\therefore$ $\angle ABC = \angle ACB = x$ (say)

Again, since sum of the angles of a triangle is 180°

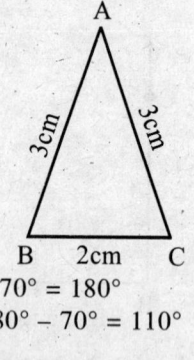

$\therefore$ $x + x + 70° = 180°$

or, $2x = 180° - 70° = 110°$

$$x = \frac{110}{2} = 55°.$$

2. Two angles are complementary to each other. If one of the angles is 40°, find the other.

Solution:

Since the two angles are complementary, therefore, their sum is equal to 90°.

Hence, other angle = $90° - 40° = 50°$.

3. In figure,

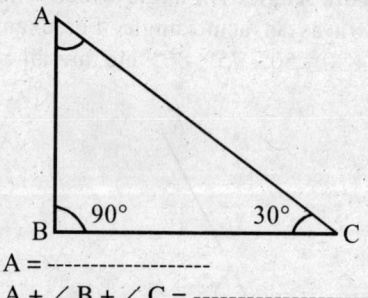

$\angle A =$ --------------------

$\angle A + \angle B + \angle C =$ ------------------------

Solution:

We know that the sum of angles of a triangle is equal to 180°.

$\therefore$ $\angle A = 180° - (\angle B + \angle C)$

$= 180° - (90° + 30°)$

$= 180° - 120°$

$= 60°$

Also, $\angle A + \angle B + \angle C =$ Sum of angles of triangle = 180°.

4. From the given figure find $\angle ABE$.

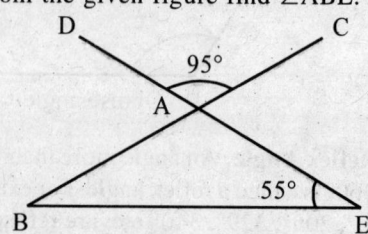

Solution:

We know from geometry

∠ DAC = ∠ BAE = 95°

∴ ∠ ABE + ∠ AEB = 85°

or, ∠ ABE = 85° − ∠ AEB

= 85° − 55° = 30°.

EXERCISE

1. Pick out the complementary angle of 45° from the list of the angle.
   A. 75°   B. 45°
   C. 90°   D. 135°

2. Spot an obtuse angle.
   A. 280°   B. 210°
   C. 170°   D. 260°

3. How many degrees are there in three right angles?
   A. 180°   B. 260°
   C. 360°   D. 270°

4. How many lines can you draw through two points?
   A. Two   B. Only one
   C. Many   D. None of these

5. For what value of x, ∠ POQ will be a straight angle?

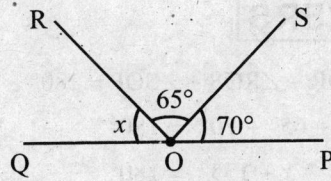

   A. 65°   B. 45°
   C. 55°   D. 40°

6. Pick out the acute angle from the following:
   A. 75°   B. 145°
   C. 155°   D. 135°

7. How many lines can you draw through one point?
   A. Two   B. One
   C. Many   D. None

8. How many lines can you draw through three non-collinear points?
   A. None   B. Three only
   C. Two only   D. Exactly one.

9. How many degrees are there in $\frac{2}{5}$ of a straight angle?
   A. 90°   B. 180°
   C. 72°   D. 60°

10. How many degrees are in $\frac{1}{10}$th of a right angle?
    A. 10°   B. 9°
    C. 40°   D. 80°

11. Find ∠ a from the given figure.

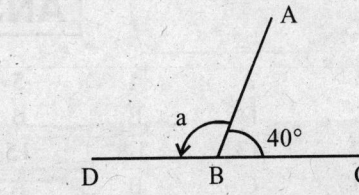

    A. 160°   B. 120°
    C. 140°   D. 90°

12. Pick out the supplementary angle of 95°.
    A. 95°   B. 15°
    C. 90°   D. 85°

13. From the given figures, find ∠ ACD.

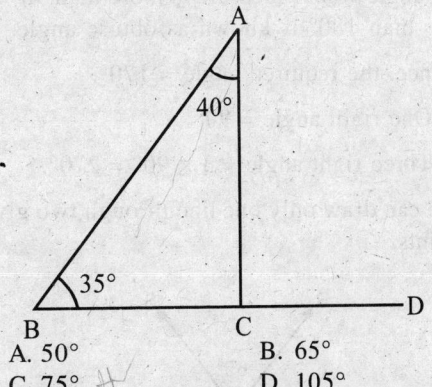

    A. 50°   B. 65°
    C. 75°   D. 105°

14. Find the complementary angle of 80°.
    A. 100°   B. 10°
    C. 75°   D. 90°

15. Find the supplementary angle of 150°.
A. 30°   B. 40°
C. 50°   D. 60°

16. Sum of three angles of a quadrilateral is 280°. Find the fourth angle of the quadrilateral.
A. 50°   B. 110°
C. 80°   D. 105°

17. Sum of two angles of a triangle is 110°. Find the third angle of the triangle.
A. 30°   B. 50°
C. 60°   D. 70°

18. Find the third angle of a triangle, if two angles are 45° and 25° respectively.
A. 105°   B. 110°
C. 95°   D. 85°

19. Two sides of a triangle are equal. The angle opposite to third side is 70°. Find the measures of other two angles.
A. 45°   B. 40°
C. 55°   D. 65°

20. In the given figure, AOB is a straight line. If ∠AOC + ∠BOD = 85°, then find the measure of ∠COD.

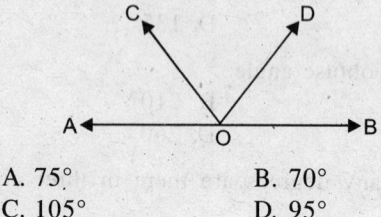

A. 75°   B. 70°
C. 105°   D. 95°

ANSWERS

1	2	3	4	5	6	7	8	9	10
B	C	D	B	B	A	C	B	C	B
11	12	13	14	15	16	17	18	19	20
C	D	C	B	A	C	D	B	C	D

EXPLANATORY ANSWERS

1. Complementary angle of 45°
= 90 – 45 ° = 45°.

2. An angle whose measure is more than 90° but less than 180° is known as obtuse angle.

Hence, the required angle = 170°.

3. ∵ One right angle = 90°

∴ Three right angle = 3 × 90° = 270°.

4. We can draw only one line through two given points.

5.

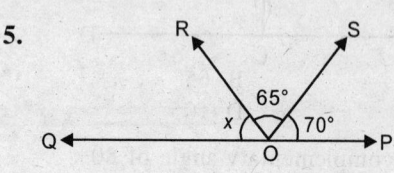

∵ ∠POQ = 180°

∴ ∠QOR + ∠ROS + ∠SOP = 180°

⇒ $x + 65° + 70°$ = 180°

⇒ $x + 135°$ = 180°

⇒ x = 180° – 135°

                     = 45°

Hence, value of x = 45°.

6. An angle whose measure is more than 0° but less than 90° is called acute angle.

Hence, the required angle = 75°.

7. We can draw many lines through one given point.

8. We can draw only three lines through three non-collinear points.

9. One straight angle = 180°

$\dfrac{2}{5}$ of a straight angle $= \dfrac{2}{5} \times 180°$

$= 2 \times 36$

$= 72°.$

10. $\because$ One right angle $= 90°$

$\therefore \dfrac{1}{10}$ of the right angle $= \dfrac{1}{10} \times 90° = 9°.$

11.

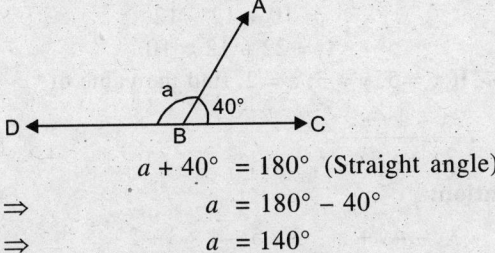

$a + 40° = 180°$ (Straight angle)

$\Rightarrow \qquad a = 180° - 40°$

$\Rightarrow \qquad a = 140°$

Hence, the value of $a = 140°.$

12. Supplementary angle of $95° = 180° - 95° = 85°.$

13.

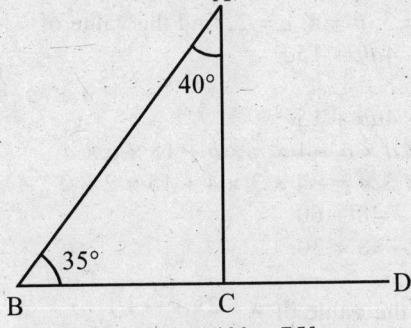

$\angle ACD = 35° + 40° = 75°$

(exterior angle is equal to sum of opposite two interior angles)

14. The complementary angle of $80°$
$= 90° - 80° = 10°$

15. The supplementary angle of $150°$
$= 180° - 150° = 30°.$

16. Sum of four angles of a quadrilateral $= 360°$
$\because$ Sum of three angles of quadrilateral $= 280°$
(given)
$\therefore$ Fourth angle $= 360° - 280° = 80°.$

17. Sum of three angles of a triangle $= 180°$
$\because$ Sum of two angles $= 110°$ (given)
$\therefore$ Third angle $= 180° - 110° = 70°.$

18. Let in a triangle ABC,
$\angle A = 45°, \angle B = 25°$
We have,
$\angle A + \angle B + \angle C = 180°$
$\Rightarrow \quad 45° + 25° + \angle C = 180°$
$\Rightarrow \qquad 70° + \angle C = 180°$
$\Rightarrow \qquad \angle C = 180° - 70°$
$= 110°$
Hence, third angle of the triangle $= 110°.$

19.

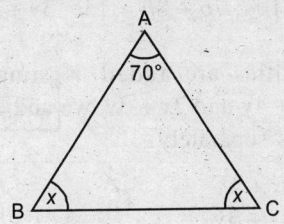

Let $\triangle ABC$, in which $AB = AC$
$\Rightarrow \qquad \angle B = \angle C = x$
$\therefore \quad \angle A + \angle B + \angle C = 180°$
$\Rightarrow \qquad x + x + 70° = 180°$
$\Rightarrow \qquad 2x = 110°$
$\Rightarrow \qquad x = 55°$
$\therefore \angle B = \angle C = 55°.$

20.

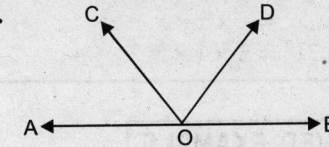

$\because \angle AOC + \angle COD + \angle DOB = 180°$
$\Rightarrow \angle AOC + \angle DOB + \angle COD = 180°$
$\Rightarrow 85° + \angle COD = 180°$
$\Rightarrow \angle COD = 180° - 85° = 95°$
Hence, the measure of $\angle COD = 95°.$

Like Arithmetic, Algebra is a science of numbers. In it, besides the figures of arithmetic the letters of the alphabet are extensively used to represent number.

Algebraic Expression: If we join two or more algebraic quantities by + or – we get algebraic expression. Thus $3x + 4y$; $7a + 8b - 4c$; $6a + 4b - 7c$ etc., are algebraic expressions.

Addition of Algebraic Expressions: We write $3x + 5x = 8x$, $6a + 4a = 10a$; $7b + 8b = 15b$, $3y + 7y = 10y$

Same type quantities are added as simple addition. If we add $3x + 4y$ and $2x + 3y$, we add the same type of quantities separately.

$$\begin{array}{r} 3x + 4y \\ 2x + 3y \\ \hline 5x + 7y \end{array}$$

Subtraction of Algebraic Expressions: Operation of subtraction is done in two steps. First we change the sign of the quantity which is to be subtracted and then we add it.

REMEMBER

$$x^2 = x \times x$$
$$x^3 = x \times x \times x$$
$$2x^2 = 2 \times x \times x$$

SOLVED EXAMPLE

1. Find the value of
   $3x + 4y$ if $x = 5$, $y = 3$

Solution:
$$3x + 4y = 3 \times x + 4 \times y$$
$$= 3 \times 5 + 4 \times 3$$
$$= 15 + 12 = 27.$$

2. If $x = 5$, $y = 4$, $z = 3$, find the value of
   $2x + 3y - 4z$.

Solution:
$$2x + 3y - 4z = 2 \times 5 + 3 \times 4 - 4 \times 3$$
$$= 10 + 12 - 12$$
$$= 22 - 12 = 10.$$

3. If $x = 5$, $y = 3$, $z = 2$, find the value of
   $$\frac{3x - 4y + z}{2x + y + z}$$

Solution:
$$\frac{3x - 4y + z}{2x + y + z} = \frac{3 \times 5 - 4 \times 3 + 2}{2 \times 5 + 3 + 2}$$
$$= \frac{15 - 12 + 2}{10 + 3 + 2} = \frac{17 - 12}{15} = \frac{5}{15} = \frac{1}{3}.$$

4. If $a = 3$, $b = 4$, $c = 2$, find the value of
   $2a^2 - 4ab + 15c^2$

Solution:
$$2a^2 - 4ab + 15c^2$$
$$= 2 \times a \times a - 4 \times a \times b + 15 \times c \times c$$
$$= 2 \times 3 \times 3 - 4 \times 3 \times 4 + 15 \times 2 \times 2$$
$$= 18 - 48 + 60$$
$$= 78 - 48 = 30.$$

5. Find the value of $x - 2y + \dfrac{x}{y} + 1$, when $x = 2$, $y = -1$

Solution:
Substituting $x = 2$, $y = -1$
$$x - 2y + \frac{x}{y} + 1 = 2 - 2(-1) + \frac{2}{-1} + 1$$
$$= 2 + 2 - 2 + 1 = 5 - 2 = 3.$$

6. Add the following:
   $2x + 3y$, $5x + 7y$, $3x + 4y$

Solution:
$$\begin{array}{r} 2x + 3y \\ 5x + 7y \\ + 3x + 4y \\ \hline 10x + 14y \end{array}$$

7. Add the following:

$8a - 7b + 6c$; $3a + 9b - 2c$

Solution:

$$\begin{array}{r} 8a - 7b + 6c \\ 3a + 9b - 2c \\ \hline 11a + 2b + 4c \end{array}$$

8. Add $(2a + 5b)$ and $(a + 7b)$

Solution:

$$\begin{array}{r} 2a + 5b \\ a + 7b \\ \hline 3a + 12b \end{array}$$

9. Add the following:

$7x - 4y$; $-3x + 9y$

Solution:

$$\begin{array}{r} 7x - 4y \\ -3x + 9y \\ \hline 4x + 5y \end{array}$$

10. If $a = 3\dfrac{6}{8}$, $b = 5\dfrac{5}{6}$ and $c = 2\dfrac{1}{3}$, then find the

value of $\left(a + b + \dfrac{b}{c} + 4 \right)$

Solution:

$$a + b + \frac{b}{c} + 4 = 3\frac{6}{8} + 5\frac{5}{6} + \frac{5\frac{5}{6}}{2\frac{1}{3}} + 4$$

$$= \frac{30}{8} + \frac{35}{6} + \frac{\frac{35}{6}}{\frac{7}{3}} + 4$$

$$= \frac{15}{4} + \frac{35}{6} + \frac{5}{2} + \frac{4}{1}$$

$$= \frac{45 + 70 + 30 + 48}{12} = \frac{193}{12} = 16\frac{1}{12}.$$

11. Add the following:

$x + 3y$; $2x + \dfrac{1}{2}y$; $\dfrac{1}{2}x + 3y$

Solution:

$$x + 3y;\ 2x + \frac{1}{2}y;\ \frac{1}{2}x + 3y$$

$$= x\left(1 + 2 + \frac{1}{2} \right) + y\left(3 + \frac{1}{2} + 3 \right)$$

$$= x\left(3 + \frac{1}{2} \right) + y\left(6 + \frac{1}{2} \right)$$

$$= \frac{7}{2}x + \frac{13}{2}y.$$

12. Subtract $2a + b - c$ from $a - b + c$

Solution.

$$\begin{array}{r} a - b + c \\ 2a + b - c \\ \underline{-\quad -\quad +} \\ -a - 2b + 2c \end{array}$$

13. Subtract $3a - 5b$ from $7a + b$

Solution:

$$\begin{array}{r} 7a + b \\ 3a - 5b \\ \underline{-\quad +} \\ 4a + 6b. \end{array}$$

14. Subtract $3x + 4y$ from $5x + 9y$

Solution:

$$\begin{array}{r} 5x + 9y \\ 3x + 4y \\ \underline{-\quad -} \\ 2x + 5y. \end{array}$$

15. Subtract $-2a + 3b$ from $2a + 3b$

Solution:

$$\begin{array}{r} 2a + 3b \\ -2a + 3b \\ \underline{+\quad -} \\ 4a. \end{array}$$

16. Multiply $(a + b)$ by c.

Solution:

$(a + b) \times c$

$= a \times c + b \times c = ac + bc.$

17. Multiply $6xy$ and $3x^2y$

Solution:

$$6xy \times 3x^2y = 6 \times 3 \times x^1 \times x^2 \times y^1 \times y^1$$
$$= 18 \times x^{1+2} \times y^{1+1}$$
$$= 18x^3 y^2.$$

18. Multiply $2a + 3b + 4c$ by $a - b + c$

Solution:

$$
\begin{array}{l}
2a + 3b + 4c \\
\times\ a - b + c \\
\hline
2a^2 + 3ab + 4ac \\
\quad\ - 2ab - 3b^2 - 4bc \\
\qquad\quad + 2ac + 3bc + 4c^2 \\
\hline
2a^2 + ab + 6ac - 3b^2 - bc + 4c^2
\end{array}
$$

19. Multiply $(2x + 3y)$ by $(3x + 4y)$

Solution:

$$
\begin{array}{l}
2x + 3y \\
\times\ 3x + 4y \\
\hline
6x^2 + 9xy \\
\quad\ + 8xy + 12y^2 \\
\hline
6x^2 + 17xy + 12y^2
\end{array}
$$

20. Multiply $(3x - 4y)$ by $(3x + 4y)$

Solution:

$$
\begin{array}{l}
3x - 4y \\
\times\ 3x + 4y \\
\hline
9x^2 - 12xy \\
\quad\ + 12xy - 16y^2 \\
\hline
9x^2 - 16y^2
\end{array}
$$

21. Divide $x^2 - 5x + 6$ by $x - 2$

Solution:

$$
\begin{array}{r}
x - 3 \\
x - 2)\overline{\smash{)}\,x^2 - 5x + 6} \\
\underline{\pm\ x^2 \mp 2x} \\
-3x + 6 \\
\underline{\mp\ 3x \pm 6} \\
\times
\end{array}
$$

$\therefore$ Hence, quotient is $(x - 3)$.

22. Divide $3x + 42$ by 3

Solution:

$$
\begin{array}{r}
x + 14 \\
3)\overline{3x + 42}(\\
\underline{3x} \\
42 \\
\underline{42} \\
\times
\end{array}
$$

$= x + 14.$

23. Divide $x^2 + 2xy + y^2$ by $x + y$

$$
\begin{array}{r}
x + y \\
x + y)\overline{x^2 + 2xy + y^2}(\\
\underline{x^2 \pm xy} \\
xy + y^2 \\
\underline{xy \pm y^2} \\
\times
\end{array}
$$

$= x + y.$

24. Find the remainder and the quotient if $x^2 + 10x + 29$ is divided by $x + 3$.

Solution:

$$
\begin{array}{r}
x + 7 \\
x + 3)\overline{x^2 + 10x + 29} \\
\underline{x^2 \pm 3x} \\
7x + 29 \\
\underline{7x \pm 21} \\
+ 8
\end{array}
$$

Remainder = 8
Quotient = $x + 7$.

EXERCISE

1. If $a = 4$, $b = 1$, find the value of $7a - 3b$
  A. 20 B. 22
  C. 25 D. 28

2. If $x = 2$, $y = 3$, find the value of $3x + 4y$.
  A. 18 B. 16
  C. 20 D. 15

3. If $x = 2$, $y = 1$, $z = 3$, find the value of $x^2 + xyz + y^2$:
  A. 8 B. 9
  C. 10 D. 11

4. If $x = 1$, $y = 2$, $z = 3$, find the value of $4x^2 + y^2 + z^2 - 3xyz + x$

A. 0   B. 1
C. 2   D. 4

5. If $a = 1$, $b = 2$, $c = 3$, find the value of $3a - 2b + 3c$
   A. 2   B. 4
   C. 5   D. 8

6. If $a = 2$, $b = 3$, $c = 4$, find the value of
   $$\frac{2a - 3b + 2c}{4a - 2b + 2c}$$
   A. $\dfrac{3}{10}$ B. $\dfrac{4}{5}$
   C. $\dfrac{7}{10}$ D. $\dfrac{8}{5}$

7. Add: $-2x - 7y + 6z$, $-5x + 4y - 2z$; $7x + 3y - 4z$
   A. 2   B. 0
   C. 4   D. 3

8. Add: $2x + 3y - z$; $-2x + 2y + z$
   A. $4x$ B. $5y$
   C. $2z$ D. 0

9. Subtract $a + b + c$ from $a + b - c$.
   A. $2a$ B. $2b$
   C. $-2c$ D. $2c$

10. Subtract $7x$ from $12x$.
    A. $19x$ B. $5x$
    C. $-5x$ D. $-19x$

11. Subtract $-3x$ from $2x$.
    A. $5x$ B. $-5x$
    C. $6x$ D. $-6x^2$

12. Multiply $2x^2$ by $8x^2$.
    A. $16x^2$ B. $10x^2$
    C. $16x^4$ D. $16x$

13. Multiply $(-4x^2)$ by $(-3x^4)$.
    A. $7x^6$ B. $-7x^6$
    C. $12x^6$ D. $-12x^6$

14. Divide $-21x^3$ by $7x^2$
    A. $3x$ B. $-3x$
    C. $3x^2$ D. $-3x^3$

15. Divide $x^2 - 9x + 14$ by $(x - 7)$
    A. $x - 2$ B. $x + 2$
    C. $x + 1$ D. $x - 1$

16. Divide $x^2 + 8x + 15$ by $(x + 5)$
    A. $x - 2$ B. $x - 3$
    C. $x + 2$ D. $x + 3$

17. Simplify: $\left(x + \dfrac{1}{x}\right)^2 - \left(x - \dfrac{1}{x}\right)^2$
    A. 2   B. 4
    C. 6   D. 8

18. Simplify: $(x + y)^2 - (x - y)^2$
    A. $2x^2$ B. $2y^2$
    C. $4xy$ D. $-4xy$

19. If $x = 2$, find $\left(x + \dfrac{1}{x}\right)^2$
    A. $\dfrac{5}{2}$ B. $\dfrac{10}{4}$
    C. $\dfrac{25}{4}$ D. $\dfrac{9}{4}$

20. Simplify: $x^2 + 11x + 18 \div (x + 2)$
    A. $x + 3$ B. $x - 3$
    C. $x - 9$ D. $x + 9$

21. What should be added to $x^2 + 7x + 10$ to make it completely divisible by $x + 4$
    A. 4   B. 2
    C. 6   D. 3

22. If $a = 1$, $b = 2$ and $c = 3$, find the value of
    $$\frac{a^2}{bc} - \frac{b^2}{ca} + \frac{c^2}{ab}$$
    A. $3\dfrac{1}{3}$ B. $2\dfrac{1}{3}$
    C. $4\dfrac{1}{3}$ D. $1\dfrac{1}{3}$

23. If $a = -2$, find the value of $\dfrac{7}{a - 2} + \dfrac{17}{a^2 + 4}$
    A. $\dfrac{5}{8}$ B. $\dfrac{7}{8}$
    C. $\dfrac{3}{8}$ D. $\dfrac{1}{8}$

24. Subtract $-4a$ from $15a$
    A. $11a$ B. $-11a$
    C. $-19a$ D. $19a$

25. Subtract 8a from 12a.
  A. $20a$ B. $-20a$
  C. $4a$ D. $-4a$

26. Simplify $(2x + 3y)(2x + 3y) - (2x - 3y)(2x - 3y)$
  A. $24xy$ B. $8x^2$
  C. $16x^2$ D. $18y^2$

27. If $a = 3$, $b = 4$, $c = 2$, find the value of $2a^2 - 4ab + 15c^2$
  A. 18   B. 20
  C. 30   D. 25

28. What will be HCF of x^3y^2, x^2y^3 and x^4y^4?
  A. x^3y^3 B. xy
  C. x^2y^2 D. x^4y^4

29. Find the LCM of $12a^3b$, $6a^2b^3$ and $4ab^4$
  A. $6a^3b^4$ B. $12a^4b^3$
  C. $8a^2b^2$ D. $12a^3b^4$

30. Find LCM of $a^2 - b^2$ and $a - b$
  A. $a^2 - b^2$ B. $a - b$
  C. $b - a$ D. $b^2 - a^2$

31. Factors of $x^2 - 25$ are:
  A. $(x - 1)(x - 25)$ B. $(x + 25)(x - 1)$
  C. $(x + 5)(x - 5)$ D. $(x - 5)(x - 5)$

32. Square of $\left(x - \dfrac{1}{x}\right)$ will be

  A. $x^2 - 2 - \dfrac{1}{x^2}$ B. $x^2 - 2 + \dfrac{1}{x^2}$

  C. $x^2 - 4 - \dfrac{1}{x^2}$ D. $x^2 - 2 + \dfrac{1}{x}$

33. Factors of $36 - 9x^2$ will be:
  A. $(6 + 3x)(6 - 3x)$
  B. $(3x - 6)(6 - 3x)$
  C. $(3x + 6)(3x - 6)$
  D. $(12x - 3x)(3 + 3x)$

34. Factors of $8x^3 + y^3$ are:
  A. $(2x + y)(4x^2 - 2xy + y^2)$
  B. $(2x + y)(4x^2 + 2xy + y^2)$
  C. $(2x - y)(4x^2 - 2xy + y^2)$
  D. $(2x + y)(4x^2 - 2xy - y^2)$

35. If the expression $x^3 + 5x^2 - 2 + k$ is completely divisible by $(x - 1)$, the value of k will be:

  A. -3 B. -8
  C. -3 D. -4

36. Find the factors of $x^2 + 3x - 10$
  A. $(x - 1)(x - 10)$ B. $(x - 2)(x + 5)$
  C. $(x + 2)(x - 5)$ D. $(x + 2)(x + 5)$

37. Factors of $1000 + C^3$ are:
  A. $(10 - c)(100 - 10c + c^2)$
  B. $(10 + c)(100 + 10c + c^2)$
  C. $(10 + c)(100 - 10c + c^2)$
  D. $(10 + c)(100 - 10c + c^2)$

38. If $x = \sqrt{3}$, the value of $x^4 + 2 + \dfrac{1}{x^4}$ will be:

  A. $\dfrac{9}{100}$ B. $\dfrac{81}{100}$

  C. $\dfrac{101}{9}$ D. $\dfrac{100}{9}$

39. Factors of $4x^2 + 8x - 5$ will be:
  A. $(2x - 1)(2x + 5)$ B. $(2x + 1)(2x + 5)$
  C. $(2x - 5)(2x - 1)$ D. $(2x + 5)(1 - 2x)$

40. If $(x - 2)$ is a factor of $x^2 + 2x - a$, the value of a will be:
  A. 8   B. 6
  C. 11   D. 3

41. Factors of $10a^2 - ab - 3b^2$ are:
  A. $(2a - b)(5a - 3b)$
  B. $(5a - 3b)(2a + b)$
  C. $(5a - 3b)(2a + b)$
  D. $(5a - 3b)(b - 2b)$

42. If $x = 3$ and $y = 4$, find the value of $256x^4 + 160x^2y^2 + 25y^4$
  A. 114967   B. 50176
  C. 103976   D. 914976

43. Factors of $a^2 - 2a^2 - 5a + 6$ are:
  A. $(a - 1)(a + 2)(a - 3)$
  B. $(a + 1)(a + 2)(a - 3)$
  C. $(a - 1)(a + 2)(a + 3)$
  D. $(a + 1)(a - 2)(a + 3)$

44. Find the HCF of x^3y^2, x^2y^3 and x^4y^4.
  A. x^3y^4 B. xy
  C. x^2y^2 D. x^4y^4

45. The LCM of $4xy^4$ and $6x^2y^2$ is:
A. $6xy^2$
B. $12x^2y^4$
C. $6x^2y^2$
D. $2xy$

46. Find the HCF of $2x^2 - 5x + 3$ and $6x^2 - 5x + 4$
A. $(2x - 3)$
B. 1
C. $(3x + 4)$
D. $(x + 1)(x + 2)$

47. The LCM of $x^3 - y^3$, $x - y$ and $x^2 + xy + y^2$ will be:
A. $(x^2 - y^2)$
B. $(x - y)$
C. $x^3 - y^3$
D. $x(x + y)$

48. Determine the LCM of $x^2 - x - 12$, $2x^2 - 11x + 15$ and $x^2 - 7x + 12$.
A. $(x - 4)(x + 3)(x - 3)(2x - 5)$

B. $(x + 2)(x - 2)(x - 4)(2x - 5)$
C. $(x + 3)(x + 4)(x - 5)$
D. $(x + 3)(x - 4)(x + 5)$

49. The H.C.F. of $x^2 - 9$, $x^3 - 27$ and $x^2 - 7x + 12$ will be:
A. $(x^2 - 9)$
B. $(x - 3)^2$
C. $(x + 3)$
D. $(x - 3)$

50. The LCM of $a^2 - 1$, $a^3 - 1$ and $a^2 + a - 2$ will be:
A. $(a + 1)(a - 1)(a - 2)(a^2 + a + 1)$
B. $(a + 1)(a - 1)(a + 2)(a^2 + a + 1)$
C. $(a + 1)(a - 1)(a + 2)(a^2 - a - 1)$
D. $(a^2 - a + 2)(a + 1)(a - 1)$

ANSWERS

1	2	3	4	5	6	7	8	9	10
C	A	D	A	D	A	B	B	C	B
11	**12**	**13**	**14**	**15**	**16**	**17**	**18**	**19**	**20**
A	C	C	B	A	D	B	C	C	D
21	**22**	**23**	**24**	**25**	**26**	**27**	**28**	**29**	**30**
B	A	C	D	C	A	C	C	D	A
31	**32**	**33**	**34**	**35**	**36**	**37**	**38**	**39**	**40**
C	B	A	A	D	B	C	D	A	A
41	**42**	**43**	**44**	**45**	**46**	**47**	**48**	**49**	**50**
C	B	A	C	B	B	C	A	D	B

EXPLANATORY ANSWERS

1. $\because a = 4, b = 1$
$\therefore$ Value of $7a - 3b = 7 \times 4 - 3 \times 1$
$= 28 - 3$
$= 25.$

2. $\because x = 2, y = 3$
$\therefore$ Value of $3x + 4y = 3 \times 2 + 4 \times 3$
$= 6 + 12$
$= 18.$

3. $\because x = 2, y = 1, z = 3$
$\therefore$ Value of $x^2 + xyz + y^2 = (2)^2 + 2 \times 1 \times 3 + (1)^2$
$= 4 + 6 + 1$
$= 11.$

4. $\because x = 1, y = 2, z = 3$
$\therefore$ Value of $4x^2 + y^2 + z^2 - 3xyz + x$
$= 4(1)^2 + (2)^2 + (3)^2 - 3(1)(2)(3) + 1$
$= 4 + 4 + 9 - 18 + 1$
$= 18 - 18$
$= 0.$

5. $\because a = 1, b = 2, c = 3$
$\therefore$ Value of $3a - 2b + 3c$
$= 3(1) - 2(2) + 3(3)$
$= 3 - 4 + 9$
$= 12 - 4$
$= 8.$

86

6. $\because a = 2, b = 3, c = 4$

$\therefore$ Value of $\dfrac{2a-3b+2c}{4a-2b+2c}$

$= \dfrac{2(2)-3(3)+2(4)}{4(2)-2(3)+2(4)}$

$= \dfrac{4-9+8}{8-6+8} = \dfrac{3}{10}.$

7. $-2x - 7y + 6z - 5x + 4y - 2z + 7x + 3y - 4z$

$= 7x - 7x + 7y - 7y + 6z - 6z$

$= 0 + 0 + 0 = 0.$

8. $2x + 3y - z - 2x + 2y + z$

$= 2x - 2x + 3y + 2y + z - z$

$= 0 + 5y + 0 = 5y.$

9. $a + b - c - (a + b + c)$

$= a + b - c - a - b - c$

$= a - a + b - b - c - c = -2c.$

10. $12x - 7x = 5x.$

11. $2x - (-3x) = 2x + 3x = 5x.$

12. $2x^2 \times 8x^2 = 2 \times 8 \times x^2 \times x^2 = 16x^4.$

13. $(-4x^2) \times (-3x^4) = 4 \times 3 \times x^2 \times x^4 = 12x^6.$

14. $-21x^3 \div 7x^2 = \dfrac{-21x^3}{7x^2}$

$= \dfrac{-7 \times 3 \times x \times x \times x}{7 \times x \times x}$

$= -3x$

15.
```
        x - 2
x - 7 ) x² - 9x + 14
        x² - 7x
        -   +
        ───────────
           - 2x + 14
           - 2x + 14
           +    -
        ───────────
              ×
```
$\therefore$ Required answer $= x - 2.$

16.
```
        x + 3
x + 5 ) x² + 8x + 15
        x² + 5x
        -   -
        ───────────
           3x + 15
           3x + 15
           -    -
        ───────────
              ×
```
$\therefore$ Required answer $= x + 3.$

17. $\left(x + \dfrac{1}{x}\right)^2 - \left(x - \dfrac{1}{x}\right)^2$

Let $x + \dfrac{1}{x} = a$ and $x - \dfrac{1}{x} = b$

$\therefore a^2 - b^2 = (a + b)(a - b)$

Putting the value of a and b

$= \left(x + \dfrac{1}{x} + x - \dfrac{1}{x}\right)\left(x + \dfrac{1}{x} - x + \dfrac{1}{x}\right)$

$= (2x)\left(\dfrac{2}{x}\right) = 4.$

18. Let $x + y = a$ and $x - y = b$

$a^2 - b^2 = (a + b)(a - b)$

$= (x + y + x - y)(x + y - x + y)$

$= (2x)(2y)$

$= 4xy.$

19. $\because x = 2$

$\therefore$ Value of $\left(x + \dfrac{1}{2}\right)^2 = \left(2 + \dfrac{1}{2}\right)^2$

$= \left(\dfrac{4+1}{2}\right)^2 = \left(\dfrac{5}{2}\right)^2$

$= \dfrac{5}{2} \times \dfrac{5}{2} = \dfrac{25}{4}.$

20.
```
         x + 9
x + 2 ) x² + 11x + 18
        x² + 2x
        ───────────
            9x + 18
            9x + 18
            -    -
        ───────────
              ×
```
$\therefore$ Required answer $= x + 9.$

21.
```
         x + 3
x + 4 ) x² + 7x + 10
        x² + 4x
        -   -
        ───────────
            3x + 10
            3x + 12
            -    -
        ───────────
              -2
```
If we add 2 in the given $x^2 + 7x + 10$ then it completely divisible by $(x + 4)$.

22. $\because a = 1, b = 2$ and $c = 3$

$\therefore$ Value of $\dfrac{a^2}{bc} - \dfrac{b^2}{ca} + \dfrac{c^2}{ab}$

$= \dfrac{1 \times 1}{2 \times 3} - \dfrac{2 \times 2}{3 \times 1} + \dfrac{3 \times 3}{1 \times 2} = \dfrac{1}{6} - \dfrac{4}{3} + \dfrac{9}{2}$

$= \dfrac{1 - 8 + 27}{6} = \dfrac{20}{6} = \dfrac{10}{3} = 3\dfrac{1}{3}.$

23. $\because a = -2$

$\therefore$ Value of $\dfrac{7}{a-2} + \dfrac{17}{a^2 + 4}$

$= \dfrac{7}{-2-2} + \dfrac{17}{(-2)^2 + 4}$

$= \dfrac{7}{-4} + \dfrac{17}{8}$

$= \dfrac{-7}{4} + \dfrac{17}{8}$

$= \dfrac{-14 + 17}{8}$

$= \dfrac{3}{8}.$

24. $15a - (-4a) = 15a + 4a$

$= 19a.$

25. $12a - 8a = 4a.$

26. $(2x + 3y)(2x + 3y) - (2x - 3y)(2x - 3y)$

$= (4x^2 + 6xy + 6xy + 9y^2) -$

$\qquad (4x^2 - 6xy - 6xy + 9y^2)$

$= (4x^2 + 12xy + 9y^2) - (4x^2 - 12xy + 9y^2)$

$= 4x^2 + 12xy + 9y^2 - 4x^2 + 12xy - 9y^2$

$= 12xy + 12xy$

$= 24xy.$

27. $\because a = 3, b = 4, c = 2$

$\therefore$ Value of $2a^2 - 4ab + 15c^2$

$= 2(3)^2 - 4(3)(4) + 15(2)^2$

$= 18 - 48 + 60$

$= 78 - 48$

$= 30.$

28. HCF of x^3y^2, x^2y^3 and x^4y^4

$= x^2y^2$ $\quad\left[\begin{array}{l}\because \text{Minimum power of } x = 2 \\ \text{Minimum power of } y = 2\end{array}\right]$

29. LCM of $12a^3b$, $6a^2b^3$ and $12a^3b^4$

LCM of 12, 6 and 12 = 12

Maximum power of $a = 3$

Maximum power of $b = 4$

$\therefore$ LCM $= 12a^3b^4.$

30. LCM of $a^2 - b^2$ and $a - b$

$= a^2 - b^2$ $\quad[\because a^2 - b^2 = (a+b)(a-b).$

31. $x^2 - 25 = (x)^2 - (5)^2$

$\qquad$ [which is of the form $a^2 - b^2$]

$= (x + 5)(x - 5).$

32. According to question:

Square of $\left(x - \dfrac{1}{x}\right) = \left(x - \dfrac{1}{x}\right)^2$

$= x^2 - 2.x.\dfrac{1}{x} + \left(\dfrac{1}{x}\right)^2$

$= x^2 - 2 + \dfrac{1}{x^2}.$

33. $36 - 9x^2 = (6)^2 - (3x)^2$

$\qquad$ [which is of the form $a^2 - b^2$]

$= (6 + 3x)(6 - 3x).$

34. $8x^3 + y^3 = (2x)^3 + (y)^3$

$\qquad$ [which is of the form $a^3 + b^3$]

$= (2x + y)[(2x)^2 - 2x.y + (y)^2]$

$= (2x + y)(4x^2 - 2xy + y^2).$

35. Since the expression $x^3 + 5x^2 - 2 + k$ is completely divisible by $(x - 1)$

$\therefore$ on substituting $x = 1$ in the given expression, its value will be zero

$i.e., (1)^3 + 5(1)^2 - 2 + k = 0 \Rightarrow 1 + 5 - 2 + k = 0$

$\Rightarrow \qquad 4 + k = 0 \Rightarrow k = -4$

Hence value of k is $-4.$

36. $\because x^2 + 3x - 10 = x^2 + 5x - 2x - 10$

$= x(x + 5) - 2(x + 5)$

$= (x - 2)(x + 5)$

37. $\because$
$$1000 + c^3 = (10)^3 + (c)^3$$
$$\text{[which is of the form } a^3 + b^3]$$
$$= (10 + c)\,[(10)^2 - 10c + (c)^2]$$
$$= (10 + c)\,(100 - 10c + c^2).$$

38. $\because$
$$x^4 + 2 + \frac{1}{x^4} = (x^2)^2 + 2.x^2.\frac{1}{x^2} + \left(\frac{1}{x^2}\right)^2$$
$$= \left(x^2 + \frac{1}{x^2}\right)^2$$

$\therefore$ On substituting $x = \sqrt{3}$
$$= \left[(\sqrt{3})^2 + \frac{1}{(\sqrt{3})^2}\right]^2$$
$$= \left(3 + \frac{1}{3}\right)^2 = \left(\frac{10}{3}\right)^2 = \frac{100}{9}.$$

39. $\because$
$$4x^2 + 8x - 5 = 4x^2 + 10x - 2x - 5$$
$$= 2x(2x + 5) - 1(2x + 5)$$
$$= (2x - 1)\,(2x + 5).$$

40. Since $(x - 2)$ is a factor of $x^2 + 2x - a$

$\therefore$ On substituting $x = 2$ in the expression, the result obtained will be zero

$\therefore$ $(2)^2 + 2.2 - a = 0$

or $4 + 4 - a = 0$

or $a = 8$

41. $\because$
$$10a^2 - ab - 3b^2 = 10a^2 + 5ab - 6ab - 3b^2$$
$$= 5a[2a + b] - 3b[2a + b]$$
$$= (5a - 3b)\,(2a + b).$$

42. $256x^4 + 160x^2y^2 + 25y^4 = (16x^2)^2 + 2 .16x^2 .$
$$5y^2 + (5y^2)^2$$
$$= (16x^2 + 5y^2)^2$$

On substituting $x = 3$ and $y = 4$,
$$(16x^2 + 5y^2)^2 = (16 \times 3^2 + 5 \times 4^2)^2$$
$$= (16 \times 9 + 5 \times 16)^2$$
$$= (144 + 80)^2$$
$$= (224)^2 = 50176$$

43. $\because$ $a^3 - 2a^2 - 5a + 6 = a^3 - a^2 - a^2 + a - 6a + 6$
$$= a^2(a - 1) - a(a - 1) - 6(a - 1)$$
$$= (a - 1)[a^2 - a - 6]$$
$$= (a - 1)[a^2 - 3a + 2a - 6]$$
$$= (a - 1)[a(a - 3) + 2(a - 3)]$$
$$= (a - 1)(a + 2)(a - 3).$$

44.
$$x^3y^2 = x^3 \times y^2$$
$$x^2y^3 = x^2 \times y^3$$
and $$x^4y^4 = x^4 \times y^4$$
$\therefore$ Required HCF $= x^2 \times y^2 = x^2y^2.$

45.
$$4xy^4 = 2^2 \times x \times y^4$$
$$6x^2y^2 = 2 \times 3 \times x^2 \times y^2$$
$\therefore$ Required LCM $= 2^2 \times 3 \times x^2 \times y^4 = 12x^2y^4.$

46.
$$2x^2 - 5x + 3 = 2x^2 - 2x - 3x + 3$$
$$= 2x(x - 1) - 3(x - 1)$$
$$= (x - 1)\,(2x - 3)$$
and $$6x^2 - 5x - 4 = 6x^2 - 8x + 3x - 4$$
$$= 2x(3x - 4) + 1(3x - 4)$$
$$= (3x - 4)\,(2x + 1)$$

Since no factor is common to two given expressions, 1 will always be a common factor.

$\therefore$ HCF of the given expressions $= 1.$

47.
$$x^3 - y^3 = (x - y)\,(x^2 + xy + y^2)$$
$$x - y = (x - y)$$
$$x^2 + xy + y^2 = (x^2 + xy + y^2)$$
$\therefore$ Required LCM $= (x - y)\,(x^2 + xy + y^2)$
$$= x^3 - y^3$$

48.
$$x^2 - x - 12 = x^2 - 4x + 3x - 12$$
$$= x(x - 4) + 3(x - 4)$$
$$= (x - 4)\,(x + 3)$$
$$2x^2 - 11x + 15 = 2x^2 - 6x - 5x + 15$$
$$= 2x(x - 3) - 5(x - 3)$$
$$= (x - 3)\,(2x - 5)$$
and $$x^2 - 7x + 12 = x^2 - 4x - 3x + 12$$
$$= x(x - 4) - 3(x - 4)$$
$$= (x - 4)\,(x - 3)$$
$\therefore$ Required LCM $= (x - 4)(x + 3)(x - 3)(2x - 5).$

49.
$$x^2 - 9 = x^2 - 3^2 = (x + 3)\,(x - 3)$$
$$x^3 - 27 = x^3 - 3^3 = (x - 3)\,(x^2 + 3x + 9)$$
and $$x^2 - 7x + 12 = x^2 - 4x - 3x + 12$$
$$= x(x - 4) - 3(x - 4)$$
$$= (x - 4)\,(x - 3)$$
$\therefore$ Required HCF $= (x - 3).$

50.
$$a^2 - 1 = (a + 1)\,(a - 1)$$
$$a^3 - 1 = (a - 1)\,(a^2 + a + 1)$$
and $$a^2 + a - 2 = a^2 + 2a - a - 2$$
$$= a(a + 2) - 1(a + 2)$$
$$= (a + 2)\,(a - 1)$$
$\therefore$ Required LCM $= (a + 1)\,(a - 1)\,(a + 2)$
$$(a^2 + a + 1).$$

INTELLIGENCE

VERBAL TEST

1 CLASSIFICATION TEST (SAME CLASS TEST)

In this group, certain groups of words are given and the Candidate is required to spot the one that does not belong to the same class or is of different class.

Solved Example

(i) Three of following four are alike in a certain way and so form a group. Which one does not belong to that group?
(a) Bud   (b) Branch
(c) Leaf   (d) Plant

Sol : All items are the parts of a plant. Hence plant does not belong to the group. So, the answer is (d).

(ii) Three of following four are alike in a certain way and so form a group. Which one does not belong to that group?
(a) Ears   (b) Hands
(c) Fingers   (d) Legs

Sol : Except fingers, all other parts of body are in pair. Hence option (c) is the correct answer.

(iii) Find the odd-man out?
(a) Ring   (b) Bangle
(c) Tyre   (d) Plate

Sol : Except (d), all items have hole in the centre. So, the answer is (d).

(iv) Three of following four are alike in a certain way and so form a group. Which one does not belong to that group?
(a) Cheese   (b) Butter
(c) Egg   (d) Curd

Sol : Except (c), all others are milk products, while the egg is laid by hen. Hence, odd one is (c).

(v) Find the odd-man out?
(a) PSRQ   (b) CGEF
(c) JMLK   (d) VYXW

Sol : The pattern used for classification is placement of alphabets in the order (+3, −1, 1). Since option (b) does not follow the pattern, it is odd in the group.

EXERCISE

Directions : *For each of the following questions, four words have been given of which three are alike in someway and one is different. Find the odd word.*

1. (a) Tiger   (b) Horse
   (c) Hyena   (d) Deer

2. (a) Gram   (b) Kilogram
   (c) Dozen   (d) Inch

3. (a) Bicycle   (b) Motor-cycle
   (c) Bus   (d) Car

4. (a) Table Tennis   (b) Badminton
   (c) Volleyball   (d) Lawn Tennis

5. (a) Weight   (b) Height
   (c) Distance   (d) Kilometre

6. (a) Star   (b) Earth
   (c) Sun   (d) Moon

7. (a) Cat   (b) Dog
   (c) Bird   (d) Elephant

8. (a) Hindi   (b) Marathi
   (c) Chinese   (d) Gujarati

9. (a) Petrol   (b) Diesel
   (c) Alcohol   (d) Kerosene Oil

10. (a) Jumping   (b) Writing
    (c) Walking   (d) Running

3

11. (a) Kerala	(b) Hyderabad	31. (a) Shorthand	(b) Morse
(c) Bangalore	(d) Kolkata	(c) Semaphore	(d) Record
12. (a) Sister	(b) Brother	32. (a) Green	(b) Violet
(c) Father	(d) Boy	(c) Brown	(d) Yellow
13. (a) Hot	(b) Cool	33. (a) City	(b) Town
(c) Fire	(d) Pain	(c) Village	(d) Home
14. (a) Circle	(b) Rectangle	34. (a) Writer	(b) Printer
(c) Square	(d) Triangle	(c) Publisher	(d) Reader
15. (a) Cow	(b) Buffalo	35. (a) Under	(b) Near
(c) Goat	(d) Hen	(c) Above	(d) Where
16. (a) Coffee	(b) Curd	36. (a) Fragrance	(b) Smell
(c) Milk	(d) Tea	(c) Aroma	(d) A foul smell
17. (a) Mango	(b) Potato	37. (a) Motorcar	(b) Tractor
(c) Orange	(d) Grapes	(c) Bus	(d) Train
18. (a) Onion	(b) Potato	38. (a) Stammer	(b) Whisper
(c) Lady-finger	(d) Banana	(c) Drawl	(d) Taunt (Speech)
19. (a) Listening	(b) Walking	39. (a) Portrait	(b) Snapshot
(c) Swimming	(d) Climbing	(c) Diagram	(d) Painting
20. (a) Ramayan	(b) Mahabharat	40. (a) Silk	(b) Fur
(c) Godan	(d) Gita	(c) Milk	(d) Rubber
21. (a) Blue	(b) Red	41. (a) Anticipate	(b) Presume
(c) Yellow	(d) Dark	(c) Expect	(d) Reckon
22. (a) Writer	(b) Actor	42. (a) Hop	(b) Dive
(c) Singer	(d) Dancer	(c) Jump	(d) Fall
23. (a) Cactus	(b) Rose	43. (a) Milk	(b) Syrup
(c) Lotus	(d) Sunflower	(c) Squash	(d) Cake
24. (a) Football	(b) Cricket	44. (a) Ink	(b) Pen
(c) Chess	(d) Hockey	(c) Pencil	(d) Chalkstick
25. (a) Sun	(b) Moon	45. (a) Cooperate	(b) Coordinate
(c) Venus	(d) Earth	(c) Correlate	(d) Combat
26. (a) Microphone	(b) Microscope	46. (a) Conscience	(b) Morality
(c) Spectacles	(d) Telescope	(c) Conduct	(d) Weight
27. (a) Artery	(b) Ventricle	47. (a) Guitar	(b) Piano
(c) Pharynx	(d) Aorta	(c) Harmonium	(d) Banjo
28. (a) Diamond	(b) Ruby	48. (a) Secretary	(b) Council
(c) Emerald	(d) Turquoise	(c) Panel	(d) Cabinet
29. (a) Crimson	(b) Scarlet	49. (a) Topple	(b) Tumble
(c) Vermilion	(d) Cardinal	(c) Slip	(d) Skip
30. (a) Swim	(b) Run	50. (a) Freeze	(b) Simmer
(c) Anticipate	(d) Dance	(c) Bake	(d) Boil

5

51. (a) Mother   (b) Sister
    (c) Brother   (d) Aunt

52. (a) Knave   (b) King
    (c) Ace   (d) Minister

53. (a) Hawk   (b) Parrot
    (c) Falcon   (d) Eagle

54. (a) Lemon   (b) Orange
    (c) Citron   (d) Banana

55. (a) Premchand   (b) Kalidas
    (c) Shakespeare   (d) G.B Shaw

56. (a) Manganese   (b) Rubber
    (c) Salt   (d) Gold

57. (a) Rectangle   (b) Rhombus
    (c) Square   (d) Circle

58. (a) Bark   (b) Cry
    (c) Chrip   (d) Roar

59. (a) Aluminium   (b) Copper
    (c) Brass   (d) Brick

60. (a) Metre   (b) Yard
    (c) Litre   (d) Inch

61. (a) Mars   (b) Jupiter
    (c) Saturn   (d) Sun

62. (a) Shimla   (b) Ooty
    (c) Dehradun   (d) Kulu

63. (a) Onion   (b) Tomato
    (c) Potato   (d) Garlic

64. (a) Moscow   (b) London
    (c) Paris   (d) New-York

65. (a) Bang   (b) Hiss
    (c) Jingle   (d) Wink

66. (a) Sparrow   (b) Parrot
    (c) Cuckoo   (d) Duck

67. (a) Gold   (b) Silver
    (c) Bronze   (d) Iron

68. (a) Sympathy   (b) Harted
    (c) Help   (d) Adoration

69. (a) Unicorn   (b) Rhino
    (c) Fox   (d) Antepole

70. (a) Milk   (b) Orange
    (c) Cotton   (d) Snow

71. (a) Blackmail   (b) Smuggling
    (c) Snobbery   (d) Forgery

72. (a) Yen   (b) Lira
    (c) Dollar   (d) Ounce

73. (a) Moon   (b) Football
    (c) Earth   (d) Bangle

74. (a) Complicated   (b) Tricky
    (c) Complex   (d) Contrast

75. (a) Book   (b) Pages
    (c) Index   (d) Chapters

76. (a) Huge   (b) Tiny
    (c) Heavy   (d) Small

77. (a) Spring   (b) Heat
    (c) Winter   (d) Summer

78. (a) Sky   (b) Star
    (c) Planet   (d) Comet

79. (a) Rigveda   (b) Yajurveda
    (c) Atharveda   (d) Ayurveda

80. (a) Teeth   (b) Tongue
    (c) Palate   (d) Chin

81. (a) Torrent   (b) Lake
    (c) River   (d) Stream

82. (a) River   (b) Earth
    (c) Aeroplane   (d) Breeze

83. (a) Misdeed   (b) Corruption
    (c) Failure   (d) Offence

84. (a) Gandhi   (b) Buddha
    (c) Mahavir   (d) Nanak

85. (a) Rickshaw   (b) Taxi
    (c) Tonga   (d) Cart

86. (a) Java   (b) Tasmania
    (c) Sri Lanka   (d) Malaysia

87. (a) Mountain   (b) Valley
    (c) Glacier   (d) Sea-coast

88. (a) Silk   (b) Cotton
    (c) Nylon   (d) Wool

89. (a) Asia   (b) Australia
    (c) America   (d) England

90. (a) Konark   (b) Madurai
    (c) Ellora   (d) Dilwara

91. (a) Trident   (b) Triumph
    (c) Tripod   (d) Trisect

92. (a) Puppet   (b) Documentary
(c) Animation   (d) Commentary

93. (a) Needle   (b) Pencil
(c) Spade   (d) Candle

94. (a) Basket   (b) Barrel
(c) Bag   (d) Barrow

95. (a) Cricket   (b) Baseball
(c) Football   (d) Billiards

96. (a) Genius   (b) Geyser
(c) Gesture   (d) Revenge

97. (a) Pew   (b) Altar
(c) Mettle   (d) Choir

98. (a) Scorpio   (b) Cancer
(c) Capricon   (d) Equator

99. (a) Camel   (b) Goat
(c) Cow   (d) Dog

100. (a) Bhils   (b) Todas
(c) Sikhs   (d) Nagas

Directions (101 – 110) : In each of the following questions four out of five alternatives contain alphabet placed in a particular form. Find the one that does not belong to the group.

101. (a) EHG   (b) JML
(c) PSR   (d) UYX
(e) TWV

102. (a) KIG   (b) ZYV
(c) NMK   (d) FEB
(e) QPM

103. (a) LNJ   (b) RTP
(c) NPK   (d) FHD
(e) WYU

104. (a) XWU   (b) QPM
(c) KJH   (d) DCA
(e) MLJ

105. (a) CAE   (b) KGM
(c) NLP   (d) YWA
(e) RPT

106. (a) NKMJ   (b) FCEB
(c) URTQ   (d) KHJG
(e) TQRP

107. (a) GT7   (b) IR9
(c) CX3   (d) MN13
(e) JP10

108. (a) J30T   (b) D22R
(c) H26R   (d) A28Z
(e) B7E

109. (a) ZYM   (b) SQN
(c) GEB   (d) MKH
(e) JHE

110. (a) NOQT   (b) DEHK
(c) BCEH   (d) RSUK
(e) JKMP

Directions (111 – 120) : In the following questions, numbers given in four out of the five alternatives have same relationship. You have to choose the one which does not belong to the group.

111. (a) 4   (b) 8
(c) 16   (d) 9
(e) 25

112. (a) 125   (b) 216
(c) 27   (d) 121
(e) 1

113. (a) 43   (b) 53
(c) 63   (d) 73
(e) 83

114. (a) 26   (b) 124
(c) 728   (d) 64
(e) 215

115. (a) 22 : 8   (b) 24 : 20
(c) 32 : 13   (d) 14 : 17
(e) 91 : 82

116. (a) 1 : 4   (b) 10 : 24
(c) 8 : 18   (d) 22 : 46
(e) 50 : 102

117. (a) 22 : 42   (b) 4 : 6
(c) 11 : 20   (d) 5 : 14
(e) 9 : 16

118. (a) 3 : 8   (b) 6 : 35
(c) 7 : 50   (d) 1 : 0
(e) 9 : 80

119. (a) 385   (b) 572
(c) 671   (d) 264
(e) 427

120. (a) 9 : 80   (b) 1 : 0
(c) 6 : 35   (d) 12 : 143
(e) 10 : 91

ANSWERS WITH EXPLANATION

1. (b) : Except (b), others are meat-eating animals while horse is a grass-eating animal.

2. (c) : Except (c), others are measures of length or weight, while dozen is a number.

3. (a) : Except (a), others are automobiles, while bicycle is peddled by feet.

4. (c) : Except (c), others are played with racket, while volleyball is played by hand.

5. (d) : Except (d), others are general measures, while kilometre is an exact measurement of length.

6. (b) : Except (b), others are heavenly bodies, while earth is a planet.

7. (c) : Except (c), all are animals which cannot fly, while the birds can fly.

8. (c) : Except (c), others are Indian languages, while Chinese is a foreign language.

9. (c) : Except (c), others are motor fuels, while alcohol is a bevergent.

10. (b) : Except (b), others are done by feet, while writing is done by hand.

11. (a) : Except (a), others are capital cities, while Kerala is a state.

12. (d) : Except (d), others show relation, while boy is a general term not showing any relation.

13. (c) : Except (c), we cannot see others while we can see fire.

14. (a) : Except (a), others contain straight lines, while circle is a curve figure.

15. (d) : Except (d), others have four legs, while hen has two legs.

16. (b) : Except (b), others are bevergents, while curd is a milk product.

17. (b) : Except (b), others are fruits, while potato is a vegetable.

18. (d) : Except (d), others are round in shape.

19. (a) : Except (a), others are exercises requiring labour, while listening needs no such labour.

20. (c) : Except (c), others are religious books, while Godan is a novel.

21. (d) : Except (d), others are colours, while dark is the attribute of a colour.

22. (a) : Except (a), others are professional workers, while writer is a creater.

23. (a) : Except (a), others are flowers, while cactus is a leafless plant.

24. (a) : Except (a), others are played by hands, while football is played by feet.

25. (b) : All the term except 'Moon' are related to the Solar system.

26. (a) : All the terms except 'Microphone' are related to the vision.

27. (c) : Except 'Pharynx' all other terms are related to heart.

28. (a) : Except 'Diamond' all the jewels contain some colour in it.

29. (d) : Except 'Cardinal' all the terms are related to colours.

30. (c) : Except 'Anticipate' all the terms are related to body movement or exercise.

31. (d) : Except 'Record' all the terms are related to secret system of sending message.

32. (c) : Except 'Brown' all the colours are present in the rainbow.

33. (d) : Except 'Home' all the terms represent different sections of area present on the earth. Home can be located in any of these sections of area.

34. (d) : All the persons work for the Readers.

35. (d) : All the terms represent the different position except Where.

36. (d) : All others terms are generally used for pleasant Smell.

37. (*b*) : All other vehicles are used to carry goods and passengers. Tractor is meant for farming.

38. (*d*) : All other terms are related to the Speech.

39. (*b*) : All other arts are hand works on the paper drawn by artist.

40. (*d*) : Only 'Rubber' is the tree product.

41. (*d*) : All other terms are related to future acts.

42. (*d*) : All other terms are related to different exercises.

43. (*d*) : All others are the drinks.

44. (*a*) : All others are the devices used for writing and painting.

45. (*d*) : All other terms are used to represent union for constructive purpose.

46. (*d*) : All other terms are used to represent human behavioural personality factors.

47. (*a*) : Guitar is the string operated musical instrument.

48. (*a*) : All other terms are related to the association of persons.

49. (*d*) : All other terms are related to the fall of something.

50. (*a*) : All other terms are related to the cooking.

51. (*c*) : All others are female relationship.

52. (*d*) : All other terms are used in the playing cards.

53. (*b*) : All others are the birds of prey.

54. (*d*) : All other fruits are source of vitamin 'C'.

55. (*a*) : Except 'Prem Chand' all others are dramatists.

56. (*b*) : Only 'rubber' is the tree product.

57. (*d*) : All other figures have edges.

58. (*b*) : This is the only sound related to human being.

59. (*d*) : All other items are metal.

60. (*c*) : All others represent the unit to measure length.

61. (*d*) : All others are the planets.

62. (*c*) : All other cities are hill-stations.

63. (*d*) : All others are vegetables. Garlic is used as spice.

64. (*d*) : Except 'New York', all others are capital of some countries.

65. (*d*) : All other terms are related with the sound.

66. (*d*) : 'Duck' is the only water bird.

67. (*c*) : 'Bronze' is the alloy (combination of two or more metals).

68. (*c*) : All other terms represent the human feelings.

69. (*a*) : 'Unicorn' is the imaginary animal.

70. (*b*) : All other articles have the white colour.

71. (*c*) : All other terms are related to the crimes.

72. (*d*) : All other terms represent the different currency.

73. (*d*) : All other items are three- dimensional figures.

74. (*d*) : All other terms are used to denote the complex nature of something.

75. (*a*) : All other items are contained in a book.

76. (*c*) : All other terms are used to denote the size.

77. (*b*) : All other terms represent the season.

78. (*a*) : All other items belong to the same class.

79. (*d*) : 'Ayurveda' is the branch of medicine. All others are Vedas.

80. (*d*) : Except 'chin' all other parts are inside the mouth.

81. (*d*) : 'Stream' is present in all forms given in other options.

82. (*d*) : Except 'Breeze' all other things can be seen. Breeze can be felt.

83. (*c*) : All others are illegal act of human being.

84. (*a*) : Except 'Gandhi' all other persons are attached with religion.

85. (*b*) : 'Taxi' is auto driven whereas other items are either man or animal driven.

86. (*d*) : 'Malaysia' is peninsula whereas other countries are island.

87. (*c*) : 'Glacier' is the mass of ice, other things are formed by land.

88. (*c*) : Only 'Nylon' is synthetic item.

89. (*d*) : Except 'England', others are continents.

90. (*c*) : 'Ellora' is famous for caves, all others are famous for temples.

91. (*b*) : Except 'Triumph', Tri stands for three in all other terms.

92. (*d*) : 'Commentary' is the description of all other shows.

93. (*d*) : Except 'Candle' all other articles have one of its ends sharp or pointed.

94. (*d*) : Barrow is man driven cart whereas others are usual containers.

95. (*d*) : Except 'Billiards' all others are outdoor games.

96. (*b*) : Only 'Geyser' is visible whereas all others are invisible.

97. (*c*) : All other things are related to the church.

98. (*d*) : Except 'Equator' all others are zodiac signs.

99. (*d*) : Except 'Dog' all others are milk yielding animals.

100. (*c*) : All others are different tribes.

101. (*d*) : In all other groups there is a gap of one letter as in the alphabet between first and third letter.

102. (*c*) : In all other groups there is a gap of two letters as in the alphabet between second and third letter.

103. (*c*) : In all other groups there is a gap of letter as in the alphabet between first and third letter.

104. (*b*) : In all other groups there is a gap of one letter as in the alphabet between second and third letter.

105. (*b*) : In all other groups there is a gap of one letter as in the alphabet between first and second letter.

106. (*e*) : In all other groups there is a gap of two letters as in the alphabet between third and fourth letter.

107. (*e*) : In all other groups first and second letters occupy the same number of position from beginning and end respectively in the alphabet as mentioned at the third place of each group.

108. (*d*) : In all other groups number in between is the sum of position of first and second letters in the alphabets.

109. (*a*) : In all other groups there is a gap of two letters as in the alphabet between second and third letter.

110. (*b*) : In all other groups of words there is a gap of one letter as in the alphabet between second and third letter.

111. (*b*) : All other numbers are square of natural numbers.

112. (*d*) : All other numbers are cubes of natural numbers.

113. (*c*) : All other numbers are prime number.

114. (*d*) : All other numbers are one less than the cube of natural numbers.

115. (*c*) : Second numbers is the sum of the square of the digits of first number.

116. (*b*) : Second number is double the one more than first number.

117. (*d*) : First number is one more than the half of second number.

118. (*c*) : In other numbers second number is one less than the square of first number.
$(3)^2 - 1 = 8, (6)^2 - 1 = 35$ . . . and so on.

119. (*e*) : Digit in the middle is the sum of the other two digits.

120. (*e*) : Second number is one less than the square of first number.

● ● ●

The term Coding-Decoding primarily relates with message sent in secret form which can not be understood by others easily. Coding, therefore, means rule or method used to hide the actual meaning of a word or group of words and decoding means the method of making out the actual message that is disguised in coding.

In question, a word (Basic word) is coded in a particular way and Candidates are asked to code other words in the same way. Questions of coding-decoding are designed to test candidate's ability to understand the rule used for the coding and then translate it quickly to find out the coding for the given word. Types of these questions are manifold which initially pose a slight problem before the student as to how to solve the questions. It is therefore, required to discuss first the various probable types of questions which may be asked in the examination, before we switch over to the methods or steps used in solving these questions.

Solved Example

(i) If in a certain language MYSTIFY is coded as NZTUJGZ, how is MEMISES coded in that code?

(a) MDLHRDR   (b) OFNJTFT
(c) ODNHTDR   (d) PGOKUGU

Sol : Clearly, in the code, each letter is the alphabet next to the corresponding letter in the word.

$$\begin{array}{c}\text{M Y S T I F Y}\\ \downarrow \\ \text{N Z T U I G Z}\end{array}$$

So, for NEMISES, N will be coded as O, E as F, M as N and so on.

∴ the answer is (b) — OFNJTFT

(ii) If TAP is coded as SZO, then how is FREEZE coded?

(a) ESDFYF   (b) GQFDYF
(c) EQDFYG   (d) EQDDYD

Sol : Clearly, each letter in the code is the alphabet before the corresponding letter in the word.

$$\begin{array}{c}\text{S} \downarrow \text{Z O}\\ \text{T A P}\end{array}$$

Thus, in FREEZE, F is coded as E, R as Q, E as D and Z as Y.

So, the answer is (d) — EQDDYD.

(iii) If CROWN is coded as BSNXM, how is BOARD coded in that code?

(a) ANZQC   (b) APZSC
(c) CPBSE   (d) CNBQE

Sol : In the given code, each letter is alternately one before and one ahead than the corresponding letter in the word.

So, B is coded as A, O as P, A as Z, R as S and D as C.

∴ the answer is (b) — APZSC

(iv) If LIGHT is coded as LJGIT, how is FLAMES coded in that code?

(a) GLBNET   (b) FKALER
(c) FMANET   (d) GLBMFS

Sol : In the code, each letter is alternately the same and one ahead than the corresponding letter in the word.

$$\begin{array}{c}\text{L I G H T}\\ \text{L J G I T}\end{array}$$

So, in FLAMES, F is coded as F, L as M, A as A, M as N, E as E and S as T.

∴ the answer is (c) — FMANET.

EXERCISE

Directions : *In each of the questions below, find out the correct answer from the given alternatives.*

1. If in a certain language, SPACE is coded as TQBDF : how is PURSE coded in that code?
   (a) QTSRF (b) OVQTD
   (c) QVSTF (d) ESRUP

2. If PLANE is coded as OKZMD in a certain language, how will TRAIN be coded?
   (a) SQZHM (b) UQBHO
   (c) SQZJM (d) USBJM

3. In a certain language GAMBLE is coded as FBLCKF, how is FLOWER coded in that code?
   (a) GKPVFQ (b) EMNXDS
   (c) GMPVDS (d) HNQYGT

4. If in a certain language NATURE is coded as MASUQE, how is FAMINE coded in that code?
   (a) FBMJND (b) FZMHND
   (c) GANIOE (d) EALIME

5. If in a certain language PEARL is coded as SHDUO, how is COVET coded in that code?
   (a) FRXHV (b) EQXHV
   (c) FRYHW (d) FNYDW

6. If in a certain language EXIST is coded as ESIXT, how is PLUTO coded in that code?
   (a) OLUTP (b) PTUOL
   (c) PULTO (d) PTULO

7. If in a certain language CURTAIN is coded as CAITURN, how is HILLOCK coded in that code?
   (a) HOCLILK (b) HCOLLIK
   (c) HKLIOC (d) HOLLICK

8. If in a certain language FASHION is coded as FOIHSAN, how is PROBLEM coded in that code?
   (a) ROBLEMP (b) PELBORM
   (c) PRBOELM (d) PELBORM

9. If in a certain language BLEMISH is coded as AODPHVG, how is CHAPTER coded in that code?
   (a) DEBOVTDR (b) BKZSSHQ
   (c) CAHTPRE (d) BGAQMFP

10. If in a certain language CHAMPION is coded as HCMAIPNO, how is NEGATIVE coded in that code?
    (a) ENAGITEV (b) NEAGVEIT
    (c) MGAETVIE (d) EGAITEVN

11. If in a certain language PENSION is coded as NEISNOP, how is FOLIAGE coded in that code?
    (a) OFILGAE (b) EOAILGF
    (c) FGLIAOE (d) EGAILOF

12. If in a certain language KINDLE is coded as ELDNIK, how is EXOTIC coded in that code?
    (a) EXOTLC (b) CXOTIE
    (c) COXITE (d) CITOXE

13. If in a certain language CASUAL is coded as GEWYEP, how is PEOPLE coded in that code?
    (a) SHRSOH (b) TISTPI
    (c) SIRTOI (d) THSTOI

14. If in a certain language SALE is coded as PAIE, how is CASUAL coded in that code?
    (a) BARUZK (b) FAVUDL
    (c) CBSVAM (d) ZAPUXL

15. If in a certain language MECHANICS is coded as HCEMASCIN, how is POSTER coded in that code?
    (a) OPTSRE (b) SOPRET
    (c) RETSOP (d) TERPOS

16. If in a certain language DISPEL is coded as IDPSLE, how is EFFECT coded in that language?
    (a) FEEFTC (b) CTFEEF
    (c) EFFETC (d) ECTEFF

17. If in a certain language HUNTER is coded as UHNTRE, how is MANAGE coded in that code?
    (a) MAANGE (b) MNAAEG
    (c) AMNAEG (d) EGNAAM

18. If RAMAYANA is coded as AMARANAY, how is TULSIDAS written?
    (a) SLUTSADI   (b) UTSLIDSA
    (c) SADISLUT   (d) SADITULS

19. If CANOE is coded as IFRRG, how is MUSIC written in that code?
    (a) NWVNI   (b) MWVMH
    (c) NTULB   (d) SZWLE

20. If TABLE is coded as GZYOV, how is JUICE coded?
    (a) OZLFJ   (b) QFRXV
    (c) HOFAD   (d) QZHMT

21. If FRIEND is coded as HUMJTK, how is CANDLE written in that code?
    (a) EDRIRL   (b) DCQHQK
    (c) FROBOC   (d) ESJFME

22. If ADVENTURE is coded as ERUTNEVDA, how is GREEN coded in that code?
    (a) NEERG   (b) ENEGR
    (c) GEREN   (d) NEEGR

23. If CAB is coded as WUV, how is DEAF coded in that language?
    (a) XYUZ   (b) UWYV
    (c) XWUY   (d) UYXZ

24. If in a certain code YELLOW is written as XFKMNX, how is COUNTRY coded?
    (a) DPVOSQX   (b) BNTMSQX
    (c) BPTMSSX   (d) AMSLRPW

25. If QUICK is coded as PSFYF, how is NEST coded?
    (a) MCPP   (b) MDQS
    (c) OGUV   (d) TESN

26. If in a certain language KNIFE is coded as IFEKN, how is DOCTOR coded in that language?
    (a) ROTCOD   (b) TORDOC
    (c) CTORDO   (d) CODTOR

27. If PEOPLE is coded as PLPOEE, how is TREND coded?
    (a) TREDN
    (b) DNERT
    (c) NDETR
    (d) TNERD

28. If FOUGHT is coded as EQRKCZ, how is MALE coded?
    (a) LCII   (b) NZMD
    (c) KCMI   (d) NBIF

29. If BATCH is coded as ABSDG, how is FORSAKE coded in that code?
    (a) ABDGS   (b) EPQTZLD
    (c) EQPZLTD   (d) GDSBA

30. In a certain code HUMIDITY is written as UHMIIDTY. How is POLITICS written in that code?
    (a) OPILITCS   (b) OPLIITCS
    (c) OPLITISC   (d) POILTISC

31. In a certain code CHAIR is written as EGCHD. How is AUDIT written in that code?
    (a) CTFHV   (b) CSFHV
    (c) BTFHV   (d) CTEHV

32. In a certain code CALANDER is written as CLANAEDR. How is CIRCULAR written in that code?
    (a) ICCRLURA   (b) CRIUCALR
    (c) CRIUCLRA   (d) ICRCLUAR

33. In a certain code language TELEPHONE is written as ENOHPELET. How is ALIGATOR written in that code?
    (a) ROTAGILE   (b) ROTAGILA
    (c) ROTEGILA   (d) ROTAGIAL

34. In a certain code, MUNICIPALITY is written as INMUAPCIYTL. How is JUDICIAL written in that code?
    (a) UJDILACI   (b) IDUJLACI
    (c) IDJULAIC   (d) IDJULACI

35. In a certain code, GOODNESS is coded as HNPCODTR. How is GREATNESS coded in that code?
    (a) HQFZUODTR   (b) HQFZUMFRT
    (c) HQFZSMFRT   (d) FSDBSODTR

36. In a certain code, RIPPLE is written as 613382 and LIFE is written as 8192. How is PILLER written in that code?
    (a) 318826
    (b) 318286
    (c) 618826
    (d) 328816

37. If ROSE is coded as 6821, CHAIR is coded as 73456 and PREACH is coded as 961473, what will be the code for SEARCH?
(*a*) 246173   (*b*) 214673
(*c*) 214763   (*d*) 216473

38. If in a certain code, TWENTY is written as 863985 and ELEVEN is written as 323039, how is TWELVE written in that code?
(*a*) 863203   (*b*) 863584
(*c*) 863903   (*d*) 863063

39. If GIVE is codes as 5137 and BAT is coded as 924, how is GATE coded?
(*a*) 5427   (*b*) 5724
(*c*) 5247   (*d*) 2547

40. If PALE is coded as 2134, EARTH is coded as 41590, how is PEARL coded in that code?
(*a*) 29530
(*b*) 24153
(*c*) 25413
(*d*) 25430

ANSWERS WITH EXPLANATION

1. (*c*) : Each letter of the given word is moved one step ahead to obtain the subsequent letter of its code.

2. (*a*) : The letter preceding each letter of the given word in the alphabets is taken as the subsequent letter of its code.

3. (*b*) : The letters preceding the first, third and fifth letters of the given word and those succeeding the second, fourth and last letters of the word in the alphabets form the code.

4. (*d*) : The letters preceding the letters at odd places in the given word are taken as the corresponding letters of the code while those at even places remain the same.

5. (*c*) : Each letter in the code is two ahead than the corresponding letter in the word.

6. (*d*) : In the code the middle three letters are put in the reverse order.

7. (*a*) : In the code, the first, the middle and the last letters of the word are kept the same. The two letters between first and middle letters are replaced by the two letters between the middle and last letters and vice-versa. Also, the mutual arrangement of each of the two letters is reversed.

8. (*d*) : In the code, the same pattern of arrangements as in 7, has been used and the letters are mutually interchanged.

9. (*b*) : In the code, the letters at odd places are one before and those at odd places are three places ahead of the corresponding letters in the word.

10. (*a*) : In the code, each of the two letters are reversed in arrangement.

11. (*b*) : In the code, first and last letters are reversed, second and second last letters are the same, third and third last letters are reversed, and middle letter is kept the same.

12. (*d*) : In the code, the arrangement of the letters in the word is wholly reversed.

13. (*b*) : In the code, each letter is the fourth alphabet after the corresponding letters in the word.

14. (*d*) : In the code, the letters in the even places are the same while those at odd places are three places before the corresponding letter in the word.

15. (*b*) : In the code the first four and the last four letters are reversed in order.

16. (*a*) : In the code, every two letters are reversed in order.

17. (*c*) : In the code, the middle two letters are kept unchanged, while on either side every two letters are mutually reversed in order.

18. (*a*) : In the code, the first four letters are reversed in arrangement and the last four letters are reversed in arrangement.

19. (*d*) : In the code, the first letter is the sixth alphabet, the second letter is the fifth alphabet, the third letter is the fourth alphabet and so on after the corresponding letter in the word.

20. (*b*) : In the word, a letter is 10th alphabet from the beginning, then in the code the correspon-ding letter is the 10th alphabet from the end.

21. (*a*) : In the code, the first letter is the second alphabet, the second letter is the third alphabet, the third letter is the fourth alphabet and so on after the corresponding letter in the word.

22. (*a*) : In the code, the first and the last letter, the second and second last letters, the third and third last letters are so on are mutually replaced.

23. (*a*) : Each letter in the code is the twentieth letter after the corresponding letter in the word.

24. (*c*) : In the code, the letters in the odd places are one before and those in the even places are one ahead than the corresponding letter in the word.

25. (*a*) : In the code, the first letter is one place, the second letter is two places, the third letter is three places and so on before the corresponding letters in the word.

26. (*c*) : The last three letters of the word are placed as it is in the first three places in the code. The remaining letters are shifted forward keeping their mutual arrangement unchanged.

27. (*d*) : In the code, keeping first and last letters the same, the second and second last, third and third last letters and so on are interchanged.

28. (*a*) : In the code, first letter is one place before, second letter is two places ahead, third

letter is two places before, fourth letter is three places ahead, and so on.

29. (*b*) : In the code, the letters at odd places are one place before and those at even place are one place after the corresponding letter in the word.

30. (*b*) : The first and second letters as well as fifth and sixth letters in the word are interchanged in the code.

31. (*a*) : In the word, the first, third and fifth letters are moved two steps forward while second and fourth letters are moved one step backward to get the code.

32. (*b*) : In the code, the second and third letters of the word are interchanged, the fourth and fifth and then sixth and seventh.

33. (*b*) : The letters of the given word are written in the reverse order in the code.

34. (*d*) : In the code, every four letters of the word are reversed in order.

35. (*b*) : In the code the letters at odd places are one alphabet ahead and those at even places are one alphabet before the corresponding letter in the word.

36. (*a*) : The alphabets are coded as shown *i.e.*, P as 3, I as 1, L as 8, E as 2 and R as 6. So, PILLER is code as 318826.

37. (*b*) : The alphabets are coded as shown *i.e.*, S as 2, E as 1, A as 4, R as 6, C as 7 and H as 3. So, SEARCH is coded as 214673.

38. (*a*) : The alphabets are coded as shown *i.e.*, T as 8, W as 6, E as 3, L as 2, and V as 0. So, TWELVE is coded as 863203.

39. (*c*) : The alphabets are coded as shown *i.e.*, G as 5, A as 2, T as 4 and E as 7. So, GATE is coded as 5247.

40. (*b*) : The alphabets are coded as shown *i.e.*, P as 2, E as 4, A as 1, R as 5 and L as 3. So, PEARL is coded as 24153.

• • •

The word Analogy stands for 'proportion to' agreement with or similarity between. Questions given in this test are based on likeness in certain aspects. In this test first two words have some relation and you have to find out the similar relation between the given choices.

Solved Example

(i) 'Page' is related to Book as Leaf is related to :
   (a) Root   (b) Green
   (c) Tree   (d) Forest

   Sol. : Page is a part of Book and in the same way we see that 'Leaf' is a part of 'Tree'. Hence, our answer is (c).

(ii) 'Goitre' is related to 'Iodine' as 'Anaemia' is related to :
   (a) Vitamin   (b) Blood
   (c) Iron   (d) Weakness

   Sol. : The above questions is based on cause and effect relationship. 'Goitre' disease is caused by the deficiency of 'Iodine'. So, if 'Goitre' is related to 'Iodine', then 'Anaemia' will be related to 'Iron' as 'Anaemia' disease is caused by the deficiency of 'Iron'. Hence, our answer is (c).

(iii) 'Doctor' is related to 'Stethoscope' in the same way as 'Painter' is related to :
   (a) Painting   (b) Brush
   (c) Exhibition   (d) Art

   Sol. : 'Stethoscope' is used by the Doctor as a tool to perform his work. Similarly a 'Painter' uses a 'Brush' as a tool to perform his work. Hence, the answer is (b).

(iv) 'Bull' is related to 'Cow' in the same way as 'Horse' is related to :
   (a) Animal   (b) Mare
   (c) Stable   (d) Meat

   Sol. : The relationship in question is a male-female relationship. So, 'Horse' is related to 'Mare'. Hence our answer is (b).

(v) 'Carpenter' is related to 'Furniture' in the same way as 'Blacksmith' is related to :
   (a) Gold   (b) Jewellery
   (c) Shoes   (d) Metal

   Sol. : 'Carpenter' makes 'Furniture'. Similarly, 'Blacksmith' makes 'Metal'. So, our answer is (d).

EXERCISE

1. 'Bank' is related to 'Money' in the same way as 'Transport' is related to :
   (a) Goods   (b) Road
   (c) Movement   (d) Speed

2. Fan is related to Wings in the same way as Wheel is related to :
   (a) Round   (b) Cars
   (c) Spokes   (d) Moves

3. 'Captain' is related to 'Soldier' in the same way as 'Leader' is related to :
   (a) Chair   (b) Follower
   (c) Party   (d) Minister

4. 'Tree' is related to 'Root' in the same way as Smoke is related to :
   (a) Cigarette   (b) Fire
   (c) Heat   (d) Chimney

5. 'Good' is related to 'Bad' in the same way as 'Roof' is related to :
   (a) Wall   (b) Pillar
   (c) Window   (d) Floor

6. 'Oval' is related to 'Circle' in the same way as 'Rectangle' is related to :
   (a) Triangle   (b) Square
   (c) Periphery   (d) Diagonal

7. 'Umpire' is related to 'Match' in the same way as 'Judge' is related to :
(a) Court   (b) Lawyer
(c) Judgement   (d) Law suit

8. 'Video' is related to 'Cassette' in the same way as 'Computer' is related to :
(a) Reels   (b) Recording
(c) Files   (d) Floppy

9. 'Hour' is related to 'Second' in the same way as 'Tertiary' is related to :
(a) Ordinary   (b) Secondary
(c) Primary   (d) Intermediary

10. 'Fire' is related to 'Ashes' in the same way as 'Explosion' is related to :
(a) Sound   (b) Debris
(c) Explosive   (d) Flame

11. 'Parliament' is related to 'Great Britain' in the same way as 'Congress' is related to :
(a) Japan   (b) India
(c) U.S.A.   (d) Netherlands

12. 'Sports' is related to 'Logo' in the same way as 'Nation' is related to :
(a) Emblem   (b) Animal
(c) Ruler   (d) Anthem

13. 'Data Processing' is related to 'Raw Data' in the same way as 'University' is related to :
(a) Teacher   (b) Building
(c) Students   (d) Principal

14. 'Braille' is related to 'Blindness' in the same way as 'Sign language' is related to :
(a) Exceptional   (b) Touch
(c) Deafness   (d) Presentation

15. 'Boat' is related to 'Oar' in the same way as 'Bicycle' is related to :
(a) Road   (b) Wheel
(c) Seat   (d) Paddle

16. 'Match' is related to 'Win' in the same way as 'Examination' is related to :
(a) Write   (b) Appear
(c) Success   (d) Attempt

17. 'Heart' is related to 'Blood' in the same way as 'Lung' is related to :
(a) Oxygen   (b) Chest
(c) Purification   (d) Air

18. 'Face' is related to 'Expression' in the same way as 'Hand' is related to :
(a) Gesture   (b) Work
(c) Handshake   (d) Waving

19. 'Wine' is related to 'Grapes' in the same way as 'Vodka' is related to :
(a) Apples   (b) Potatoes
(c) Oranges   (d) Flour

20. 'England' is related to 'Atlantic Ocean' in the same way as 'Greenland' is related to :
(a) Pacific Ocean   (b) Atlantic Ocean
(c) Arctic Ocean   (d) Antarctica Ocean

21. 'Eye' is to 'See' in the same way as 'Ear' is to :
(a) Ring   (b) Sound
(c) Hear   (d) Smell

22. 'Mountain' is related to 'Valley' in the same way as 'Enemy' is related to :
(a) Cruel   (b) Stranger
(c) Country   (d) Friend

23. 'Horse' is related to 'Hoof' in the same way as 'Eagle' is related to :
(a) Claw   (b) Clutch
(c) Leg   (d) Foot

24. 'Cube' is related to 'Square' in the same way as 'Square' is related to :
(a) Plane   (b) Triangle
(c) Line   (d) Point

25. 'Much' is related to 'Many' in the same way as 'Measure' is related to :
(a) Count   (b) Calculate
(c) Quantity   (d) Weighs

26. 'Jungle' is related to 'Zoo' in the same way as 'Sea' is related to :
(a) Harbour   (b) Water
(c) Aquarium   (d) Fishery

27. 'Needle' is related to 'Clock' in the same way as 'Wheel' is related to :
(a) Drive   (b) Vehicle
(c) Circular   (d) Move

28. 'Liberty' is related to 'Slavery' in the same way as 'Danger' is related to :
(a) Safety   (b) Dangerous
(c) Anger   (d) Stability

29. 'Blood' is related to 'Vein' in the same way as 'Oil' is related to :
    (a) Car
    (b) Engine
    (c) Pipelines
    (d) Petrol

30. 'Success' is the 'Failure' as Big is to :
    (a) Great
    (b) Good
    (c) Small
    (d) Rig

31. 'Pen' is to 'Pencil' as 'Hockey' is to :
    (a) Football
    (b) Ground
    (c) Team
    (d) Players

32. 'Dog' is related to 'Kennel' in the same way as 'Bird' is related to :
    (a) Tree
    (b) Nest
    (c) Chirp
    (d) Cage

33. 'Book' is to 'Open' as 'Door' is to :
    (a) House
    (b) Shut
    (c) Close
    (d) Wood

34. 'Usual' is to 'Common' as 'Light' is to :
    (a) Bright
    (b) Black
    (c) Dark
    (d) Glow

35. 'Uneasy' is to 'Quiet' as 'Fit' is to :
    (a) Proper
    (b) Suitable
    (c) Pertinent
    (d) Unfit

36. 'Trap' is to 'Net' as 'Trade' is to :
    (a) Earning
    (b) Money
    (c) Profit
    (d) Pursuit

37. 'Marriage' is to 'Divorce' as 'True' is to :
    (a) Truth
    (b) Story
    (c) Fiction
    (d) False

38. 'Fish' is related to 'water' in the same way as 'Bird' is related to :
    (a) Water
    (b) Food
    (c) Sky
    (d) Air

39. 'Tree' is related to 'Forest' in the same way as 'Soldier' is related to :
    (a) Battle
    (b) Army
    (c) Gun
    (d) General

40. 'Crime' is related to 'Police' in the same way as 'Flood' is related to :
    (a) Rain
    (b) River
    (c) Dam
    (d) Reservoir

ANSWERS WITH EXPLANATION

1. (a) : 'Bank' is the institute which deals with transaction of 'Money'. Likewise, 'Transport' deals with the movement of Goods.

2. (c) : 'Wings' are the parts of 'Fan'. Likewise, 'Spokes' are the parts of 'Wheel'.

3. (b) : 'Captain' is supposed to lead the battalion of 'Soldiers' in the same way.

4. (b) : 'Tree' originates from 'Root'. Likewise, 'Smoke' originates from 'Fire'.

5. (d) : 'Good' is the word opposite in meaning to 'Bad'. Similarly, 'Floor' is the antonym of 'Roof'.

6. (b) : 'Oval' is the figure which is similar to the 'Circle'. Likewise, 'Rectangle' is related to 'Square', as both of them have four corners.

7. (d) : 'Umpire' is required to give decision in 'Match'. Likewise, 'Judge' is required to give decision in 'Law Suit'.

8. (d) : 'Cassette' is used as a software in the 'Video'. Similarly, 'Floppy' is used as a software in the 'Computer'.

9. (c) : 'Second' is the third position after 'Hour' in time measurement. Likewise, 'Tertiary' is the third position after 'Primary' in the order of ranking.

10. (b) : 'Fire' reduces anything to 'Ashes' in the same way as 'Explosion' reduces anything to 'Debris'.

11. (c) : Law assembly of 'Great Britain' is known as 'Parliament', in the same way law assembly of U.S.A. is known as 'Congress'.

12. (*a*) : The symbol 'Logo' is related to 'Sports'. Likewise 'Emblem' is related to 'Nation'.

13. (*c*) : 'Data processing' is the process of using 'Raw data' to shape it in the final product. Likewise, 'University' is the place which is used to shape the 'Students' for their career.

14. (*c*) : 'Braille' is the system of reading and writing for the blind persons. Similarly, 'Sign-language' is the system of reading and writing for Deaf persons.

15. (*d*) : 'Oar' is a device used to push a 'Boat'. Likewise, 'Paddle' is used to push the 'Bicycle'.

16. (*c*) : One of outcomes of 'Match' is 'Victory'. Likewise, 'Success' is one of the outcomes of 'Examination'.

17. (*a*) : 'Heart' is the organ which deals with the pumping and flow of 'Blood'. In the same way, 'Lungs' deals with the storage and flow of Oxygen.

18. (*a*) : 'Expression' of a person is read from the 'Face'. Likewise, 'Gesture' of a person is read from the position of 'Hand'.

19. (*d*) : 'Wine' is made from 'Grapes' and 'Vodka' is made from 'Flour'.

20. (*c*) : England is situated in 'Atlantic Ocean'. 'Greenland' is situated in 'Arctic Ocean'.

21. (*c*) : The function of 'Eye' is to 'See' and that of 'Ear' is to 'Hear'.

22. (*d*) : 'Mountain' is antonym of 'Valley'. Likewise, 'Friend' is the antonym of 'Enemy.'

23. (*a*) : The lower part of the feet of 'Horse' is known as 'Hoof'. In the same way, lower part of feet of 'Eagle' is known as 'Claw'.

24. (*c*) : 'Cube' comprises 'Square' on all of its surfaces. In the same way, 'Square' comprises 'Line' on all of its sides.

25. (*a*) : 'Much' is synonym of 'Many'. Similarly, 'Measure' is synonym of 'Count'.

26. (*a*) : 'Zoo' is the small form of 'Jungle' used for the shelter of animals. Similarly, 'Harbour' is the part of 'Sea' used as a place for shelter of ships.

27. (*b*) : 'Needle' is a part of 'Clock' in the same way, as 'Wheel' is a part of 'Vehicle'.

28. (*a*) : 'Liberty' is opposite to 'Slavery' and 'Danger' is opposite to 'Safety'.

29. (*c*) : 'Blood' flows in 'Vein' in the same way, as 'Oil' flows in 'Pipelines'.

30. (*c*) : 'Success' is opposite to 'Failure'. In the same way opposite to 'Big' is 'small'.

31. (*a*) : 'Pen' and 'Pencil' are the articles to write and 'Hockey' and 'Football' are the items to play.

32. (*d*) : 'Kennel' is place where pet 'Dogs' are kept and 'Cage' is the place where pet 'Birds' are kept.

33. (*b*) : A 'Book' is 'opened' before reading it. Likewise, movement of 'Door' is called 'Shut' for the purpose of closing it.

34. (*d*) : 'Usual' and 'Common' are the words conveying the same meaning. Similarly, 'Light' and 'Glow' are synonym to each other.

35. (*d*) : 'Uneasy' and 'Quiet' are opposite to each other. Likewise, 'Fit' and 'Unfit' are opposite to each other.

36. (*b*) : 'Net' is required to 'Trap' and 'Money' is required for 'Trade'.

37. (*d*) : 'Divorce' is the antonym of 'Marriage'. Likewise, 'False' is the antonym of 'True'.

38. (*c*) : 'Fish' swims in 'Water' and Bird flies in the 'Sky'.

39. (*b*) : 'Tree' is a part of 'Forest'. Likewise, 'Soldier' is a part of 'Army'.

40. (*c*) : 'Police' is meant to check 'Crime' and 'Dam' is constructed to prevent 'Flood'.

• • •

4

ARTIFICIAL VALUES AND MISSING NUMBERS

Playing with numbers and mathematical skills are needed to attempt these type of tests. The candidates have to work out the right combination of arithmetical symbols to arrive at the answer options which will take the place of the interrogation sign in the given questions.

Solved Example

1. Select the right option which can be placed at the sign of interrogation?

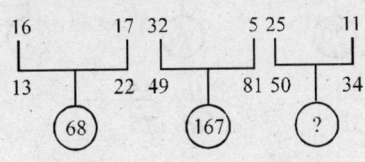

(a) 65
(b) 120
(c) 116
(d) 192

Ans. (b) : The number inside the circle is the sum of the other four numbers, i.e.,
16 + 17 + 13 + 22 = 68

32 + 5 + 49 + 81 = 167, similarly
25 + 11 + 50 + 34 = 120

2. Which one number can be placed at the sign of interrogation?

(a) 6
(b) 8
(c) 7
(d) 3

Ans. (a) : The difference between two opposite numbers is 4, i.e.,
23 – 19 = 4 and 16 – 12 = 4
14 – 10 = 4 and 12 – 8 = 4, similarly
9 – 5 = 4 and 6 – 2 = 4.

There are no definite rules to reach the right answer. Try solving the questions in the exercise given below to learn more about the different ways of getting the correct answer.

EXERCISE

Directions : *In each question given below which one number can be placed at the sign of interrogation?*

1.

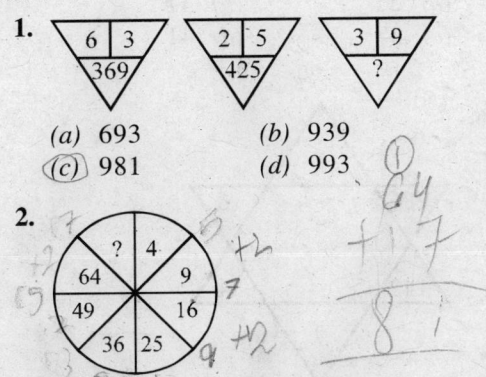

(a) 693
(b) 939
(c) 981
(d) 993

2.

(a) 68
(b) 100
(c) 72
(d) 81

3.

```
   23              20×4         2
7   201 16 8      12 21    46   4 25
  Y       Y              Y    184
   207      80          ?
```

(a) 425
(b) 184
(c) 241
(d) 210

4.

```
  3   5     4   7     3   5
    39         51         ?
  6   3     5   4     5   4
```

(a) 35
(b) 37
(c) 45
(d) 48

19

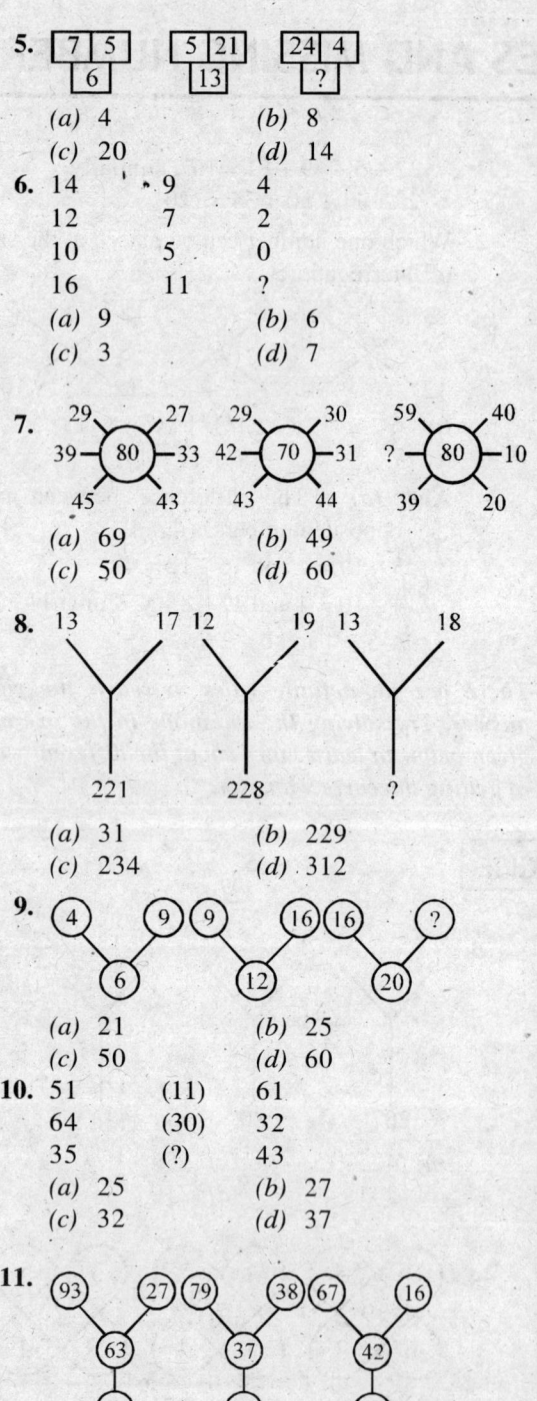

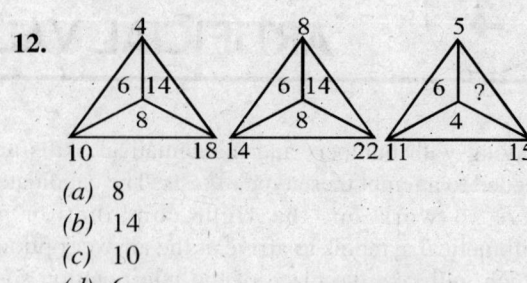

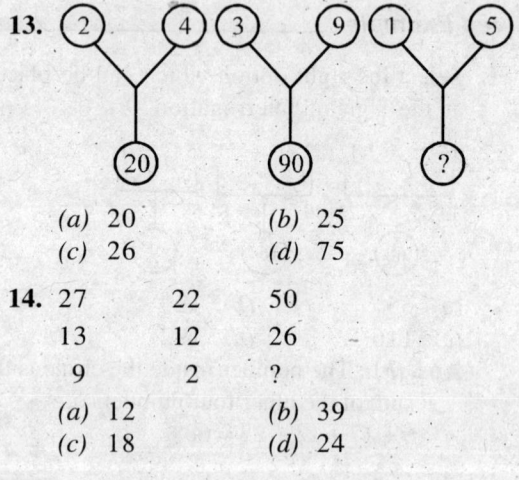

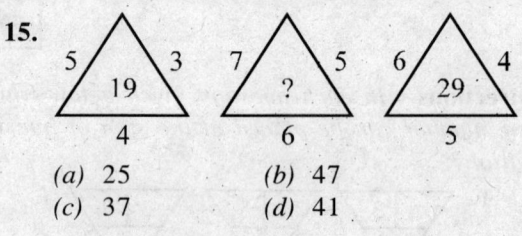

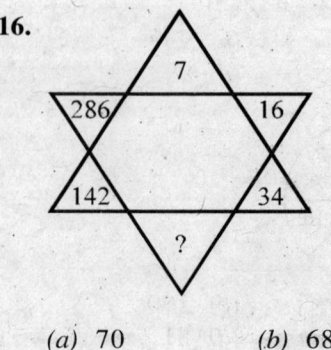

20

5.

7	5

| 6 | |

5	21

| 13 | |

24	4

| ? | |

(a) 4   (b) 8
(c) 20   (d) 14

6.

14	9	4
12	7	2
10	5	0
16	11	?

(a) 9   (b) 6
(c) 3   (d) 7

7.

(a) 69   (b) 49
(c) 50   (d) 60

8.

221   228   ?

(a) 31   (b) 229
(c) 234   (d) 312

9.

(a) 21   (b) 25
(c) 50   (d) 60

10.

51	(11)	61
64	(30)	32
35	(?)	43

(a) 25   (b) 27
(c) 32   (d) 37

11.

(a) 5   (b) 6
(c) 8   (d) 9

12.

(a) 8
(b) 14
(c) 10
(d) 6

13.

(a) 20   (b) 25
(c) 26   (d) 75

14.

27	22	50
13	12	26
9	2	?

(a) 12   (b) 39
(c) 18   (d) 24

15.

(a) 25   (b) 47
(c) 37   (d) 41

16.

(a) 70   (b) 68
(c) 56   (d) 92

17.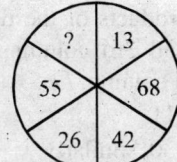

(a) 41 (b) 37
(c) 29 (d) 25

18.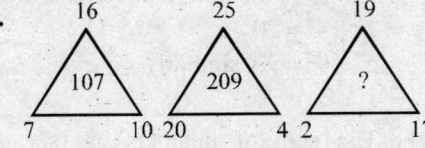

(a) 72 (b) 68
(c) 82 (d) 96

19. 42 (21) 22
78 (?) 84
162 (18) 99

(a) 12 (b) 13
(c) 60 (d) 72

20.

(a) 68 (b) 93
(c) 175 (d) 217

21.

(a) 960 (b) 628
(c) 830 (d) 492

22.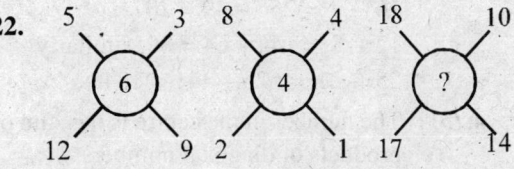

(a) 18 (b) 10
(c) 36 (d) 24

23.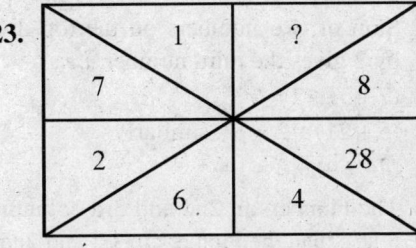

(a) 24 (b) 10
(c) 32 (d) 12

24. 6 (40) 4
3 (12) 3
7 (?) 2

(a) 51 (b) 36
(c) 22 (d) 4

25.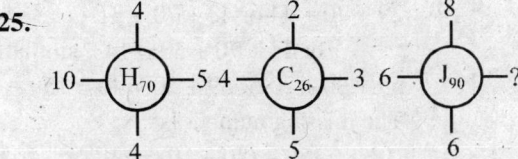

(a) 5
(b) 4
(c) 2
(d) 1

ANSWERS WITH EXPLANATION

1. (c) : The squares of two numbers on the top placed side by side gives the number inside the bottom triangle, i.e.,
6^2 and $3^2 = 369$
2^2 and $5^2 = 425$, similarly
3^2 and $9^2 = 981$.

2. (d) : Starting from number 4 the numbers are the squares of numbers in natural order i.e., $2^2 = 4, 3^2 = 9, 4^2 = 16 \ldots \ldots 9^2 = 81$

3. (b) : The number at the bottom is the difference of the squares of two numbers at the top, i.e.,

$16^2 - 7^2 = 256 - 49 = 207$
$12^2 - 8^2 = 144 - 64 = 80$, similarly
$25^2 - 21^2 = 625 - 441 = 184$

4. (b) : The number in the centre is the sum of the products of diagonal numbers, *i.e.,*
$(3 \times 3) + (5 \times 6) = 39$
$(4 \times 4) + (7 \times 5) = 51$, similarly
$(3 \times 4) + (5 \times 5) = 37$

5. (d) : Sum of two numbers on the top divided by 2 gives the third number, *i.e.,*
$(7 + 5) \div 2 = 6$
$(5 + 21) \div 2 = 13$, similarly
$(24 + 4) \div 2 = 14$

6. (b) : The numbers in 2nd and 3rd columns are 5 less than the nunbers in 1st and 2nd columns respectively, *i.e.,*
$14 - 5 = 9$ and $9 - 5 = 4$
$12 - 5 = 7$ and $7 - 5 = 2$, . . . similarly
$16 - 5 = 11$ and $11 - 5 = 6$.

7. (a) : The sum of 3 numbers in each line in one figure is same, *i.e.,*
$29 + 80 + 43$ or $39 + 80 + 33$
    or $45 + 80 + 27 = 152$
$29 + 70 + 44$ or $42 + 70 + 31$
    or $43 + 70 + 30 = 143$, similarly
$59 + 80 + 20$ or $39 + 80 + 40 = 159$.
The missing number is :
    $159 - (80 + 10) = 69$

8. (c) : The number at the bottom is the product of two numbers at the top, *i.e.,*
$13 \times 17 = 221$
$12 \times 19 = 228$, similarly
$13 \times 18 = 234$

9. (b) : Square of number at the bottom is equal to the product of two numbers at the top, *i.e.,*
$6^2 = 4 \times 9$, *i.e.,* 36
$12^2 = 9 \times 16$, *i.e.,* 144,
similarly
$20^2 = 16 \times ?$, *i.e.,* 400.

The missing number is $400 \div 16 = 25$

10. (b) : The sum of the products of the digits of numbers in 1st and 3rd columns is the number in the 2nd column, *i.e.,*
$(5 \times 1) + (6 \times 1) = 11$
$(6 \times 4) + (3 \times 2) = 30$, similarly
$(3 \times 5) + (4 \times 3) = 27$

11. (d) : The sum of numbers on right and centre subtracted from the number on the left gives the number at the bottom, *i.e.,*
$93 - (27 + 63) = 3$
$79 - (38 + 37) = 4$, similarly
$67 - (16 + 42) = 9$

12. (c) : The number inside each triangle is the difference of the numbers at its base *i.e.*
$10 - 4 = 6$, $18 - 4 = 14$ and $18 - 10 = 8$
$14 - 8 = 6$, $22 - 8 = 14$ and $22 - 14 = 8$, similarly
$11 - 5 = 6$, $15 - 5 = 10$ and $15 - 11 = 4$.

13. (c) : The sum of squares of two numbers at the top gives the third number below, *i.e.,*
$2^2 + 4^2 = 20$
$3^2 + 9^2 = 90$, similarly
$1^2 + 5^2 = 26$

14. (a) : The sum of numbers in 1st and 2nd column plus 1 is the number in the 3rd column, *i.e.,*
$27 + 22 + 1 = 50$
$13 + 12 + 1 = 26$, similarly
$9 + 2 + 1 = 12$

15. (d) : The product of numbers on either side of the triangle plus the number at the base is the number inside the triangle, *i.e.,*
$(5 \times 3) + 4 = 19$
$(6 \times 4) + 5 = 29$, similarly
$(7 \times 5) + 6 = 41$

16. (a) : Clockwise starting from number 7, the next number is obtained by doubling the number and adding 2, *i.e.,*
$(7 \times 2) + 2 = 16$
$(16 \times 2) + 2 = 34$ . . . , similarly
$(34 \times 2) + 2 = 70$
$(70 \times 2) + 2 = 142$
$(142 \times 2) + 2 = 286$

17. (c) : The difference between the numbers in opposite sectors is 13, *i.e.,*

$26 - 13 = 13$

$68 - 55 = 13$, similarly

The missing number is $42 - 13 = 29$

$(42 + 13 = 55$ is not given as option)

18. (b) : The number at the bottom is obtained by subtracting the sum of two numbers in the centre grid line from the square of the number at the top, *i.e.,*

$7^2 - (2 + 7) = 40$

$5^2 - (8 + 3) = 14$, similarly

$9^2 - (7 + 6) = 68$

19. (b) : The number inside the brackets is obtained by multiplying the number on the left by 2 and then dividing the product by the sum of digits of number on the right, *i.e.,*

$(42 \times 2) \div (2 + 2) = 21$

$(162 \times 2) \div (9 + 9) = 18$, similarly

$(78 \times 2) \div (8 + 4) = 13$

20. (a) : Subtracting the sum of squares of two numbers at the base from the square of number at the apex gives the number inside the triangle, *i.e.,*

$16^2 - (7^2 + 10^2) = 107$

$25^2 - (20^2 + 4^2) = 209$, similarly

$19^2 - (2^2 + 17^2) = 68$

21. (c) : The number in the centre is the product of all the 4 numbers minus 10, *i.e.,*

$(3 \times 5 \times 2 \times 6) - 10 = 170$

$(8 \times 1 \times 4 \times 9) - 10 = 278$, similarly

$(10 \times 6 \times 7 \times 2) - 10 = 830$

22. (d) : The number inside the circle is the product of difference of two numbers above and difference of two numbers below, *i.e.,*

$(5 - 3)(12 - 9) = 6$

$(8 - 4)(2 - 1) = 4,$

similarly

$(18 - 10)(17 - 14) = 24$

23. (a) : Starting from number 1 anticlockwise the number in the diagonally opposite section is its multiplication by 4, *i.e.,*

$1 \times 4 = 4$, $7 \times 4 = 28$, $2 \times 4 = 8$, similarly $6 \times 4 = 24$

24. (a) : Square of the number on the left plus the number on the right is the number within brackets, *i.e.,*

$6^2 + 4 = 40$

$3^2 + 3 = 12$, similarly

$7^2 + 2 = 51$

25. (b) : Letter H is 8th in order of alphabetical series. Taking the sum of numbers placed vertically outside the circle + 8; multiplying it by the number on the right; then subtracting from the product the number on the left, gives the number inside the circle, *i.e.,*

Step I → $4 + 8 + 4 = 16$

Step II → $16 \times 5 = 80$

Step III → $80 - 10 = 70$

Letter C is 3rd in order, so

Step I → $2 + 3 + 5 = 10$

Step II → $10 \times 3 = 30$

Step III → $30 - 4 = 26$

Similarly, J is 10th in order, so

Step I → $8 + 10 + 6 = 24$

Step II → $24 \times ?$

Step III → $(24 \times ?) - 6 = 90$

Simplifying the above equation :

$24 \times ? = 90 + 6$, *i.e.,* 96

$? = 96 \div 24 = 4$

• • •

In these type of tests, the directions in questions needs to be perceived. Such questions are based on the direction chart.

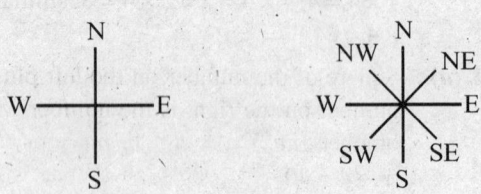

N = North S = South E = East W = West

The sense of the different directions are guided by the left and right turns or angular turns.

Solved Example

1. A person is walking in the North direction. He turns right two times and continues to walk. In which direction is he walking now ?
   (a) North   (b) South
   (c) East   (d) West

   Ans. (b) :

   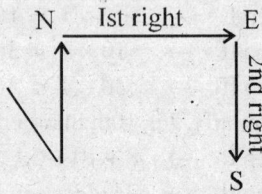

   By following the direction chart it is clear that the person is walking in South direction.

2. A person is walking in the East direction. He turns 45° left and then 90° right. In which direction is he now ?
   (a) North
   (b) North-West
   (c) North-East
   (d) West

Ans. (c) :

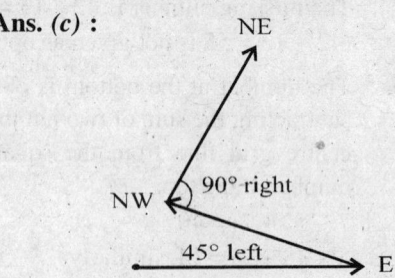

The 45° turn escapes from the straight direction to the coupled direction. 90° turn also follows the coupled direction from North-West to North-East.

The directions to be followed for changing one direction to another can also be routed by making proper use of the direction sense. The distances can also be measured easily.

3. Maya is travelling towards South. Which of the following directions should she take in order to travel towards North ?
   (a) right, left, right, right
   (b) left, right, right
   (c) right, right, left
   (d) left, left, left, left

   Ans. (a) : Maya's first right turn is towards West, second turn to the left turns her to South again. The third turn to the right takes her to the West once again, but by taking the final right turn, she is going towards North.

   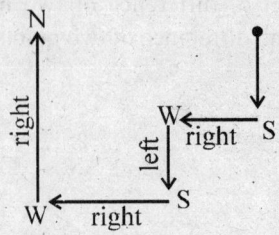

EXERCISE

Directions : *In the following questions, select the right answer from the given options to depict the correct direction/distance.*

1. Kittu walks towards East and then towards South. After walking some distance he turns towards West and then turns to his left. In which direction is he walking now?
   (a) North   (b) South
   (c) East   (d) West

2. A person is driving towards West. What sequence of directions should he follow so that he is driving towards South?
   (a) left, right, right
   (b) right, right, left
   (c) left, left, left
   (d) right, right, right

3. Richa drives 8 km to the South, turns left and drives 5 km. Again, she turns left and drives 8 km. How far is she from her starting point?
   (a) 3 km   (b) 5 km
   (c) 8 km   (d) 13 km

4. Dingi runs 40 km towards North then turns right and runs 50 km. He turns right and runs 30 km, and once again turns right and runs 50 km. How far is he from his starting point?
   (a) 90 km   (b) 50 km
   (c) 10 km   (d) 5 km

5. Debu walks towards East then towards North and turning 45° right walks for a while and lastly turns towards left. In which direction is he walking now?
   (a) North   (b) East
   (c) South-East   (d) North-West

6. If North is called North-West, North-West is called West, West is called South-West and so on. What will South-East be called?
   (a) East   (b) West
   (c) North-East   (d) South-East

7. I went 15 m to the North, then I turned West and covered 10 m, then I turned South and covered 5 m, and then turned East and covered 10 m. In which direction am I from the starting point?
   (a) East   (b) West
   (c) North   (d) South

8. I travel in North direction and then turn left. After travelling for some time I turn left again and then right. Later in the journey I turn left and left once again. What is the direction I am facing?
   (a) North   (b) South
   (c) East   (d) West

9. Raj is walking towards West. He takes three turns while walking, all at an angle of 45° towards right, right and left. What direction is he facing now?
   (a) North-East   (b) South-East
   (c) East   (d) West

10. Jatin leaves his house and walks 12 km towards North. He turns right and walks another 12 km. He turns right again, walks 12 km more and turns left to walk 5 km. How far is he from his home and in which direction?
    (a) 7 km East   (b) 10 km East
    (c) 17 km East   (d) 24 km East

11. A lady runs 12 km towards North, then 6 km towards South and then 8 km East. How far is she from her starting point and in which direction?
    (a) 5 km North-East
    (b) 5 km East
    (c) 10 km North-East
    (d) 10 km West.

12. Diva journeys 10 km to East then 10 km to South-West. He turns again and journeys 10 km to North-West. Which direction is he in from the starting point?
    (a) South   (b) North
    (c) West   (d) East

13. Manu goes 40 km North, turns right and goes 80 km, turns right again and goes 30 km. In the end he turns right again and goes 80 km. How far is he from his starting point if he goes straight ahead another 50 km and turns left to go his last 10 km?
(a) 10 km   (b) 30 km
(c) 40 km   (d) 50 km

14. I walked 18 km towards North, then turned left and having walked another 4 km, I turned right and walked for 12 km more. How far have I walked from the starting point and in which direction?
(a) 8 km North   (b) 10 km West
(c) 16 km South   (d) 34 km North

15. Ravi drives 12 km towards West. He turns South and drives 3 km. He again turns East and drives 8 km. How far is he from his starting point?
(a) 3 km   (b) 5 km
(c) 7 km   (d) 11 km

16. A child crawls 20 feet towards North, turns right and crawls 30 feet, turns right again and crawls 35 feet. He turns left now and crawls 15 feet. He turns left again and crawls 15 feet. Finally he turns to his left to crawl another 15 feet. How far is he from his starting point and in which direction?
(a) 45 feet North-East (b) 30 feet East
(c) 30 feet West   (d) 15 feet West

17. A man travels 100 km towards South. From there he turns right and travels 100 km and again turns right to travel 50 km. Which direction is he in from his starting point?
(a) North   (b) North-East
(c) East   (d) South-West

18. A train runs 120 km in West direction, 30 km in South direction and then 80 km in east direction before reaching the station. In which direction is the station from the train's starting point?
(a) South-West   (b) North-West
(c) South-East   (d) South

19. Facing the West direction, Priya jogs for 20 m, turns left and goes further 40 m. She turns left again and jogs for 20 m. Then she turns right to go 20 m to reach the park. How far is the park from her starting point and in which direction?
(a) 20 m South   (b) 40 m West
(c) 60 m South   (d) 100 m East

20. If all the directions are rotated, *i.e.*, if North is changed to West and East to North and so on, then what will come in place of North-West?
(a) South-West
(b) North-East
(c) East-North
(d) East-West

ANSWERS WITH EXPLANATION

1. (b) :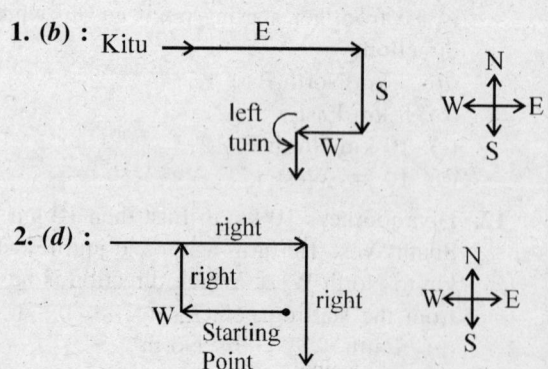

3. (b) :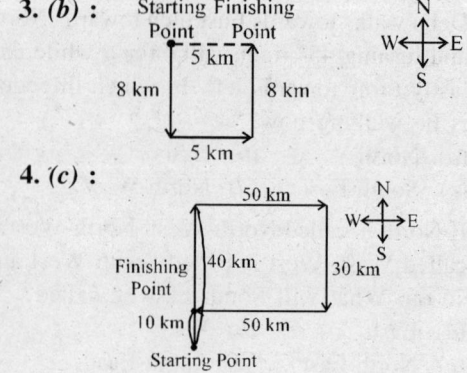

4. (c) :

5. (d) :

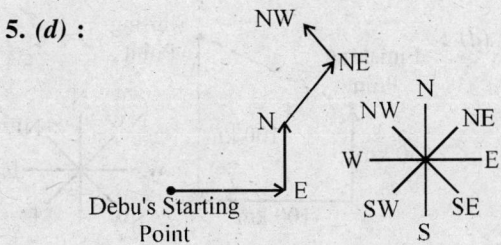

6. (a) :

Original Directions

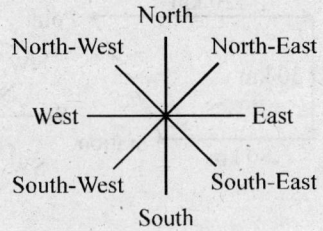

Changed Directions

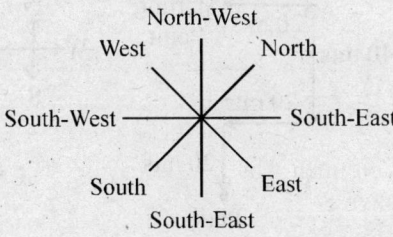

7. (c) :

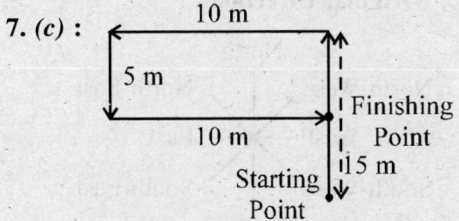

Finishing Point is at 10 m North from Starting Point

8. (c) :

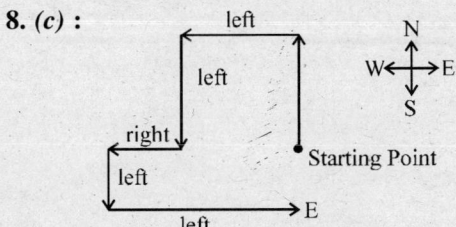

9. (a) :

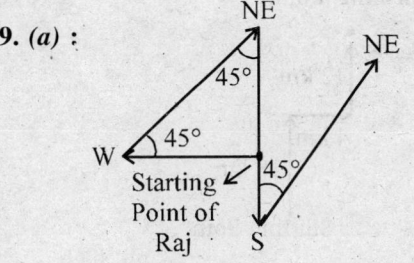

10. (c) : (12 km + 5 km = 17 km)

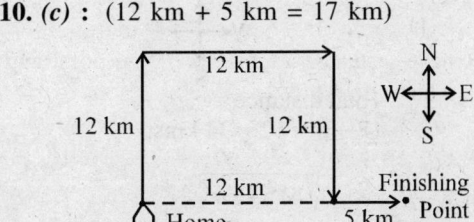

11. (c) : $ab = \sqrt{ac^2 + bc^2}$

$? = \sqrt{8^2 + 6^2} = \sqrt{64 + 36} = \sqrt{100}$

$= 10$

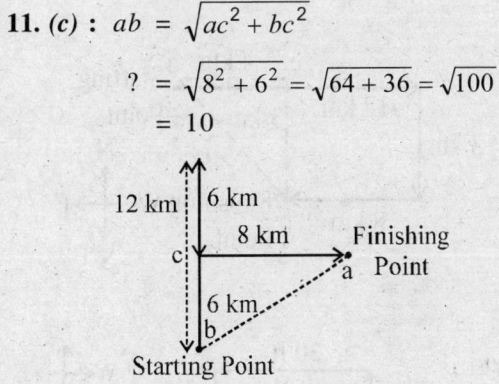

12. (c) :

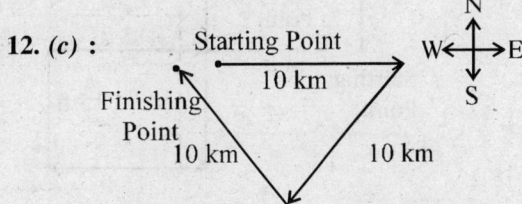

13. (d) :

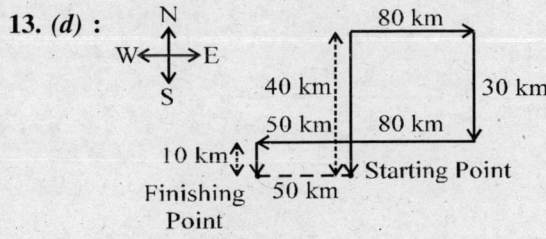

14. (d) : Finishing Point

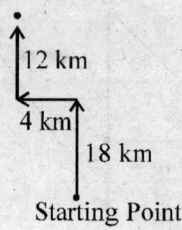

12 km

4 km

18 km

Starting Point

N
W ← → E
S

Total distance =
18 + 4 + 12 = 34 kms.

15. (b) : $ab = \sqrt{bc^2 + ca^2}$

$? = \sqrt{3^2 + 4^2} = \sqrt{9 + 16} = \sqrt{25} = 5$

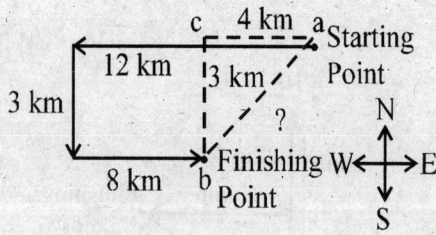

c   4 km a Starting
12 km   3 km   Point
3 km
8 km   b Finishing W ← → E
Point

N
W ← → E
S

?

16. (b) :

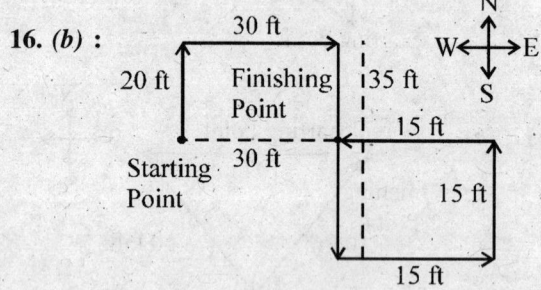

30 ft
20 ft   Finishing   35 ft
Point   15 ft
Starting   30 ft
Point   15 ft
15 ft

N
W ← → E
S

17. (d) :

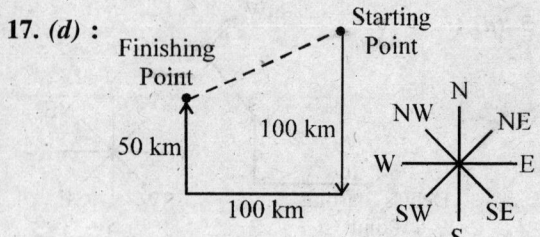

Finishing Point   Starting Point
50 km   100 km
100 km

N
NW   NE
W ← → E
SW   SE
S

18. (a) :

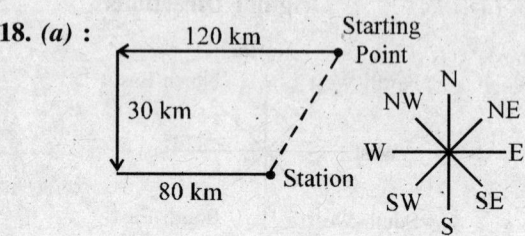

120 km   Starting Point
30 km
80 km   Station

N
NW   NE
W ← → E
SW   SE
S

19. (c) : (40 + 20) = 60 metres South

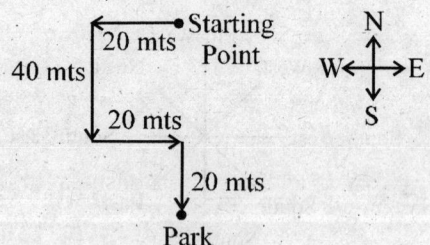

20 mts   Starting Point
40 mts
20 mts
20 mts
Park

N
W ← → E
S

20. (a) : Original Directions

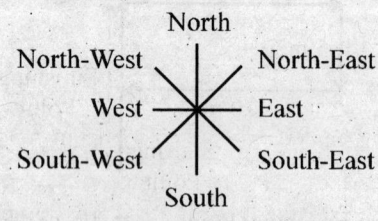

North
North-West   North-East
West   East
South-West   South-East
South

Changed Directions

● ● ●

6 BLOOD RELATIONSHIPS

While attempting questions on blood relations, one should be clear of all the relation patterns that can exist between any two individuals. These type of questions are given mainly to test one's relationship ability.

Very well known relations are :

Mother	Grandmother
Father	Grandfather
Son	Grandson
Daughter	Granddaughter
Brother	Brother-in-law
Sister	Sister-in-law
Niece	Father-in-law
Nephew	Mother-in-law
Uncle	Son-in-law
Aunt	Daughter-in-law
Husband	Cousin
Wife	

The patterns of some relationships which help in solving questions in these tests are :

Father's *or* Mother's Father	—	Grandfather (Paternal *or* Maternal)
Father's *or* Mother's Mother	—	Grandmother (Paternal *or* Maternal
Father's *or* Mother's Son	—	Brother
Father's *or* Mother's Daughter	—	Sister
Father's Brother	—	Paternal Uncle
Father's Sister	—	Paternal Aunt
Mother's Brother	—	Maternal Uncle
Mother's Sister	—	Maternal Aunt
Uncle *or* Aunt's Son *or* Daughter	—	Cousin
Son's Wife	—	Daughter-in-law
Daughter's Husband	—	Son-in-law
Husband's *or* Wife's Brother	—	Brother-in-law
Husband's *or* Wife's Sister	—	Sister-in-law
Brother's Wife	—	Sister-in-law
Sister's Husband	—	Brother-in-law
Brother's Son	—	Nephew
Brother's Daughter	—	Niece

Solved Example _____

1. Pointing to a photograph, a woman said, "This man's son's sister is my mother-in-law". How is the woman's husband related to the man in the photograph?

   (a) Son   (b) Grandson
   (c) Nephew   (d) Son-in-law

   Ans. (b) : The relationship chart based on the given problem can be worked out as given below :

   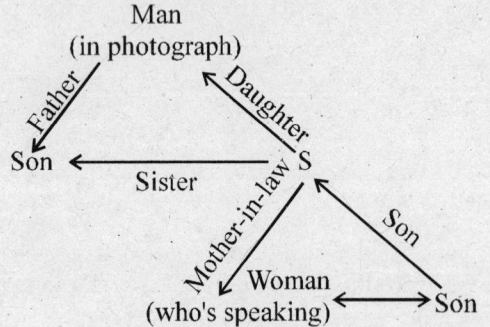

   Man's son's sister (supposed as 'S'), will be man's daughter. If this sister 'S' is the mother-in-law of the woman, who's speaking, then the woman is married to S's son. Mother of the man who is also the husband of the woman is S and S is the daughter of man in photograph. Therefore woman's husband is grandson of the man in the photograph.

2. 'X' is the wife of 'Y' and 'Y' is the brother of 'Z'. 'Z' is the son of 'P'. How is 'P' related to 'X'?

   (a) Sister   (b) Aunt
   (c) Brother   (d) Father-in-law

   Ans. (d) : The relationship chart, based on the given problem can be worked out as given below :

   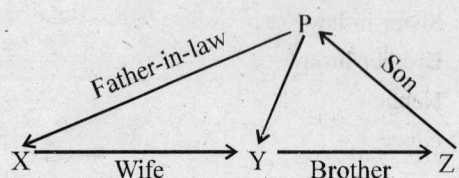

'Y' is the brother of 'Z' who is son of 'P'. So 'Z' is also the son of 'P'. When 'P' is the father of 'Y' and 'X' is the wife of 'Y', then 'P' is the father-in-law of 'X'.

3. How many daughters does M have? To answer the above question, which of the following informations given in the statements (A) and (B) is/are sufficient?

   (A) B is sister of R.
   (B) K, who is married to M, is mother of B and D.

   (a) Both A and B together are needed
   (b) Both A and B together are not sufficient
   (c) Either A or B is sufficient
   (d) Only B is sufficient

   Ans. (b) : The relationship chart that is drawn on the basis of information in both the statements is given below :

   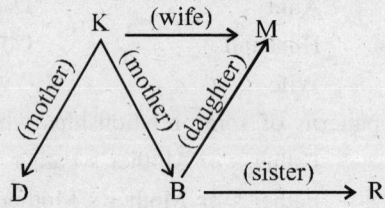

   Only the Sex of B is depicted. Sex of D and R is not given. So, it is not possible to conclude the number of daughters M has. As such, both the statements, A and B together are not sufficient to get the right information.

4. (a) : If R × S means 'R' is the sister of S, Y÷T means 'Y' is the mother of 'T', V + W means 'V' is the wife of 'W', S – Y means 'S' is the husband of 'Y' and W = T means W is the brother of 'T', which of the following would mean 'Y' is the mother-in-law of 'V'?

   (a) V – Y+W   (b) W + Y = V
   (c) Y÷W – V   (d) W = Y + V

   Ans. (c) : The relationship chart, based on the given problem can be worked out as given below :

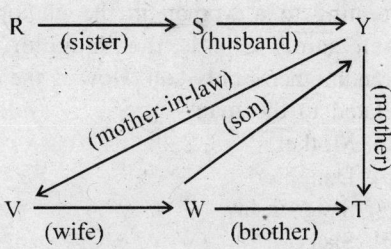

'Y' is the mother of 'T' and 'W' is the brother of 'T'. So, 'W' is the son of 'Y',

Y ÷ W means 'Y' is the mother of 'W' and

W – V means 'W' is the husband of 'V'. So, 'Y' is the mother-in-law of 'V'.

(b) : In the above question which of the given statements can be dispensed with to arrive at the answer?

(a) R × S   (b) S – Y
(c) V + W   (d) Y ÷ T

Ans. (a) : R × S, *i.e.*, 'R' is the sister of 'S' is the only statement which can be dispensed with.

EXERCISE

Directions : *In each of the following questions keenly study the relationship mentioned between the persons, and then from the given options select the right relationship as the answer.*

1. 'A' is the father of 'B' and 'C'. 'B' is the son of 'A' but 'C' is not the son of 'A'. What is 'C's' relation with 'A'?
   (a) Daughter   (b) Son
   (c) Niece   (d) Nephew

2. A lady said, "The person standing there is my grandfather's only son's daughter". How is the lady related to the standing person?
   (a) Sister   (b) Mother
   (c) Aunt   (d) Cousin

3. Ravi is the brother of Amit's son's son. What is Amit's relation to Ravi?
   (a) Cousin   (b) Father
   (c) Grandfather   (d) Son

4. Mayank said, "My mother is the sister of Rajat's brother." What is Rajat's relation with Mayank?
   (a) Cousin   (b) Maternal uncle
   (c) Uncle   (d) Brother-in-law

5. Introducing Lily, Raghav said, "Her father is my mother's only son". How is Lily related to Raghav?
   (a) Aunt   (b) Daughter
   (c) Mother   (d) Sister

6. Ajay is the brother of Vijay. Mili is the Sister of Ajay. Sanjay is the brother of Rahul and Mehul is the daughter of Vijay. Who is Sanjay's Uncle?
   (a) Rahul   (b) Ajay
   (c) Mehul   (d) Data inadequate

7. Adity is Bhavi's brother, Bharat is Jayant's father. Ella is Bhavi's mother. Aditya and Jayant are brothers. What is Ella's relationship with Bharat?
   (a) Sister   (b) Mother
   (c) Daughter   (d) Wife

8. A man introduced the boy coming with him as "He is son of the father of my wife's daughter". What relation did the boy bear to the man?
   (a) Son-in-law   (b) Son
   (c) Brother   (d) Father

9. A and B are two brothers. C is sister of B. D is sister of E. E is son of A. Who is D's uncle?
   (a) D   (b) E
   (c) B   (d) C

10. Varun said pointing towards Arun, "He is my sister's only brother's son". How is Arun related to Varun?
    (a) Son
    (b) Brother
    (c) Nephew
    (d) Data insufficient

11. Pointing to a man, a lady said, "His brother's father is my grandfather's only son." How is the lady related to the man?
    (a) Mother   (b) Sister
    (c) Daughter   (d) Aunt

12. Vidya is the wife of Gopi and Gopi is the brother of Akhil. Akhil is the uncle of Vijay. What is Vijay's relation with Vidya?
    (a) Son
    (b) Nephew
    (c) Brother-in-law
    (d) Brother

13. If Amit's father is Billoo's father's only son and Billoo has neither a brother nor a daughter, what is the relationship between Amit and Billoo?
    (a) Uncle - Nephew
    (b) Father- Daughter
    (c) Father - Son
    (d) Cousins

14. A is the sister of B. B is the son of C, and E is the daughter of D, and sister of A. What is D to C?
    (a) Brother
    (b) Husband
    (c) Wife
    (d) Data is inadequate

15. A Man said to a lady, "Fagu's mother is the only daughter of your father". How is the lady related to Fagu?
    (a) Daughter   (b) Sister
    (c) Wife   (d) Mother

16. Pointing to a man, a woman said, "He is the only son of my mother's mother". How is the woman related to the man?
    (a) Aunt   (b) Daughter
    (c) Niece   (d) Sister

17. If B's mother was A's mother's daughter, how was A related to B?
    (a) Uncle or Aunt
    (b) Brother
    (c) Sister
    (d) Data is insufficient

18. Pointing to a woman in the photograph a man said, "She is the daughter of my grandmother's only son. How is the woman related to the man?
    (a) Mother
    (b) Daughter
    (c) Sister-in-law
    (d) Sister

19. A man and a woman are sitting in a room. Man's mother-in-law and woman's mother-in-law are mother and daughter respectively. Man is the .... of the woman.
    (a) Father
    (b) Father-in-law
    (c) Uncle
    (d) Grandfather-in-law

20. Pointing to Suman, Amit said, "He is my sister's only brother's son". How is Suman related to Amit?
    (a) Grandson
    (b) Son
    (c) Nephew
    (d) Cannot be determined

21. Pointing to someone, I said, "She is my father's sister and she is the only daughter". How many children did my paternal grandparents have in all?
    (a) Two sons
    (b) One daughter
    (c) One son and one daughter
    (d) Cannot be determined

22. Pointing to a photograph, a woman said, "She is the only daughter of my mother's father." How is the woman related to the person in the photograph?
    (a) Mother
    (b) Grandmother
    (c) Daughter
    (d) Cannot be determined

23. Sandip's mother is the only daughter of Rekha's father. How is Rekha's husband related to Sandip?
    (a) Uncle   (b) Brother
    (c) Grandfather   (d) Father

ANSWERS WITH EXPLANATION

1. (a) :

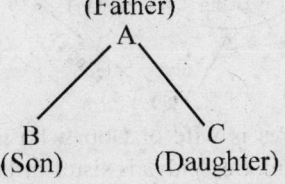

'C' is not the son of 'A', but 'A' is the father of 'C'. So, 'C' is the daughter of 'A'.

2. (a) :

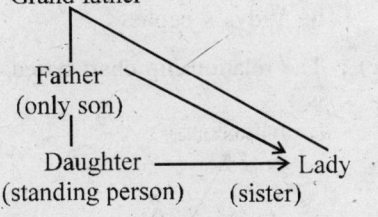

Lady's grandfather's son is lady's father and father's daughter will only be lady's sister.

3. (c) :

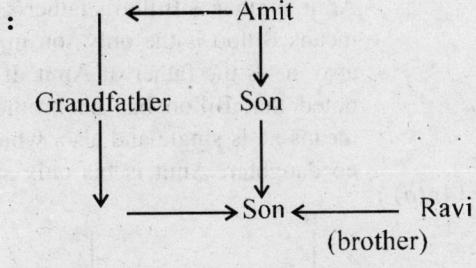

Amit's son's son is Amit's grandson. Ravi is the brother of Amit's son's son. So, Amit is also the grandfather of Ravi.

4. (b) :

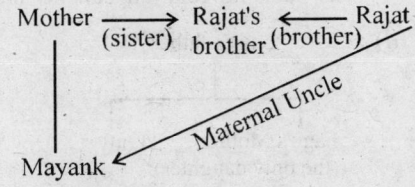

Mayank's mother is the sister of Rajat's brother. So Rajat is also the brother of Mayank's mother. Relation of the brother with his sister's child is maternal. So Rajat is Mayank's maternal uncle.

5. (b) : The relation is :Mother

$\uparrow$ (Son)

Raghav

$\downarrow$ (Father)

Lily (Daughter)

'My mother's only son' means Raghav himself. 'Her father' means Lily's father; *i.e.* Raghav and so, Lily is Raghav's daughter.

6. (d) :

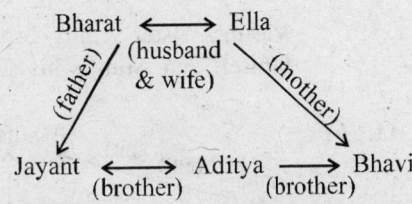

There are two sets of relationship. Information given is incomplete and no relation can be established between the two sets.

7. (d) : The relationship chart based on problem is :

Bharat ⟷ Ella
(husband & wife)
(father) (mother)

Jayant ⟷ Aditya ⟶ Bhavi
(brother) (brother)

Jayant and Aditya are brothers. If Aditya is Bhavi's brother, then Jayant is also Bhavi's brother. If Bharat is Jayant's father, then he is also the father of Aditya and Bhavi. If Ella is Bhavi's mother, then she is also the mother of Aditya and Jayant. This means Bharat and Ella are husband and wife and the parents of three.

8. (b) : The relationship chart based on problem is :

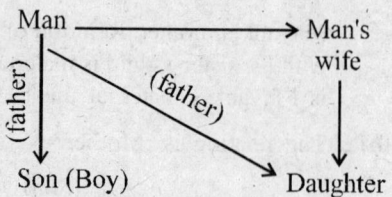

'Father of the man's wife's daughter' is the man himself and the boy in question is the man's son.

9. (c) : The relationship chart based on the problem is :

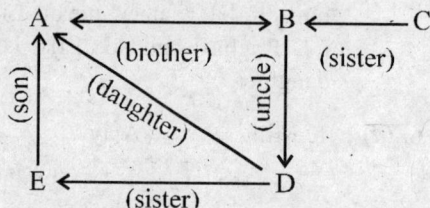

When D is sister of E, who is son of A then D is daughter of A. Brother of A is B and so, B is D's uncle.

10. (a) :

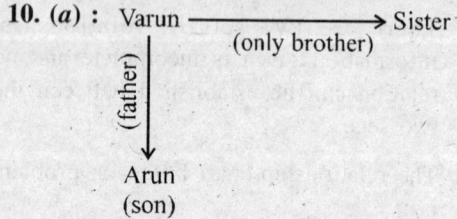

Varun's sister's only brother is Varun himself and Arun is his son.

11. (b) :

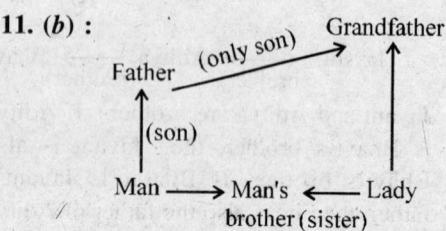

Man's brother's father is also the lady's father as he is the only son of lady's grandfather. So, the lady is man's sister.

12. (b) : The relationship chart based on problem is :

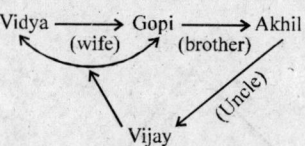

Vidya is wife of Gopi who is brother of Akhil. So, Vidya is sister-in-law of Akhil. If Akhil is uncle of Vijay then Gopi will naturally be the uncle of Vijay as it is not specified that any of the mentioned persons are Vijay's parents. Now, when Vijay is Gopi's nephew then he will also be Vidya's nephew.

13. (c) : The relationship chart based on problem is :

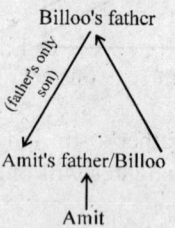

Amit's father is Billoo's father's only son means Billoo is the only son in question also, he is the father of Amit. It must be noted that Billoo has no brother which means he is single and also, when he has no daughter, Amit is his only son.

14. (d) :

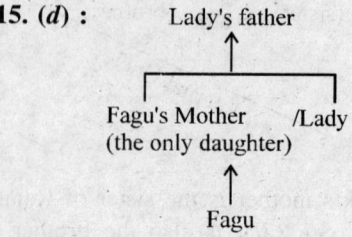

Information about 'D' and 'C' is not given as such no relation can be specified.

15. (d) :

Lady's father

Fagu's Mother   /Lady
(the only daughter)

Fagu

The only daughter of Lady's father is Fagu's mother.

16. (c) :

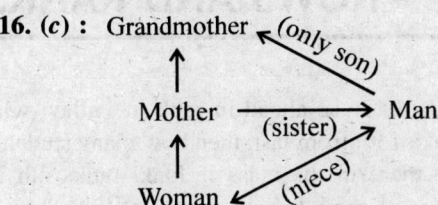

The man is the brother of the woman's mother. So, the woman is man's niece.

17. (a) :

A's mother

(daughter)

B's mother   A

B

18. (d) :

Man's Grandmother

Grandmother's only son
A

Man (sister) Daughter

'My grandmother's only son' is the father of the man, and 'daughter of my grand-mot'er's only son' is the sister of the man.

19. (b) :

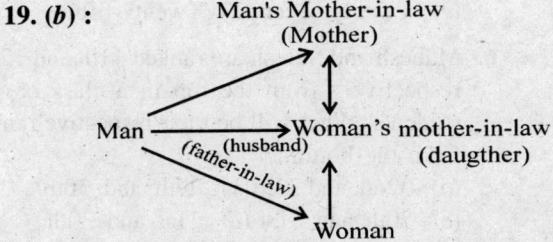

Woman's mother-in-law is the daughter of Man's mother-in-law. So, the man is

the husband of woman's mother-in-law and the father-in-law of the woman.

20. (b) :

Amit ⟷ Amit's Sister
(only brother)
↓
Son (Suman)

'My sister's only brother's is Amit himself and 'Sister's only brother's son' is the son of Amit *i.e.*, Suman is the son of Amit.

21. (d) :

My father ⟵ Father's sister
↗   (only daughter)
Myself

Nothing can be determined from this information.

22. (c) :

Woman's mother's father
⇕
Person in photograph
(woman's mother/only daughter)
↑ (daughter)
Woman

'Only daughter of my mother's father' is the person in the photograph and she is also the mother of the woman. So, the woman is the daughter of the person in the photograph.

23. (d) :

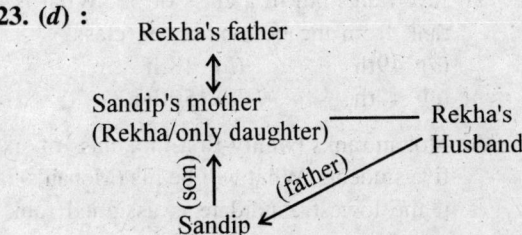

'Only daughter of Rekha's father's is Rekha who is also Sandip's mother. And so, Rekha's husband is the father of Sandip.

7 ROWS AND RANKS

These type of problems need easy calculations to find out the number of objects in a row, lane or queue or to find a person's rank in a class of certain number of students; or to find the total number of students.

Solved Example

1. In a row of trees, one tree is 8th from one end and 3rd from the other. How many trees are there in the row?
   (a) 11   (b) 9
   (c) 10   (d) 12
   (e) None of these

   Ans. (c) : The number of trees in the row is:

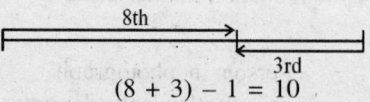

$$(8 + 3) - 1 = 10$$

2. If Janki is 12 ahead in rank of Pallavi who ranks 15th from last, then how many students are there in the class if Janki ranks 4th in order of merit?
   (a) 23   (b) 27
   (c) 31   (d) 33
   (e) None of these

   Ans. (c) : After calculations the answer will be :

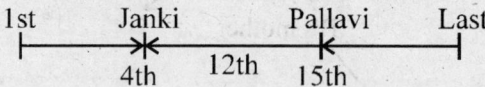

The total number of students are :

$$4 + 12 + 15 = 31$$

EXERCISE

1. In a row of trees, one tree is fifth from either end of the row. How many trees are in the row?
   (a) 11   (b) 8
   (c) 10   (d) 9

2. Jaya ranks 5th in a class of 53. What is her rank from the bottom in the class?
   (a) 49th   (b) 48th
   (c) 47th   (d) 50th

3. Mohan ranks twenty-first in a class of sixty-five students. What will be his (Mohan's) rank if the lowest candidate is assigned rank 1?
   (a) 44th   (b) 45th
   (c) 46th   (d) Data inadequate

4. If Rahul finds that he is 12th from the right in a line of boys and 4th from the left, how many boys should be added to the line such that there are 28 boys in the line?
   (a) 12   (b) 14
   (c) 20   (d) 13

5. In a row of boys, Rajan is tenth from the right and Suraj is tenth from the left. When Rajan and Suraj interchange their positions, Suraj will be twenty-seventh from the left. Which of the following will be Rajan's position from the right?
   (a) Tenth   (b) Twenty-sixth
   (c) Twenty-seven (d) Twenty-fifth

6. Mahesh and Suresh are ranked 11th and 12th respectively from the top in a class of 41 students. What will be their respective ranks from the bottom?
   (a) 32nd and 33rd (b) 29th and 30th
   (c) 30th and 31st (d) 31st and 30th

7. Uma ranked 8th from the top and 37th from bottom in a class. How many students are there in the class?
   (a) 47   (b) 44
   (c) 45   (d) 48

8. In a queue, Sadiq is 14th from the front and Joseph is 17th from the end, while Jane is in between Sadiq and Joseph. If Sadiq be ahead of Joseph and there be 48 persons in the queue, how many persons are there between Sadiq and Jane?

(a) 5   (b) 6
(c) 7   (d) 8

9. Rohan ranked eleventh from the top and twenty-seventh from the bottom among the students who passed the annual examination in a class. If the number of students who failed in the examination was 12, how many students appeared for the examination?

(a) 48
(b) 49
(c) 50
(d) Cannot be determined

10. Some boys are sitting in a row. P is sitting fourteenth from the left and Q is seventh from the right. If there are four boys between P and Q, how many boys are there in the row?

(a) 19   (b) 21
(c) 25   (d) 23

11. There are five different houses, A to E, in a row. A is to the right of B and E is to the left of C and right of A, and B is to the right of D. Which of the houses is in the middle?

(a) B   (b) A
(c) D   (d) E

12. Madhav ranks seventeenth in a class of thirtyone. What is his rank from the last?

(a) 13   (b) 14
(c) 15   (d) 16

13. Veena ranks 73rd from the top in a class of 182. What is her rank from the bottom if 22 students have failed the examination?

(a) 88   (b) 108
(c) 110   (d) 90

14. Rakesh ranked 9th from the top and 38th from the bottom in a class. How many students are there in the class?

(a) 47   (b) 45
(c) 46   (d) 48

15. John ranks 19th in class and is 36th from the last. How many students are there in the class?

(a) 53   (b) 54
(c) 51   (d) 50

ANSWERS WITH EXPLANATION

1. (d):

Tree
5th

Total number of trees in the row are :
(5 + 5) −1 = 9

2. (a) :

Jaya 53rd
5th

Jaya's rank from the bottom is :
(53 − 5) + 1 = 49th.

3. (b) :

1st   Mohan   65th
21st
65th   ?   1st

Note : Mohan's rank from the last or the question asked means the same.
Mohan's rank is (65 − 21) +1 = 45th

4. (d) :

4th   Rahul   12th

The number of boys in the line are :
(4 + 12) − 1 = 15

To make a line of 28 boys, (28 −15) *i.e.*
13 more boys are needed.

5. (c) :

L   Suraj   Rajan   R
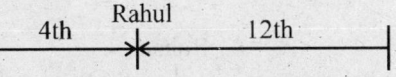
10th   10th

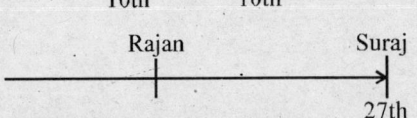
Rajan   Suraj
27th

As the position of boys is equal from both ends, Rajan will also be 27th from the right after changing positions.

6. (d) :

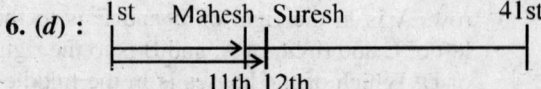

Mahesh's position from bottom is :
(41 – 11) + 1 = 31st

Suresh's position from bottom is :
(41 – 12) +1 = 30th

7. (b) :

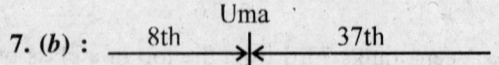

Total number of students in the class are :

(8 + 37) – 1 = 44

8. (c) :

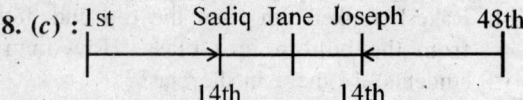

Sadiq's position from last is :

(48 – 14) + 1 = 35th

Number of persons between Sadiq and Joseph are (35 – 17) – 1 = 17

Jane is in-between Sadiq and Joseph *i.e.,* she's at 9th position from both the boys.

∴ there are 8 persons between Sadiq and Jane.

Note : (8 + 8) – 1 = 17

9. (b) :

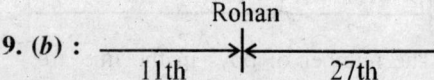

Number of students who passed the examination (11+ 27) – 1 = 37
Those who failed = 12
Total number of students who appeared in the examination = 37 + 12 = 49.

10. (c) :

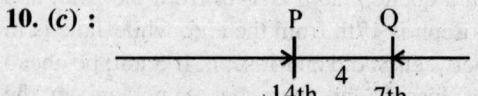

The number of boys in the row are :
(14 + 4 + 7) = 25

11. (b) : The houses in the row are :
D B A E C

12. (c) :

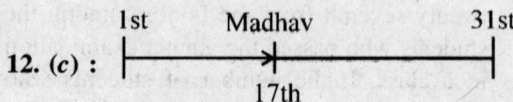

Madhav's rank from the last is :
(31 – 17) + 1 = 15th

13. (a) :

1st   Veena   182nd
73th

Number of students who failed is 22.
Number of students who passed
= 182–22
= 160.
So Veena's rank from the bottom will be:
(160 – 73) + 1 = 88th

14. (c) :

Rakesh
9th   38th

Number of students in the class is :
(9 + 38) – 1 = 46

15. (b) :

John
19th   36th

Number of students in the class is :
(19 + 36) – 1 = 54

● ● ●

Number problems consists of number sequences, problems with algebraic expressions, mathematical calculations and other compatiable problems.

Solved Example

1. How many such 7s are there in the following number sequence which are immediately followed by 4 but not immediately preceded by 8?

   5 4 7 8 9 7 4 3 8 7 5 7 4 8 7 4 1 2 7 4 5 7 9 4
   (a) Two
   (b) Three
   (c) Four
   (d) Five
   (e) None of these

   Ans. (b) : Number of 7s which are immediately followed by 4 but not immediately preceded by 8 are :
   5 4 7 8 9 <u>7 4</u> 3 8 7 <u>5 7 4</u> 8 7 4 1 <u>2 7 4</u> 5 7 9 4
             1   2   3

2. A number is 9 times twice the other number. The sum of two numbers is 133. The two numbers are :

   (a) 9, 124   (b) 11, 122
   (c) 17, 166   (d) 7, 126
   (e) 27, 136

   Ans. (d) : If the smaller number is x, then
   $$x + (2x \times 9) = 133$$
   $$x + 18x = 133$$
   $$19x = 133$$
   $$x = 133 \div 19 = 7$$
   If one number is 7, the other number is :
   $$133 - 7 = 126$$

3. If all the numbers from 1 to 28 which are exactly divisible by 3 are arranged in descending order, which would come at the sixth place from the top?
   (a) 12   (b) 21
   (c) 15   (d) 18
   (e) 24

   Ans. (a) : The numbers divisible by 3 in descending order are : 27, 24, 21, 18, 15, 12, 9, 6, 3 and the number at the sixth place is 12.

EXERCISE

1. How many 6's are there in the following series of numbers which are preceded by 7 but not immediately followed by 9?
   6 7 9 5 6 9 7 6 8 7 6 7 8 6 9 4 6 7 7 6 9 5 7 6 3
   (a) One   (b) Two
   (c) Three   (d) Four

2. In a chess tournament each of six players will play every other player exactly once. How many matches will be played during the tournament?
   (a) 12   (b) 15
   (c) 30   (d) 36

3. How many 4's are there in the following series which are preceded by 7, but are not preceded by 8?
   3 4 5 7 4 3 7 4 8 5 4 3 7 4 9 8 4 7 2 7 4 1 3 6
   (a) 1   (b) 2
   (c) 3   (d) 4

4. How many even numbers are there in the following series of numbers, each of which is immediately preceded by an odd number, but not immediately followed by an even number?
   5 3 4 8 9 7 1 6 5 3 2 9 8 4 3 5

(a) Nil   (b) 1

(c) 2   (d) 3

5. If all the numbers from 1 to 51 which are exactly divisible by 3 are arranged in descending order, which of the following numbers will come at the seventh and tenth places from the top?

(a) 33 & 27   (b) 33 & 21

(c) 21 & 30   (d) 33 & 24

6. Nitin was counting down from 32. Shasank was counting upwards, the numbers starting from 1 and he was calling out only the odd numbers. Which common number will they call out at the same time if they were calling out at the same speed?

(a) 21

(b) 22

(c) 19

(d) They will not call out the same number

7. In the following list of numerals, how many 3s are followed by 3, but NOT preceded by 3?

2 4 6 3 3 1 5 7 8 3 3 3 4 6 2 3 3 3 3 9 7 2 3

(a) 1   (b) 2

(c) 3   (d) 4

8. If in a given number 5 8 9 4 3 2 7 6 1 4, we interchange the first and the second digits, the third and the fourth, the fifth and the sixth and so on, then counting from the right end, which digit will be sixth?

(a) 3   (b) 2

(c) 4   (d) 5

9. Aparna cuts a cake into two halves and cuts one-half into smaller pieces of equal size. Each of the small pieces is twenty grams in weight. If she has seven pieces of the cake in all with her, how heavy was the original cake?

(a) 140 grams

(b) 280 grams

(c) 240 grams

(d) 120 grams

10. In the following number sequence how many such even numbers are there which are exactly divisible by its immediate preceding number but not exactly divisible by its immediate following number?

3 8 4 1 5 7 2 8 3 4 8 9 3 9 4 2 1 5 8 2

(a) Two   (b) Three

(c) Four   (d) More than four

11. How many 7s are there in the following series which are not immediately followed by 3 but immediately preceded by 8?

8 9 8 7 6 2 2 6 3 2 6 9 7 3 2 8 7 2 7 7 8 7 3 7 7 9 4

(a) Nil   (b) One

(c) Two   (d) Three

12. How many 9's are there in the following sequence which are neither preceded by 6 nor immediately followed by 3?

9 3 8 6 9 9 5 9 3 7 8 9 9 9 3 9 6 3 9

(a) One   (b) Two

(c) Three   (d) Four

13. If a number is five times as great as another number which is four less than forty, then the number is :

(a) 220   (b) 180

(c) 144   (d) 200

14. If 2/3rd of a number is 96, what will be the 3/4th of that number?

(a) 108   (b) 198

(c) 128   (d) 48

15. If such numbers which are divisible by 5, and also those which have 5 as one of the digits are eliminated from the numbers 1 to 60, how many numbers would remain?

(a) 53   (b) 47

(c) 40   (d) 45

16. How many 8's are there in the following number series which are exactly divisible by its immediately preceding and also exactly divisible by immediately succeeding numbers?

8 2 4 5 1 7 2 8 4 8 4 2 2 8 2 6 9 8 4 5 4 8 3 2 8 4 3 1 8 3

(a) 1   (b) 2

(c) 3   (d) 4

ANSWERS WITH EXPLANATION

1. (c): 6 7 9 5 6 <u>9 7</u> 6 8 7 6 7 8 6 9 4 <u>6 7</u> 7 6 9
5 7 6 3
         1   2   3

2. (b): When all the players have to play with each other then the method of calculating the number of matches to be played is $\dfrac{n(n-1)}{2}$ where 'n' is the number of players playing the match. So, the number of matches played will be :
$(6 \times 5) \div 2 = 30 \div 2 = 15$

3. (d): 3 4 5 <u>7 4</u> 3 <u>7 4</u> 8 5 4 3 <u>7 4</u> 9 8 4 7 2 <u>7 4</u> 1 3 6
         1   2   3   4

4. (c): 5 3 4 8 9 7 <u>1 6 5</u> <u>3 2 9</u> 8 4 3 5
                1   2

5. (d): The numbers divisible by 3 in descending order are :
51, 48, 45, 42, 39, <u>36</u>, 33, 30, 27, <u>24</u>, 21,
                          7th   10th
18, 15, 12, 9, 6, 3.

6. (d): When Nitin is on count 22, Shasank is on 21 and when Nitin is on count 21, Shasank is on 23.

7. (c): 2 4 <u>6 3</u> 3 1 5 7 <u>8 3 3</u> 3 4 6 <u>2 3 3</u> 3 3 9 7 2 3
         1   2   3

8. (b): The new number after interchanging the digits is :
8 5 4 9 2 3 6 7 4 1
          ↑
        6th

9. (c): There is one bigger piece and six smaller pieces. One small piece weighs 20 gm. Total weight of six smaller speices is 120 gm.
∴ Weight of the bigger piece = 120 gm
∴ Weight of the original cake = 240 gm

10. (a): 3 8 4 1 5 7 <u>2 8 3</u> 4 <u>8 9</u> 3 9 4 2 1 5 8 2
               1   2

11. (c): 8 9 <u>8 7</u> 6 2 2 6 3 2 6 9 7 3 2 <u>8 7</u> 2 7 7 8 7 3 7 7 9 4
         1   2

12. (d): 9 3 8 6 <u>9 9 5</u> 9 3 7 <u>8 9 9 9</u> <u>3 9 6</u> 3 9
             1   2 3   4

13. (b): Number four less than forty is $40 - 4 = 36$
Five times the number is $= 36 \times 5 = 180$

14. (a): If the number is x, then
$$\frac{2}{3}x = 96$$
$$x = \frac{96 \times 3}{2} = 144$$
$\dfrac{3}{4}$ th of the number is $144 \times \dfrac{3}{4} = 108$

15. (c): The eliminated twenty numbers are : 5, 10, 15, 20, 25, 30, 35, 40, 45 and 50 to 60. The remaining numbers are $60 - 20 = 40$.

16. (d): 8 2 4 5 1 7 <u>2 8 4</u> 8 4 2 2 <u>8 2</u> 6 9 8 4 5 4 8
              1   2   3
3 <u>2 8</u> 4 3 1 8 3
    4

In this type of series small letters of the alphabet are used to make a set of letters which are repeated. The candidate has to find the set of letters which will fit the blanks left in the given series in such a manner that one section of the series is further repeated in the same manner.

Solved Example

1. Which of the following groups of letters will complete the given series?

   ba_b_aab_a_b

   (a) baab   (b) abba
   (c) abaa   (d) babb
   (e) bbab

Ans. (b) : The series is baab, baab, baab. Here the section 'baab' is repeated in the series.

Solving steps : The candidate has to look for clues to solve such series pattern. 'aab' in the Series indicates that 'b' in this series is preceded by two 'a' so, the first blank and the last blank will be filled by 'a'.

Now the first set is formed, *i.e.,* 'baab' in the beginning. This set is repeated, so the second and third blanks will have 'b' filling them. Now, solve the exercise given below to know the different ways in which these series are formed.

EXERCISE

Directions : *Which of the following groups of letters will complete the given series?*

1. ab__b_bbaa
   (a) babba   (b) abaab
   (c) abbab   (d) baaab
   (e) ababa

2. aa_ab__aaa_a
   (a) baaa   (b) abab
   (c) aaab   (d) aabb
   (e) bbaa

3. _baa_aab_a_a
   (a) baab   (b) abab
   (c) aaba   (d) aabb
   (e) baba

4. _a cca_ccca_accccc_aaa
   (a) ccaa   (b) acca
   (c) caac   (d) caaa
   (e) ccca

5. c_bbb__abbbb_abbb_
   (a) abccb   (b) bacbb
   (c) aabcb   (d) abacb
   (e) bacba

6. ac_cab_baca_aba_acac
   (a) bcbb   (b) aacb
   (c) babb   (d) acbc
   (e) cbcc

7. __aba__ba_ab
   (a) abbab   (b) bbaba
   (c) baabb   (d) abbba
   (e) aabab

8. __babbba_a__
   (a) bbaba   (b) babbb
   (c) baaab   (d) ababb
   (e) abbba

9. k_mk_lmkkl_kk_mk
   (a) lklm   (b) lkmk
   (c) lkmm   (d) lkml
   (e) lmkm

10. abc_d_bc_d_b_dd
    (a) decdb   (b) dadac
    (c) cdabe   (d) bacde
    (e) abcde

11. b_abbc_bbca_bcabb_ab
   (*a*) acba   (*b*) acaa
   (*c*) cacc   (*d*) cabc
   (*e*) baca

12. aca_ac__a_ac
   (*a*) babc   (*b*) aaac
   (*c*) cacc   (*d*) caca
   (*e*) acac

13. ba_cb_b_bab_?
   (*a*) acbb   (*b*) bcaa
   (*c*) cabb   (*d*) bacc
   (*e*) baca

14. ab_aa_caab_aab_a
   (*a*) bcbc   (*b*) bbca
   (*c*) cbcc   (*d*) caba
   (*e*) acbc

15. _bbcaa_bcaa_bc_a_bca
   (*a*) bacab   (*b*) abbab
   (*c*) abcba   (*d*) bcaab
   (*e*) abcab

16. a_bccb_ca_cca_baab_c
   (*a*) accab   (*b*) abcaa
   (*c*) bacaa   (*d*) ababc
   (*e*) aabbc

17. b_dabbcd_b_c_ab
   (*a*) cabd   (*b*) bcad
   (*c*) dcba   (*d*) acbd
   (*e*) abcd

18. a_ba_caacb_bc_
   (*a*) acbb   (*b*) cbab
   (*c*) cbaa   (*d*) cbba
   (*e*) acba

19. c_baa_aca_cacab_acac_bca
   (*a*) acbaa   (*b*) cbaac
   (*c*) bccab   (*d*) bbcaa
   (*e*) acabc

20. _bcc_ac_aabb_ab_cc
   (*a*) bacab   (*b*) abaca
   (*c*) aabca   (*d*) bcaca
   (*e*) bacac

21. ab_ccca_bccc_bbcc_
   (*a*) abbc   (*b*) bbac
   (*c*) bbca   (*d*) cabc
   (*e*) acba

22. _cbc_a_bcaac_ca
   (*a*) aaba   (*b*) caab
   (*c*) bcab   (*d*) aacb
   (*e*) abca

23. ab_ba__ba_
   (*a*) abba   (*b*) baab
   (*c*) baba   (*d*) abab
   (*e*) abba

24. yx_yx_yxz_xz_y_zyxz
   (*a*) zzyx   (*b*) xxzy
   (*c*) yyzx   (*d*) yzxz
   (*e*) xyzx

25. xxxy_y_xxy_yxx_
   (*a*) xyxy   (*b*) yxyx
   (*c*) yyxx   (*d*) xxyy
   (*e*) None of these

26. aa_aabb_b_aa_aabb_bb
   (*a*) abbab   (*b*) bbbaa
   (*c*) babba   (*d*) aabbb
   (*e*) ababa

27. ab_aabc_abc_
   (*a*) aab   (*b*) caa
   (*c*) bca   (*d*) cba
   (*e*) abc

28. c_abca_b_aab
   (*a*) bbc   (*b*) bca
   (*c*) aac   (*d*) cab
   (*e*) cba

29. cc_bac_bbacc_baccb_a
   (*a*) cbca   (*b*) bcbc
   (*c*) bcbb   (*d*) bbbc
   (*e*) bbcb

30. aaab_aaaaba_a_abaa
   (*a*) baa   (*b*) aaa
   (*c*) aba   (*d*) bba
   (*e*) bab

31. nl_n_mn_m_lm
   (*a*) mlnn   (*b*) lnnm
   (*c*) mlnl   (*d*) mlln
   (*e*) lmnl

32. lm_nnll_mn_llmm_nl
   (*a*) lmmn   (*b*) lnnm
   (*c*) mmnn   (*d*) mnll
   (*e*) nnml

33. aba_caab__cca_bac_a
- (a) cbac
- (b) caac
- (c) bccb
- (d) abcb
- (e) cabc

34. _cd_bc_ab_dabc_a
- (a) badcd
- (b) ccddb
- (c) abccd
- (d) ccbab
- (e) None of these

35. _cabcc_bc_abcca_
- (a) babc
- (b) acac
- (c) cacb
- (d) bacc
- (e) abcc

36. mn_om_oom_oo_noo
- (a) onnm
- (b) nmmo
- (c) mnoo
- (d) nmon
- (e) None of these

37. _lmn_ll_nol_mno
- (a) nlmo
- (b) mnoo
- (c) omlm
- (d) loml
- (e) lomn

38. xx_zzx_yzz_xyz_
- (a) xyzx
- (b) zyxx
- (c) yxxy
- (d) yxxz
- (e) xzyx

39. y_xx_yxx_yyx_xy
- (a) xyxx
- (b) xxxy
- (c) yxxy
- (d) xxyx
- (e) xyxy

40. a_bab__b_abb
- (a) abab
- (b) bbab
- (c) aabb
- (d) babb
- (e) baba

41. aa_bbb_ccaaab_bc_c
- (a) acbc
- (b) acbc
- (c) accb
- (d) cbac
- (e) abcb

42. aba_a_acab_caba_
- (a) cbac
- (b) bbcc
- (c) abab
- (d) cacb
- (e) abca

43. l_nnlm_nlmn_lmn_
- (a) lmnn
- (b) nnml
- (c) mlnm
- (d) mnnn
- (e) None of these

44. ll_mnnl_mm_nllm_nn
- (a) nlmn
- (b) mlnm
- (c) mnln
- (d) lmmn
- (e) None of these

45. _ba_baa_ab_a
- (a) babb
- (b) baab
- (c) abbb
- (d) aaba
- (e) abba

46. ab_da_cd_bc_
- (a) abdc
- (b) cbad
- (c) bcad
- (d) acbd
- (e) abcd

47. _yyx_xxyx_yxyx_y
- (a) yxxy
- (b) xyxy
- (c) yxyx
- (d) xyyx
- (e) None of these

48. a_ba_bb_ab_a
- (a) abab
- (b) baab
- (c) baba
- (d) abbb
- (e) aaab

49. x_yyx_y__xyy
- (a) xyyy
- (b) yyyx
- (c) xyxy
- (d) xxyx
- (e) xxxy

50. _bcbc_caba__
- (a) aabc
- (b) abac
- (c) caab
- (d) baba
- (e) abca

ANSWERS WITH EXPLANATION

1. (d) : The series is abbaab, abbaab
2. (c) : The series is aaaaba, aaaaba
3. (b) : The series is aba, aba, aba, aba

4. (d) : The series is c,a,cc,aa, ccc, aaa, cccc, aaaa
5. (a) : The series is cabbbb, cabbbb, cabbbb
6. (b) : The series is acac, abab, acac, abab, acac

7. (*a*) : The series is ab, ab, ab, ab, ab, ab

8. (*b*) : The series is bababb, bababb

9. (*d*) : The series is klmk, klmk, klmk, klmk

10. (*b*) : The series is abcdd, abcdd, abcdd

11. (*d*) : The series is bcab, bcab, bcab, bcab, bcab

12. (*c*) : The series is ac, ac, ac, ac, ac, ac

13. (*d*) : The series is babc, babc, babc

14. (*c*) : The series is abca, abca, abca, abca

15. (*b*) : The series is abbca, abbca, abbca, abbca

16. (*d*) : The series is aabcc, bbcaa, ccabb, aabcc

17. (*a*) : The series is bcdab, bcdab, bcdab

18. (*c*) : The series is acbabca, acbabca

19. (*a*) : The series is cabaac, acabca, cabaac, acabca

20. (*a*) : The series is bbccaa, ccaabb, aabbcc.

21. (*b*) : The series is abbccc abbccc.

22. (*d*) : The series is acbca acbca acbca.

23. (*d*) : The series is ab ab ab ab ab.

24. (*a*) : The series is yxz yxz yxz yxz yxz yxz.

25. (*b*) : The series is xxx yyy xxx yyy xxx.

26. (*a*) : The series is aaaaa bbbbb aaaaa bbbbb.

27. (*b*) : The series is abca abca abca.

28. (*c*) : The series is caab caab caab.

29. (*c*) : The series is ccbba ccbba ccbba ccbba.

30. (*b*) : The series is aaabaa aaabaa aaabaa.

31. (*d*) : The series is nlm, nlm, nlm, nlm.

32. (*c*) : The series is lmmnnl lmmnnl lmmnnl.

33. (*b*) : The series is abacca abacca abacca.

34. (*a*) : The series is bcda bcda bcda bcda.

35. (*c*) : The series is ccab ccab ccab ccab.

36. (*a*) : The series is mnoo mnoo mnoo mnoo.

37. (*d*) : The series is llmno llmno llmno.

38. (*d*) : The series is xxyzz xxyzz xxyzz.

39. (*a*) : The series is yxxxy yxxxy yxxxy.

40. (*b*) : The series is abb abb abb abb.

41. (*b*) : The series is aaa bbb ccc aaa bbb ccc.

42. (*a*) : The series is abac abac abac abac.

43. (*d*) : The series is lmnn lmnn lmnn lmnn.

44. (*b*) : The series is ll mm nn ll mm nn ll mm nn.

45. (*c*) : The series is ababba ababba.

46. (*b*) : The series is abcd abcd abcd.

47. (*d*) : The series is xyyx yxxy xyyx yxxy.

48. (*b*) : The series is abba abba abba.

49. (*d*) : The series is xxyy xxyy xxyy.

50. (*a*) : The series is abc bca cab abc.

● ● ●

In number analogy also, the relationship between the given numbers is detected and then applied to the second part to find the missing numbers. This relationship between the numbers can be based on any of the following patterns :

  (i) numbers can be odd/even/prime numbers;
 (ii) numbers can be multiples of one number;
(iii) numbers can be squares/cubes of different numbers;
(iv) some numbers can be added to/subtracted from/multiplied to/divided into the first number to get the second number;
 (v) the second number can be the sum/product/ difference of the digits of first number; and
(vi) combinations of any mathematical calculations given above can apply to the relationship between the two given numbers.

Solved Example

Directions : *Which number will come in the place of question mark?*

1. 25 : 81 : : 36 : ?
   (a) 121
   (b) 93
   (c) 65
   (d) 103
   (e) 114

Ans. (a) : All the numbers are squares of different numbers.

$$25 \quad : \quad 81 \quad :: \quad 36 \quad : \quad 121$$
$$\downarrow \qquad \downarrow \qquad \downarrow \qquad \downarrow$$
$$5^2 \qquad 9^2 \qquad 6^2 \qquad 11^2$$

2. 36 : 18 : : 72 : ?
   (a) 164   (b) 134
   (c) 94   (d) 14
   (e) 27

Ans. (d) : The second number is the product of digits of the first number.

$$36 \quad : \quad 18 \quad :: \quad 72 \quad : \quad 14$$
$$\underset{3 \times 6}{\underline{\qquad\qquad}} \qquad \underset{7 \times 2}{\underline{\qquad\qquad}}$$

EXERCISE

Directions : *In the following questions, select the number from the given options which follows the same relationship as shared between the first two numbers.*

1. 1 : 11 : : 2 : ?
   (a) 20   (b) 22
   (c) 24   (d) 44
   (e) 42

2. 18 : 27 : : 22 : ?
   (a) 42   (b) 39
   (c) 33   (d) 54
   (e) 46

3. 14 : 20 : : 16 : ?
   (a) 23   (b) 10
   (c) 48   (d) 32
   (e) 64

4. 8 : 27 : : 64 : ?
   (a) 277   (b) 125
   (c) 250   (d) 99
   (e) 120

5. $\dfrac{1}{7} : \dfrac{1}{14} : : \dfrac{1}{9} : ?$

   (a) $\dfrac{1}{88}$ (b) $\dfrac{1}{80}$

   (c) $\dfrac{1}{81}$ (d) $\dfrac{1}{18}$

   (e) None of these

6. 0.16 : 0.0016 : : 1.02 : ?
   (*a*) 10.20   (*b*) 0.102
   (*c*) 0.0102   (*d*) 1.020
   (*e*) None of these

7. 5 : 24 : : 8 : ?
   (*a*) 65   (*b*) 63
   (*c*) 62   (*d*) 64
   (*e*) 66

8. 23 : 53 : : 8 : ?
   (*a*) 66   (*b*) 57
   (*c*) 27   (*d*) 19
   (*e*) 21

9. 6 : 9 : : 7 : ?
   (*a*) 4   (*b*) 14
   (*c*) 10   (*d*) 28
   (*e*) 18

10. 7 : 28 : : 2 : ?
   (*a*) 8   (*b*) 16
   (*c*) 24   (*d*) 12
   (*e*) 28

11. 65 : 30 : : 44 : ?
   (*a*) 79   (*b*) 62
   (*c*) 28   (*d*) 16
   (*e*) 23

12. 99 : 76 : : 24 : ?
   (*a*) 1   (*b*) 13
   (*c*) 9   (*d*) 7
   (*e*) 8

13. 11 : 35 : : 17 : ?
   (*a*) 3   (*b*) 22
   (*c*) 58   (*d*) 10
   (*e*) 16

14. 663 : 884 : : 221 : ?
   (*a*) 332   (*b*) 554
   (*c*) 773   (*d*) 442
   (*e*) 552

15. 16 : 0.16 : : ?
   (*a*) 2 : 0.02
   (*b*) 7 : 0.007
   (*c*) 1.3 : 0.13
   (*d*) 0.01 : 0.001
   (*e*) None of these

16. $3 : \frac{1}{3}$: : ?
   (*a*) 6 : 12
   (*b*) 5 : 2/15
   (*c*) 8 : 1/8
   (*d*) 9 : 27
   (*e*) None of these

17. 43 : 34 : : 52 : ?
   (*a*) 49   (*b*) 25
   (*c*) 36   (*d*) 64
   (*e*) 26

18. 65 : 13 : : 180 : ?
   (*a*) 93   (*b*) 36
   (*c*) 133   (*d*) 102
   (*e*) 45

19. 882 : 447 : : 881 : ?
   (*a*) 444   (*b*) 445
   (*c*) 446   (*d*) 447
   (*e*) 448

20. 125 : 27 : : 343 : ?
   (*a*) 729   (*b*) 64
   (*c*) 216   (*d*) 512
   (*e*) 81

21. 30 : 42 : : 56 : ?
   (*a*) 92   (*b*) 21
   (*c*) 38   (*d*) 72
   (*e*) 40

22. 190 : 10 : : 102 : ?
   (*a*) 4   (*b*) 7
   (*c*) 3   (*d*) 5
   (*e*) 6

23. 95 : 38 : : 167 : ?
   (*a*) 110   (*b*) 120
   (*c*) 113   (*d*) 134
   (*e*) 130

24. 4 : 36 : : 6 : ?
   (*a*) 63   (*b*) 54
   (*c*) 35   (*d*) 30
   (*e*) 48

25. 6 : 12 : : 20 : ?
   (*a*) 50   (*b*) 30
   (*c*) 42   (*d*) 38
   (*e*) 36

26. 6 : 18 : : 4 : ?
  (*a*) 2   (*b*) 6
  (*c*) 8   (*d*) 16
  (*e*) 12

27. 10 : 20 : : 30 : ?
  (*a*) 45   (*b*) 60
  (*c*) 50   (*d*) 70
  (*e*) 40

28. 92 : 69 : : 46 : ?
  (*a*) 57   (*b*) 23

  (*c*) 31   (*d*) 19
  (*e*) 29

29. 63 : 9 : : 49 : ?
  (*a*) 12   (*b*) 3
  (*c*) 36   (*d*) 7
  (*e*) 16

30. 2 : 11 : : ?
  (*a*) 6 : 17   (*b*) 8 : 43
  (*c*) 5 : 41   (*d*) 7 : 35
  (*e*) None of these

ANSWERS WITH EXPLANATION

1. (*b*) : The first number is repeated to obtain the second number.

2. (*c*) : In the given set, the numbers are multiples of 9 and in the second set, multiples of 11.

  18 : 27 : : 22 : 33
  9×2 9×3 11×2 11×3

3. (*a*) : The relationship between the numbers is :

  14 : 20 : : 16 : 23
  7×2 $(7 \times 3) -1$ 8×2 $(8 \times 3) -1$

4. (*b*) : The numbers are cubes of different numbers.

  8 : 27 : : 64 : 125
  2^3 3^3 4^3 5^3

5. (*d*) : The first fraction is multiplied by half to obtain the second fraction.

  $\dfrac{1}{7}$: $\dfrac{1}{14}$: : $\dfrac{1}{9}$: $\dfrac{1}{18}$
  $\times \dfrac{1}{2}$ $\times \dfrac{1}{2}$

6. (*c*) : The decimals are divided by 100.

  0.16 : 0.0016 : : 1.02 : 0.0102
  $\div 100$ $\div 100$

7. (*b*) : The second number is square of first number minus 1.

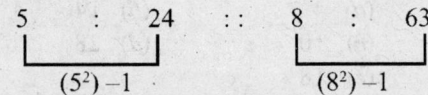

  5 : 24 : : 8 : 63
  $(5^2) -1$ $(8^2) -1$

8. (*d*) : All the numbers are prime numbers.

9. (*c*) : The second number is three more than the first number.

  6 : 9 : : 7 : 10
  $+3$ $+3$

10. (*a*) : The second number is four times the first.

  7 : 28 : : 2 : 8
  $\times 4$ $\times 4$

11. (*d*) : The second number is the product of digits of first number.

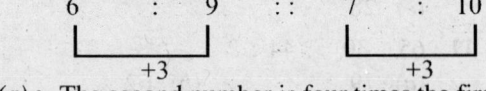

  $\dfrac{65:30}{(6 \times 5)}$: : $\dfrac{44:16}{(4 \times 4)}$

12. (*a*) : The second number is 23 less than the first number.

  99 : 76 : : 24 : 1
  -23 -23

13. (*a*) : All the numbers are odd numbers.

14. (*d*) : The digits at tens and hundreds place is same but the digit at the units place is half the other identical digits.

  66 3 : 88 4 : : 22 1 : 44 2

15. (*a*) : Of the two related numbers, the second number is the result of first number divided by 100.

16. *(c)* : Of the two related numbers, the second number is the part fraction of the first number, *i.e.* 3 is related to one-third $\left(\dfrac{1}{3}\right)$.

Similarly, 8 will be related to one-eighth $\left(\dfrac{1}{8}\right)$.

17. *(b)* : The digits are written in reverse order in the second number.

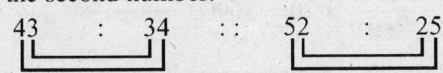

18. *(b)* : The first number is divided by 5 to get the second number.

$$65 \quad : \quad 13 \quad :: \quad 180 \quad : \quad 36$$
$$\div 5 \qquad\qquad \div 5$$

19. *(c)* : The relationship between two numbers is :

$$88\,2 \quad : \quad 44\,7 \quad :: \quad 88\,1 \quad : \quad 44\,6$$
$$\div 2 \qquad\qquad \div 2$$
$$+5 \qquad\qquad +5$$

20. *(a)* : The numbers are cubes of different odd numbers.

$$125 \quad : \quad 27 \quad :: \quad 343 \quad : \quad 729$$
$$\downarrow \qquad \downarrow \qquad \downarrow \qquad \downarrow$$
$$5^3 \qquad 3^3 \qquad 7^3 \qquad 9^3$$

21. *(d)* : The numbers are squares of different numbers plus the number itself.

$$30 \quad : \quad 42 \quad :: \quad 56 \quad : \quad 72$$
$$\downarrow \qquad \downarrow \qquad \downarrow \qquad \downarrow$$
$$5^2 + 5 \qquad 6^2 + 6 \qquad 7^2 + 7 \qquad 8^2 + 8$$

22. *(c)* : The second number is the sum of digits of first number.

$$\underset{(1 + 9 + 0)}{190 : 10} \quad :: \quad \underset{(1 + 0 + 2)}{102 : 3}$$

23. *(a)* : The second number is 57 less than the first number.

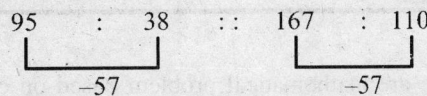

24. *(b)* : The second number is 9 times the first number.

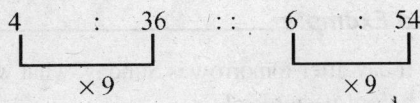

25. *(b)* : The numbers are squares of different numbers minus the number itself.

$$6 \quad : \quad 12 \quad :: \quad 20 \quad : \quad 30$$
$$\downarrow \qquad \downarrow \qquad \downarrow \qquad \downarrow$$
$$3^2 - 3 \qquad 4^2 - 4 \qquad 5^2 - 5 \qquad 6^2 - 6$$

26. *(c)* : Half the square of first number is the second number.

$$6 \quad : \quad 18 \quad :: \quad 4 \quad : \quad 8$$
$$6^2 \div 2 \qquad\qquad 4^2 \div 2$$

27. *(b)* : The second number is double the first number.

$$10 \quad : \quad 20 \quad :: \quad 30 \quad : \quad 60$$
$$\times 2 \qquad\qquad \times 2$$

28. *(b)* : The difference between the two numbers is 23.

$$92 \quad : \quad 69 \quad :: \quad 46 \quad : \quad 23$$
$$-23 \qquad\qquad -23$$

29. *(d)* : The first number is divided by 7 to get the second number.

$$63 \quad : \quad 9 \quad :: \quad 49 \quad : \quad 7$$
$$\div 7 \qquad\qquad \div 7$$

30. *(c)* : The sum of the digits of the second number is equal to the first number

$$2 \quad : \quad 11 \quad :: \quad 5 \quad : \quad 41$$
$$(1 + 1) \qquad\qquad (4 + 1)$$

CALENDAR, CLOCK, TIME, DISTANCE

These are mathematical problem based on calculations of time by a clock or calendar and computations of speed or distances.

Solved Example

1. If day-after-tomorrow is Sunday, what was day-before-yesterday?
   (a) Wednesday   (b) Thursday
   (c) Friday   (d) Saturday

   Ans. A :
   Day-after-tomorrow   —   Sunday
   Tomorrow   —   Saturday
   Today   —   Friday
   Yesterday   —   Thursday
   Day-before-yesterday   —   Wednesday

2. If the next day after 3rd Monday in a month is 16th, what will be the date on day before 5th Monday?
   (a) 27   (b) 28
   (c) 29   (d) 30

   Ans. (b) : Next day after 3rd Monday is 16th
   So Monday is 15th
   4th Monday is 22nd.... (15 + 7)
   5th Monday is 29th .... (15 + 14) or (22 + 7)
   So, date on day before 5th Monday is 28th

3. How many times in 12 hours the hands of a clock will be at right angles?
   (a) 12   (b) 16
   (c) 18   (d) 24

   Ans. D : In every hour the hands are at right angles twice.

4. If a train runs at a speed of 92.7 km/hr, then the distance covered in metres in 20 minutes will be :
   (a) 3009   (b) 308.9
   (c) 309   (d) 30900

   Ans. D : Speed of the train is 92.7 km/hr *i.e.* 92700 metres in 60 minutes
   In 20 minutes the distance covered will be :
   $$\frac{92700}{60} \times 20 = 30900 \text{ metres}$$

5. Prabhat remembers that his mother's birthday is after seventeenth April but before twenty-first April, whereas his sister Urmila remembers that their mother's birthday is after nineteenth but before twenty-fourth April. Which of the following days in April is definitely their mother's birthday?
   (a) Nineteenth   (b) Twenty-first
   (c) Twenty-second   (d) Twentieth

   Ans. D : Mother's birthday in the month of April :

   According to Prabhat: is from
   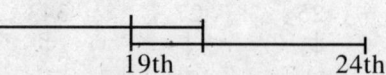

   According to Urmila: is from
   It is clear that the mother's birthday is between 19th and 21st April and so the definite date is 20th April.

EXERCISE

1. If the day before yesterday was Thursday, when will Sunday be?
   (a) Tomorrow   (b) Day after tomorrow
   (c) Today
   (d) Two days after today

2. If the seventh day of a month is three (3) days earlier than Friday, what day will it be on the nineteenth day of the month?
   (a) Sunday   (b) Monday
   (c) Wednesday   (d) Friday

50

(951) Intelligence—7-II

3. Radha remembers that her father's birthday is after 16th but before 21st of March, while her brother Mangesh remembers that his father's birthday is before 22nd but after 19th of March. On which date is the birthday of their father?

(a) 19th

(b) 20th

(c) 21st

(d) Cannot be determined

4. A man is three (3) years older than his wife and four (4) times as old as his son. If the son attains an age of fifteen (15) years after three (3) years, what is the present age of the mother?

(a) 60 years　　　(b) 51 years

(c) 48 years　　　(d) 45 years

5. A clock is so placed that at 12 noon its minute hand points towards north-east. In which direction does its hour hand point at 1.30 P.M.?

(a) East　　　(b) West

(c) North　　　(d) South

6. If in the above question clock is turned through an angle of 135° in an anticlockwise direction, in which direction will its minute hand point at 8.45 P.M.?

(a) East　　　(b) West

(c) North　　　(d) South

7. A couple married in 1980 had two children, one in 1982 and the other in 1984. Their combined ages will equal the years of the marriage in?

(a) 1986　　　(b) 1985

(c) 1987　　　(d) 1988

8. Manoj left home for the bus stop 15 minutes earlier than the usual time. It takes 10 minutes to reach the stop. He reached the stop at 8.40 a.m. What time does he usually leave home for the bus stop?

(a) 8.30 a.m.　　　(b) 8.55 a.m.

(c) 8.45 p.m.　　　(d) None of these

9. Mamuni went to the movies nine days ago. She goes to the movies only on Thursday. What day of the week is today?

(a) Sunday　　　(b) Tuesday

(c) Thursday　　　(d) Saturday

10. If Thursday was the day after the day before yesterday five days ago, what is the least number of days ago when Sunday was three days before the day after tomorrow?

(a) Two days ago　　　(b) Three days ago

(c) Four days ago　　　(d) Five days ago

11. 1.12.91 is the first Sunday. Which is the fourth Tuesday of December 91?

(a) 31.12.91　　　(b) 24.12.91

(c) 17.12.91　　　(d) 26.12.91

12. If the third day of a month is Monday, which of the following will be the fifth day from 21st of that month?

(a) Tuesday　　　(b) Monday

(c) Wednesday　　　(d) Thursday

13. If 15 horses eat 15 bags of gram in 15 days, in how many days will one horse eat one bag of grain?

(a) 15 days　　　(b) 1/15 days

(c) 1 day　　　(d) 30 days

14. A century leap year is divisible by :

(a) 4　　　(b) 16

(c) 40　　　(d) 400

15. If the fifth day of a month is Friday, which of the following will be the Seventh day from 10th of that month?

(a) Tuesday　　　(b) Monday

(c) Wednesday　　　(d) Thursday

ANSWERS

1	2	3	4	5	6	7	8	9	10
(a)	(a)	(b)	(d)	(a)	(d)	(a)	(c)	(d)	(a)

11	12	13	14	15
(b)	(c)	(a)	(d)	(c)

52

ANSWERS WITH EXPLANATION

1. Thursday —Day-before-yesterday
Friday —Yesterday
Saturday —Today
Sunday — Tomorrow

2. 7th day is 3 days earlier than Friday so, 10th day is Friday, so also is 17th.
   ∴ 19th day will be 2nd day ahead of Friday, *i.e.,* Sunday.

3. Father's birthday

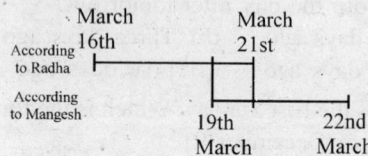

∴ Their father's birthday is on 20th March.

4. Present age of son is 15-3 = 12 years. Age of the man is 4 times the age of son,
   i.e., 12 × 4 = 48 years
   Man is 3 years elder to his wife/son's mother. So Age of the mother is 48 − 3 = 45 years

5.

At 12 noon

At 1.30 p.m. the hour hand will point towards East.

6.

After rotating the clock in earlier question, its minute hand will point towards South at 8:45 p.m.

7. 1982 —   2 years later — 1st child
   1984 —   4 years later — 2nd child
   Total age of children — 2 years.

1985 — 5 years later — Total age of children : 4 years.
1986 — 6 years later — Total age of children : 6 years.

8. Manoj reached the bus stop at 8.40 a.m. He left his home at 8:40 − 10 minutes = 8:30 a.m. He left 15 minutes earlier than usual, so his actual time of leaving home is 8:30 am + 15 minutes = 8:45 a.m.

9. Mamuni goes to the movies on Thursday, so nine days ago was Thursday.
   ∴ Two days ago was also Thursday. So, today is Saturday.

10. Day after the day-before-yesterday five days ago is the 6th day which is Thursday. And so, the 3rd day will be Sunday. Three days before the day-after-tomorrow is Yesterday which is the 1st day of the five days. So, two days ago was Sunday.

11. First Sunday is on 1st December
    First Tuesday is on 3rd December
    3 weeks later, Fourth Tuesday will be on 3 + (7 × 3) = 24th December.

12. 3rd day of the month is Monday
    5th day from 21st is 26th
    26 − 3 = 23 days
    23 days later, 23/7 leaves 2 days.
    So, two days ahead of Monday will be Wednesday.

13. 15 horses eat 15 bags of grain in 15 days
    15 horses eat 1 bag of grain in 1 day
    1 horse eats 1 bag of grain in 15 days

14. A leap year is divisible by 4 and a century leap year is divisible by 400.

15. Seventh day from 10th is 17th.
    5th day is Friday. Next Friday is on 12th 17 − 12 = 5, 5 days ahead of Friday will be Wednesday. So, 17th is Wednesday.

MIRROR IMAGES

These type of problems are based on the mirror images or reflections of number, letters and figures. While attempting such questions one must be able to visualise clearly the questioned reflections, be they on vertical plane or on horizontal plane. Study the chart and information given below. The visualisation of letters and numbers is easier than the visualisation of figures for the simple reason that the figures have many forms and all cannot be summed up.

Horizontal Mirror Images (HMI) of Numbers

Number	HMI	Number	HMI
0	0	5	5
1	1	6	6
2	2	7	7
3	3	8	8
4	4	9	9

Note : HMI of 0 and 8 remain unchanged

Vertical Mirror Images (VMI) of Numbers

Numbers : 0 1 2 3 4 5 6 7 8 9

VMI : 0 1 2 3 4 5 6 7 8 9

Note : VMI of 0, 3 and 8 remain unchanged. Exceptions in style need caution. Example 3 will be 3, or 8 will be 8.

Horizontal Mirror Images of Capital Letters

Letter	HMI	Letter	HMI	H letter	HMI
A	A	J	J	S	S
B	B	K	K	T	T
C	C	L	L	U	U
D	D	M	M	V	V
E	E	N	N	W	W
F	F	O	O	X	X
G	G	P	P	Y	Y
H	H	Q	Q	Z	Z
I	I	R	R		

Note : HMI of A, H, I, M, O, T, U, V, W, X and Y remain unchanged.

Exceptions in style need caution. Example : A will be A, or X will be X.

Vertical Mirror Images of Capital Letters

Letters : A B C D E F G H I J K L M
VMI : A B C D E F G H I J K L M
Letters : N O P Q R S T U V W X Y Z
VMI : N O P Q R S T U V W X Y Z

Note : VMI of C, D, E, H, I, K, O and X remain unchanged.

Horizontal Mirror Images of Small Letters

Letter	HMI	Letter	HMI	Letter	HMI
a	a	j	j	s	s
b	d	k	k	t	t
c	c	l	l	u	u
d	b	m	m	v	v
e	e	n	n	w	w
f	f	o	o	x	x
g	g	p	p	y	y
h	h	q	q	z	z
i	i	r	r		

Note : HMI of o, v, w and x remain unchanged.

Vertical Mirror Images of Small Letters

Letter : a b c d e f g h i j k l m
VMI : a b c d e f g h i j k l m
Letter : n o p q r s t u v w x y z
VMI : n o p q r s t u v w x y z

Note : VMI of c, o and x remain unchanged. Letter l has exceptions: if it is a straight vertical line – 1 then it remains unchanged.

53

Horizontal Mirror Images of Some Geometrical Shapes

	GS	HMI		GS	HMI
1.	○	○	2.	◠	◠
3.	D	C	4.	C	D
5.	◿	◺	6.	▽	▽
7.	◿	◺	8.	◹	◸
9.	▷	◁	10.	△	△
11.	◸	◹	12.	◹	◸
13.	△	△	14.	◁	▷
15.	□	□	16.	◇	◇
17.	▱	▱	18.	▱	▱
19.	⬠	⬠	20.	⬡	⬡
21.	⬡	⬡	22.	⬡	⬡
23.	⬡	⬡	24.	▱	▱
25.	▱	▱	26.	◺	◺

Vertical Mirror Images of Some Geometrical Shapes

Gs :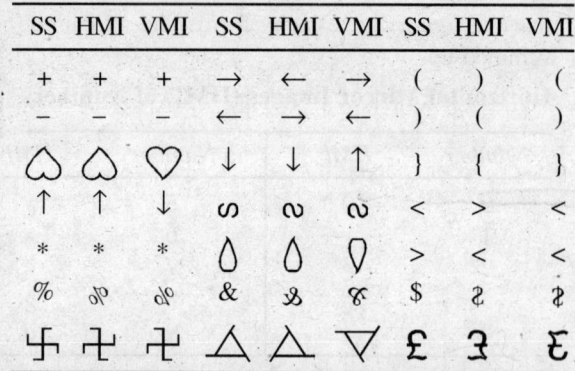

Gs :

Horizontal and Vertical Mirror Images of some Signs and Symbols (SS)

SS	HMI	VMI	SS	HMI	VMI	SS	HMI	VMI
+	+	+	→	←	→	(	)	(
–	–	–	←	→	←	)	(	)
♡	♡	♡	↓	↓	↑	}	{	}
↑	↑	↓	⌒	⌒	⌒	<	>	<
*	*	*	♦	♦	♦	>	<	<
%	%	%	&	&	&	$	$	$
⊹	⊹	⊹	△	△	▽	£	£	£

Note that the problems may be on numbers or letters or figures or signs or they may be a combination of all the above.

EXERCISE

Directions (Qs. 1 to 20) : *In each question given below which one would be the mirror image of the given figure when the mirror is placed along the line shown in each figure.*

1. Problem Figure

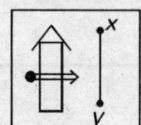

Answer Figures

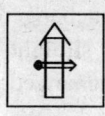 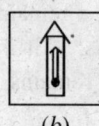  

(a) (b) (c) (d)

2. Problem Figure

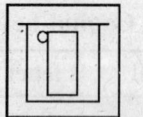

Answer Figures

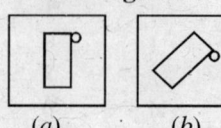 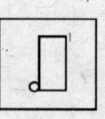 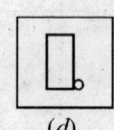

(a) (b) (c) (d)

3. Problem Figure

Answer Figures

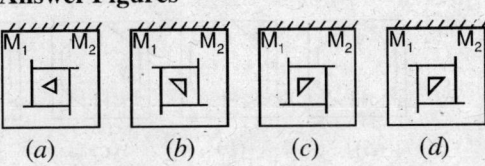

(a) (b) (c) (d)

4. Problem Figure

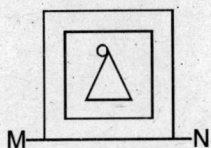

Answer Figures

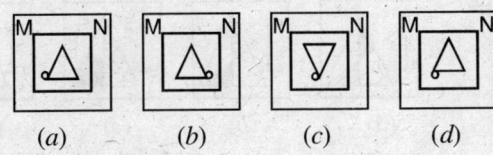

(a) (b) (c) (d)

5. Problem Figure

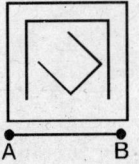

Answer Figures

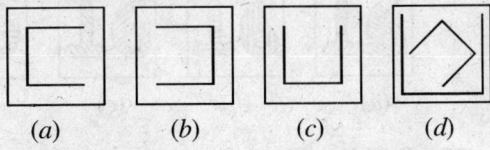

(a) (b) (c) (d)

6. Problem Figure

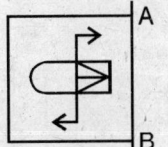

Answer Figures

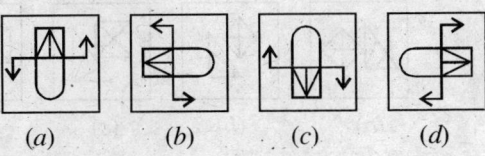

(a) (b) (c) (d)

7. Problem Figure

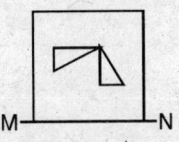

Answer Figures

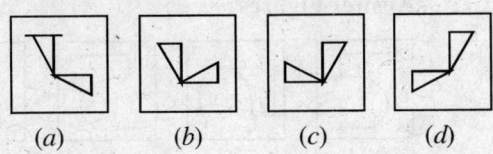

(a) (b) (c) (d)

8. Problem Figure

Answer Figures

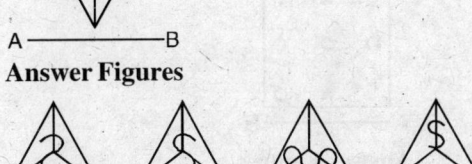

(a) (b) (c) (d)

9. Problem Figure

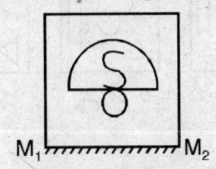

Answer Figures

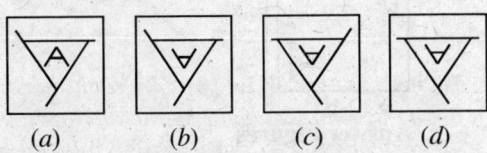

(a) (b) (c) (d)

10. Problem Figure

Answer Figures

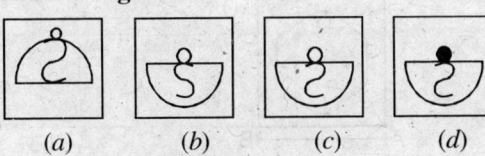

(a) (b) (c) (d)

11. Problem Figure

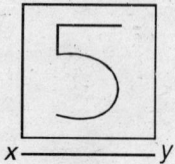

x ——————— y

Answer Figures

   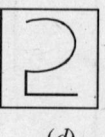

(*a*)　　　　(*b*)　　　　(*c*)　　　　(*d*)

12. Problem Figure

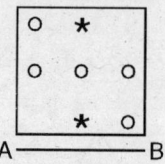

A ——————— B

Answer Figures

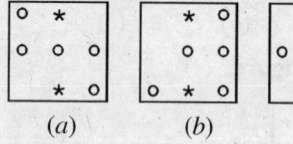 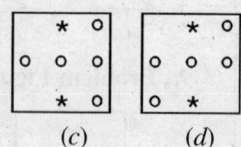

(*a*)　　　　(*b*)　　　　(*c*)　　　　(*d*)

13. Problem Figure

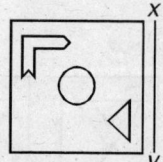

Answer Figures

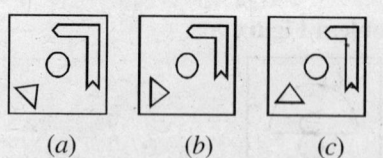

(*a*)　　　　(*b*)　　　　(*c*)　　　　(*d*)

14. Problem Figure

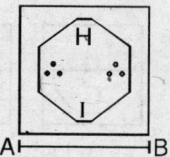

Answer Figures

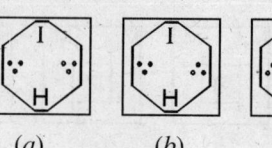

(*a*)　　　　(*b*)　　　　(*c*)　　　　(*d*)

15. Problem Figure

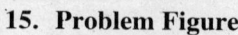
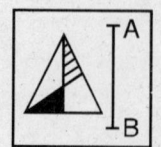

Answer Figures

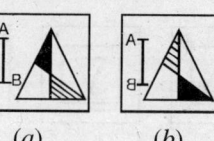 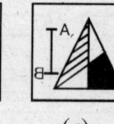 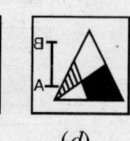

(*a*)　　　　(*b*)　　　　(*c*)　　　　(*d*)

16. Problem Figure

Answer Figures

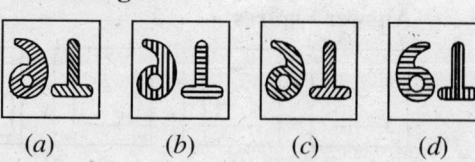

(*a*)　　　　(*b*)　　　　(*c*)　　　　(*d*)

17. Problem Figure

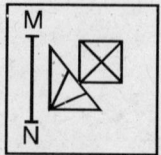

Answer Figures

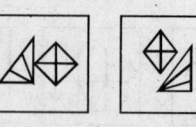  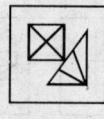 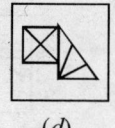

(*a*)　　　　(*b*)　　　　(*c*)　　　　(*d*)

18. Problem Figure

Answer Figures

(*a*)   (*b*)   (*c*)   (*d*)

19. Problem Figure

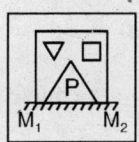

Answer Figures

  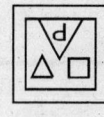 

(*a*)   (*b*)   (*c*)   (*d*)

20. Problem Figure

Answer Figures

(*a*)   (*b*)   (*c*)   (*d*)

ANSWERS

1	2	3	4	5	6	7	8	9	10
(*d*)	(*c*)	(*b*)	(*c*)	(*d*)	(*b*)	(*c*)	(*a*)	(*b*)	(*c*)

11	12	13	14	15	16	17	18	19	20
(*d*)	(*a*)	(*b*)	(*a*)	(*b*)	(*c*)	(*c*)	(*d*)	(*a*)	(*b*)

● ● ●

NUMBER OF SHAPES

In these problems one has to count the geometrical figures in a given complex figure. A little bit of systematic approach is needed to get the correct number of the asked figure. The shapes of all geometrical figures must be clear in mind.

Solved Example

1. How many straight lines are used to make the figure given below?

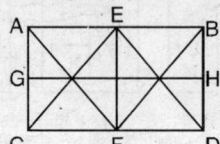

(a) 8   (b) 6
(c) 10   (d) 12
(e) 14

Answer (c) : The method of counting is given below.

The horizontal lines are AB, GH and CD i.e. – 3 lines, the vertical lines are AC, EF and BD i.e. – 3 lines, the diagonal lines are CE, FB, AF and ED i.e. – 4 lines, therefore the total number of straight lines is 3 + 3 + 4 = 10

2. How many square are there is this figure?

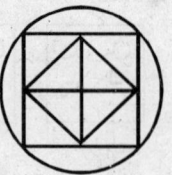

(a) 4   (b) 6
(c) 8   (d) 5
(e) 7

Answer (b) : The squares are counted in this manner.

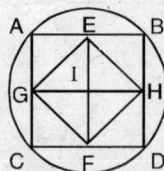

There is one main square ABCD divided into four parts by lines EF and GH. So, all the 5 squares are ABCD, AEGI, GICF, EBIH and IHFD. The square in the middle is EGHF. The total number of squares are 5 + 1 = 6

EXERCISE

1. How many triangles are there in the figure given below?

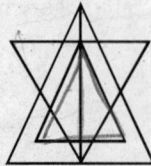

(a) 24   (b) 27
(c) 25   (d) 26
(e) 22

2. How many parallelograms are there in this figure?

(a) 9   (b) 13
(c) 15   (d) 18
(e) 20

3. How many triangles are there in this figure?

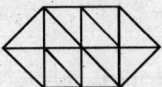

(a) 16   (b) 17
(c) 18   (d) 19
(e) 15

4. The number of rectangles in this figure are.

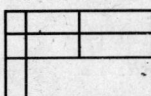

(a) 21   (b) 24
(c) 23   (d) 25
(e) 20

5. How many squares are hidden in this figure?

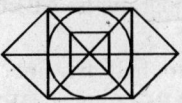

(a) 7   (b) 8
(c) 9   (d) 10
(e) 6

6. The number of triangles in this figure are.

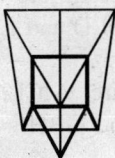

(a) 19   (b) 16
(c) 21   (d) 15
(e) 12

7. How many squares are there in the figure given below?

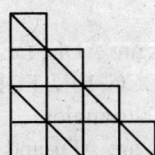

(a) 10   (b) 11
(c) 13   (d) 14
(e) 12

8. The number of circles in this figure is

(a) 6   (b) 5
(c) 2   (d) 3
(e) 4

9. How many triangles are there in the figure given below?

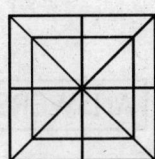

(a) 28   (b) 36
(c) 24   (d) 32
(e) 20

10. How many straight lines are needed to draw the figure in question 9?
(a) 10   (b) 12
(c) 11   (d) 13
(e) 8

11. How many squares are there in this figure?

(a) 15   (b) 11
(c) 8   (d) 3
(e) 10

12. The number of squares in the figure below is

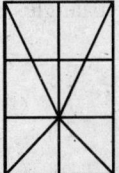

(a) 6   (b) 10
(c) 8   (d) 12
(e) 14

13. How many hexagons are there in the figure given below?

(a) 1   (b) 2
(c) 4   (d) 5
(e) 3

14. The number of parallelograms in this figure is

(a) 11   (b) 12
(c) 9   (d) 10
(e) 14

15. The number of squares in the figure given below is

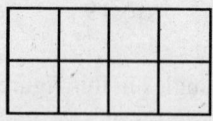

(a) 8   (b) 10
(c) 11   (d) 12
(e) 13

ANSWERS WITH EXPLANATION

1. (a) :

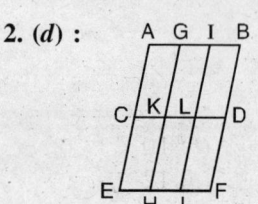

- The main triangles making the figure are ABC, DEF and GHI i.e., – 3 triangles
- The simplest triangles are AJG, AGK, KEM, DJL, NHP, PQF, QFR and ORI i.e., – 8 triangles
- The triangles formed by the bisecting line AF are ABF, AFC, GHQ, GQI, DGF and GFE i.e., – 6 triangles
- The triangles formed inbetween the three triangles
  AJK, ALF, AMF, DGN, DGF, LBF, MFC, GEO, GNF and GOF – i.e., 10 triangles
- So, the total number of triangles is
  3 + 8 + 6 + 10 = 27

2. (d) :

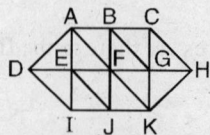

- The main parallelogram is ABEF i.e., 1 parallelogram
- When divided into half by line CD the main figure has ABCD and CDEF i.e., 2 parallelograms
- When further lines GH and IJ are drawn, the parallelograms are AGEH, GIJH and IBJF i.e., – 3 parallelograms.
- The simplest parallelogram are AGCK, CKEH, GIKL, KLHJ, IBLD and LDJF i.e. – 6 parallelograms

  Other parallelograms are AICL, CLEJ, GBKD, KDHF, AIEJ and GBHF – i.e., 6 parallelograms

  So, the total number of parallelograms is
  1 + 2 + 3 + 6 + 6 = 18

3. (a) :

The simplest triangles are ADE, DEI, AEF, ABF, EIJ, EFJ, BFG, BCG, FJK, FGK, CGH and GHK – i.e., – 12 triangles

The bisected triangles are ADI and CHK – i.e. – 2 triangles

Other triangles are AIK and ACK i.e., – 2 triangles

So, the total number of triangles is
12 + 2 + 2 = 16

4. (c) :

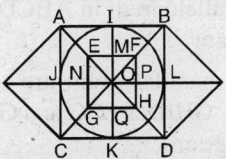

The main rectangle is ABCD – *i.e.,* – 1 rectangle

The simplest rectangles are AIEJ, ILJM, LBMF, EJGK, JMKN, MFNH, GKCO and KHOD *i.e.* – 8 rectangles.

The rectangles which have two parts are ALEM, IBJF, EMGN, JFKH, AIGK, IKLN, LBNH, EJCO and GHCD *i.e.* – 9 rectangles.

The rectangles which have three parts are AICO, ABEF and EFGH *i.e.* – 3 rectangles

The rectangles which have four parts are ALGN and IBKH *i.e.* – 2 rectangles

So, the total number of rectangles
1 + 8 + 9 + 3 + 2 = 23

5. (d) :

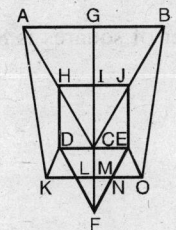

The main squares are ABCD and EFGH *i.e.,* – 2 squares

The simplest outer squares are AIJO, IBOL, JOCK and OLKD *i.e.,* – 4 squares

The simplest inner square are EMNO, NOGQ, MFOP and OPQH *i.e.,* – 4 squares

There are no other squares formed in the figure

So, the total number of squares is
2 + 4 + 4 = 10

6. (b) :

The main triangles are : ABC, DEF, LNF, and HJC *i.e.* 4 triangles

The simplest triangles are : HIC, IJC, HDC, JCE, DKL, LMF, MFN and NOE *i.e.* – 8 triangles

Other triangles are : AGC, GBC, DCF and CEF – *i.e.* 4 triangles

So, the total number of triangles is 4 + 8 + 4 = 16

7. (c) :

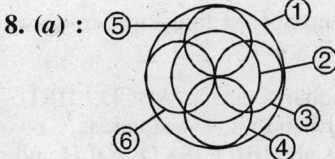

The simplest squares are : ABCD, CDFG, DEGH, FGJK, GHKL, HILM, JKOP, KLPQ, LMQR and MNRS *i.e.* – 10 squares.

Other squares are : CEJL, FHOQ and GIPR *i.e.* – 3 squares

So, the total number of squares is 10 + 3 = 13

8. (a) :

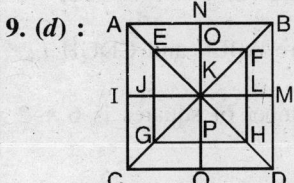

There are two main circles and four smaller circles intersecting each other.

So, the total number of circles is 2 + 4 = 6

9. (d) :

The larger triangles are : ABC, BCD, ABD and ACD *i.e.* – 4 triangles

The smaller triangles are : EFH, EGH, EFG and FGH *i.e.* – 4 triangles.

The simplest triangles are : EJK, EOK, OFK, JKG, FKL, KLH, KGP and KPH *i.e.* – 8 triangles

The bisected triangles are: AKC, ABK, CKD, KBD, EKG, EKF, KHG, KHF, i.e., –8 triangle.

Other triangles are : ANK, NKB, KBM, KMD, KQD, KQC, KCI, IKA *i.e.* – 8 triangles.

So, the total number of triangles is 4 + 4 + 8 + 8 + 8 = 32

10. (b) :

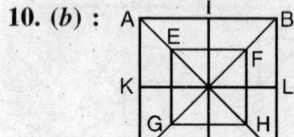

The horizontal lines are : AB, EF, KL, GH and CD *i.e.* – 5 lines.

The vertical lines are AC, EG, IJ, FH and BD *i.e.* – 5 lines.

The diagonal lines are : AD and BC *i.e.* – 2 lines.

So, the total number of lines used to draw this figure is 5 + 5 + 2 = 12

11. (c) : The main squares are : ABCD, IJKL, MNPQ and EFHG *i.e.* – 4 squares.
Other squares are. EIJO, IFKO, JOLH and OKGL *i.e.* – 4 squares
So, the total number of squares is 4 + 4 = 8

12. (c) : The simplest squares are : AICK, CKEM, EMGN, IBKD, KDMF ad MFNH *i.e.* – 6 squares
Other squares are ABEF and CDGH *i.e.* – 2 squares.
So, the total number of squares is 6 + 2 = 8

13. (c) :

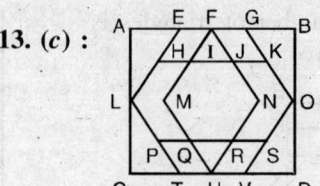

The larger hexagon is : EG – GO – GV – VT – TL – LE *i.e.* – 1 hexagon.

The smaller hexagons are : IJ – JN – NR – RQ – QM – MT, HJ – JN – NR – RP – PL – LH and IK – KO – OS – SQ – QM – MI, *i.e.*, –3, hexagons. So, the total number of hexagons is 1 + 3 = 4

(Hexagon is a figure having six side of equal length.)

14. (a) :

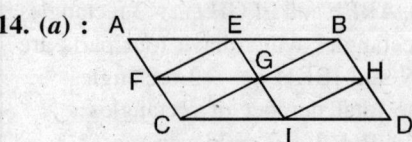

The main parallelogram in ABCD – *i.e.* – 1 parallelogram

The simplest parallelogram are : AEFG, FGCI, EBGH, GHID, FECG and GBIH *i.e.* – 6 parallelograms

Other parallelograms are : ABFH, FHCD, AECI and EBID *i.e.* – 4 parallelograms

So, the total number of parallelograms is 1 + 6 + 4 = 11

15. (c) : The simplest squares are ABFG, FGKL, BCGH, GHLM, CDHI, HIMN, DEIJ and IJNO *i.e.* – 8 squares.

Other squares are ACKM, BDLN and CEMO i.e., 3 squares

So, the total number of squares is 8 + 3 = 11 squares

• • •

NON-VERBAL TEST

These tests are based on figures or matrices. It com-prises of many types of tests based on figures. Only a few types of tests are asked in the Sainik School Entrance Examination. The Verbal tests are based on language. One who has got a command over the language may have more advantages over the one who has less knowledge of language. In non-verbal tests difficulty of language does not arise at all.

The questions of Non-Verbal Tests are asked in the form of figures, designs and drawings. The questions are generally of the following three types : (i) Classification Test, (ii) Series Test, (iii) Analogies Test.

1

FIGURE CLASSIFICATION

This test is presented in only problem figures denoted by A, B, C, D and E. Four of these figures are alike in some way but the fifth one in an outcaste, because it does not fit in the space assigned to it.

Solved Example

1. Problem figures

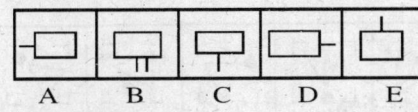

Ans. (B)

Explanation : Clearly figure 'B' differs from the other figures because there are two small straight lines coming out form the rectangle in the each figure except 'B'.

2. Problem figures

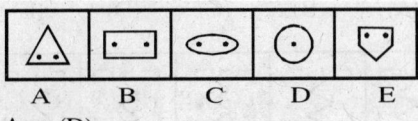

Ans. (D)

Explanation : Every figure contains two dots except figure 'D'. Hence the answer is 'D'.

3. Problem figures

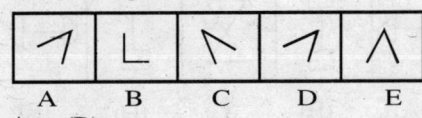

Ans. (B)

Explanation : All the angles are acute angled except that of drawn in the figure 'B'. Hence, 'B' will be the answer.

4. Problem figures

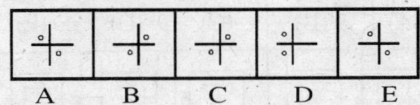

Ans. (D)

Explanation : In figures A, B, C and E small circles are drawn on the opposite quadrants but in the figure 'D' circle do not lie in opposite quadrants. The circles lie in adjacent quadrants. Hence, answer will be 'D'.

5. Problem figures

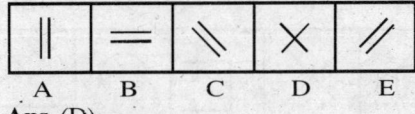

Ans. (D)

Explanation : In figures A, B, C and E lines do not cut each other but in figure D the lines cut each other. Hence, the answer is 'D'.

EXERCISE

PROBLEM FIGURES

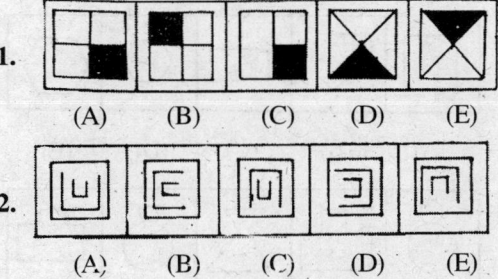

64

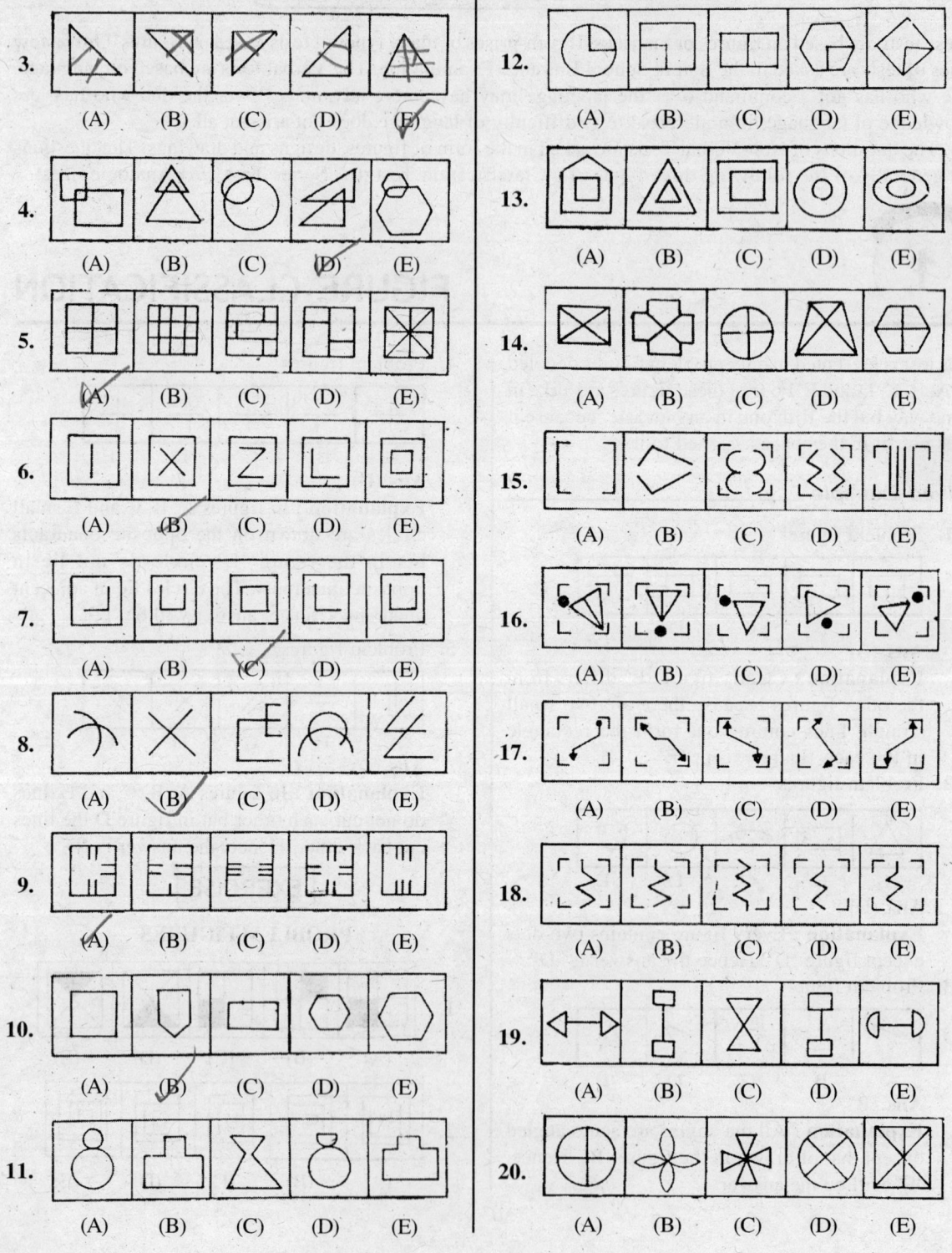

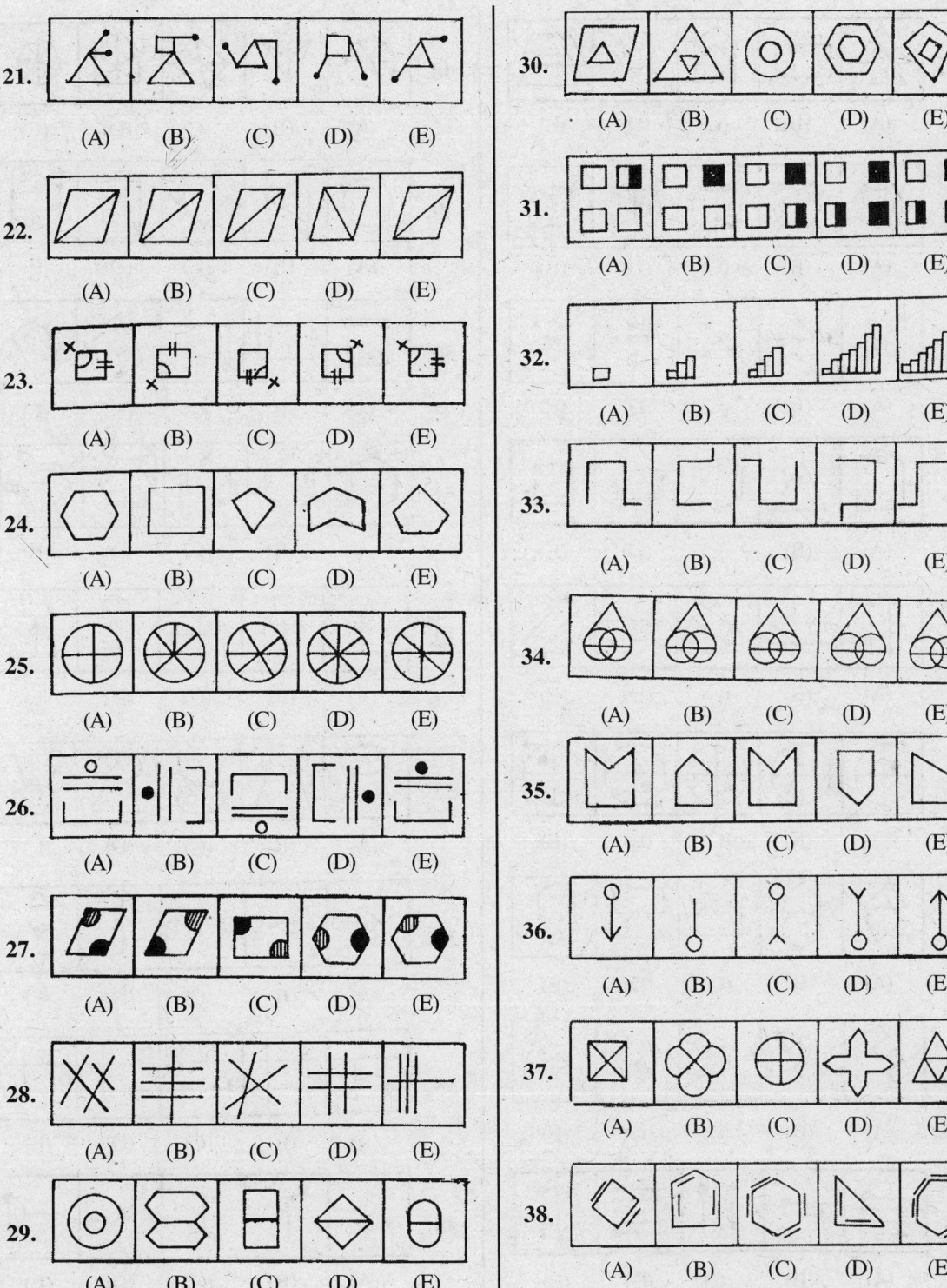

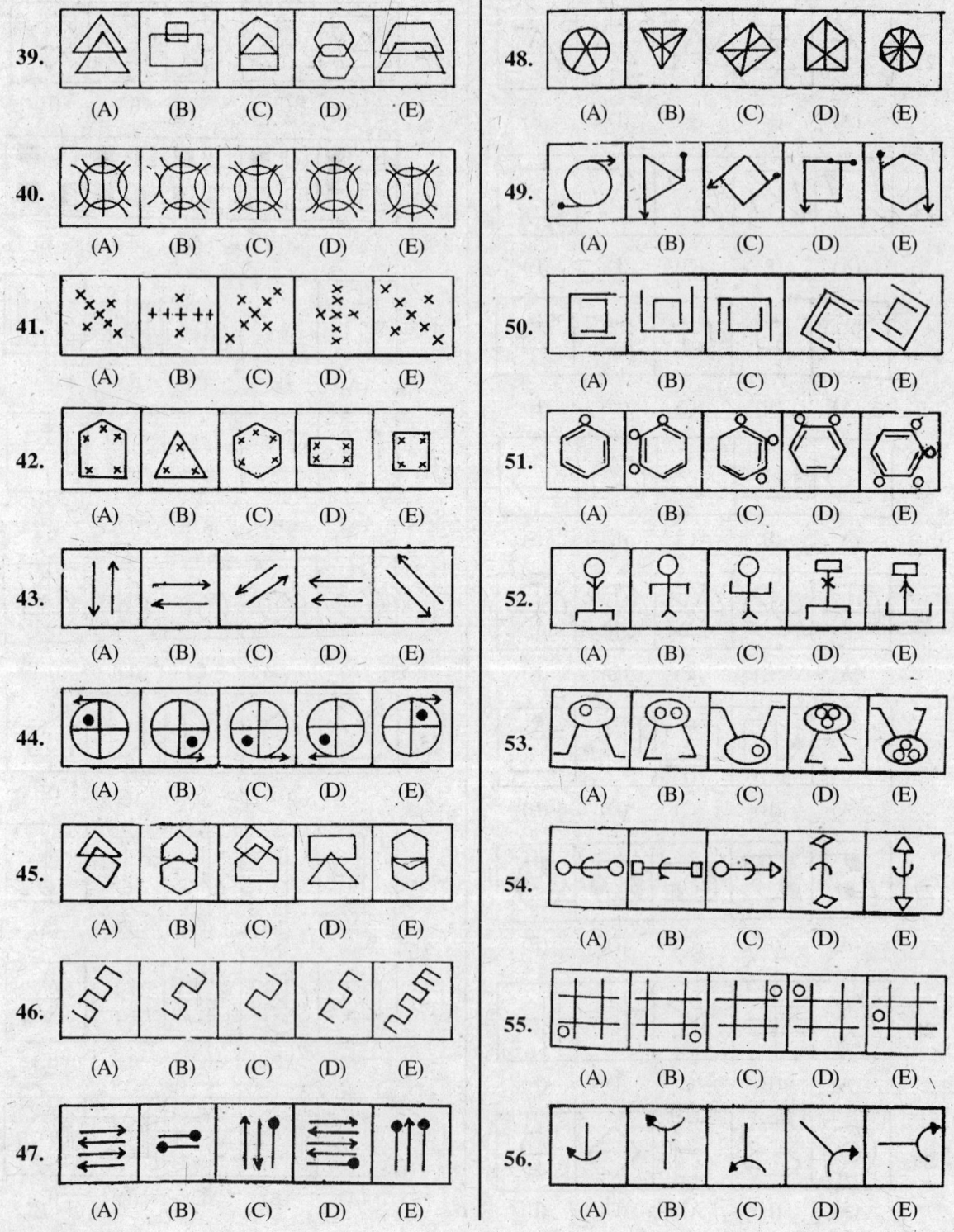

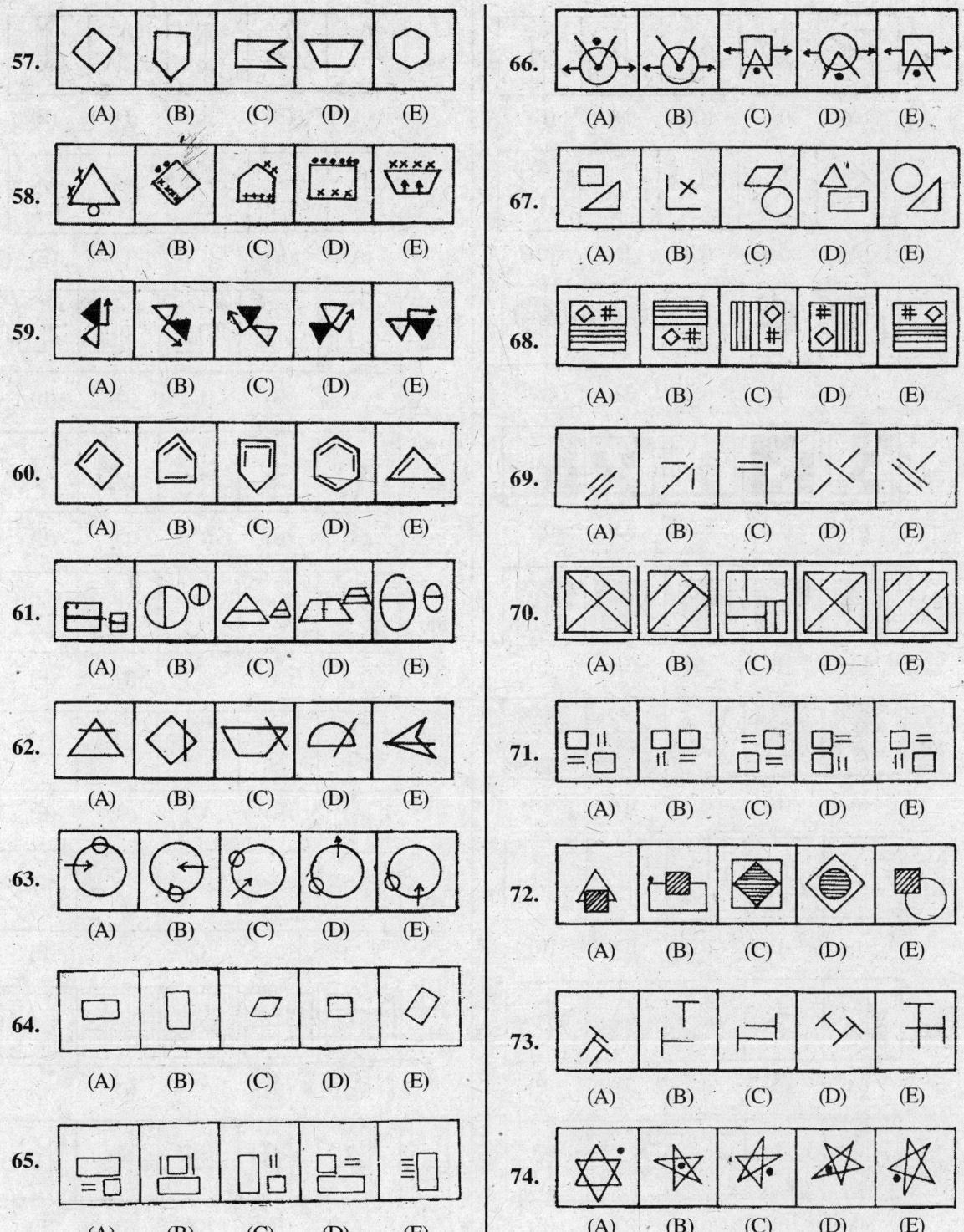

68

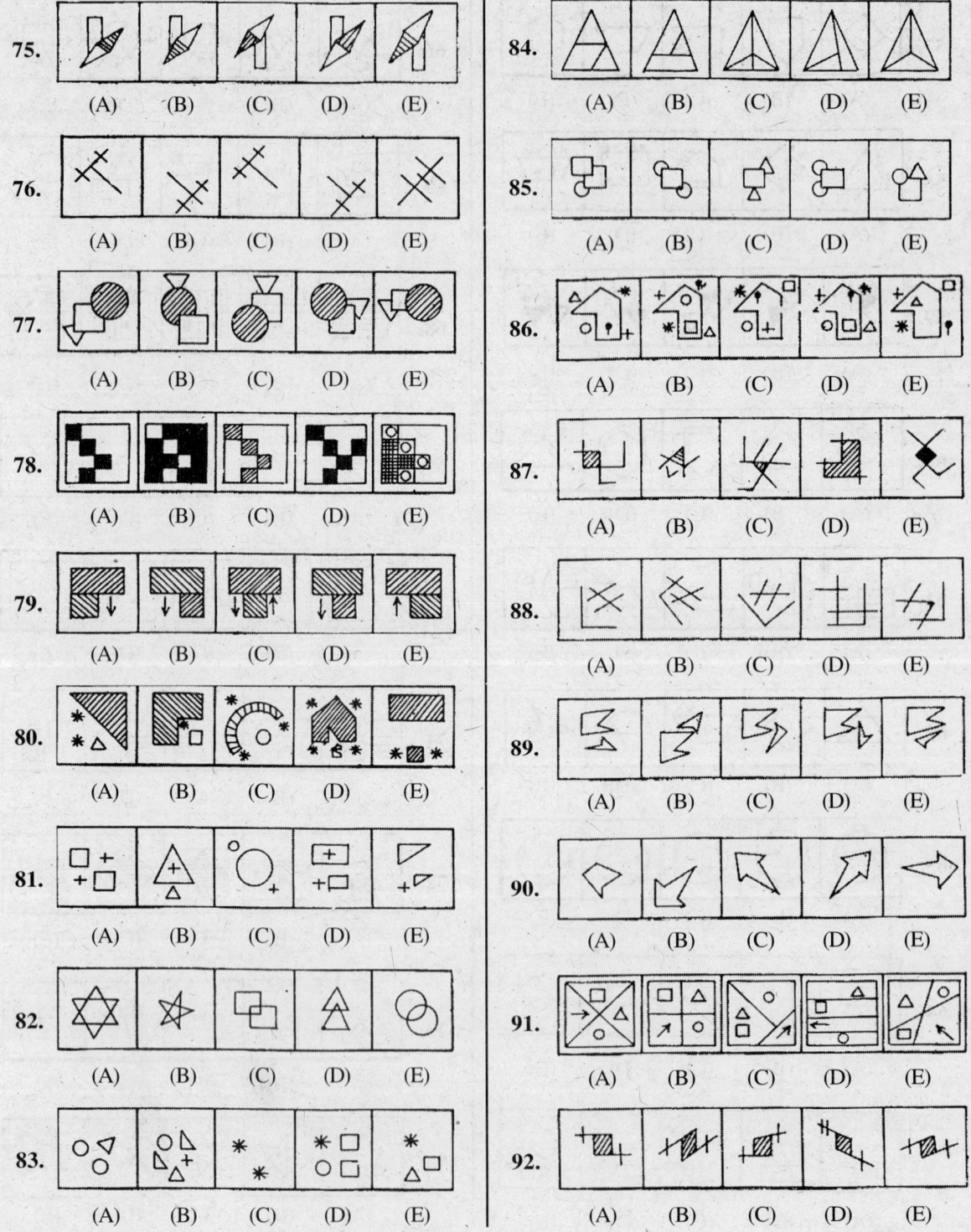

69

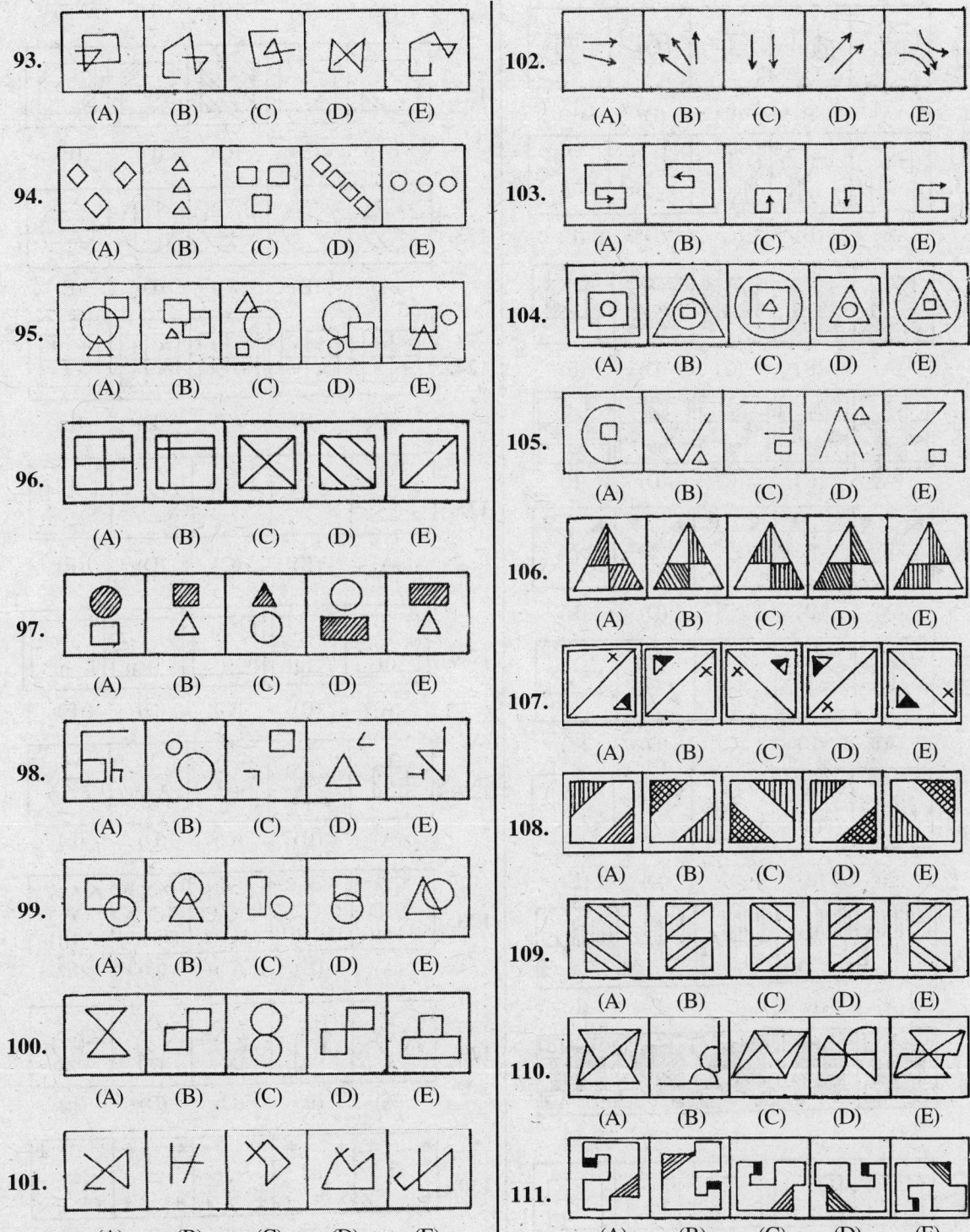

93. (A) (B) (C) (D) (E)

94. (A) (B) (C) (D) (E)

95. (A) (B) (C) (D) (E)

96. (A) (B) (C) (D) (E)

97. (A) (B) (C) (D) (E)

98. (A) (B) (C) (D) (E)

99. (A) (B) (C) (D) (E)

100. (A) (B) (C) (D) (E)

101. (A) (B) (C) (D) (E)

102. (A) (B) (C) (D) (E)

103. (A) (B) (C) (D) (E)

104. (A) (B) (C) (D) (E)

105. (A) (B) (C) (D) (E)

106. (A) (B) (C) (D) (E)

107. (A) (B) (C) (D) (E)

108. (A) (B) (C) (D) (E)

109. (A) (B) (C) (D) (E)

110. (A) (B) (C) (D) (E)

111. (A) (B) (C) (D) (E)

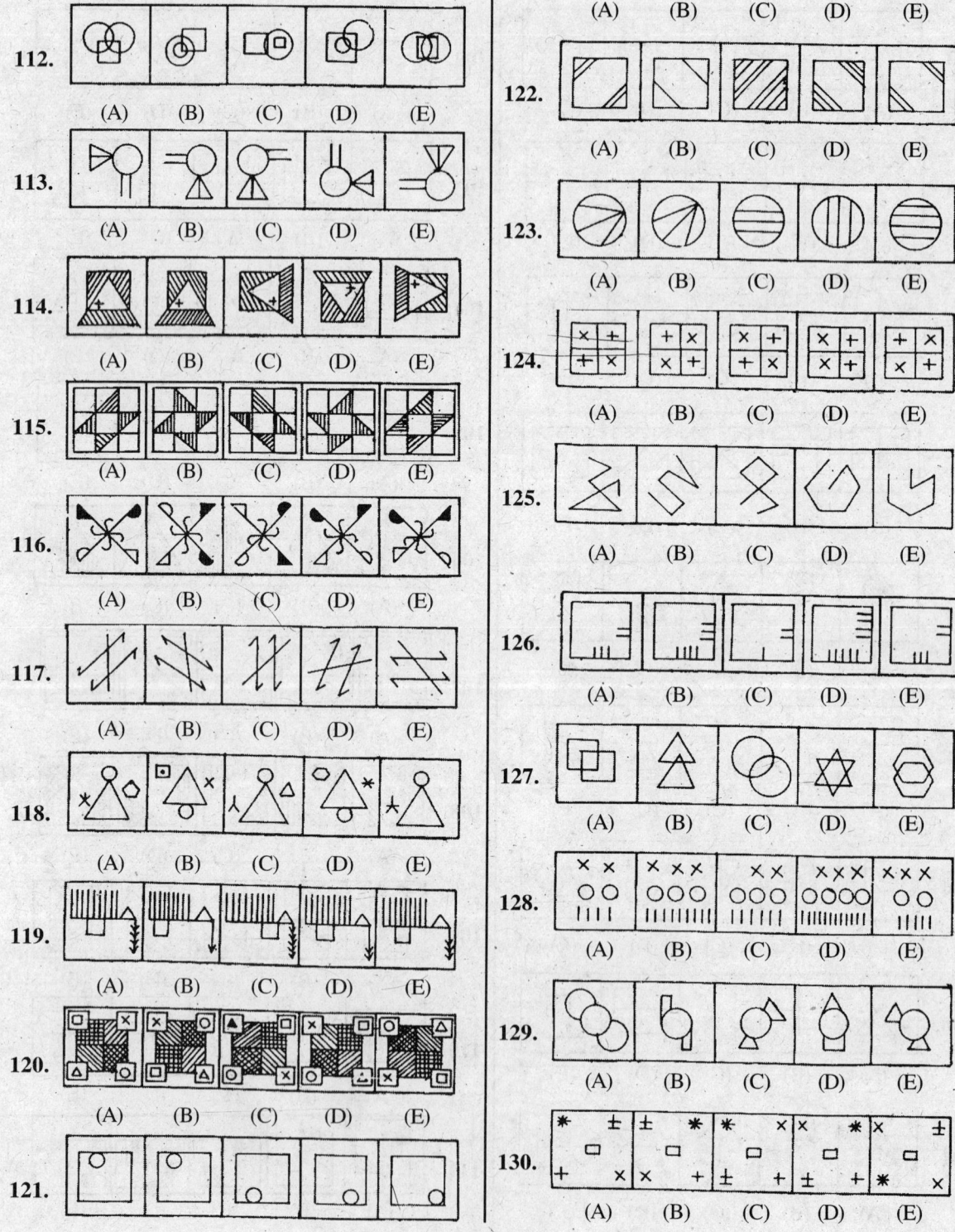

71

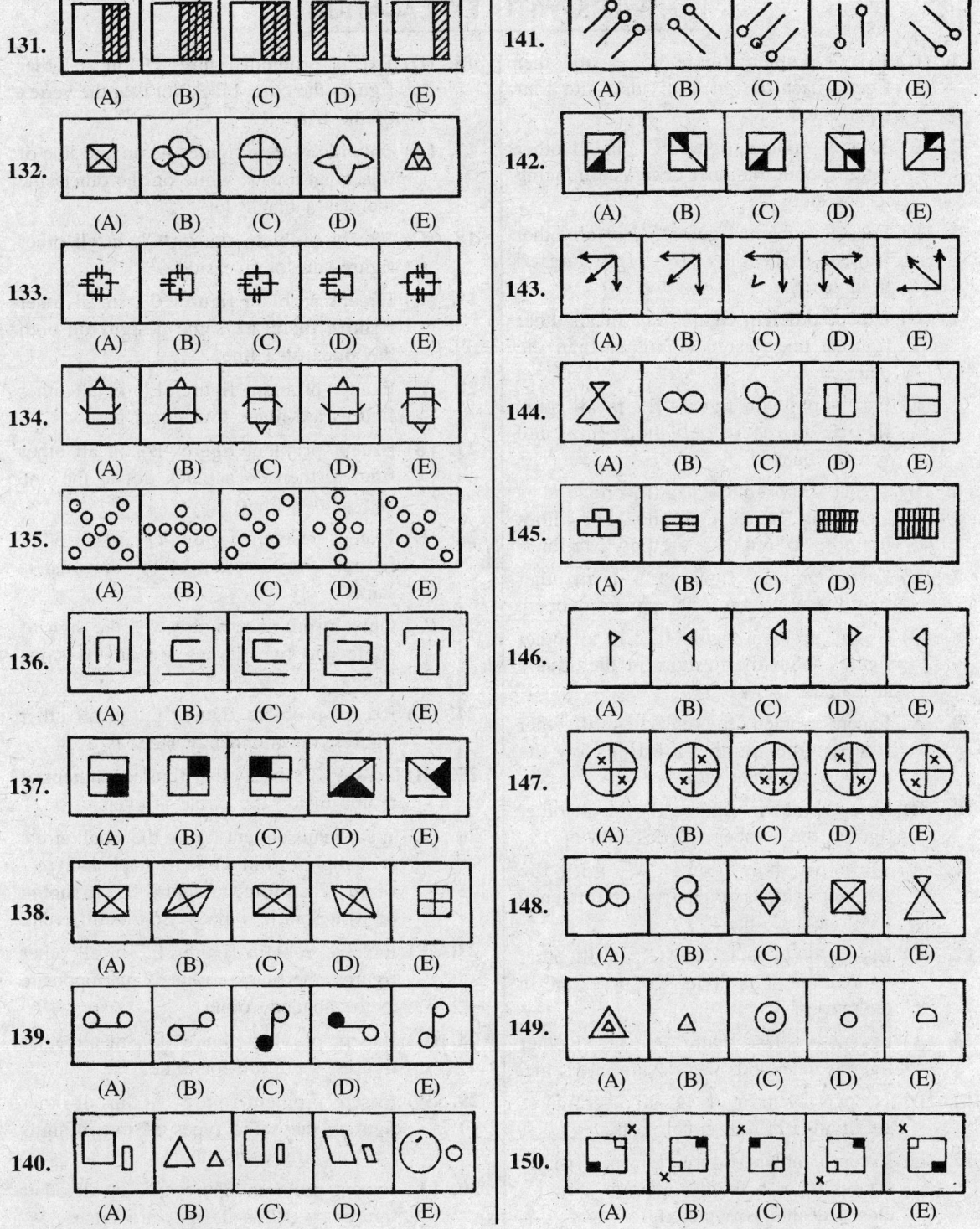

ANSWERS WITH EXPLANATION

1. **(C)** Except problem figure 'C' in all other figure, each design is divided into four equal parts.

2. **(C)** Except problem figure 'C', in all other figures, both the inner designs are facing to one side.

3. **(E)** Except problem figure 'E', in all other figures, triangles are right-angled triangles.

4. **(D)** Except problem figure 'D', in all other figures, one design is bigger than the other.

5. **(E)** Except problem figure 'E', in all other figures, there are only horizontal and vertical lines.

6. **(D)** In each subsequent figure one line is increasing., Hence, there should be 4 lines in figure 'D' but there are only two lines.

7. **(C)** Except problem figure 'C', in all other figures, the design in the square is open.

8. **(D)** Except problem figure 'D', in all other figures, both the designs in the square are same.

9. **(A)** Except problem figure 'A', in all other figures, the number of lines on the opposite sides are same.

10. **(B)** Except problem figure 'B', in all other figures, the number of sides is even.

11. **(A)** Only problem figure 'A', both the complete and same designs are attached with one and other.

12. **(C)** Except problem figure 'C', in all other figures, the parts divided by lines are in the ratio of 3 1.

13. **(A)** Except problem figure 'A', in all other figures, inner and outer designs are same.

14. **(D)** Except problem figure 'D', all other figures are divided in four equal parts.

15. **(E)** Except problem figure 'E', in all other figures, if both the designs are joined a closed design is obtained.

16. **(D)** Except problem figure 'D', in all other figures the outer black dot is at the vertex of the triangle.

17. **(A)** Only in problem figure 'A' on one side of line is an arrow, while on the other side there is a black dot.

18. **(C)** Except problem figure 'C', in all other figures are of five sides.

19. **(C)** Except problem figure 'C', in all other figures, there are same designs on both the sides of a line.

20. **(E)** Except problem figure 'E', in all other figures are made four equal parts.

21. **(B)** Except problem figure 'B', in all other figures, there is a black dot at the one end of two lines.

22. **(D)** Except problem figure 'D', in all other figures, the direction of the diagonal is same.

23. **(C)** Only in problem figure 'C', the sign of angle and two dashes are on the same line.

24. **(E)** Except problem figure 'E', in all other figures, the number of sides is even.

25. **(B)** Except 'B', in all other figures, number of radius inside the circle is even.

26. **(E)** In each subsequent figure the small circle is changing from white to black and *vice-versa*. Therefore, in figure 'E' it should be white but it is black. So it is different.

27. **(E)** Except problem figure 'E', in all other figures, the black corner is just opposite to the shaded corner.

28. **(C)** Except problem figure 'C', in all other figures, there are four lines.

29. **(A)** Except problem figure 'A', in all other figures, the same types of two designs are touching each other.

30. **(A)** Except problem figure 'A', in all other figures, both the designs are same.

31. **(D)** Except problem figure 'D', in all other figures, starting from right top, the square gets darkened by 1/2, 1, $1\frac{1}{2}$, 2 etc., while this pattern is not followed in problem figure 'D'.

32. **(C)** Except in problem figure 'C', the number of rectangles in other figures are odd, while in problem figure, the number of rectangles are even (form).

33. **(E)** Each problem figure is obtained from previous problem figure by rotating the figure anti-clockwise through 90°, while problem figure 'E' does not follow this rule.

34. **(E)** Except in problem figure 'E', the common area between two intersecting circles is diminishing, while it is not so in problem figure 'E'.

35. **(E)** Except 'E', in all other figures, the number of sides is five.

36. **(B)** Except problem figure 'B', in all other figures, the line head has no arrow.

37. **(D)** Only problem figure 'D', is the interior of figure having no straight line.

38. **(D)** Except problem figure 'D', in all other figures, the difference between the interior and exterior lines is two.

39. **(B)** Only in problem figure 'B' the size of the upper figure is smaller than that of the lower figure.

40. **(B)** Only in problem figure 'B'. One are completely lines outside.

41. **(B)** Except problem figure 'B', all the remaining figures are alike.

42. **(C)** Except problem figure 'C', in all other figures, the number of the inside figures is equal to the number of sides in the outside figures.

43. **(D)** Only in problem figure 'D' the arrows point in the same direction while such is not the case with other figures.

44. **(C)** Except problem figure 'C', in all other figures, the arrow and the black circle belong to the same quadrant.

45. **(D)** Except in problem figure 'D', upper figure has one side less than that sides of the lower figure, while in problem figure 'D' upper figure has one side more than the sides of the lower figure.

46. **(E)** Except problem figure 'E', in all other figures, the erect and the inverted regions occur alternately.

47. **(E)** Only in problem figure 'E' all the units point to same direction.

48. **(E)** Except in problem figures 'E', the number of inner divisions in all other figures is six.

49. **(D)** Only in PF/'D' the lines attached on the sides of this figure are neither parallel nor face opposite direction.

50. **(D)** Only in problem figure (PF) 'D' the inner and outer designs of this figure point towards the same direction.

51. **(C)** Except in PF/'C' in all other figures, the short line stationed within reappears on the other side with a gap of one.

52. **(B)** Only in PF/'B', the upper and the lower lines are in the same direction.

53. **(E)** Except in PF/'E', the bent portions in all the remaining figures are oppositely faced.

54. **(C)** Only in PF/'C', the terminal units of the line are different from each other.

55. **(E)** Except in PF/'E', all other figures can be equally obtained by turning.

56. **(A)** Only in PF/'A', a straight line is formed form the concave side of the arrowed arc.

57. **(C)** Only in PF/'C', the two lines are inclined within this figure in this column.

58. **(A)** Except in PF/'A', all other figures have inner and outer units, while PF/'A' has only outer units.

59. **(D)** Only in PF/'D' the arrows in this figure do not lie towards the black portion.

60. **(A)** Except PF/'A' in all other figures, there exists a difference of two between the number of inner short lines and the number of sides of the outer design.

61. **(D)** Only in PF/'D' the direction of the inner line of the first unit is different from the inner line of the second unit.

62. **(E)** Only in PF/'E', a straight line divides an angle and a side.

63. **(D)** Only in PF/'D', the arrow points outward.

64. **(C)** Except in PF/'C', all other figures are either rectangular or squares, while in PF/'C' is a rhombus.

65. **(E)** Except problem figure /'E'. All other figures have square.

66. **(B)** Except problem figure 'B', in all other figures have a dark dot outside the figure, while problem figure 'B' has a dark dot within the circle.

67. **(B)** Except problem figure 'B', all other figures have two closed figures.

68. **(E)** Except in problem figure 'E' the symbol # is to the right of the symbol ◊, while in problem figure 'E', the symbol is on the left side.

69. **(A)** Except problem figure 'A', on other figure has all the three lines parallel.

70. **(C)** Except problem figure 'C', in other figures at least one line starts from corner.

71. **(C)** Except problem figure 'C', the parallel lines in other figures are vertical and horizontal, while in problem figure 'C', all the parallel lines are horizontal.

72. **(C)** Except problem figure 'C', other figures have different kinds of figures, while problem figure 'C', has same kind of figures, inside and outside.

73. **(A)** Except in problem figure 'A', both the Ts are not in the same direction.

74. **(A)** Except PF/'A', all figures have 5 corners.

75. **(B)** Except PF/'B', other figures can be obtained by turning problem figure 'A'.

76. **(E)** Except in PF/'E', the longer line is in the centre, while in PF/'E' shorter lines is in the centre.

77. **(B)** Except PF/'B' other figures have complete circle.

78. **(D)** Except problem figure 'D', other figures have four blocks, while problem figures 'D' has 5 blocks.

79. **(C)** Except PF/'C', there is one arrow in other figures.

80. **(C)** Except PF/'C', other figures are made of straight lines.

81. **(A)** Except PF/'A', other figures have unequal units, but PF/'A' has equal units.

82. **(B)** Except PF/'B', other figures are made of 2 units.

83. **(C)** Except PF/'C', other figures have two units the same, while PF/'C' has all units different.

84. **(C)** Except PF/'C', other figures have three segments while PF/'C', has 4 segments.

85. **(E)** Except problem figure 'E', others have two units same, while PF/'E' has no units common.

86. **(A)** Except problem figure 'A' other figures have a square, while problem figure 'A' has no square.

87. **(D)** Exception in problem figure 'D', shaded portion is enclosed by three or four lines, while the shaded portion of PF/'D' is enclosed by six lines.

88. **(E)** Except in problem figure 'E', one line intersects the other two lines.

89. **(B)** Except in problem figure 'B', small unit is given downwards.

90. **(A)** Except problem figure 'A', other figures are made of 6 lines, while problem figure 'A' is made of 5 lines.

91. **(C)** Except PF/'C', other figures are divided into four segments, while PF/'C' is divided into three segments.

92. (D) Except problem figure 'D' other figures are made of 6 lines.

93. (A) Except problem figure 'A', other figures are open, while PF/'A' is closed.

94. (D) Except PF/'D', other figures have three units, while PF/'D' has 4 units.

95. (A) Except in problem figure 'A' all the three units are not cutting each other.

96. (E) Except problem figure 'E', other figures are divided into 4 segments, while problem figure 'E' is divided into 2 segments.

97. (D) Except in problem figure 'D', the upper unit is shaded, while in problem figure 'D' lower unit is shaded.

98. (B) Except problem figure 'B', others are made of straight lines, while problem figure 'B' is made of circles.

99. (C) Except problem figure 'C', in other figures, two units are cutting each other, while in problem figure 'C', units are touching each other.

100. (E) Except in PF/'E', there are two similar figures joining each other.

101. (B) Except in PF/'B', part of the figures is closed, while in PF/'B' no part of the figures is closed.

102. (E) Except PF/'E', other figures consist of straight lines, while problem figure 'E', consists of curved lines.

103. (E) Except PF/'E', arrow is pointing inside the figure, while in problem figure 'E' arrow is pointing outside the figure.

104. (A) Except problem figure 'A', the inner and outer figure does not consist of same figure.

105. (A) Except problem figure 'A', the other figures do not consist of one unit inside the other.

106. (B) Except problem figure 'B', the lines in upper and lower sectors are parallel.

107. (B) Except problem figure 'B', the half-shaded triangle is on the left of cross (×).

108. (A) Except problem figure 'A', all other figures have crossed corner with mutually perpendicular lines.

109. (B) Except in problem figure 'B', the lower pair of lines touches the middle line in one point only, while in PF/'B', the touch is at two points.

110. (B) Except in PF/'B', the other figures have triangles, while PF/'B', has no triangle.

111. (E) Except in problem figure 'E', the other figures have 4 lines in the corner, while problem figure 'E', has 5 lines in the corner.

112. (C) Except in PF/'C', the other figures have two circles and one square, while PF/'C', has two square and one circle.

113. (B) Except in PF/'B', the pair of lines are to the right of triangle, while in PF/'B' they are to the left of the triangle.

114. (B) Except in PF/'B', the other figures can be rotated into PF/'A'.

115. (E) Except in PF/'E', there are vertical lines adjoining the blank square, while in PF/'E' there are horizontal lines adjoining the blank square.

116. (D) Except in PF/'D', the shaded portions are not in the same direction.

117. (A) Except in PF/'A', the motion of the arrows is in the anti-clockwise direction, while in PF/'A', it is in clockwise direction.

118. (E) Except PF/'E' in no other figure, outer units are at the corners of the triangle.

119. (C) Except in PF/'C', the rectangle is joined to the parallel lines, while in PF/'C', the rectangle is joined to the middle of the parallel lines.

120. (C) Except in PF/'C', the internal interval is blank, while in PF/'C', it is shaded.

121. (E) Except PF/'E', in all other figures, the circle is touching only one side of the square.

122. **(A)** Except PF/'A', in all other figure, the distance between the lines is equal.

123. **(E)** Except PF/'E', in all other figures, there are three lines inside the circle.

124. **(D)** Except PF/'D', in all other figures, the pairs of '+' and '×' are not along diagonals.

125. **(C)** Except PF/'C', in all other figures, the design is made of six lines.

126. **(C)** Except PF/'C', in all other figures, the number of vertical lines is one more than the number of horizontal lines.

127. **(D)** Except PF/'D', in all other figures, both the units are exactly same but in PF/'D' one triangle is reverse of the other.

128. **(E)** Except PF/'E', in all other figures, the number of circles is not less than the number of crosses.

129. **(A)** Except PF/'A', in all other figures, rectilinear figures are attached with circle, while in PF/'A' circles are attached with circle.

130. **(E)** Except PF/'E', in all other figures, all the four outer units are different, while in PF/'E' two are same.

131. **(D)** Except problem figure 'D' in all other figures, the shaded portion is at the right side, while in PF/'D' it is at the left hand side.

132. **(D)** Except PF/'D', in all other figures, there are four inner designs, while in PF/'D', it is one.

133. **(E)** Except in PF/'E', the number small lines on opposite sides of a square are not same.

134. **(B)** Except PF/'B', in all other figures, if inclined lines are increased to the back side, the point of intersection lines to the opposite side of the vertex of the triangle.

135. **(A)** Except PF/'A', in all other figures, the number of circles is 7, while it is 9 in PF/'A'.

136. **(C)** Except PF/'C', in all other figures, the inner units are in opposite directions.

137. **(C)** Except PF/'C', in all other figures, the square is divided into 3 parts, while in PF/'C' square is divided into 4 parts.

138. **(E)** Except PF/'E', in all other figures, diagonals are straight.

139. **(A)** Except PF/'A', in all other figures, the circles are on opposite sides of the lines, while in problem figure 'A' they are on the same side.

140. **(A)** Except PF/'A', in all other figures, the inner units are of same shape.

141. **(D)** Except in PF/'D', in all other figures, the small circles are on the same side on a line.

142. **(B)** Except PF/'B', the figures can be rotated into each other, while it is not so in PF/'B'.

143. **(C)** Except PF/'C', in all other figures, the number of arrows is 3.

144. **(A)** Except PF/'A', in all other figures, both the units are of same size.

145. **(A)** Except PF/'A', in all other figures, either the number of units above is same as below or there is no design above.

146. **(C)** Except PF/'C', in all other figures, the vertex of the triangle is outward.

147. **(C)** Except PF/'C', in all other figures, the signs of cross are vertically opposite.

148. **(E)** Except PF/'E', in all other figures, both the units are of same size.

149. **(E)** Except PF/'E', in all other figures, there are full geometrical units, while in PF/'E' it is semi-circle.

150. **(C)** Except problem figure 'C', in all other figures the sign of cross is near the white small square.

● ● ●

FIGURE ANALOGIES

Analogy is case of parallel reasoning. The figures in the first set bear a certain analogy (relation) to each other. The same analogy must be reflected in the second unit also. The candidate has to choose from given answer figures what would be best substitute of the sign of interrogation, thus establishing the required analogy.

Solved Example

Problem Figures

1.

Answer Figures

(A)   (B)   (C)   (D)

Answer (C): Problem figure 2 is obtained from problem figure 1 by moving its units (Small circles) to the right and adding one similar unit to the left in a set order.

Similarly, Answer figure 'C' is obtained from problem figure 3.

EXERCISE

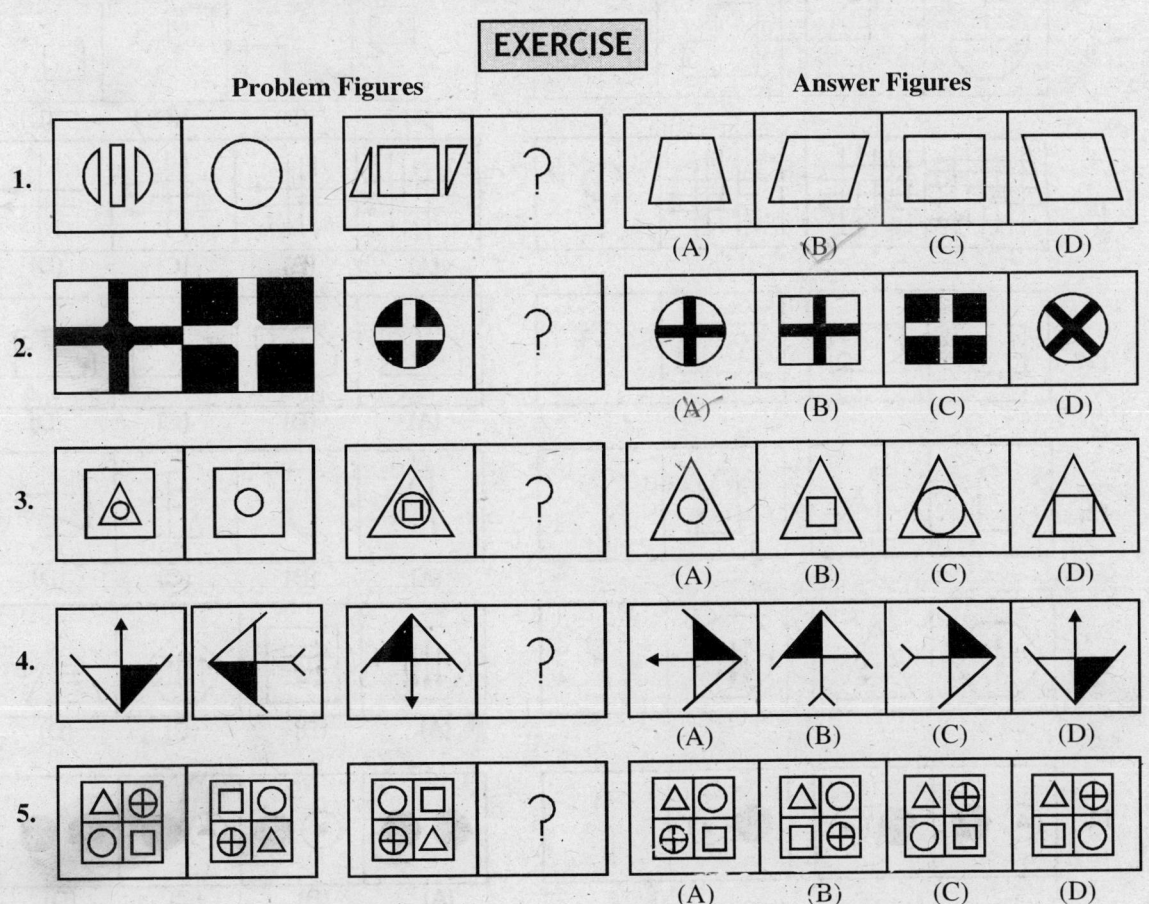

Problem Figures   **Answer Figures**

1.   (A)   (B)   (C)   (D)

2.   (A)   (B)   (C)   (D)

3.   (A)   (B)   (C)   (D)

4.   (A)   (B)   (C)   (D)

5.   (A)   (B)   (C)   (D)

78

Problem Figures   **Answer Figures**

6.

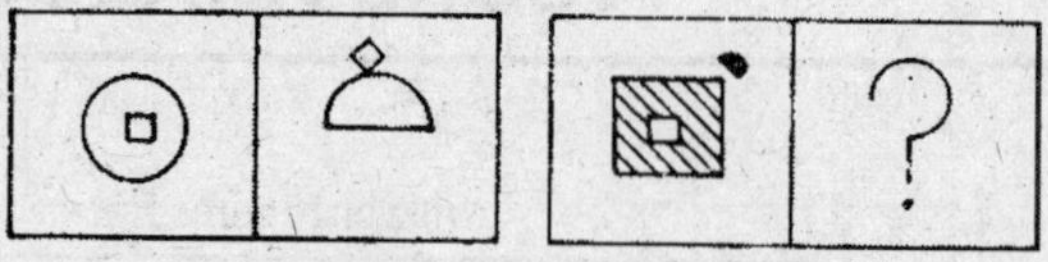

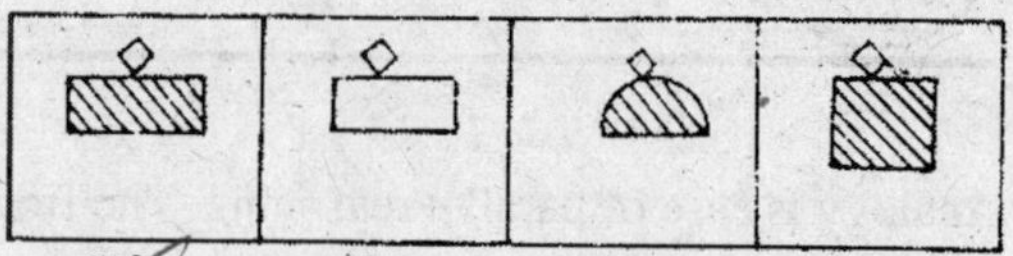

(A)   (B)   (C)   (D)

7.

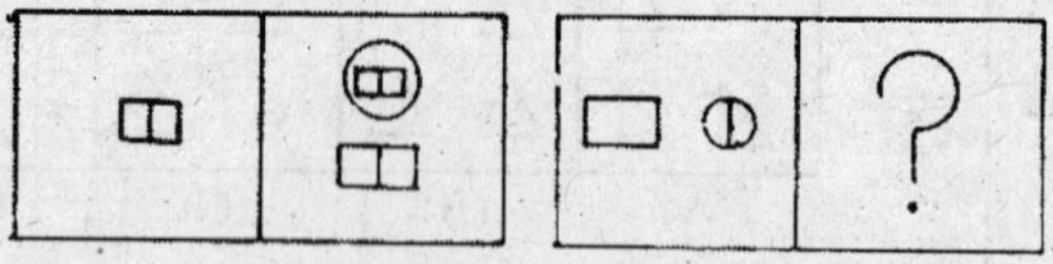

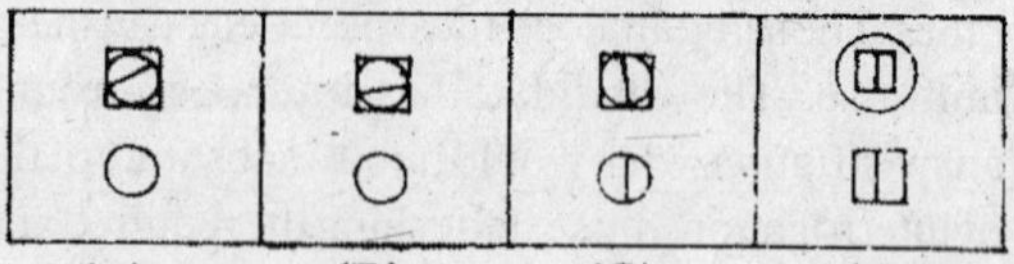

(A)   (B)   (C)   (D)

8.

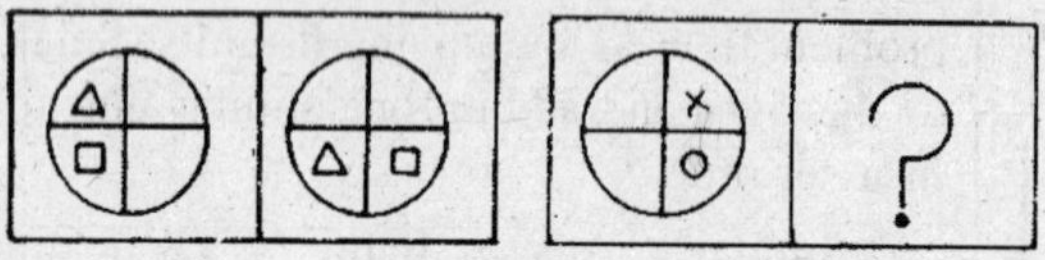

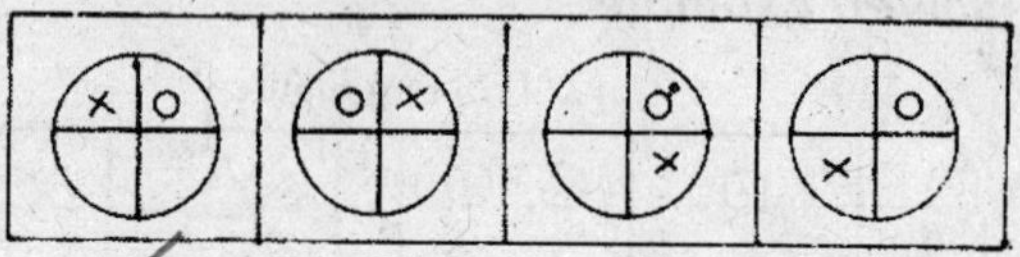

(A)   (B)   (C)   (D)

9.

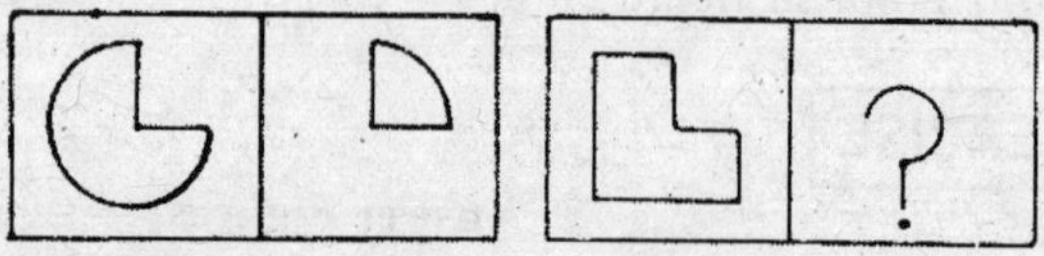

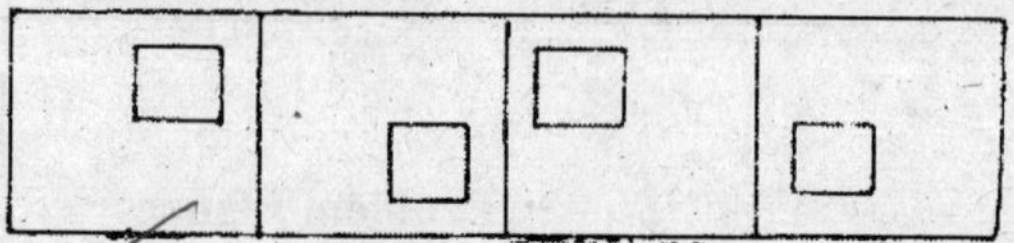

(A)   (B)   (C)   (D)

10.

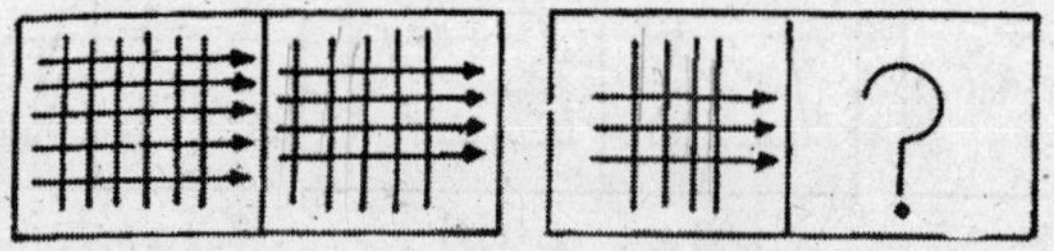

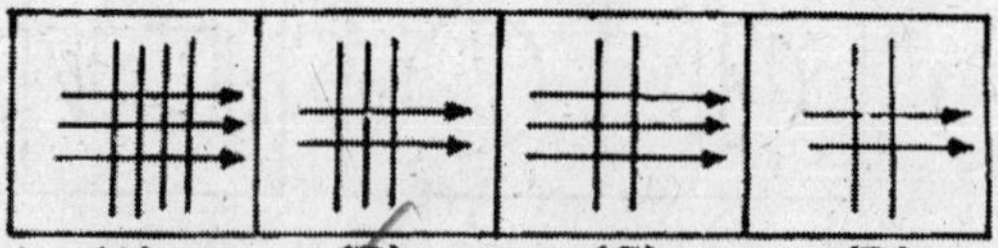

(A)   (B)   (C)   (D)

11.

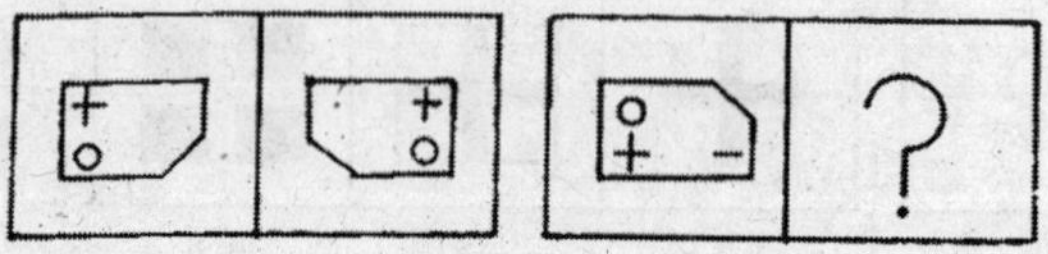

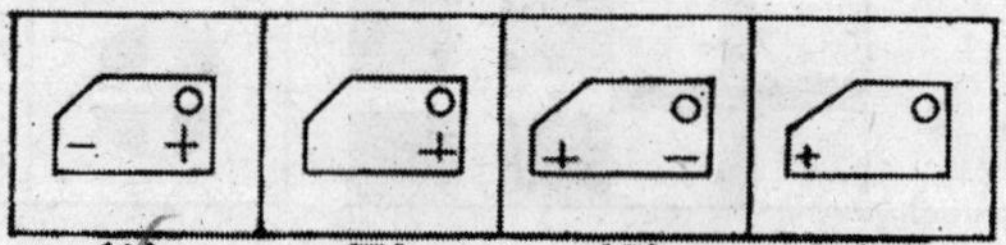

(A)   (B)   (C)   (D)

12.

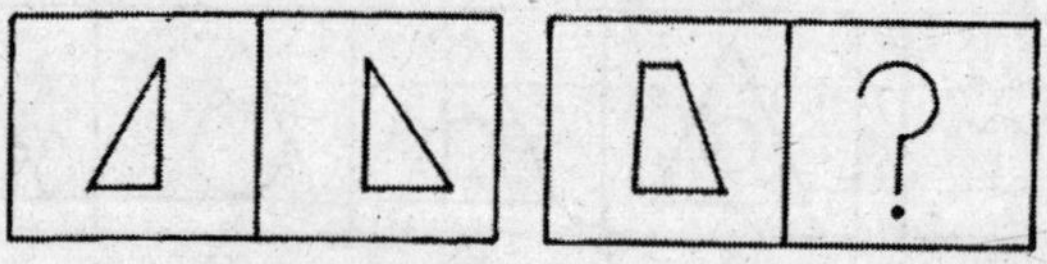

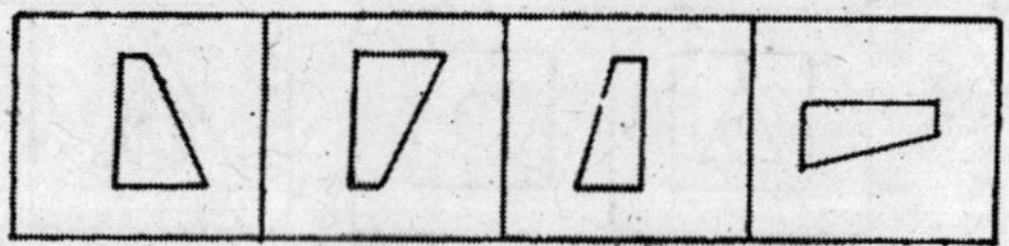

(A)   (B)   (C)   (D)

13.

(A)   (B)   (C)   (D)

14.

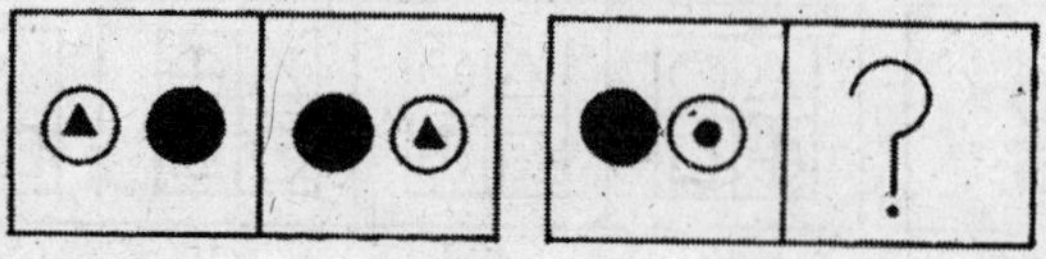

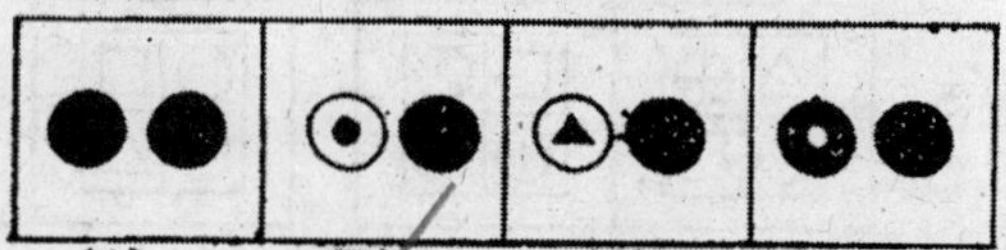

(A)   (B)   (C)   (D)

Problem Figures   **Answer Figures**

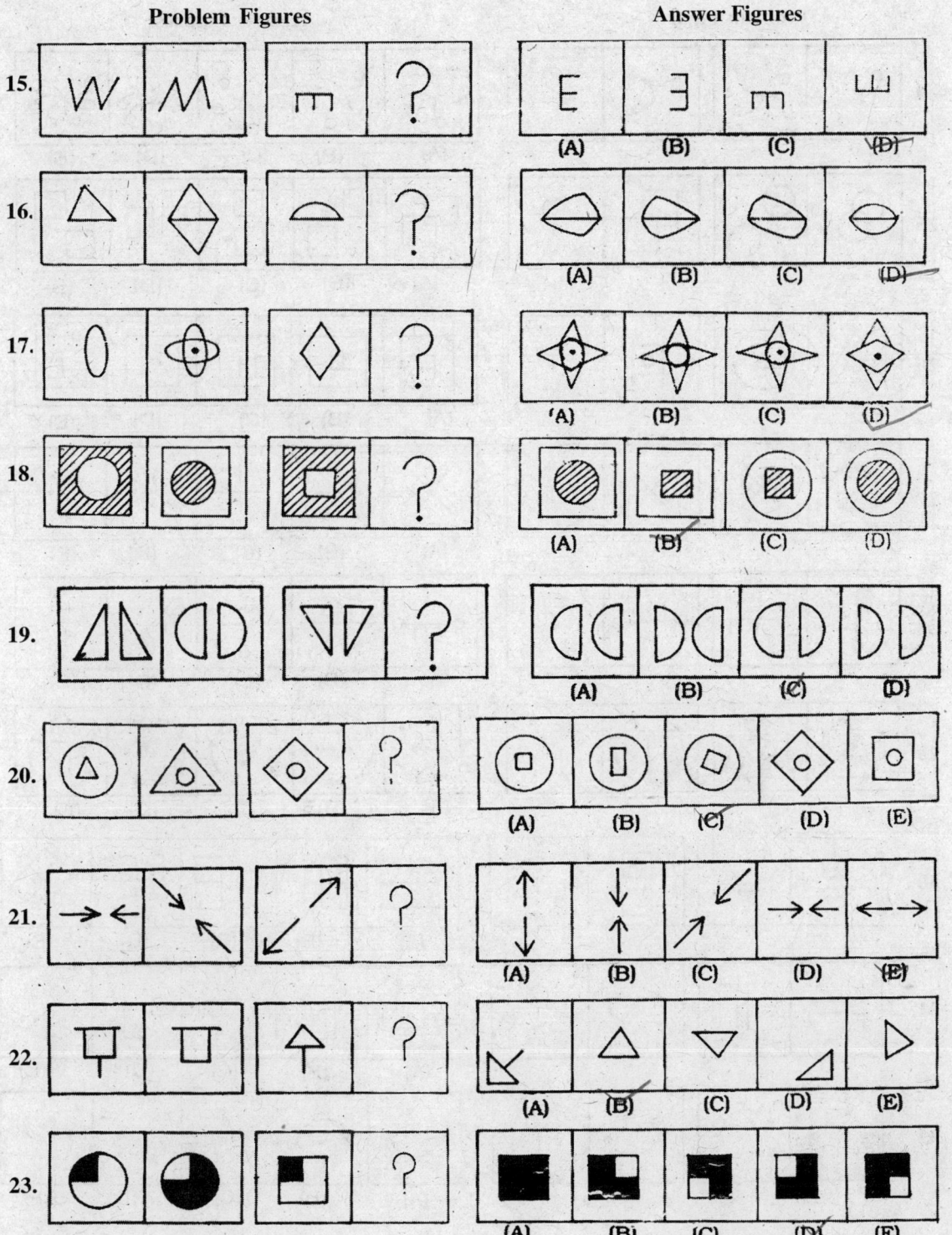

80

Problem Figures   **Answer Figures**

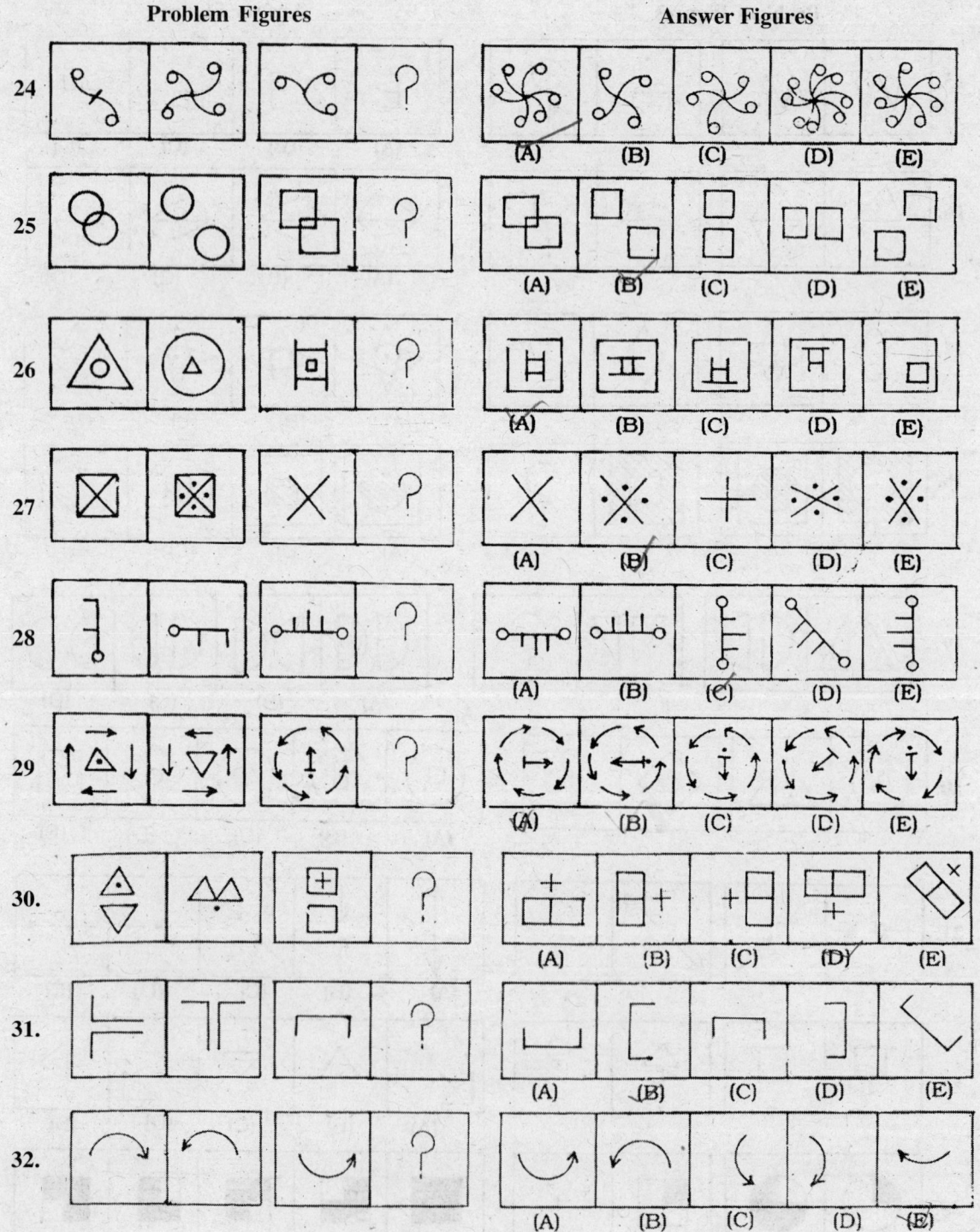

Problem Figures

Answer Figures

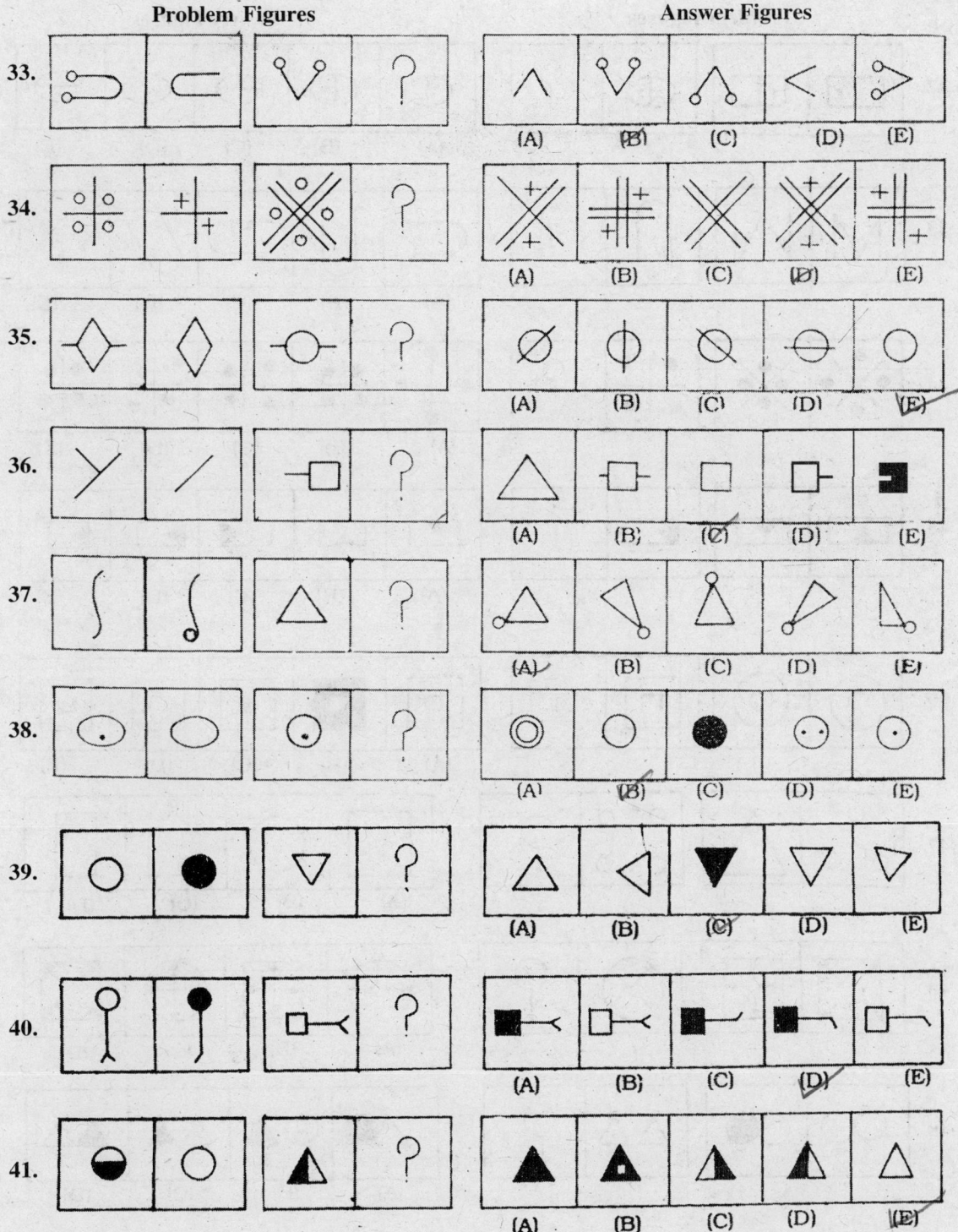

Problem Figures   **Answer Figures**

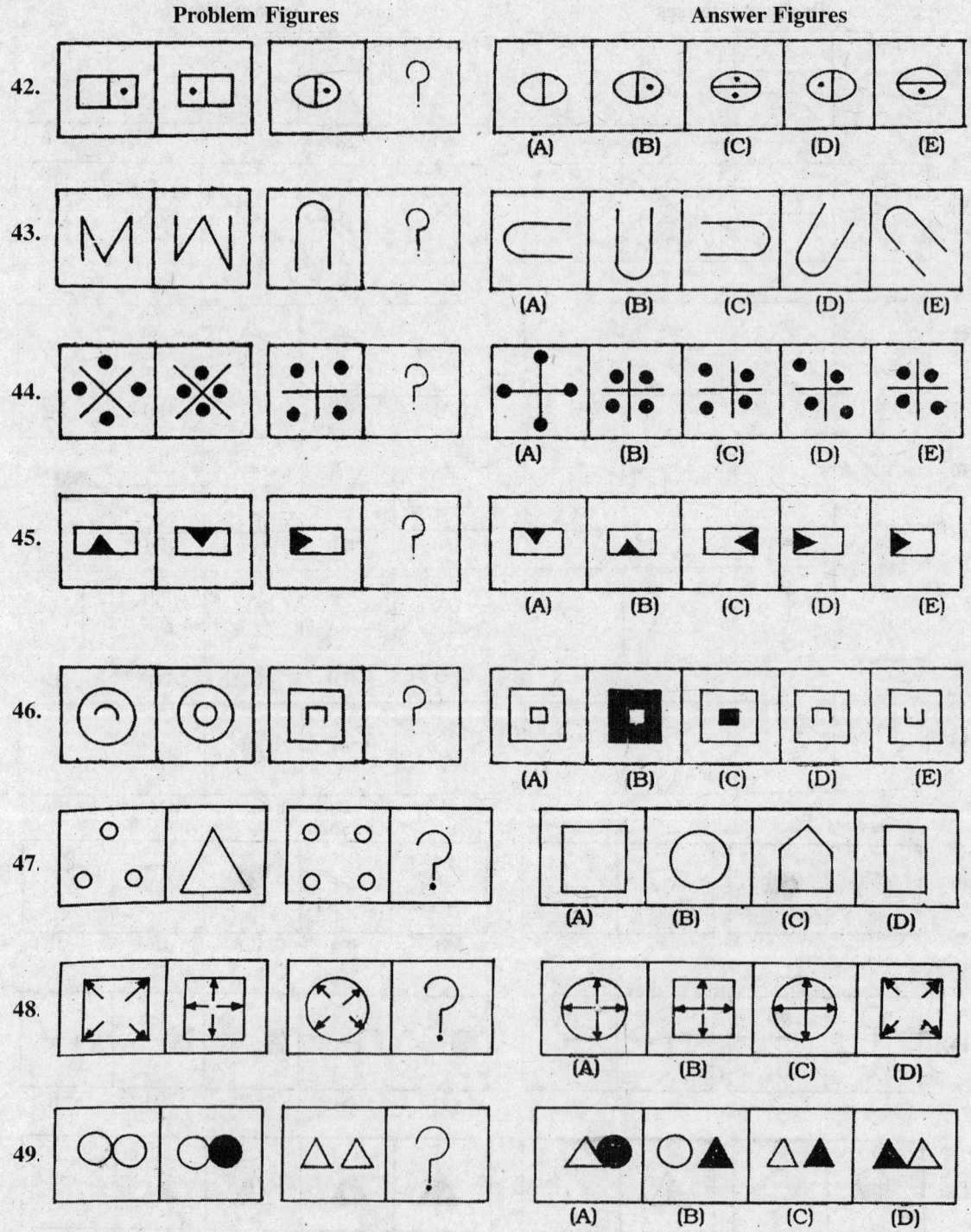

Problem Figures　　　　　　　　　　　　**Answer Figures**

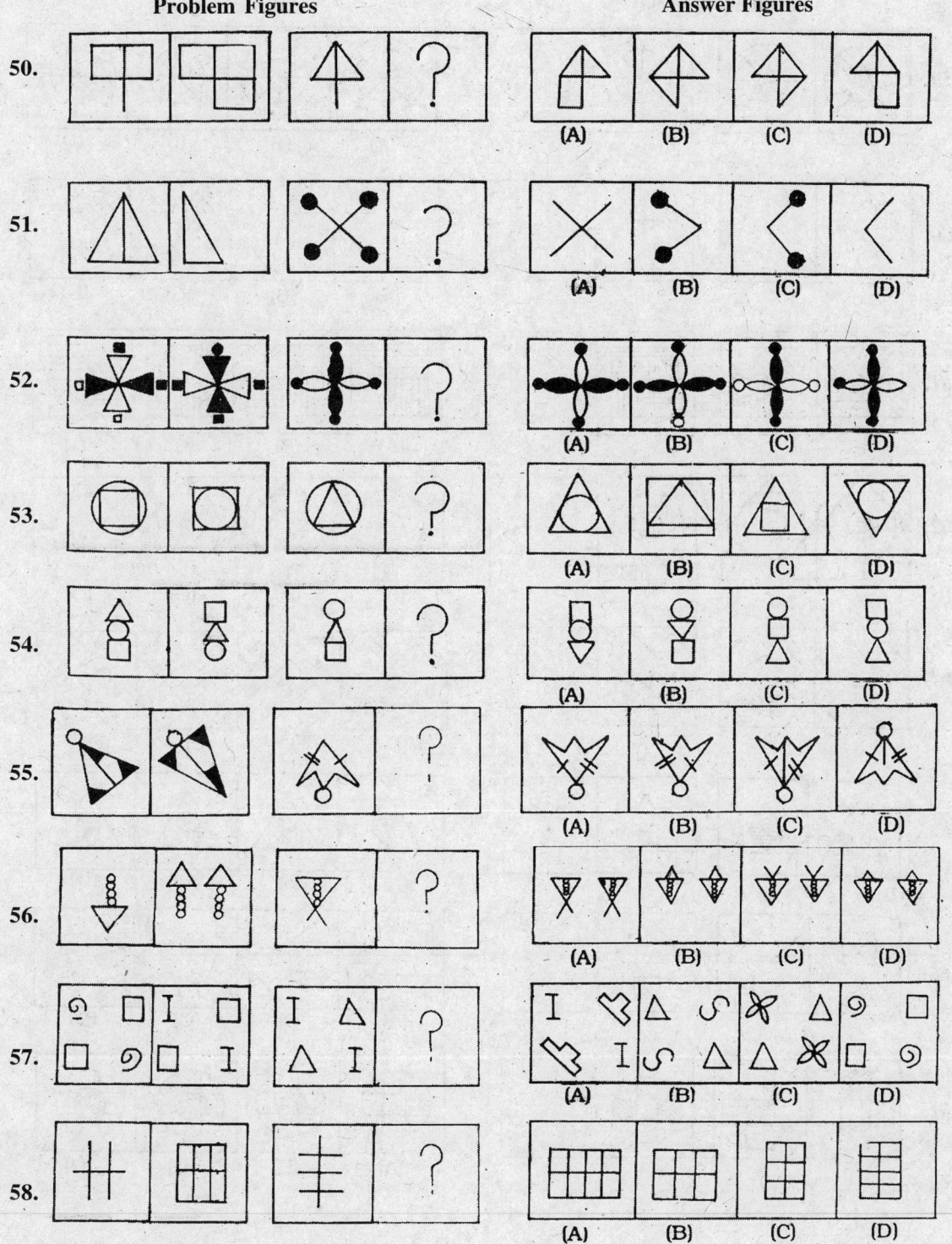

84

Problem Figures

Answer Figures

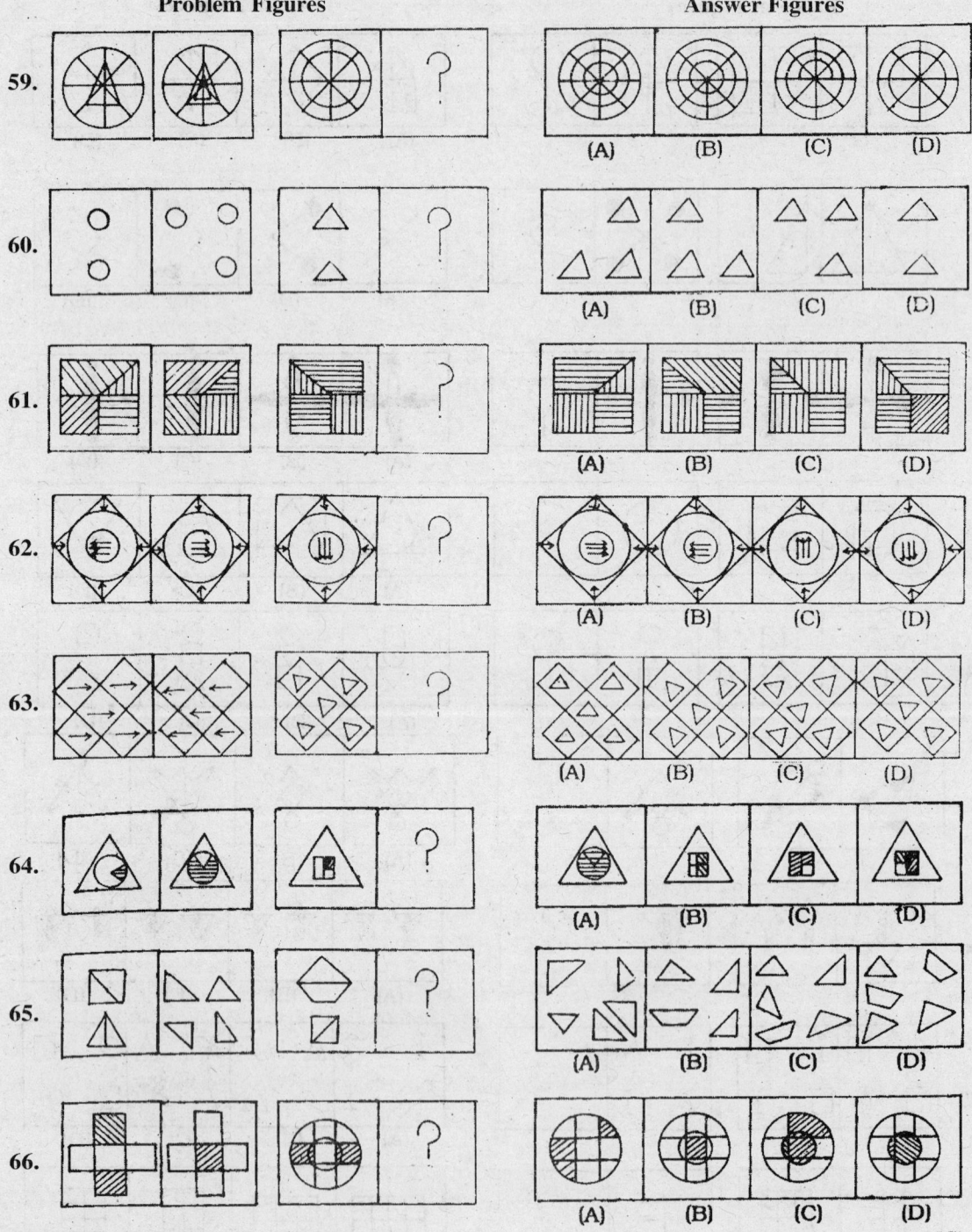

ANSWERS WITH EXPLANATION

1. **(B)** Problem figure 2 is obtained from problem figure 1 by uniting the three sections to obtain a circle. Similarly, Answer figure 'B' is obtained from problem figure 3.

2. **(A)** Problem figure PF 2 is obtained from PF/1 by turning the black cross (+) into the white cross. Similarly, Answer figure (AF) 'A' is obtained from PF/3 by turning white cross into black cross.

3. **(B)** PF/2 is obtained from PF/1 by removing the middle figure (triangle). Similarly, AF/B is obtained from PF/3.

4. **(C)** PF/2 is obtained from PF/1 by rotating it clockwise through 90°. Similarly, AF 'C' is obtained from PF/3.

5. **(D)** PF/2 is obtained from PF/1 by moving the symbols (units) to the vertical opposite square. Similarly, AF/'D' is obtained from PF/3.

6. **(A)** PF/2 is obtained from PF/1 by removing the lower half circle and moving the internal small square edge on to the top. Similarly, AF/'A' is obtained from PF/3.

7. **(C)** PF/2 is obtained from PF/1 by removing the small circle on the left and doubling the number of squares. Two squares are placed within a circle and two squares are placed below it. Similarly, AF/'C' is obtained from PF/3.

8. **(A)** PF/2 is obtained from PF/1 by rotating it clockwise through 90°. Similarly, we can obtain AF/'A' from PF/3.

9. **(A)** PF/2 is obtained from PF/1 by taking out only one (top right) quadrant. Similarly, we can obtain AF/'A' from PF/3.

10. **(B)** PF/1 has 6 vertical and 5 horizontal lines (arrows). PF/2 has 5 vertical and 4 horizontal lines (arrows) that is one less each way. Similarly, AF/'B' is obtained from PF/3.

11. **(C)** PF/2 is the lateral inversion of PF/1. Similarly, AF/'C' is the lateral inversion of PF/3.

12. **(C)** PF/2 is the lateral inversion of PF/1. Similarly, AF/'C' is the lateral inversion of PF/3.

13. **(B)** PF/2 has half the number of sides and double the number of parallel horizontal arrows. Similarly, we obtain AF/'B' from PF/3.

14. **(B)** PF/2 is obtained by interchanging the position of units in PF/1. Similarly, we obtain AF/'B' from PF/3.

15. **(D)** PF/2 is obtained by inverting PF/1. Similarly, we get AF/'D' from PF/3.

16. **(B)** PF/2 is obtained by placing another figure like it below the base as shown. Similarly, we obtain AF/B from PF/3.

17. **(D)** PF/2 is obtained from PF/1 by placing an identical figure horizontally across the PF/1 and putting a dot at the centre. Similarly, we obtain AF/'D' from PF/3.

18. **(B)** PF/2 is obtained from PF/1 by shading the inner unit and clearing the shade of the area outside the inner figure. Similarly, AF/'B' is obtained from PF/3.

19. **(C)** PF/2 is obtained from PF/1 by changing the base and hypotenuse of each triangle into a semicircle. Similarly, AF/C is obtained from PF/3.

20. **(C)** PF/2 is obtained from PF/1 by enlarging the internal figure triangle and enclosing it by shortening the outer circle. Similarly, AF/C is obtained from PF/3.

21. **(E)** PF/2 is obtained from PF/1 by rotating it clockwise through 45°. Similarly, AF/E is obtained from PF/3.

22. **(B)** PF/2 is obtained from PF/1 by removing the lower line similarly, AF/B is obtained from PF/3.

23. **(D)** PF/2 is obtained form PF/1 by darkening the white portion and whitening the black portion. Similarly, AF/D is obtained from PF/3.

24. **(A)** PF/2 is obtained from PF/1 by doubling the numbering of branches. Similarly, AF/A is obtained from PF/3.

25. **(B)** PF/2 is obtained from PF/1 by separating the intersecting circles. Similarly, AF/B is obtained from PF/3.

26. **(A)** PF/2 is obtained from PF/1 by enlarging the inner figure circle and enclosing it by the outer figure triangle. Similarly, AF/A is obtained from PF/3.

27. **(B)** PF/2 is obtained from PF/1 by adding four dots near the crossing. Similarly, AF/B is obtained from PF/3.

28. **(E)** PF/2 is obtained from PF/1 by rotating it clockwise through 90°. Similarly, AF/E is obtained from PF/3.

29. **(E)** PF/2 is obtained from PF/1 by reversing the direction of arrows and inverting the internal figure. Similarly, AF/E is obtained from PF/3.

30. **(D)** PF/2 is obtained from PF/1 by bringing the dot outside and reverting the lower triangle and placing it by the side of the upper triangle. Similarly, AF/'D' is obtained from PF/3.

31. **(D)** PF/2 is obtained from PF/1 by rotating it clockwise through 90°. Similarly, AF/D is obtained from PF/3.

32. **(E)** PF/2 is obtained from PF/1 by reversing the direction of its arrow. Similarly, AF/'E' is obtained from PF/3.

33. **(A)** PF/2 is obtained from PF/1 by reversing the direction and removing the small circles. Similarly, AF/A is obtained from PF/3.

34. **(D)** PF/2 is obtained from PF/1 by replacing the four small circles with two plus (+) signs. Similarly, AF/D is obtained from problem figure 3.

35. **(E)** PF/2 is obtained from PF/1 by removing its small side lines. Similarly, AF/E is obtained from PF/3.

36. **(C)** PF/2 is obtained from PF/1 by removing the perpendicular. Similarly, AF/'C' is obtained from PF/3.

37. **(A)** PF/2 is obtained from PF/1 by attaching a small ring at its end. Similarly, AF/'A' is obtained from PF/3.

38. **(B)** PF/2 is obtained from PF/1 by removing dot. Similarly, AF/B is obtained from PF/3.

39. **(C)** PF/2 is obtained from PF/1 by darkening the circle. Similarly, AF'C' is obtained from PF/3 by darkening the triangle.

40. **(D)** PF/2 is obtained from PF/1 by darkening the face and removing the right leg. Similarly, AF/D is obtained from PF/3.

41. **(E)** PF/2 is obtained from AF/1 by whitening the dark portion. Similarly, AF/E is obtained from PF/3.

42. **(D)** PF/2 is obtained from PF/1 by shifting the dot from the right portion to the left portion. Similarly, AF/D is obtained from PF/3.

43. **(B)** PF/2 is obtained from PF/1 by inverting it. Similarly, AF/B is obtained from PF/3.

44. **(B)** PF/2 is obtained from PF/1 by bringing the dots near the crossing. Similarly, AF/B is obtained from PF/3.

45. **(C)** PF/2 is obtained from PF/1 by rotating it clockwise through 90° Similarly, AF/C is obtained from PF/3.

46. **(A)** PF/2 is obtained from PF/1 by completing the internal half circle. Similarly, AF/A is obtained from PF/3

47. **(A)** PF/2 is obtained from PF/1 by converting the three rings into three sides of the triangle. Similarly, AF/A is obtained from PF/3.

48. **(A)** PF/2 is obtained from PF/1 by changing the sign of multiplication (×) into a plus sign (+). Similarly, AF/A is obtained from PF/3.

49. **(C)** PF/2 is obtained from PF/1 by blackening its right hand figure. Similarly, AF/C is obtained from PF/3.

50. (C) PF/2 is obtained from PF/1 by adding an equal size section on the right below the horizontal line. Similarly, AF/C is obtained from PF/3.

51. (C) PF/2 is obtained from PF/1 by removing its left side. Similarly, AF/C is obtained from PF/3.

52. (A) PF/2 is obtained from PF/1 by rotating the entire figure clockwise through 90°. Similarly. AF/A is obtained from PF/3.

53. (A) PF/2 is obtained from PF/1 by enlarging the inner figure (Square) to enclose the outer figure (circle). Similarly, AF/A is obtained from PF/3.

54. (D) PF/2 is obtained from PF/1 by removing the figures in cycle order. Similarly, AF/D is obtained from PF/3.

55. (B) PF/2 is obtained from PF/1 by inverting the triangle and keeping circle in tact. Similarly, Answer figure B is obtained from PF/3.

56. (C) PF/2 is obtained from PF/1 by inverting it and adding a similar unit on its right hand side. Similarly, AF/C is obtained from PF/3.

57. (C) PF/2 is obtained from PF/1 by replacing the upper left and bottom right units by new units. Similarly AF/C is obtained from PF/3.

58. (D) PF/2 is obtained from PF/1 by joining the ends of the lines by parallel horizontal and vertical lines to complete the figure. Similarly, AF/D is obtained from PF/3.

59. (A) PF/2 is obtained from PF/1 by adding a similar unit within the internal unit. Similarly, AF/A is obtained from PF/3.

60. (C) PF/2 is obtained from PF/1 by moving its units (Small circles) to the right and adding one similar unit to the left in a set order. Similarly, AF/C is obtained from PF/3.

61. (C) PF/2 is obtained from PF/1 by rotating its lines clockwise through 90°. Similarly, AF/C is obtained from PF/1.

62. (C) PF/2 is obtained from PF/1 by rotating its arrows clockwise through 90°. Similarly, AF/C is obtained from PF/3.

63. (A) PF/2 is obtained from PF/1 by rotating its arrows clockwise through 180°. Similarly, AF/A is obtained from PF/3 by rotating its triangles through 180°.

64. (C) PF/2 is obtained from PF/1 by rotating the inner unit anti – clockwise through 90° and unshading the shaded portion and shading the unshaded portion. Similarly, AF/C is obtained from PF/3 by rotating internal unit clockwise through 90° and unshading the shaded portion and shading the unshaded portion.

65. (B) PF/2 is obtained from PF/1 by separting the internal units into two parts. Similarly, AF/B is obtained from PF/3.

66. (B) PF/2 is obtained from PF/1 by shifting the shaded portion to the centre. Similarly, AF/B is obtained from PF/3.

• • •

In this test two sets of figures pose the problem. These sets are called problem Figures and Answer Figures. Each problem figure undergoes certain change with respect to the preceding figure. The Answer Figure contain four figures A, B, C and D from the Answer Figures you are to choose the one which would best continue the series.

Solved Example

1. Ex.

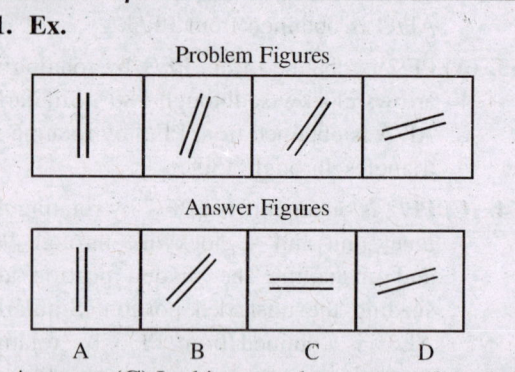

Answer: (C) In this example as you go from left to right. You find that the line across the problem figures is falling down. In the first figure line is vertical *i.e.,* standing upright, in the second figure onwards the line is gradually falling down.

Now look at the Answer Figures. You find that such a line is shown by Answer Figure 'C'. Therefore, your answer to this problem is 'C'.

2. Ex.

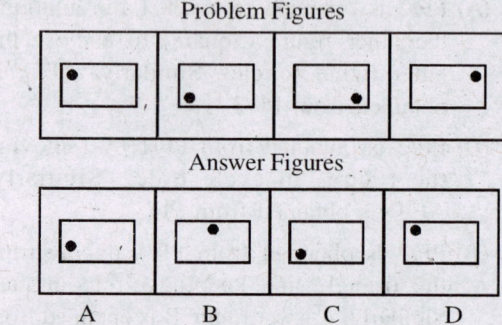

Answer: (D) Study the position of the dots in all the problem figures. Note that the dot keeps on moving around the square. It always moves in the anti clockwise direction. The dot would come back to the upper corner, therefore, Answer figure 'D' is the answer.

EXERCISE

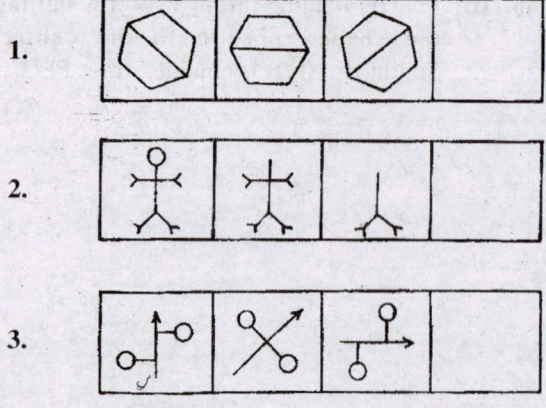

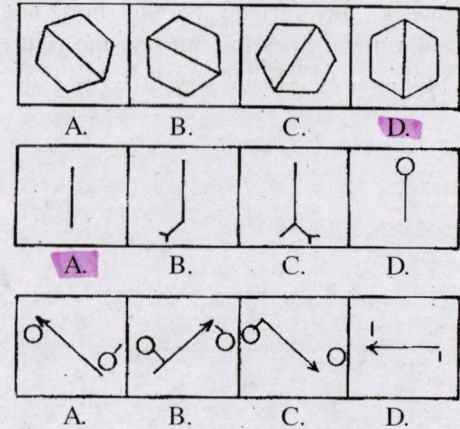

(951) Intelligence—12

Problem Figures   **Answer Figures**

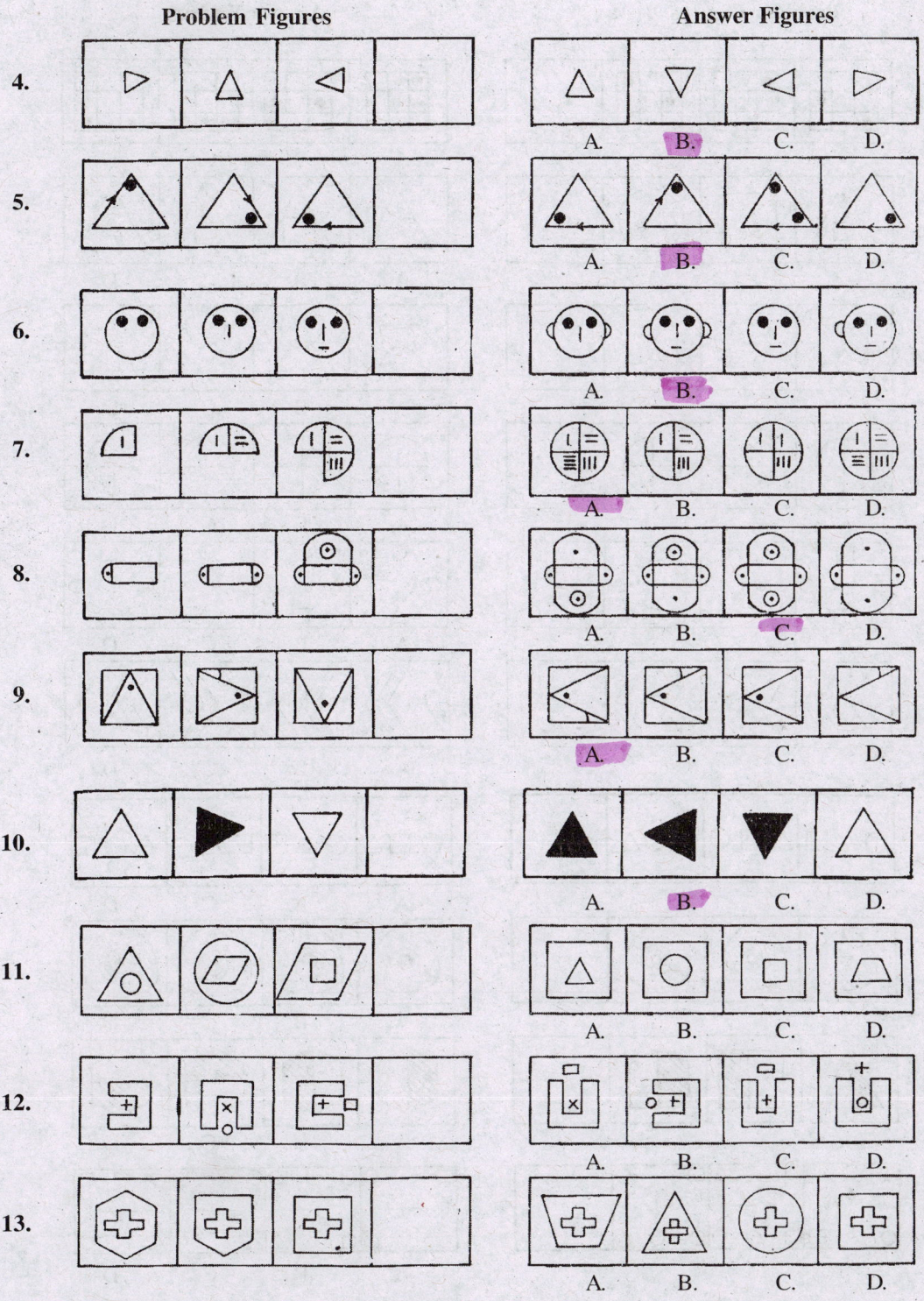

4.   A.   B.   C.   D.

5.   A.   B.   C.   D.

6.   A.   B.   C.   D.

7.   A.   B.   C.   D.

8.   A.   B.   C.   D.

9.   A.   B.   C.   D.

10.   A.   B.   C.   D.

11.   A.   B.   C.   D.

12.   A.   B.   C.   D.

13.   A.   B.   C.   D.

90

Problem Figures

Answer Figures

14.

A. B. C. D.

15.

A. B. C. D.

16.

A. B. C. D.

17.

A. B. C. D.

18.

A. B. C. D.

19.

A. B. C. D.

20.

A. B. C. D.

21.

A. B. C. D.

22.

A. B. C. D.

23.

A. B. C. D.

Problem Figures   **Answer Figures**

24.

A.   B.   C.   D.

25.

A.   B.   C.   D.

26.

A.   B.   C.   D.

27.

A.   B.   C.   D.

28.

A.   B.   C.   D.

29.

A.   B.   C.   D.

30.

A.   B.   C.   D.

31.

A.   B.   C.   D.

32.

A.   B.   C.   D.

33.

A.   B.   C.   D.

Problem Figures

Answer Figures

34.

A.   B.   C.   D.

35.

A.   B.   C.   D.

36.

A.   B.   C.   D.

37.

A.   B.   C.   D.

38.

A.   B.   C.   D.

39.

A.   B.   C.   D.

40.

A.   B.   C.   D.

41.

A.   B.   C.   D.

42.

A.   B.   C.   D.

43.

A.   B.   C.   D.

Problem Figures   **Answer Figures**

44.

A.   B.   C.   D.

45.

A.   B.   C.   D.

46.

A.   B.   C.   D.

47.

A.   B.   C.   D.

48.

A.   B.   C.   D.

49.

A.   B.   C.   D.

50.

A.   B.   C.   D.

51.

A.   B.   C.   D.

52.

A.   B.   C.   D.

53.

A.   B.   C.   D.

ANSWERS WITH EXPLANATION

1. **(D)** Problem figure/2 is obtained from problem figure 1 by rotating the entire figure anti – clockwise through 45°. Similarly, Answer figure 'D' is obtained from Problem figure 3. Hence, Answer figure 'D' completes the series.

2. **(A)** First the head of problem figure 1 has disappeared in problem figure 2, then arms have disappeared in problem figure 3, now in, Answer figure 'A' legs also have disappeared. Hence, Answer figure 'A' completes the series.

3. **(C)** The nail on the right side of the arrow gradually shifts to the left (away from the arrowhead) and the nail on the left side of the arrow moves towards the arrowhead. Answer figure 'C' completes the series.

4. **(B)** Problem figure PF/2 is obtained from PF/1 by rotating it anti – clockwise through 90°. Similarly, Answer figure (AF) 'B' is obtained from problem figure 3. Hence, AF/'B' completes the series.

5. **(B)** PF/2 is obtained from PF/1 by moving the arrows from side to side and dot from corner to corner. Similarly, AF/'B' is obtained from PF/3. Hence, AF/B completes the series.

6. **(B)** PF/2 is obtained from problem figure 1 by adding one nose. Similarly, AF/B is obtained from PF/B by adding two ears. Hence, AF/B completes the series.

7. **(A)** PF/2 is obtained from PF/1 by adding one quadrant and two horizontal lines. Similarly AF/'A' is obtained from PF/3. Hence, AF/'A' completes the series.

8. **(C)** PF/2 is obtained from PF/1 by adding similar dot and semi – circle on the right hand side. Similarly, AF/'C' is obtained from PF/3 by adding similar unit below the figure. Hence, AF/'C' completes the series.

9. **(A)** PF/2 is obtained from PF/1 by moving the entire figure clockwise through 90° and adding one small line. Similarly, AF/'A' is obtained from PF/3. Hence AF/'A' completes the series.

10. **(B)** PF/2 is obtained from PF/1 by rotating it clockwise through 90° and shading it. Similarly, AF/'B' is obtained from PF/3. Hence, AF/'B' complete the series.

11. **(D)** PF/2 is obtained from PF/1 by taking out circle and enclosing a new figure in it. Similarly, AF/'D' is obtained from PF/3. Hence, AF/'D' complete the series.

12. **(A)** PF/2 is obtained from PF/1 by turning the units through 90° anti – clockwise and changing the internal unit from + and ×. Similarly, AF/'A' is obtained from PF/3 by rotating it through 90° anti – clockwise. Hence, AF/'A' completes the series.

13. **(B)** PF/2 is obtained from PF/1 by removing one side of the hexagon, keeping the internal unit the same. Similarly, AF/'B' is obtained from PF/3. Hence, AF/'B' completes the series.

14. **(C)** PF/2 is obtained from PF/1 by moving the dot clockwise from one corner to another and moving the star anti – clockwise diagonally through the small square. Similarly, AF/'C' is obtained form PF/3. Hence, AF/'C' complete the series.

15. **(C)** PF/2 is obtained from PF/1 by taking out the inner geometrical figure outside and putting a new figure inside. Similarly, AF/'C' is obtained from PF/3. Hence, AF/'C' completes the series.

16. **(B)** PF/2 is obtained from PF/1 by rotating the figure clockwise through 90° and removing one diameter. Similarly, AF/'B' is obtained from PF/'B'. Hence, AF/'B' completes the series.

17. **(C)** PF/2 is obtained from PF/1 by rotating it anti – clockwise through 90°. Similarly, AF/'C' is obtained from PF/3. Hence, AF/'C' completes the series.

18. **(C)** PF/2 is obtained from PF/1 by rotating it clockwise through 90°. Similarly, AF/'C' is obtained from PF/3. Hence, AF/'C' completes the series.

19. **(A)** PF/2 is obtained from PF/1 by removing one '>' symbol to the right. Similarly, AF/A is obtained from PF/3. Hence, AF/A completes the series.

20. **(B)** PF/2 is obtained from PF/1 by moving its symbols to the left in cyclic order. Similarly AF/'B' is obtained from PF/3. Hence, AF/B completes the series.

21. **(C)** PF/2 is obtained from PF/1 by moving the bud clockwise from one vertex to another and adding one small circle at the centre. Similarly, AF/'C' is obtained from PF/3. Hence, AF/'C' completes the series.

22. **(B)** PF/2 is obtained from PF/1 by increasing one side to the figure and shading the right side of the new figure (Square) formed. Similarly, AF/'B' is obtained from PF/3. Hence, AF/'B' completes the series.

23. **(C)** PF/2 is obtained from PF/1 by rotating all the four geometrical figures clockwise through 90° and the arrow anti-clockwise through 90°. Similarly, AF/'C' is obtained from PF/3. Hence, AF/'C' completes the series.

24. **(B)** PF/1 is obtained from PF/2 by removing the rings and crosses from the middle two rows. Similarly, AF/'B' is obtained from PF/3. Hence, AF/'B' completes the series.

25. **(A)** PF/2 obtained from PF/1 by rotating symbol in the circle anti-clockwise through 45° and the blank ring clockwise through 90°. Similarly, AF/'A' is obtained from PF/3. Hence, AF/'A' completes the series.

26. **(C)** PF/2 is obtained from PF/1 by adding one line in a set manner. Similarly, AF/'C' is obtained from PF/3. Hence, AF/'C' completes the series.

27. **(D)** PF/2 is obtained from PF/1 by rotating the die clockwise through 180° through 180° and adding one dot. Similarly, AF/'D' is obtained from PF/3. Hence, AF/'D' completes the series.

28. **(A)** PF/2 is obtained from PF/1 by removing one arc from the right and one arc from the left. Similarly, AF/'A' is obtained from PF/3. Hence, AF/'A' completes the series.

29. **(B)** PF/2 is obtained from PF/1 by moving the internal units clockwise through length side of the square and replacing them by equal number of new units. Similarly, AF/'B' is obtained from PF/3. Hence, AF/'B' completes the series.

30. **(B)** PF/2 is obtained from PF/1 by inverting its internal unit and moving it to the opposite side. Similarly, AF/'B' is obtained from PF/3. Hence, AF/'B' completes the series.

31. **(D)** PF/2 is obtained from PF/1 by rotating its internal units anti-clockwise through 90° and rotating its lines anti-clockwise through 45°. Similarly, AF/'D' is obtained from PF/3. Hence, AF/'D' completes the series.

32. **(C)** PF/3 is obtained from PF/1 by inverting it. Similarly, AF/'C' is obtained from PF/2 by inverting it. Hence, AF/'C' completes the series.

33. **(D)** PF/2 is obtained from PF/1 by moving each unit clockwise through length-side of the square and adding a new unit. Similarly, AF/'D' is obtained from PF/3. Hence, AF/'D' completes the series.

34. **(C)** PF/2 is obtained from PF/1 by interchanging the upper unit and moving the bottom left unit clockwise through length-side of the square and bringing a new unit at bottom left corner. Similarly, AF/'C' is obtained from PF/3. Hence, AF/'C' completes the series.

35. **(D)** PF/2 is obtained from PF/1 by moving top left unit to the centre and central unit to the bottom right and bringing a

new unit at top left. Similarly, AF/'D' is obtained from PF/3. Hence, AF/'D' completes the series.

36. **(B)** PF/2 is obtained from PF/1 by moving the bottom unit at the centre, central unit at the top and top unit at the bottom. Similarly, AF/'B' is obtained from PF/3. Hence, AF/'B' completes the series.

37. **(B)** PF/2 is obtained from PF/1 by keeping top left unit fixed; moved top right unit clockwise through length-side of the square and moving bottom left unit to the opposite corner, and replacing it by a new unit. Similarly, AF/'B' is obtained from PF/3 by bottom right unit fixed moving bottom left unit clockwise through length-side of the square and moving the top right unit to the opposite corner and replacing it by a new unit. Hence, AF/'B' completes the series.

38. **(B)** PF/2 obtained from problem figure 1 by rotating it clockwise through 45°. Similarly, AF/'B' is obtained from PF/3. Hence AF/'B' completes the series.

39. **(C)** PF/2 is obtained from PF/1 by rotating it clockwise through 45°. Similarly, AF/'C' is obtained from PF/3. Hence, AF/'C' completes the series.

40. **(B)** Corners of the lower inverted triangle is shaded turn by turn. No part of the upper triangle is shaded. AF/'B' which is similar to PF/1. completes the series.

41. **(B)** The size of the dark (end) figure increases continuously and the line in this figure rotates anti-clockwise through 45° each time. Hence, AF/'B' completes the series.

42. **(B)** PF/2 is obtained from PF/1 by rotating the hexagon through 90° and adding one line inside it. Similarly, AF/'B' is obtained from PF/3. Hence, AF/'B' completes the series.

43. **(B)** With every turn a quarter of the square is shed off clockwise, AF/'B' completes the series.

44. **(D)** PF/2 is obtained form PF/1 by rotating it anti-clockwise through 45°. Similarly, AF/'D' is obtained from PF/3. Hence AF/'D' completes the series.

45. **(B)** The mouths of the problem figure open more and more. PF/'B' complete the series.

46. **(B)** Every time a ball on the arc is added a little circle appears in the next figure when another little line is already ready. AF/'B' completes the series.

47. **(C)** PF/3 is obtained from PF/1 by rotating one unit clockwise through 90° and the other unit anti-clockwise through 90°. Similarly, AF/'C' is obtained from PF/3. Hence, AF/'C' completes the series.

48. **(C)** PF/3 is obtained from PF/1 by adding 2 big circles and one small circle in a set order. Similarly, AF/'C' is obtained from PF/3. Hence. AF/'C' completes the series.

49. **(B)** PF/3 is obtained from PF/1 by inverting it and adding one angle (A) in a set order. Similarly, AF/'B' is obtained from PF/3. Hence, AF/'B' completes the series.

50. **(B)** PF/3 is obtained by PF/1 by moving the triangle and small circle downward through half the length of the side of arrow. Similarly AF/'B' is obtained from PF/3. Hence, AF/'B' completes the series.

51. **(A)** Each problem figure is obtained from its previous problem figure by rotating it clockwise through 90° and removing half line in a set order. Similarly, AF/'A' is obtained from PF/4. Hence, AF/'A' complete the series.

52. **(C)** PF/3 is obtained from PF/1 by inverting and bringing two lines in it at right angle in a set order. Similarly, AF/'C' is obtained from PF/3. Hence, AF/'C' completes the series.

53. **(B)** PF/3 is obtained from PF/1 by rotating one arrow clockwise through 90° and the other arrow anti-clockwise through 90°. Similarly, AF/'B' is obtained from PF/3. Hence, AF/'B' completes the series.

•••

General Knowledge
(Sc & SST)

2

Indian History

INDUS VALLEY CIVILISATION (2500-1750 BC)

- The earliest excavations in the Indus valley were done at Harappa in the West Punjab and Mohanjodaro in Sindh. Both places are now in Pakistan.

Important Sites

- The most important sites are Kot Diji in Sindh, Kalibangan in Rajasthan, Ropar in the Punjab, Banawali in Haryana, Lothal, Surkotada and Dhaulavira, all the three in Gujarat.
- Mohanjodaro is the largest of all the Indus cities and it is estimated to have spread over an area of 200 hectares.

Salient Features of the Harappan Culture

- The Harappan Civilization was primarily Urban.
- Mohanjodaro and Harappa were the planned cities.
- The large-scale use of burnt bricks in almost all kinds of constructions are the important characteristics of the Harappan culture.
- Another remarkable feature was the underground drainage system connecting all houses to the street drains which were covered by stone slabs or bricks.
- The most important public place of Mohanjodaro is the Great Bath measuring 39 feet length, 23 feet breadth and 8 feet depth.
- Agriculture was the most important occupation. In the fertile soils, farmers cultivated two crops a year. They were the first who had grown paddy.
- Wheat and barley were the main crops grown besides sesame, mustard and cotton.
- Animals like sheep, goats and buffalo were domesticated. The use of horse is not yet firmly established.
- Bronze and copper vessels are the outstanding examples of the Harappan metal craft.
- A large number of seals numbering more than 2000 have been discovered.

Social Life

- Jewelleries such as bangles, bracelets, fillets, girdles, anklets, ear-rings and finger rings were worn by women. These ornaments were made of gold, silver, copper, bronze and semi precious stones.
- Fishing was a regular occupation while hunting and bull fighting were other pastimes.
- Manufacture of terracotta (burnt clay) was a major industry of the people.
- Figures of animals such as sacred bull and dove were discovered. The figures of Mother Goddesses were used for religious purposes.
- Most of the inscriptions were engraved on seals. It is interesting to note that the Indus script has not yet been deciphered.
- The Pipal tree was used as a religious symbol.
- The origin of the 'Swastika' symbol can be traced to the Harrapan Civilization.
- The chief male deity was Pasupati, (proto-Siva) represented in seals as sitting in a yogic posture with three faces and two horns.

4

THE VEDIC PERIOD

RIG VEDIC AGE (1500 - 1000 B.C.)

- The Early Vedic period is known from the *Rig Veda*.
- The Rig Veda refers to Saptasindhu or the land of seven rivers. This includes the five rivers of the Punjab, namely, Jhelum, Chenab, Ravi, Beas and Sutlej along with the Indus and Saraswathi.
- Historians view that the Aryans came from Central Asia. They entered India through the Khyber pass between 2000 B.C. and 1500 B.C. They first settled in seven places in the Punjab region which they called Sapta Sindhu. Slowly, they moved towards the Gangetic Valley.
- The Aryan Civilisation was a rural civilisation.

Vedic Literature

- The word 'Veda' is derived from the root 'vid', which means to know and signifies 'superior knowledge'.
- The Vedic literature consists of the four Vedas – Rig, Yajur, Sama and Atharva.
- The *Rig Veda* is the earliest of the four Vedas divided into 10 mandalas and it consists of 1028 hymns. The hymns were sung by *Hotri* in praise of various gods.
- The *Yajur Veda* consists of various details of rules to be observed at the time of sacrifice. Its hymns were recited by *Adharvayus*.
- The *Sama Veda* is set to tune for the purpose of chanting during sacrifice. It is called the book of chants and the origins of Indian music are traced in it. Its hymns were recited by *Udgatri*.
- The *Atharva Veda* contains details of rituals.
- Besides the Vedas, there are other sacred works like the Brahmanas, the Aranyakas, the Upanishads, and the epics Ramayana and Mahabharata.

Political Organisation

- During this period, the kingdom was tribal in character. Each tribe formed a separate kingdom.
- The basic unit of political organisation was *kula* or family.
- The highest political unit was called *jana* or tribe.

- There were several tribal kingdoms during the Rig Vedic period such as Bharatas, Matsyas, Yadus and Purus. The head of the kingdom was called as *rajan* or king.
- There were two popular bodies called the *Sabha* and *Samiti*. The former seems to have been a council of elders and the latter, a general assembly of the entire people.

Social Life

- Family was the basis of the society.
- The head of the family was known as *grihapathi*.

Economic Condition

- The Rig Vedic Aryans were pastoral people and their main occupation was cattle rearing. Their wealth was estimated in terms of their cattle.
- Carpentry was another important profession.

Religion

- The important Rig Vedic gods were Prithvi (Earth), Agni (Fire), Vayu (Wind), Varuna (Rain) and Indra (Thunder).
- Indra was the most popular among them during the early Vedic period.
- There were also female gods like Aditi and Ushas. There were no temples and no idol worship during the early Vedic period.

LATER VEDIC PERIOD (1000–600 B.C.)

- This age is also called as the Epic Age because the two great epics the Ramayana and Mahabharata were written during this period.
- The Sama, Yajur, Atharva Vedas, Brahmanas, Aranyakas, Upanishads and the two epics are the sources of information for this period.

Political Organisation

- Larger kingdoms were formed during the later Vedic period.
- The king performed various rituals and sacrifices to strengthen his position. They include Rajasuya (consecration ceremony), Asvamedha (horse sacrifice) and Vajpeya (chariot race).
- Kingship became hereditary.
- Kings assumed titles like Ekrat, Samrat and Sarvabauma.

Economic Condition

- Iron was used extensively in this period and this enabled the people to clear forests and to bring more land under cultivation. Agriculture became the chief occupation.
- Taxes like Pali, Sulk and Bhaga were collected from the people.
- Wealth was calculated in terms of cows.

Social Life

- The four divisions of society (Brahmins, Kshatriyas, Vaisyas and Sudras) or the Varna system was thoroughly established during the Later Vedic period.
- The Ashrama system was formed to attain 4 purusharthas. They were *Dharma*, *Artha*, *Kama* and *Moksha*.

Religion

- Gods of the Early Vedic period like Indra and Agni lost their importance. Prajapathi (the creator), Vishnu (the protector) and Rudra (the destroyer) became prominent during the Later Vedic period.

JAINISM AND BUDDHISM

JAINISM

- Jainism originated in the 6th century B.C. It rejected Vedic religion and avoided its rituals.
- Founded by Rishabha Deva. Rishabha Deva was succeeded by 23 Thirthankaras (prophets). Mahavira was the 24th Thirthankara.

Vardhamana Mahavira (540-468 B.C.)

- Vardhamana was born in a village called Kundagrama near Vaishali in Bihar.
- His father was *Siddhartha*. He was the head of a famous Kshatriya clan.
- His mother was *Trisala*. She was a princess of the Lichchhavi clan. She was the sister of the ruler of Vaishali.
- Vardhamana was married to Yasoda, a princess. They had a daughter.
- At the age of 30, he left his home and family. He became an ascetic (monk). He wandered from place-to place in search of truth for 12 years.
- In the 13th year of his penance, he attained the highest spiritual knowledge called Kevalya Jnana.

Thereafter, he was called Mahavira and Jina. His followers were called Jains and his religion Jainism.

- He died at the age of 72 in 468 B.C. at a place called Pavapuri near modern Rajgir.

Teachings of Jainism

- The three principles of Jainism, also known as Triratnas (three gems), are:
  1. right faith.
  2. right knowledge.
  3. right conduct.
- Mahavira preached his disciples to follow the five principles. They are:
  1. Ahimsa—not to injure any living beings
  2. Satya—to speak the truth
  3. Asteya—not to steal
  4. Tyag—not to own property
  5. Brahmacharia—to lead a virtuous life.

Spread of Jainism

- Mahavira preached his religion in Prakrit language which was the language of the masses.
- Chandragupta Maurya, Kharavela of Kalinga and the royal dynasties of south India such as the Gangas, the Kadambas, the Chalukyas and the Rashtrakutas patronised Jainism.
- Jainism was divided into two sects after Vallabhi Council, namely *Svetambaras* (wearing white dresses) under Sthulbhadra and *Digambaras* (naked) under Bhadrabahu.
- The first Jain Council was convened at Pataliputra by Sthulabahu, the leader of the *Digambaras*, in the beginning of the 3rd century B.C.
- The second Jain Council was held at Valabhi in 5th century A.D. The final compilation of Jain literature called Twelve Angas was completed in this council.

BUDDHISM

Gautama Buddha (563-483 B.C.)

- Buddha's original name was *Siddhartha*.
- Siddhartha was born in the Lumbini Garden near Kapilavastu in Nepal. His father was Suddhodana. He was a Sakya chief of Kapilavastu. His mother, Mayadevi, died when Siddhartha was only seven days old. He was brought up by his step mother Mahaprajapati Gauthami.

- At the age of sixteen Siddhartha, married Yasodhara and gave birth to a son, Rahul.
- The sight of an old man, a diseased man, a corpse and an ascetic turned him away from worldly life. He left home at the age of twenty-nine in search of Truth.
- He wandered for seven years and at last, he sat under a bodhi tree at Bodh Gaya and did intense penance, after which he got Enlightenment (Nirvana) at the age of thirty-five. Since then, he became known as the Buddha or 'the Enlightened One'.
- Buddha delivered his first sermon at Sarnath near Banaras (now Varanasi).
- He died at the age of 80 in 483 B.C. at Kushinagar in Uttar Pradesh.

Teachings of Buddha

- The Four Noble Truths of Buddha are:
  1. The world is full of suffering.
  2. The cause of suffering is desire.
  3. If desires are get rid off, suffering can be removed.
  4. This can be done by following the Eightfold Path.
- The Eightfold Path consists of:
  1. Right Thought.
  2. Right Belief.
  3. Right Speech.
  4. Right Action.
  5. Right Living.
  6. Right Efforts.
  7. Right Knowledge.
  8. Right Meditation.

DYNASTIES OF ANCIENT INDIA

HARYANKA DYNASTY

- Bimbisara was the founder of Haryanka Dynasty.
- He was a contemporary of both Vardhamana Mahavira and Gautama Buddha.
- During his rule, Darius I, the Achaemenian emperor, conquered the Indus Valley area.
- Ajatasatru imprisoned his father Bimbisara.
- The first Buddhist Council was convened by Ajatasatru at Rajgir.
- The immediate successor of Ajatasatru was Udayin.

- Udayin laid the foundation of the new capital at Pataliputra situated at the confluence of the two rivers, the Ganges and the Son.
- Shishunaga was the founder of Shishunaga dynasty.
- After Shishunaga, the mighty empire began to collapse. His successor was Kakavarman or Kalasoka. During his reign, the second Buddhist Council was held at Vaishali.
- Kalasoka was killed by the founder of the Nanda dynasty.

NANDAS

- The fame of Magadha scaled new heights under the Nanda dynasty.
- Mahapadmananda was the founder of Nanda rule in Magadha.
- The last Nanda ruler was Dhana Nanda. Alexander invaded India during his rule.

MAURYAN EMPIRE

CHANDRAGUPTA MAURYA (322–298 B.C.)

- Chandragupta Maurya was the founder of the Mauryan Empire. He overthrew Nanda dynasty with the help of Chanakya.
- Chandragupta defeated Seleukos Nikator, the Greek general of Alexander, in a battle in 305 B.C.
- Seleukos sent Megasthenes as Greek Ambassador to the Court of Chandra-gupta. Megasthenes wrote *Indica*.
- Chandragupta was a follower of Jainism.
- He came to Sravana Belgola, near Mysore with a Jain monk called Bhadrabahu. The hill in which he lived until his death is called Chandragiri.
- Chanakya served as prime minister during the reigns of Chandragupta and Bindusara.

BINDUSARA (298–273 B.C.)

- Chandragupta Maurya was succeeded by his son Bindusara.
- Bindusara was called by the Greeks as "*Amitragatha*" meaning, slayer of enemies.

ASHOKA (273–232 B.C.)

- Ashoka was the most famous ruler of the Mauryan dynasty.
- The most important event of Ashoka's reign was his victorious war with Kalinga in 261 B.C.

- Ashoka convened the Third Buddhist Council at Pataliputra around 250 B.C. in order to strengthen the *Sangha*. It was presided over by Moggaliputta Tissa.
- Ashoka's edicts and inscriptions were deciphered by James Prinsep in 1837.
- The last Mauryan king, Brahadratha was killed by his minister Pushyamitra Sunga. It put an end to the Mauryan Empire.

SUNGAS

- The founder of the Sunga dynasty was *Pushyamitra Sunga*, who was the commander-in-chief under the Mauryas.
- He ascended the throne of Magadha in 185 B.C.
- Pushyamitra was a staunch follower of Brahmanism. He performed two asvamedha sacrifices.
- After the death of Pushyamitra, his son Agnimitra became the ruler.
- Agnimitra was a great conqueror. He was also the hero of the play Malavikagnimitram written by Kalidasa.

KANVA

- The last Sunga ruler was Devabhuti, who was murdered by his minister Vasudeva Kanva, the founder of the *Kanva dynasty*.
- The Kanva dynasty ruled for 45 years. After the fall of the Kanvas, the history of Magadha was a blank until the establishment of the Gupta dynasty.

SATAVAHANAS

- The founder of the Satavahana dynasty was Simuka.
- The greatest ruler of the Satavahana dynasty was *Gautamiputra Satakarni*.
- The greatest port of the Satavahanas was Kalyani on the west Deccan. Gandakasela and Ganjam on the east coast were the other important seaports.
- The fine painting at Amaravathi and Nagarjunakonda caves belong to this period.

GUPTA PERIOD

- The Gupta period is considered as the *Golden Age* in the history of India because this period witnessed all round developments in Religion, Literature, Science, Art and Architecture.

CHANDRAGUPTA I (320-334 A.D.)

- In the beginning of the 4th Century A.D., Sri Gupta established a small Kingdom at Pataliputra. He is considered as the founder of the Gupta dynasty.
- The first notable ruler of the Gupta dynasty was Chandragupta I. He assumed the title *Maharajadhiraja*. The Meherauli Iron Pillar inscription mentions his extensive conquests.
- Chandragupta I is considered to be the founder of the Gupta era which starts with his accession in A.D. 320.

SAMUDRAGUPTA (335-380 A.D.)

- Samudragupta was the greatest of the rulers of the Gupta dynasty. The Allahabad Pillar inscription provides a detailed account of his reign.

Gold Coins of Samudragupta

- Because of his military achievements, Samudragupta was hailed as *'Indian Napoleon'*.

CHANDRAGUPTA II (380-414 A.D.)

- Samudragupta was succeeded by his son Chandragupta II Vikramaditya.
- The greatest of the military achievements of Chandragupta II was his war against the Saka *satraps* of western India.
- The famous Chinese pilgrim, Fahien visited India (A.D. 399 - A.D. 414) during the reign of Chandragupta II.

SUCCESSORS OF CHANDRAGUPTA II

- Kumaragupta (415-455) was the son and successor of Chandragupta II. His reign was marked by general peace and prosperity.
- Kumaragupta was the founder of the Nalanda University.
- Kumaragupta was followed by *Skandagupta* who ruled from A.D. 456 to A.D. 468.
- After Skandagupta's death, many of his successors like Purugupta, Narasimhagupta, Buddhagupta and Baladitya could not save the Gupta empire from the Huns. Ultimately, the Gupta power totally disappeared due to the Hun invasions and later by the rise of Yasodharman in Malwa.

MEDIEVAL INDIA

SULTANATE PERIOD

SLAVE DYNASTY (1206-1290)

- The Slave dynasty was also called Mamluk dynasty. Mamluk was the Quranic term for slave.

Qutb-ud-din Aibak

- Qutb-ud-din Aibak was a slave of Muhammad Ghori, who made him the Governor of his Indian possessions.
- After the death of Ghori in 1206, Aibak declared his independence. He assumed the title Sultan and made Lahore his capital.
- Muslim writers call Aibak Lakh Baksh or giver of lakhs because he gave liberal donations to them.
- He built the famous Quwat-Ul-Islam mosque at Delhi. He began the construction of the famous Qutb Minar at Delhi but did not live long to complete it. It was later completed by Iltutmish.

Iltutmish (1210-1236 A.D.)

- Iltutmish belonged to the Ilbari tribe and hence his dynasty was named as Ilbari dynasty.
- He shifted his capital from Lahore to Delhi.
- He organised the *Iqta system* and introduced reforms in civil administration and army.

Raziya (1236-1240 A.D.)

- She appointed an Abyssinian slave Yakuth as Master of the Royal Horses.
- In 1240, Altunia, the governor of Bhatinda revolted against her. She went in personally to suppress the revolt but Altunia killed Yakuth and took Raziya prisoner.
- Bahram Shah, son of Iltutmish killed her.

Balban (1266-1286 A.D.)

- Balban introduced rigorous court discipline and new customs such as prostration and kissing the Sultan's feet to prove his superiority over the nobles.
- He also introduced the Persian festival of *Nauroz* to impress the nobles and people with his wealth and power.
- He established a separate military department - *diwan-i-arz* – and reorganized the army.

KHILJI DYNASTY (1290-1320 A.D.)

- The founder of the Khilji dynasty was Jalaluddin Khilji.
- Ala-ud-din Khilji was the greatest ruler of the Khilji Dynasty.
- He was the first Muslim ruler to extend his empire right upto Rameshwaram in the South.
- The Sultan had built a new city called Siri near Delhi.
- Amir Khusrau the great Persian poet, patronised by Balban, continued to live in Ala-ud-din Khilji's court also.
- He introduced the system of *dagh* (branding of horses) and prepared *huliya* (descriptive list of soldiers).
- Ala-ud-din Khilji maintained a large permanent standing army and paid them in cash from the royal treasury.

TUGHLAQ DYNASTY

- Ghiyas-ud-din Tughlaq was the founder of the Tughlaq dynasty.
- To have the capital at the centre of the empire and safe from the Mongol raids, Tughlaq chose Devagiri as his new capital in A.D. 1327. The Sultan renamed the new capital Daulatabad.
- In 1329-30, Muhammad-bin-Tughlaq introduced a token currency.
- Firoz Shah Tughlaq became Sultan after the death of Muhammad-bin-Tughlaq in A.D. 1351.
- He was the first Sultan to impose irrigation tax.
- He had built new towns of Firozabad, Jaunpur, Hissar and Firozpur.
- Timur Mongol leader of Central Asia, ordered general massacre in Delhi (AD 1398) at the time of Nasiruddin Mahmud (later Tughlaq king).

SAYYID DYNASTY

- Before his departure from India, Timur appointed Khizr Khan as governor of Multan. He captured Delhi and founded the Sayyid dynasty in 1414.
- Mubarak Shah, Mohammed Shah and Alam Shah were some of the other important noteworthy rulers of Sayyid Dynasty.

LODI DYNASTY

- The Lodis were Afghans.
- Bahlol Lodi was the first Afghan ruler while his predecessors were all Turks. He died in 1489 and was succeeded by his son, Sikandar Lodi.
- In 1504, Sikandar Lodi founded the city of Agra and transferred his capital from Delhi to Agra.
- Babar marched against Delhi and defeated and killed Ibrahim Lodi in the first battle of Panipat (1526).

MUGHAL EMPIRE
(1526-1707 AD)

BABAR (1526-1530 AD)

- Babar was the founder of the Mughal Empire in India.
- On 21st April, 1526 the first Battle of Panipat took place between Babar and Ibrahim Lodi, who was killed in the battle.
- Babar was the first one to use guns or artillery in a battle on the Indian soil.
- Babar defeated Rama Sanga of Mewar in the battle of Kanwah in A.D. 1527.
- Babar was a soldier-scholar and wrote his own autobiography called Babar Nama in Turkish language.

HUMAYUN (1530-1556 AD)

- Sher Shah defeated Humayun at *Chausa in A.D. 1539* and again at Kannauj in A.D. 1540.
- After losing his kingdom, Humayun became an exile for the next fifteen years.
- In 1555, Humayun defeated the Afghans and recovered the Mughal throne. After six months, he died in 1556 due to his fall from the staircase of his library.
- *Gulbadan Begum*, Humayun's half-sister wrote *Humayun-nama*.

SHER SHAH SURI

- The founder of the Sur dynasty was Sher Shah, whose original name was Farid.
- Sher Shah became the ruler of Delhi in 1540.
- Sher Shah organized a brilliant administrative system. The central government consisted of several departments.

- He built a new city on the banks of the river Yamuna near Delhi. Now the old fort called Purana Quila and its mosque is alone surviving.
- He built a Mausoleum at Sasaram, which is considered as one of the master pieces of Indian architecture.

AKBAR (1556-1605 AD)

- When Akbar ascended the throne in A.D. 1556 he was only 14 years old. His guardian Bairam Khan served him as a faithful minister and tutor.
- Bairam Khan, along with Akbar met Hemu in the second Battle of Panipat in 1556. Hemu was initially successful, but lost his consciousness after an arrow hit him. Akbar killed him.
- The Battle of Haldighati was fought between Rana Pratap and Mughal army led by Man Singh in 1576. Some historian say that this battle was indecisive but some say that Rana Pratap was defeated.
- Akbar abolished the pilgrim tax and in 1562, he abolished Jaziya.
- Akbar evolved a new faith called Din-i-Illahi or Divine Faith.

JAHANGIR (1605-1627 AD)

- When Akbar died, Prince Salim succeeded with the title Jahangir (Conqueror of World) in 1605.
- Jahangir's eldest son, Khusrau, rebelled against him. He was arrested and put into prison. *Guru Arjun Dev, the fifth Sikh Guru* was executed by Jahangir.
- In 1611, Jahangir married Mehrunnisa who was known as Nurjahan (Light of World).
- Jahangir died in A.D. 1627.

SHAHJAHAN (1628-1658 AD)

- The reign of Shahjahan is generally considered as the *Golden Age* of the Mughal period.
- Shahjahan is called as the *Prince of Builders*. He had built the Jama Masjid and *Red Fort* in Delhi and Taj Mahal in Agra.
- Fine arts like painting, music and literature reached high level of development during Shahjahan's time.

AURANGAZEB (1658-1707 AD)

- Aurangazeb was the last great Mughal ruler. He ascended the throne after killing his three brothers Dara, Shuja and Murad in a fratricidal war.
- Aurangazeb defeated Sikandar Shah of Bijapur and annexed his kingdom.

- Aurangazeb was against the Sikhs and he executed the ninth Sikh Guru Tegh Bahadur.
- He was called *Darvesh* or a *Zinda Pir*. He forbade *Sati*. Conquered Bijapur (AD 1686) and Golconda (AD 1687) and reimposed Jaziya and Pilgrim tax in AD 1679.
- He built *Biwi ka Makbara* on the tomb of his queen *Rabaud-Durani* at Aurangabad; *Moti Masjid* within Red Fort, Delhi; and the Jami or Badshahi Mosque at Lahore.
- Aurangazeb died in A.D. 1707.

THE MARATHAS

SHIVAJI (1627-1680 AD)

- Shivaji was born at Shivner in 1627. His father was Shahji Bhonsle and mother Jija Bai.
- His religious teacher was Samarth Ramdas and guardian was Dadaji Kondadev.
- In 1674, Shivaji crowned himself at Raigarh and assumed the title Chatrapathi.

- *Ashtapradhan* (eight ministers) helped in administration. These were Peshwas, Sar-i-Naubat (Military), Mazumdar or Amatya (Accounts); Waqenavis (Intelligence); Surnavis (Correspondence); *Dabir* or *Sumanta* (Ceremonies); *Nyayadhish* (Justice); and *Panditrao* (Charity).
- Successors of Shivaji were Shambhaji, Rajaram and *Shahu* (fought at Battle of Khed in AD 1708).

THE PESHWAS

- Balaji Vishwanath was the first Peshwa. He began his career as a small revenue official and became Peshwa in 1713.
- Baji Rao I was the eldest son of Balaji Vishwanath. He was considered as the "greatest exponent of guerilla tactics after Shivaji".
- It was during reign of Balaji Baji Rao (Nanasaheb) when the Marathas lost the Third Battle of Panipat.
- Baji Rao II (last Peshwa) was the first Maratha to have fled from the British attacks instead of fighting with them. Baji Rao II surrendered to Sir John Malcom.

MODERN INDIA

THE ADVENT OF THE EUROPEANS

THE PORTUGUESE

- Vasco-da-Gama, a Portuguese explorer, sailed through the route of cape of Good Hope and reached near Calicut on 20th May 1498 A.D. during the reign of King Zamorin (Hindu King of Calicut).
- Vasco-da-Gama founded a factory at Cannanore on his second visit to India in 1501. In due course, Calicut, Cochin and Cannanore became the Portuguese trading centres.
- Francisco Almeida came to India in 1505. He was the first Governor of Portuguese possessions in India.
- The real founder of Portuguese power in India was *Alfonso de Albuquerque*. He captured Goa from the rulers of Bijapur in 1510. It was made their headquarters.

THE DUTCH

- The United East India Company of the Netherlands founded a factory at Masulipatnam in 1605. They built their first fort on the main land of India at Pulicut in 1609, near Madras (Chennai). They captured Nagapattinam from the Portuguese.
- They made Agra, Surat, Masulipatnam and Chinsura in Bengal as their trading centres.

THE DANES

- The Danish East India Company was established in 1616 in Denmark.
- They came to South India and founded a factory at Tranquebar (Tharangambadi) in 1620. They also made settlements at Serampore near Calcutta (Kolkata).

THE ENGLISH

- The English East India Company was formed in 1599 under a charter granted by Queen Elizabeth in 1600.
- The East India Company sent Sir William Hawkins to the court of the Mughal Emperor Jahangir in 1609 to obtain permission to erect a factory at Surat.
- In 1615, Sir Thomas Roe, another British merchant, came to Jahangir's court. He stayed for

- three years and succeeded in getting permission to set up their trading centres at Agra, Surat, Ahmedabad and Broach.
- In 1690, the British got permission from Aurangazeb to build a factory on the site of Calcutta. In 1696 a fort was built at that place. It was called Fort William.

THE FRENCH
- The French East India Company was established in 1664 under the inspiring and energetic leadership of Colbert, the economic adviser of the French King Louis XIV.
- In 1667, the first French factory was established at Surat by Francis Caron who was nominated as Director-General.
- French were defeated by English in *Battle of Wandiwash* (1760).

NATIONAL MOVEMENT (1885-1947)

INDIAN NATIONAL CONGRESS (1885)
- Allan Octavian Hume, a retired civil servant in the British Government took the initiative to form an all-India organization. Thus, the Indian National Congress was founded and its first session was held at Bombay in 1885. W.C. Banerjee was its first president. It was attended by 72 delegates from all over India.
- The second session was held in Calcutta in 1886 and the third in Madras in 1887.
- Between 1885 and 1905, the Congress leaders were moderates. The Moderates had faith in the British justice and goodwill. They were called moderates because they adopted peaceful and constitutional means to achieve their demands.
- In 1905, Gopal Krishna Gokhale founded the Servants of India Society to train Indians to dedicate their lives to the cause of the country.

Partition of Bengal (1905)
- By Lord Curzon on 16th October, 1905 through a royal proclamation, reducing the old province of Bengal in size by creating East Bengal and Assam out of the rest of Bengal.
- The partition of Bengal in 1905 provided a spark for the rise of extremism in the Indian National Movement.

- Curzon's real motives behind this partition were:
  - To break the growing strength of Bengali nationalism since Bengal was the base of Indian nationalism.
  - To divide the Hindus and Muslims in Bengal.
  - To show the enormous power of the British Government in doing whatever it liked.

Swadeshi Movement (1905)
- The Swadeshi Movement involved programmes like the boycott of government service, courts, schools and colleges and of foreign goods. It was both a political and economic movement.
- Lal, Bal, Pal and Aurobindo Ghosh played an important role.

Muslim League (1906)
- In December 1906, Muslim delegates from all over India met at Dacca for the Muslim Educational Conference.
- Taking advantage of this occasion, Nawab Salimullah of Dacca proposed the setting up of an organisation to look after the Muslim interests. The proposal was accepted.
- The All-India Muslim League was finally set up on December 30, 1906.

Minto Morley Reforms (1909)
- Minto, the Viceroy and Morley, the Secretary of State for India jointly proposed reforms to the Indian Councils. An Act, called the Indian Councils Act or the Minto-Morley Reforms Act was passed in 1909.
- A separate communal electorate was introduced for the Muslims.

The Lucknow Pact (1916)
- During the 1916 Congress session at Lucknow two major events occurred. The divided Congress became united. An understanding for joint action against the British was reached between the Congress and the Muslim League and it was called the Lucknow Pact.
- The signing of the Lucknow Pact by the Congress and the Muslim League in 1916 marked an important step in the Hindu-Muslim unity.

The Home Rule Movement (1916)
- Two Home Rule Leagues were established, one by B.G. Tilak at Poona in April 1916 and the other by Mrs. Annie Besant at Madras in September 1916.

- While Tilak's Movement concentrated on Maharashtra, Annie Besant's Movement covered the rest of the country.

Rowlatt Act (1919)

- In 1917, a committee was set up under the presidentship of Sir Sydney Rowlatt to look into the militant Nationalist activities. On the basis of its report the Rowlatt Act was passed in March 1919 by the Central Legislative Council. As per this Act, any person could be arrested on the basis of suspicion. No appeal or petition could be filed against such arrests.
- This Act was called the Black Act and it was widely opposed. An all-India hartal was organized on 6 April, 1919.

Jallianwala Bagh Massacre (13 April, 1919)

- On 13th April, the Baisakhi day (harvest festival), a public meeting was organized at the Jallianwala Bagh (garden). Gen. Dyer marched in and without any warning opened fire on the crowd. The firing continued for about 10 to 15 minutes and it stopped only after the ammunition exhausted.
- According to official report 379 people were killed and 1137 wounded in the incident. There was a nationwide protest against this massacre and Rabindranath Tagore renounced his knighthood as a protest.

Khilafat Movement (1920)

- The chief cause of the Khilafat Movement was the defeat of Turkey in the First World War.
- The Muslims in India were upset over the British attitude against Turkey and launched the Khilafat Movement.
- Ali brothers, *Mohd Ali* and *Shaukat Ali* started this movement. It was jointly led by the Khilafat leaders and the Congress.

Non-Co-operation Movement (1920-22)

- Mahatma Gandhi announced his plan to begin Non-Cooperation with the government as a sequel to the Rowlatt Act, Jallianwala Bagh massacre and the Khilafat Movement. It was approved by the Indian National Congress at the Nagpur session in December, 1920.
- The Congress observed the Non-Co-operation movement in 1920. The main aim of this movement was to attain Swaraj through non-violent and peaceful means.

- The whole movement was abruptly called off on 11th February, 1922 by Gandhi following the Chauri-Chaura incident in the Gorakhpur district of U.P. Many top leaders of the country were stunned at this sudden suspension of the Non-Co-operation Movement.
- On 5th February an angry mob set fire to the police station at *Chauri-Chaura* and twenty two police men were burnt to death.

Swaraj Party

- Leaders like Motilal Nehru and Chittranjan Das formed a separate group within the Congress known as the Swaraj Party on 1 January, 1923.
- The Swarajists wanted to contest the council elections and wreck the government from within.

Simon Commission (1927)

- The Act of 1919 included a provision for its review after a lapse of ten years. However, the review commission under the chairmanship of Sir John Simon was appointed by the British Government two years earlier of its schedule in 1927.
- Indian leaders opposed the commission, as there were no Indians in it, they cried *Simon Go Back*.
- The government used brutal repression and at Lahore, *Lala Lajpat Rai* was severely beaten in lathi-charge.

Lahore Session (1929)

- On Dec. 19, 1929, under the Presidentship of J.L. Nehru, the INC, as its Lahore session, declared Poorna Swaraj (Complete Independence) as its ultimate goal.
- On Dec. 31, 1929, the newly adopted tricolour flag was unfurled and Jan. 26, 1930 was fixed as the First Independence Day, which was to be celebrated every year.

Dandi March (1930)

- On 12th March, 1930, Gandhi began his famous March to Dandi with his chosen 79 followers to break the salt laws. He reached the coast of Dandi on 5 April, 1930 after marching a distance of 200 miles and on 6 April formally launched the Civil Disobedience Movement by breaking the salt laws.

Civil Disobedience Movement

- Countrywide mass participation by women.
- The Garhwal soldiers refused to fire on the people at Peshawar.

Round Table Conference

- The first Round Table Conference was held in November 1930 at London and it was boycotted by the Congress.
- On 8 March, 1931 the Gandhi-Irwin Pact was signed. As per this pact, Mahatma Gandhi agreed to suspend the Civil-Disobedience Movement and participate in the Second-Round Table Conference.
- In September 1931, the Second Round Table Conference was held at London. Mahatma Gandhi participated in the Conference but returned to India disappointed.
- In January 1932, the Civil-Disobedience Movement was resumed.

Poona Pact (1932)

- The idea of separate electorate for the depressed classes was abandoned, but seats reserved for them in the provincial legislature were increased.
- Thus, Poona Pact agreed upon a joint electorate for upper and lower castes.

Cripps Mission (1942)

- The British Government in its effort to secure Indian co-operation in the Second World War sent Sir Stafford Cripps to India on 23 March, 1942. This is known as Cripps Mission.
- The main recommendations of Cripps was the promise of Dominion Status to India.
- Congress rejected it. Gandhi called Cripp's proposals as a "Post-dated Cheque".

Quit India Movement (1942-1944)

- The All India Congress Committee met at Bombay on 8 August, 1942 and passed the famous Quit India Resolution. On the same day, Gandhi gave his call of 'do or die'.
- On 8th and 9th August, 1942, the government arrested all the prominent leaders of the Congress. Mahatma Gandhi was kept in prison at Poona. Pandit Jawaharlal Nehru, Abul Kalam Azad, and other leaders were imprisoned in the Ahamednagar Fort.
- Quit India Movement was the final attempt for country's freedom.

Indian National Army (INA)

- On July 2, 1943, Subhash Chandra Bose reached Singapore and gave the rousing war cry of 'Dilli Chalo'. He was made the President of Indian Independence League and soon became the supreme commander of the Indian National Army. He gave the country the slogan of Jai Hind.
- INA had three fighting brigades names after Gandhi, Azad and Nehru. Rani of Jhansi Brigade was an exclusive women force. INA headquarters at Rangoon and Singapore.

Cabinet Mission (1946)

- The Cabinet Mission put forward a plan for solution of the constitutional problem. A proposal was envisaged for setting up an Interim Government, which would remain in office till a new government was elected on the basis of the new Constitution framed by the Constituent Assembly.
- Elections were held in July 1946 for the formation of a Constituent Assembly.
- Muslim league observed the *Direct Action Day* on 16 August, 1946.
- An Interim Government was formed under the leadership of Jawaharlal Nehru on 2 September, 1946.

Mountbatten Plan (1947)

- On 20 February 1947, Prime Minister Atlee announced in the House of Commons the definite intention of the British Government to transfer power to responsible Indian hands by a date not later than June 1948.
- Lord Mountbatten armed with vast powers became India's Viceroy on 24 March, 1947. The partition of India and the creation of Pakistan appeared inevitable to him.
- After extensive consultation Lord Mountbatten put forth the plan of partition of India on 3 June, 1947. The Congress and the Muslim League ultimately approved the Mountbatten Plan.

Indian Independence Act, 1947

- The salient features of this Act was the partition of the country into India and Pakistan would come into effect from 15 August, 1947.
- On 15th August, 1947 India, and on the 14th August Pakistan came into existence as two independent states.
- Lord Mountbatten was made the first Governor General of Independent India, whereas Mohammad Ali Jinnah became the first Governor General of Pakistan.
- C. Rajagopalachari became the first and last Indian Governor-General of India. When India became a Republic on 26 January, 1950 Dr. Rajendra Prasad became the first President of our country.

Geography

THE UNIVERSE

- Existing matter and energy are together known as **Universe.**

GALAXY

- A galaxy is a huge system of billions of stars and clouds of dust and gases.
- Our solar system is a part of *MilkyWay* galaxy.
- There are millions of galaxies that make the Universe.

STARS

- Stars account for 98 per cent of the matter in a galaxy. The stars nearest to the earth are *Proxima Centauri, Alpha Centauri, Barnard's Star, Sirius* and so on. Of these, *Sirius* is the brightest.

LIGHT YEAR

- Light year is the distance travelled by light in one year at a speed of 2,99,792.5 km. per second.

SOLAR SYSTEM

- The Sun, eight planets, satellites and some other celestial bodies known as asteroids and meteoroids form the solar system.

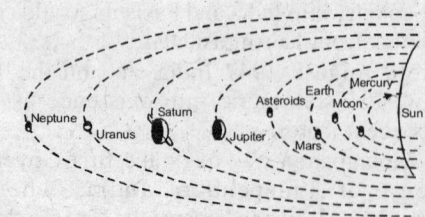

SUN

- The Sun is in the centre of the solar system.

- The Sun is a mixture of gases. It consists of 92% hydrogen, 7.8% helium and 0.2% other gases.
- The Sun is about 150 million km away from the earth.
- The sun is an ultimate source of energy for life on Earth.
- Sunlight takes 8 min 16.6 sec to reach earth.

☞ **Facts about Planets**

Closest to Sun	*Mercury*
Farthest from Sun	*Neptune*
Heaviest	*Jupiter*
Hottest	*Venus*
Inner	*Mercury, Venus, Earth, Mars*
Largest	*Jupiter*
Smallest	*Mercury*
Moons, None	*Mercury, Venus*
Moon; Largest	*Ganymede (Jupiter), larger than Mercury*
Nearest to Earth	*Venus*
Orbits; Order	*Mercury (closest to Sun), Venus, Earth, Mars, Jupiter, Saturn, Uranus, Neptune.*
Rings/largest number	*Saturn*
Spin; Backwards	*Venus (East to West)*

COMETS

- It has a head and a tail. Its tail originates only when it gets closer to the sun. The tail can be 20-30 million km long. It always point away from the sun because of the force exerted by solar wind and radiation on the cometory material.

THE EARTH

- The earth is the third nearest planet to the Sun.

14

- From the outer space, the earth appears blue because its two-thirds surface is covered by water. It is, therefore, called a blue planet.
- It is the densest of all planets.
- Rotation is the movement of the earth on its axis. Due to this rotation, day and night occur.
- The earth takes about 23 hours 56 minutes and 4 seconds to complete one rotation around its axis.
- Earth takes 365¼ days (one year) to revolve around the sun.

THE MOON

- Earth has only one satellite, that is, the moon.
- Its diameter is only one-quarter that of the earth. It is about 3,84,400 km away from us.
- The moon moves around the earth in about 27 days. It takes exactly the same time to complete one spin. As a result, only one side of the moon (only 59% of its surface) is visible to us on the earth.
- Moonlight takes 1.3 sec. to reach earth.

LATITUDE

- Imaginary lines drawn parallel to the equator. Measured as an angle whose apex is at the centre of the earth.
- The equator represents 0° latitude, while the North Pole is 90°N and the South Pole 90°S.
- 23½°N represents Tropic of Cancer while 23½°S represents Tropic of Capricorn.

LONGITUDE

- It is the angular distance measured from the centre of the earth. On the globe the lines of longitude are drawn as a series of semicircles that extend from the North Pole to the South Pole through the equator. They are also called meridians.
- The distance between any two meridians is not equal. At the equator, 1 degree = 111 km. At 30°N or S, it is 96.5 km. It goes on decreasing this way until it is zero at the poles.

INTERNATIONAL DATE LINE

- It is the 180° meridian running over the Pacific Ocean, deviating at Aleutian Islands, Fiji, Samoa and Gilbert Islands.
- Travellers crossing the Date Line from west to east repeat a day and travellers crossing it from east to west lose a day.

INDIAN STANDARD TIME (IST)

- Indian Standard Time is calculated on the basis of 82.5°E longitude which passes through Uttar Pradesh, Madhya Pradesh, Odisha, Chattisgarh and Andhra Pradesh.

ATMOSPHERE

- Atmosphere is a mixture of different gases and it envelopes the earth all round. It contains life-giving gases like oxygen for humans and animals and carbon dioxide for plants.

☞ **Permanent Gases of the Atmosphere**

Constituent	Formula	Percentage by Volume
Nitrogen	N_2	78.08
Oxygen	O_2	20.95
Argon	Ar	0.93
Carbon dioxide	CO_2	0.036
Neon	Ne	0.002
Helium	He	0.0005
Krypton	Kr	0.001
Xenon	Xe	0.00009
Hydrogen	H_2	0.00005

WINDS

- Due to horizontal differences in air pressure, air flows from areas of high pressure to areas of low pressure. **Horizontal movement** of the air is called wind.

  Classification of winds: Winds may be classified into 4 types:
  1. Permanent or Planetary winds
  2. Periodic or Seasonal winds
  3. Variable winds
  4. Local winds

☞ **Major Producers of Crops, Minerals and Industrial goods**

Coal	China, USA, India, Australia, Indonesia, Russia
Coffee	Brazil, Vietnam, Columbia, Indonesia
Copper	Chile, Peru, China, USA
Cotton	China, India, USA, Pakistan, Brazil
Gold	China, Australia, Russia, USA, Canada
Manganese	China, South Africa, Australia
Petroleum	USA, Russia, Saudi Arabia, Iraq
Rice	India, China, Indonesia, Bangladesh
Silk	China, India, Uzbekistan, Thailand
Steel	China, Japan, India, USA
Wheat	China, India, USA, France, Russia

INDIAN GEOGRAPHY

AREA AND LOCATION

- India is in the southern parts of the Asian continent. In the west of India lies the Arabian Peninsula while in the east lies the Indo-China Peninsula.
- India extends between 8°4' N and 37°6' N latitudes and between 68°7' E and 97°2' E longitudes.
- India, has a total geographic area of 32,87,263 sq. km. This is only 2.42 % of the total geographic area of the world but holds 17.5 per cent of the world's population.
- The 23½°N, which is the Tropic of Cancer, runs across the country.
- India has a length of 3214 km from north to south and 2933 km from east to west. It has a land frontier of 15200 km.
- The total length of the coastline of the mainland, Lakshadweep Islands and Andaman and Nicobar Islands is 7,516.6 km.
- India ranks seventh among the countries of the world, in terms of the geographical extent.
- India is bordered on three sides by water and on one by land, it is also a peninsula.
- India shares its common border with Afghanistan and Pakistan in the north-west, China and Bhutan in the north, and Bangladesh in the east. In the south, Sri Lanka is separated from India by a strait, known as the Palk Strait.
- There are 28 States, and 7 (after merger of Daman & Diu and Dadra & Nagar Haveli in 2020) Union Territories and 1 National Capital Territory (Delhi) in India.
- 82°30' E longitude is considered as the Indian Standard Meridian. The local time of this longitude is taken as the Indian Standard Time (IST). This is 5½ hours ahead of the Greenwich Mean Time.

☞ **Heighest Mountain Peaks of India**

Peaks	Elevation' (in mts.)
Godwin Austin (K2)	8611*
Kanchenjunga	8598
Nanga Parvat	8126*
Gasherbrum	8068*
Broad Peak	8047*
Dastegil	7885*
Masherbrum (East)	7821*
Nanda Devi	7817
Masherbrum (West)	7806*
Rakoposhi	7788*
Kamet	7756
Saser Kangdi	7672

• *Above mean sea level in metres.*
* *Situated in Pak occupied Kashmir (PoK).*

CLIMATE

- The climate of India may be described as tropical monsoon. On the basis of variations of monsoon the year is divided into four seasons.
  1. Winter Season (Mid December to Mid March).
  2. Summer Season (Mid March to May).
  3. Rainy Season (June to September).
  4. Retreating South-West Monsoon or North-East Monsoon (October to Mid December).

SOILS OF INDIA

- Soils is the layer of the earth surface made up of tiny rock debris and it is called 'soil'. In the soil, there are minerals, decomposed vegetation and bacteria.
- Indian soil has been divided into four categories, viz., Alluvial soil, Black soil, Red soil and Laterite soil. The Indian soil when compared with soil of any other country, is comparatively dry and requires an adquate supply of water for the purpose of cultivation.

☞ **Major Indian Crops**

Crops	States where Produced
Rice	West Bengal, Uttar Pradesh, Punjab
Wheat	Uttar Pradesh, Madhya Pradesh, Punjab
Maize	Maharashtra, Karnataka, Madhya Pradesh
Gram	Mahdya Pradesh, Maharashtra, Rajasthan
Tur	Maharashtra, Karnataka, Madhya Pradesh
Groundnut	Gujarat, Rajasthan, Andhra Pradesh
Soyabean	Madhya Pradesh, Maharashtra, Rajasthan
Sunflower	Karnataka, Odisha, Andhra Pradesh
Sugarcane	Uttar Pradesh, Maharashtra, Karnataka
Cotton	Maharashtra, Gujarat, Telangana
Jute & Mesta	West Bengal, Bihar, Assam

☞ **Mineral Wealth at a Glance (Metallic Minerals)**

Mineral	Chief Producers
Bauxite	Odisha, Gujarat, Jharkhand
Chromite	Odisha, Karnataka
Coal	Chhattisgarh, Odisha, Jharkhand
Copper	Madhya Pradesh, Rajasthan
Diaspore	Uttar Pradesh, Madhya Pradesh
Gold	Karnataka
Iron	Odisha, Karnataka, Goa
Lead	Rajasthan, Andhra Pradesh
Lignite	Tamil Nadu
Manganese	Madhya Pradesh, Maharashtra
Natural Gas	Gujarat, Assam
Petroleum	Gujarat, Assam, Andhra Pradesh
Silver	Rajasthan, Andhra Pradesh, Jharkhand
Tungsten	Rajasthan
Zinc	Rajasthan, W. Bengal

TRANSPORT

RAILWAYS

Important Facts

- Indian Railways are the biggest national undertaking.
- The first Indian railway train rolled on its 34 km track from Bombay to Thane on April 16, 1853.
- Indian Railway System is fourth largest railway system in the world after America, China and Russia.
- The number of stations, till 31st March 2020, is 7,325.
- The total length of Indian railways till 31st March 2020 is 67,956 km.
- Till 31st March 2020, Indian railways have 12,729 locomotives, 76,608 passenger coaches and 2,93,077 wagons.
- Rail Budget has been merged in Union Budget since 2017-18.
- The first electric train rolled on from Mumbai to Kurla on 3rd February, 1925.
- Kolkata Metro Rail is the first underground rail.
- The longest railway journey which takes 82.30 hours is from Dibrugarh to Kanyakumari (4,286 km).

- The longest railway platform of the world is Gorakhpur. Its length is 1335.4 mtrs.
- The longest tunnel of Indian railways between Banihal and Gazigund stations in J&K is 11.21 km long.
- Indian Railway Board was established in 1905.
- Indian Railways have three gauges—Broad gauge, metre gauge and narrow gauge.
- Rapid metro train has been started in Gurugram (Haryana) on 14th November, 2013.
- Nehru Setu is the longest river railway bridge built on river Sone.

ROAD TRANSPORT

Important Facts

- The road network in India is one of the largest in the world. The total length of roads, till 31st March 2019 is 63.86 lakh km.
- The total length of National Highways is 1,34,440 km, State Highways is 1,86,528 and other roads is 60,63,329 km.
- The Central Government owns the responsibility of 1,34,440 km long national highways.
- Border Road Organisation was established in 1960.
- Though the national highways do not constitute even 2 per cent of the total road length of the country, they bear about 40% of the traffic.
- National Highways Development Project has been launched to link the four corners of the country by four or six lanes in a network. The four major cities—Kolkata, Delhi, Chennai and Mumbai will be linked by 5,882 km long roads in golden quadrilateral.
- Indian roads have been divided into three parts—
  (a) National Highways
  (b) State Highways
  (c) Border Roads.
- **NH44** is the longest highway of India.
- **NH47A** is the smallest highway of India.

SHIPPING

Important Facts

- India has 7,516 km long coast line.
- Mumbai is the biggest port in the country. It is a natural harbour and handles more than one-fifth of the total traffic of the parts.

- The public sector company, The Shipping Corporation of India Limited was established on 2nd October, 1961.
- India has the largest merchant shipping fleet among the developing countries and ranks 16th in the world in shipping tonnage.
- There are 13 major ports in the country apart from about 200 minor ports. Major ports are under Central Government and others are maintained by State Governments.

Major Ports of Country

- 1. Kolkata, 2. Mumbai, 3. Nhava Sheva (J.L. Nehru Port), 4. Tuticorin, 5. Chennai, 6. Mormugao, 7. New Mangalore, 8. Paradeep, 9. Kandla, 10. Vishakhapatnam, 11. Cochin, 12. Haldia, 13. Ennore.

CIVIL AVIATION

- Beginning of civil aviation in India may be traced to 1877 when Joseph Lin flew to a height of 5000 feet in a balloon from Lal Bagh in Mumbai. The World War II gave a fillip to air transport and 11 passengers and cargo aviation companies started operations in the country. All the air routes and companies were nationalised in 1953.
- **Privatization of Air India:** On January 27, 2022 the Government of India successfully handed over Air India to the Tata Group, nearly 69 years after it was taken from TATAs. The Tata Group, as part of the deal are also handed over the Air India express and a 50% stake in the ground handling arm of Air India SATS. Air India will be the third airline brand in Tata's stable as the conglomerate holds a majority interest in Air Asia India and Vistara. Tata Group chairman N. Chandrashekhar witnessed the formal transfer of the Air India to Tata Group. The Government of India on October 8, 2021 had announced the sale of the national carrier to its original developer–the salt-to-software conglomerate Tata Group at an enterprise value of ₹ 18,000 crore. This is the first major privatisation step in about two decades.
- **Airports Authority of India:** It was constituted on April 1, 1995 by merging the International Airports Authority of India and the National Airports Authority. It owns and maintains AAI manages 115 airports including 23 civil enclave and also provides CNS-ATM facilities at 11 other airports. AAI has been bestowed with the responsibility to manage the entire Indian airspace measuring around 2.8 million nautical square mile area covering the Bay of Bengal and the Arabian Sea, as designated by ICAO for provisioning of Air Traffic Services in the said air space.
- **Pawan Hans Limited:** Set-up in October 1985 and renamed Pawan Hans Helicopters Limited, it provides helicopter support service to petroleum sector in off-shore operations and to inaccessible areas and difficult terrains.

☞ **Major International Airports in India**

International Airports	*City*
Indira Gandhi International Airport	Delhi
Anna International Airport	Chennai
Sri Guru Ram Dass Jee International Airport	Amritsar
Rajiv Gandhi International Airport	Hyderabad
Calicut International Airport	Kozhikode
Chhatrapati Shivaji International Airport	Mumbai
Kempegowda International Airport	Bengaluru
Dabolim Airport in Vasco di Gama City	Goa
Netaji Subash Chandra Bose International Airport	Kolkata
Thriuvananthapuram International Airport	Thiruvananthapuram
Lokpriya Gopinath Bordoloi International Airport	Guwahati
Sardar Vallabhbhai Patel International Airport	Ahmedabad

INDIAN POLITY

INDIAN CONSTITUTION

- Demand for a constituent Assembly composed of the people of India officially asserted by the Congress for the first time in 1935.
- The election for Indian Constitution Assembly held in 1946 according to the *Cabinet Mission Plan*.
- The first session of the Assembly was held in New Delhi on December 9, 1946. *Sachidanand Sinha* was elected provisional chairman of the session.
- On December 11, 1946, Dr. Rajendra Prasad was elected as the Permanent Chairman of the Constituent Assembly.
- The Constitution was framed by the Constituent Assembly of India, set-up in December 1946, in accordance with the Cabinet Mission Plan, under the Chairmanship of Sachidanand Sinha, initially.
- The total membership of Constituent Assembly was 299, when 70 were representatives from the Indian states and others from British India.
- The Chairman of the Drafting Committee was **Dr. BR Ambedkar**, also called the Father of the Constitution.
- The Constituent Assembly took 2 years, 11 months and 18 days to complete the Constitution.
- The Constitution, adopted on 8th November, 1949, contained 395 Articles and Schedules.
- The Constitution was delayed till 26th January because, in 1929, on this day Indian National Congress demanded Poorna Swaraj in Lahore Session under JL Nehru.
- Indian Constitution is a comprehensive document and it is the lengthiest written Constitution in the World.

THE PREAMBLE

- *The Preamble of the Constitution:* "We the people of India, having solemnly resolved to Constitute India into a Sovereign, Socialist, Secular Democratic Republic and to secure to all its citizen:
  Justice, Social, economic and political;
  Liberty of thought, expression, belief, faith and worship;
  Equality of status and of opportunity; and to promote among them all;
  Fraternity assuring the dignity of the individual and the unity and integrity of the nation;
  In our Constituent Assembly, this twenty-sixth day of November, 1949, do hereby adopt, enact and give to ourselves this constitution."

☞ **Foreign Sources of Indian Constitution**

Foreign Sources	Subject
Britain	Parliamentary system, collective responsibilities of Cabinet
America	Fundamental right, Citizenship, Independent Judiciary, Judicial review
Canada	Division of powers
Ireland	Directive principles
Germany	Emergency provisions
Russia	Fundamental duties
Australia	Concurrent list

MAIN FEATURES

- It is perhaps the bulkiest written Constitution.
- It combines rigidity with flexibility.
- Envisages parliamentary system of government, both at the centre and the states, real executive, power with the council of Ministers.
- It provides a federal system of government with a unitary bias.
- It declares India a secular state.
- An elaborate list of Fundamental Rights and Duties is given in the Constitution.
- It lays down Directive Principles of State Policy. It provides for single citizenship.

19

- It makes special provision for the protection of backward classes.
- It grants rights to vote to all adults above the age of 18 years without any distinction.

UNION AND ITS TERRITORIES

- The Constitution says, "India, that is Bharat, shall be a Union of States".
- Parliament has the power to create any State, reduce it, change the name of boundaries of any State.

CITIZENSHIP

- The Constitution provides for a single Citizenship.
- *Indian Citizenship can be acquire:*
  1. by birth
  2. by descent
  3. by registration
  4. by naturalisation
  5. by incorporation of territory
- *Indian Citizenship can be lost by:*
  1. renunciation;
  2. termination — it takes place if a citizen of India voluntary acquires the citizenship of another country; and
  3. deprivation — if the Government terminates the citizenship.

FUNDAMENTAL RIGHTS

- Following fundamental rights are enjoyed by every Indian citizen, irrespective of caste, colour, creed and sex:
  1. *Right to Equality:* No special privileges, no distinction on grounds of religion, caste, creed and sex.
  2. *Right to Freedom:* The right to freedom of expression and speech, the right to choose one's own profession, the right to reside in any part of the Indian Union.
  3. *Right to Freedom to Religion:* Except when it is in the interest of public order, morality, health or other conditions, everybody has the right to profess, practice and propagate his religion freely.
  4. *Cultural and Educational Rights:* The Constitution provides that every community

can run its own institutions to preserve its own culture and language.
  5. *Right against Exploitation:* Traffic in human beings and forced labour and the employment of children under 14 years in factories or mines, are punishable offences.
  6. *Rights to Constitutional Remedies:* When a citizen finds that any of his fundamental rights has been encroached upon, he can move the Supreme Court, which has been empowered to safeguard the fundamental rights of a citizen (Article 32).

DIRECTIVE PRINCIPLES OF STATE POLICY

Directive principles are not enforceable through courts. Main aim of Directive principles is to provide social and economic base of a genuine democracy.

Some Important Directive Principles:

- Provisions for adequate means of livelihood for all citizens (Art. 39).
- Right to work (Art. 41).
- Right to human condition of work and maternity relief (Art. 42).
- Right to a living wage and condition of work ensuring decent standard of life of worker (Art. 43).
- Common Civil Code (Art. 44).
- Prohibit consumption of liquor (Art. 47).
- Prevent slaughter of useful cattle (Art. 48).
- Organise Panchayati Raj (Art. 40).
- Separate the judiciary from the executive (Art. 50).
- Protect and maintain places of historic monuments (Art. 49).
- International peace (Art. 51).

FUNDAMENTAL DUTIES

- The fundamental duties for the Indian citizens have been incorporated in the Constitution through the Constitution (42nd) Amendment Act, 1976. These duties are:
  1. to abide by the Constitution and respect its ideals and institutions, the National Flag and the National Anthem;
  2. to cherish and follow the noble deeds which inspired our national struggle for freedom;

3. to uphold and protect the sovereignty, unity and integrity of India;

4. to defend the country and render national service when called upon to do so;

5. to promote harmony and the spirit of common brotherhood amongst all the people transcending religious, regional or sectional diversities and to renounce practices derogatory to the dignity of women;

6. to value and preserve the rich heritage of our composite culture;

7. to protect and improve natural environment including forests, lakes, rivers and wildlife, and to have compassion for living creatures;

8. to develop the scientific temper, humanism and the spirit of inquiry and reform;

9. to safeguard public property and to abjure violence;

10. to strive towards excellence in all spheres of individual and collective activity so that the nation constantly rises to higher levels of endeavour and achievement.

11. who is parent or guardian to provide opportunities for education to his child or, as the case may be, ward between age of six and fourteen years.

UNION

The President

- The President is the Constitutional head of the Republic of India. He is more or less the titular head of the executive.

- He is the constitutional head but not the real executive. The real power is vested in the hands of the Council of Ministers.

- President is the first citizen of India.

- *Qualifications:* (i) Indian citizen, (ii) age not less than 35 years, (iii) should have qualification for election to Lok Sabha, (iv) should not hold any office of profit, (v) should not be a Member of Parliament or State Legislature.

- *Election:* Indirectly elected through Electoral College consisting of elected members of both the Houses of the Parliament and elected members of the Legislative Assemblies of the States.

- According to the 70th Amendment Act, 1992, the expression 'States' include the National Capital Territory of Delhi and the Union Territory of Puducherry. Members of the Legislative Councils have no right to vote in the Presidential election.

- *Powers:* He makes appointments to all the constitutional posts.

- He can address either House of Parliament and dissolve Lok Sabha.

- All Bills passed by Parliament must receive his assent to become an Act.

- He issues ordinances when Parliament is not in session. No Money Bill can be introduced in Lok Sabha without his recommendation.

- He appoints 12 members of special repute in the Rajya Sabha.

- He has the power of *Pardon* to a criminal in special cases.

- The President holds the office for a period of five years. He is eligible for re-election.

- He is also entitled to rent free official residence called Rashtrapati Bhawan.

Vice-President

- *Article 63* of the Constitution stipulates a Vice-President for India.

- The Vice-President acts as the ex-officio Chairman of the Council of States (Rajya Sabha).

- He is elected by an electoral college consisting of the members of both Houses of Parliament in accordance with the system of proportional represen-tation by means of the single transferable vote.

- He must be a citizen of India, not less than 35 years of age, and should be eligible for election as a member of the Council of States.

- Disputes in connection with election of a president or a vice-president are to be dealt with in accordance with Article-71. Such disputes shall be decided by the Supreme Court.

UNION LEGISLATURE

- The Legislature of the Union, which is called 'Parliament' Consists of the President and the two Houses of Parliament known as the Council of states (Rajya Sabha) and the House of the People (Lok Sabha).

RAJYA SABHA

- The Rajya Sabha is the Upper House of the Parliament and it is constituted of representatives from the States or the Constituent units of the Indian Union.
- It is a permanent body, one third of its members retiring after every two years.
- Its maximum strength is 250. Out of these, twelve members are nominated by the President from well-known personalities in the realm of Science, Art, Literature and Social Service. Rest of 238 representatives of the States and Union Territories are elected.
- Currently, the strength of the Rajya Sabha is 245.

LOK SABHA

- The Lok Sabha whose life is five years, is the Lower House of Parliament and comprises of members directly elected by the people.
- The House of the people (Lok Sabha) at present consists of 543 members elected from the states and Union Territories. (By the 104th amendment of the constitution the reservation for two members of Anglo-Indian community nominated by President have been abolished)
- The House of the People shall continue for five years (unless sooner dissolved) from the date of its meeting and no longer and the expiry of the said period of 5 years shall operate as dissolution of the House.

SUPREME COURT

- The Constitution provides for the Supreme Court, which consists of Chief Justice and 33 judges. They are appointed by the President of India.

Qualification and Tenure

- Eligibility conditions for a judge of the Supreme Court are that he must be : (i) a citizen of India; (ii) a judge of a high court for a minimum period of 5 years; or (iii) an advocate of a high court for at least ten years or a distinguished jurist.

- Judges hold office till the age of 65.
- They can resign earlier or can be removed by the President on the recommendation of the two Houses of the Parliament by 2/3rd majority of the members present and voting.

Powers

- *Original jurisdiction:* Cases involving Government of India and the states or cases involving the enforcement of Fundamental Rights fall under original jurisdiction.
- *Appellate Jurisdiction:* In cases which are brought to it in the form of appeals against the judgement of the lower courts—It hears appeals in civil and criminal cases.
- *Advisory functions:* the Supreme Court advises the President on the constitutionality of a particular legal matter. However, its advice is not binding on the President. *Other Powers:*
  1. it is a court of record and can punish for contempt of itself;
  2. it can make rules for regulating the practice and procedure of courts with the approval of the President; and
  3. it can recommend to the President the removal of chairman and members of the UPSC. Supreme Court enjoys the power of judicial review (right of the court which declares as unconstitutional, the laws passed by the legislature and orders issued by executive) though it is not specifically mentioned in the Constitution.
- The first Chief Justice of India was H.J. Kania (1950-51).

THE STATES

THE GOVERNOR

- The Governor is appointed by the President and holds office during the pleasure of the President.
- Apart from the power to appoint the council of ministers, if the governor finds that the government of state cannot be carried on in accordance with the provisions of the constitution (Art. 356), he may send his report to the President who may assume to himself the functions of the government of the state. (This is popularly known as 'President's Rule').

- Article 161 gives the Governor the power to grant pardons, reprieves, remission of punishment to persons convicted under the state law.
- Article 171 states that the States where Legislative Councils exists, the Governor can nominate some members from amongst those distinguished in literature, science, arts, cooperative movement and social service.

STATES LEGISLATURE

- The state legislature consists of Governor and legislative assembly.
- In some state like *Bihar, Maharashtra, Andhra Pradesh, Karnataka, Uttar Pradesh and Telangana* have a legislative council.
- The membership of the council should not be more than *one-third* of the legislative assembly but not less than 40.
- The legislative assembly of each state shall be composed of members chosen by direct election on the basis of adult suffrage and the number of members shall not be more than 500 or less than 60.
- The assembly of Sikkim, Goa, Puducherry and Mizoram have less than 60 members.

HIGH COURTS

- The High Court stands at the apex of the State Judiciary.
- As per the Constitution, there shall be a High Court in each State. But there may be a common High Court for two or more States and Union Territory, if it is provided by a law of the Parliament. For example, the Madras High Court has its Jurisdiction over the State of Tamil Nadu and the Union Territory of Puducherry.
- The State Government has no control over it.
- There are 25 High Courts in India.
- The Calcutta High Court, established in 1862, is the oldest High Court in India.

THE PANCHAYATS

- Panchayati Raj was introduced in India with a view to associated the people with administration at grass-root level.
- It is a three-tier system as recommended by Balwant Rai Mehta Committee.
- Introduced by the 73rd Amendment Act, 1992 which envisaged a three tier system of local governance.
  These are:
  1. Gram Panchayat at the village level
  2. Panchayat Samiti at the block level
  3. Zila Parishad at the district level.

THE MUNICIPALITIES

- Big cities have municipal corporations headed by the elected Mayor.
- For small towns there are elected boards or councils, in turn, elect their Presidents.
- Introduced by the 74th Amendment Act, 1993 which envisages three types of urban local bodies, namely, municipality (nagar palika), city council (nagar panchayat).
- Municipal governance in India was first introduced in Madras in 1688.

Indian Economy

NATIONAL INCOME

- National income is a flow concept not a stock concept.
- In India, National income estimates are related with the financial year (April 1 to 31st March).
  1. **GNP (Gross National Product):** GNP refers to the money value of total output or production of final goods and services produced by the nationals of a country during a given period of time, generally a year.
  2. **NNP (Net National Product):** NNP is obtained by subtracting depreciation value from GNP. NNP can be calculated in two ways: (a) at market prices of goods and services and (b) at factor cost.
  3. **National Income:** When NNP is obtained at factor cost, it is known as National Income. National Income is calculated by subtracting net indirect taxes from NNP at market prices. The obtained value is known as NNP at factor cost or National income.
  4. **Personal Income:** Personal income is that income which is actually obtained by nationals. Personal income is obtained by subtracting corporate taxes and payments made for social securities provisions from national income and adding to it government transfer payments, business transfer payments and net interest paid by the government.
- For measuring national income in India, in 1868, the first attempt was made by *Dada Bhai Nauroji*. He, in his book, *"Poverty and Un-British Rule in India"*, estimated Indian per capita annual income at a level of ₹ 20.
- After independence, the Government of India appointed the National Income Committee in August, 1949, under the Chairmanship of Prof. P.C. Mahalanobies, to compile authoritative estimates of national income.
- National income includes the contribution of three sectors—Primary sector, Secondary sector, Tertiary sector.
- Under Primary Sector—Agriculture, Forest, Fisheries and allied sector are included.
- Under Secondary Sector—Manufacturing, Construction, Electricity, Gas and Water Supply are included.
- Under Teritiary Sector—Trade, Transport, Communication, Banking, Insurance, Real Estate, Community and Personal Services are included.
- At present estimation of national income is based on the base year of 2011-12.

POPULATION

- Every year 11th July is celebrated as the World Population Day.
- The first census of India was done in 1872 during the reign of Viceroy Lord Mayo. But a series of census (After every ten years) was adopted in 1881 during the reign of Viceroy Lord Ripon.
- 2011 census is the 15th census of India, and the 7th census of free India.

☞ **2011 Census Highlights**
- *Population of India*—Total Indian population is 17.7% of total world population—1,21,08,54,977 (Male: 62,32,70,258; Female: 58,75,84,719)
- *Decadal Growth (2001-2011)*—17.7 per cent (Males: 17.1 per cent; Females: 18.3 per cent)
- *Highest Decadal Growth (State-wise)*—Meghalaya (27.9 per cent)
- *Lowest Decadal Growth (State-wise)*—Nagaland (–0.6 per cent)
- *Most populous State*—Uttar Pradesh (16.17 per cent of National Population)

- *Density of population*—382 persons per sq. km.
- *Most densly populated State*—Bihar : 1106 per sq. km
- *Sex Ratio*—943 females per 1000 males
- *Total Literacy Rate*—73% (Males – 80.9%) (Females – 64.06%)
- *Highest Literacy (State-wise)*—Kerala (94%)
- *Lowest Literacy (State-wise)*—Bihar (61.8)

POVERTY

- Poverty can be defined as a social phenomenon in which a section of society is unable to fulfil even the basic necessities of life.
- In India, the generally accepted definition of poverty emphasises minimum level of living rather than a reasonable level of living.
- An expert group of planning commission, defined poverty line on a nutritional norm of per capita daily intake of 2400 calories in rural areas and 2100 calories for urban areas. A person who fails to obtain this minimum level of calories is treated as being below the poverty line.
- There are two types of common standards in economic literature for the measurement of poverty:

1. *Absolute Poverty:* In the absolute standard, minimum physical quantities of cereals, pulses, milk, butter, etc. are determined for a subsistence level and then the price quotations converted into monetary terms the physical quantities.

2. *Relative Standard:* According to the relative standard, income distribution of the population in different fractile groups is estimated and a comparison of the levels of living of the top 5 to 10 per cent with the bottom 5 to 10 per cent of the population reflects the relative standards of poverty.

- As per the Tendulkar Committee Report, the national poverty line at 2004-05 prices was a monthly per capita consum-ption expenditure of ₹ 446.68 in rural and ₹ 578.80 in urban areas in 2004-05.

☞ **Poverty Ratios (per cent)**

	Earlier estimates (URP) based on the Lakdawala methodology		Estimates, (MRP) based on the Tendulkar methodology	
	1993-94	2004-05	1993-94	2004-05
Rural	37.3	28.3	50.1	41.8
Urban	32.4	25.7	31.8	25.7
Total	36.0	27.5	45.3	37.2

☞ **Various Employment Generations Programmes**

Programme	Year of beginning
Community Development Programme (CDP)	1952
Command Area Development Programme (CADP)	1974-75
Antyodaya Yojana	1977-78
Training Rural Youth for Self-Employment (TRYSEM)	Aug. 15, 1979
Integrated Rural Development Programme (IRDP)	Oct. 2, 1980
National Rural Employment Programme (NREP)	1980
Development of Women and Children in Rural Areas (DWCRA)	Sept. 1982
Rural Landless Employment Guarantee Programme (RLEGP)	Aug. 15, 1983
Self-Employment to the Educated Unemployed Youth (SEEUY)	1983-84
National Fund for Rural Development (NFRD)	February 1984
Council for Advancement of People's Action and Rural Technology (CAPART)	Sept. 1, 1986
Self-Employment Programme for the Urban Poor (SEPUP)	Sept. 1986
Jawahar Rozgar Yojana	April 1989
Scheme of Urban Wage Employment (SUWE)	1990
Employment Assurance Scheme (EAS)	Oct. 2, 1993
Prime Minister's Integrated Urban Poverty Eradication Programme (PMIUPEP)	Nov. 18, 1995
Swarna Jayanti Shahari Rozgar Yojana (SJSRY)	Dec. 1997
Swarna Jayanti Gram Swarozgar Yojana	April 1999 Yojana
Mahatma Gandhi National Rural Employment Guarantee Act (MNREGA)	Feb. 2, 2006
Standup India	5 April, 2016
Pradhan Mantri Kaushal Vikas Yojana	15 July, 2015
National Career Service (NCS)	20 July, 2015

AGRICULTURE

- Agriculture is an important sector of the economy. Though the share of agriculture in national income has come down since the inception of planning era in the economy but still it has substantial share in GDP.
- As per the provisional estimates of national income released by CSO on 29th May, 2020, the share of agriculture and allied sectors in Gross Value Added (GVA) of the country at current prices is 17.8 per cent for the year 2019-20. The share of agriculture and allied sectors in GVA of the country has declined from 18.2 per cent in 2014-15 to 17.8 per cent in 2019-20, an inevitable outcome of a development process in which the relative performance of non-agricultural sectors becomes more dominant.
- Agriculture accounted for about 48.9 per cent employment in the country according to census 2011.
- Agriculture provides raw materials to various industries and other agro-based industries. Cotton and Jute textile industries, Sugar, Vanaspati industry etc. are directly dependent on agriculture.

LAND REFORM PROGRAMMES

- Land reform programme in India include:
  1. Elimination of intermediaries.
  2. Tenancy Reform.
  3. Determination of ceiling of holding per family and to distribute surplus land among landless people.
  4. Consolidation of holdings.

INDUSTRY

- After independence, the first industrial policy was declared on April 6, 1948 by then Union Industry Minister Mr. Shyama Prasad Mukherjee.
- Under this first industrial policy established a base for Mixed and Controlled Economy in India and clearly divided the industrial sector into private and public sectors.
- Second Industrial Policy Resolution declared on April 30, 1956 with the basic objective of establishing 'Socialistic Pattern of Society' in the country.

- In line with the liberalisation measures announced during the 1980s, the government announced a New Industrial Policy on July 24, 1991. This new policy de-regulates the industrial economy in a substantial manner. The major objectives of the new policy are "to build on the gains already made, correct the distortions or weaknesses that might have crept in, maintain a sustained growth in productivity and gainful employment, and attain international competitiveness."
- During the second five year plan (1956-61) a major task in industry was building up of three steel plants in the public sector—Rourkela Steel Plant in Odisha (then Orissa), Bhilai Steel Plant in Chhattisgarh (then Madhya Pradesh) and Durgapur Steel Plant in West Bengal. The three steel plants came into operation in stage between 1959 and 1962.
- Bokaro steel plant was established in third five year plan.
- In 1973, the Steel Authority of India Limited (SAIL) was created and was made responsible for the development of steel industry.
- Globally, India is the largest producer and second largest exporter of jute goods. There are 78 jute mills in the country of which 61 are in West Bengal, 3 each in Bihar and Uttar Pradesh, 7 in Andhra Pradesh and one each in Assam, Odisha, Tripura and Chhattisgarh.
- Sugar industry occupies an important place among agriculture based industries. This industry took a shape of a large industry in the beginning of 20th century. Sugar industry in the second largest industry after cotton textile industry among agriculture based industries of the country.
- India is the second largest producer of cement in the world after China. The cement industry was delicensed in 1991.
- The small and medium sector has been defined as micro, small and medium enterprises with effect from October 2, 2006 (the Act defined the medium enterprises for the first time). Further, separate investment limits have been prescribed for manufacturing and service enterprises.

ECONOMIC PLANNING

☞ **Five Year Plans in India**

Plans	Period	Investment (Rs. Crore)	Objectives
First Plan	April 1, 1951-March 31, 1956	1,960	Priority to agriculture, electricity and irrigation.
Second Plan	April 1, 1956—March 31, 1961	4,672	Development of basic and heavy industries.
Third Plan	April 1, 1961—March 31, 1966	8,577	Long term development of India's economy.
Annual Plan	April 1, 1966—March 31, 1967	2,137	
Annual Plan	April 1, 1967—March 31, 1968	2,205	
Annual Plan	April 1, 1968—March 31, 1969	2,283	
Fourth Plan	April 1, 1969—March 31, 1974	15,779	Enlarge the income of rural population and supply of goods of mass consumption.
Fifth Plan	April 1, 1974—March 31, 1979	39,426	Attain increased self-reliance and employment avenues.
Annual Plan	April 1, 1979—March 31, 1980	12,176	
Sixth Plan	April 1, 1980—March 31, 1985	1,09,292	Removal of unemployment
Seventh Plan	April 1, 1985—March 31, 1990	2,18,730	Food work and productivity were the basic priorities.
Eighth Plan	April, 1992—March 31, 1997	4,95,670	Raising employment
Ninth Plan	April 1, 1997—March 31, 2002	9,41,041	Agriculture and rural development
Tenth Plan	April 1, 2002—March 31, 2007	14,91,610	Growth rate 7.8 percent per annum.
Eleventh Plan	April 1, 2007—March 31, 2012	36,44,718	Literacy, Employment, Rural development & Transport development.
Twelfth Plan	April 1, 2012–March 31, 2017	43,30,000	Longterm development of India's economy.

15-YEAR VISION PLANE

With the end of the Twelfth Plan in March 2017 the era of five year plans came to an end. NITI Aayog has come forward with a draft 15- year vision plan to catapult the country's economy to more than three times as compared to the present day. The new plan is set to replace the centralised five-year plans the country has been following for decades. The new plan is accompanied by shorter sub-plan—a seven-year strategy for 2017-24, and a three-year 'Action Agenda' from 2017-18 to 2019-20. No less than 300 specific action points covering a wide range of sectors points covering a wide range of sectors have been drawn up as part of the 15-year vision.

MONEY AND BANKING

RESERVE BANK OF INDIA

- Reserve Bank of India (RBI) is the central bank of the country.
- Reserve Bank of India was established on April 1, 1935 under Reserve Bank of India Act, 1934 with a authorised capital of ₹ 5 crore.
- The Reserve Bank of India was nationalised on January 1, 1949.
- The general administration and direction of RBI is managed by a Central Board of Directors consisting of 20 members which includes 1 Governor and 4 Deputy Governors.
- The head office of the Reserve Bank of India is in Mumbai.

☞ **Establishment Years of Major Financial Institutions in India**

❑ Imperial Bank of India	1921	
❑ Reserve Bank of India (Nationalisation of RBI took place on January 1, 1949)	April 1, 1935	
❑ Industrial Finance Corporation of India (IFCI)	1948	
❑ State Bank of India (SBI)	July 1, 1955	
❑ Unit Trust of India (UTI)	Feb. 1, 1964	
❑ IDBI	July 1964	
❑ NABARD	July 12, 1982	
❑ SIDBI	1990	
❑ EXIM Bank	January 1, 1982	
❑ National Housing Bank (NHB)	July 1988	
❑ Life Insurance Corporation (LIC)	Sept. 1956	
❑ General Insurance Corporation (GIC)	Nov. 1972	
❑ Regional Rural Banks (RRBs)	Oct. 2, 1975	
❑ Risk Capital and Technology Finance Corporation Ltd.	March 1975	
❑ Housing Development Finance Corporation Ltd. (HDFC)	1977	

General Science

PHYSICS

PHYSICAL QUANTITIES

Physical quantities may be divided in two classes:
1. Scalar Quantities
2. Vector Quantities

A scalar quantity is one which has only magnitude.

A vector quantity has both magnitude and direction.

Force, Velocity, Momentum, Acceleration are examples of vector quantities.

Mass, length, time, volume, speed, energy, work are examples of scalar quantities.

UNITS

All measurements in physics require standard units.

In 1960, the General Conference of Weights and Measures recommended that a metric system of measurements called the International System of Units, abbreviated as SI units, be used.

Some Important Units

S.No.	Units	Quantity
1.	Metre	Length
2.	Kilogram	Mass
3.	Second	Time
4.	Ampere	Electric Current
5.	Candela	Luminous Intensity
6.	Newton	Force
7.	Joule	Workdone
8.	Watt	Power
9.	Coulomb	Quantity of Electricity
10.	Volt	Potential Difference
11.	Ohm	Electrical Resistance
12.	Farad	Capacitance
13.	Henry	Inductance
14.	Lumen	Luminous Flux

Very small distances are measured in micro-meters or (microns) (μm), angstroms (Å), nanometers (nm) and femtometres (fm).

MOTION

When a body changes its position with respect to something else as time goes on, we say the body is in motion.

There are two types of motion— translational (linear) and rotational (spin).

The motion of a car on a road is translational whereas the motion of a top, spinning on its axis is rotational.

SPEED

It is a scalar form of velocity and is defined as the distance travelled in one second.

$$\text{Speed} = \frac{\text{distance travelled}}{\text{time required}}$$

SI unit of speed is m/s.

VELOCITY

The distance covered by an object in a specified direction in unit time interval is called velocity.

The SI unit of velocity is m/s.

Velocity is a vector quantity.

ACCELERATION

The velocity of a body changes due to change in its speed or direction or both. The rate of change of the velocity of a body is called its acceleration.

$$\text{Acceleration} = \frac{\text{change in velocity}}{\text{time}}$$

FORCE AND MOTION

GRAVITATIONAL FORCE

It is the force of attraction between two masses.

It is gravitational force that holds the moon in its orbit round the earth and the earth in its orbit round the sun.

- *Newton's Law of Universal Gravitation* states that every particle in the universe attracts every other particle with a force that is directly proportional to the product of their masses and inversely proportional to the square of the distance between them.
- The value of G is 6.67×10^{-11} SI units.

CENTRIPETAL FORCE

- The force acting towards the centre on a particle executing uniform circular motion is called centripetal force and is given by

$$F = \frac{mv^2}{r}$$

where, m = Mass of the object

v = Speed

r = Radius of the Circular Path
- In case of the moon, gravitational force between the earth and the moon acts as the centripetal force.
- Centripetal force always acts on the particle performing circular motion.

CENTRIFUGAL FORCE

- The pseudo force that balances the centripetal force in uniform circular motion is called centrifugal force.
- Centrifugal force is directed away from the centre along the radius.
- The centrifugal force is zero exactly at the poles and maximum at the equator.

WEIGHT

- The weight of a body is the force with which the earth attracts the body towards its centre.
- The mass of a body is a constant quantity whereas its weight varies slightly from place-to-place on the earth.
- The weight of a body is maximum at the poles and minimum at the equator. This variation in weight is due to:
  1. the shape of the earth.
  2. the rotation of the earth about its axis.
- The weight of an object is less at high elevations than at sea level.
- At the centre of the earth, the weight of a body would be zero.

- An astronaut feels weightless in a spaceship because he is not pushing against anything.

NEWTON'S LAWS OF MOTION

First Law

- Every object continues in its state of rest or of uniform motion in a straight line if no net force acts upon it. It is also known as *law of inertia*.
- **Examples:** 1. An unwary passenger in a fast-moving bus falls forward when it stops suddenly. This happens because the feet of the passenger come to rest suddenly whereas his body continues to be in motion. 2. A person getting down from a moving bus has to run some distance, in the direction of the bus, before stopping. If he does not run he is bound to fall because his feet come to rest whereas his body continues to be in motion.

Momentum

- The momentum of a body is defined as the product of its mass and velocity.

Second Law

- This law states that "the rate of change of momentum of a body is proportional to the applied force and takes place in the direction of the force."
- If we express force (F) in Newtons, mass (m) in kilograms and acceleration (a) in metres per second squared, we can write the second law as; $F = ma$.
- In travelling the same distance, a car consumes more fuel on a crowded road than on a free road. This happens because the car has to stop and start quite often on a crowded road. The repeated acceleration requires a force (second law), which ultimately comes from the fuel. On a free road the car runs at almost uniform speed requiring fewer accelerations and hence less fuel consumption.

Third Law

- This law states that "to every action there is an equal and opposite reaction."
- When a bullet is fired from a gun, equal and opposite forces are exerted on the bullet and the gun.
- The engine in a jet aeroplane works on the same principle as a rocket but there is a difference in the method of obtaining the high velocity as jet.

WORK, POWER AND ENERGY

WORK

Whenever a force acting on a body displaces it, work is said to be done. Work = Force × Distance moved in the direction of force.

Work is a scalar quantity and its SI unit is Joule (J).

POWER

Power is defined as the rate of doing work.

$$\text{Power} = \frac{\text{Work done}}{\text{Time taken}}$$

The SI unit of power is Watt (W) and is also measured in horse power.

1 HP = 746 W

ENERGY

Energy is defined as the capacity to do work.

DENSITY AND RELATIVE DENSITY

DENSITY

The mass per unit volume of a substance is called its density.

$$\text{Density} = \frac{\text{Mass}}{\text{Volume}}$$

The SI unit of density is kilogram per metre cubed (kg/m³).

The relative density of a substance is the ratio of the density of the substance to the density of water. Relative density has no unit.

PRESSURE

Pressure is defined as force acting per unit area.

$$\text{Pressure} = \frac{\text{Force}}{\text{Area}}$$

The SI unit of pressure is newton per metre squared or pascal.

Broad wooden sleepers are placed below the rails to reduce the pressure exerted by the weight of a train.

The pressure of water increases with depth, therefore bottom of a dam is made much thicken than the top.

The pressure exerted on an enclosed liquid at one place is transmitted equally throughout the liquid. This is called Pascal's Principle.

Hydraulic presses, hydraulic brakes, hydraulic door closers, etc. are applications of the Pascal's Principle.

At high attitudes where atmosphere pressure is less nose bleeding may occur due to the greater pressure of blood.

In an aircraft flying at high altitude, normal atmospheric pressure is maintained by the use of air pumps. If this were not done, the crew and passengers would experience difficulty in breathing and consequently face dangers.

Atmospheric pressure is measured with an instrument called the *Barometer*.

HEAT

Heat is that form of energy which flows from one body to other body due to difference in temperature between the bodies. The amount of heat contained in a body depends upon the mass of the body.

TEMPERATURE

The temperature of a body is the quantity that tells how hot or cold it is with respect to some standard body.

MEASUREMENT OF TEMPERATURE

Temperature is measured by a thermometer.

A thermometer may be graduated in following scales—

1. The upper and lower points of centigrade scale are 100°C and 0°C.
2. The upper and lower points of Fahrenheit scale are 212°F and 32°F.
3. The upper and lower points of Reaumur scale are 80°R and 0°R.
4. The upper and lower points of Kelvin scale are 373K and 273K.
5. The upper and lower points of Rankine scale are 672° Ra and 460° Ra.

At −40 degrees both celsius and Fahrenheit scales will show identical readings.

Water cannot be used in a thermometer becaues it freezes at 0°C and also because of its irregular expansion.

TRANSMISSION OF HEAT

There are three ways of heat transmission:
1. Conduction; 2. Convection; 3. Radiation.

Conduction

- In this process, heat is transferred from one place to other place by the successive vibration of the particles of the medium without bodily movement of the particles of the medium.
- Conduction takes place mainly in solids.
- Air is a very bad conductor of heat. The good insulating properties of wool, cotton, etc. are mainly due to the air spaces they contain.

Convection

- In this process, heat is transferred by the actual movement of particles of the medium from one place to other place.
- In liquids and gases heat is transmitted by convection.

Radiation

- In this mode of heat transmission heat is transferred from one place to another without effecting the intervening medium.

LIGHT

- Light is a form of energy which is propagated as electromagnetic waves.
- Light is a transverse wave.
- Speed of light in vacuum is 3×10^8 m/s.
- Light takes 8 minute 16.6 second to reach from sun to earth.

REFLECTION

- When light is incident upon a surface, part of it is reflected. But certain surfaces like mirrors and polished metals reflect almost all the light incident upon them.
- The law of reflection states that the angle of incidence is equal to the angle of reflection.
- To see his full image in a plane mirror, a person requires a mirror of at least half of his height.

INCLINED MIRROR (No. of Images)

- When an object is placed between two inclined mirrors, several images of the object are formed.

CURVED MIRRORS

- There are two types of curved spherical mirrors—1. Concave Mirror, 2. Convex Mirror.
- Concave mirror can concentrate the sun's radiation falling on it at one point, it can be used as a burning glass.

- Concave mirrors are also used in solar cookers.
- Large concave mirrors are used in reflecting telescopes for observing and photographing distant stars and other heavenly bodies.
- Concave mirror is also used as a shaving or make-up mirror.
- Small concave mirrors are used by dentists for examining teeth.
- Concave parabolic mirrors are used in searchlight and headlamps of cars.
- Convex mirrors are also used as rear view mirrors in vehicles.

REFRACTION

- When a ray of light passes from one medium to other it suffers a change in direction at the boundary of separation of two media. This phenomenon is called refraction.
- When a ray passes from one medium to another optically denser medium, e.g., from air to water or glass, it bends towards the normal. Conversely, a ray passing from water or glass into air is bent away from the normal.
- Rivers appear shallow, coin in a beaker filled with water appears raised, due to refraction.
- Another effect of refraction is the apparent upward bending of the immersed portion of a stick when dipped in water.

DISPERSION

- White light consists of seven colours—violet, indigo, blue, green, yellow, orange and red. These colours are called the spectrum of the white light.
- Violet has the minimum wavelength (or maximum frequency) and red the maximum wavelength (or minimum frequency).
- Due to different speeds, the colours are refracted through different angles and therefore, when a narrow beam of white light passes through a glass prism, it is split up into its constituent colours. This separation of light into colours is called dispersion.

COLOUR OF OBJECTS

- We see objects because of the light they reflect.
- When a rose is viewed in white light, its petals appear red and the leaves appear green, because the petals reflect the red part of the white light

and leaves reflect the green part. The remaining colours are absorbed. When the same rose is viewed in green light, the petals will appear black and the leaves green. In blue or yellow light both the petals and leaves will appear black.

- Red, blue and green and primary colours.

LENSES

- There are mainly two types of lenses:
  1. Convex or Converging Lens
  2. Concave or Diverging Lens
- Converging or convex lens is used as a magnifying glass.
- SI unit of power of lens is dioptre (D).
- The power of a converging lens is positive and that of a diverging lens is negative.
- For all positions of the object, the images formed by diverging (concave) lens are virtual, erect and diminished.

EYE

- The light entering the eye is focused by the eye-lens to form an image on the retina.
- In front of the eye lens is the coloured part of eye, called the iris, which auto-matically adjusts the size of the pupil to the intensity of light falling on it.
- In bright light the iris automatically shuts tighter, reducing the amount of light entering the pupil. This protects the retina from getting damaged.
- When a person enters a dark room after being in bright light, he is not able to see clearly for a while because the iris is unable to dilate the pupil immediately.
- Least distance of distinct vision is 25 cm.

DEFECTS OF VISION

- A person suffering from long sight (hyper-metropia) can clearly see objects at infinity but cannot see near objects clearly. This defect is caused by the eyeball being too short and can be corrected by wearing converging lenses.
- In the case of a person suffering from short sight (myopia), the eye ball is too long and distant objects are focused in front of the retina. This defect can be corrected by wearing diverging lenses.
- *Astigmatism:* Curvature of cornea becomes irregular and image is not clear. Cylindrical lens is used.

SCATTERING OF LIGHT

- When light falls on atoms and molecules, it is scattered in all directions.
- Scattering of light is maximum for violet colour and minimum for red colour.
- Blue colour of sky is due to scattering of light.
- In the evening, the sun is lower in the sky and its light has to traverse a longer path through the atmosphere to reach an observer. Thus, at sunset, blue, green and other colours having been scattered only red and some orange light reach us and the sun appears a deep orange-red.
- In outerspace, i.e., beyond the atmosphere, there is nothing to scatter the sunlight and therefore the sky appears dark and stars are visible even in the presence of the sun.

SOUND

- Sound waves are longitudinal and cannot travel in vacuum. The transmission of sound requires a medium: air, liquid or solid.
- The longitudinal mechanical waves which lie in the frequency range 20 Hz to 20,000 Hz are called audible or sound waves. These waves are sensitive to human ear.
- The longitudinal mechanical waves having frequencies less than 20 Hz are called Infrasonic. These waves are produced by sources of bigger size such as earthquakes, volcanic eruptions, ocean waves etc.
- The longitudinal waves having frequencies greater than 20,000 Hz are called ultrasonic waves. Human ear cannot detect these waves. But some animals such as cats, dogs, bats can detect these waves.

PITCH

- The pitch (shrillness of a sound depends on its frequency.
- A sound of higher frequency has a higher pitch.
- The pitch of a woman's voice is higher than that of a man.

LOUDNESS

- The relative loudness of a sound is measured in decibels (db).
- All stringed instruments, such as the violin, sitar, guitar, etc. have sound boxes attached to increase the loudness.

SPEED OF SOUND

- The presence of water vapour in the air increases the speed of sound.
- Sound travels faster through warm air than through cold air. The speed of sound is higher on a hot day than on a cold day.
- Thunder is heard much after the flash of lighting is seen because of the wide difference in the speeds of light and sound.

ELECTRICITY

- Electricity produced by friction between two dissimilar objects is known as static electricity. Depending on the nature of the objects, one acquires a positive charge and the other an equal negative charge. For example, if a glass rod is rubbed with silk, the rod acquires positive charge and the silk an equal negative charge.
- *Lightning* is a gigantic electric discharge occurring between two charged clouds or between a charged cloud and the earth.

CONDUCTOR

- Conductors are those materials which allow electricity (charge) to pass through themselves.
- Metals conduct electricity because they have a large number of conduction or free electrons.

INSULATORS

- Insulators are those materials which do not allow electricity to flow through themselves. Insulators have no free electrons.

SUPER CONDUCTORS

- The resistance of metals to flow of electricity reduces with decreasing temperature. At temperatures near absolute zero, metals have almost zero resistance and became super conductors.

SEMI-CONDUCTORS

- Certain materials, such as silicon and germanium, have electrical resistivity intermediate between those of conductors and insulators. These materials are termed as semi-conductors.
- Semi-conductors are good insulators in their pure crystalline form but their conductivity increases when small amounts of impurities are added to them.

ELECTRIC CURRENT

- Electric current is simply the flow of electric charge. In solid conductors the flow of electrons and in fluids the flow of ions as well as electrons constitute the current.
- SI units of electric current is Ampere (A).

ELECTRICAL RESISTANCE

- When electric current flows through a conductor, e.g., a metallic wire, it offers some obstruction to the current. This obstruction offered by the wire is called its electrical resistance.
- SI unit of Resistance is ohm.

OHM'S LAW

- If physical conditions like temperature, intensity of light etc. remains unchanged then electric current flowing through a conductor is directly proportional to the potential difference across its ends.

MAGNETISM

- A magnet attracts and holds pieces of iron but does not attract pieces of copper.
- Iron, cobalt, nickel and certain alloys are strongly magnetic whereas copper, wood, glass, etc. are non-magnetic.
- Our earth behaves as a powerful magnet whose south pole is near the geographi-cal north pole and whose north pole is near the geographical south pole.

☞ **IMPORTANT INVENTIONS**

Name of Invention	Inventor	Nationality	Year
Aeroplane	Orville & Wilbur Wright	U.S.A.	1903
Ball-Point Pen	John J. Loud	U.S.A.	1888
Barometer	Evangelista Torricelli	Italy	1644
Bicycle	Kirkpatrick Macmillan	Britain	1839-40
Bifocal Lens	Benjamin Franklin	U.S.A.	1780
Car (Petrol)	Karl Benz	Germany	1888
Celluloid	Alexander Parkes	Britain	1861

Name of Invention	Inventor	Nationality	Year
Cinema	Nicolas & Jean Lumiere	France	1895
Clock (mechanical)	I-Hsing & Liang Ling-Tsan	China	725
Diesel Engine	Rudolf Diesel	Germany	1895
Dynamo	Hypolite Pixii	France	1832
Electric Lamp	Thomas Alva Edison	U.S.A.	1879
Electric Motor (DC)	Zenobe Gramme	Belgium	1873
Electric Motor (AC)	Nikola Tesla	U.S.A.	1888
Electro-magnet	William Sturgeon	Britain	1824
Electronic Computer	Dr. Alan M. Turing	Britain	1943
Film (moving outlines)	Louis Prince	France	1885
Film (musical sound)	Dr. Le de Forest	U.S.A.	1923
Fountain Pen	Lewis E. Waterman	U.S.A.	1884
Gramophone	Thomas Alva Edison	U.S.A.	1878
Helicopter	Etienne Oehmichen	France	1924
Jet Engine	Sir Frank Whittle	Britain	1937
Laser	Charles H. Townes	U.S.A.	1960
Lift (Mechanical)	Elisha G. Otis	U.S.A.	1852
Locomotive	Richard Trevithick	Britain	1804
Machine Gun	James Puckle	Britain	1718
Microphone	Alexander Graham Bell	U.S.A.	1876
Microscope	Z. Janssen	Netherlands	1590
Motor Cycle	G. Daimler	Germany	1885
Photography (on film)	John Carbutt	U.S.A.	1888
Printing Press	Johann Gutenberg	Germany	c.1455
Razor (safety)	King C. Gillette	U.S.A.	1895
Refrigerator	James Harrison & Alexander Catlin	U.S.A.	1850
Safety Pin	Walter Hunt	U.S.A.	1849
Sewing machine	Barthelemy Thimmonnier	France	1829
Ship (steam)	J.C. Perier	France	1775
Ship (turbine)	Hon. Sir C. Parsons	Britain	1894
Skyscraper	W. Le Baron Jenny	U.S.A.	1882
Slide Rule	William Oughtred	Britain	1621
Steam Engine (condenser)	James Watt	Britain	1765
Steel Production	Henry Bessemer	Britain	1855
Steel (stainless)	Harry Brearley	Britain	1913
Submarine	David Bushnell	U.S.A.	1776
Tank	Sir Ernest Swinton	Britain	1914
Telegraph	M. Lammond	France	1787
Telegraph Code	Samuel F.B. Morse	U.S.A.	1837
Telephone (perfected)	Alexander Graham Bell	U.S.A.	1876
Television (mechanical)	John Logie Baird	Britain	1926
Television (electronic)	P.T. Farnsworth	U.S.A.	1927
Thermometer	Galileo Galilei	Italy	1593
Transformer	Michael Faraday	Britain	1831
Transistor	Bardeen, Shockley & Brattain	U.S.A.	1948
Washing Machine (elec.)	Hurley Machine Co.	U.S.A.	1907
Zip Fastener	W.L. Judson	U.S.A.	1891

CHEMISTRY

ELEMENTS

- An element may be defined as a substance which is made by same type of atoms and it can neither be broken into, nor built from two or more simpler substances by any known physical or chemical methods, e.g., copper, silver, hydrogen, carbon, oxygen, nitrogen, gold, iron etc.

COMPOUNDS

- A compound may be defined as a substance which contains two or more elements combined in some fixed proportion by weight and which can be decomposed into two or more elements by any suitable method.
- The properties of a compound are entirely different from those of the elements from which it is made.
- Some common examples of compounds are water, sugar, salt, aspirin, chloroform, alcohol and ether.

MIXTURES

- A material containing two or more elements or compounds in any proportion is a mixture.
- The components of a mixture can be separated by physical means like filtration, sublimation and distillation.

ATOMIC STRUCTURE

ATOM

- Atom is the smallest part of the element that takes part in a chemical reaction. Atom of an element can not be changed into that of another element by a chemical or physical means. It odes not exist in free state.

MOLECULE

- A molecule is the smallest part of an element or compound that is capable of existing independently.

ATOMIC WEIGHT (OR ATOMIC MASS)

- The atomic mass of an element is the number of times its atom is heavier than 1/12th of the mass of carbon (C^{12}) atom.
- The unit used to measure atomic mass called atomic mass unit, i.e., amu.

ELECTRON

- The electron is a fundamental particle of an atom which carries a unit negative charge. It was discovered by J.J. Thomson in 1897.

PROTON

- It is a fundamental particle of an atom carrying a unit positive charge. It was discovered by Rutherford and Goldstein in 1886.

NEUTRON

- It is a fundamental particle of an atom carrying no charge. It was discovered by Chadwick in 1932.

ISOTOPES

- The atoms of the same element having different mass numbers are called isotopes.

ISOBARS

- Elements having the same atomic mass but differ in atomic number are called isobars.

ISOTONES

- Elements having the same number of neutrons are called isotones.

OXIDATION AND REDUCTION

- Oxidation is a process in which a substance adds on oxygen or loses hydrogen. In modern terms, oxidation is the process in which a substance loses electrons.
- Reduction is a process in which a substance adds on hydrogen or loses oxygen. In modern terms, reduction is the process in which a substance gains electrons.
- Oxidation and reduction always occur simultaneously. If one substance is oxidised, another is reduced. The reaction in which this oxidation-reduction process occurs is called a redox reaction.
- Oxidising agents are substances which bring about the oxidation of other substances, e.g., Potassium Permanganate, Potassium Dichromate, Nitric Acid, Hydrogen Peroxide, etc.
- Reducing agents are substances which bring about the reduction of other substances, e.g., hydrogen sulphide, hydrogen, carbon, sulphur dioxide, etc.

METALLURGY

- Metals occur in nature, in the native (in free state) as well as in the combined state.
- Naturally occurring materials containing metals are called minerals.
- A mineral from which a given metal is obtained economically is called an ore.
- The process of extraction of a metal in a pure state on a large scale from its ore by Physical and Chemical means is called metallurgy.
- The rocky and siliceous matter that associated with the ore is known as gangue.
- Substance that is added to ore to remove the gangue is known as flux.
- The process of removal of gangue from the ore is known as concentration.
- Calcination is the heating of the ore in the absence of air. This method is employed for obtaining the metal oxides from carbonates and hydroxides.
- Roasting is the heating of the ore in the presence of air. On roasting, part of the ore is oxidised to form an oxide. This oxide is then reduced to the metal.
- The industrial reduction process for obtaining metal from the treated ore is called smelting.

AMALGUM
- An alloy in which one of the component metals is mercury is known as amalgum.

IRON AND STEEL
- Iron is extracted from its ores by the blast furnace process.
- Iron obtained from blast furnace is called pig iron or cast iron containing about 5% carbon.
- Pure iron is called wrought iron which does not contain carbon more than 0.2%, or any other impurities or constituents.
- Steel contains 0.25% – 2% carbon and varying amounts of other elements.

CARBON AND ITS COMPOUNDS

ALLOTROPY
- Such substances which having the same chemical properties, but differ in physical properties, known as allotropes and this property is called allotropy.

DIAMOND
- Diamond is the purest form of carbon.
- It is non-conductor of heat and electricity.
- It is the hardest natural substance.
- It burns in air at 900°C and gives out CO_2.

GRAPHITE (BLACK LEAD)
- It is good conductor of heat and electricity.
- Graphite is used in making lead pencils.
- Graphite is also used as electrodes, lubricant, moderators, electrotyping and carbon arc.

AMORPHOUS FORMS OF CARBON
1. Wood Charcoal – Obtained from wood
2. Sugar Charcoal – Obtained from cane sugar
3. Bone or Animal Charcoal – Obtained from animal bones
4. Coke Charcoal – Obtained from coal

CARBON MONOXIDE (CO)
- Carbon monoxide is an active poison and is very dangerous as it is a colourless and odourless gas and cannot, therefore, be easily detected.
- The extremely poisonous nature of carbon monoxide is a result of its combining with the haemoglobin of the blood to form carboxyhaemoglobin, which is not decompassed by any of the processes in the body.

HYDROCARBONS
- Compounds of carbon and hydrogen are called hydrocarbon.
- A natural source of hydrocarbon is petroleum obtained from sedimentary rocks.
- Compounds having the same molecular formula but differ in properties due to different structural formula known as isomers and this property is called isomerism.

Saturated Hydrocarbons (Alkanes)
- Containing single covalent bonds only.
- Such compounds are, in general, called alkanes for instance, Methane, Ethane, Propane, Butane.

Unsaturated Hydrocarbons
- Containing multiple bonds.
- Compounds with double bonds are called alkenes, e.g. ethylene, propyene etc and triple bond containing compounds are called alkynes, e.g. acetylene, propyne etc.

- Benzene is an unsaturated cyclic hydrocarbon with the structure.
- Compounds derived from benzene are called aromatic compounds.

FUELS

Solid Fuels

- These contain carbon and, during combustion, form mainly carbon dioxide and carbon monoxide with a large amount of heat.
- Examples of solid fuels are wood, coal, coke and paraffin wax.

Liquid Fuels

- These are basically mixtures of several hydrocarbons. During combustion, they form carbon dioxide and water.

- Liquid fuels are obtained as different fractions during the distillation of petroleum.
- Examples of liquid fuels are kerosene oil, petrol, diesel oil and alcohol.

Gaseous Fuels

- Gaseous fuels do not leave ash on burning and have high content of heat.
- The main gaseous fuels are liquefied petroleum gas (LPG, mainly a mixture of propane and butane and used in homes for cooking, water gas ($CO + H_2$), producer gas ($CO + N_2$), coal gas (mixture of hydrogen, methane ethylene, carbon monoxide, nitrogen, oxygen and carbon dioxide) and natural gas (mixture of methane, ethane, propane and butane with traces of higher hydrocarbons obtained from oil well, above petroleum).

BIOLOGY

CELL THEORY

- Cell is the basic unit of structure of all living organisms. According to the cell theory, all organism are composed of cells and cell products and growth and development results from the division and differentiation of cells.
- Cells membrane surrounds all living cells.
- Nucleus is the most important cell orgallelle which controls and coordinates all cell activities and also concerned with the transmission of heredity characters.
- Mitochondria, ribosomes, Iysosomes and dictyosomes are present in plant and animal cells.
- Only plant cells have cell wall, chloroplast and vacuole.
- Viruses constitute a difficulty since in many ways they are intermediate between living and dead matter.
- The cell is said to be made up of a substance called Protoplasm which has two main constituents cytoplasm and nucleus, and is bounded by a cell membrane on outside.
- Cells take up the raw materials for metabolism through the cell membrane from extracellular fluid surrounding them.

- Cytoplasm inside is responsible for maintaining the internal distribution of organelles and also for free cell move-ments.
- Mitochondria inside provides energy for reactions inside the cell. Ribosomes are responsible for the synthesis of proteins.
- The Endoplasmic Reticulum helps in addition of other sugar units to proteins and their transportation to other parts of the cell.

FOOD

- It is a nutritive substance taken by an organism for growth, work, repair and maintaining life processes. It provides energy to do work and maintain body heat, provides materials for the growth of the body, makes necessary materials for reproduction and provides materials for the repair of damaged cells and tissues of our body.
- **Carbohydrates:** For a normal person, 400 to 500 gms of carbohydrates are required daily but for sportspersons, growing children and nursing mothers, it is on higher side.
- **Proteins:** They are complex organic com-pounds made up of carbon, hydrogen, oxygen and nitrogen. The building blocks of Protein are Amino acids and there are large number of amino acids.

- Proteins are essential for the growth of children and teenagers, and for maintenance and making good the wear and tear of the body tissues in adults.
- An adult needs about 1 gm of protein per kg of body weight.
- **Fats:** They are esters of long chain fatty acids and an alcohol called glycerol. Fats also contain atoms of carbon, hydrogen and oxygen.
- The main function of fats in the body is to provide a steady source of energy and for this purpose, they are deposited within the body.
- One gm of fat gives 37 kilojoules of energy which is more than double of that given by carbohydrates.
- Fats, the richest source of energy to our body, can be stored in the body for subsequent use. Fats,

soluble in organic solvents and insoluble in water, also supply fat-soluble vitamins to our body.
- **Minerals:** Some of the important minerals needed by our body are — iron, iodine, calcium, phosphorus, sodium, potassium, zinc, copper, magnesium, chloride, fluoride and sulphur.
- We get most of the minerals in combined form from plant sources. Deficiency of these minerals causes many diseases.
- **Vitamins:** They act as catalysts in certain chemical reactions of metabolism in our body.
- They don't provide energy to our body nor form body tissues.
- More than 15 types of vitamins are known and only 2 vitamins — D and K can be formed in our body.

Vitamin	Necessity	Source
Vitamin A	For maintaining healthy eyesight, normal skin and hair	Cod liver oil, fish, eggs, milk, carrot, leafy vegetables.
Vitamin B$_1$	For growth, carbohydrate metabolism, functioning of heart, nerves and muscles.	Milk, soya-food, meat, whole cereals, green vegetables.
Vitamin C	For keeping teeth, gums and joints healthy, for increasing resistance of body to infection	Citrus fruits, guava, tomatoes.
Vitamin D	For normal growth of bones and teeth	Milk, eggs, butter, cod liver oil, sun light.
Vitamin E	For normal reproduction, functioning of muscles and protection of liver	Green leafy vegetables, milk, butter, tomato.
Vitamin K	For normal clotting of blood and normal functioning of liver	Green leafy vegetables, soyabean, tomato.

- **Roughage:** Though it does not provide any energy to the body, yet keeps the digestive system in order, by helping in retaining water in the body and preserving constitution.
- The main source of roughage are salads, cabbage, corn cob, porridge, vegetables and fruits with stems.

DISEASES

COMMUNICABLE DISEASES

- They are the diseases which can be transmitted from reservoirs of infection or infected person to the healthy but susceptible persons.
- The disease causing agent or the pathogen can be transmitted directly or indirectly.

...CIENCY DISEASES

occur due to deficiency of some nutrients
...et or some hormone due to hypo activity
... to endocrine glands.

Diet Deficiency	Disease
Protein	Kwashiorkor
Protein-energy malnutrition	Marasmus
Vitamin A	Night-blindness, Xerophthalmia
Vitamin B$_1$	Beri-Beri
Vitamin B$_2$	Cheilosis
Vitamin B$_5$	Pellagra
Vitamin C	Scurvy
Vitamin D	Rickets (in children), (in adult) Osteomalacia
Vitamin K	Hypothrombinemia
Iron	Anaemia
Iodine	Goitre
Fluoride	Dental caries
Calcium and phosphorus	Affects formation of bones and teeth

Hormone Deficiency	Disease
Insulin	Diabetes
Thyroxine	Cretinism (child), Goitre
STH	Dwarfism, Gigantism

☞ Internal Security Organisations of India

S.No.	Name of Organisation	Year of Creation	Headquarters
1.	Assam Rifles (A.R.)	1835	Shillong
2.	Central Reserve Police Force (CRPF)	1939	New Delhi
3.	Territorial Army	1948	In different States
4.	Indo-Tibetan Border Police	1962	New Delhi
5.	Home Guard	1962	In different States
6.	Coast Guard	1978	New Delhi
7.	Border Security Force (B.S.F.)	1965	New Delhi
8.	Central Industrial Security Force (CISF)	1969	New Delhi
9.	National Security Guard	1984	New Delhi
10.	Police	—	In different States

First in the World

* First Chinese visitor to India — *Fahien*
* First foreign invader of India — *Alexander, the Great (Greek)*
* First person to climb Mt. Everest — *Tenzing Norgay (India) and Edmund Hillary (New Zealand) (1953)*
* First atom bomb dropped at ___ — *Hiroshima (Japan)*
* First man in the space — *Yuri Gagarin (former USSR)*
* First woman in the space — *Valentina Tereshkova (former USSR)*
* First person to walk in the space — *Alexei Leonov (former USSR)*
* First person to land on the moon — *Neil Armstrong (USA)*
* First and the only woman to have climbed Mt. Everest twice — *Santosh Yadav (Indian; May 12, 1992; May 10, 1993)*
* First person on Mt. Everest without oxygen — *Phu Dorjee (Indian; May 9, 1984)*
* First person to climb Mt. Everest twice — *Nawang Gombu*
* First person to climb Mt. Everest maximum times — *Chhewang Nima Sherpa (19 times)*
* First President of the USA — *George Washington*
* First woman Prime Minister — *Sirimavo Bandaranaike (Sri Lanka)*
* First person to swim across English Channel — *Mathew Webb*
* First woman to swim across English Channel — *Gertrude Caroline Ederle*
* First woman to climb Mt. Everest — *Junko Tabei (Japan)*
* First woman to climb Mt. Everest alone and without oxygen supplies — *Alison Hargreaves (Briton: May 13, 1995)*
* First Aeroplane to fly around the world without refuelling — *Voyager (Dec. 1986)*
* First test-tube Baby — *Louise Brown (UK; 1978)*
* First all-talking Film — *Jaz Singer (1927)*
* First Secretary-General of the UN — *Trygve Lie (Norway: 1946-53)*
* First woman President of the UN General Assembly — *Vijayalakshmi Pandit (India: 1953)*
* First woman to reach North Pole — *Ann Bancroft (1986)*
* First person to reach North Pole — *Robert Peary*
* First person to reach South Pole — *Amundsen (1911)*
* First woman to command Spacecraft in Space — *Ellin Collins*

Capital and Currencies

Country	Capital	Currency	Country	Capital	Currency
Afghanistan	Kabul	Afghani	Germany	Berlin	Euro
Albania	Tirana	Lek	Ghana	Accra	Cedi
Algeria	Algiers	Dinar	Greece	Athens	Euro
Angola	Luanda	New Kwanza	Guatemala	Guatemala City	Quetzal
Argentina	Buenos Aires	Peso	Guyana	George Town	Dollar
Armenia	Yeravan	Dram	Hungary	Budapest	Forint
Australia	Canberra	Dollar	Iceland	Reykjavik	Krona
Austria	Vienna	Euro	India	New Delhi	Rupee
Azerbaijan	Baku	Manat	Indonesia	Jakarta	Rupiah
Bahrain	Manama	Dinar	Iran	Teheran	Rial
Bangladesh	Dhaka	Taka	Iraq	Baghdad	Dinar
Barbados	Bridgetown	Dollar	Ireland	Dublin	Euro
Belarus	Minsk	Ruble	Israel	Jerusalem	Shekel
Belgium	Brussels	Euro	Italy	Rome	Euro
Benin	Porto Novo	Franc	Jamaica	Kingston	Dollar
Bhutan	Thimphu	Ngultrum	Japan	Tokyo	Yen
Bolivia	La paz	Dollar	Jordan	Amman	Dinar
Botswana	Gaborone	Pula	Kazakhstan	Akmola	Tenge
Brazil	Brasilia	Real	Kenya	Nairobi	Shilling
Bosnia Herzegovina	Sarajevo	Dinar	Korea (S)	Seoul	Won
Bulgaria	Sofia	Lev	Korea (N)	Pyongyang	Won
Cambodia	Phnom-Penh	Riel	Kyrgyzstan	Bishkek	Som
Canada	Ottawa	Dollar	Kuwait	Kuwait City	Dinar
Chile	Santiago	Peso	Laos	Vientiane	Kip
China	Beijing	Yuan	Latvia	Riga	Lats
Colombia	Bogota	Peso	Lebanon	Beirut	Pound
Congo	Brazzaville	Franc	Liberia	Monrovia	Dollar
Croatia	Zagreb	Kuna	Libya	Tripoli	Dinar
Cuba	Havana	Peso	Lithuania	Vilnius	Litas
Cyprus	Nicosia	Pound	Luxembourg	Luxembourg	Euro
Czech Republic	Prague	Koruna	Macedonia	Skopje	Dinar
Denmark	Copenhagen	Krone	Malawi	Lilongwe	Kwacha
Ecuador	Quito	Sucre	Malaysia	Kuala Lumpur	Ringgit
Egypt	Cairo	Pound	Maldives	Male	Rufiyaa
Estonia	Tallinn	Kroon	Mali	Bamako	Franc
Ethiopia	Addis Ababa	Birr	Mauritius	Port Louis	Rupee
Fiji	Suva	Dollar	Mexico	Mexico City	Peso
Finland	Helsinki	Euro	Moldavia	Chisinau	Leu
France	Paris	Euro	Mongolia	Ulan Bator	Tugrik
Georgia	Tbilisi	Lari	Morocco	Rabat	Dirham
			Mozambique	Maputo	Metical

Country	Capital	Currency
* Myanmar (Burma)	Nay Pyi Taw	Kyat
* Namibia	Winohoek	Dollar
* Nepal	Kathmandu	Rupee
* Netherlands	Amsterdam	Euro
* New Zealand	Wellington	Dollar
* Nigeria	Abuja	Naira
* Norway	Oslo	Krone
* Oman	Muscat	Rial
* Pakistan	Islamabad	Rupee
* Panama	Panama City	Balboa
* Peru	Lima	New Sole
* Philippines	Manila	Peso
* Poland	Warsaw	Zloty
* Portugal	Lisbon	Euro
* Qatar	Doha	Riyal
* Romania	Bucharest	Leu
* Russia	Moscow	Ruble
* Saudi Arabia	Riyadh	Rial
* Senegal	Dakar	Franc
* Slovakia	Bratislava	Koruna (Crown)
* Spain	Madrid	Euro
* Sri Lanka	Colombo	Rupee
* Sudan	Khartoum	Dinar
* Suriname	Paramaribo	Guilder
* Sweden	Stockholm	Krona

Country	Capital	Currency
* Switzerland	Berne	Swiss Francs
* Syria	Damascus	Pound
* South Africa	Capetown (Legislative) Pretoria (Administrative)	Rand
* Tadzhikistan	Dushanbe	Ruble
* Taiwan	Taipei	Dollar
* Tanzania	Dodoma	Shilling
* Thailand	Bangkok	Baht
* Tunisia	Tunis	Dinar
* Turkey	Ankara	Lira
* Turkmania	Ashikabad	Manat
* Uganda	Kampala	Shilling
* Ukraine	Kiev	Hyrvnia
* United Arab Emirates	Abu Dhabi	Dirham
* U.K.	London	Pound Sterling
* U.S.A.	Washington	Dollar
* Uruguay	Montevideo	Peso
* Uzbekistan	Tashkent	Som
* Venezuela	Caracas	Bolivar
* Vietnam	Hanoi	Dong
* Yemen	Sana'a	Rial
* Zimbabwe	Harare	Dollar
* Congo (Zaire)	Kinshasa	Zaire
* Zambia	Lusaka	Kwacha

First in India

* The first Indian to get the Nobel Prize for Literature — Rabindra Nath Tagore
* The first Indian to get the Nobel Prize for Physics — C.V. Raman
* The first Indian to get the Nobel Prize for Peace — Mother Teresa
* The first Indian to get the Nobel Prize for Economics — Amartya Sen
* The first Indian to get Special Oscar award (1992) — Satyajit Ray
* The first and the last Indian Governor-General of free India — C. Rajagopalachari
* The first woman to become the Governor of a State — Smt. Sarojini Naidu
* The first Indian Chief of the Army Staff — General K.M. Cariappa
* The first ever woman to become the Chief Minister of a State — Smt. Sucheta Kripalani
* The first Indian woman President of UN General Assembly — Smt. Vijaylakshmi Pandit
* The first Indian to become the President of International Court of Justice — Dr. Nagendra Singh
* The first Indian woman to swim across the English Channel — Ms. Aarti Saha

* The first Indian girl to become Miss Universe — *Miss Sushmita Sen*
* The first Indian girl to become Miss World — *Rita Faria*
* The first Indian to swim across the English Channel — *Mihir Sen*
* The first Field Marshal — *S.H.F.J. Manekshaw*
* The first Indian recipient of Victoria Cross — *Khudadad Khan*
* The first Indian to conquer Mt. Everest — *Sherpa Tenzing (May 29, 1953)*
* The first Indian Cosmonaut (man) — *Rakesh Sharma (April 3, 1984)*
* The first Indian Cosmonaut (woman) — *Kalpana Chawla (Nov. 19, 1997)*
* The first woman to climb Mt. Everest — *Miss Bachendri Pal (May 23, 1984)*
* The first ICS — *Satyendranath Tagore*
* The first to address the UN General Assembly in Hindi — *Atal Bihari Vajpai*
* The first Newspaper — *Bengal Gazette (Jan 27, 1780)*
* The first Postage Stamp issued — *In 1852*
* The first Telegraph line laid *(Calcutta-Diamond Harbour)* — *In 1851*
* The first Railways run — *April 16, 1853 (Bombay-Thane)*
* The first Electric Train run — *1925 (Bombay-Kurla)*
* The first Atomic Power Station — *Tarapore (Maharashtra)*
* The first passenger-cum-cargo ship made in India — *Harshavardhan*
* The first Satellite — *Aryabhatta (1975)*
* The first President of the Indian National Congress — *W.C. Banerjee*
* The first President of Indian Republic — *Dr. Rajendra Prasad*
* The first woman judge of the Supreme Court — *Ms Fatima Bibi*
* The first to climb Everest without oxygen — *Phu Dorjee (1987)*
* The first film (movie) — *Raja Harishchandra*
* The first film (talkie) — *Alam Ara*
* The first Metro Railway — *Calcutta Metro Railway*
* The first Test-tube baby, scientifically documented — *Born on August 6, 1986 at K.E.M. Hospital, Bombay*

* The first TV Centre — *At Delhi*
* The first Indian to get an Oscar — *Bhanu Athaiya*
* The first woman pilot in IAF — *Ms Harita Kaur Deol*
* The first woman to get Olympic Medal — *Karnam Malleswari*
* The first woman Foreign Secretary — *Chokila Iyer*

Superlatives (India)

Highest, Biggest, Largest and Longest in India

* Award for Gallantry, highest — *Param Vir Chakra*
* Award, highest civilian — *Bharat Ratna*
* Bank, with largest number of branches — *State Bank of India*
* Road Bridge, Longest — *Bhupen Hazarika Setu Across Lohit at Assam (9.15 km.)*
* Cattle Fair, Largest — *Sonepur (Bihar)*
* City, Most Populous — *Mumbai metropolis*

✶ Corridor, Longest	*Rameshwaram Temple corridor (4,000 ft.)*
✶ Desert, Largest	*Thar (Rajasthan)*
✶ Dam, Longest	*Hirakud Dam (Odisha)*
✶ Delta, Largest	*Sunderban's Delta*
✶ Dome, Largest	*Gol Gumbaj (Bijapur)*
✶ Dam, Highest	*Tehri Dam (855 ft.)*
✶ Gateway, Highest	*Buland Darwaja at Fatehpur Sikri (176 ft.)*
✶ Lake, Largest (Fresh water)	*Wular Lake (Kashmir)*
✶ Literacy, Highest	*Kerala*
✶ Museum, Largest	*Indian Museum (Kolkata)*
✶ Mosque, Biggest	*Jama Masjid (Delhi)*
✶ Peak, Highest**	*K-2 (Pak-Occupied Kashmir)*
✶ Platform, Longest	*At Gorakhpur, NE Railway (1335.4 mtrs)*
✶ Railway Bridge, longest	*Vembanad Bridge, Kerala (4.6 km)*
✶ Railway route, longest	*Passenger train-Dibrugarh to Kanyakumari (4,286 km).*
✶ Road-Rail Longest Bridge	*Bogibeel bridge, Assam (4.94 km)*
✶ River, Longest***	*The Ganges (2525 Km)*
✶ Rainfall, Highest (annual mean)	*Mowsynram near Cherrapunji (1178 cm)*
✶ Road Longest	*Grand Trunk Road (1,500 miles)*
✶ State, with maximum forest cover	*Madhya Pradesh*
✶ State, with maximum density of population	*Bihar*
✶ Tunnel, Longest (Road)	*Chenani Nashri Tunnel (J&K 9.28 kms)*
✶ Tunnel, Longest (Railway)	*Banihal—Gazigund Railway Tunnel (J&K, 11 km)*
✶ Tower, Highest	*Qutub Minar (Delhi 72.5 m.)*
✶ Waterfall, Highest	*Gersoppa Waterfall (Karnataka: 960 ft.)*
✶ Zoo, Largest	*Zoological Gardens (Kolkata)*

** *Highest peak in the world is Mount Everest, which is in Nepal. K-2 is the second highest peak in the world. It is 8,611 metres high.*
*** *Indus and Brahmaputra (each 2900 km). Both of them, however, cover a long distance outside India.*

Important Dates and Days of the Year

✶ JANUARY ✶

5-11 Road Safety Week
12 National Youth Day
15 Army Day
15-21 Pin Code Week
23 National Day of Patriotism
26 Republic Day
30 Martyr's Day

✶ FEBRUARY ✶

1-14 Oil Conservation Fortnight
14 Valentine's Day

✶ MARCH ✶

4 National Safety Day
8 International Women's Day
15 Consumers' Day
21 World Forest Day
22 World Day for Water
24 World Meteorological Day
1-7 Preservation of Blindness Week

✶ APRIL ✶

7 World Health Day
7-13 Handloom Week

14-20 Fire Service Week   *April*
18 World Heritage Day
22 World Earth Day

✱ MAY ✱

1 May Day
5 National Labour Day
8 World Red Cross Day
11 National Technology Day
15 International Day of the Family
17 World Telecommunication Day
24 Commonwealth Day
31 World No-Tobacco Day

✱ JUNE ✱

5 World Environment Day
21 International Day of Yoga
26 International Day against Drug Abuse and Illicit Trafficking

✱ JULY ✱

11 World Population Day

✱ AUGUST ✱

1-7 World Breast feeding Week
10 Sanskrit Divas
15 Independence Day
20 Sadbhavana Divas

✱ SEPTEMBER ✱

1-7 National Nutrition Week
5 Teachers' Day
8 International Literary Day
14 Hindi Diwas

23 World Deaf Day
27 World Tourism Day

✱ OCTOBER ✱

2 ✱ Gandhi Jayanti
  ✱ International Day of Non Violence
  ✱ Anti-Leprosy Day
4 World Animal Day
6 World Habitat Day (*1st Monday*)
8 Indian Air Force Day
14 World Standard Day
15 International Day of Rural Women
16 World Food Day
24 United Nations Day
27 Infantry Day
28 World Thrift Day
31 Anti-Terrorism Day

✱ NOVEMBER ✱

2 All Saints Day
14 Children's Day
15-21 National Cooperative Week
19-25 Quami Ekta Week
20 Child Rights Day
26 Constitution Day

✱ DECEMBER ✱

1 World AIDS Day
3 World Day for the Disabled
4 Naval Day
7 Flag Day
8 SMRC Day
10 Human Rights Day
14 National Energy Conservation Day

National Sports of Some Countries

Country	National Sport	Country	National Sport
Australia	Cricket	Malaysia	Badminton
Canada	Lacrose (Ice Hockey)	Scotland	Rugby/Football
China	Table Tennis	Spain	Bull Fighting
England	Cricket	USA	Baseball
Japan	Sumo		

Important Sport Terms

Sport	Terms
Basketball	Dunk, Front court, Lay up, Held ball, Pivot, Rebound, Steel
Cricket	Bye, Draw, Googly, Topspin, Over throw, Duck, Hit Wicket, Cut, Pull, Full Toss
Football	Bend dribble, Dissent, Dummy, Fient, Free kick, Header, Red card, Throwins
Hockey	Bully, Striking, Circke, Post back
Chess	Castle, Diagonaes, Files, Pawns, Peices, Promote, Gambit, Pawn
Boxing	Jab, laying on Knock, Second out habbit punch, Upper cut
Badminton	Loab, Let, Drive, Drop, Love
Polo	Chuker, Bunker
Baseball	Diamond, home run, Put out, Strike; Ant-rubber
Rifle Shooting	Target, Muzzle fulb, Bulls eye
Wrestling	Hold Sager, Rebuts, Hal, Nelson, Free Style
Golf	Fore some, Stymie, T, Put hole, Caddy, Nib lick, Iron, The green, Bunkeer
Billiards	Jigger, Pot, Break pot, In off, Cans, Bolting, Long, Hazard, Cue
Swimming	Breast Stroke, Twist, Butterfly, Crawl, Spring Board
Volley Ball	Antennae, Attack bit, Libero, Service, Set up, Blocking, Dribbling
Lawn Tennis	Advantage, Ace, Dence, Volley, Foot Foult, Smash, Grand-Slam, Slice, Love
Table Tennis	End line, Flat hit, Foil, Service, Phnholder grip, Reverse, Top-spin, Couter-hitting, Let

Important cups and Trophies

Sport	Cup and Trophy
Cricket	Irani Trophy, Duleep Trophy, Ranji Trophy, Vijay Hazare Trophy, Asia Cup, Deodhar Trophy, CK Naidu Trophy, Cooch-Behar Trophy, Gandhi-Mandela Series, The Ashes Series etc.
Football	Durand Cup, Nizam Gold Cup, Rovers Cup, Sanjay Gold Cup, Santosh Trophy, Subroto Mukherjee Cup, Vittal Trophy, Nehru Gold Cup.
Hockey	Agha Khan Cup, Azlan Shah Cup, Nehru Trophy Dhyanchand Trophy, Beighton Cup, Scindia Gold Cup, Modi Gold Cup, Indra Gandhi Gold Cup, Rangaswami Cup, Khan Abdul Gaffar Cup.
Golf	Canada Cup, Muthian Gold Cup, Ryder Cup, Walker Cup
Table Tennis	Corbillion Cup (women), Jayalaxmi Cup (women), Swaythling Cup (men)
Lawn Tennis	Davis Cup, Hamlet Cup, Australian Open, French Open, Wimbledon, US Open
Badminton	Thomas Cup (men), Uber Cup (women), Narang Cup, Malaysian Open
Boxing	Aspy Adjania Trophy
Rowing	Wellington Trophy
Bridge	Ruia Trophy
Polo	Ezra Cup, Winchestor Cup, Radha Mohan Cup, West Chester Cup

United Nations (UN)

- The United Nations (UN) is a world level organisation formed in 1945. It came into existence after World War II, when the leaders of the world, including American President Roosevelt and British Prime Minister Churchil, decided to create a world level organisation that would help to ensure peace.

- The original membership of 51 nations has grown to 193 members. The 193rd member being the newly created South Sudan. The United Nation's Headquarters is in New York City. The US also has offices in Geneva, (Switzerland), and Vienna, (Austria).

- Six official languages are spoken and used in documents at the United Nations: Arabic, Chinese, English French, Russian and Spanish.

- **The General Assembly:** The General Assembly is the main place for discussions and policy making in the United Nations. All the members of the UN are the members of General Assembly.

- **The Security Council:** The Security Council has primary responsibility for the maintenance of international peace and security. The Security Council is made up of 15 members.

- This comprise of 5 permanent and 10 non permanent member. India is a non-permanent members. There are five permanent members of the Security Council-China, France, Russia, United Kingdom and USA.

- The International Court of Justice (ICJ), located in The Hague, Netherlands, is the primary judicial organ of the United Nations, established in 1945 by the United Nations Charter, the Court began work in 1946, as the successor to the Permanent Court of International Justice.

☞ **United Nations Secretary Generals**

Name	Tenure	Country	Resigned/Retired
Trygve Lie	1946-53	Norway	Resigned
Dag Hammarsk jold	1953-61	Sweden	Died in plane crash in Northern Rhodesia (now Zambia)
U Thant	1961-71	Myanmar	Declined to consider a third term
Kurt Waldheim	1972-81	Austria	China vetoed his third term
Javier Perez	1982-91	Peru	Refused to be considered for a third term
Boutros Ghali	1992-96	Egypt	The United States vetoed his second term
Kofi Annan	1997-06	Ghana	Retired after two full terms
Ban ki-Moon	2007-2016	South Korea	Retired after two full terms
Antonio Guterres	2017—	Portugal	Incumbent

☞ **United Nations Agencies and Headquarters**

Name of Agency	Estd in	Headquarter	Objective
International Labour Organisation (ILO)	1919	Geneva	To improve conditions and living standard of workers.
International Monetary Fund (IMF)	1945	Washinton DC	Promotes international monetary cooperation.
Food and Agricultural Organisation (FAO)	1945	Rome	To improve living conditions of rural population.
International Bank for Reconstruction and Development (IBRD)	1944	Washington DC	To provide funds from different sources.
United Nations Internation Children's Emergency Fund (UNICEF)	1946	New York	To promote children's welfare all over the world.

Name of Agency	Estd in	Headquarter	Objective
United Nations Educational, Scientific and Cultural Organisation (UNESCO)	1945	Paris	To promote collaboration among nations through education, science and culture.
Internation Telecommunication Union (ITU)	1965	Geneva	Sets international regulations for radio telegraph, telephone and space radio communications.
International Civil Aviation Organisation (ICAO)	1947	Montreal, Canada	It condifies the principles and techniques of international air navigation and fosters the planning and development of international air transport to ensure safe and orderly growth.
World Health Organisation (WHO)	1948	Geneva	Attainment of highest possible level of health by all people.
International Atomic Energy Agerncy (IAEA)	1957	Vienna	To promote peaceful uses of atomic energy.
International Development Association (IDA)	1960	Washington DC	An affiliate of the World Bank, aims to help under developed countries raise living standards.
United Nations Development Programme (UNDP)	1965	New York	Helps developing countries increase the wealth producing capabilities of their natural and human resources.
United Nations Environmental Programme (UNEP)	1972	Nairobi	Promote international cooperation in human environment.
World Trade Organisation (WTO)	1995	Geneva	Setting rules for world trade to reduce tariffs.

Multiple Choice Questions

1. The Constitution of India was adopted on:
   A. 15 August, 1947
   B. 26 January, 1950
   C. 26 November, 1949
   D. 15 August, 1950

2. Who administers the oaths of office to the Vice-President?
   A. Chief Justice of India
   B. President of India
   C. Speaker of the Lok Sabha
   D. Attorney-General of India

3. Who among the following is not appointed by the President?
   A. Chairman of UPSC
   B. Governor of State
   C. Judge of a High Court
   D. Vice-President

4. The President can dissolve the Lok Sabha before expiry of its term, on the advice of:
   A. Prime Minister
   B. Speaker
   C. Vice-President
   D. Election Commissioner

5. A presidential ordinance remains in force for:
   A. three months   B. one month
   C. six months   D. till it is revoked

6. The idea of Fundamental Duties is derived from:
   A. Russian Constitution
   B. British Constitution
   C. American Constitution
   D. German Constitution

7. Whether the bill in the Parliament, is a money bill or not, is decided by:
   A. Prime Minister
   B. Speaker
   C. President
   D. Comptroller and Auditor General

8. Which of the following is presided over by a non-member:
   A. Lok Sabha
   B. Rajya Sabha
   C. Vidhan Sabha
   D. Joint sitting of Lok Sabha and Rajya Sabha

9. The official language of Jammu and Kashmir is:
   A. Dogri   B. Kashmiri
   C. Urdu   D. Hindustani

10. The minimum age to qualify for the membership of Rajya Sabha is:
    A. 18 years   B. 21 years
    C. 25 years   D. 30 years

11. A minister, who is not a member of either house of the Parliament must get himself elected within:
    A. a year   B. six months
    C. three months   D. two months

12. By convention, the Governor of a state generally belongs to:
    A. ruling party in the state
    B. opposition party of the state
    C. IAS cadre of the state
    D. some other state

13. Constitution describes India as a:
    A. Federation of states
    B. Quasi-federation
    C. Union of states
    D. Dominion of free states

14. Minimum age to qualify for the President's post is:
A. 21 years　　B. 25 years
C. 30 years　　D. 35 years

15. In case of unavailability of the President and Vice-President, the duties of the President are discharged by:
A. Prime Minister
B. Speaker of the Lok Sabha
C. Senior-most Cabinet Minister
D. Chief Justice of India

16. Which Fundamental Right can be described as the soul and heart of the Constitution:
A. Right to equality
B. Right to prosperity
C. Right to constitutional remedies
D. Right to freedom of speech

17. Ordinances are promulgated by:
A. Prime Minister
B. Lok Sabha Speaker
C. President
D. Rajya Sabha Chairman

18. Indian states have been constituted on the basis of:
A. geographical continuity
B. language
C. administrative convenience
D. economic conditions

19. The Chief Election Commissioner can be removed by:
A. Prime Minister
B. President
C. Supreme Court's Chief Justice
D. Parliament

20. Speaker of the Lok Sabha can only:
A. adjourn the house
B. prorogue the house
C. summon the house
D. dissolve the house

21. Membership of state assembly range from:
A. 30 to 300
B. 40 to 400
C. 50 to 600
D. 60 to 500

22. Salaries of Supreme Court judges are drawn from:
A. Law Ministry Grants
B. Consolidated Fund of India
C. Home Ministry Grants
D. Parliamentary Grants

23. The need of establish Panchayati Raj institutions is prescribed in:
A. Directive Principles
B. Fundamental Rights
C. Preamble
D. Seventh Schedule

24. The quorum in Lok Sabha is:
A. 50
B. 55
C. one-fourth of the strength
D. one-tenth of the strength

25. The seventh schedule consists of:
A. List of national languages
B. List of oaths and affirmations
C. List of subjects
D. List of States and Union Territories

26. The retirement age for Supreme Court judges is:
A. 58 years　　B. 60 years
C. 62 years　　D. 65 years

27. One can be disqualified from voting, only on the grounds of:
A. Age　　B. Sex
C. Religion　　D. Education

28. Governors of states are:
A. appointed by Chief Ministers
B. appointed by the President
C. elected by members of Legislative Assembly
D. elected by people

29. First General elections in the country were held in:
A. 1948　　B. 1950
C. 1949　　D. 1952

30. A total of ...... members can be nominated by the President of Rajya Sabha.
A. 6　　B. 12
C. 15　　D. 18

31. The Union executive is responsible to:
    A. Lok Sabha   B. Rajya Sabha
    C. President   D. Supreme Court

32. Attorney-General of India is appointed by:
    A. UPSC   B. President
    C. Prime Minister
    D. Lok Sabha Speaker

33. Time gap between two sessions of Parliament cannot exceed:
    A. 3 months   B. 6 months
    C. 1 year   D. no fixed gap

34. Supreme Commander of defence forces is:
    A. Army Chief   B. Defence Minister
    C. Prime Minister   D. President

35. The only President to be elected twice is:
    A. Rajendra Prasad
    B. Radhakrishnan
    C. V.V. Giri
    D. Neelam Sanjeeva Reddy

36. Vice-President can submit his resignation to:
    A. President
    B. Prime Minister
    C. Chief Justice of India
    D. Deputy Chairman of Rajya Sabha

37. The Chairman of the drafting committee of the Constitution was:
    A. Rajendra Prasad   B. Jawaharlal Nehru
    C. B.R. Ambedkar   D. Sardar Patel

38. Which one is not a national duty?
    A. Respect the Constitution
    B. Respect the President
    C. Defend the country
    D. Protect natural environment

39. President does not appoint:
    A. Prime Minister
    B. Lok Sabha Speaker
    C. Election Commissioner
    D. Comptroller and Auditor-General

40. Prime Minister of India, at the time of appointment, need not be:
    A. citizen of India
    B. above 25 years of age
    C. Member of Parliament
    D. of sound mind

41. Vice-President is ex-officio:
    A. Member of Rajya Sabha
    B. Chairman of Rajya Sabha
    C. Member of Lok Sabha
    D. Speaker of Lok Sabha

42. Official language of the Union is:
    A. Hindi in Devanagri script
    B. Hindi in Roman script
    C. English in Roman script
    D. Hindi and English

43. Indian citizenship cannot be terminated by:
    A. Renunciation   B. Termination
    C. Deprivation   D. Imprisonment

44. Finance Commission is constituted by:
    A. Parliament
    B. President
    C. Prime Minister
    D. Lok Sabha Speaker

45. Indus Valley Civilisation people did not probably know about the use of:
    A. cow   B. bull
    C. horse   D. dog

46. Among the four Vedas, the first one was:
    A. Rig Veda   B. Sama Veda
    C. Yajur Veda   D. Atharva Veda

47. The Ramayana was written by:
    A. Ved Vyas   B. Tulsidas
    C. Dronacharya   D. Valmiki

48. Vardhman Mahavir was the .... Tirthankar of Jainism.
    A. first   B. second
    C. third   D. twenty fourth

49. The forces of Alexander and Porus fought on the banks of river:
    A. Ravi   B. Jhelum
    C. Sutlej   D. Indus

50. At the time of Alexander's invasion, Magadha was being ruled by:
    A. Nanda Kings   B. Gupta Kings
    C. Maurya Kings   D. Vardhana King

51. The Satavahans ruled mostly in:
    A. Avadh   B. Andhra
    C. Central India D. Magadh

52. Ashoka belonged to:
    A. Gupta dynasty   B. Maurya dynasty
    C. Kushan dynasty D. Saka dynasty

53. Vikramaditya was the name given to:
    A. Chandragupta Maurya
    B. Bindusar
    C. Chandragupta II
    D. Samudragupta

54. Harshavardhana, the last great Hindu King
    of Northern India ruled in the:
    A. 2nd century AD   B. 4th century AD
    C. 7th century AD   D. 10th century AD

55. The slave dynasty was established by:
    A. Balban
    B. IItutmish
    C. Razia Begum
    D. Outb-ud-din Aibak

56. Razia Begum was the daughter of:
    A. IItutmish
    B. Balban
    C. Alauddin Khilji
    D. Ghayasuddin Tughlak

57. Tughlaq dynasty occupied Delhi throne after
    decline of:
    A. Lodi dynasty   B. Khilji dynasty
    C. Slave dynasty   D. Suri dynasty

58. The King, known for transferring the capital
    from Delhi to Daulatabad was:
    A. Firoz Tughlaq
    B. Ghyasuddin Tughlaq
    C. Muhammad Tughlaq
    D. Muhammad Bin Oasim

59. In the first battle of Panipat, Babar fought
    against:
    A. Sher Shah Suri   B. Firoz Tughlaq
    C. Humayun   D. Ibrahim Lodi

60. Fatehpur Sikri has been built by:
    A. Babur   B. Aurangzeb
    C. Akbar   D. Jahangir

61. Khurram was the original name of:
    A. Akbar   B. Jahangir
    C. Shahjahan   D. Shah Alam

62. Din-I-Ilahi was launched by:
    A. Akbar   B. Humayun
    C. Babur   D. Jahangir

63. Sher Shah defeated which Mughal King:
    A. Babur   B. Humayun
    C. Akbar   D. Aurangzeb

64. The last Mughal King was:
    A. Shah Alam
    B. Muhammad Shah Rangeela
    C. Bahadur Shah Zafar
    D. Dost Muhammad

65. Which battle proved crucial in giving
    foothold to the British in India?
    A. Battle of Plassey
    B. Battle of Buxar
    C. Third Battle of Panipat
    D. Battle of Mysore

66. Sati was abolished by:
    A. Lord Comwallis B. Lord Clive
    C. Lord Wellesley D. Lord Bentinck

67. The partition of Bengal was carried out by:
    A. Lord Minto   B. Lord Curzon
    C. Lord Canning   D. Lord Ripon

68. At the time of independence, the Governor
    General of India was:
    A. Lord Mountbatten B. Lord WaveII
    C. Rajgopalachari   D. Lord Linlithgow

69. Krishnadeva Rai was the great:
    A. Chola King
    B. Pallava King
    C. Rashtrakuta King
    D. King of Vijayanagar empire

70. The Sikh guru to be beheaded by Mughal
    King was:
    A. Guru Gobind Singh
    B. Guru Tegh Bahadur
    C. Guru Angad Dev
    D. Guru Arjan

71. Who was not involved in 1857 rebellion:
    A. Nana Saheb   B. Kunwar Singh
    C. Ranjit Singh   D. Rani Jhansi

72. People of Ongese tribe live in:
    A. Andaman Islands B. Bihar
    C. Nilgiri hills   D. Meghalaya

73. Rajput King Rana Pratap fought the Mughal forces in the:
    A. Battle of Khanwah
    B. Battle of Haldighati
    C. Battle of Thanesar
    D. Battle of Wandiwash

74. Chand Bibi is known for:
    A. Participating in 1857 revolt
    B. Social religious reforms process
    C. Valiantly fighting the Mughal forces
    D. None of the above

75. Simon Commission came to India in:
    A. 1927   B. 1928
    C. 1929   D. 1930

76. The Congress split among the extremists and the moderates in:
    A. 1906   B. 1915
    C. 1907   D. 1927

77. Chauri-Chaura incident led to the suspension of:
    A. Civil Disobedience Movement
    B. Quit India Movement
    C. Khilafat Agitation
    D. Non-Cooperation Movement

78. The Congress participated in which Round Table Conference:
    A. First only   B. Second only
    C. First and Third   D. All three

79. At the time of Indian independence, Britain was being ruled by:
    A. Labour party
    B. Conservative party
    C. Liberal party
    D. National government

80. Delhi was made capital by the British government in:

A. 1892   B. 1905
C. 1911   D. 1927

81. Permanent settlement of Bengal was introduced in:
    A. 1757   B. 1763
    C. 1793   D. 1858

82. The first President of the Congress was:
    A. A.O. Hume   B. S.N. Banerjee
    C. D.B. Naoroji   D. W.C. Banerjee

83. The Grand Trunk Road was built by:
    A. Chandragupta   B. Sher Shah Suri
    C. Jahangir   D. Lord Bentinck

84. Balban belonged to:
    A. Khilji dynasty   B. Tughlaq dynasty
    C. Slave dynasty   D. Suri dynasty

85. Which among the following was not a Rajput dynasty?
    A. Solankis   B. Rashtrakutas
    C. Chauhans   D. Chandelas

86. Aryabhatta was the famous:
    A. Gupta King
    B. astronomer and mathematician
    C. poet
    D. spy

87. Hieun Tsang came to India during the reign of:
    A. Ashok   B. Chandragupta
    C. Skandagupta   D. Harshavardhana

88. Who among the following was an expert in medicine?
    A. Banabhatta   B. Ashvaghosha
    C. Charaka   D. Satkarni

89. The favourite pastime of the early Aryans was:
    A. Chariot racing
    B. playing dice
    C. painting
    D. dancing and music

90. Poet Amir Khusro lived during the reign of:
    A. Balban
    B. Qutub-ud-din Aibak
    C. IItutmish
    D. Alau-din Khilji

91. Chinese pilgrim Fa-hien visited India during:
    A. 3rd century BC   B. 4th century BC
    C. 5th century AD   D. 4th century AD

92. Sufi saints mostly belonged to:
    A. Islam   B. Hinduism
    C. Christianity   D. Buddhism

93. Who among the following is known as the Indian Napoleon?
    A. Chandragupta Maurya
    B. Samudragupta
    C. Chandragupta Vikramaditya
    D. Bindusar

94. The Bahmani Kingdom existed in the:
    A. 13th century   B. 14th century
    C. 15th century   D. 16th century

95. English was made medium of higher education in India by:
    A. Lord Mayo   B. Lord Chelmsford
    C. Lord Rippon   D. Lord Bentinck

96. First Indian to be Governor-General was:
    A. C. Rajagopalachari
    B. Pt. Nehru
    C. Sardar Patel
    D. Rajendra Prasad

97. Nadir Shah invaded and sacked Delhi in the year:
    A. 1645   B. 1695
    C. 1739   D. 1752

98. Brahmo Samaj was founded by:
    A. Devendranath Tagore
    B. A.O. Hume
    C. Dayanand Saraswati
    D. Raja Ram Mohan Roy

99. The battle of Wandiwash was fought between:
    A. the English and the French
    B. the English and Tipu Sultan
    C. the English and the Dutch
    D. the English and the Mughal emperor

100. The reign of which Mugal emperor is called the golden age of the Mughal dynasty?
    A. Humayun   B. Akbar
    C. Shahjahan   D. Aurangzeb

101. Banaras Hindu University was founded by:
    A. C.R. Das
    B. Pt. J.L. Nehru
    C. Madan Mohan Malviya
    D. Vivekananda

102. Gandhara School of Art flourished during:
    A. Ashoka
    B. Kanishka
    C. Chandragupta Maurya
    D. Samudragupta

103. Treaty of Seringapatam was signed between:
    A. Tipu Sultan and Nawab of Hyderabad
    B. Tipu Sultan and the French
    C. Tipu Sultan and the English
    D. Tipu Sultan and Hyder Ali

104. Which of the following happened first?
    A. Simon Commission
    B. Jallianwala Bagh tragedy
    C. Resolution of Purna Swaraj
    D. Non-Cooperation Movement

105. The first woman President of the Congress was:
    A. Annie Besant
    B. Sarojini Naidu
    C. Indira Gandhi
    D. Vijaya Lakshmi Pandit

106. Who among the following was an extremist leader in the early phase of the Congress?
    A. Dadabhai Naoroji
    B. Gopal Krishna Gokhale
    C. C. Rajgopalachari
    D. Bal Gangadhar Tilak

107. The main aim of the Swaraj party was:
    A. to launch Non-Cooperation Movement
    B. to support the extremist
    C. to take part in the legislative council meetings and voice the problems of India and the Indians
    D. Boycott the foreign goods

108. "Delhi Chalo" was the slogan of:
    A. Bhagat Singh
    B. Subhash Chandra Bose
    C. Mahatma Gandhi
    D. Lala Lajpat Rai

109. 'Sardar' was the title given to Vallabh Bhai Patel by:
   A. Mahatma Gandhi
   B. the British government
   C. M.L. Nehru
   D. G.K. Gokhale

110. Annual festivals in memory of Shivaji and Lord Ganesha were started by:
   A. G.K. Gokhale   B. A.A. Pandurang
   C. B.R. Ambedkar   D. B.G. Tilak

111. 'Champaran Movement' was meant for:
   A. securing rights of lower castes
   B. separate electorate of Muslims
   C. solving problems of Indian farmers
   D. protest against the government's education policy

112. Who among the following died due to hunger strike in prison?
   A. Lala Lajpat Rai   B. Sukhdev
   C. Jatin Das   D. Mangal Pandey

113. The Non-Cooperation Movement was suspended in:
   A. 1921   B. 1922
   C. 1929   D. 1930

114. Lala Lajpat Rai suffered fatal injuries while protesting against:
   A. Cripps Mission
   B. Simon Commission
   C. Cabinet Commission
   D. Bengal Partition

115. The Quit India Movement was launched in:
   A. 1939   B. 1941
   C. 1942   D. 1945

116. Muslim League for the first time gave a call for a separate state in:
   A. 1916   B. 1929
   C. 1937   D. 1940

117. Gandhiji launched his first mass movement in India in:
   A. Champaran   B. Wardha
   C. Sabarmati   D. Bardoli

118. Kuka Movement was started by:
   A. the Congress
   B. the Muslim League
   C. the Army
   D. the Sikhs

119. The Home Rule Movement was started by:
   A. Mrs Annie Besant
   B. Mahatma Gandhi
   C. G.K. Gokhale
   D. MA Jinnah

120. Civil Disobedience Movement was launched in:
   A. 1920   B. 1928
   C. 1930   D. 1932

121. Dandi March marked the beginning of:
   A. Non Cooperation Movement
   B. Civil Disobedience Movement
   C. Quit India Movement
   D. Split in the Congress

122. In the 1937 provincial elections, the Congress party got majority in:
   A. only one assembly
   B. no assembly
   C. all assemblies
   D. most of the assemblies

123. The British government reacted to the Poona Pact by:
   A. accepting the agreement
   B. rejecting the agreement
   C. accepting the modifications
   D. none of the above

124. The main demand of the Congress resolution in Wardha in 1942 was:
   A. release of all political leaders
   B. universal franchise
   C. unconditional withdrawal by the British
   D. elections to the provincial legislatures

125. The Shimla conference was held in:
   A. 1942   B. 1943
   C. 1944   D. 1945

126. The Cabinet Mission was led by:
   A. Pethick Lawrence
   B. Stafford Cripps
   C. AV. Alexander
   D. Attlee

127. Bhagat Singh and B.K. Dutta threw bomb in the Central legislative assembly in the year:
 A. 1925　　　　　B. 1927
 C. 1929　　　　　D. 1931

128. Bhagat Singh was hanged in the year:
 A. 1928　　　　　B. 1931
 C. 1932　　　　　D. 1935

129. All India States People's Conference was formed to:
 A. demand independence of states
 B. demand reforms in princely states
 C. demand integration of states
 D. none of the above

130. Which of the following leader attended the Congress of oppressed nationa-lities at Brussels?
 A. J.L. Nehru
 B. Subhash Chandra Bose
 C. Mahatma Gandhi
 D. C. Rajgopalachari

131. Who among the following was implicated in Alipore bomb case?
 A. SA Dange
 B. Aurobindo Ghosh
 C. Khudiram Bose
 D. M.N. Roy

132. The Prarthana Samaj was mostly active in:
 A. Mysore　　　　B. Bengal
 C. Punjab　　　　D. Maharashtra

133. Who was implicated in the Meerut conspiracy case?
 A. M.N. Roy　　　B. Chandra Sekhar
 C. S.A. Dange　　D. Bhagat Singh

134. The dual system of governance was introduced by which Governor General?
 A. Lytton　　　　B. Clive
 C. Rippon　　　　D. Wellesley

135. Which of the following does not come under the public sector?
 A. TISCO
 B. IISCO
 C. SAIL
 D. Ordnance factories

136. Term loans to industry is provided by:
 A. RBI　　　　　B. EXIM Bank
 C. IDBI　　　　　D. NABARD

137. Among the steel plants, following has been built with Russian assistance:
 A. Rourkela　　　B. Bhillai
 C. Durgapur　　　D. Kothagudam

138. The "Cafeteria approach" for family planning was put forward during:
 A. Third plan　　　B. Emergency
 C. Annual plans　　D. Janata party rule

139. The Monopolies and Restrictive Trade Practice Act was passed in:
 A. 1968　　　　　B. 1969
 C. 1970　　　　　D. 1971

140. Inflation is caused by:
 A. decrease in general spending
 B. decrease in money supply
 C. increase in industrial and agriculture output
 D. increase in general spending or money supply

141. Among the following, quasi-governmental institution is:
 A. EXIM Bank　　B. IDBI
 C. ICICI　　　　　D. UTI

142. The main purpose of UTI is:
 A. mobilise and channelise small investors' savings
 B. regulate the mutual fund industry
 C. act as a stabilising agent in the share market
 D. coordinate activities of other financial institution

143. White revolution refers to:
 A. Cement industry
 B. Dairying
 C. Cotton textile industry
 D. Marble industry

144. In India, the major means of irrigation is:
 A. Wells & Tubewalls
 B. Canals
 C. Tanks
 D. Animal drought

145. The major function of the Food Corporation of India is:
A. to distribute high yielding variety seeds
B. to extend credit to farmers
C. to control the demand side of foodgrains
D. to check the fluctuation in foodgrain prices by controlling supply

146. The largest population among the states is in:
A. Bihar B. Bengal
C. Uttar Pradesh D. Madhya Pradesh

147. Which of the following is referred as Sunrise industry?
A. Coffee B. Hi-technology
C. Small scale D. Heavy Industries

148. Which of the following is not a measure of economic growth?
A. Per capita income
B. Gross National Product
C. Net Domestic Product
D. Money in circulation

149. Among the following, least revenue comes from:
A. Income tax B. Excise duty
C. Custom duty D. Wealth tax

150. A blue chip company is called so because:
A. it produces computer hardware
B. it produces computer software
C. it gives high rains and has low risk
D. it exports most of its produce

151. The Command Area Development Programme was a major step in the field of:
A. irrigation
B. plant protection measures
C. farm mechanisation
D. high yield variety seeds

152. Poverty line is defined on the basis of:
A. living conditions of people
B. the number of children per family
C. per capita family income
D. the requirement of calories per person

153. The oldest large scale industry of India is in the field of:

A. iron and steel sector
B. jute sector
C. cotton textile sector
D. sugar sector

154. Seasonal unemployment is maximum in:
A. Industrial sector
B. Agricultural sector
C. Service sector
D. Handloom sector

155. The oldest trade union organisation in India is:
A. Hind Mazdoor Sabha
B. Indian National Trade Union Congress
C. All India Trade Union Congress
D. Central Industrial Trade Union

156. Sindri, Haldia and Paradip have:
A. Sea-ports
B. Steel plants
C. Big Multipurpose dams
D. Fertilizer plants

157. The Export-Import Bank was set up in:
A. 1969 B. 1980
C. 1982 D. 1985

158. Which among the following is India's biggest trade partner?
A. USA
B. UAE
C. China
D. Germany

159. Which of the following does not contribute to the development of the Indian economy?
A. Rising industrial output
B. Exports' share decreased; imports' share increased; Modern technology
C. Exports' and imports' share increased; Green Revolution
D. Population growth

160. Which of the following has largest share in India's export?
A. Manufactured goods
B. Ores and minerals
C. Agriculture and allied products
D. Others

161. Which of the following has largest share in India's imports?
A. Food and allied products
B. Capital goods
C. Fertilizers
D. Fuel

162. Special Economic Zone Act was passed on:
A. February 2004   B. May 2006
C. May 2005   D. February 2007

163. The first steel project city in India was established at
A. Bhilai   B. Jamshedpur
C. Kolkata   D. Bokaro

164. Rupee was made convertible on current account in:
A. 1991   B. 1994
C. 1995   D. 1997

165. The Reserve Bank of India was established in—
A. 1927   B. 1947
C. 1935   D. 1949

166. The foodgrain production is more during:
A. Rabi season
B. Kharif season
C. Between Kharif and Rabi season
D. No fixed season

167. Where is India's most prized tea grown?
A. Jorhat   B. Darjeeling
C. Nilgiris   D. Munnar

168. The ideal NPK ratio for fertilizers utilisation is:
A. 2 : 4 : 1   B. 2 : 1 : 4
C. 4 : 2 : 1   D. 1 : 2 : 4

169. Telangana was carved out of which state?
A. Andhra Pradesh   B. Bihar
C. Karnataka   D. Tamil Nadu

170. The growth rate of population in 2001-11 has been:
A. 1.93%   B. 21.43%
C. 17.7%   D. 14.46%

171. The state with lowest literacy rate is:
A. Arunachal Pradesh
B. Rajasthan
C. Bihar
D. Uttar Pradesh

172. Planning Commission was constituted in—
A. March 1950   B. June 1949
C. October 1951   D. January 1952

173. Which among the following is new WPI series?
A. 1993-94   B. 1995-96
C. 1999-2000   D. 2011-12

174. Which is not having the status of 'Maha Ratna'?
A. NTPC   B. NHPC
C. ONGC   D. SAIL

175. "Green Revolution" began in India during the year—
A. 1972-73   B. 1977-78
C. 1967-68   D. 1980-81

176. The major source of revenue in India is through—
A. Internal Borrowings
B. Indirect Taxes
C. Direct Taxes
D. External Borrowings

177. The currencies has the highest value in terms of rupee is—
A. Pound   B. Dollar
C. Euro   D. Saudi Rial

178. VAT is related to—
A. Business Tax System
B. Life Insurance
C. Banking Service
D. Social Services

179. The maximum revenue comes from:
A. Excise duty
B. Customs duty
C. Income and Corporation Tax
D. Sales tax

180. Which amidst the following is not a credit rating agency?
A. CRISIL   B. CARE
C. ICRA   D. IFCI

181. The Capital of Malaysia is:
    A. Bangkok
    B. Abu Dhabi
    C. Kuala Lumpur
    D. Doha

182. Which unit of valuation is known as "Paper gold"?
    A. Euro dollar   B. Petro dollar
    C. GDK   D. SDR

183. The crops grown after the summer monsoon are called?
    A. Rabi   B. Kharif
    C. Annual   D. Seasonal

184. During which plan, annual compound growth rates was maximum?
    A. Second plan   B. Sixth plan
    C. Fourth plan   D. Seventh plan

185. The maximum number of shares are being traded at:
    A. BSE   B. NSE
    C. OTCEI   D. DSE

186. Which is the crop of the longest duration?
    A. Gram   B. Sugarcane
    C. Barley   D. Millet

187. When was the National Small Scale Industries Corporation formed?
    A. 1951   B. 1961
    C. 1965   D. 1955

188. The finance minister to present five successive budgets was:
    A. S.B. Chavan
    B. Pranab Mukherjee
    C. Man Mohan Singh
    D. S.N. Patel

189. Charge on a particle cannot be:
    A. Positive
    B. Negative
    C. Neutral
    D. Partly positive, partly negative

190. Current is nothing but a flow of:
    A. Atoms   B. Molecules
    C. Electrons   D. Neutrons

191. Like charges:
    A. Attract each other
    B. Repel each other
    C. Don't affect each other
    D. Depends on the charge

192. Which among the following is an insulator?
    A. Iron   B. Pure water
    C. Nickel   D. Silver

193. Which material is used to form semi-conductors?
    A. Silicon   B. Gold
    C. Aluminium   D. Gallium

194. Current passing through a conductor cannot cause:
    A. Heating effect
    B. Gravitational effect
    C. Magnetic effect
    D. Chemical effect

195. Lead is added to the petrol to:
    A. Increase calorific value
    B. Reduce pollution
    C. Decrease Cracking
    D. Provide lubrication to mobile parts

196. The purest form of iron is:
    A. Wrought iron   B. Cast iron
    C. Stainless steel D. Pig iron

197. Rusting is a special case of corrosion, applied to:
    A. Nickel   B. Tin
    C. Iron   D. Silver

198. Age of a tree is calculated by:
    A. Measuring its thickness
    B. Measuring its length
    C. Measuring the number of annual rings
    D. Measuring the number of branches

199. J.G. Mendel is known for his work in the field of:
    A. Biotechnology
    B. Genetics
    C. Parasitology
    D. Medical engineering

200. Sound travels fastest in:
    A. Air   B. Water
    C. Vacuum   D. Iron

201. The maximum displacement of the particle in a wave motion is called:
A. Phase
B. Frequency
C. Amplitude
D. Time period

202. Each magnet has _____ poles:
A. 2
B. 3
C. 4
D. 5

203. pH factor is used to measure:
A. Colour of a liquid
B. Acidity of a liquid
C. Density of a liquid
D. Turbidity of a liquid

204. The common salt contains:
A. Sodium and sulphate
B. Sodium and nitrate
C. Sodium and chloride
D. Calcium and sulphate

205. Brass contains the metals of:
A. Copper and zinc
B. Copper and iron
C. Copper and tin
D. Sodium and iron

206. Goitre is caused by the malfunctioning of:
A. Liver
B. Brain
C. Spleen
D. Thyroid

207. The blood pressure of a normal man is:
A. 1,00,150 mm Hg
B. 50,100 mm Hg
C. 80,120 mm Hg
D. 200,300 mm Hg

208. Deficiency of Vitamin B causes:
A. Rickets
B. Scurvy
C. Beri-Beri
D. Night blindness

209. The largest organ in the human body is:
A. Kidney
B. Liver
C. Heart
D. Pancreas

210. Largest number of satellites belong to the planets
A. Mercury
B. Saturn
C. Jupiter
D. Neptune

211. Time taken by light to travel from sun to earth is:
A. About 8 minutes
B. About 17 seconds
C. About 129 years
D. About 6 months

212. The planet nearest to the sun is:
A. Mars
B. Venus
C. Mercury
D. Earth

213. Comets are heavenly bodies, known for their:
A. Brilliant shine
B. Tails
C. Position near polar star
D. Frequency of appearance

214. The first satellite to go into space was:
A. Explorer
B. Luna
C. Sputnik
D. Challenger

215. The first women to go in space was:
A. Yuri Gagrin
B. Nadio Comonseshki
C. Rita Phillips
D. Valentina Tareshkova

216. The first man reached moon in:
A. 1961
B. 1965
C. 1969
D. 1971

217. India joined the space club in:
A. 1975
B. 1978
C. 1979
D. 1982

218. India's range of geostationary satellite is:
A. IRS
B. INSAT
C. Rohini
D. Bhaskara

219. Green colour of the leaves is due to:
A. Mitochondria
B. ATP
C. Chlorophyll
D. Vacuole

220. Glucose belongs to the category of:
A. Carbohydrates
B. Proteins
C. Vitamins
D. Fats

221. Number of pairs of chromosomes in man is:
A. 6
B. 17
C. 20
D. 23

222. Which among the following belongs to mammals category?
A. Sparrow
B. Peacock
C. Bat
D. Pigeon

223. Photosynthesis, is the process by which?
   A. Plants take fresh air
   B. Plants produce food
   C. Plants suck water
   D. Plants transport food

224. Reflex actions of body are controlled by:
   A. Brain   B. Heart
   C. Pituitary gland   D. Spinal cord

225. The heartbeat of a normal adult is:
   A. 18   B. 72
   C. 80   D. 120

226. Oranges are good source of:
   A. Vitamin A   B. Vitamin B
   C. Vitamin C   D. Vitamin D

227. Gland to be called master gland is:
   A. Thyroid   B. Pancreatic
   C. Lymph   D. Pituitary

228. The lens in our eyes is:
   A. Concave   B. Convex
   C. Double convex D. Double concave

229. Antipyretics are medicines used for:
   A. Controlling fever
   B. Controlling heart beat
   C. Controlling blood pressure
   D. Controlling viral infection

230. Which disease is caused by the bite of insects:
   A. Cholera   B. Smallpox
   C. Measles   D. Malaria

231. Penicillin is produced from a:
   A. Bacteria   B. Virus
   C. Fungi   D. Algae

232. Which class of animals can live in water as well as land:
   A. Mammals   B. Amphibians
   C. Anthropoids   D. Reptiles

233. Organic chemistry is the study of compounds of:
   A. Oxygen
   B. Nitrogen
   C. Carbon
   D. Sulphur

234. Dry ice is:
   A. Ordinary ice at $-30°C$
   B. Compressed CO_2
   C. Compressed CI_2
   D. Water under pressure

235. Permanent hardness of water is due to:
   A. Chlorides and sulphates of calcium and magnesium
   B. Bicarbonates of calcium and Magnesium
   C. Carbonates of calcium and sodium
   D. Nitrates of calcium, magnesium and sodium

236. Amalgam is an alloy, containing:
   A. Magnesium   B. Iron
   C. Calcium   D. Mercury

237. Metal that floats on water is:
   A. Iron   B. Sodium
   C. Calcium   D. Potassium

238. PVC is made from:
   A. Ethene   B. Propene
   C. Vinyl-chloride D. Butane

239. Which is the biggest planet?
   A. Venus   B. Mars
   C. Mercury   D. Jupiter

240. Which is the smallest continent in the world?
   A. Greenland   B. Australia
   C. South America D. Europe

241. Which is the lowest body of water in the world?
   A. Black Sea   B. Dead Sea
   C. Adriatic Sea   D. Red Sea

242. Which is the highest volcano of the world?
   A. Cameroon   B. Mauna Loa
   C. Kluchevaskaya D. Cotopaxi

243. Which is the largest island sea in the world?
   A. Caribbean Sea
   B. Mediterranean Sea
   C. Red Sea
   D. Beaufort Sea

244. Which is the largest continent of the world?
   A. Asia   B. Africa
   C. Australia   D. North America

245. Name the highest peak in the Indian sub-continent:
   A. Nanda Devi
   B. Everest
   C. Trishul
   D. Kanchanjunga

246. Which is the largest island in the world?
   A. New Guinea
   B. Brneo
   C. Madagascar
   D. Greenland

247. Which is the world's tallest free-standing structure?
   A. Sky Tree, Japan
   B. Eiffel Tower
   C. Qutab Minar
   D. C.N. Tower (Toronto)

248. Which is the biggest ocean?
   A. Pacific Ocean
   B. Atlantic Ocean
   C. Antarctic Ocean
   D. Indian Ocean

249. Which is the largest peninsula in the world?
   A. Pacific
   B. India
   C. Bangladesh
   D. Africa

250. Which is the largest Archipelago in the world?
   A. Indonesia
   B. Malaysia
   C. New Zealand
   D. Malta

251. Which is the deepest ocean in the world?
   A. Arctic
   B. Atlantic
   C. Pacific
   D. Indian

252. What do you name as the Holy Land?
   A. Palestine
   B. Amritsar
   C. Vatican
   D. Jerusalem

253. What does the 17th Parallel line separate?
   A. South and North America
   B. North and South Korea
   C. South and North Yemen
   D. South and North Vietnam

254. Which continent/portion of the world is uninhabited?
   A. Antarctica
   B. Rajasthan
   C. Australia
   D. Gobi

255. Land of the Golden Fleece is:
   A. Bhutan
   B. Japan
   C. Canada
   D. Australia

256. Which mountains are called the Blue Mountains?
   A. Nilgiri Mountains
   B. The Alps
   C. Mount Everest
   D. The Himalayas

257. Name the countries which lie on either side of Durand Line?
   A. India and Pakistan
   B. Indian and Bangladesh
   C. Afghanistan and Pakistan
   D. Iran and Iraq

258. Which is the largest lake in the world?
   A. Caspian (C.I.S., Iran)
   B. Lake Huron (Canada, U.S.)
   C. Nyanza (Tanzania-Kenya)
   D. Lake Superior (U.S.A. Canada)

259. Name the countries which lie on either side of MacMohan Line?
   A. South Vietnam and North Vietnam
   B. India and China
   C. India and Ceylon
   D. France and Germany

260. Which is the largest Gulf in the world?
   A. Gulf of Aqaba
   B. Gulf of Bengal
   C. Gulf of Mexico
   D. Gulf of Aden

261. Which country is called the "Land of Morning Calm"?
   A. Sweden
   B. Netherlands
   C. Norway
   D. Korea

262. Which is called the Dark Continent?
   A. Africa
   B. Australia
   C. Greenland
   D. South America

263. What does the 38th Parallel Line separate?
   A. India from Bangladesh
   B. India from China
   C. North Korea from South Korea
   D. India from Pakistan

264. The Panama Canal Connects:
   A. The Pacific and Atlantic Oceans
   B. The Pacific and Arctic Oceans
   C. The Atlantic and Arctic Oceans
   D. The Atlantic and Indian Oceans

265. What is the habitable portion of the world land area?
    A. Less than 35%
    B. Less than half of it
    C. 50%
    D. About 75%

266. The largest of all the peninsulas in the world is the:
    A. Arabian peninsula
    B. Iberian peninsula
    C. Indian peninsula
    D. Kamehaika peninsula

267. Forbidden City is:
    A. Rome   B. Lhasa (Tibet)
    C. Jerusalem   D. Beijing

268. Rome is the:
    A. Eternal city   B. Forbidden city
    C. City of palaces   D. Cleanest city

269. The capital of Israel is:
    A. Palestine   B. Jerusalem
    C. Vatican   D. Tel Aviv

270. The City of Seven Hills is:
    A. Rome   B. Athens
    C. Cairo   D. Tokyo

271. Laplands is a group of countries located in:
    A. Europe   B. Australia
    C. Asia   D. America

272. Zanzibar is called:
    A. Island of cloves B. Eternal city
    C. Holy land   D. Land of spices

273. The Himalayas constitute the natural boundary between :
    A. China and India
    B. China and Afghanistan
    C. India and Nepal
    D. India and Myanmar

274. Hermit Kingdom is:
    A. Korea   B. Palestine
    C. Rome   D. Haridwar

275. The highest of all the plateaus in the world is the:
    A. Deccan Plateau
    B. Bolivian Plateau
    C. Tibetan Plateau
    D. Colombian Plateau

276. Eternal City is:
    A. Kolkata   B. Rome
    C. Athens   D. Bangkok

277. The city of Khartoum is situated on the banks of:
    A. Hudson   B. Nile
    C. Tiber   D. Seine

278. In which continent some of its parts are over 1500 miles from the sea and in which the hottest as well as the coldest climates of the world are to be found:
    A. America   B. Asia
    C. Europe   D. Australia

279. Paris is situated on the river:
    A. Tibea
    B. Seine
    C. Danube
    D. None of the above

280. Name the place where Blue and White Nile Rivers effect a confluence:
    A. Cairo
    B. Constantinople (except Greenland)
    C. Khartoum
    D. Teheran

281. Which place in the world is known for the least amount of rainfall?
    A. Cairo (Egypt)   B. Yarkand (China)
    C. Atacama (Chile)   D. Thar (Rajasthan)

282. Australia is the:
    A. only continent in the Southern Hemisphere
    B. island continent
    C. smallest continent
    D. all the above points are true

283. Name the place where Rhine and Spree rivers meet in Europe:
    A. Lyons   B. Paris
    C. Hamburg   D. Berlin

284. Moscow is situated on the bank of:
    A. Moskva   B. Spree
    C. Volga   D. Tagus

285. The country Congo is in the ..... continent:
    A. European   B. Australian
    C. Asian   D. African

286. China's Sorrow is:
    A. Lin Piao   B. Sinkiang
    C. Hwang-ho   D. I'sang Ho

287. Sugar Bowl of the world is:
    A. Manila   B. Japan
    C. Cuba   D. Havana

288. The City of Palaces is:
    A. Peru   B. Rome
    C. Kolkata   D. Bangkok

289. The highest peak in Europe is:
    A. Mont Blanc   B. Andes
    C. Monte Rosa   D. Elburz

290. Land of the Rising Sun is:
    A. Japan   B. Norway
    C. Assam   D. Myanmar

291. Where was electricity supply first introduced in India?
    A. Darjeeling   B. Kolkata
    C. Mumbai   D. Delhi

292. Name the largest island in the world:
    A. New Guinea   B. Greenland
    C. Madagascar   D. Great Britain

293. Land of the Midnight Sun is:
    A. Japan   B. Myanmar
    C. Norway   D. Manipur

294. The longest river in the world is:
    A. Nile
    B. Amazon
    C. Yangtze
    D. Missouri-Mississippi

295. The Island Continent is:
    A. Asia   B. America
    C. Africa   D. Australia

296. Suez Canal joins:
    A. London to Paris
    B. Tokyo to Osaka
    C. Mediterranean to the Red Sea
    D. Rangoon to Philippines

297. The Radcliffe Line was drawn on 15th August, 1947 between:
    A. India and Myanmar (Burma)
    B. Pakistan and China
    C. Pakistan and India
    D. Pakistan and Nepal

298. New York is situated on the river bank of:
    A. Rhine   B. Thames
    C. Hudson   D. Amazon

299. Which place is called the land of Golden Fleece?
    A. Australia   B. Cuba
    C. Austria   D. Myanmar

300. Kiel is a:
    A. renowned explorer
    B. American antelope
    C. big American sea bird
    D. shipping canal between London and Baltic Sea

301. USA Consists of so many States:
    A. 30   B. 50
    C. 20   D. 40

302. The Turan Type of Regions have the climate of extremes because:
    A. These lie in the interior ports of the continent
    B. These have either too much or too less rain
    C. These are either on hills or near the deserts
    D. None of the above

303. Which country tops in the mining of gold:
    A. U.S.A.   B. Canada
    C. China   D. India

304. The largest Fresh water lake is:
    A. Lake Superior
    B. Caspian Sea
    C. Lake Baikal
    D. Hind Sea

305. ..... is the most important occupation of the people in the Monsoon Lands:
    A. Forestry   B. Agriculture
    C. Industry   D. Mining

306. There is the great variations of vegetation in the Monsoon Region because of:
A. It depends on nearness to forests, oceans, mountains
B. Variation in the amount of rainfall in different places
C. The effect of rainfall is different in different regions.
D. None of the above

307. In the Amur Valley of the Russia ..... is the most important economic activity:
A. agriculture   B. animal rearing
C. mining   D. industry

308. Which is the Land of White Elephants?
A. Korea   B. Japan
C. Thailand   D. Tanzania

309. The most important occupation of the people in the Turan Type of Regions is .....
A. agriculture
B. cattle and animal rearing
C. mountaineering
D. industry

310. Which is the City of Magnificent Buildings?
A. Tokyo   B. New York
C. Washington   D. Rome

311. In the West European Type of Regions, the summer temperature hardly exceeds ..... °C.
A. 10°C   B. 16°C
C. 7°C   D. 8°C

312. The extensive treeless tracts of North America, which are covered with tall coarse grass, are called:
A. Savanna   B. Tundras
C. Pampas   D. Prairies

313. ....., ... and ..... are the important animal products of the Iran Type of Regions.
A. Skins and hides
B. Meat canning and export
C. Wool, meat and skins
D. Wool and hides

314. Which is the largest country of the world (in area)?

A. U.S.A.   B. Russia
C. China   D. Canada

315. The Lakshadweep Islands are situated in :
A. Indian Ocean
B. Bay of Bengal
C. Arabian Sea
D. None of these

316. The second highest peak in the world is:
A. Kanchanjunga   B. K-2
C. Himalayas   D. Andes

317. Which state in the world occupies the smallest area:
A. Bermuda   B. Peru
C. Monaco   D. Vatican

318. Which is the highest volcano of the world:
A. Cotopaxi   B. Cameroon
C. Kluchevskaya   D. Mount Wrangell

319. Match the following columns:
(a) Tin   1. Chile
(b) Copper   2. Brazil
(c) Iron   3. China
(d) Mica   4. Russia
                5. Malaysia

	(a)	(b)	(c)	(d)
A.	1	2	4	5
B.	2	3	5	4
C.	5	1	3	2
D.	3	4	2	1

320. Korba is famous for
I. Thermal power plant
II. Aluminium plant
III. Hydroelectric power plant
The correct answer out of these is
A. I only   B. II only
C. I and II only   D. I, II and III

321. India's biggest multi-purpose river valley scheme is
A. Kosi
B. Hirakud
C. Bhakra Nangal
D. Nagarjunasagar

322. Match the following columns:
(a) Spain   1. Madrid
(b) Finland   2. Oslo
(c) Lebanon   3. Helsinki
(d) Norway   4. Beirut

	(a)	(b)	(c)	(d)
A.	1	3	4	2
B.	1	4	3	2
C.	4	1	2	3
D.	2	1	4	3

323. Arrange the following states in the descending order of their respective population?
1. West Bengal 2. Uttarakhand 3. Maharashtra
A. 1, 2, 3   B. 3, 1, 2
C. 2, 3, 1   D. 1, 3, 2

324. From which of the following places is Kathmandu nearest by air route?
A. Patna   B. Gorakhpur
C. Varansi   D. Kolkata

325. Chota Nagpur region in Jharkhand is famous for:
A. oil refinery   B. fertile soil
C. lac industry   D. textiles

326. Which of the following pairs is correct?
A. Bhilai—Bihar
B. Bokaro—Madhya Pradesh
C. Durgapur—Karnataka
D. Rourkela—Orissa

327. India earns maximum foreign exchange through the export of:
A. jute   B. coffee
C. cotton textile   D. tea

328. Khetri is famous for
A. copper complex
B. gold fields
C. aluminium complex
D. fertilisers

329. Savana grasslands are found in—
A. Australia
B. East Asia
C. South America
D. Africa

330. Which of the following ports is not a major port in India?
A. Marmugao   B. Cochin
C. Kozhikode   D. Kandla

331. Which of the following is associated with the creation of a Third World news agency?
A. NAMEDIA
B. CHOGM
C. COMECON
D. NAM

332. Which of the following ports has a free trade zone?
A. Kandla   B. Cochin
C. Chennai   D. Tuticorin

333. Approximately how many kilometres are represented by $1°$ of latitude?
A. 421 km   B. 111 km
C. 91 km   D. 211 km

334. Which state in India has the largest area?
A. Assam
B. Uttar Pradesh
C. West Bengal
D. Rajasthan

335. Which of the following winds cause rainfall in Tamil Nadu?
A. Cyclonic winds in the Bay of Bengal
B. South-West monsoons
C. North-East monsoons
D. Retreating monsoons

336. 'Aeroflot' is the name of the airline of:
A. Germany   B. Thailand
C. Indonesia   D. Russia

337. The water of which of the following seas is most saline?
A. Black Sea   B. Dead Sea
C. Baltic Sea   D. Red Sea

338. Which is the highest mountain peak in India?
A. Nanda Devi   B. Kanchanjunga
C. Annapurna   D. Mount Everest

339. The last Governor-General of British-India was
A. Lord Wavell   B. Lord Mountbatten
C. Lord Simon   D. Lord Irwin

340. The great Indian saint who said, "There is neither a Hindu nor a Muslim: only man" was
A. Guru Nanak
B. Kabir
C. Sheikh Farid
D. Swami Vivekananda

341. The most important feature of the Indian culture is
A. its continuity
B. healthy attitude towards all life
C. toleration
D. unity in diversity

342. Home Rule Movement was started by
A. Bal Gangadhar Tilak
B. Mahatma Gandhi
C. Vivekananda
D. Annie Besant

343. The Harappan civilisation belongs to
A. Bronze Age   B. Neolithic Age
C. Paleolithic Age   D. Iron Age

344. Hiuen-Tsang, the Chinese Pilgrim visited India during the reign of
A. Ashoka the Great
B. Chandragupta I
C. Harshavardhana
D. Chandragupta Maurya

345. Raja Rammohan Roy was the founder of
A. Arya Samaj
B. Brahmo Samaj
C. Ramakrishna Mission
D. Prarthana Samaj

346. Areawise, the biggest State in India is
A. Rajasthan   B. Uttar Pradesh
C. Andhra Pradesh   D. Arunachal Pradesh

347. The call for "total revolution" was given by
A. Mahatma Gandhi
B. Bhagat Singh
C. B. R. Ambedkar
D. Jayprakash Narayan

348. The southern-most tip of India is in
A. Kanya Kumari
B. Andaman and Nicobar Islands
C. Thiruvananthapuram
D. Lakshadweep

349. The President of India is the
A. Head of the State
B. Head of Government
C. Head of State as well as Government
D. None of these

350. The first woman to become the Prime Minister in the world was
A. Smt. Indira Gandhi
B. Smt. Margaret Thatcher
C. Smt. Srimavo Bhandarnaike
D. Smt. Kim Campbell

351. Who was the Political guru of Gandhiji?
A. Dadabhai Nauroji
B. Gopalkrishna Gokhale
C. Bal Gangadhar Tilak
D. Lala Lajpat Rai

352. The Headquarters of Asian Development Bank is at
A. Paris
B. Washington
C. Manila
D. Canberra

353. Which was the first metal used by the man?
A. Copper   B. Silver
C. Bronze   D. Brass

354. Dolly is the name of the
A. first cloned sheep   B. first cloned monkey
C. first test-tube baby D. first human fossil

355. The mammal that lays eggs is
A. kangaroo
B. duck-billes platypus
C. opossum
D. otter

356. The capital of Haryanka King Bimbisara was
A. Vaishali
B. Ujjain
C. Rajgira or Girivraja
D. Champa

357. The principal patrons of Gandhara art were
A. Mauryas
B. Satavahanas
C. Sakas and Kushanas
D. None of these

358. Which foreign country is closest to Andaman Islands?
A. Sri Lanka   B. Indonesia
C. Myanmar   D. Pakistan

359. The pioneer of the Bhakti Movement in India was
A. Kabir   B. Ramanand
C. Tukaram   D. Shankaracharya

360. Kuchipudi is the dance drama of which State?
A. Uttar Pradesh   B. Karnataka
C. Andhra Pradesh   D. Rajasthan

361. The river Jhelum has its source from
A. Mount Kailash   B. Rohtang
C. Verinag   D. Tibat

362. Which is the capital of Sikkim?
A. Kothar   B. Gangtok
C. Naroli   D. Kavaratti

363. Name the place where Gautam Buddha was born
A. Bodh Gaya   B. Kushinagar
C. Lumbini   D. Pavapuri

364. Which is the largest sea in the world?
A. South China Sea
B. Mediterranean Sea
C. Black Sea
D. Red Sea

365. Scholar Amir Khusro was patronised by the ruler
A. Akbar
B. Ghias-ud-din Tughlak
C. Shahjahan
D. Babur

366. Which is the largest animal in the world?
A. Blue Whale   B. Rhinoceros
C. Hippopotamus   D. Elephant

367. Name the instrument used for measuring humidity
A. barometer   B. thermometer
C. hygrometer   D. hydrometer

368. First Battle of Panipat took place in the year
A. 1518   B. 1526
C. 1556   D. 1761

369. The last Governor-General of Indian Union was
A. Lord Louis Mountbatten
B. Lord Irwin
C. Sachchidanand Sinha
D. C Rajagopalachari

370. "Lightyear" is the unit of measuring
A. distance   B. time
C. light intensity   D. light power

371. What is the average adult pulse rate?
A. 140-150   B. 115-125
C. 72-80   D. 60

372. Which one of the following does not pollute atmospheric air?
A. Carbon monoxide
B. Hydrogen sulphide
C. Nitrogen
D. Carbon dioxide

373. The characteristic symptom of vitamin K deficiency is
A. haemorrhage   B. heart problems
C. soft bones   D. redness of skin

374. The National Flower of India is
A. Rose   B. Lotus
C. Sunflower   D. Champa

375. Homer was the greatest poet of the language namely:
A. Greek   B. Latin
C. English   D. Spanish

376. The first US President who visited India was
A. Kennedy
B. Eisenhower
C. Jimmy Carter
D. George Washington

377. The headquarters of the UN University is located at
A. Geneva   B. Bonn
C. Tokyo   D. New York

378. Who was the first recipient of Nehru Award for International Understanding?
A. Martin Luther King
B. Mother Teresa
C. U. Thant
D. Dr. Jonas Salk

379. The first person who sailed around the world was
A. Robert Piere   B. Magellan
C. Captain Cook   D. None of these

380. 'ELISA' test is done for detection of
A. AIDS   B. Kalazar
C. Cancer   D. Diabetes

381. With which of the following periods do we associated the "Microleoth" implements?
A. Palaeolithic   B. Mesolithic
C. Neolithic   D. Chalcolithic

382. The Harappans worshipped
A. Shiva and Parvati
B. Mother Goddess and Pashupati
C. Vishnu and Mother Goddess
D. Pashupati and Vishnu

383. Research Designs & Standards Organisation is situated at
A. Nagpur   B. Lucknow
C. Ranchi   D. Bangalore

384. Which of the following is not an Indus Valley Civilisation site?
A. Alamgirpur   B. Lothal
C. Kaushambi   D. Balakot

385. Deep blue colour is imparted to glass by the presence of
A. cupric oxide   B. iron oxide
C. cobalt oxide   D. nickel oxide

386. The stone age people had the first domestics?
A. Asses   B. Dogs
C. Horses   D. Sheeps

387. The largest living bird is
A. Duck   B. Ostrich
C. Peacock   D. Dodo

388. What is the name of the organisation founded by Mother Teresa?
A. Mother House
B. SOS Village
C. Missionary of Charity
D. Nirmala Niketan

389. The term 'Bunker' is associated with which of the following sports?
A. Boxing   B. Polo
C. Shooting   D. Karate

390. Which of the following is the currency of Japan?
A. Dinar   B. Pound
C. Taka   D. Yen

391. O_2 released in the process of photoshynthesis comes from
A. CO_2 B. Sugar
C. Water   D. Pyruric

392. Fundamental Rights in Indian Constitution have been taken from the
A. Russian Constitution
B. US Constitution
C. English Constitution
D. Act of 1935

393. The greatest contribution of the Romans to the world civilisation has been
A. architecture   B. irrigation system
C. literature   D. code of laws

394. Rana Pratap Sagar is associated with
A. hydroelectricity   B. solar energy
C. irrigation   D. nuclear power

395. The Kamakhya temple is situated in:
A. Guwahati in Asom
B. Madurai in Tamil Nadu
C. Trichur in Kerala
D. Halebid in Karnataka

396. Baku is famous for the production of
A. Copper   B. Iron ore
C. Mica   D. Petroleum

397. Which one of the following acids is present in Vitamin C?
A. Citric acid   B. Ascorbic acid
C. Lactic acid   D. Folic acid

398. Which country is called the "Sick Man of Europe"?
A. Germany   B. France
C. Italy   D. Turkey

399. Which state in India has the lowest literacy percentage according to Census Data of 2011?
A. Arunachal Pradesh   B. Bihar
C. Rajasthan   D. Uttar Pradesh

400. Which is the longest river in the world?
A. Amazon
B. Mississippi Missouri

C. Nile
D. Zaire

401. Who wrote "Sare Jahan Se Achcha"?
   A. Bismil   B. Ashfaq-ullah
   C. Iqbal   D. Firaq

402. To which mountain range do the Nilgiris belong?
   A. Eastern Ghats   B. Sahayadri
   C. Satpura   D. Vindhyas

403. Which is the highest plateau in the world?
   A. Pamir   B. Tibet
   C. Ladakh   D. Gilgit

404 Where did Gautam Buddha attain "Nirvana"?
   A. Bodh Gaya   B. Kushinagar
   C. Nalanda   D. Sarnath

405. Which gland of the human body produces insulin?
   A. Pituitary   B. Thyroid
   C. Pancreas   D. Spleen

406. Rickets is caused by the deficiency of
   A. Vitamin A   B. Vitamin B
   C. Vitamin C   D. Vitamin D

407. Which of the following is a book written by Dr. A.P.J. Abdul Kalam?
   A. Indian Modernity
   B. The Transparent Mind
   C. A Brief History of Time
   D. Wings of Fire

408. Which state is the greatest beneficiary from the Sardar Sarovar Dam?
   A. Madhya Pradesh   B. Gujarat
   C. Maharashtra   D. Rajasthan

409. Who among the following is regarded as the "Father of Russian Revolution"?
   A. Kerensky   B. Trotsky
   C. Karl Marx   D. Lenin

410. The Supreme Court of India was set up by the
   A. Regulating Act, 1773
   B. Pitts India Act, 1784
   C. Charter Act, 1813
   D. Charter Act, 1833

411. Kumar Gandharva earned a distinction in which of the following fields?
   A. Classical dance B. Drama
   C. Literature   D. None of these

412. Pongal is a popular festival of which state?
   A. Tamil Nadu   B. Kerala
   C. Karnataka   D. Andhra Pradesh

413. The famous Rock Garden is located in which city?
   A. Shimla   B. Jaipur
   C. Udaipur   D. Chandigarh

414. The Khasi, Garo and Jaintia tribes are mostly inhabited in which state?
   A. Andhra Pradesh   B. Sikkim
   C. Mizoram   D. Meghalaya

415. Corbett National Park is in
   A. Bihar   B. Madhya Pradesh
   C. Uttarakhand   D. Himachal Pradesh

416. Which of the following is classical dance form of Kerala?
   A. Bharatanatyam   B. Kathak
   C. Kuchipudi   D. Kathakali

417. The Parliament of which country is known as "National Panchayat"?
   A. Nepal   B. Russia
   C. Bhutan   D. England

418. Who among the following is known as Father of the Indian Constitution?
   A. Dr. Rajendra Prasad
   B. Dr. B. R. Ambedkar
   C. Dr. S. Radhakrishnan
   D. M. K. Gandhi

419. Which one of the following is the chief constituent of biogas?
   A. Butane   B. Methane
   C. Ethane   D. Propane

420. Glavkosmos is a space agency of
   A. China   B. Ukraine
   C. Russia   D. Georgia

421. Silk is produced by
   A. larva of silkworm
   B. pupa of silkworm
   C. egg of silkworm
   D. insect itself

422. The Cellular Jail is a major tourist attraction in
   A. Pune
   B. Vellore
   C. Nagpur
   D. Port Blair

423. Bauxite is the ore for the extraction of
A. Magnesium   B. Aluminium
C. Boron   D. Barium

424. Who among the foreign travellers was the first to visit India?
A. Hieun Tsang   B. Ibn-Batutah
C. Marco Polo   D. Fahien

425. Most of the Ajanta paintings were completed during the rule of the
A. Vardhanas   B. Sakas
C. Satvahanas   D. Guptas

426. Malik Kafur was a general of
A. Sikander Lodi
B. Qutb-ud-din-Aibak
C. Ala-ud-din-Khilji
D. Humayun

427. Who was the Governor-General of India during the Sepoy Mutiny?
A. Dalhousie   B. Uttar Lytton
C. Hardinge   D. Canning

428. Garba dance is a folk dance of ..... State, India.
A. Tamil Nadu   B. Punjab
C. Gujarat   D. Manipur

429. Which is the headquarters of Dadra & Nagar Haveli and Daman & Diu?
A. Kothar   B. Naroli
C. Randhu   D. Daman

430. Who was the founder of Arya Samaj?
A. Dayanand Saraswati
B. Ram Tirtha
C. Raja Rammohan Roy
D. Swami Vivekananda

431. In which Indian State the percentage of Christian population is the highest?
A. Goa   B. Kerala
C. Mizoram   D. Nagaland

432. Name the place where Gautam Buddha was born.
A. Bodh Gaya   B. Lumbini
C. Kushinagar   D. Rajgrih

433. The 'Atala Devi Masjid' is situated in
A. Kanpur   B. Jodhpur
C. Jaunpur   D. Jaipur

434. Name the first woman Governor of an Indian State.
A. Lakshmi N. Menon
B. Padmaja Naidu
C. Sarojini Naidu
D. Sucheta Kripalani

435. Which State in the Indian Union is the smallest in area?
A. Assam   B. Goa
C. Nagaland   D. Sikkim

436. The Mughal dynasty in India was found in
A. 1526   B. 1536
C. 1546   D. 1556

437. In which State is Chilka, the largest brackish water inland lake in Asia, located?
A. Assam   B. Bihar
C. Odisha   D. Tripura

438. The largest botanical garden in Asia is located in
A. Srinagar   B. Mysore
C. Kolkata   D. Bangalore

439. The seven sacred rivers of India are known as
A. Saptavahini   B. Saptateertha
C. Saptasindhu   D. Saptakshetra

440. Which is the longest Indian National Highway?
A. NH 1   B. NH 3
C. NH 5   D. NH 44

441. Name the place where the only rock-cut Jain Temple exists in South India.
A. Annavasal   B. Sittannavasal
C. Srirangam   D. Vaikundam

442. Who painted Mona Lisa?
A. Leonardo da Vinci   B. Michelangelo
C. Pablo Picasso   D. Vincent Van Gogh

443. Which is the brightest planet in the Solar System?
A. Jupiter   B. Mercury
C. Uranus   D. Venus

444. Asia's largest vaulted hall called the Bada Imambara is situated at
A. Agra   B. Bijapur
C. Lucknow   D. Mathura

445. Which is the oldest Veda?
A. Yajur   B. Sama
C. Rig   D. Atharva

ANSWERS

1	2	3	4	5	6	7	8	9	10
C	B	D	A	C	A	B	B	C	D

11	12	13	14	15	16	17	18	19	20
B	D	C	D	D	C	C	B	D	A

21	22	23	24	25	26	27	28	29	30
D	B	A	D	C	D	A	B	D	B

31	32	33	34	35	36	37	38	39	40
A	B	B	D	A	A	C	B	B	C

41	42	43	44	45	46	47	48	49	50
B	A	D	B	A	A	D	D	B	A

51	52	53	54	55	56	57	58	59	60
B	B	C	C	D	A	B	C	D	C

61	62	63	64	65	66	67	68	69	70
C	A	B	C	A	D	B	A	D	B

71	72	73	74	75	76	77	78	79	80
C	A	B	C	B	C	D	B	A	C

81	82	83	84	85	86	87	88	89	90
C	D	B	C	B	B	D	C	A	D

91	92	93	94	95	96	97	98	99	100
C	A	B	B	D	A	C	D	A	C

101	102	103	104	105	106	107	108	109	110
C	B	C	B	A	D	C	B	A	D

111	112	113	114	115	116	117	118	119	120
C	C	B	B	C	D	A	D	A	C

121	122	123	124	125	126	127	128	129	130
B	D	A	C	D	A	C	B	B	A

131	132	133	134	135	136	137	138	139	140
B	D	C	B	A	C	B	D	B	D

141	142	143	144	145	146	147	148	149	150
C	A	B	A	D	C	B	D	D	C

151	152	153	154	155	156	157	158	159	160
A	D	C	B	C	D	C	C	D	A

161	162	163	164	165	166	167	168	169	170
D	C	D	B	C	A	B	C	A	C

171	172	173	174	175	176	177	178	179	180
C	A	D	B	C	B	D	A	C	D

181	182	183	184	185	186	187	188	189	190
C	D	B	B	A	B	D	C	D	C

191	192	193	194	195	196	197	198	199	200
B	D	A	B	C	A	C	C	B	D

201	202	203	204	205	206	207	208	209	210
C	A	B	C	A	D	C	C	B	B

211	212	213	214	215	216	217	218	219	220
A	C	B	C	D	C	A	B	C	A

221	222	223	224	225	226	227	228	229	230
D	C	B	D	B	C	D	C	A	D
231	232	233	234	235	236	237	238	239	240
C	B	C	B	A	D	D	C	D	A
241	242	243	244	245	246	247	248	249	250
B	D	B	A	B	D	A	A	B	A
251	252	253	254	255	256	257	258	259	260
B	A	D	A	D	A	C	A	B	C
261	262	263	264	265	266	267	268	269	270
D	A	C	A	B	C	B	A	D	A
271	272	273	274	275	276	277	278	279	280
A	A	A	A	C	B	B	B	B	B
281	282	283	284	285	286	287	288	289	290
C	D	A	A	D	C	C	C	D	A
291	292	293	294	295	296	297	298	299	300
A	B	C	A	D	C	C	C	A	D
301	302	303	304	305	306	307	308	309	310
B	A	C	A	B	B	A	C	B	C
311	312	313	314	315	316	317	318	319	320
B	D	C	B	C	B	D	A	C	A
321	322	323	324	325	326	327	328	329	330
C	A	B	A	C	D	C	A	D	C
331	332	333	334	335	336	337	338	339	340
A	A	B	D	D	D	B	B	B	B
341	342	343	344	345	346	347	348	349	350
D	D	A	C	B	A	D	B	A	C
351	352	353	354	355	356	357	358	359	360
B	C	A	A	D	C	C	C	D	C
361	362	363	364	365	366	367	368	369	370
C	B	C	A	B	A	C	B	D	A
371	372	373	374	375	376	377	378	379	380
C	D	A	B	A	B	C	C	B	A
381	382	383	384	385	386	387	388	389	390
C	B	B	C	C	D	A	C	B	D
391	392	393	394	395	396	397	398	399	400
C	B	D	D	A	D	B	D	B	C
401	402	403	404	405	406	407	408	409	410
C	B	A	A	C	D	D	B	D	A
411	412	413	414	415	416	417	418	419	420
D	A	D	D	C	D	A	B	B	C
421	422	423	424	425	426	427	428	429	430
B	D	B	D	D	C	D	C	D	A
431	432	433	434	435	436	437	438	439	440
D	B	C	C	B	A	C	C	B	D
441	442	443	444	445					
B	A	D	C	C					

2204